ETHNOGRAPHY AND HUMAN DEVELOPMENT

Context and Meaning in Social Inquiry

EDITED BY

Richard Jessor, Anne Colby,
and Richard A. Shweder

THE UNIVERSITY OF CHICAGO PRESS / CHICAGO & LONDON

Richard Jessor is director of the Institute of Behavioral Science at the University of Colorado, Boulder. **Anne Colby** is director of the Henry A. Murray Research Center at Radcliffe College. **Richard Shweder** is chair of the Committee on Human Development at the University of Chicago.

The University of Chicago Press, Chicago 60637
The University of Chicago Press, Ltd., London
© 1996 by The University of Chicago
All rights reserved. Published 1996
Printed in the United States of America
09 08 07 06 05 04 03 02 01 00   2 3 4 5 6

ISBN: 0-226-39902-8 (cloth)
ISBN: 0-226-39903-6 (paper)

The University of Chicago gratefully acknowledges a subvention from the John C. and Catherine T. MacArthur Foundation in partial support of the costs of production of this volume.

Library of Congress Cataloging-in-Publication Data

Ethnology and human development: context and meaning in social
  inquiry/edited by Richard Jessor, Anne Colby, and Richard A.
  Schweder.
        p. cm.—(The John D. and Catherine T. MacArthur Foundation
series on mental health and development)
    Papers presented at a conference entitled Ethnographic Approaches
to the Study of Human Development, held June 9–13, 1993, Oakland,
Calif.
    Includes bibliographical references (p.   ) and index.
    ISBN 0-226-39902-8.—ISBN 0-226-39903-6 (pbk.)
    1. Ethnology-Methodology—Congresses. 2. Ethnology—Philosophy—
Congresses. 3. Human behavior—Congresses. 4. Developmental
psychology—Congresses. 5. Social epistemology—Congresses.
I. Jessor, Richard. II. Colby, Anne, 1946– . III. Schweder,
Richard A. IV. Series.
GN345.E74   1996
305.8′001—dc20   95-52027
                                                     CIP

∞ The paper used in this publication meets the minimum requirements of the American National Standard for Information Sciences—Permanence of Paper for Printed Library Materials, ANSI Z39.48-1992.

In memory of our friend and colleague
Donald T. Campbell
Whose larger vision inspired us all

CONTENTS

Preface

RICHARD JESSOR, ANNE COLBY, AND RICHARD A. SHWEDER

This volume is part of—and reflects—the resurgent interest in ethnographic methods in contemporary social science. The idea for the volume had its provenance in a collaborative, interdisciplinary research program trying to illuminate the process of development among youth growing up in contexts that place them at risk—contexts of poverty and disadvantage, limited opportunity, and racial and ethnic marginality. The research addresses a key question: How is it, despite the adversity and malignity of everyday experience, that so many young people nevertheless manage to "make it"? In their attempts to advance understanding of development under such circumstances, the researchers found themselves seeking a firmer grasp on the settings in which the transactions of daily life took place, and on the meanings those transactions and settings had for the young people involved. The reach of traditional surveys and formal face-to-face interviews for such purposes is limited, so there was impetus to explore more observational and interpretive procedures that might supplement those already in hand. That impetus, in turn, raised issues far beyond the immediate needs of the research enterprise—issues about qualitative methods more generally, about their methodological and epistemological status, about their relation to the more quantitative, objective, "mainstream" procedures, about their application to developmental study, and about their contribution to research on social problems.

It seemed important to engage those issues quite directly and, through good fortune, an opportunity to do so materialized. The MacArthur Foundation's Research Network on Successful Adolescent Development among Youth in High-Risk Settings was able to join with the Henry A. Murray Research Center for the Study of Lives, at Radcliffe, to organize a conference for just that purpose. The directors of those respective units,

Richard Jessor and Anne Colby, began a planning process that soon included Richard Shweder and which eventuated in the conference Ethnographic Approaches to the Study of Human Development, held at the Claremont Resort in Oakland, California, 9–13 June 1993. The chapters in this volume are revised versions of presentations made at that conference. The intellectual exchange during the meeting was lively, stimulating, and consistently provocative, and we hope that that sense of engagement with issues of importance for both science and society will be apparent to the readers of the chapters that follow.

Organized and sponsored by the MacArthur Foundation Research Network on Successful Adolescent Development and the Murray Research Center, the conference received additional funding from the William T. Grant Foundation, the Russell Sage Foundation, the Social Science Research Council, the MacArthur Foundation Program on Mental Health and Human Development, the MacArthur Foundation Research Network on Successful Midlife Development, and the MacArthur Foundation Research Network on Human Development and Criminal Behavior. We are grateful to each of those organizations and to their directors for their generous support.

Early on we received helpful advice and suggestions about the conference from Patti Adler, William Damon, Tony Earls, Robert LeVine, Dennis McGilvray, Joy Osofsky, and Paul Shankman, among others.

Marilyn Sena, the administrator of the Research Network on Successful Adolescent Development at the University of Colorado, was responsible for the logistics of the conference and for putting the final manuscripts together. Evelyn Liberatore, at the Murray Research Center, coordinated communication with authors and compilation of chapters, and Katia Mitova, at the University of Chicago, did the same. We are indebted to them all for their exceptionally dedicated assistance; the effort could not have succeeded without their sustained contributions.

Completion of the volume was facilitated by the Center for Advanced Study in the Behavioral Sciences, where editors Jessor and Shweder were privileged to be in residence as fellows. They appreciate the financial support provided by the John D. and Catherine T. MacArthur Foundation and the William T. Grant Foundation for Richard Jessor, and by the John D. and Catherine T. MacArthur Foundation for Richard Shweder.

It seems to be a propitious time for an undertaking such as this. If the volume helps to advance interest in and incorporation of ethnographic methods in social inquiry, it will have fulfilled the aspirations we had when we set out on what has been for us a most enlightening and gratifying endeavor.

Contributors

Kevin Allison, Populations Issues Research Center, Pennsylvania State University

Howard S. Becker, Department of Sociology, University of Washington

Linda M. Burton, Populations Issues Research Center, Pennsylvania State University

Donald T. Campbell, Department of Sociology and Anthropology, Lehigh University

Anne Colby is director of the Henry A. Murray Research Center at Radcliffe College

William A. Corsaro, Department of Sociology, Indiana University

William Damon, Department of Education, Brown University

Norman K. Denzin, Department of Sociology, University of Illinois, Urbana

Shirley Brice Heath, Department of English, Stanford University

Mardi J. Horowitz, Center for the Study of Neuroses, University of California, San Francisco

Richard Jessor is director of the Institute of Behavioral Science at the University of Colorado, Boulder

Margaret Lock, Department of Humanities and Social Studies in Medicine, McGill University

Raymond P. McDermott, School of Education, Stanford University

Constance Milbrath, Center for the Study of Neuroses, University of California, San Francisco

Peggy J. Miller, Department of Speech Communication, University of Illinois, Urbana

Elliot G. Mishler, Department of Psychiatry, Harvard Medical School, at the Cambridge Hospital

John Modell, Department of History, Carnegie Mellon University

Katherine Newman, Department of Anthropology, Columbia University

Dawn A. Obeidallah, Populations Issues Research Center, Pennsylvania State University

Geoffrey B. Saxe, Graduate School of Education, University of California, Los Angeles

Richard A. Shweder is chair of the Committee on Human Development at the University of Chicago

Charles Stinson, Center for the Study of Neuroses, University of California, San Francisco

Mercer L. Sullivan, Senior Research Fellow, Vera Institute of Justice

Hervé Varenne, Teachers College, Columbia University

Thomas S. Weisner, Departments of Psychology and Anthropology, University of California, Los Angeles

PART 1

Epistemology and Ethnographic Representation

1 Ethnographic Methods in Contemporary Perspective

RICHARD JESSOR

Although still emerging from the thrall of positivism, social inquiry has for some time been undergoing a profound and searching reexamination of its purpose and its methods. Canonical prescriptions about the proper way of making science are increasingly being challenged, and a more catholic perspective on the quest for knowledge and understanding is gaining wider acceptance. The honorific status accorded particular research methods—the laboratory experiment, the large-sample survey—has less influence on working social scientists than before, and there is a growing commitment to methodological pluralism and more frequent reliance on the convergence of findings from multiple and diverse research procedures. This openness of the postpositivist climate in the final decades of the twentieth century has presented the social disciplines with the opportunity to think anew about what it is they are really after and how best to achieve those objectives.

Such salutary changes in orientation toward the making of science can be traced to several sources. One is the work in the history of science (for example, Kuhn 1962; Hanson 1958) that shattered long-held notions about how advances in knowledge were in fact produced. It is quite clear now that positivist reconstructions of scientific advance were highly idealized, based largely on deductions from the outcomes or end products of research rather than reflecting the actual process of inquiry that yielded those outcomes. A second source is the newer analyses in the philosophy of science that revealed the untenability of earlier thinking about the definition of concepts and the nature of confirmation and disconfirmation (Kaplan 1964; Polanyi 1964). These two sources of influence are, however, external to the social sciences themselves. The third source, from within the social disciplines, was widespread dissatisfaction with scientific accomplishment; that dissatisfaction was—and is—responsible for much of the changing climate of postpositive social science.

Most of the social science disciplines have experienced the eruption of internal "crises" over the past several decades: agonizing self-appraisals about the impoverished state of scientific accomplishment; worries about the shallowness or surface quality of the usual findings; and apprehension about the failure of research findings to cumulate or tell a story that has coherence, broad applicability, and permanence (Ring 1967; Blalock 1984). These various disciplinary crises appear to have several themes in common. To many in the disciplines, social scientific knowledge seems to have had only limited relevance for understanding societal problems, whether those involve social behavior such as school learning and interpersonal violence, or community and institutional conditions such as poverty, unemployment, and racial segregation. Another common theme—of particular concern in psychology—has been the *a*contextual character of research findings, the fact that the accumulated body of knowledge tends not to be situated, not to be conceptually and empirically connected to the properties and texture of the social settings in which it was obtained. A third theme reflecting discontent in the social sciences is the failure to accommodate human subjectivity in inquiry and to attend to the role of meaning in behavior, in development, and in social life. There has been a tendency to ignore subjectivity or to leave matters of the inner life to the humanities.

Fourth, there is frustration over the inability to recover persons—to retrieve their individuality—from the matrix of relationships that continue to be established among variables of scientific interest (see Elliott Mishler's essay in this volume). The absence of a person focus, and the continued emphasis on relations among variables, has yielded a body of knowledge in which persons in all of their complexity—actors managing the uncertainties and vicissitudes of daily life—are difficult to discern. In this regard, Abbott has admonished us that "our normal methods . . . attribute causality to the variables . . . rather than to agents; variables do things, not social actors" (1992:428). Finally, there is widely shared concern about the tenuous purchase of contemporary social/behavioral science on the dynamics and the course of individual, institutional, and societal change. The obvious difficulties of carrying out longitudinal research are, of course, recognized, but there are more subtle and recondite factors at work here—the surprising paucity of conceptualizations that are truly developmental; the inattention to long-unit notions like "career" that can help to capture the time-extended organization of lives; and the seemingly ingrained preference for large-sample research over detailed studies of development in individual cases in particular settings.

Despite a continuing sense of crisis, the openness of the postpositivist era, the compelling logic of methodological pluralism, and the troubled sense that established approaches to social inquiry have yielded a less than bountiful harvest have all created a new context in which there is keen interest in shifting the orientation and enlarging the armamentarium of social research.

The Turn to Qualitative Methods

That interest has been most evident, perhaps, in the renewed attention to ethnographic or qualitative approaches (the terms are interchangeable as used here) in contemporary studies of social behavior and development. Although long-established in the tool kit of emic anthropology, symbolic interactionist and social constructionist sociology, and phenomenological psychology, ethnographic or qualitative methods have generally been given only limited respect, and they have never been able to attain the scientific status accorded the so-called objective or quantitative methods. Although acknowledged for their usefulness in the exploratory or preliminary phases of an investigation, that is, in the "context of discovery," they have been viewed with great skepticism when employed to establish valid, generalizable knowledge, that is, when used in the "context of justification." This marginalization of qualitative methods in the social science enterprise is precisely what has been changing in the postpositivist climate of epistemological openness and methodological pluralism.

The reintroduction of ethnographic approaches into mainstream social science has been stimulated especially by the sense that such methods speak directly to many of the central themes in the crises with which the social disciplines have been struggling. Ethnographers do, after all, concern themselves with extensive, naturalistic description of settings and contexts, with interpreting the meaning of social behavior and interaction, with understanding the perspective of the actor, the subjectivity of the Other, and with being able to narrate a coherent "story" of social life in which it is persons who have agency and who adapt and change with time and circumstances. Each of these aspects of qualitative inquiry can be seen as responsive to one or another of the felt shortcomings of mainstream research, and it is probably that fact which accounts for much of the recent renewal of interest in ethnography.

The Quantitative-Qualitative Antinomy

The terms *ethnography* and *qualitative method* refer to a congeries of approaches and research procedures rather than to any singular, self-contained, unique method. Their coherence—whether participant observation, unstructured interview, informal survey, case study, or the hermeneutic analysis of text—derives from a common concern with the interpretation of meaning and with understanding the point of view of the Other. Qualitative and quantitative methods are often cast as an irreconcilable antinomy, with each the polar opposite of the other, but such a contrast is inherently misleading. It is not only how data are collected but how they are used—for example, counted versus interpreted—that determines whether a study is more qualitative or more quantitative. And, of course, qualitative data lend themselves to being quantified, and quantitative data can be interpreted. As Hammersley concluded in *What's Wrong with Ethnography?* "the distinction between qualitative and quantitative is of limited use and, indeed, carries some danger" (1992:159). A similar conclusion, phrased somewhat differently, is reached by Weisner (this volume): "all studies have an 'ethnographic' component embedded in them, even if ethnography was not done."

Insofar as no sharp distinction can be drawn between ethnographic approaches and those more conventionally relied upon in formal investigations, the a priori restriction of qualitative method only to the "context of discovery" would seem difficult to defend. The role that ethnography can play in the "context of justification," though still relatively less explored, could well be an important instrumentality for advancing the frontiers of social knowledge, and *joint* reliance on qualitative and quantitative procedures, producing kinds of information that are complementary and converging, can now be seen as a powerful strategy for enriching the understanding of social life.

Ethnography and Epistemology

Notwithstanding the postpositivist welcoming of methodological pluralism and current recognition of the inferential compatibility of qualitative and quantitative data, the epistemological status of ethnography continues to be challenged. On one front it remains beleaguered by the legacy of positivism, especially by its traditional concerns about validity and objectivity. On another front it is under siege by the postmodernists for not carrying its intrinsic reliance on subjectivity to the logical extreme, namely, the denial of empirical reality. Reflecting on these sorts of epistemological challenges, as well as on the moral and political questions now being raised about contemporary ethnographic work, Geertz has expressed alarm that "the very right to write . . . ethnography seems at risk" (1988:133); "its goals, its relevance, its motives, and its procedures all are questioned" (139).

In the essays that follow in this section, and indeed in the others throughout this volume, the critical epistemological issues are dealt with both directly and indirectly. The combination of logical argument in some of those essays, and the demonstrably rich ethnographic yield in others, makes it clear that epistemology no longer provides a secure haven for critics of qualitative work. The consensus that emerges, instead, is that qualitative and quantitative methods of social inquiry, though often asking different kinds of questions, share a common epistemological foundation and a common philosophy of science.

One of the epistemological tensions surrounding ethnographic work has had to do with presuppositions about an empirical world, conventional science assuming its existence and postmodernists insisting that the constructionist perspective of ethnography permits only skepticism and doubt (see chapter 6, by Norman Denzin, in this volume). It is interesting in this regard to reexamine a foundational work in sociological ethnography, namely, Blumer's classical exegesis on symbolic interactionism, in which he is explicit that "an empirical science presupposes the existence of an empirical world" (1969:21). The same position for cultural anthropology has been expressed—in perhaps a more literary style—by Geertz: "Whatever else ethnography may be . . . it is above all a rendering of the actual, a vitality phrased" (1988:143). Hammersley's methodological exploration of ethnography also accepts "the idea that research investigates independent, knowable phenomena" (1992:52), and Campbell (chapter 7 in this volume) decries the efforts of those "ontological nihilists" in postmodern scholarship to "deny to language any degree of competent reference to a nonlinguistic world." In this volume, only Denzin seems willing to consider postmodern doubt about an empirical world seriously. An earlier exchange about this very issue between Denzin and Plummer, another postmodern interactionist, is instructive. In the end, Plummer finds himself unwilling to go as far as Denzin: "I cannot leave the empirical world" (1990:159) is his almost plaintive conclusion.

Obviously, this ongoing ontological debate is unlikely to be resolved in any final way, and postmodern scholarship in the sciences and humanities remains a forceful presence in discourse about social reality (see Denzin's essay in this volume). Nevertheless, it seems clear from the essays in this volume that ethnography, notwithstanding its interactionist perspective and its commitment to social constructionism, remains closely allied to quantitative method, both having their epistemological feet set firmly in an empirical world.

The ethnographic insistence on grasping the perspective of the actor, on seeing the world as it appears to someone else, on understanding the subjectivity of the Other, has been another source of epistemological tension, this time challenged from the positivist rather than the postmodern flank. Shweder's notion of a "true ethnography" does, indeed, call for it "to represent the qualia of 'otherness,' of other 'minds,' of other 'ways of life.' It aims to make insiders intelligible to outsiders" (chapter 2 in this volume). Beyond positivism's resistance to subjectivity in general there is a special reluctance about claims that the subjectivity of the observer can reach and represent the subjectivity of the Other. How is it possible to know other minds?

In one sense, the knowing of other minds can be seen as a particular aspect of the larger ethnographic enterprise of coming to know the social world. That enterprise rests, as we have seen, on inherently subjective, interpretive practices of social and personal construction. But the problematics of knowing and representing other minds have generated additional and special assumptions about the commonality of human nature. Campbell (in this volume) calls attention in this regard to Quine's "principle of charity" (1960), the assumption that the Other is in many ways like ourselves. Similarly Shweder (chapter 2 in this volume) argues for assuming a "universal original multiplicity" underlying a potential for unity among human beings. That assumption undergirds the process of "mind reading" that is so critical in Shweder's vision of a true ethnography: "the construction of an account about what it is like to be a differently situated, differently motivated human being." The knowing of other minds, then, becomes feasible not only as part of the larger constructionist effort but resting also on the additional assumption that other minds are like our own in imaginative capability, an assumption that permits inquiry to proceed beyond the otherwise impenetrable barrier of solipsism.

Related to both of these issues—the existence of an empirical world and the knowability of other minds—is yet a third problematic issue, the place of "validity" in ethnographic representation. In quantitative approaches in mainstream social science, validity has always been an issue of central concern, but the charge is often made that there is no way to establish the validity or the truth value of scientific claims or observations in qualitative work.

Here again it is instructive to consult Blumer's exposition of the methodological position of symbolic interactionism to see how central the concern for validity actually has been. For Blumer, empirical validation comes from direct "examination of the empirical social world"; "the merit of naturalistic study [ethnography] is that it respects and stays close to the empirical domain" (1969:32, 46; see also Becker's essay in this volume). In this perspective, validity is safeguarded by procedures for close, careful, accurate, and extensive observation, procedures that can yield a coherent, credible, and internally consistent account. This is a somewhat different perspective on validity from the traditional discourse about "interobserver agreement" and "correlation with external criteria," but it is consonant with the implications of more recent notions such as "construct validity" that emphasize conceptual embeddedness, and with current emphases on the "plausibility" and "credibility" of scientific accounts (Hammersley 1992), on their "ring of authenticity" (Shweder, chapter 2), and on "validation as the social discourse through which trustworthiness is established" (Mishler 1990:420).

The very complexity of the validity notion in contemporary inquiry precludes any simplistic resolution that would apply across the various investigative procedures and diversity of circumstances of social research. What does seem clear, however, is that validity remains an essential and inescapable concern for qualitative study and that the interpretive products of ethnographic inquiry are, like any other scientific products, subject to appraisal for validity. Even the hermeneutic turn does not automatically permit evasion of such appraisal; Campbell's call for "a validity-seeking hermeneutics" (1986:109) is a noteworthy caution about just this obligation.

Ethnography and the Larger Enterprise of Social Science

The foregoing considerations and the essays in this volume provide strong endorsement for an ecumenical orientation to social inquiry—a stance that embraces a diversity of research methods. Fundamental epistemological differences between qualitative and quantitative methods no longer seem compelling, and there is a growing sense that, used together, they can be mutually enriching while providing alternative ways of converging on the same set of inferences. In addition, ethnographic approaches speak directly to much of the discontent with mainstream, quantitative accomplishment.

Conclusions such as these—if widely shared—could have reverberating implications for the larger social science enterprise, not just for the design of research efforts but also for the scientific "culture" in which those efforts are embedded. Values that are now attached to methods might more appropriately be connected to the significance of the questions asked or the topics addressed. Graduate training in the methodology of research might try to encompass qualitative in addition to quantitative approaches so that every cohort of graduate students would not first have to exorcise the legacy of positivism before discovering for itself the advantages of methodological pluralism. A more pervasive legitimation of ethnographic approaches in both training and application might entail other changes as well, for example, changes in the norms and regulatory processes that influence the making of science—the kind of evaluative criteria employed by journal editors and by research review panels. And the scientific societies and journals that now celebrate honorific methods in their very titles—*Journal of Experimental Whatever*—might seek labels or titles that focus on substantive issues and topical concerns instead.

Changing a culture—even that of a field of science—is notoriously difficult. Yet it seems that that is precisely what is called for if there is indeed to be a "deep incorporation" (see Weisner's essay in this volume) of qualitative approaches in the study of social behavior and human development. Happily, the essays in this volume suggest that change is well underway in the culture of social inquiry.

The Essays in This Section

The essays in this section speak for themselves—with vigor, with logic, with wisdom, and with commitment. All deal, in one way or another, with the critical epistemological issues in the ethnographic enterprise. Since two of the essays, Denzin's and Campbell's, were prepared as commentaries on the other chapters, only brief, additional comment is warranted here.

Richard Shweder's far-reaching effort to characterize "true ethnography," presented as the keynote address at the conference, ranges from how we know other minds, to what the concept of "culture" entails, to whether there are plural prescriptive norms for development (that is, whether developmental outcomes are differentially valued in different social and historical contexts).

Elaborating the position that a true ethnography is a "mind read," Shweder argues forcefully that other minds are, indeed, accessible, and that the meanings of social action can be comprehended and represented. In mind reading, a process of interpretation is applied to what someone says and does, and mental state concepts are invoked to model what that Other "has in mind." This interpretive process is, of course, fundamental to all ethnographic inquiry, and its application to knowing other minds engages cultural psychology in the larger constructionist enterprise.

True ethnography views culture as analytically separate from behavior; theoretically important, such a perspective provides for a problematic relation between the two, thereby conserving culture as an explanatory resource in accounting for variation in behavior and development. For Shweder, culture is a conceptual model of the preferences and constraints that characterize a "moral community," one whose members are each other's reference group. This gives culture a "local" character that enables it to play a proximal explanatory role in relation to the patterns of ordinary social life. Its local character also implies that, for any complex society, it will be more useful to entertain multiple cultures than to seek one that is overarching and sovereign.

Most provocative, perhaps, is Shweder's exploration of the relation of culture to human development. In raising the issue of plural *prescriptive* norms for development, he is proposing that desired developmental out-comes may be context dependent, variable, or different—depending on time, setting, and circumstance—rather than autochthonous or inherent. Some developmentalists may not find this easy to accommodate, while social contextualists will most likely welcome it. Among the latter, Dan-nefer has emphasized "the irreducibly social dynamics of individual devel-opment" and pointed to "the pervasive impact of social structure as an organizer of development" (1984:106).

Overall, Shweder's vision of true ethnography will have to be reckoned with by future scholars venturing to represent "what it is like to be a differently situated . . . human being."

Howard Becker (chapter 3 in this volume) rejects any fundamental epis-temological difference between qualitative and quantitative research. In-deed, he is impatient about the fact that "the issue does not go away . . . this continuing inability to settle the question." In "further thoughts" at the end of his chapter, he suggests that it is the status differential between the quantitative research community and the qualitative research com-munity that sustains the ongoing tension—a reflection of the politics of science rather than of any difference in philosophy of science.

Seeing epistemology in its prescriptive mode as a negative discipline, Becker is more concerned with empirical practice, with the relation between what is actually done in research and the compellingness of the inferences it yields. This "practical epistemology" is, in fact, entirely consonant with the emphasis of recent work in the sociology and history of science.

Qualitative work, according to Becker, does differ from quantitative work in other ways—in being more interested in specific cases than ag-gregate relationships, in more accurately grasping the point of view of the actor, in yielding more contextually situated understanding, and in providing fuller—"thicker," "broader"—description of the phenomena of interest. His contrast serves as a critique of quantitative or "objective" methods and illuminates some of their limitations in achieving the shared goals of social inquiry. The typical social survey, for example, necessitates and thereby imposes costly simplification on the complexity of the world of everyday life and social action.

In dealing with the validity issue as a matter of "credibility" based on the accuracy, precision, and breadth of the data gathered, Becker joins with the other authors in this section. This interpretation of validity is in the Blumerian tradition and is a reaffirmation of the centrality of validity concerns in qualitative research.

Elliot Mishler undertakes a rather heroic task—to recover the "missing persons" in so much of mainstream social research. Scholars in both sociology (for example, Abbott 1992) and psychology (Magnusson and Bergman 1988) have again reminded us that inferences drawn from aggregate data may not apply to all—or even to any—of the individuals making up the aggregate, and that individual variability in such aggregate data, instead of being dealt with, is usually dismissed as error. Arguing "the incommensurability of group and individual analyses," Mishler (chapter 4 in this volume) proposes an alternative paradigm to the nomothetic, population-based model that dominates contemporary research, namely, case-based research in which individual cases—persons, cultures, organizations, or institutions—are the units of study and analysis.

The compatibility of a case-based orientation to research with the ethnographic tradition in social inquiry is apparent. It is an approach that lends itself to Blumer's "close observation," or, as Mishler notes, "that privileges the accumulation of details," and it obviously enhances the accommodation and representation of context. However, the key commonality, according to Mishler, lies in the shared concern for *cases* as the unit of analysis rather than in any common preference for qualitative over quantitative methods. Indeed, a contribution of the chapter is the exploration of quantitative approaches to the patterns and structures that emerge in case-based analyses.

The person-centered rather than variable-centered thrust of Mishler's chapter reflects his theoretical preoccupation with the concept of agency, and his essay is an attempt to restore agency to persons, an objective that is, of course, central in current developmental science. The application of case-based analysis to narratives about "careers" illustrates the role of agency in long-term developmental change. Mishler's conclusion that "case-based analytic methods are now on the agenda in the human sciences" portends a scientific future in which "missing persons" may well be easier to find.

In a penetrating exploration about the nature and locus of disability, R. P. McDermott and Hervé Varenne (chapter 5 in this volume) grapple with epistemological issues involving the social construction of reality, the meaning and signification of action, and the contribution of context to understanding the course and outcome of development. Relying exclusively on case study—the deaf on Martha's Vineyard; a learning disabled child named Adam; and illiterate adults among pest exterminators in New York City—they argue that the social (and political) construction of disability, the way a "difference is noticed, identified, and made consequential," is more influential than the disability itself.

The place of "culture" in these case studies is central. Indeed, in explicating their perspective on culture *as* disability, disability is located in the culture rather than the person: cultures "actively organize ways for persons to be disabled." In their view, persons are "acquired" by already framed, cultural notions of disability. This treatment of culture as a construction analytically separate from behavior is consonant with that in Shweder's true ethnography, and the close, detailed, contextually embedded observation such case studies permit reinforces Becker's and Mishler's calls for case-based study and analysis. The complex role of culture in shaping the course and setting the outcomes of development is also apparent in these exemplars. As the authors conclude, "in organizing a science of development, it may be necessary to begin with the recognition that life in any culture gives us much to fall short of."

The essays by Norman Denzin and Donald Campbell were invited as commentaries on the other chapters, and they fulfill that charge brilliantly. Unable to attend the conference, Denzin prepared his discussion on the basis of early drafts of the various papers. He provides an intensely interesting and challenging postmodernist or post-structuralist perspective on the ethnographic project, one much more radical than that of any of the other contributors. Despite his ontological differences with the other authors, however, Denzin sees researchers as "bricoleurs" and qualitative work as "bricolage," yet another way of urging the methodological pluralism about which a growing consensus has already been noted. His ultimate interest in "cultural studies"—critical analyses of cultural representations of everyday experience in film, sports, music, and so on—as an approach to studying youth development in high-risk settings does promise to enhance the bricolage by delineating further the quiddities of experience in everyday life settings.

Campbell's essay creates a valuable dialectic with Denzin's. As noted earlier, Campbell remains committed to efforts to improve the competence of scientific belief, and he rejects what he labels "ontological nihilism," the denial in post-structuralism of the possibility of valid reference to an independent reality. Acknowledging the "worldview embeddedness of all observations" and the social construction of social reality, he argues nevertheless for a science in which validity remains a guiding objective to be pursued even if never likely to be fully achieved. The obstacles to the latter that he singles out for discussion—methodological cultural relativism and the failure of communication—have important ramifications for the process of trying to understand other cultures and other minds.

Campbell urges us to learn from successful exemplars in our efforts to extend ethnographic methodology, and he refers specifically to the substantive chapters that appear later on in this volume. With that positive appraisal of what lies ahead, we can turn to the essays in this section to see, in detail, what their authors have to tell us about the epistemology of ethnographic research.

References

Abbott, A. 1992. "From Causes to Events: Notes on Narrative Positivism." *Sociological Methods and Research* 20:428–55.

Blalock, H. M., Jr. 1984. *Basic Dilemmas in the Social Sciences.* Beverly Hills, Calif.: Sage.

Blumer, H. 1969. *Symbolic Interactionism: Perspective and Method.* Englewood Cliffs, N.J.: Prentice-Hall.

Campbell, D. 1986. "Science's Social System of Validity-Enhancing Collective Belief Change and the Problems of the Social Sciences. In *Metatheory in Social Science: Pluralisms and Subjectivities.* Ed. D. W. Fiske and R. A. Shweder. Chicago: University of Chicago Press.

Dannefer, D. 1984. "Adult Development and Social Theory: A Paradigmatic Reappraisal." *American Sociological Review* 49:100–116.

Denzin, N. K. 1990. "The Spaces of Postmodernism: Reading Plummer on Blumer." *Symbolic Interaction* 13:145–54.

Geertz, C. 1988. *Works and Lives: The Anthropologist as Author.* Stanford, Calif.: Stanford University Press.

Hammersley, M. 1992. *What's Wrong with Ethnography? Methodological Explorations.* London: Routledge.

Hanson, N. R. 1958. *Patterns of Discovery.* Cambridge: Cambridge University Press.

Kaplan, A. 1964. *The Conduct of Inquiry: Methodology for Behavioral Science.* San Francisco: Chandler.

Kuhn, T. S. 1962. *The Structure of Scientific Revolutions.* Chicago: University of Chicago Press.

Magnusson, D., and L. R. Bergman. 1988. "Individual and Variable-Based Approaches to Longitudinal Research on Early Risk Factors." In *Studies of Psychosocial Risk: The Power of Longitudinal Data.* Ed. M. Rutter, 45–61. Cambridge: Cambridge University Press.

Mishler, E. G. 1990. "Validation in Inquiry-Guided Research: The Role of Exemplars in Narrative Studies." *Harvard Educational Review* 60:415–42.

Polanyi, M. 1964. *Personal Knowledge: Towards a Post-Critical Philosophy.* New York: Harper and Row.

Plummer, K. 1990. "Staying in the Empirical World: Symbolic Interactionism and Postmodernism—A Response to Denzin." *Symbolic Interaction* 13:155–60.

Quine, W. V. 1960. *Word and Object.* New York: Wiley.

Ring, K. 1967. "Experimental Social Psychology: Some Sober Questions about Some Frivolous Values." *Journal of Experimental Social Psychology* 3:113–23.

2 True Ethnography: The Lore, the Law, and the Lure

RICHARD A. SHWEDER

Anthropologist Sir Evans-Pritchard, in a postscript to his book *Witchcraft, Oracles and Magic among the Azande* (1937), reminisces about his disciplinary training in methodology. As a young student in London about to set off for Central Africa, he sought tips about ethnographic procedure from more experienced hands in the field. He went to his teacher Charles Seligman, who told him to "take 10 grains of quinine every night and keep off women." He went to Edward Westermarck who told him "don't converse with an informant for more than twenty minutes because if you aren't bored by that time, he will be." He went to the famous Malinowski who told him "not to be a bloody fool." Evans-Pritchard (E. P., as he was known in the profession) then went off to the field and wrote a classic ethnography.

It is not just the British who offer such a rigorous training in ethnographic method. Most American anthropology departments follow the tradition by refusing to require any courses at all in methodology. There are even significant theoretical trends in the philosophy of science which are explicitly "against method." Methodological advice in anthropology comes more in the form of "lore" than "laws," of the sort Evans-Pritchard passed on to his readers after returning from the field and writing about what it is like to hunt for a witch in Central Africa: "You cannot have a renumerative, even intelligent, conversation with people about something they take as self-evident if you give them the impression you regard their belief as an illusion." Now that is a useful and important piece of advice but not quite the kind of advice that is sought by those who are "for method."

Many anthropologists are "for ethnography," which they don't necessarily think is the same as being "for method." They harbor the suspicion that methodological pursuits actually get in the way of participating in the flow of life of a community. They think that if you are really serious and want to get to know a place well then the most important thing you can do is just "muck around" a lot like a good journalist, and follow your nose.

Some anthropologists are neither for method nor against it, but simply innocent of it. Indeed, more than a few Ph.D. candidates in anthropology have had the experience described by Dennis McGilvray in a lecture delivered at the University of Chicago on the occasion of the twenty-fifth anniversary of the university's Committee on South Asian Studies. Reminiscing about his training as an anthropology graduate student at Chicago in the late 1960s, McGilvray recounted how he arrived in a remote area of Sri Lanka only to discover that his theoretically sophisticated and fashionable thesis proposal (Erving Goffman's dramaturgy was the rage of the day) was irrelevant to the mundane realities of the local scene, that he had learned the wrong dialect of Tamil, and that he was not going to be able to select his informants. Instead they were going to select him. He wrote his ethnography relying heavily on conversations with his cook, and his postman, and with a few young unmarried men in the community who were eager to talk to him and had nothing better to do.

McGilvray and I were in graduate school in the same era, although at different institutions. Let me report that at Harvard University in the late 1960s the methodological scene in anthropology was a bit more complicated than at Chicago, or at least a bit more conflicted. I remember how in those days two professors on the admissions committee could never agree on which students to admit to the Harvard anthropology program. The first professor wanted students with a high mathematical IQ and a strong background in formal methods—componential analysis, statistics, experimental design and sampling procedures. He liked people who could count and decompose complex things into simple elements. The second professor wanted students with a high verbal IQ and a strong background in history, philosophy, languages, and literature. He liked people who could write, easily pick up the local language, and synthesize their field experiences into compelling narratives.

The first professor thought that one day there would be a manual or rule book for doing ethnography. I think he believed that anthropology could develop mechanical knowledge production procedures (some people call this the scientific method) and that, armed with an artificial intelligence, anyone should be able to write a true and literal description of another culture, the way the other "really is." As far as I know, he never did write an ethnographic book.

The second professor preferred insight over technique, imagination over procedure. With an educated contempt for methical inquiry, off to the field on a vision quest went his literate and well-read students. Invariably they managed to return with a revelation, or a metaphor, about a faraway place. Thinking back I wish less time had been spent in graduate school arguing whether it is scientists or humanists who make the best ethnographers. I wish more time had been spent spelling out the character of a "true ethnography."

Characterizing "true ethnography" is, of course, a hopeless, hazardous, and thankless task. It is sort of like trying to define true love. I am going to try my hand at it in this essay. If the process of getting there is half the fun, and half as much fun as they say, I am willing to settle for that, while braving the anticipated wave of antiessentialist criticism. Along the way I will have some things to say about a series of other issues central to the ethnographic project in anthropology: plural norms (what they are, whether they exist, and how you might go about studying them), the role of authority and power in the maintenance of norms, and the place of mind reading in the construction of an account about what it is like to be a differently situated, differently motivated human being. At the very least I hope this essay will encourage others to wonder about the aims of fieldwork, and about the nature of the regulative ideals that we ought to share as a community of scholars committed to the study and representation of "others." So here goes. The lecture I didn't get (or perhaps didn't attend) when I was in graduate school.

Somewhere Between Solipsism and Superficiality

True ethnography resides somewhere between solipsism and superficiality. Its mission is to gain access to other minds and other ways of life so as to represent what it is like to be a differently situated human being. Its practitioners are people willing to hazard border crossings in pursuit of differences that make a difference for the way lives are lived, developed, and experienced, and for the way competence, excellence, virtue, and personal well-being are defined. Its theories tell us what it means to be differently situated—what it is like to have different preferences (values, goals, tastes, desires, ideals of personal well-being and of developmental competence) and/or what it is like to live with different constraints (information, causal beliefs, abilities, dispositions, resources, technology, systems of domination or control). Its methods make use of the things people say and do to each other in everyday life, as well as the things they strategically and deliberately say and do to us on special "scientific" occasions (for example, when we ask them to answer questions in an interview or to narrate a life history), to construct a plausible and intelligible account about what it is like to be someone else. Yet true ethnography also aims to deepen our understanding of "otherness" and to move us beyond the cover stories, idealized self-representations, well-rehearsed verbal modes of public image management, and strategic manipulations of those whose lives we seek to understand.

True ethnography confronts us with alternative worlds of value and meaning, with different universes of preference and constraint. It tests the limits of our capacity to suspend our disbelief and to access hidden, unconscious, or marginalized aspects of our own subjectivity. It draws us a picture of moral communities where people have different ideas about the desirable states of functioning for human beings.

True ethnography aims to represent otherness in such a way that "we," who are outside the relevant situation, can imagine what it is like to be in it. It tells us, for example, what it is like to be a midlife Oriya Brahman woman whose culturally categorized childhood ("pila") ended with an arranged marriage, whereupon she took up residence in her mother-in-law's house. It tells us what it is like for her to have lived her entire life within the walls of a patriarchal extended joint family compound in a sanctified temple town in India. It helps us understand why she might look forward to the midlife years with the greatest anticipation of satisfaction, why she is relatively indifferent to the physical signs of aging (including menopause), why she is so finely attuned to matters of honor and social prestige, and why she measures her sense of well-being not in terms of autonomy and the liberty to do the things she wants but rather in direct proportion to the magnitude of the social responsibilities she has shouldered, the intensity of the sacrifices she has endured, and the respect she receives from others in exchange for the service she has done as a dutiful daughter-in-law, mother, and wife. It lets us hear her "voice" and her complaints. It forces us to acknowledge the terms (*her* chosen terms, not ours) by which she deeply values a way of life that we may find difficult to value, at least at first blush (Menon and Shweder 1994; Shweder, Mahapatra, and Miller 1990; and Shweder, Much, Mahapatra, and Park, in press; I have done fieldwork among Oriya Brahmans since 1968 and shall make reference to that community throughout this essay).

Such an ethnography tells us provocatively that within the Brahmanical wards of Hindu temple towns in Orissa, India, moral "goods" or "values" such as duty, hierarchy, interdependency, sanctity, and ritual purity count for more than liberty, autonomy, and equality (Mahapatra 1981; Shweder 1990, 1991; Shweder and Much 1991; Shweder, Much, Mahapatra, and Park, in press; and Menon and Shweder 1994, in press). It tells us that most members of such communities prefer certain constraints on their choices in life, such as a taboo against a "love marriage," against divorce, and against widow remarriage (Shweder, Mahapatra, and Miller 1990).

It tells us that most women in those communities actively constrain their preferences in such a way that they develop a taste for modesty and downcast eyes and idealize the behavior of the "shrinking violet" as a feminine virtue. It informs us that while downcast eyes, "modesty," and the behavior of a shrinking violet are associated in the minds of contemporary middle-class Anglo-Americans with concepts such as *meek, timid, shy, bashful, mousy, sheepish, shrinking, embarrassed, self-deprecating, not ego-enhanced, ashamed, humiliated, degraded,* and *weak,* this is not true in all moral communities. In Orissa, India, for example, downcast eyes, modesty, and the behavior of a shrinking violet elicits a quite different set of associations: *unpretentious, unobtrusive, reserved, self-restrained, quiet, having humility, coy, demure, self-effacing, not brazen, decent, elegant, delicate, undefiled, unsullied, powerful, virtuous,* and *good* (see Shweder 1993; Menon and Shweder, in press; Shweder and Menon 1993). True ethnography challenges our willingness to transcend our own habitual modes of moral judgment and emotional reaction. It dares us to view the world in a different light.

True Ethnography: The Culture Concept

A true ethnography is about something called a culture. As everyone knows, there are many definitions of *culture.* The definition I was taught as a "mantra" in 1963 in my first undergraduate course in anthropology was "patterns of behavior that are learned and passed on from generation to generation" (a "pattern of behavior" was meant to include any kind of habit, "standard operating procedure" or symbolic action—shaking hands, addressing your father as "Sir," reading the *New York Times* every morning—that had some history or "tradition" behind it and thus could be thought of as having an identity of its own over and above the intentionality and experience of any one individual).

At the time I did not think to ask why the individuals who carry on a tradition would be motivated to simply replicate patterns of behavior, or why they would care to "pass on" their traditions to others. I did not think to ask whether the perpetuators of a tradition were "rational agents" doing what they did because what they did seemed to them, in light of their causal beliefs, to be an efficient or effective way to accomplish some set of worthy goals. The very idea of worthy goals and other questions about the relationship of tradition to the moral order or to a rational order never really came up. It was simply presupposed that the agents of culture have a taste or a propensity to form habits and do traditional things, and that children are inculcated with culture and readily shaped by the desire for external rewards or the fear of external punishment to "internalize" whatever a group defines as "traditional."

A bit later, in graduate school, I discovered that Sir Edward Tylor's late nineteenth-century definition of culture (as all the inclinations, skills, values, knowledge, and mental states acquired by an individual by virtue of being a member of a group) was still in vogue, although by the late 1960s, under the influence of the cognitive revolution, Tylor's definition was given an "informational" twist: culture was all the information you needed to know to pass or get along competently as a "native." At least that was the intellectual fashion at Harvard, Stanford, Yale, and Penn (although probably not at Chicago, where the cognitive revolution never did arrive).

In more recent times, after several other "revolutions" (the post-structural revolution, the symbolic revolution, the rational choice revolution) and a few "turns" (the interpretive turn, the deconstructive turn, the turn to pragmatics and toward praxis), I have been teaching my own students that a culture is "a reality lit up by a morally enforceable conceptual scheme composed of values (desirable goals) and causal beliefs (including ideas about means-ends connections) that is exemplified or instantiated in practice." Members of a culture are members of a moral community who work to coconstruct a shared reality and who act as though they were parties to an agreement to behave rationally within the terms of the realities they share. In this essay I am going to develop a case for the truth and usefulness of that particular conception of culture.

To get things started, allow me to suggest that we think about the thing called a culture as nothing other than a plausible hypothetical model, articulated in a mental-state language (intelligible to the ethnographer's interpretive audience), which represents the shared and relatively enduring preferences and constraints exhibited in the observable behavior of a designated network of individuals who are tied to each other as members of some self-sanctioning moral community. Accordingly, the methods of true ethnography are designed to reveal things called preferences and constraints, including those that may be taken for granted by members of a moral community, that may be implicit in their behavior, difficult for them to notice, or socially undesirable for them to articulate or disclose under even the most ideal of communicative circumstances.

True ethnography takes time. It requires some degree of rapport and a good deal of trust. Its methods aim to reveal assessments about the value of life that have a ring of authenticity. Because true ethnography is about the structure of other minds, and because it takes time, it resides, quite naturally, somewhere in between solipsism and superficiality, in the vicinity of the discourse and praxis of members of some designated moral community.

In the context of social science methodologies, superficiality can be principled, sophisticated, and predictively useful, and when it is I shall refer to it as superficialism. Superficialism insists that upon demand and "off the top of their heads" the natives tell what they know, know what they are talking about, and keep their answers short. All of us engage in the practice of "superficialism" (for example, whenever limitations of time, resources, access, or courage lead us to rely on interviews to elicit reports from "native" participants about what they think and do, and why, rather than doing it the hard way, by gaining access to the mental states of others through real time participant observation.)

I shall have more to say about superficialism later, when I discuss the way human beings respond to social science survey probes such as, "How satisfied are you with your life on a ten point scale?" or "How would you rate your overall health (excellent, very good, good, fair, poor)?" or "Do you believe in God (very much, a moderate amount, a little, not at all)?" First, however, I want to examine the doctrine of solipsism and its implications for true ethnography.

Solipsism in Ethnography: "Let's Talk about Me for a While"

I learned something about solipsism a few years ago, from a conversation I had with Claude Lévi-Strauss. I met Lévi-Strauss for the first time in Paris in 1990, and part of our conversation went like this. Lévi-Strauss told me that he hears the term *postmodern* all the time but does not understand what it means. He told me he would have preferred to live in the past, before the twentieth century, before the postmodern era. "But where in the world would you have preferred to live in the past," I asked, thinking of Athens in the fifth century B.C., India at the time of the Buddha, and all of those cultures of the world—the Nuer, the Trobriand Islanders, the Samoans, the Ifaluk—studied and thereby made famous by anthropologists. "In France, of course," Lévi-Strauss replied. "Why France?" I asked. "Because French subjectivity is the only subjectivity I can ever understand," he replied. "But what about all those other cultures you have studied all your life? Can't you enter into their subjectivity?" "No," Lévi-Strauss replied, "I can only understand other cultures as objects, not as subjects."

Solipsism is the view that the only mental life you can ever really know is your own. This view can be derived from two premises: that the only way to understand something that has a mental life is by getting "inside its head," and that the only head you can ever really get inside is your own. The solipsistic approach to ethnographic method is well represented by the story being told these days in anthropological circles about the postmodern ethnographer who arrives at a remote field site, recruits an informant, sits her down by a campfire, and says, "Now let's talk about me for a while." The implication is that the only way you can ever get to know what it is like to be someone else is by understanding his or her mental life, and that is impossible. Ironically, despite Lévi-Strauss's apparent antipathy for postmodern thought, it is precisely the postmodern ethnographer who agrees with him that the only subjectivity you can ever understand is your own.

The postmodern "native" seems to agree with Lévi-Strauss as well. I recently had dinner at a storefront restaurant in Chicago, which is owned and run by a Thai family. Prominently displayed on the wall of the restaurant was a poster describing the homeland. It read, "Thailand: The Most Exotic Country in Asia."

Now many of you are probably familiar with the anthropologist's assumption that native peoples experience their own beliefs, desires, and practices as routine, transparent, and commonsensical. That assumption has become old-fashioned. In these postmodern times of cable television, international travel, a global economy, metaphysical jet lag, and hyper-reflexivity, the native peoples of the world are more up-to-date. They know all about the international market in solipsism. They have a canny recognition of the taste of others for impenetrability. They have even come to see themselves, through the eyes of others, as strange and alien. And they are ready to trade on the limits of understanding and to publicize themselves as hidden and mysterious. This keeps the westerners coming. "Thailand: The Most Exotic Country in Asia."[1]

Perhaps there is nothing new in this self-conscious representation by others of themselves as puzzling and inaccessible, as a black hole beyond the reach of the mental telescope of the West. Perhaps the native peoples of the world have always been a step ahead of their principal investigators. The history of the encounters of the indigenous peoples of the East and South with the indigenous peoples of the West and North (so-called explorers and other anthropological aliens) has been sufficiently bizarre and inhumane that the natives may have (quite understandably) judged themselves to be impervious to the gaze of the westerner and unintelligible to a Northern subjectivity. Perhaps long ago the "natives" of the world decided to turn exoticism to their advantage and to collaborate with Lévi-Strauss on the thesis that French subjectivity is the only subjectivity that a French anthropologist can ever understand.

It is also possible that they read Descartes. For it is Descartes who managed to draw almost everyone's attention to the quite mysterious appearance and nature of consciousness in the natural world. It is no secret that Descartes reasoned that mental states (beliefs and desires, the experience of seeing red, the feeling of being in pain) are strangers in the natural world. Given that most other things in the world are material, open (in principle) to direct and public sensory inspection and governed by physical laws of causal determination, it is perhaps not too surprising that mental states have the appearance of a singular nonnatural quality: immaterial, inherently private, self-justifying, and bound to a first-person point of view. Whether one refers to this alien spirit lost on a material world as "consciousness," *qualia,* or the phenomenological side of experience, the subjective states that are the *qualia* of life are not open, even in principle, for others to directly observe or inspect. Only one person—you—has potential sensory access to your own experienced states of mind. Your conscious experiences qua states of consciousness are indubitable. They are shielded against criticism and against the external objective standards of the third-person point of view.

There is, for example, no objective neurological or biochemical measure, no "external standard" of pain by which to assess the character of the experience you label "pain" or even to gauge its intensity. In most medically investigated cases of reported headaches, backaches, or chest pains, the brain scan, treadmill test, or X-ray is negative and the clinician has nothing in the natural world to point to as an explanation of, or rationale for, the experience that you named "pain." Typically, the clinician can't even come up with a meager biochemical or neurological (material) correlate of your announced pain. In most cases all the clinician has in his or her hands are your ineffable words uttered in some language ("I have a pain in my chest"), referring to some invisible experience. How can the clinician know whether you use your mental-state words the same way he or she does? What is it you experience? Do you experience a lot of it or only a moderate amount? There is nothing there to grasp or lay hold of except your words, and even they, as words, are immaterial and must be interpreted and translated? Your first-person experience (for example, of pain) is as hermetically sealed as it is self-certifying. Like some mystical experience it provides a sufficient warrant for its own authenticity, but only for the person who experiences it. You can never be wrong that you had the experience you had, and we can never quite be sure that you had an experience, or that we really know what that subjective experience was, if you truly had one. In other words, the only subjectivity that Lévi-Strauss can ever really know is his own. Forget about other Frenchmen. Or so the well-known argument in favor of solipsism goes.

Descartes made us aware of the discrepancy between the essential indubitability of our own experienced states of mind, which no one else can experience, and the essentially contestable character of our speculations and projections about what it is like to be a state in another mind, which only it can experience. "Cosmic exile" is the phrase used by anthropologist Ernest Gellner to characterize this heightened and somewhat terrifying form of solipsistic self-consciousness in which everyone is exotic to everyone else and separated by a valley of doubt.

If "true ethnography" is possible, then either solipsism is wrong or ethnographic authority is not really threatened by radical doubts about the existence and character of other minds. That is because true ethnography aims to represent the *qualia* of otherness, of other minds, of other ways of life. It aims to make insiders intelligible to outsiders. It tries to remove the "veil of ignorance" that obscures the view between differently situated human beings and makes each seem peculiar and alien to the eyes of the other. A true ethnography does not lead us to gaze upon the other only as a material object or a thing. Nor does it shroud the other in mystery. Nor, quite crucially, does it seek to replace the veil of ignorance with a mirror, turning the other into an all too familiar, all too easily recognized reflection of the self (as the subaltern antiorientalists, who are so hostile to anthropology and are so uniformitarian and monistic in their moral assumptions, would have it). A true ethnography deprives us of neither our differences nor our humanity. It only deprives us of our oddness. Given such goals—to represent the other as different but not odd, as intelligible and fully human but human in a different sort of way—it is hardly surprising that some scholars think it is impossible to construct a true ethnography and that the aims of true ethnography are hopelessly incoherent.

If true ethnography is possible, then either solipsism must be wrong, or else ethnographic authority is compatible with radical doubt. But what is wrong with solipsism? I do not think the problem with solipsism is with the premise that the only head you can ever get inside is your own. That seems true enough. I do not even think it is wrong to argue that the only mental life you will ever really understand is your own, as long as you recognize that your own mental life is very complex, and that major aspects of your mental life are hidden from your view and direct experience, and stand in desperate need of anthropological excavation. The same is true of the mental life of others. The unity of human beings is not to be found in that which makes us common and all the same, but rather in a universal original multiplicity, which makes each of us so variegated that others become accessible and imaginable to us through some aspect of our own complex self. I like to dub this last proposition the "principle of original multiplicity" (Shweder 1991, 1993c). It is the principle of original multiplicity that makes true ethnography possible. An alternative way to phrase the principle, indeed its slogan, is "universalism without the uniformity."

An Antisolipsistic Mentalism

According to the principle of original multiplicity it is not really worrisome if the only head you can ever get inside is your own, as long as the only head you can get inside is complex enough to contain within it everyone else's head as well. The real problem with solipsism, as I see it, is the premise that the only way to understand the mental life of something that has a mental life is by getting inside *its* head, by experiencing it or observing it directly. I think this point of criticism is what Clifford Geertz (1984) had in his mind when he said that one does not have to be an empath to be a true ethnographer. True ethnography can stand on the assumption that it is possible to understand what it is like to be a differently situated human being precisely because to understand the mental life of a differently situated human being one does not have to get inside his or her head. That is the conclusion drawn by such philosophers as Wittgenstein and Ryle, who are sometimes described as philosophical behaviorists. That is the conclusion drawn by those anthropologists (such as Geertz) who were influenced by Wittgenstein and Ryle.

I hasten to point out that philosophical behaviorism is not the same as psychological behaviorism. There is black magic in the word *behaviorism.* So beware of the illusions produced through associations with the wrong history of the term.

Witness, for example, the difficulty that arose back in 1981 at a planning meeting for a conference on culture theory (Shweder and LeVine 1984:7–8) when Roy D'Andrade and Clifford Geertz fooled us all by seeming to be at loggerheads over the role of the study of behavior and conceptual schemes (or ideas) in the analysis of culture. D'Andrade made the following historical and ontogenetic observation:

> When I was a graduate student [in the late 1950s] one imagined people *in* a culture; ten years later, culture was all in their heads. The thing went from something out there and very large to something that got placed inside. . . . We went from "Let's try to look at behavior and describe it" to "Let's try to look at ideas." Now how you were to look at ideas was a bit of a problem—and some people said, "Look at language." That notion, that you look at idea systems, was extremely general in the social sciences. On, I think, the same afternoon in 1957 you have papers by [Noam] Chomsky and [George] Miller and in anthropology, Ward Goodenough. All signal an end to the era of "Let's look at behavior and see what they do." Before 1957 the definition of culture was primarily a behavioral one—culture was patterns of behavior, action and customs. The same behavioral emphasis was there in

linguistics and psychology. The idea that cognition is where it's at struck all three fields at the same time. . . . I think it was a nice replacement. . . . But the thing is now breaking . . . and we each have different ideas about how it is breaking up.

Clifford Geertz responded as follows:

At the same time the revolution was going on where people were putting things inside people's heads a counterrevolution was going the other way—criticizing the whole myth of inner reality, the whole myth of private language. The one thing that anthropologists hadn't said about culture is that it is a conceptual structure . . . it's not a psychological phenomenon in the first place. It's a conceptual structure—and that is what the whole depsychologizing of the concept of sense, of meaning, was all about and still is about.

Looking back on this exchange a decade later it seems to me that D'Andrade and Geertz were talking past each other because they are speaking for and against two different types of behaviorisms. D'Andrade was speaking against the antimentalistic doctrine of psychological behaviorism, which tried to circumvent the scientific use of a mental-state language (references to beliefs, desires, plans, wants, emotions, goals, feelings) through the study of the behavior of organisms. Geertz, on the other hand, was speaking in favor of the antisolipsistic doctrine of philosophical behaviorism, which tried to defend the use of a mental-state language by insisting that mental states are not primarily the inherently inaccessible and private experiences of this or that person's consciousness, but rather derive their meaning from the "external" (and hence intersubjectively accessible) concepts that are exhibited in practices and in the observable "forms of life" that lend meaning to a behavior. For the philosophical behaviorist the study of behavior is not a way of getting rid of mental state concepts. It is rather a way to identify them without having to get inside someone's head. In fact, D'Andrade tacitly accepted this antisolipsistic philosophical behaviorism with his acknowledgement that perhaps the best way to get at a latent unobservable thing such as an idea or concept is through the observation of linguistic behavior. And Geertz tacitly rejected antimentalistic psychological behaviorism when he defined culture as a conceptual scheme.

The two revolutions (antisolipsism and promentalism) can be joined by insisting that true ethnography is the interpretive study of the sanctionable behavior (the "normal" discourse and praxis) of members of a moral community. The two revolutions can be joined by insisting that the first and most fundamental interpretive act in the study of sanctionable behavior (discourse and praxis) is the application of mental-state concepts (beliefs, desires) to render such behavior intelligible. For example, to add some concreteness to the idea of the sanctionable behavior of a moral community, in urban middle-class Anglo-America, exclusive husband-wife sleeping arrangements, the family meal, and saying "thank you" are sanctionable behaviors. In rural Hindu India they are not. In rural Hindu India, menstrual seclusion and husband-wife avoidance in public places are sanctionable behaviors. In urban middle- class Anglo America they are not. The first and foremost interpretive act in the study of such sanctionable behavior is to understand the beliefs about persons, society, and nature, as well as the worthy and unworthy motives, desires, and goals that get conveyed to competent members of a moral community by the things other members of the community say and do to each other in everyday life (D'Andrade and Strauss 1992).

The Mind Reading of Mental States

That is not to suggest that the interpretive act called true ethnography is an easy act to follow. It is merely to suggest that the application of mental-state concepts to render the behavior of others intelligible is the only act in town, if we are to understand others as "persons." Precisely how difficult it can be to write a true ethnography is best illustrated with simple materials. Consider, for example, the relatively commonplace anthropological observation that in some culture's (among Tahitians, Oriyas, and Chinese, for example) people can be observed responding to apparent "loss" not (as the anthropologist expects them to respond) with expressions of sadness but rather with various kinds of bodily distress such as fatigue, backaches, or sickness. (See Kleinman 1986, Levy 1984, and Lazarus 1991 for a discussion of this type of case; see also Shweder 1993b, a response to Lazarus from which this discussion is drawn.) How do we represent what it is like to be such a people?

I think the way we do it is not by getting inside the other's head but by mind reading. Mind reading begins with conceptual analysis. We begin with an analysis of the concept of a person, which leads us to the concept of a mental life (symbolic capacity, self, will, belief, desire, rationality, feeling, and so on), which leads us to the concept of emotions (self-relevant feelings), which leads us to the concept of sadness, which leads us to the concept of loss. We observe the death of a child followed by the observation that his father or mother are evincing bodily distress but not evincing sadness. Constrained by a framework of meanings internal to our language for persons, mental states, emotions, and sadness, we go beyond what we have observed to generate a series of interpretive possibilities.

One possible interpretation is that the absence of sadness is only apparent, not real. According to this mind read the other has experienced a serious irreversible loss of something that is highly valued and therefore must be experiencing sadness, but either denies it, defends against it via some hypothesized process called somatization, or does not have a vocabulary for describing it or a nonverbal means of expressing it.

A second possible interpretation is that the loss was only apparent, not real. In the ethnographic literature the appraisal of loss is typically a judgment made by the observing anthropologist who has witnessed a circumstance (for example, death of a newborn infant) which he or she thinks of as loss. According to this mind read the other did not appraise things the way the anthropologist did (Scheper-Hughes 1990).

A third possible interpretation is that the loss was real but the other does not respond to loss emotionally. Several kinds of mind reads are possible here. Perhaps others do not respond to loss emotionally because: (1) they are not persons but rather some kind of being midway between robots and persons who can experience fatigue, sickness, and bodily distress but have no mental life (this is not a mind read that anthropologists are prone to make); (2) they are suffering from some kind of psychopathology that has switched off the causal connection between information processing and emotional experience; or (3) in their society a good way to cope with loss is to switch off the processes that bring emotional experiences online, much the way some people in my subculture are able to become fearless, emotionless, and focused when confronted with a sudden and very real threat to their life. (Perhaps in their society derealization or dissociation is a normal or realized state of mind.) One mind read we are blocked from making is that among others, irreversible loss is a context for the experience of pride or joy. We are blocked from making that interpretation by the limits of coherency established by the logic of our own mental-state concepts and language.

Notice that in constructing a true ethnography the other's self-report is neither a necessary nor sufficient datum for weeding out these interpretive possibilities. If the other should explicitly deny appraising the death of a child as a loss, that is grist for our interpretive mill, but we are also free to discount the testimony. If the other explicitly confirms appraising his or her circumstances as loss but claims to experience no sadness and gives off no evidence of experiencing sadness, again that is grist for our interpretive mill. We are free to either mind read an experience of sadness that is not expressed, or to take the other at his or her word, while either suspecting some form of pathology or some form of mental discipline that keeps the other from emotionalizing encounters with the world. Whichever interpretation we settle upon, a true ethnography is a mind read in which we rely on our mental state concepts to interpret the discourse and praxis of members of some moral community. Whatever interpretation we settle upon, we do not treat what people tell us in an interview as an incorrigible representation of their inner life but rather as one more piece of information to be made use of, as we construct a model of the mental state concepts exhibited in their behavior.

Building Conceptual Models

What does it mean for a concept or an idea to be exhibited in behavior and for an ethnographer to spell out the concept? Minimally what it means is that ethnography is the attempt to establish a correspondence between behaviors and something exhibited in those behaviors that is *analytically* external to and separable from the behaviors themselves. I say analytically external to the behaviors themselves because it is in the nature of cultural things in everyday life that often no analytic separation is made between a behavior and its meaning. The interpretation goes through rapidly and unself-consciously, and the behavior is apprehended as though it were ready-made. We see *in* the behavior (shaking hands) that which it exhibits (politeness). The vehicle of meaning becomes its meaning and it seems as though there is nothing to explain.

To clarify this point, let us assume for a moment that behaviors can be analyzed as alternatives in some choice set. Consider a person who is faced with two choice sets, (x,y) and (x,y,z), and chooses x from the first set and y from the second set. Arguing against the idea of "revealed preferences," economist Amartya Sen (1993:498–99) has pointed out that in and of themselves, acts of choice are not like statements, "which can contradict, or be consistent with, each other." He argues that the choice of x from the first set and y from the second set are not contradictory or inconsistent choices. They only become contradictory when we try to understand these choices in the light of some idea of what the person is trying to do, which means we invoke a frame of reference (motives, goals, concepts, principles) external to the choice. The choices only become contradictory or inconsistent choices once we interpret them as though they implied two statements of a particular kind, with the first choice entailing the statement "x is a better alternative than y" and the second choice entailing the statement "y is a better alternative than x." It is Sen's point that "being consistent or not consistent is not the kind of thing that can happen to choice functions without interpretation—without a presumption about the context that takes us beyond the choices themselves."

Indeed, the context may take us far beyond the behavior itself into the pragmatic meanings of the event. Thus Sen notes that while the statement

"x is a better alternative than y" is inconsistent with the statement "y is a better alternative than x," the pragmatic action of actually *saying* or *uttering* both statements "may not be really inconsistent in the way the two statements themselves are. . . . For example, the person making the statements may want to be taken as mentally unsound to establish diminished responsibility, or be taken as unfit to stand trial. Or simply want to confound the observer. Or check how people react to apparently contradictory statements." The aims of true ethnography are to construct a model of those statements and purposes that are exhibited in behavior and to turn that behavior into an action that must be read and interpreted, however rapidly, routinely, or unconsciously that reading is done.

Building a Conceptual Model: The Case of "Who Sleeps by Whom?"

Consider for example the universal system of behavior known as sleeping and the praxis of arranging the locations where members of a family sleep at night. "Who sleeps by whom" is not only a classic, if under-studied, problem for ethnographers. It is also a universal moral issue that is resolved in quite different ways around the world. Caudill and Plath's (1966) seminal research on Japanese sleeping arrangements revealed that from birth to death members of a Japanese family rarely sleep in a location or room of their own, and that they prefer not to do so, even when space is available. The praxis is an expression of their preferences and not a by-product of a resource constraint. Solitary sleeping (the kind of sleeping pattern forced upon young children by middle-class Anglo-American adults) is emotionally and mentally disturbing to the Japanese.

Sleeping arrangements are one of many practices of concern in my ongoing research on the moral basis of family life and life-span development in Bhubaneswar, Orissa, India (Shweder, Jensen and Goldstein 1995; Shweder 1991; Shweder, Mahapatra, and Miller 1990; Shweder, Much, Mahapatra, and Park 1994, in press). It is not feasible or permissible for outsiders to enter the interior spaces of Hindu family compounds to photograph who sleeps by whom, or to directly witness in what order, like peas in a pod, family members arrange themselves on cots or mats. What one can do is collect reports from members of households in which informants are asked in detail about where everyone had slept the night before. The ethnographic goal, however, is not only to document the praxis but to spell out the concepts or principles implicit in the choices being made about how to arrange family members in a common sleeping space.

We have recently constructed a cultural model of the concepts and principles implicit in Oriya sleeping practices in the temple town of Bhubaneswar (Shweder, Jensen, and Goldstein 1995). Although a record of actual sleeping patterns was at hand, we did not initially try to induce the cultural model from records of behavior. Actual families differ in size and in their age and sex structure, which makes the task of induction quite complex. It proved more fruitful to select a representative hypothetical family consisting of seven members (father, mother, son 15 years of age, son 11, son 8, daughter 14, daughter 3) and to ask insiders (Oriyas) and outsiders (Anglo-Americans in Hyde Park, the Chicago neighborhood in which the University of Chicago is located) to arrange and rearrange members of the family into sleeping spaces under different hypothetical resource constraints. You have one sleeping space. How would you arrange the seven family members? You have two sleeping spaces. You have three sleeping spaces. And so forth through seven sleeping spaces. The number of the sleeping spaces available is the resource constraint.

Although I do not have space to discuss the details of the Shweder, Jensen,and Goldstein (1995) analysis, I would make the following summary methodological remarks. First, it turns out upon logical analysis that there is a large number of ways to sort seven family members into up to seven sleeping spaces. Of course, there is only one way to sort seven people in one sleeping space, and only one way to sort them into seven sleeping spaces. But there are sixty-three ways to sort them into two sleeping spaces. A particular three-sleeping-space solution, for example— father, mother; son 15, son 11, son 8; daughter 14, daughter 3—is only one of 301 possible ways to sort the members of the family into three sleeping spaces. Overall there are 877 logically possible ways to sort the seven family members into one to seven sleeping spaces.

Second, of the 877 logically possible solutions very few, less than forty, are ever selected by any single Oriya or Anglo-American informant. Fewer than fifteen are selected by more than one informant. The solutions are highly constrained, and the task of the ethnographer is to explain all the missing cells by reference to as small a set of moral principles as possible. This is one way to get at "values"—not by asking directly (although direct questioning can sometimes be instructive), but by positing principles to make sense of actual choices.

Third, Shweder, Jensen, and Goldstein (1995) discover that a small set of moral concepts help explain both the missing cells in the hypothetical seven-person sleeping arrangements task, and the arrangements of family members (who slept by whom) in actual families in the temple town. For Oriyas there are four moral concepts implicit in their praxis, which can be listed in a precedence order as follows: incest avoidance, care of the dependent young (children do not sleep alone), female chastity anxiety (sexualized women do not sleep alone), hierarchical deference for males (mature males do not sleep with other males who must defer to them because there is an implication of disrespectful familiarity; status and familiarity drive each other out). For the Anglo-Americans there are three moral concepts implicit in their praxis, which can be listed in precedence order as follows: incest avoidance, the sacred couple, and autonomy.

Fourth, Shweder, Jensen, and Goldstein discover both dramatic similarities and dramatic differences in the moral concepts and principles implicit in this praxis in rural Hindu India and urban middle-class Anglo-America. For example, the single most important principle in both cultures is the same, incest avoidance. Thus, sexualized family members of different genders (father, daughter 14; son 15, daughter 14; mother, son 15) do not sleep together. All the other moral concepts implicit in their sleeping practices differentiate the cultures. Thus the second most important principle for the Anglo-Americans can be dubbed "the sacred couple." According to this principle, the husband and wife must sleep together and alone. This principle plays no part whatsoever in the choices made in Oriya culture about where people sleep, and it is a principle that is rarely acknowledged on a worldwide scale. The sacred couple principle places great constraints on possible solutions to the seven-person family problem (it rules out 92 percent of the possibilities), and indeed Anglo-Americans can conceive of fewer solutions than the Oriyas. For example, many Oriyas are willing to accept a two-sleeping-space solution that divides the males from the females and honors the incest avoidance rule. But this arrangement violates the sacred couple principle for Anglo-Americans and most of them find this "solution" entirely unacceptable. Many Anglo-Americans can come up with no solution under a two-sleeping-space constraint.

Finally, the research makes it easy to see why in constructing a true ethnography it is imperative to analytically distinguish preferences from constraints. On the ground, under particular resource constraints, the behavior of two communities may look more similar than an analysis of their cultural preferences would reveal. Thus, for example, rural Hindus and urban Anglo-Americans tend to converge in their solutions to the three-sleeping-space problem, despite the fact that their choices are regulated by somewhat different moral concepts and principles. Under a three-sleeping-space constraint Anglo-Americans strongly favor father and mother in one sleeping space; son 15, son 11, and son 8 in another; and daughter 14 and daughter 3 in the third. This is consistent with the two most important Anglo-American principles (incest avoidance and the sacred couple). Under the three-sleeping-space constraint, most Anglo-Americans are willing to compromise on the autonomy of the children. It is noteworthy that a plurality of Oriyas find this solution acceptable as well. This is because this solution is consistent with their top three principles (incest avoidance, care of the dependent young, chastity anxiety). Under the three-sleeping-space constraint, Oriyas are willing to compromise the hierarchical deference of males. It is true that even under the three-sleeping-space constraint, Oriyas do generate solutions that Anglo-Americans reject (for example, mother, daughter 14, daughter 3; father, son 8; son 15, son 11). Nevertheless, if one were to only observe the behavior of the two cultures at that (three sleeping spaces) resource level, one might be misled into thinking the two cultures were more or less the same. Only when one looks at behavior across a variety of resource constraints are true differences in cultural preferences (values, goals, and so on) revealed.

Evaluative Discourse and Praxis

In a recent essay called "A Theory of Culture for Demography," Eugene Hammel (1990) takes up the cause of true ethnography. Hammel, an anthropologist and a demographer, has the following things to say about true ethnography. He suggests that the social sciences would benefit from a "greater reliance on comparative studies of relatively small social units, however large and complex may be the societies within which these are embedded." He suggests that more information about social processes can be gathered by intensive investigation of a few cases than by the superficial examination of many. He suggests that cultural communities need not correspond to interest groups or even geographical units.

Hammel suggests that members of a cultural community acquire their culture through praxis; in other words, they resonate to, activate, or absorb unarticulated concepts and principles through exposure to behavior.[2] Hammel does suggest that ethnographers can make progress by collecting commentaries about actual behavioral events from focal participants. He suggests that members of the same culture share not only a language and specific customary behaviors but also an "evaluative discourse," and that the "value of culture for social analysis is not so much that the informants speak to the investigator, but that they speak to one another and can be overheard." He cautions ethnographers to make sure that what informants tell us about their behavior is what they tell one another (again the need for participant observation). Most importantly, Hammel suggests a definition of culture as the principles exhibited in the everyday evaluative discourse and behavior of members of some small-scale moral community (for example, a household).[3]

The Moral Community

An important implication of Hammel's essay is that a central aim of ethnographic theory is to identify the relevant moral communities that are embedded within any complex society. Members of a genuine moral community take an interest in sanctioning and regulating each other's behavior. They are usually conscious of themselves, and of their honor, prestige, and well-being as a moral community. As Greenwood has argued, true "social collectivities" (genuine moral communities) are "composed of individuals who are parties to sets of arrangements, conventions, and agreements," and they must be distinguished from mere "aggregate groups" (for example, all Americans who happen to be of Mexican descent).

It can generally be assumed that members of a household are networked in such way that they are members of the same moral community. Beyond that, as one moves to the level of neighborhoods or politically/economically motivated interest groups or census bureau categories, it is best not to assume. In the United States today global ethnic labels such as African American, Latino, West Indian, Jewish, White Anglo-Saxon Protestant, or non-Hispanic white are not likely to correspond to moral communities in the relevant ethnographic sense. The contemporary "tribes" of North America have yet to be properly identified.

It is the wager of many ethnographers in anthropology interested in life-span development that human development outcomes are mediated by behavior and that most systems of behavior are regulated by the norms of some local moral community. For example, it is well known that Mormons and Seventh Day Adventists and other puritanical and abstemious moral communities live about six years longer than other Americans. It is likely that this is the result of certain "right practices" or constrained preferences (such as taboos on smoking cigarettes and drinking alcohol) sanctioned by the moral community which have as their unintended consequence and secondary gain a reduction in levels of lung cancer or cirrhosis of the liver.

Or, to cite a second example, the Hindu moral community in rural India sanctions premarital chastity, arranged marriages, and joint family living in the ancestral household of the father of the groom. It is mandated that the bride shift her kinship affiliation and loyalties as she moves into her "mother-in-law's house" ("sasu gharo") and is inducted into the formal and highly ritualized status hierarchy of the residential kinship group of her husband. This kinship group (the "joint family") may well consist of several coresident brothers ranked by age across and within three generations, along with their status-conscious wives, mothers, and children. The status hierarchy is so ritualized that patterns of interpersonal contact in

the family are explicitly regulated by patterns of avoidance and stereotyped joking. A young married woman, for example, must never talk to
or be in the presence of her husband's older brothers, father, or father's
brothers. Indeed, she is not supposed to be witness to interpersonal contact between her husband and the higher-status males in the family, to
whom he must defer and show respect. While this is an effective way to
protect the self-esteem of the husband, in effect it means that a woman
and her husband avoid each other in the "public spaces" of the joint family compound.

Although it is not difficult to construct a plausible and intelligible model
of preferences and constraints to explain these marriage and residential
practices, it has been observed by anthropologists that young brides are
prone to displays of dissociative states such as spirit possession, list-
lessness, seizures (the kinds of behaviors that get you labeled as a "hys-
teric" in the pathologizing discourse of Western psychiatry). These young
brides have entered a well-marked social status or life stage ("jouvana")
that the moral community in Hindu society explicitly recognizes as a vulnerable, burdensome, and rather sad period in life. During this life stage
there is a major loss of autonomy, control, power, and social support.
Stereotyped weeping songs accompany the marriage rituals. Headaches
and other somatic complaints are common among mothers of brides. The
young bride, now living in her husband's ancestral home, is cut off from
her natal home and family and assumes a social position at the very bottom of the elaborate and explicit female (and male) prestige hierarchy.
This prestige hierarchy is a central reality of family life in rural India. It
confers shape, meaning, and dignity to the communal life of these three
generational patriarchal families (Menon and Shweder 1995).

In the tradeoff between autonomy and hierarchical community, women
in the community value community over autonomy. Yet in the early years
of married life they suffer the psychological consequences of this radical
reduction of personal control. They suffer whether the official culture
explicitly values autonomy and control or not, although, as Usha Menon's
recent research reveals so clearly (Menon 1995), they suffer without losing
a sense of the meaning and moral fabric of their lives.

There are other stresses as well. In the context of a moral community
that lives by the tenets of a communitarian ethic there is a value placed
on contributing to the group, which means that for Hindu women, fertility
can be a fearsome responsibility. Infertility or the wrong kind of fertility
produces great collective misery. The young daughter-in-law is well aware
that her future success and status in the family is closely connected to
reproductive success and to the realization of everyone's socially constrained preference for male children who will man the ancestral estate

and reap the benefits (rather than suffer the considerable costs) of the dowry system.

Recently Menon and I have been examining the lives of women in joint family households in the Hindu temple of Bhubaneswar (Menon and Shweder 1995). This is a community in which I have conducted anthropological research since 1968, with a special emphasis in recent years on the moral basis of family life practices. The research on women's lives has been carried out in connection with the activities of the MacArthur Foundation Research Network on Successful Midlife Development (MIDMAC), on ethnic and cross-cultural variations in the social and psychological context of health, happiness, and social responsibility in middle-aged adults.

One of the more striking discoveries from this research is that moral concepts that have been enshrined in Western academic theories of moral development (for example, autonomy, individual rights, justice as equality) play a rather secondary role in the moral psychology of Oriya Brahmans (Shweder 1990, 1991, 1994; Shweder, Mahapatra, and Miller 1990; Shweder and Much 1991; Shweder, Much, Mahapatra, and Park, in press). It is not that moral concepts such as rights and justice (as equality) are totally absent, but they are overshadowed by other far more elaborated and salient moral concepts. Indeed, on the basis of this research several of my associates and I have posited a "big three" theory of conceptual domains for moral reasoning and behavioral regulation. We refer to the big three moral domains as autonomy, community, and divinity (Shweder, Much, Mahapatra, and Park, forthcoming; Shweder 1990; Shweder and Haidt 1993; Haidt, Koller, and Dias 1993; Jensen 1995; Much 1992).

The morality of autonomy is quite puffed up and elaborated in the discourse and praxis of highly individualistic subcultures such as our own. Ideas such as freedom of choice and individual rights, and the moral and legal protection given to the satisfaction of personal wants, needs, and desires make it almost seem natural that every child should be given a room of his or her own or that parents should ask children what they want to eat for dinner before preparing the family meal. Within the framework of a morality of autonomy one of the very best reasons for having something is simply that you want it, and it is precisely that kind of reason that is often cultivated and advanced in individualistic subcultures. That is what the folk and philosophical doctrine of utilitarianism is all about.

However, within the context of family life in Orissa, India, it is the other two moralities that are elaborated in discourse and practice. The morality of community is concerned with obligations of station, social position, or role; its stress is upon the connection between social and personal identity and the embeddedness of the self within a larger community or team. Duty, sacrifice, loyalty, and respect are its central themes. The morality of divinity is concerned with concepts such as purity, sin, and the sacred order; its stress is upon the self as a spiritual entity able to approach divinity, able to be on speaking terms with God. Dignity and degradation, sanctity and pollution are its central themes.

Our ethnographic methods for studying the morality of family and social life in India have relied heavily on the observation of praxis, the analysis of various kinds of discourses about praxis, and the construction of hypothetical models representing in a mental-state language the principles exhibited in discourses about praxis, and in praxis itself. Manamohan Mahapatra, Nancy Much, Usha Menon, Lena Jensen, Jon Haidt, and others who have worked on moral evaluation in Bhubaneswar have listened to the voices of insiders expressed in well-known texts, in structured and unstructured interviews conducted by insiders and by outsiders, and in everyday household talk. The research goal is to make sure that ideas and concepts that are exhibited when informants talk to researchers are also exhibited when they talk to each other and when they speak with their actions as well as with their words.

The Idea of Plural Norms

The claim that there exist alternative moral goods (for example, autonomy, community, divinity) or a heterogeneous base set of moral ideals (justice, sympathy, fidelity, gratitude, respect) raises the question, What precisely do we mean when we speak about the existence of plural norms for human development? The aims of any true ethnography will be deeply influenced by the answer one gives to that perplexing question. The question is perplexing for the following reasons.

The idea of a norm is routinely analyzed into a descriptive sense (a report about what typically is the case) and a prescriptive sense (a report about what justifiably ought to be the case). A descriptive norm is a summary report made by some observer about what is regularly (or typically) the case for some designated population; for example, that in Bangladesh most villagers in endemic malaria areas do not sleep under mosquito nets, that in the United States wives do a greater share of the housework than do their husbands regardless of who earns a greater share of the family income, that 70 percent of African-American youths have had sexual intercourse by age fifteen, that among the Samburu people of Kenya it is commonplace for adults to perform clitoridectomies on adolescent girls, that marriages are arranged in India, that the slaughter of large mammals is prevalent among the Newars of Nepal for the sake of ritual sacrifice and among Anglo-Americans for the sake of food consumption.

The idea of the plural, of course, implies more than one, and, as everyone knows, the anthropological literature is in large measure a record of the existence of plural norms in the descriptive sense. It is a standard feature of anthropological research to document the existence of two or more populations, each with a different typical pattern of behavior (for example, arranged marriage versus love marriage), or to demonstrate that within a single population there is a bimodal or multimodal distribution of behaviors of a certain kind (for example, college-educated husbands in the United States differ from other married men in the amount of housework they do).

The anthropological documentation of plural norms in the descriptive sense has sometimes been extended to include documentation of plurality in the prescriptive norms of different populations. Prescriptive norms (the "ought" statements of some local authority: a parent, chief, government, or God) can, of course, be readily examined from a descriptive norm point of view. For example, some investigator might report that when it comes to stated ideas about what is right or wrong, good or bad, correct or incorrect, desirable or undesirable, a majority of adult Samburu women in Kenya think it is good or desirable for Samburu girls to be circumcised during adolescence, or that a majority of upper middle-class Anglo-American husbands assert that husbands and wives ought to equally share the burden of housework, or that ascetic fasting is judged to be pathological by the American Psychiatric Association.

But notice that when prescriptive norms are studied only from a descriptive point of view, claims about plural norms amount to little more than the proposition that there is variety in things that are desired by different people in different times and places. Such a proposition does not come close to touching on the far more controversial topic that is definitive of moral studies and at the heart of the very idea of prescriptive norms, namely, whether there is plurality in what is *desirable,* not just in what is *desired.* Critics of pluralism will be quick to point out that just because there is diversity in what people do or desire to do does not mean there is diversity in what is desirable or in what people justifiably ought to do.

Here we enter a territory of critical moral discourse that positivistically oriented anthropologists (the pure descriptivists) have often tried to avoid. The preferred positivistic strategy of restricting one's interest to the study of plural norms only in the descriptive sense may work tolerably well for the study of language diversity or diversity in systems of kinship classification, but it fails miserably when it comes to the comparative study of human development.

It fails because the very idea of human development implies some desirable state of functioning (a goal or end state) that is not immediately or readily available to human beings but must be achieved or cultivated by means of some process or practice. Notice that the idea of human development can be applied to any domain of human functioning—somatic functioning (physical health), emotional, motivational, intellectual, moral, or spiritual functioning (mental health), interpersonal or social functioning (social health). Notice too that the idea of human development does not permit the reduction of prescriptive norms to mere descriptive or positivistic study. Quite the contrary, the idea of human development privileges the prescriptive sense of the normative. Thus within the terms of the idea of human development the descriptive study of human development becomes the study of means or processes for promoting some desirable end state, which presupposes (at the very least) the identification of some prescriptively desirable end state for healthy functioning.

This is true as well of the idea of plural norms for human development, which may be used prescriptively to suggest that there is no uniform or singular account that can be given of the states of functioning that are desirable for all human beings. This prescriptive pluralistic claim amounts to a defense of the proposition that what human beings justifiably ought to strive for in somatic, emotional, moral, intellectual, and spiritual development varies across time (history), space (population or culture), social position (for example, class) and gender.

Of course, the idea of plural norms for human development may be used in a subordinate descriptive sense. As a pure descriptive claim the idea of plural norms for human development merely suggests that across time, space, social position, and gender the processes and practices that in fact work best as a means for promoting some desirable end state can be given no uniform or singular account. But notice here that in the absence of a prior prescriptive pluralistic claim (that there exists variety in the end states that human beings justifiably ought to strive to develop), this descriptive pluralistic claim reduces to the noncontroversial conception of a world in which there are many means to the same end, many roads that lead to Rome.

The idea of taking context into account often amounts to a descriptive pluralistic claim of that sort; for example, that in a tropical rain forest the best way to deliver protein to a young child is through three years of breast feeding, while this may not be the best way in Boston; or that the best way to develop literacy skills in an upper middle-class Anglo-American classroom is with teaching techniques that are laissez-faire and egalitarian, while this may not be the best way in a working-class Mexican-American classroom; or that the best way to develop senses of loyalty, gratitude, and justice in West Africa is through ordeals and hardships imposed on children, while this may not be the best way in Scarsdale, New York; or that a good way to avoid heart disease in Norway is by giving up cigarette smoking, while this makes little difference in Japan. Notice that in each example the pluralistic claim is a descriptive claim about variety in effective means. Such descriptive claims can be provocative, for they may imply that different treatment conditions should be applied to different persons or peoples to promote their developmental competence. But notice as well that in each example it is a unitary rather than pluralistic prescriptive norm for physical, intellectual, or moral health (the same prescriptive norm for all human beings) that is presupposed by the descriptive claim that there are alternative means to the same (desirable) end.

It is, of course, fascinating and important to document cases where processes and practices for promoting desirable states of somatic, emotional, intellectual, moral, or social functioning are effective for one population but not for another, where different peoples flourish under different treatment conditions, and where aggregate human development is diminished by treating everyone alike. There is, however, a deeper and far more controversial meaning to the idea of plural norms for human development, which arises whenever the idea is used in its prescriptive sense.

I suspect that many ethnographers would like to use the idea of plural norms for human development in its more controversial, prescriptive sense. I suspect they would like to propose that the end states that are truly desirable for human beings cannot be specified in the abstract and without qualification by reference to time, place, social position, or gender; that states of functioning that are pathological for one people may be healthy for another; that states of emotional, social, and motivational functioning that justifiably ought to be promoted in Japan or China are not necessarily those that ought to be promoted in other times or places; that, for example, it might be healthy for Chinese mothers to shame and tease their children or for Japanese parents to sleep with their children until adolescence, while this would not be healthy or desirable for Anglo-American parents.

For the sake of the theoretical development of a defensible prescriptive pluralism it is important for ethnographers to realize that it is not going to be easy to defend such propositions. At the very least ethnographers are going to have to ponder the profound question, What justifies the "ought" implicit in the idea of human development? At the very least they are going to have to show that the plurality of norms that so fascinates them is really a plurality of ends and not just of means (shaming and teasing in China, for example, might be interpreted or represented as merely an alternative means to some unitary and justifiable "higher" end, which the Western anthropologist and the Chinese parent both acknowledge as a "common good"). They are going to have to show that plurality is a terminal (rather than an intermediary) state of moral reality. One strategy for defending the idea of plural norms in the prescriptive sense can be found in Shweder and Haidt (1993), where it is argued that what human beings have in common is a base set of plural goods or virtues (like justice, beneficence, fidelity, loyalty, gratitude, and so on). Yet those multiple goods, which everyone in the world recognizes as goods, at least in the abstract, are inherently in conflict and cannot be activated at the same time or in the same social practices. Much more work is needed to add force and substance to the proposition that what is truly desirable is not the same around the world. Extreme and unqualified formulations of a prescriptive pluralistic proposition are not likely to be cogent, which is why, speaking as a pluralist, I believe we need to reformulate the idea of psychic unity along the lines of the principle of original multiplicity, as discussed earlier. We are multiple from the start. It is that original multiplicity that constitutes our common humanity. It is that original multiplicity which makes mutual sympathetic understanding of differences possible.

Power and the Idea of Moral Authority

So far I have been discussing culture as a characteristic of a moral community. Now I want to clarify the relationship between power and moral authority, and make the point that while a moral community is never merely a power order, any social ordering of human beings that is a moral ordering must be a power ordering as well. In other words, with due respect to those culture critics (Marxist, feminist, deconstructionist) who think otherwise, *power* is not necessarily a dirty word.

Try to imagine a society lacking both power and moral authority. The thought experiment is not difficult because all one has to do is imagine a society of fully developed and autonomous human beings in which each and every member of society recognizes that he or she is fully developed and autonomous and that everyone else is as well. In such an ideal society everyone is fully developed and autonomous in the sense that everyone pursues worthy goals, possesses accurate knowledge about how to reach those goals, and controls the means or instrumentalities for doing so. In such a society there is no place for the exercise of power or moral authority because there is no need or capacity for any one to be under any one else's governance.

So much for the thought experiment. The societies that anthropologists study are always peopled by vulnerable and only partially developed human beings whose autonomy (in the sense just described) is always compromised to some greater or lesser degree. Real human beings do not always know what is in their true interests or how to accomplish their goals.

They act under duress, lacking perfect foresight or information about the consequences of their actions. More often than not they lack total control over the resources they need to get what they want or ought to have. It is largely because human beings are vulnerable and only partially developed (in the sense just described) that the social order has evolved as a moral order, and as a power order as well.

Between power and moral authority, power is the more encompassing and general notion. Power is defined by a person's ability to get others to do what one wants regardless of the means used to get others to do it. The means might include intimidation, muscling, bribery, or other means for creating and manipulating the emotion of fear. It is conceivable that the force associated with power is ultimately explainable in terms of a theory of human emotions. Indeed, it would be fascinating to classify forms of power on the basis of the type of emotion (fear, shame, guilt, humiliation, sympathy) that ultimately motivates one person to comply with the wants of powerful others.

Moral authority can be distinguished from power, but the distinction is not one of opposition or contrast. Moral authority is a specific or particular type of instantiation of power, because when you have moral authority you can get others to do what you want, and that is what power is all about. Moral authority, however, is that special form of power that is empowered by virtue of its connection to ideas about what is right and good. That means there is an asymmetry between moral authority and power. Not all forms of power have moral authority, because some forms of power are unconnected to acknowledged ideas about what is right and good. (It should be noted, however, that even moral authority may work most effectively when it is connected to emotions such as fear, shame, disgust, and guilt).

To the extent a true ethnography is a characterization of both preferences and constraints it must take account of the power system of a community. Although these systems vary in numerous ways, at least the following three types of power orders can be conceptualized, which I shall label "pure moral authority," "paternalism" (or "parentalism"), and "authoritarianism."

Pure moral authority refers to a power order where agents do what others with moral authority want them to do because agents recognize that it is in their own true interest to do so. In such a case, the power of the person with moral authority derives from his or her ability to augment the development and autonomy of others, and such power of moral authority is held by virtue of the recognition of others that this is so. Moral authority comes from knowing things others do not know or being able to make available to others resources or instrumentalities that others do not control. The idea of expertise (the expert is the prototype of a person with pure moral authority) is relevant here. Also relevant is the forthright recognition, so commonplace in many of the world's religious traditions, of the limits of one's own power and knowledge and the need for complementarity and interdependence in social life.

A paternalistic power order contrasts with a power order based on pure moral authority. Paternalism refers to a power order where agents do not do what others with moral authority want them to do, because agents do not recognize others as having moral authority, even though they do. In such a system those with moral authority are in fact in a position to promote the "true interests" of others; those with paternalistic power have the power to force others "against their will" to do what is right and good. If you are a paternalistic moral authority then you have two choices vis-à-vis those who refuse to acknowledge you as a pure moral authority: coercion (you can strong arm others to do what is in their true interests) and benign neglect (you can allow others to act against their own true interests, with the hope that they will come to recognize the limits of their own autonomy and ultimately freely choose to augment their capacities in various ways, perhaps even by acknowledging the pure moral authority of those who have it).

Finally there is authoritarianism. Authoritarianism refers to a power order where agents do not do what others want them to do because those with power do not have the agents' true interests in mind and the agents know it. In other words, those in power lack moral authority; they act to negate rather than augment the autonomy and development of others. In authoritarian power orders, those in power act in such a way that only their own interests are served, and no one can stop them from doing so.

Notice that the very idea of pure moral authority, paternalism, and authoritarianism as categories of power rests on the presupposition that it is reasonable to distinguish between a person's true interests and a person's mere wants or preferences. For a social or cultural theorist to even conceptualize such power categories and distinctions between forms of power and authority, he or she must assume that not all wants and preferences are good or worthy. He or she must reject the claim that merely wanting something is a good reason for having it. To the extent that true ethnography provides an account of power at all it must do so by first putting forward some moral conception of the good, some moral conception of the worthy goals of life. In other words, the analysis of culture as a moral order and the analysis of culture as a power order are not hostile enterprises. Quite the contrary, they depend on each other.

Life Satisfaction in Another Cultural World

What is it like to live in another cultural world, with a different set of preferences, under a different set of constraints? Alas, only a true ethnography can answer that question. The best I can do in this essay is talk about true ethnography rather than produce one. I would mention in passing, however, one aspect of some research Usha Menon and I have been conducting on life satisfaction and successful adult development among women in rural India (Menon and Shweder forthcoming; Menon, 1995).

The most satisfying periods of life for women are patterned somewhat differently in India and in the United States. In Hindu moral communities in rural India, at least among high-caste communities, the taboo on divorce is a preferred constraint (despite the laws of the land). Thus women have a more secure license to engage in conflicts with their husbands. By the time a reproductively successful woman has reached the culturally specified life stage of mature adulthood ("prauda") (approximately thirty-five to sixty years of age), she has moved up in the family prestige hierarchy and has gained considerable control over her life and the lives of other women. She is deeply embedded in family social networks, the value of which she perceives to more than compensate her for the culturally acknowledged "sadness" produced by the intense social constraints on her mobility and autonomy during the earlier life stage of "jouvana" (the stage between marriage and mature adulthood).

A typical Oriya housewife in a Brahmanical joint family compound is acutely self-conscious about matters of social standing and social position and far less concerned about matters of physical appearance and psychological well-being. Indeed, the life course tends to be defined into five stages primarily on the basis of the kinship-based social statuses and responsibilities associated with fertility, marriage, childbearing, and family management.

One big life-course divide is between life in my father's house ("bapa gharo") and life in my mother-in-law's house ("sasu gharo"). Life in my father's house is divided into life before versus life after the time (approximately seven to nine years of age) when a child begins to pray for itself and knows the difference between right and wrong. At that time the undisciplined child ("pila") becomes a morally formative youth ("kishoro"). Life in my mother-in-law's house begins as a newly wed daughter-in-law ("jouvana") and ends with the explicit social markings and restrictions of widowhood ("briddha"). The burdens and social responsibilities of life peak in young adulthood. Widowhood is a socially formalized period of perpetual mourning and ascetic renunciation. Remarriage is prohibited. No cosmetics and only white saris are worn. A series of food taboos are imposed; there are prohibitions against fish, meat, garlic, onions, or any other food that might (by the lights of the local theory of hot and cold foods) stimulate the senses or arose feelings of sensuality. Life is spent in penance and prayer and in absolving oneself of spiritual debts (or what we call sins).

Mature adulthood ("prauda") contrasts sharply with the burdens of early adulthood and the penance of widowhood. In between a period of monotonous drudgery and fateful asceticism is a stage of life where one is likely to be an experienced mother-in-law, with a high standing in the prestige hierarchy and with the capacity to manage and control the family and to be somewhat withdrawn from the laborious demands of the daily family routine.

Oriya women in extended family households have idyllic memories of life in their father's house. Indeed, I would predict that a surprising number of them would say that six to ten years of age is the very best age to be. Aside from early childhood, however, it is the years of mature adulthood, after raising children and before sixty years of age, that they view as the most satisfying and happiest years in a life.

The reverse seems to be true for Anglo-American women. In the United States the autonomy and freedom of young married life is frequently followed by a period of vulnerability associated with foreboding signs of aging and an intense concern about attractiveness. Given the absence of any major social constraints concerning divorce, there is for many women a sense of anxiety and disappointment over the lack of reliability and loyalty of middle-aged males. For others there is the sense of isolation from children and other kin. There are the mental and physical costs of divorce. For midlife Anglo-American women in the United States, self-esteem is measured against many yardsticks, but not typically or primarily against the yardstick of social responsibility within a hierarchy of coresiding kin. This contrasting trajectory of perceived life satisfactions between Oriya and Anglo-American women can be seen in figure 1.

If solipsism makes ethnography seem impossible, superficialism makes it appear far easier than it really is. Superficialism is the view that the only way you can ever know anything about someone who has a mental life is by asking him or her the same English question that you are going to ask everyone else in the world, and by insisting that the responses be kept short. In figure 1 I engage in a bit of superficialism, which I hope can now be deepened or thickened or fattened up by all the contextualizations and local meanings I have tried to provide in my very brief summary of the moral world of Hindu joint family life.

In the course of conducting very detailed and intimate interviews with sixty-six Oriya women of various ages, Usha Menon asked them to assess

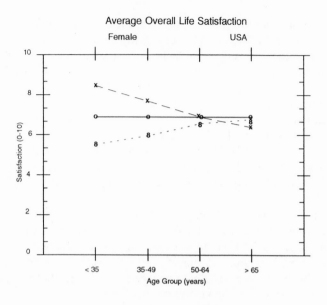

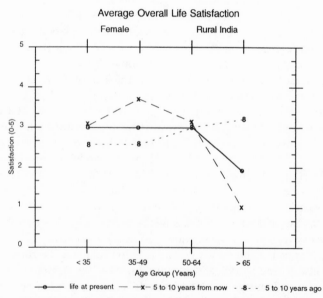

Figure 1. The American data were collected and analyzed by Paul Cleary and his associates at Harvard University. I am grateful for the opportunity to use this unpublished material as a point of comparison with the data from India.

their past, present, and future life satisfaction on a five-point scale. She asked about the ratio of positive and negative events in their lives five to ten years ago, now, and as anticipated five to ten years hence. Comparable data, surveying American women about past, present, and future life satisfaction (how satisfied are you with your life on a ten-point scale) had been previously collected by Paul Cleary and his associates at the Harvard Medical School.

The American findings (fig. 1) suggest that (on the average) adult women report the same level of life satisfaction (seven on a ten-point scale) no matter what age they are. Female adults less than fifty years of age remember a past that was less satisfying than the present and anticipate a future that is more satisfying than the present. The younger the female adult the greater is the discrepancy between past, present, and future life satisfaction. The promise of the future in comparison to the present slowly declines in a linear fashion until, somewhere between fifty and sixty-four years of age, the past is no longer remembered as worse than the present and the future is no longer anticipated with optimism. I want to use these unpublished results from Cleary's research as a point of comparison with the local Oriya scene.

The data on Oriya women are based on very small samples compared to the American survey research. Nevertheless, a very suggestive pattern is revealed that highlights both similarities and differences with the American results. The pattern makes good cultural sense, given all the things I have said about what it is like to be an Oriya housewife in a traditional joint family household.

The results in figure 1 suggest that, just like American women, Oriya women less than fifty years of age remember a past that was less satisfying than the present and anticipate a future that will be more satisfying than the present. And just like American women, they eventually stop looking toward the future with optimism somewhere between fifty and sixty-four years of age. That much is the same across the two cultural worlds.

Nevertheless, two striking differences appear in the life-course phenomenology of these Oriya women. For one thing, Oriya women do not exhibit a linear decline in anticipated future life satisfaction as they move from their twenties into their thirties and forties. Quite the contrary, it is the period of mature adulthood that excites the greatest anticipation of positive life satisfaction. Second, the Oriya women exhibit a dramatic decline in both present and anticipated life satisfaction as they enter old age. Given all that I have said about the burdens and responsibilities of low-status brides and about the culturally marked and elaborated requirements of a mournful ascetic widowhood, it should be possible to contextualize these results. It should also be possible to suggest that evaluations of personal well-being are not driven only by the universal reality of aging, but are driven as well by the institutions and meanings of one's local moral community.

The Native's Point of View

In this essay I have suggested that a true ethnography is a hypothetical model representing the preferences and constraints exhibited in the behavior (discourse and praxis) of members of a moral community. This is not to say that a true ethnography must adduce good reasons for the customs of others which they cannot adduce for themselves. Long before any ethnographer arrives and tries to move in, members of most moral communities have constructed models of and for their own behavior, which they display to one another through that common form of behavior that Hammel and many others have labeled "evaluative discourse." By means of evaluative discourse members of most moral communities comment on their preferences and constraints, socialize and sanction their members, and seek to maintain their honor, prestige, and well-being. The observation of everyday evaluative discourse by members of a moral community offers the ethnographer a glimpse of the official cultural model constructed by insiders to represent to themselves and (sometimes) to others the meanings exhibited in their own behavior. So it is a mistake to assume that insiders cannot speak for themselves.

On the other hand, it is also a mistake to assume that the official cultural model constructed by insiders must be the best or only way to model the preferences and constraints exhibited in the behavior of members of a moral community. While the insider is entitled to the first say (and may well turn out to be an expert at constructing a model of the preferences and constraints exhibited in observed behavior), not all members of a moral community are experts about their own way of life.

In one recent study of narrated meanings about a core religious icon in Bhubaneswar, Menon and Shweder (1994) discovered that knowledge about the Great Goddess of Hinduism is culturally structured yet quite unevenly distributed across ninety-two members of the temple town community.

The meanings were culturally structured in the following sense. The twenty-five most frequently mentioned meanings associated with the icon of the Goddess Kali formed a rather neat Guttman scale. That is to say, it was possible to predict which meanings would be mentioned by any particular narrator by simply knowing how many meanings were mentioned, and those meanings which were mentioned by the fewest narrators were mentioned by precisely those narrators who knew the most about the icon.

Yet the meanings were also unevenly distributed. Less than 25 percent of the members of this rather close-knit community were highly expert in the meanings of one of the most important symbols in their local moral world.

In other words, when it comes to representing the "native's point of view," there is no solipsistic privilege accorded to what insiders say. Like the thing called culture itself, the native's point of view is nothing more than a theoretical model, articulated in a mental-state language (a folk psychologese) intelligible to the ethnographer, and constructed as a theoretical representation of the hypothesized preferences and constraints exhibited in the observed behavior of some "other."

It is the native's point of view because it is the native's behavior that is being modeled, not the ethnographer's. That model of the native's behavior is mentalistic. It personifies and represents the other as a subject, not as an object. The model is derived from a theory of true ethnography that is antisolipsistic and promentalistic. The native's point of view is a construction. No one has to actually climb inside anyone else's head to understand that point of view. It does not really matter who constructs the model, us or them, as long as it provides a plausible and intelligible account of the concepts and ideas exhibited in the behavior of a designated moral community.

Every attempt to understand what it is like to be another person or people runs the risk of going too far in the direction of solipsism, or, alternatively, too far in the direction of superficiality. A truly true ethnography stays on course between a self-indulgent narcissism and a shallow humanism, making it possible for us to contemplate the meaning of life in a premodern frame of mind. A true ethnography may even make it possible for a French anthropologist to understand what it is like to live outside a Gallic world.

Acknowledgment

An earlier version of this essay was presented as the keynote address at the meeting entitled "Meaning and Context: A Conference on Ethnographic Approaches to the Study of Human Development," organized by Richard Jessor and Anne Colby, 9–13 June 1993, at the Claremont Resort, Oakland, California. The essay was prepared with support from the Mac-Arthur Foundation Research Network on Adolescence, and the Mac-Arthur Foundation Research Network on Successful Midlife Development (MIDMAC), for which I am deeply grateful. My observations about Evans-Pritchard and graduate school training in anthropology at Harvard University were previously published in Shweder (1986).

Notes

1. Alas, there is this deep irony inherent in the ethnographic enterprise, for one is likely to become bored with otherness as soon as the other is so well understood that his or her behavior, which once seemed astonishing, comes to seem common-sensical, commonplace, and merely routine. Fortunately for ethnography, one can never be everyone at once—otherness will never be in short supply.

2. Perhaps it is for this reason that one would not want to construct a grammar of a language by relying on what speakers of a language might tell you about their grammar. That would be data for the study of ethnogrammatical "theories" but not necessarily data for the study of the grammar of their language. To get the latter type of data one would want to go through some type of dialectical process whereby spoken sentences were judged for grammatical "acceptability" by "competent" speakers, while at the same time speakers were judged for grammatical competence by reference to sentences known to be grammatically acceptable. Yes, the process is circular, but not necessarily vicious.

3. Recent research conducted in Zaire by Robert Aunger (1994) on the reliability of repeated interviews about food taboos provides some justification for a heavy reliance in data collection on the interpersonal and linguistic skills of insiders. A visiting anthropologist may not be as good as indigenous native interviewers at eliciting stable and reliable verbal responses. Aunger discovers that the information provided by indigenous folk about their food taboos in two repeated identically formatted interview sessions is more likely to be the same information when the interviewer is a cultural compatriot rather than an anthropologist. On the other hand, I would suggest that the role of "outsider" may have certain benefits in that informants may be willing to disclose to a temporary visitor information that would threaten their reputation if offered to a cultural compatriot.

References

Aunger, R. 1994. "Sources of Variation in Ethnographic Interview Data: Food Avoidances in the Ituri Forest, Zaire." *Ethnology* 33:65–99.

Caudill, W., and D. W. Plath. 1966. "Who Sleeps by Whom? Parent-Child Involvement in Urban Japanese Families." *Psychiatry* 29:344–66.

D'Andrade, R. G., and C. Strauss, eds. 1992. *Human Motives and Cultural Models.* New York: Cambridge University Press.

Evans-Pritchard, E. E. 1937. *Witchcraft, Oracles and Magic among the Azande.* Oxford: Clarendon Press.

Geertz, C. 1984. "From the Native's Point of View." In *Culture Theory: Essays on Mind, Self and Emotion.* Ed. R. A. Shweder and R. A. LeVine, 123–36. New York: Cambridge University Press.

Greenwood, J. D. Unpublished. "Durkheim, Weber, and the Demarkation of the Social." Available from John D. Greenwood, 29 Sheppard Ln., Stony Brook, NY 11790.

Haidt, J., S. H. Koller, and M. G. Dias. 1993. "Affect, Culture, and Morality, or,

Is It Wrong to Eat Your Dog?" *Journal of Personality and Social Psychology* 65:613–25.

Hammel, E. 1990. "A Theory of Culture for Demography." *Population and Development Review* 16:455–85.

Jensen, L. 1995. "Habits of the Heart Revisited: Autonomy, Community, and Divinity in Adults' Moral Language." *Qualitative Sociology* 18:71–86.

Kleinman, A. 1986. *Social Origins of Distress and Disease.* New Haven, Conn.: Yale University Press.

Levy, R. I. 1984. "Emotion, Knowing and Culture." In *Culture Theory: Essays on Mind, Self and Emotion.* Ed. R. A. Shweder and R. A. LeVine. New York: Cambridge University Press.

Lazarus, R. S. 1991. *Emotion and Adaptation.* New York: Oxford University Press.

Mahapatra, M. 1981. *Traditional Structure and Change in an Orissan Temple.* Calcutta: Punthi Pustak.

Menon, U. 1995. "Receiving and Giving: Distributivity as the Source of Women's Well-Being." Ph.D. diss., University of Chicago.

Menon, U., and R. A. Shweder. 1994. "Kali's Tongue: Cultural Psychology and the Power of 'Shame' in Orissa, India." In *Emotion and Culture.* Ed. H. Markus and S. Kitayama, 241–84. Washington, D.C.: A.P.A. Publications.

———. Forthcoming. "The Return of the White Man's Burden: The Encounter Between the Moral Discourse of Anthropology and the Domestic Life of Oriya Women." In *Midlife and Other Cultural Fictions.* Ed. R. A. Shweder. Chicago: University of Chicago Press.

Much, N. C. 1992. "Analysis of Discourse as Methodology for a Semiotic Psychology." *American Behavioral Scientist* 36:52–72.

Scheper-Hughes, N. 1990. "Mother Love and Child Death in Northeastern Brazil." In *Cultural Psychology: Essays on Comparative Human Development.* Ed. J. Stigler, R. A. Shweder, and G. Herdt, 542–65. New York: Cambridge University Press.

Sen, A. 1993. "Internal Consistency of Choice." *Econometrica* 61:495–521.

Shweder, R. A. 1986. "Storytelling among the Anthropologists." *New York Times Book Review,* 21 Sept., 1, 38–39.

———. 1990. "In Defense of Moral Realism." *Child Development* 61:2060–68.

———. 1991. *Thinking through Cultures: Expeditions in Cultural Psychology.* Cambridge, Mass.: Harvard University Press.

———. 1993a. "The Cultural Psychology of the Emotions." In *The Handbook of Emotions.* Ed. M. Lewis and J. Haviland. New York: Guilford Publications.

———. 1993b. "Everything You Ever Wanted to Know About Cognitive Appraisal Theory without Being Conscious of It: A Review of Lazarus, R. S., *Emotion and Adaptation.*" *Psychological Inquiry* 4:322–42.

———. 1993c. "Why Do Men Barbecue? and Other Ironies of Growing Up in the Decade of Ethnicity." *Daedalus* 122:279–308.

———. 1994. Are Moral Intuitions Self-Evident Truths?" *Criminal Justice Ethics* 13:24–31.

Shweder, R. A., and J. Haidt. 1993. "The Future of Moral Psychology: Truth, Intuition, and the Pluralist Way." *Psychological Science* 4:360–65.

Shweder, R. A., L. Jensen, and W. M. Goldstein. 1995. "Who Sleeps by Whom Revisited: A Method for Extracting the Moral Goods Implicit in Practice." In *Cultural Practices as Contexts for Development.* Ed. J. Goodnow, P. Miller, and F. Kessel. San Francisco: Jossey-Bass.

Shweder, R. A., and R. A. LeVine, eds. 1984. *Culture Theory: Essays on Mind, Self and Emotion.* Cambridge: Cambridge University Press.

Shweder, R. A., M. Mahapatra, and J. G. Miller. 1990. "Culture and Moral Development." In *The Emergence of Moral Concepts in Early Childhood.* Ed. J. Kagan and S. Lamb, 130–204. Chicago: University of Chicago Press.

Shweder, R. A., U. Menon. 1993. "The Story of Kali's 'Shame' and the Authority of 'Original Texts'; or, Tales 'You Can Find in the Puranas' Which Are Not Really There." Unpublished.

Shweder, R. A., and N. C. Much. 1991. "Determinations of Meaning: Discourse and Moral Socialization." In Shweder, *Thinking through Cultures: Expeditions in Cultural Psychology.* Cambridge, Mass.: Harvard University Press, 186–240.

Shweder, R. A., N. C. Much, M. Mahapatra, and L. Park. Forthcoming. "The 'Big Three' of Morality (Autonomy, Community, Divinity), and the 'Big Three' Explanations of Suffering." In *Morality and Health.* Ed. A. Brandt and P. Rozin. New York: Routledge.

3 The Epistemology of Qualitative Research

HOWARD S. BECKER

Qualitative and Quantitative

It is rhetorically unavoidable, discussing epistemological questions in social science, to compare qualitative and ethnographic methods with those which are quantitative and survey: to compare, imaginatively, a field study conducted in a community or organization with a survey of that same community or organization undertaken with questionnaires, self-administered or put to people by interviewers who see them once, armed with a printed form to be filled out. The very theme of this conference assumed such a division.

Supposing that the two ways of working are based on different episte-mological foundations and justifications leads to asking the question posed to me by the conference's organizers: What's the epistemology of qualitative research? To me, it's an odd question. I'm an intellectual de-scendant of Robert E. Park, the founder of what has come to be called the Chicago school of sociology. Park was a great advocate of what we now call ethnographic methods. But he was equally a proponent of quantitative methods, particularly ecological ones. I follow him in that, and to me, the similarities between these methods are at least as, and probably more, important and relevant than the differences. In fact, I think that the same epistemological arguments underlie and provide the warrant for both.

How so? Both kinds of research try to see how society works, to de-scribe social reality, to answer specific questions about specific instances of social reality. Some social scientists are interested in very general de-scriptions, in the form of laws about whole classes of phenomena. Others are more interested in understanding specific cases, how those general statements worked out in this case. But there's a lot of overlap.

The two styles of work do place differing emphasis on the understanding of specific historical or ethnographic cases as opposed to general laws of social interaction. But the two styles also imply one another. Every analysis of a case rests, explicitly or implicitly, on some general laws, and every general law supposes that the investigation of particular cases would show that law at work. Despite the differing emphases, it all ends up with the same sort of understanding, doesn't it?

That kind of ecumenicism clearly won't do, because the issue does not go away. To point to a familiar example, although educational researchers have done perfectly good research in the qualitative style for at least sixty years, they still hold periodic conferences and discussions, like this one, to discuss whether it's legitimate and, if it is, why it is. Surely there must be some real epistemological difference between the methods that accounts for this continuing inability to settle the question.

Some Thoughts About Epistemology

Let's first step back and ask about epistemology as a discipline. How does it see its job? What kinds of questions does it raise? Like many other philosophical disciplines, epistemology has characteristically concerned itself with "oughts" rather than "is's," and settled its questions by reasoning from first principles rather than by empirical investigation. Empirical disciplines, in contrast, have concerned themselves with how things work rather than what they ought to be, and settled their questions empirically.

Some topics of philosophical discussion have turned into areas of empirical inquiry. Scholars once studied biology and physics by reading Aristotle. Politics, another area philosophers once controlled, was likewise an inquiry in which scholars settled questions by reasoning rather than by investigation. We can see some areas of philosophy, among them epistemology, going through this transformation now, giving up preaching about how things should be done and settling for seeing how they are in fact done.

Aesthetics, for instance, has traditionally been the study of how to tell art from nonart and, especially, how to tell great art from ordinary art. Its thrust is negative, concerned primarily with catching undeserving candidates for the honorific title of art and keeping such pretenders out. The sociology of art, the empirical descendant of aesthetics, gives up trying to decide what should and shouldn't be allowed to be called art, and instead describes what gets done under that name. Part of its enterprise is exactly to see how that honorific title—art—is fought over, what actions it justifies, and what users of it can get away with (Becker 1982:131–64).

Epistemology has been a similarly negative discipline, mostly devoted to saying what you shouldn't do if you want your activity to merit the title of science, and to keeping unworthy pretenders from successfully appropriating it. The sociology of science, the empirical descendant of epistemology, gives up trying to decide what should and shouldn't count as science, and tells what people who claim to be doing science do, how the term is fought over, and what people who win the right to use it can get away with (Latour 1987).

So this chapter will not be another sermon on how we ought to do science, and what we shouldn't be doing, and what evils will befall us if we do the forbidden things. Rather, it will talk about how ethnographers have produced credible, believable results, especially those results which have continued to command respect and belief.

Such an enterprise is, to be philosophical, quite Aristotelian, in line with the program of the *Poetics,* which undertook not to legislate how a tragedy ought to be constructed but rather to see what was true of tragedies which successfully evoked pity and terror, producing catharsis. Epistemologists have often pretended to such Aristotelian analysis, but more typically deliver sermons.

Why Do We Think There's a Difference?

Two circumstances seem likely to produce the alleged differences between qualitative and quantitative epistemologists of social science make so much of. One is that the two sorts of methods typically raise somewhat different questions at the level of data, on the way to generalizations about social life. Survey researchers use a variant of the experimental paradigm, looking for numerical differences between two groups of people differing in interesting ways along some dimension of activity or background. They want to find that adolescents whose parents have jobs of a higher socioeconomic status are less likely to engage in delinquency, or more likely, or whatever—a difference from which they will then infer other differences in experience or possibilities that will "explain" the delinquency. The argument consists of an "explanation" of an act based on a logic of difference between groups with different traits (see Abbott 1992).

I don't mean to oversimplify what goes on in such work. The working out of the logic can be, and almost always is, much more complicated than this. Researchers may be concerned with interaction effects, and with the way some variables condition the relations between other variables, in all this striving for a complex picture of the circumstances attending someone's participation in delinquency.

Fieldworkers usually want something quite different: a description of the organization of delinquent activity, a description which makes sense of as much as possible of what they have seen as they observed delinquent youth. Who are the people involved in the act in question? What were their relations before, during, and after the event? What are their relations to the people they victimize? To the police? To the juvenile court? Fieldworkers are likewise interested in the histories of events: How did this start? Then what happened? And then? And how did all that eventually end up in a delinquent act or a delinquent career? And how did this sequence of events depend on the organization of all this other activity?

The argument rests on the interdependence of a lot of more or less proved statements. The point is not to prove, beyond doubt, the existence of particular relationships so much as to describe a system of relationships, to show how things hang together in a web of mutual influence or support or interdependence or what have you, to describe the connections between the specifics the ethnographer knows by virtue of having been there (Diesing 1971). Being there produces a strong belief that the varied events you have seen are all connected, which is not unreasonable since what the fieldworker sees is not variables or factors that need to be "related" but people doing things together in ways that are manifestly connected. After all, it's the same people and it's only our analysis that produces the abstract and discrete variables which then have to be put back together. So fieldwork makes you aware of the constructed character of "variables." (Which is not to say that we should never talk variable talk.)

A second difference which might account for the persistent feeling that the two methods differ epistemologically is that the situations of data gathering present fieldworkers, whether they seek it or not, with a lot of information, whether they want it or not. If you do a survey, you know in advance all the information you can acquire. There may be some surprises in the connections between the items you measure, but there will not be any surprise data, things you didn't ask about but were told anyway. A partial exception to this might be the use of open-ended questions, but even such questions are usually not asked in such a way as to encourage floods of unanticipated data suggesting new variables. In fact, the actual workings of survey organizations discourage interviewers from recording data not asked for on the forms (see Peneff 1988).

In contrast, fieldworkers cannot insulate themselves from data. As long as they are "in the field" they will see and hear things which ought to be entered into their field notes. If they are conscientious or experienced enough to know that they had better, they put it all in, even what they think may be useless, and keep on doing that until they know for sure that they will never use data on certain subjects. They thus allow themselves to become aware of things they had not anticipated which may have a bearing on their subject. They expect to continually add variables and ideas to their models. In some ways, that is the essence of the method.

Many Ethnographies

The variety of things called ethnographic aren't all alike, and in fact may be at odds with each other over epistemological details. In what follows, I will concentrate on the older traditions (for example, participant observation, broadly construed, and unstructured interviewing) rather than the newer, more trendy versions (for example, hermeneutic readings of texts), even though the newer versions are more insistent on the epistemological differences. What I have to say may well be read by some as less than the full defense of what they do that they would make. So be it. I'll leave it to less middle-of-the-road types to say more. (I will, however, talk about ethnographers or fieldworkers somewhat indiscriminately, lumping together people who might prefer to be kept separate.)

A lot of energy is wasted hashing over philosophical details, which often have little or nothing to do with what researchers actually do, so I'll concentrate less on theoretical statements and more on the way researchers work these positions out in practice. What researchers do usually reflects some accommodation to the realities of social life, which affect them as much as any other actor social scientists study, by constraining what they can do. Their activity thus cannot be accounted for or explained fully by referring to philosophical positions (see Platt). In short, I'm describing practical epistemology, how what we do affects the credibility of the propositions we advance. In general, I think that the arguments advanced by qualitative researchers have a good deal of validity, but not in the dogmatic and general way they are often proposed. So I may pause here and there for a few snotty remarks on the excesses ethnographers sometimes fall into.

A few basic questions seem to lie at the heart of the debates about these methods. First, must we take account of the viewpoint of the social actor and, if we must, how do we do it? And how do we deal with the embeddedness of all social action in the world of everyday life? And how thick can we and should we make our descriptions?

The Actor's Point of View: Accuracy

One major point most ethnographers tout as a major epistemological advantage of what they do is that it lets them grasp the point of view of the actor. This satisfies what they regard as a crucial criterion of adequate social science. "Taking the point of view of the other" is a wonderful example of the variety of meanings methodological slogans acquire. For some, it has a kind of religious or ethical significance: if we fail to do that we show disrespect for the people we study. Another tendency goes further, finding fault with social science which "speaks for" others, by giving summaries and interpretations of their point of view. In this view, it is not enough to honor, respect, and allow for the actors' points of view. One must also allow them to express it themselves.

For others, me among them, this is a technical point best analyzed by Herbert Blumer: all social scientists, implicitly or explicitly, attribute a point of view and interpretations to the people whose actions we analyze (Blumer 1969). That is, we *always* describe how they interpret the events they participate in, so the only question is not whether we should, but how accurately we do it. We can find out, not with perfect accuracy, but better than zero, what people think they are doing, what meanings they give to the objects and events and people in their lives and experience. We do that by talking to them, in formal or informal interviews, in quick exchanges while we participate in and observe their ordinary activities, and by watching and listening as they go about their business; we can even do it by giving them questionnaires which let them say what their meanings are or choose between meanings we give them as possibilities. To anticipate a later point, the nearer we get to the conditions in which they actually do attribute meanings to objects and events, the more accurate our descriptions of those meanings are likely to be.

Blumer argued that if we don't find out from people what meanings they are actually giving to things, we will still talk about those meanings. In that case, we will, of necessity, invent them, reasoning that the people we are writing about must have meant this or that, or they would not have done the things they did. But it is inevitably epistemologically dangerous to guess at what could be observed directly. The danger is that we will guess wrong, that what looks reasonable to us will not be what looked reasonable to them. This happens all the time, largely because we are not those people and do not live in their circumstances. We are thus likely to take the easy way and attribute to them what we think we would feel in what we understand to be their circumstances, as when students of teenage behavior look at comparative rates of pregnancy, and the correlates thereof, and decide what the people involved "must have been" thinking in order to behave that way.

The field of drug use, which overlaps the study of adolescence, is rife with such errors of attribution. The most common meaning attributed to drug use is that it is an "escape" from some sort of reality the drug user is said to find oppressive or unbearable. Drug intoxication is conceived as an experience in which all painful and unwanted aspects of reality recede into the background so that they need not be dealt with. The drug user replaces reality with gaudy dreams of splendor and ease, unproblematic pleasures, perverse erotic thrills and fantasies. Reality, of course, is understood to be lurking in the background, ready to kick the user in the ass the second he or she comes down.

This kind of imagery has a long literary history, probably stemming from De Quincey's 1856 *Confessions of an English Opium Eater* (a wonderful nineteenth-century American version is Fitz Hugh Ludlow's 1857 *The Hashish Eater*). These works play on the imagery analyzed in Edward Said's dissection of *orientalia,* the Orient as mysterious other (Said 1978). More up-to-date versions, more science-fiction, less oriental, and less benign, can be found in such works as William Burroughs's *Naked Lunch* (1966).

Such descriptions of drug use are, as could be and has been found out by generations of researchers who bothered to ask, pure fantasy on the part of the researchers who publish them. The fantasies do not correspond to the experiences of users or of those researchers who have made the experiments themselves. They are concocted out of a kind of willful ignorance.

Misinterpretations of people's experience and meanings are commonplace in studies of delinquency and crime, of sexual behavior, and in general in studies of behavior foreign to the experience and lifestyle of conventional academic researchers. Much of what anthropological and ethnographic studies have brought to the understanding of the problems of adolescence and growing up is the correction of such simple errors of fact, replacing speculation with observation.

But "don't make up what you could find out" hardly requires being dignified as an epistemological or philosophical position. It is really not much different from a more conventional, even positivist, understanding of method (see Lieberson 1992), except in being even more rigorous, requiring the verification of speculations that researchers will not refrain from making. So the first point is that ethnography's epistemology, in its insistence on investigating the viewpoint of those studied, is indeed like that of other social scientists, just more rigorous and complete. (I find it difficult, and don't try very hard, to avoid the irony of insisting that qualitative research is typically more precise and rigorous than survey research, ordinarily thought to have the edge with respect to those criteria.)

One reason many researchers who would agree with this in principle nevertheless avoid investigating actors' viewpoints is that the people we study often do not give stable or consistent meanings to things, people, and events. They change their minds frequently. Worse yet, they are often not sure what things *do* mean; they make vague and woolly interpretations of events and people. It follows from the previous argument that we ought to respect that confusion and inability to be decisive by not giving things a more stable meaning than the people involved do. But that makes the researcher's work more difficult, since it is hard to describe, let alone measure, such a moving target.

An excellent example of the instability of "native" meanings is given in Bruno Latour's (1987) analysis of science. Conventionally, social scientists accord a special status to the knowledge created by scientists, treating it as better than conventional lay knowledge, as being more warranted. Latour notes this paradox: scientists themselves don't always regard science that way. Sometimes they do, treating a result as definitive and "black-boxing" it. But scientists often argue with each other, trying to keep others from putting a result in a black box or, worse yet, opening black boxes everyone thought were shut for good. His rule of method is, we should be as undecided as the actors we study. If they think a conclusion, a finding, or a theory is shaky, controversial, or open to question, then we should, too. And we should do that even if what we are studying is a historical controversy whose outcome we now know, even though the actors involved at the time couldn't. Conversely, if the actors involved think the piece of science involved is beyond question, so should we.

People who write about science prescriptively—epistemologists—could avoid misconstruing the ideas of those they study if they followed the simple rules anthropologists have invented for themselves about fieldwork. It was once thought good enough to visit your tribe for a month or two in the summer and to get all your information from informants interviewed with the help of translators. No one thinks that any more, and now there is a minimum standard—know the native language, stay a year to eighteen months, use some sort of rudimentary sampling techniques. Applied to the study of science, these rules would require that epistemologists learn the native language fully, not just the high church version trotted out on formal occasions but the language of daily work as well, not just the views of "eminent scientists" and those who speak for the science, but of the ordinary scientists who actually do the work. Which is what Latour and the other students of "shop-floor practice" in science have done (and what Diesing [1971], an unusual epistemologist, did), and many other sociologists of science did not.

Epistemologically, then, qualitative methods insist that we should not invent the viewpoint of the actor, and should only attribute to actors ideas about the world they actually hold, if we want to understand their actions, reasons, and motives.

The Everyday World: Making Room for the Unanticipated

A second point, similar to the emphasis on learning and understanding the meanings people give to their world and experiences instead of making them up, is an emphasis on the everyday world, everyday life, the *quotidian*. This catch phrase appears frequently in ethnographic writing, often referring to the ideas of Alfred Schutz. In Schutz's writings (see Schutz 1962), and in the elaborations of those ideas common among ethnomethodologists, the everyday world typically refers to the taken-for-granted understandings people share which make concerted action possible. In this, the idea resembles the notion of culture one finds in Redfield—"shared understandings made manifest in act and artifact" (1941:132)—and the similar emphasis on shared meanings in Meadian (George Herbert Mead, that is) thought as interpreted by Blumer.

The general idea is that we act in the world on the basis of assumptions we never inspect but just act on, secure in the belief that when we do, others will react as we expect them to. A version of this is the assumption that things look to me as they would look to you if you were standing where I am standing. In this view, "everyday understandings" refers not so much to the understandings involved, say, in the analysis of a kinship system—that this is the way one must behave to one's mother's brother's daughter, for instance—but to the deep epistemological beliefs that undergird all such shared ideas, the meta-analyses and ontologies we are not ordinarily aware of that make social life possible.

Much theoretical effort has been expended on this concept. I favor a simpler, less controversial, more workaday interpretation, either as an alternative or simply as a complement to these deep theoretical meanings. This is the notion of the everyday world as the world people actually act in every day, the ordinary world in which the things we are interested in understanding actually go on. As opposed to what? As opposed to the simpler, less expensive, less time-consuming world the social scientist constructs in order to gather data efficiently, in which survey questionnaires are filled out and official documents consulted as proxies for observation of the activities and events those documents refer to.

Most ethnographers think they are getting closer to the real thing than that, by virtue of observing behavior *in situ* or at least letting people tell about what happened to them in their own words. Clearly, whenever a social scientist is present, the situation is not just what it would have been without the social scientist. I suppose this applies even when no one knows that the social scientist is a social scientist doing a study. Another member of a cult who believes flying saucers from other planets are about to land is, after all, one more member the cult would not have had otherwise and, if the cult is small, that increase in numbers might affect what the observer is there to study.

But given that the situation is never exactly what it would have been otherwise, there are degrees of interference and influence. Ethnographers pride themselves on seeing and hearing, more or less, what people would have done and said had the observers not been there. One reason for supposing this to be true is that ethnographers observe people when all the constraints of their ordinary social situation are operative. Consider this comparatively. We typically assure people to whom we give a questionnaire or who we interview that no one will ever know what they have said to us, or which alternatives on the questionnaire they have chosen. (If we can't make that assurance, we usually worry about the validity of the results.) This insulates the people interviewed from the consequences they would suffer if others knew their opinions. The insulation helps us discover people's private thoughts, the things they keep from their fellows, which is often what we want to know.

But we should not jump from the expression of a private thought to the conclusion that that thought determines the person's actions in the situation to which it might be relevant. When we watch someone as they work in their usual work setting or go to a political meeting in their neighborhood or have dinner with their family—when we watch people do things in the places they usually do them with the people they usually do them with—we cannot insulate them from the consequences of their actions. On the contrary, they have to take the rap for what they do, just as they ordinarily do in everyday life. An example: when I was observing college undergraduates, I sometimes went to classes with them. On one occasion, an instructor announced a surprise quiz for which the student I was accompanying that day, a goof-off, was totally unprepared. Sitting nearby, I could easily see him leaning over and copying answers from someone he hoped knew more than he did. He was embarrassed by my seeing him, but the embarrassment didn't stop him copying, because the consequences of failing the test (this was at a time when flunking out of school could lead to being drafted, and maybe being killed in combat) were a lot worse than my potentially lowered opinion of him. He apologized and made excuses later, but he did it. What would he have said about cheating on a questionnaire or in an interview, out of the actual situation that had forced him to that expedient?

Our opinions or actions are not always regarded as inconsequential by people we study. Social scientists who study schools and social agencies regularly find that the personnel of those organizations think of research as some version of the institutional evaluations they are constantly subject to, and take measures to manipulate what will be discovered. Sometimes the people we find it easiest to interview are on the outs with their local society or culture, hoping to escape and looking to the ethnographer for help. But although these exceptions to the general point always need to be evaluated carefully, ethnographers typically make this a major epistemological point: when they talk about what people do they are talking about what they saw them do under the conditions in which they usually do it, rather than making inferences from a more remote indicator such as the answer to a question given in the privacy of a conversation with a stranger. They are seeing the "real world" of everyday life, not some version of it created at their urging and for their benefit, and this version, they think, deserves to be treated as having greater truth value than the potentially less accurate versions produced by other methods, whatever the offsetting advantages of efficiency and decreased expense.

A consequence of finding out about the details of everyday life is that many events and actions turn out to have mundane explanations seldom accounted for in our theories. A student in a fieldwork class I taught in Kansas City studied letter carriers. Under my prodding, he tried to find out what sorts of routes the carriers preferred, which parts of town they chose to work in when they had a chance to make a choice. Having done his research, he invited his fellow students to guess the answer and, budding social scientists that they were, their guesses centered on social class: the carriers would prefer middle-class areas because they were safer; the carriers would prefer working-class areas because the inhabitants would be on fewer mailing lists and thus there would be less mail to carry; and so on. All these clever, reasonable guesses were wrong. What the carriers he talked to preferred (and this is not to say that other carriers elsewhere might not have different preferences and reasons for them) were neighborhoods that were flat. Kansas City is hilly and the carriers preferred not to climb up and down as they moved from street to street. This is not an explanation that would make sense from a "stratification" point of view; a follower of Bourdieu, for instance, might not think to include such an item in a survey. But that was the reason the carriers gave, a homely reason waiting to be discovered by someone who left room for it to come out.

Full Description, Thick Description: Watching the Margins

Ethnographers pride themselves on providing dense, detailed descriptions of social life, the kind Geertz (1974) has taught us to recognize as "thick." Their pride often implies that the fuller the description, the better, with no limit suggested. At an extreme, ethnographers talking of reproducing the "lived experience" of others.

There is something wrong with this on the face of it. The object of any description is not to reproduce the object completely—why bother when we have the object already?—but rather to pick out its relevant aspects, details which can be abstracted from the totality of details that make it up so that we can answer some questions we have. Social scientists, for instance, usually concentrate on what can be described in words and numbers, and thus leave out all those aspects of reality that use other senses, what can be seen and heard and smelled. (How many monographs deal with the smell of what is being studied, even when that is a necessary and interesting component—and when isn't it? [cf. Becker 1986:121–35].)

Ethnographers usually hail "advances" in method which allow the inclusion of greater amounts of detail: photographs, audio recording, video recording. These advances never move us very far toward the goal of full description; the full reality is still a long way away. Even when we set up a video camera, it sits in one place at a time, and some things cannot be seen from that vantage point; adding more cameras does not alter the argument. Even such a small technical matter as the focal length of the camera's lens makes a big difference: a long lens provides close-up detail, but loses the context a wide-angle lens provides.

So full description is a will-o'-the-wisp. But, that said, a fuller description is preferable to, and epistemologically more satisfying than, a skimpy description. Why? Because, as with the argument about the actor's point of view, it lets us talk with more assurance about things than if we have to make them up—and, to repeat, few social scientists are sufficiently disciplined to refrain from inventing interpretations and details they have not, in one way or another, observed themselves. Take a simple example. We want to know if parents' occupations affect the job choices adolescents make. We can ask them to write down the parents' occupations on a line in a questionnaire; we can copy what the parents have written down somewhere, perhaps on a school record; or we can go to where the parents work and verify by our own observation that this one teaches school, that one drives a bus, the other one writes copy in an advertising agency.

Is one of these better than another? Having the children write it down on a form is better because it is cheap and efficient. Copying it from a record the parents made might be better because the parents have better knowledge of what they do and better language with which to express it than the children do. Seeing for ourselves would still be open to question—maybe they are just working there this week—but it leaves less room for slippage. We don't have to worry about the child's ignorance or the parents' desire to inflate their status. Epistemologically, I think, the observation which requires less inference and fewer assumptions is more likely to be accurate, although the accuracy so produced might not be worth bothering with.

A better goal than "thickness"—one fieldworkers usually aim for—is "breadth": trying to find out something about every topic the research touches on, even tangentially. We want to know something about the neighborhood the juveniles we study live in, and the schools they go to, and the police stations and jails they spend time in, and dozens of other things. Fieldworkers pick up a lot of incidental information on such matters in the course of their participation or lengthy interviewing but, like quantitative researchers, they often use "available data" to get some idea about them. They usually do that, however, with more than the usual skepticism.

It is time to mention, briefly, the well-known issue of "official statistics" or, put more generally, the necessity of looking into such questions as why records are kept, who keeps them, and how those facts affect what's in them. (None of this is news to historians, who would think of this simply as a matter of seeing what criticisms the sources they use have to be subjected to.) As Bittner and Garfinkel (1967) told us years ago, organizations don't keep records so that social scientists can have data but, rather, for their own purposes. This is obvious in the case of adolescents, where we know that school attendance records are "managed" in order to maximize state payments; behavioral records slanted to justify actions taken toward "difficult" kids; and test scores manipulated to justify tracking and sorting. Similarly, police records are kept for police purposes, not for researchers' hypothesis testing.

Ethnographers therefore typically treat data gathered by officials and others as data about what those people did: police statistics as data about how police keep records and what they do with them, data about school testing as data about what schools and testers do rather than about student traits, and so on. That means that ethnographers are typically very irreverent, and this makes trouble.

It makes trouble where other people don't share the irreverence but take the institution seriously on its own terms. Qualitative researchers are often, though not necessarily, in a kind of antagonistic relationship to sources of official data, who don't like to be treated as objects of study but want to be believed (I have discussed this elsewhere under the heading of the "hierarchy of credibility" [Becker 1967]).

Coda

There's not much more to say. Practitioners of qualitative and quantitative methods may seem to have different philosophies of science, but they really just work in different situations and ask different questions. The politics of social science can seduce us into magnifying the differences. But it needn't, and shouldn't.

Further Thoughts

After the foregoing had been discussed at the conference, some people felt that there were still unresolved questions that I ought to have dealt with. The questions were ones that are often raised and my answers to them are not really "answers," but rather responses which discuss the social settings in which such questions are asked rather more than the questioners may have anticipated.

One question had to do with how one might combine what are sometimes called the two modalities, the qualitative and quantitative approaches to social research. There is a little literature on this question, which generally ends up suggesting a division of labor, in which qualitative research generates hypotheses and quantitative research tests them. This question is invariably raised, and this solution proposed, by quantitative researchers, who seem to find it an immense problem, and never by qualitative researchers, who often just go ahead and do it, not seeing any great problem, in that following the lead of Robert E. Park, as I suggested above.

Well, why don't qualitative researchers think it's a problem? They don't think it's a problem because they focus on questions to be answered rather than on procedures to be followed. The logic of this is laid out in enormous detail in a book that is not about sociology at all, George Polya's *Mathematics and Plausible Reasoning* (1954), in which he shows how one combines information of all kinds in assessing the reasonableness of a conclusion or idea.

And how do researchers actually go about combining these different kinds of data? This is not an easy matter to summarize briefly, because qualitative researchers have been doing this for a very long time, and there are many examples of it being done in many parts of the literature. Thomas Kuhn (1970) noted that scientists learn their trade not by following abstract procedural recipes but rather by examining exemplars of work in their field commonly regarded as well done. The best way to see how data of these various kinds can be combined is to examine how they were combined in exemplary works. This was obviously too large a task for the conference paper.

But I will cite three well-known works and suggest that analysis of the methods used in them and in other such works be undertaken by those who want to see the answer to the question. Horace Cayton and St. Clair Drake's *Black Metropolis* (1945) is a monumental study of the black areas of the south side of Chicago in the late thirties. It contains data of every kind imaginable, some statistical, some observational, all pointed toward answering questions about the organization of that community. *Boys in*

White (1961), the study of medical students several of us conducted in the 1950s, relied on observation and unstructured interviews to generate data, but presented the results both in an ethnographic form and in simple tables which were, somewhat to the surprise of qualitative zealots, "quantitative," though we did not use any tests of significance, the differences we pointed to being gross enough to make such tests an unnecessary frill. Jane Mercer's *Labeling the Mentally Retarded* (1973) is the nearest of these three to the standard combination often recommended; she used community surveys, official records of several kinds, as well as unstructured interviews, to arrive at her conclusions about the social character of mental retardation.

A second question dealt with validity, noting that my paper did not speak to that question, but instead talked (following the lead of Polya, already referred to) about credibility. Do I really think that that's all there is to it, simply making a believable case? Isn't there something else involved, namely, the degree to which one has measured or observed the phenomenon one claims to be dealing with, as opposed to whether two observers would reach the same result, which was one of the ways some people interpreted my analysis of credibility?

We come here to a difference that is really a matter not of logic or scientific practice but of professional organization, community, and culture. The professional community in which quantitative work is done (and I believe this is more true in psychology than in sociology) insists on asking questions about reliability and validity, and makes acceptable answers to those questions the touchstone of good work. But there are other professional communities for whose workers those are not the major questions. Qualitative researchers, especially in sociology and anthropology, are more likely to be concerned with the kinds of questions I raised in the body of my paper: whether data are accurate, in the sense of being based on close observation of what is being talked about or only on remote indicators; whether data are precise, in the sense of being close to the thing discussed and thus being ready to take account of matters not anticipated in the original formulation of the problem; whether an analysis is full or broad, in the sense of being based on knowledge about a wide range of matters that impinge on the question under study, rather than just a relatively few variables. The paper contains a number of relevant examples of these criteria.

Ordinarily, scholarly communities do not wander into each other's territory, and so do not have to answer to each other's criteria. Operating within the paradigm accepted in their community, social scientists do what their colleagues find acceptable, knowing that they will have to answer to their community for failures to adhere to those standards. When, however, two (at least two, maybe more) scholarly communities meet, as they did in this conference, the question arises as to whose language the discussions will be conducted in, and what standards will be invoked. It is my observation over the years that quantitative researchers always want to know what answers qualitative researchers have to *their* questions about validity and reliability and hypothesis testing. They do not discuss how they might answer the questions qualitative researchers raise about accuracy and precision and breadth. In other words, they want to assimilate what others do to their way of doing business and make those other ways answer their questions. They want the discussion to go on in their language and the standards of qualitative work translated into the language they already use.

That desire—can I say "insistence"?—presumes a status differential: *A* can call *B* to account for not answering *A*'s questions properly, but *B* has no such obligation to *A*. But this is a statement about social organization, not about epistemology, about power in hierarchical systems, not about logic. When, however, scholarly communities operate independently, instead of being arranged in a hierarchy of power and obligation, as is presently the case with respect to differing breeds of social science, their members need not use the language of other groups; they use their own language. The relations between the groups are lateral, not vertical, to use a spatial metaphor. One community is not in a position to require that the other use its language.

That has to some extent happened in the social sciences, as the growth of social science (note that this argument has a demographic base) made it possible for subgroups to constitute worlds of their own, with their own journals, organizations, presidents, prizes, and all the other paraphernalia of a scientific discipline.

Does that mean that I'm reducing science to matters of demographic and political weight? No, it means recognizing that this is one more version of a standard problem in relations between culturally differing groups. To make that explicit, the analogies to problems of translation between languages and cultures (neatly analyzed, for instance, in Talal Asad's essay, "The Concept of Cultural Translation in British Social Anthropology" [1986]) are close. Superordinate groups in situations of cultural contact (for example, colonial situations) usually think everything should be translated so that it makes sense in *their* language rather than being translated so that the full cultural difference in the concepts in question is retained. They are very often powerful enough, at least for a while, to require that that be done.

This problem of translation between culturally differing groups is what Kuhn called attention to in noting that when there is a substantial paradigm difference, as in the case of a paradigm shift, the languages in which scientific work is conducted cannot be translated into one another. If the groups are in fact independent, then there is a translation problem and the same dynamic—the question, you might say, of whose categories will be respected—comes into play.

So what seem like quite reasonable requests for a little clarification are the playing out of a familiar ritual, which occurs whenever quantitative workers in education, psychology, and sociology decide that they will have to pay attention to work of other kinds and then try to coopt that work by making it answer to their criteria, criteria like reliability and validity, rather than to the criteria I proposed, commonly used by qualitative workers. I would say that I wasn't *not dealing* with validity, but *was,* rather, *dealing* with something else that seems as fundamental to me as validity does to others.

This will all sound at odds with my fundamental belief, expressed in the paper, that the two styles of work actually share the same, or a very similar, epistemology. I do believe that's true. But I also think that some workers get fixated on specific procedures (not the same thing as epistemology), act as I have described with respect to those procedures, and have this same feeling that other styles of work must be justified by reference to how well they accomplish what those procedures are supposed to accomplish.

Finally, some people asked how one could tell good from bad or better from worse in qualitative work. I've suggested one answer in the criteria already discussed. Work that is based on careful, close-up observation of a wide variety of matters that bear on the question under investigation is better than work which relies on inference and more remote kinds of observations. That's a criterion. One reason *Street Corner Society* (Whyte 1981) is widely recognized as a masterwork of social science research is that it satisfies this criterion; William Foote Whyte knew what he was talking about, he had observed the social organization he analyzed in minute detail over a long time, and had looked not only at the interactions of a few "corner boys" but also at the operation of much larger organizations in politics and crime, which impinged on the corner boys' lives.

But something else needs to be said. Many people who are quick to recognize the quality of Whyte's work or of Erving Goffman's studies of social organization are just as quick to say that this kind of thing can only be done by specially gifted people, that only *they* can get these remarkable results and, thus, that the methods they have used are not suitable for the development of a science. This recognizes what must be recognized—quality that everyone knows is there—while marginalizing the enterprise that made that quality possible. Goffman was indeed a gifted social scientist, but his gifts expressed themselves within a tradition of thinking and fieldwork that extended from Durkheim through Radcliffe-Brown to Lloyd Warner, as well as from Simmel to Park to Hughes and Blumer. The tradition made his work possible.

That is, however, true of good work in every branch of social science, qualitative or quantitative. Stanley Lieberson, for instance, is a gifted quantitative researcher, but what makes his work outstanding is not that he uses some particular method or that he follows approved procedures correctly, but that he has imagination and can smell a good problem and find a good way to study it. Which is to say that telling good from bad is not as simple as it appears. It's easy enough to tell work that's done badly, and to tell how it was done badly, and where it went off the track. But that in no way means that it is possible, in any version of social science, to write down the recipe for doing work of the highest quality, work that goes beyond mere craft. That's another story. Physicists, who so many social scientists think to imitate, know that. How come we don't?

So these are matters that are deeper than they seem to be, in a variety of ways, and mostly, I think, in organizational ways. I haven't, for reasons I hope to have made clear, answered these questions as the people who asked them hoped. I've explained things in my terms, and I guess they will have to do the translating.

References

Abbott, Andrew. 1992. "What Do Cases Do? Some Notes on Activity in Sociological Analysis." In *What Is a Case? Exploring the Foundations of Social Inquiry.* Ed. Charles C. Ragin and Howard S. Becker, 53–82. New York: Cambridge University Press.

Asad, Talal. "The Concept of Cultural Translation in British Social Anthropology." In *Writing Culture: The Poetics and Politics of Ethnography.* Ed. James Clifford and George E. Marcus, 141–64. Berkeley: University of California Press.

Becker, Howard S. 1967. "Whose Side Are We On?" *Social Problems* 14 (Winter):239–47.

———. 1982. *Art Worlds.* Berkeley: University of California Press.

———. 1986. *Doing Things Together.* Evanston, Ill.: Northwestern University Press.

Becker, Howard S., Blanche Geer, Everett C. Hughes, and Anselm L. Strauss. 1961. *Boys in White: Student Culture in Medical School.* Chicago: University of Chicago Press.

Bittner, Egon, and Harold Garfinkel. 1967. "'Good' Organizational Reasons for 'Bad' Organizational Records." In Harold Garfinkel, *Studies in Ethnomethodology,* 186–207. Englewood Cliffs, N.J.: Prentice-Hall.

Blumer, Herbert. 1969. *Symbolic Interactionism*. Englewood Cliffs, N.J.: Prentice-Hall.

Burroughs, William. 1966. *Naked Lunch*. New York: Grove Press.

De Quincey, Thomas. 1856 [1971]. *Confessions of an English Opium Eater*. Ed. Aletha Hayter. Harmondsworth: Penguin.

Diesing, Paul. 1971. *Patterns of Discovery in the Social Sciences*. Chicago: Aldine-Atherton.

Drake, St. Clair, and Horace Cayton. 1945. *Black Metropolis*. New York: Harcourt, Brace.

Geertz, Clifford. 1974. *The Interpretation of Cultures*. New York: Basic Books.

Kuhn, Thomas. 1970. *The Structure of Scientific Revolutions*. 2d ed. Chicago: University of Chicago Press.

Latour, Bruno. 1987. *Science in Action*. Cambridge, Mass.: Harvard University Press.

Lieberson, Stanley. 1992. "Einstein, Renoir, and Greeley: Some Thoughts About Evidence in Sociology." *American Sociological Review* 57 (Feb.): 1–15.

Ludlow, Fitz Hugh. 1857 [1975]. *The Hashish Eater*. Ed. Michael Horowitz. San Francisco: Level Press.

Mercer, Jane. 1973. *Labeling the Mentally Retarded*. Berkeley: University of California Press.

Peneff, Jean. 1988. "The Observers Observed: French Survey Researchers at Work." *Social Problems* 35 (Dec.):520–35.

Platt, Jennifer. "Theory and Practice in the Development of Sociological Methodology." Unpublished.

Polya, George. 1954. *Mathematics and Plausible Reasoning*. Princeton, N.J.: Princeton University Press.

Redfield, Robert, *The Folk Culture of Yucatan,* Chicago: University of Chicago Press, 1941.

Said, Edward. 1978. *Orientalism*. New York: Pantheon.

Schutz, Alfred. 1962. *The Problem of Social Reality*. Vol. 1 of *Collected Papers*. The Hague: M. Nijhoff.

Whyte, William Foote. 1981. *Street Corner Society: The Social Structure of an Italian Slum*. 3d ed. Chicago: University of Chicago Press.

4 Missing Persons: Recovering Developmental Stories/Histories

ELLIOT G. MISHLER

A Paradox

About fifteen years ago, George Miller (1977) reported some puzzling findings. Summarizing Joyce Weil's study (1977) of a hypothesis, proposed earlier by Eve Clark, that children's understanding of linguistic connectives progresses through "stages," he observed:

> Tests of *before* and *after* were given four times during the school year; each of these four assessments can be looked at as a separate cross-sectional study. When the data are analyzed in this manner, Clark's hypothesis is confirmed . . . . however, it is also possible to look at the data longitudinally . . . . [to] ask whether a child whose errors fitted Stage I on an early assessment later moved on to Stages II or III. When the same data were analyzed longitudinally, no evidence could be found that these were successive stages in the development of any individual child's understanding. (Miller 1977:137–38)

Noting his prior "suspicion that cross-sectional data seldom tell the whole story," Miller recommended "minilongitudinal studies" to complement them:

> Cross-sectional studies tell us what to expect on the average, but not what individual children do; they provide an envelope, but inside the envelope we may find many individual differences. The only way to determine if individual minds follow the same course of development as the group mind is to track individual minds over a period of time—and that is precisely what minilongitudinal studies are designed to do. (139)

Several years later, when I came across this report, the findings seemed to me like Kuhnian anomalies (Kuhn 1970) that might lead to a paradigm shift in a scientific community. And Miller's recommendation pointed in that direction. I was surprised and puzzled by the discrepancy between cross-sectional and longitudinal findings. However, developmental researchers with whom I discussed the problem were apparently neither surprised or concerned. Acknowledging that such inconsistencies happened all the time, they tended to view them either as trivial, since the average or "group mind" could still be studied, and/or as random noise routinely dealt with as error in statistical analyses. Further, they did not consider it a productive problem since methods were not available for comparative analysis of multiple, variable patterns of change.

Nonetheless, the "Weil-Miller paradox" continued to puzzle me, and served as the stimulus for this chapter. My initial aim was to understand how cross-sectional and longitudinal analyses differed, to account for and explore implications of their discrepant findings. I came to view this paradox as only one variant of a larger problem, namely, a distinction between case-based and population-based analytic approaches. I discovered that other researchers in developmental psychology and the experimental study of learning, before and after Weil and Miller, recognized the incommensurability of longitudinal and cross-sectional analyses and demonstrated that inferences to individual behavior could not be made from average, group trends.[1] Still others, for example, in sociology and comparative history, addressed the related difference between group/ aggregate and individual units of analysis.[2] Further, the value of case-oriented research is now under active reconsideration in many fields, and various systematic methods have been developed for comparative study of individual growth curves, career trajectories, and other sequential and temporally ordered patterns of change.[3]

Although it is still too early to suggest that these new directions of inquiry and argument signal the paradigm shift I expected, we seem to have entered a period of critical reflection about the role and significance of case studies and case-based analyses for theory and research in the human sciences. This chapter both reflects and enters into a discussion already well underway.[4] I will focus on the implications of different assumptions and features of case- and population-based approaches for theory and research in human development. My bias will be evident: I will be arguing the case for case-based conceptual models and methods that retain individual histories and narratives as units of analysis.

Paradox Lost and (Re)Discovered: A Chronicle

The puzzling findings that initiated my inquiry are iatrogenic, to borrow a term from medicine. It refers to unanticipated negative consequences of therapeutic interventions focused on relieving one symptom while ignoring its full biological, psychological, and sociocultural context. Physicians and biomedical researchers tend to discount and trivialize this problem, labeling occurrences that do not fit their theories or match their expectations as side effects. Developmental researchers, as I noted earlier, tend to treat individual departures from average developmental norms in much the same way, but their term of dismissal is *error*.

Briefly, individual variability is dismissed since it does not fit with and cannot be incorporated within the dominant framework for legitimate scientific inquiry in psychology, Kuhn's "normal science." Such pervasive concepts as mean, norm, error, and development (in the singular) are not neutral terms pointing to "objective" reality but are defined within and, in turn, specify this framework. They are topics and themes of a model of scientific research that includes such key elements as the search for universal causal laws, an emphasis on quantitative measurement and experimentation, and assumptions of linearity and continuity in development. If we begin with different assumptions—focusing on particularity and variation, on qualitative and naturalistic methods of inquiry, and on the significance of recursions, detours, and regressions in development—we would not have a trouble-free science, but it would be one with a very different set of troubles.

Of course, the domain of developmental studies is not monolithic. But alternative approaches have been and continue to be marginalized and subordinated to the positivist model of science. This results in an odd tension between theory-building and research practices. The grand hall of theorists within the developmental Pantheon includes busts of Freud, Piaget, Lewin, Erikson, and Skinner. Cutting across their theoretical diversity is a remarkable unity of approach: all developed their theories through the study of individual cases.[5] Despite their theoretical significance, case studies are devalued within the research sector of this "knowledge community" (Fleck 1979). The irony of this is recognized among developmental researchers—one of my colleagues remarked, "Everyone knows it's all right to study individual cases to develop theory, but that's not how we're supposed to do scientific research."

Lewin, in his well-known article on Aristotelian versus Galilean modes of thought, asserts instead that theory cannot be based on statistical generalizations but is dependent on analyses of individual cases. Arguing against a supposed "antithesis" between "individuality and lawfulness,"

Lewin concludes that the "general validity of the law and concreteness of the individual case are not antitheses, and that reference to the totality of the concrete whole situation must take the place of reference to the largest possible historical collection of frequent repetitions" (1935:42).

Differences between individual and group analyses of developmental change were recognized well before Weil's findings. For example, in an early 1940s text on child development reflecting a Lewinian orientation, Olson and Hughes report both individual and average growth curves along a number of dimensions. They argue that one of the "basic, systematic limitations to the portrayal of a coherent story of child growth and development . . . [was] imposed upon data and generalizations by examining large groups of children on a single occasion, thus obscuring, except by statistical inference, the life history of any given child over a significant age span" (1943:199). In the same volume, Freeman and Flory report both individual and "composite" group curves for intellectual growth and recommend their method as a way to analyze "changes in the relative intelligence of different individuals" (1943:148).

These views did not represent the generally accepted position within developmental psychology, neither then nor now. An equally influential text from the same period that aligns itself within the dominant paradigm, the first edition of *The Manual of Child Psychology,* opens with a chapter on methods by Anderson. Recognizing the "practical value in guiding and treating children" of collecting information on single cases, he then states, "When, however, such material is published and conclusions are drawn for a universe of children, the individual case is to be regarded as a design at the lower limit of possible design. As such, it is to be treated in the light of the scientific information it yields, which is obviously very little since N in every formula is 1" (1946:33).

Anderson's view prevailed, but its success depends on the suppression of information about individual variation. Neither observed nor recorded in standard cross-sectional designs, it is dismissed as error when it occasionally surfaces. However, in the experimental study of learning, the problem of relating group and individual learning curves was recognized in the early to mid-1950s as significant and fundamentally intractable.[6] Sidman's essay is the key document. Addressing the problem that "intraorganism variability may be so great as to obscure any lawful relation," that is, "functional relations between behavior and its controlling variables" (1952:263), he notes that experimenters turn to group data, using different groups to determine each point on a learning curve—a direct analogue to cross-sectional designs in developmental studies.

Beginning with the observation that "the mean curve obtained by [use of group data] is not necessarily of the same shape as the inferred individual curves" (263), he then demonstrates through hypothetical examples and a mathematical exposition that a "mean curve may approximate . . . any one of a large number of other forms [of individual curves]" (268). He concludes that "the mean curve cannot be of the same form as the individual curves except under special conditions. Furthermore, given a particular mean curve, the form of the individual curves is not uniquely specified. It appears, then, that when different groups of subjects are used to obtain the points determining a functional relation, the mean curve does not provide the information necessary to make statements concerning the function for the individual" (268). Although he tries to salvage some usefulness for group data under very restrictive assumptions about the "general lawfulness of individual behavior," as does Estes (1956) in his response to this essay, Sidman's final, recommended alternative "is to develop techniques which will produce lawful individual functions and to present the data without averaging" (269).

With rare exceptions (for example, Wohlwill 1970), these definitive demonstrations of the incommensurability of group and individual analyses (see also note 6) have, until recently, had no discernible impact on developmental studies. Weil's findings came as a surprise—to her, Miller, and later to me—only because the dominant research paradigm excluded case-based data. Cross-sectional designs were legitimized by the assumption that findings from group data could be used to construct theories about individual functioning and development—an assumption that is clearly untenable. Further, the methodological counterpart to this assumption—that a sample of individual curves would correspond to a singular group curve—could not be tested since individual longitudinal data were not collected. Without such data, the Weil-Miller paradox is invisible, dissolved magically, or more precisely, by sleight of hand, by the assumptions and methods of cross-sectional studies. It is in this sense that the paradox is iatrogenic.

Recentering Developmental Research: Case-Based Models

The disjunction between case-based theory and population-based research findings reflects the neglect of individual agency in conceptualizations of development. This is a fundamental problem, since theoretical statements about psychological change—learning as well as development—must refer to dynamics and processes at the level of the individual actor. We are not really concerned with theorizing about an abstract "group mind" since this is not a meaningful psychological concept.

The learning theorists cited earlier were clear about this. For example, in his effort to salvage some usefulness for averaged data, Estes (1956) specifies the issue as a problem of "inference," that is, a test of whether a derived group curve fits a sample of actual individual curves. This contrasts to the essentially indeterminate approach in cross-sectional studies where hypothetical individual curves are "deduced" (or assumed) from an average curve. To make deductions about psychological processes from studies of average tendencies and population-based statistical analyses, a way must be found to insert a model of individual functioning into the chain of reasoning.[7]

Developmental researchers accomplish this necessary task, the deductive shift between levels, by assuming that a mean score for a sample of cases represents the ideal or typical child. The mean is reified, treated as if it is the ideal child that would have been available for study in the best of all possible worlds—if it were not for all the messiness of inter- and intraindividual variation resulting from a host of uncontrolled and unknown sources. This is a rather remarkable inversion of reality and abstraction. The mean that does not represent any single individual is conceptually redefined as the real reality, and individuals' actual scores become the abstractions.

This Platonic conception, where a presumed, underlying, invisible "reality" displaces our observations of acting human agents, provides the necessary bridge between empirical average findings and theoretical statements about individuals. In this perspective, the real child is a defective version of an ideal one. Statistical methods are applied to eliminate these defects, namely, error. This permits inferences to an idealized, universal child. Variability disappears. Developmental differences among children, reflecting contingencies and particularities of individual biographies, are excluded from theoretical attention. In this way, the circle of deduction from average data to individual functioning is completed.

The aim of case-based approaches is to break out of this circle. This requires methods that retain individuals as units of observation and analysis so that empirical findings more closely match theoretical concerns. The distinction between case and population/aggregate models and methods has often been made, in psychology and other fields, where the former tends to be defined in contrast to the latter, dominant approach.[8] Among various ways in which this contrast might be defined and developed, I am emphasizing the fundamental importance of units of analysis, since I believe this is the critical link between theory and research practices.[9]

Further, by focusing on the implications of whether analytic units refer to individuals or population aggregates, we may avoid oversimplified characterizations of methods as qualitative versus quantitative, or nonexperimental versus experimental. These contrasts are not only invidious but are largely irrelevant to various case-based methods. Finally, this perspective may lead to more direct comparisons among case-based approaches, which merit consideration in their own terms rather than only by how they contrast with the dominant model.

In searching for such methods for human development studies, it may be useful to turn to fields that focus on historical processes—on the temporal ordering of events in complex systems—for example, literature and history as well as those disciplines in the biological and natural sciences informed by evolutionary theory. Surely, cognitive and linguistic development, learning and socialization, are as complex as processes through which the structure of DNA is expressed in physiology and behavior. And their study must just as surely require more appropriate methods than those based on experimental designs and statistical analyses developed to measure effects of fertilizer on average yields of corn or soybeans.[10]

Abbott, a comparative historian/sociologist, develops an argument for case-based approaches that is particularly germane to developmental studies. He addresses the implications of two different views of historical processes or "careers": in terms of "causality" or as "narrative pattern." In the former, the temporal ordering of events is treated as accidental, an "appearance rather than a reality." It is the "realization" of an underlying stochastic "process of causes or choices" (1990:140) that is assumed to be the reality. Studies from this perspective focus on outcomes at particular points, as in path analysis or event-history analyses—and in cross-sectional developmental studies. From a narrative pattern perspective, a "career is a reality, a whole, not simply the list of successive realizations of an underlying stochastic process" (141). Rather than emphasizing causes where "initiative and action . . . belong to the variables, not to the cases," where variables "do things" and cases "merely endure," in the "narrative or typical-pattern view of careers, the social world is made up of subjects who participate in events" (141).

In population-based developmental research, such as cross-sectional studies of cognitive or linguistic development, variables "do" all the work: they are the focus of measurement and statistical analysis, and the key terms in our statements of causal relationships. Typically, we compare average levels or values of single variables across different ages. In this way, individuals are stripped of agency; they "endure" but have no initiative, they are sites with measurable attributes but do not "participate" in or actively produce the events of interest.

Terms like *actor, agent, agency,* and *history* assume some type of coherence in human experience and action. This does not mean specific attributes or dimensions cannot be studied. But it does argue that we must study their relations to each other, at the same or different points in time. This shifts our focus from analyses of significant differences between measures of single attributes to analyses of structures and trajectories. Case-based models are designed for this task of restoring agency to individuals in our research and our theories. They grant them unity and coherence through time, respecting them as subjects with both histories and intentions. This is no less scientific a form of inquiry than population-based, variable-centered approaches. The task is to develop methods for systematic research within this agent-centered perspective.

Turning to this task in the following sections, I describe and illustrate two quite different methods. The first, optimal matching, compares degrees of resemblance or similarity among sequentially ordered events. It is a quantitative case-based approach that can be applied to large samples of individual trajectories with many distinctive events. A method for analyzing the narrative structure of life history accounts is then presented. This is a qualitative example but, as will be shown, it permits comparisons across cases and its findings may provide the primary data for optimal matching analysis.

Development as Career: Optimal Matching

In a series of essays notable for their mix of theoretical cogency and methodological sophistication, Andrew Abbott develops an argument for case-based approaches to research on individual and social histories, which he refers to as careers. (Abbott 1983–1992b) To solve the problem at the heart of the present essay, namely, how individual trajectories can be retained as analytic units in large-sample studies, he adopts a "simple dynamic programming technique called optimal matching . . . widely known in natural science" (Abbott and Hrycak 1990:152; see also Sankoff and Kruskal 1983 for a mathematical exposition and several applications). It specifies a way to measure degrees of "sequence resemblance" among cases and may be applied to any "data consisting of ordered sequences of potentially repeating events," that is, to any "'history' that can be expressed as a sequential list of events" among which are "the life cycles of individuals or families" (Abbott and Hrycak 1990:144–45).

Detailed procedures and empirical studies may be found in Kruskal (1983) and in reports of Abbott's research group (Abbott and Forrest 1986; Abbott and Hrycak 1990; Forrest and Abbott 1990). Briefly, the first step is to define and calculate a measure of "minimal distance" between two sequences. Referred to as the Levenshtein distance (Kruskal 1983:18), this "optimal" measure of sequence resemblance is the smallest number of changes—substitutions, insertions, and deletions—required to transform one sequence into another. Each sequence is compared with every other one; for large data sets, computer programs are available for this task.

This procedure produces a set of intermediate "interval-level measures of resemblance between sequences" (Abbott and Hrycak 1990:152), which may then serve as inputs to clustering or multidimensional scaling analyses to determine typical sequence patterns.

I will illustrate the first steps in optimal matching—calculating and comparing resemblance scores among a set of sequences—with data from McCabe and Peterson's (1990) longitudinal study of the development of narrative competence. Extending their earlier large-scale, cross-sectional study of children's narratives (Peterson and McCabe 1983), they collected stories told to their parents of a small sample of ten children, at each half-year point between the ages of three and one-half and six.

In their analyses they focus on the relative frequencies of seven different "types" or structures of stories told by each child at each age: for example, whether a story includes only one, two, or three events, or ends "prematurely at the climactic high point"; is a simple chronology, or "a full-blown 'classic' narrative." The latter—which I selected as the focus for this exercise—represents "the upper limits of performance, which might be termed a kind of competence." It begins "by orienting listeners to when, where, and who and what was involved in some incident, proceeds to build an action sequence culminating in some emotional high point, and briefly resolves this crisis" (3).

From their age x child frequency distributions of narrative types (their table 2), I computed a measure of the relative dominance of "classic" to other narratives told by each child at each age. This is an ordinal case-based scale, that is, an intraindividual measure, based on each child's own distribution of stories among types, rather than an interindividual one. It refers to whether the number of classic narratives told by a child at each age is at the median (M) of the distribution of all types of stories that child tells at that age, or above (H) or below (L) it.[11] These scores are presented in table 1. Their sequential order across the age range might be thought of as an individual's narrative-competence trajectory or "career." The cases are grouped in terms of degrees of similarity among resemblance scores reported below.

After specifying a set of sequences, the next step is to calculate optimal resemblance scores. Briefly, the aim is to transform a "source" sequence into a "target" one by the smallest number of changes (see Kruskal 1983 for alternative approaches). For this introductory example, the simplest procedure is to count differences at each point in the sequence between each pair. For example, cases CL and ND differ by one rank at ages 4.0 and 6.0. Their resemblance score is 2. CL and SL differ by one rank at each of the five age points between 3.5 and 5.5, and by two ranks at 6.0. Their resemblance score is 7. The matrix of resemblance scores among all

Table 1   Intraperson Levels of Classic Narratives Relative to Seven Narrative Types by Age Above (H), At (M), Below (L) Person × Age Medians

	AGE					
CASE	3.5	4.0	4.5	5.0	5.5	6.0
CL	M	M	M	M	M	H
ND	M	L	M	M	M	M
CA	M	L	L	M	H	M
PA	L	M	L	M	M	M
HT	L	L	L	M	L	M
KL	L	L	L	L	M	L
LH	L	L	M	L	M	L
SL	L	L	L	L	L	L
GY	L	L	L	L	L	L
TY	L	L	L	L	L	L

Source: Based on and adapted from data in McCabe and Peterson 1990 and used with their permission.

Note: These median levels (H, M, L) are intraperson by age scores. They refer to the relative number of classic narratives produced by a child at each age of testing, within that child's distribution of McCabe and Peterson's seven different narrative types.

sequences is presented in table 2, with cases arranged to display more clearly the clusters of most similar and most different sequences.

Scores range from 0 to 7, the end points representing highly similar and dissimilar sequence pairs. From these "optimal resemblance" scores and examination of the actual sequences, we might hypothesize a typology of four patterns of narrative competence acquisition. SL, GY, and TY form one type—scores of 0 mark them as identical to each other. From table 1 we see that none produces even a moderate level of "classic" narratives by age 6. KL and LH are a second type, with a score of 1. Their sequences suggest early low levels of narrative competence with unstable movement to a moderate level. PA and HT, linked by a 2 score, move from low levels to more stable moderate levels after age 5. CL, ND, and CA—with scores of 2 and 3—show early variable signs of moderate competence which then stabilizes, CL and CA reaching high levels at ages 6 and 5.5.

This typology is a hypothesis based on a small number of cases, assessed at a few points over a restricted age-span at a relatively early stage in linguistic development—ten children, half-yearly, from two and one-half to six years of age. Further, the children's stories were told to parents in "natural," nonlaboratory settings. The components or "occurrences" that

Table 2   Matrix of Resemblance Scores among Age-Ordered Sequences for Levels of Narrative Competence

	CL	ND	CA	PA	HT	KL	LH	SL	GY	TY
CL		_2_	4	3	5	6	5	7	7	7
ND			_2_	3	3	4	3	5	5	5
CA				3	3	4	5	5	5	5
PA					_2_	3	4	4	4	4
HT						3	4	_2_	_2_	_2_
KL							_1_	_1_	_1_	_1_
LH								_2_	_2_	_2_
SL									_0_	_0_
GY										_0_
TY										

Note: Numbers underlined and in **boldface** indicate strongest cluster resemblances (**0–2**); numbers without underlining in **boldface** (**3**) indicate moderate ties between cases.

specify the temporally ordered sequences are derived ordinal scores—case-based, intraindividual measures reflecting the level of "classic" narratives relative to other narrative types at each age for each individual child or case. These trajectories of narrative-competence development are the individual units of analysis that are central to case-based approaches. I have been arguing that such units are required for theories about the dynamics of linguistic or cognitive development.

   The small number of cases, the contexts in which stories were elicited, and the original categorization of narrative types all place constraints on interpretations and generalizations, but I would argue that they are neither different from nor greater than constraints on generalizations from large-sample, cross-sectional, and other population-based studies. In the latter, statistical analyses treat these sources of variability as error, as an assemblage of unaccounted-for variance. This gives us the illusion of a "group mind," but optimal matching offers the "look inside the envelope" that Miller recommended.

   Finally, the proposed typology gives no weight to some of the high-resemblance scores: the 1 scores between KL and the SL-GY-TY triplet, and the 2 scores between the latter and both HT and LH. In grouping the sequence patterns in table 1 to construct the typology, I also took into account—in addition to the overall scores—whether a level of moderate competence (M) was achieved, which it was not for cases in the SL-GY-TY type. And, if this level was achieved, whether it seemed to stabilize toward the end of the period—as it does for the PA-HT pair, but not for the KL-LH pair. Thus the typology reflects judgment and theoretical considerations as well as the distribution of resemblance scores.

With larger samples and more extended sequences, there are ways to more systematically assess the adequacy of such proposed typologies and their assumptions. Resemblance scores may serve as data for further statistical analyses. For example, the significance of differences between within- and between-group distance scores, such as the four clusters in our typology, can be tested by various procedures; multidimensional scaling and other types of analysis can more precisely define the clusters and evaluate hypotheses about specific mechanisms that might account for the findings (Abbott and Forrest 1986; Abbott and Hrycak 1990). In short, these measures of complex individual developmental sequences—case-based, qualitative, descriptive categories—are amenable to various forms of systematic "quantitative" analysis.

Abbott and Hrycak observe that "the chief strength of optimal matching is its ability to directly measure sequence resemblance. It provides a way of addressing such fundamental questions as whether there is or are common sequential patterns among data" (1990:171). Among various methods for comparing sequentially ordered series of events, optimal matching has several features that make it particularly attractive for developmental studies.[12] First, it may be applied either to continuous variables or to discrete, qualitative categories such as developmental stages, social or occupational careers (Abbott and Hrycak 1990), or historical changes in cultural forms such as dance movements (Abbott and Forrest 1986). Second, large numbers of cases pose no problem: Abbott and Hrycak begin with a data set of 595 musicians' careers over 160 years, which they then reduce to a sample of 279 to focus on the subset of individuals who held only one job at a time.

Third, and most importantly, by retaining individual sequences as units of analysis, optimal matching opens up an alternative approach to theorizing about development and other forms of temporally ordered change. Rather than focusing on causation as a general, underlying relation between abstract variables, the method aligns us more closely with historians who "write their narratives to follow the causal action" (Abbott 1990:143). This unitary, holistic view of careers and trajectories allows and encourages investigation of whether the timing and relevance of presumed "causes" are the same for all cases.

Finally, a recent report by developmental biologist Esther Thelen (cited and summarized in Sacks 1993) of the "development of motor skills— walking, reaching for objects—in infants" suggests that the potential contribution of such a shift in perspective about causation is more than a pious hope. Emphasizing the centrality of individual differences in the "evolution of unique motor patterns," she states that the development of motor skills

> follows no single programmed or prescribed pattern. Indeed there is great variability among infants at first, with many patterns of reaching for objects; but there then occurs, over the course of several months, a competition among these patterns, a discovery or selection of workable patterns, or workable motor solutions. These solutions, though roughly similar, . . . are always different and individual, adapted to the particular dynamics of each child, and they emerge by degrees, through exploration and trial. . . . The child is forced to be original, to create its own solutions. (47)

Thelen's work is consistent with the analysis of narrative competence development presented in this section. It also provides strong support for my general argument for case-based longitudinal studies of temporally ordered sequences.[13]

Development as Life History: Narrative Analysis

Although Abbott distinguishes between two different conceptual models of careers, as either "causality" or "narrative pattern," his view of narrative is historical and sociological rather than psychological. Whether cases are individuals, for example, musicians' careers, or the course of riots and collective disturbances (Abbott and Forrest 1986), he focuses both theoretically and empirically on social and cultural categories.

My study of how individuals construct their life stories applies a case-based method of narrative analysis that more directly addresses questions of psychological interest. The method differs in other respects as well from optimal matching, but the two approaches are conceptually similar in focusing on structural descriptions of individual cases as units of analysis. This opens up possibilities for combining the two approaches, that is, life-history narratives might serve as sequences for optimal matching analysis.

I interviewed a small number of contemporary craftspersons—furniture makers, potters, and others—asking them about how they began doing what they do, how their work developed, what problems they had making a living and sustaining their work. Interviews were unstructured, from one and one-half to three hours in length. Topics were initiated by respondents and pursued through open-ended questions that varied from interview to interview. The extended life history accounts produced by the respondents are the primary data for this analysis (Mishler 1990, 1992, 1994).

I developed a two-stage model for analyzing the narrative structure of

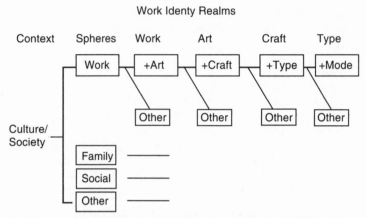

Figure 1.   The Structure of Crafts Work Identities: Realms and Choices (from Mishler 1992). This decision tree represents a set of logical hierarchically ordered choices among successive realms within the sphere of Work. Achievement of a work identity as an artist-craftsperson is marked as a sequence of positive choices (that is, +Art, +Craft, +Type, +Mode).

respondents' accounts of their work histories. First, based on the interviews, I specified a set of analytic categories that reflected culturally defined occupational choices for individuals with established work identities as artist-craftspersons. Conceptualized as a hierarchically ordered set of different "realms" of work—art, craft, type of craft, mode of craft work—the categories are logically related to each other (fig. 1). For example, whether one is a studio potter or makes one-of-a-kind pieces are alternative modes of work within ceramics, one type of a larger category of crafts that are viewed by these respondents as among the arts.

From the full interviews I selected those sections where respondents described aspects of their work history: training and education, jobs and types of work, decisions about and timing of job changes. I arranged these episodes in their real-time chronological order, thereby constructing their work-history narratives. In Goodman's terms, my reconstruction represented the "order of the told" rather than the "order of the telling" (1981:799). The analytic categories of work realms in figure 1 serve as a framework for representing and interpreting the temporally ordered narratives. Figure 2 shows the relationship between the two for one artist-furniture maker.

It is apparent that his work history is not linear, developing progressively through the hierarchically ordered work realms, but involves detours or "off-line" choices. This back-and-forth movement with shifts from crafts into noncrafts work in the arts is his work trajectory. We can repre-

Work Sphere

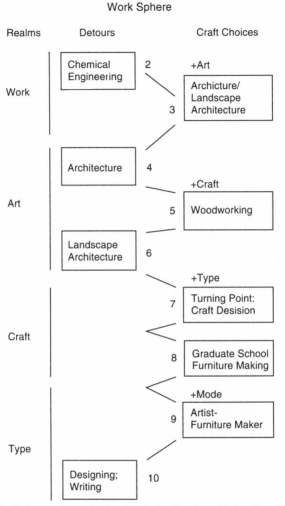

Figure 2.   The Path to a Craft Identity: An Artist–Furniture Maker (from Mishler 1992). The work history of an artist–furniture maker is shown as a sequence of choices between and within different work identity realms. "Detours" are "off" the path to his current identity; "craft choices" are "on-line."

sent his "career" as a sequence of moves: [−work] > [+art] > [−art] > [+craft] > [−art] > [+type] > [+type] > [+mode] > [−mode]. Trajectories of other respondents also appear to follow a nonlinear course but vary in their particulars. Each can be represented similarly as a sequence of moves, but they would have different patterns.

Abbott refers to sequences where the same acts or episodes may be repeated as "recurrent" and distinguishes between "events" that refer to theoretical categories, here the analytic work realms, and "occurrences"— the actual choices made by individuals (Abbott 1988). These structural descriptions of work-history narratives correspond to the developmental and career trajectories to which optimal matching was applied. Thus there is no serious methodological or theoretical obstacle to using that procedure to search for typical patterns within larger samples of life-history narratives, or other equally complex sequences of individual and social behavior.[14]

Coda

The central aim of this chapter is limned in its title: the "recovery" of individual stories/histories in developmental studies. This is one specification of a fundamental task in the human sciences, namely, to recenter theory and research on human agency. Linking this task to an epistemological stance, I have argued that case-based analyses might resolve anomalies and paradoxes in developmental inquiry that reflect a disjunction between theoretical models of individual functioning and population-based methods of empirical research.

To explore the implications of this perspective, I focused on studies of temporally ordered sequences. Comparison of population-based, cross-sectional, variable-oriented analyses to case-based, longitudinal, structure-oriented analyses showed that they were incommensurate and generated inconsistent findings and interpretations. To illustrate what might be learned from case-based analyses, I selected two exemplars that retain individual sequential patterns as units of analysis—optimal matching of sequence resemblances, applied to longitudinal data on the development of narrative competence; and the structural analysis of one individual's work-history narrative.

The dominant variable-centered, population-based research paradigm in psychology and the social sciences marginalizes case-based approaches by denying their claim to scientific legitimacy (Mishler 1979, 1990). I focused on methods and presented worked-out although brief examples in order to move beyond programmatic statements and stale controversies about qualitative versus quantitative methods or nonexperimental versus experimental research. By documenting what can be learned from systematic case-based methods, I hope to have shown that they lead to new and interesting questions about human development.

Several problems bypassed in the chapter require brief comment although they cannot be examined here in detail: the significance of temporally ordered sequences as a topic for theory and research; different approaches to longitudinal and sequential analysis; conceptions of agency; and the relation of ethnography to methods of case-based analysis presented here.

Temporally ordered sequences—careers, histories, narratives—are fundamental features of personal and social life. Nonetheless, the dynamic force of temporal processes, the structuring impact of earlier on later events, is neglected in both theory and research in psychology and the social sciences. For example, experimental approaches attend primarily to the temporal markers "before" and "after," and the logical structure of abstract theories tends to treat "causality" as if it were a simultaneous relation between variables in a mathematical equation. By focusing on analyses of temporally ordered sequences, this chapter joins the recent effort among a number of investigators to "make processes the fundamental building blocks of sociological [and other types of] analysis," reflecting the view that "social reality happens in sequences of actions . . . It is a matter of particular actors, in particular social places, at particular social times" (Abbott 1992a:428).

Among the variety of methods for longitudinal or sequential analysis (for example, see notes 3 and 12), many continue to rely on the variable-oriented model, aggregating individual measures at different points in a sequence, thus deleting individual cases as units of analysis. They differ in this important respect from the two exemplar case-based methods presented here. The relevance and implications of alternative longitudinal methods for developmental theory depends on a careful assessment of the stage in the analysis where individual measures are aggregated. The earlier the aggregation, the more severe the constraints on inferences to the dynamics of individual change. Despite these constraints, I would argue that all longitudinal approaches that preserve individual trajectories as units of analysis to some degree provide a more grounded and reasonable basis for theory building than cross-sectional approaches.

The notion of agency that is central to my perspective merits more unpacking and specification than can be given here. It is a value-laden shibboleth in proposals for alternative, anti- and postpositivist models of science and has various shades of meaning. By treating it primarily as a "unit of analysis" problem, I have not directly addressed such issues as the agent's point of view or subjectivity that are critical in many types of case-study research: biographies, ethnographies, histories.

I believe these are important issues. However, attributions of agency and subjectivity to actors—a constellation of related terms—are located within theoretical and interpretive frameworks. They are not simply descriptors of real persons (see note 13). The brunt of my argument, in this respect, is that case-based analytic methods are requisite for agency-centered theories. We need methods that focus on "initiative and action" as located in cases rather than on variables as "causes," to recite Abbott. And, of course, "cases" may be cultures, institutions, and other social units and processes where "subjectivity" is not an applicable term. This orientation to agency allowed for treating both optimal matching and narrative analysis as appropriate agency-oriented, case-based methods, though the former does not depend on actors' intentions while the latter does.

I suggested at an earlier point that a concern with agency was a link between case-based analytic methods and ethnography. However, there are also important distinctions between the approaches I have proposed and case studies. The tradition of case studies in anthropology, history, medicine, psychiatry, and other fields tends to focus on the "holistic" description of a particular culture, historical period, clinical case, and so on. To this end, many different methods and types of data are used—within one and across different case studies. These may, where appropriate and available, include a mixture of observations, assessment of written records, interpretation of cultural artifacts and life-history interviews. The case study is not a method, but an orientation toward an object that privileges the accumulation of details and their assemblage into a coherent "full" picture.

In contrast, optimal matching and the form of narrative analysis I described are specific methods that make no claims for holistic description of individual cases. Instead, their strength lies in their applicability to a series of cases. They are directed to the comparative analysis of patterns. The aim is to determine the range of variability among "cases" theoretically defined as of the same type, that is, to assess degrees of similarity and difference among trajectories or structures.

The holistic emphasis in the case study tradition has been accompanied by a neglect of variability. The latter is central to case-based analytic methods. More attention to variability would, I believe, lead to the development of more complex theories in which attention would be given to the many alternative ways in which human agency exhibits itself in the world. There is always more than one picture, however detailed it may be.

Case-based analytic methods are now on the agenda in the human sciences. They have attained sufficient legitimacy to warrant serious discussion, as is attested by sources cited here. There are many questions that remain. I am moderately optimistic that a growing community of researchers engaged in an alternative practice will extend and deepen the discussion. We may already have passed the point where we have to begin each report of a case-based analysis by contrasting it with the dominant paradigm. We can then turn our attention more fully to problems and questions that are specific to different forms of case-based analyses.

Acknowledgment

Vicky Steinitz's comments on successive earlier drafts markedly improved this chapter. The editors' suggestions and John Modell's critique of the conference draft led to a clarification of my argument. I wish to acknowledge the collegial generosity of Allyssa McCabe and Joyce Weil, who shared and gave me permission to use unpublished data from their respective studies. The latter are not included in this revision but played an important role in its history. Bill McMullin's elegant graphs of growth curves, prominent in the conference draft, have also been omitted but I wish to thank him for his skills and effort.

Notes

1. I am indebted here to Dick Jessor, who first mentioned Estes's work to me, and to Aline Sayer, who gave me a copy of Estes's paper (1956), and an essay by Wohlwill (1970), who proved an exception to the general indifference of developmental psychologists to this problem. It turns out, as I report in the text, that Estes was responding to Sidman's (1952) earlier demonstration of the independence between individual and group curves. See also Bakan 1954, Hayes 1953, and the grandmaternal source of these analyses, Margaret Merrell (1931).

2. The history of concern about this problem in sociology and social research, like other "histories" discussed here, is neither continuous or linear. Robinson's (1950) demonstration that "ecological correlations" bore no necessary relationship to the "behavior of individuals" was an influential, early statement. The multilevel approach to data analysis Nancy Waxler and I developed for our study of family interaction and schizophrenia (Mishler and Waxler 1968) reflected Robinson's work and drew on Riley's comprehensive model (1963). During this same period, Galtung proposed a general framework for distinguishing among different "units" and "levels" of analysis, labeling the "too simple inferences" from groups to individuals and vice versa as the "fallacy of the wrong level" (1967:45). The "fallacy" is ubiquitous in psychological and social research. (For example, see Mishler 1984 for a critique of coding procedures used in observation and interview studies, and Whitley's (1992) reanalysis of a social psychology experiment using Galtung's model.)

Rueschemeyer provides an instructive example in comparative social history of the different implications of population-based "quantitative cross-national research" and case-based "qualitative comparative historical studies." Comparing studies of "conditions of democracy and its relation to capitalist development," he finds that "results of these two modes of research diverge as much as their methods" and are "contradictory": "Quantitative cross-national comparisons of many countries have found consistently a positive correlation between development and democracy. They thus come to relatively optimistic conclusions about the chances of democracy in the developing countries of today. By contrast, comparative historical studies that emphasize qualitative examination of complex sequences tend to trace the rise of democracy to a favorable historical constellation of conditions in early capitalism. Their conclusions are therefore far more pessimistic about today's developing countries" (1991:9–11).

3. For example, two recent edited volumes attest to the active reconsideration in sociology of the value of case studies and other case-oriented approaches: Feagin, Orum, and Sjoberg 1991; Ragin and Becker 1992. Alternative models and methods for analyses of sequential and temporally ordered patterns of change include: Abbott 1983, 1990; Abbott and Forrest 1986; Abbott and Hrycak 1990; Collins and Horn 1991; Corsaro and Heise 1990; Griffin 1992, 1993; Heise 1988, 1989; Ragin 1987; Sankoff and Kruskal 1983; Willett 1994; Willett and Sayer 1993. Parallel to but independent of these developments, a positive reevaluation is underway of the utility of case-based models of reasoning, that is, casuistry, for understanding judgment and inference processes in, for example, bioethics (Davis 1991; Jonsen and Toulmin 1988), clinical training and practice (Hunter 1991), and the validation of scientific theories (Mishler 1990).

4. The current discussion is the latest episode in a long story that began with the beginnings of the human sciences. In this still unresolved debate, ethnography's voice, or rather its plurality of voices, has been prominent. The relation between ethnographic approaches and case-based models informing my argument is indirect, mediated primarily by our shared perspective on the significance of human agency and our respective emphases on cases—persons, cultures, institutions—as analytic units. In these respects, we are aligned on the same side of the great divide separating proponents of positivist from anti- or postpositivist views of science.

Nonetheless, our approaches differ in many important respects. The limited focus of this essay precludes systematic discussion of these differences, though that is an important task. Its complexities may be suggested by a recent complaint of Laura Nader, an anthropologist, about a collection of "ethnographies" by sociologists. Dismissing their claim to this label, she argues, "the concept 'ethnography' has been gradually reduced in meaning in recent years and in proportion to its popularity . . . [it] is a special kind of description, not to be confused with qualitative and descriptive studies of another kind," and asserts that "ethnographic is not ethnography" (1993: 7). Her idealized and somewhat monolithic view elides the extraordinary ferment in anthropology about "what" ethnographies are that has been generated by feminist and postmodern critiques of the field—controversies that caution against a direct or innocent transfer of "new ethnographic approaches" to another area of inquiry. See, for example, Clifford and Marcus 1986; Marcus and Fischer 1986; Wolf 1992.

5. A further twist of irony was brought to my attention by Eleanor Duckworth, the distinguished educator and Piaget scholar. She observes that after three books based on longitudinal case studies, Piaget shifted to cross-sectional research: "Never again has he looked at the detail of how one child's actions or thoughts

evolve" (Duckworth 1987:42). There are, of course, other notable exceptions to the dominant view of "normal science," for example, the well-known case studies that track language development (Brown 1973; Halliday 1975; Nelson 1986, 1989).

6. In an earlier draft prepared for the conference I included a hypothetical example showing how a mean curve could represent any of a large number of sets of individual curves. Thus, the $N!$ expansion for six individuals measured on one dimension at six different points in time produces 4,320 sets of curves—all of which have the same mean curve. Estes makes the same point, expanding possibilities to infinity: "Just as any mean score for a group of organisms could have arisen from sampling any of an infinite variety of populations of scores, so also could any given mean curve have arisen from any of an infinite variety of populations of individual curves" (1956:134).

This restates Sidman's point (1952) in a paper Bakan refers to as "a devastating criticism of a great deal of current and historical psychological research" (1954:63). (See also Hayes 1953.) The independence of average and individual growth curves was demonstrated much earlier by Margaret Merrell, a biostatistician. Noting that "it is clear, therefore, that individual curves and their average do not of necessity exhibit the same characteristics," she shows that the characteristics of an average curve may be "primarily due to the mathematical process of averaging and may not be present in individuals." She concludes that "when observations on any biological form are taken on different individuals of varying ages and the description of growth is given in terms of the averages of these observations, the form of the growth of these averages cannot be assumed to be characteristic of the growth of the individual organism" (1931:40, 53, 68).

In the light of these precursors, another demonstration seemed redundant. I have, therefore, deleted from this revision both my hypothetical example and my reanalysis of Joyce Weil's data reported in her unpublished study (1977).

7. Abbott makes a related point about how users of stochastic models who claim that "causality resides in variables" turn out in the end to rely on "narration as the final form of social explanation. . . . careful reading shows that the language of 'variables causing things' is merely a short-hand; stochastic writers fall back on stories or 'plausible mechanisms,' when they must defend or support particular assertions about the variables. Narrative is the fundamental recourse" (1990:143).

8. Allport's (1937, 1940) idiographic-nomothetic distinction is well-known. Runkel (1990), focusing on their respective implications for theory, refers to the "two grand methods of psychology," as "testing specimens" or "casting nets." Nesselroade (1991) specifies the difference between intra- and interindividual patterns of variability and change in terms of selections made from a "data box" of persons, occasions, and variables. Ragin (1991), a comparative social historian, compares case-oriented and variable-oriented studies of social and political change.

9. Ragin discusses the problem of the dual reference for units of analysis as "data categories" and "theoretical categories," and the confusion of failing to distinguish between these "two very different metatheoretical constructs" (1987:7). He notes that the "tension between the two meanings of unit of analysis has bedeviled the comparative social science literature" and led to various terminological distinctions: "data units" versus "analytical units"; "units of observation" versus

"units of inference"; "research sites" versus "theoretical units"; "levels of observation" versus "levels of analysis" (8). The choice of terms is not important, but the attention given the problem in comparative social science studies supports my argument about its importance for clarifying relationships between theory and research in human development.

10. In their scholarly and instructive history of the concept of probability, Gigerenzer et al. analyze changes over time in its meaning and in how it was applied in various models of statistical reasoning. Describing the "vigorous" and often rancorous debate among contending theorists of the modern period, they point to the problematic consequences of R. A. Fisher's triumph over his rivals. Fisher's great contribution was to make "systematic discussion of general causal claims possible" by his "unification of experiment and statistical analysis," achieved through the principle of randomization, the analysis of variance, and reliance on a particular conception of tests of statistical significance. That this model became paradigmatic in the social sciences and psychology "has been highly troubling to some thoughtful observers. In psychology, for example, the idea of what an experiment is was strikingly narrowed to fit the Procrustean Bed of Fisherian statistics. . . . The experimental psychology that relies on Fisherian experimental design is often associated with an abandonment of the search for universal psychological phenomena that apply equally to all people. It concentrates on establishing general causal statements, with their implicit reference to a population, that require only an increase in the incidence of the effect when the cause is present. Since these claims do not necessarily apply to the individual, they are of foremost interest to the state and its administrators" (1989:89–90).

11. It is important to note that this is a different measure than the one I used in the early draft of this paper. The latter was an interindividual measure that referred to the rank ordering of persons on their relative rates of production of "classic" narratives. On further reflection I developed the intraindividual measure used here since it is more appropriate for the case-based analyses I am proposing.

12. A variety of alternative models for sequential analysis are presented in Collins and Horn (1991), including item-response theory; random effects growth and structural equation models; time series and P-technique factor analyses; mixed longitudinal and cross-sectional designs. Covariance structure analysis has been applied to developmental changes in "tolerance of deviance" (Willett and Sayer 1993), Boolean algebra to studies in comparative social history (Ragin 1987), and multivariate information analysis to social interaction (Mishler and Waxler 1975). Abbott (1992) provides a critical review of stochastic models used in historical and sociological studies.

13. Responding to the conference draft of this chapter, John Modell in a personal communication raised two important questions about the optimal matching analysis of developmental trajectories. First, he argues that teleology is one of the "immanent qualities" of histories and narratives, and that optimal matching fails to address it. The critical difference between us centers on his assumption of immanence, that is, that certain features are inherent to and reside "in" development or history. I, on the other hand, view such teleological features as goal directedness and progressive development as theoretical constructs. When we use these terms,

we are not simply describing what is out "there" in reality. We are ascribing such terms to interpret, that is, to give theoretical meaning to patterns in our data produced by our methods. Optimal matching is teleologically agnostic, but no more or less so than other methods. Its advantage lies in its focus on individual cases, to which teleological ascriptions are more meaningful and appropriate than they are to population aggregates.

Second, he points to a serious methodological problem in my optimal matching analysis of sequences based on age-interval scores, that is, the group-based average measures used in the earlier draft. In a hypothetical simulation of my analysis, he shifted the ages at which children were tested—from three and one-half and four to three and three-quarters and four and one-quarter, and so on. Calculating new scores by extrapolation, he found different patterns of resemblance than I did. His demonstration is irrefutable. Further, it seems to me that his critique applies generally to any study relying on age-interval measurements, which includes the vast majority of developmental studies.

Both the timing and number of measurements are typically arbitrary, depending more on practical than theoretical considerations. And the lines we draw between points, that is, "growth curves" assume a steady rate of change between them. The critical problems raised for analysis and interpretation are rarely examined. Thus Cohen refers to this as a "neglected problem" and points out that although "the ideal design would include repeated measures at many closely spaced intervals," that "this design imperative is hardly ever followed" (1991:19–20; see also Collins and Graham 1991). Clearly, it was not followed in the McCabe-Peterson study from which I adapted data to illustrate optimal matching. The intraperson by age measures used in my revised analysis are equally vulnerable to Modell's criticism since they depend on the same age interval data. This suggests additional caution about the typology of sequence patterns reported here, but it is a caution that has equal relevance to studies of change using any method.

14. Describing "further applications of optimal matching methods," Forrest and Abbott recognize this possibility, foreshadowing this suggestion. They reexamine sixty-seven of the eighty-six versions of a particular folktale collected and analyzed by an anthropologist to test his hypothesis that all versions "can be grouped into seven categories." They partially confirm his analysis but clarify it, pointing out that optimal matching allows them "to make finer discriminations and to see how 'bridges' may form between versions of the tale" (1990:165–67).

References

Abbott, A. 1983. "Sequences of Social Events: Concepts and Methods for the Analysis of Order in Social Processes." *Historical Methods* 16:129–47.

———. 1984. "Event Sequence and Event Duration: Colligation and Measurement." *Historical Methods* 17:192–204.

———. 1988. "Transcending General Linear Reality." *Sociological Theory* 6:169–86.

———. 1988. "Workshop on Sequence methods." Unpublished.

———. 1990. "Conceptions of Time and Events in Social Science Methods." *Historical Methods* 23:140–50.

———. 1992a. "From Causes to Events: Notes on Narrative Positivism." *Sociological Methods and Research* 20:428–54.

———. 1992b. "What Do Cases Do? Some Notes on Activity in Sociological Analysis." In *What Is a Case?* Ed. C. Ragin and H. Becker. New York: Cambridge.

Abbott, A., J. Forrest. 1986. "Optimal Matching Methods for Historical Sequences." *Journal of Interdisciplinary History* 16:471–94.

Abbott, A., A. Hrycak. 1990. "Measuring Resemblance in Sequence Data: An Optimal Matching Analysis of Musicians' Careers." *American Journal of Sociology* 96:144–85.

Allport, G. W. 1937. *Personality: A Psychological Interpretation.* New York: Holt.

———. 1940. "The Psychologist's Frame of Reference." *Psychological Bulletin* 37:1–28.

Anderson, J. E. 1946. "Methods of Child Psychology." In *Manual of Child Psychology.* Ed. L. Carmichael. New York: Wiley.

Bakan, D. 1954. "A Generalization of Sidman's Results on Group and Individual Functions, and a Criterion." *Psychological Bulletin* 51:63–64.

Barker, R. G., J.S. Kounin, and H. F. Wright, eds. 1943. *Child Behavior and Development: A Course of Representative Studies.* New York: McGraw-Hill.

Brown, R. 1973. *A First Language: The Early Stages.* Cambridge, Mass.: Harvard University Press.

Carmichael L., ed. 1946. *Manual of Child Psychology.* New York: Wiley.

Clifford, J. and G. E. Marcus, eds. 1986. *Writing Culture: The Politics and Poetics of Ethnography.* Berkeley: University of California Press.

Cohen, P. 1991. "A Source of Bias in Longitudinal Investigations of Change." In *Best Methods for the Analysis of Change: Recent Advances, Unanswered Questions, Future Directions.* Ed. L. M. Collins and J. L. Horn. Washington, D.C.: American Psychological Association.

Collins, L. M., and J. L. Horn, eds. 1991. *Best Methods for the Analysis of Change: Recent Advances, Unanswered Questions, Future Directions.* Washington, D.C.: American Psychological Association.

Collins, L. M., and J. W. Graham. 1991. Comments on P. Cohen, "A Source of Bias in Longitudinal Investigations of Change." In *Best Methods for the Analysis of Change: Recent Advances, Unanswered Questions, Future Directions.* Ed. Collins and J. L. Horn. Washington, D.C.: American Psychological Association.

Corsaro, W. A., and D. R. Heise. 1990. "Event Structure Models from Ethnographic Data." In *Sociological Methodology.* Ed. C. Clogg. London: Blackwell.

Davis, D. S. 1991. "Rich Cases: The Ethics of Thick Description." *Hastings Center Report* (July-Aug.):12–17.

Duckworth, E. 1987. *"The Having of Wonderful Ideas" and Other Essays on Teaching and Learning.* New York: Teachers College Press.

Estes, W. K. 1956. "The Problem of Inference from Curves Based on Group Data." *Psychological Bulletin* 53:134–40.

Feagin, J. R., A. M. Orum, and G. Sjoberg, eds. 1991. *A Case for the Case Study.* Chapel Hill: University of North Carolina Press.

Fleck, L. 1979. *Genesis and Development of a Scientific Fact.* Chicago: University of Chicago Press.

Forrest, J., A. Abbott. 1990. "The Optimal Matching Method for Studying Anthropological Sequence Data: An Introduction and Reliability Analysis." *Journal of Quantitative Anthropology* 2:151–70.

Freeman, F. N., and C. D. Flory. 1943. "Growth in Intellectual Ability." In *Child behavior and development: A course of representative studies.* Ed. R. G. Barker, J. S. Kounin, and H. F. Wright. New York: McGraw-Hill.

Galtung, J. 1967. *Theory and Methods of Social Research.* New York: Columbia University Press.

Gigerenzer, G., et al. 1989. *The Empire of Chance: How Probability Changed Science and Everyday Life.* New York: Cambridge University Press.

Goodman, N. 1981. "Critical Response: The Telling and the Told." *Critical Inquiry* 7:799–801.

Griffin, L. J. 1992. "Temporality, Events, and Explanation in Historical Sociology: An Introduction." *Sociological Methods and Research* 20:403–27.

Griffin, L. J. 1993. "Narrative, Event-Structure Analysis, and Causal Interpretation in Historical Sociology." *American Journal of Sociology* 98:1094–1133.

Halliday, M. A. K. 1975. *Learning How to Mean: Explorations in the Development of Language.* London: Edward Arnold.

Hayes, K. J. 1953. "The Backward Curve: A Method for the Study of Learning." *Psychological Review* 60:269–75.

Heise, D. 1988. "Computer Analysis of Cultural Structures." *Social Science Computer Review* 6:183–96.

———. 1989. "Modeling Event Structures." *Journal of Mathematical Sociology* 14:139–69.

Hunter, K. M. 1991. *Doctor's Stories: The Narrative Structure of Medical Knowledge.* Princeton, N.J.: Princeton University Press.

Jonsen, A. R., and S. Toulmin. 1988. *The Abuse of Casuistry: A History of Moral Reasoning.* Berkeley: University of California Press.

Kruskal, J. B. 1983. "An Overview of Sequence Comparison." In *Time Warps, String Edits, and Macromolecules: The Theory and Practice of Sequence Comparison.* Ed. D. Sankoff and J. B. Kruskal. Reading, Mass.: Addison-Wesley.

Kuhn, T. S. 1970. *The Structure of Scientific Revolutions.* 2d ed. Chicago: University of Chicago Press.

Lewin, K. 1935. "The Conflict between Aristotelian and Galileian Modes of Thought in Contemporary Psychology." In Lewin, *A Dynamic Theory of Personality: Selected Papers.* New York: McGraw-Hill.

Marcus, G. E., and M. J. Fischer. 1986. *Anthropology as Cultural Critique: An Experimental Moment in the Human Sciences.* Chicago: University of Chicago.

McCabe, A., and C. Peterson. 1990. "Keep Them Talking: Parental Styles of Interviewing and Subsequent Child Narrative Skill." Presented at the Fifth International Congress of Child Language, Budapest, Hungary, 16 July.

Merrell, M. 1931. "The Relationship of Individual Growth to Average Growth." *Human Biology* 3:37–70.

Miller, G. A. 1977. *Spontaneous Apprentices: Children and Language.* New York: Seabury Press.

Mishler, E. G. 1979. "Meaning in Context: Is There Any Other Kind?" *Harvard Educational Review* 49:1–19.

———. 1984. *The Discourse of Medicine: Dialectics of Medical Interviews.* Norwood, N.J.: Ablex.

———. 1990. "Validation in Inquiry-Guided Research: The Role of Exemplars in Narrative Studies." *Harvard Educational Review* 60:415–42.

———. 1992. "Work, Identity, and Narrative: An Artist-Craftsman's Story." In *Storied Lives: The Cultural Politics of Self-Understanding.* Ed. G. C. Rosenwald and R. L. Ochberg. New Haven, Conn.: Yale University Press.

———. Forthcoming. "Narrative Accounts in Clinical and Research Interviews." In *The Construction of Professional Discourse.* Ed. B-L. Gunnarsson, P. Linell, and B. Nordberg.

Mishler, E. G., and N. E. Waxler. 1968. *Interaction in Families: An Experimental Study of Family Processes and Schizophrenia.* New York: Wiley.

———. 1975. "The Sequential Patterning of Interaction in Normal and Schizophrenic Families." *Family Process* 14:17–50.

Nader, L. 1993. "Paradigm Busting and Vertical Linkage." *Contemporary Sociology* 22:6–7.

Nelson, K. 1986. *Event Knowledge: Structure and Function in Development.* Hillsdale, N.J.: Erlbaum.

Nelson, K., ed. 1989. *Narratives from the Crib.* Cambridge, Mass.: Harvard University Press.

Nesselroade, J. R. 1991. "Interindividual Differences in Intraindividual Change." In *Best Methods for the Analysis of Change: Recent Advances, Unanswered Questions, Future Directions.* Ed. L. M. Collins and J. L. Horn. Washington, D.C.: American Psychological Association.

Olson, W. C., B. O. Hughes. 1943. "Growth of the Child as a Whole." In *Child Behavior and Development: A Course of Representative Studies.* Ed. R. G. Barker, J. S. Kounin, and H. F. Wright. New York: McGraw-Hill.

Peterson, C., and A. McCabe. 1983. *Developmental Psycholinguistics: Three Ways of Looking at a Child's Narrative.* New York: Plenum.

Ragin, C. C. 1987. *The Comparative Method: Moving Beyond Qualitative and Quantitative Strategies.* Berkeley: University of California Press.

———. 1991. "Introduction: The Problem of Balancing Discourse on Cases and Variables in Comparative Social Science." *International Journal of Comparative Sociology* 32:1–8.

Ragin, C. C., and H. S. Becker, eds. 1992. *What Is a Case? Exploring the Foundations of Social Inquiry.* New York: Cambridge University Press.

Riley, M. W. 1963. *Sociological Research.* Vol. 1, *A Case Approach.* New York: Harcourt, Brace.

Robinson, W. S. 1950. "Ecological Correlations and the Behavior of Individuals." *American Sociological Review* 15:351–57.

Rueschemeyer, D. 1991. "Different Methods, Contradictory Results? Research on Development and Democracy." *International Journal of Comparative Sociology* 32:9–38.

Runkel, P. J. 1990. *Casting Nets and Testing Specimens: Two Grand Methods of Psychology.* New York: Praeger.

Sacks, O. 1993. "Making Up the Mind." *New York Review of Books* 40, no. 7:42–49.

Sankoff, D., and J. B. Kruskal, eds. 1983. *Time Warps, String Edits, and Macromolecules: The Theory and Practice of Sequence Comparison.* Reading, Mass.: Addison-Wesley.

Sidman, M. 1952. "A Note on Functional Relations Obtained from Group Data." *Psychological Bulletin* 49:263–69.

Weil, J. 1977. "Lexical Development: A Minilongitudinal Approach." Unpublished.

Whitley, B. E. 1992. "Units of Analysis, Measurement Scales, and Statistics: A Comment on Kerwin and Shaffer." *Personality and Social Psychology Bulletin* 18:680–84.

Willett, J. B. Forthcoming. "Measuring Change More Effectively by Modeling Individual Growth Over Time." In *The International Encyclopedia of Education.* Ed. T. Husen and T. N. Postlethwaite. 2d ed. Oxford: Pergamon.

Willett, J. B., and A. G. Sayer. Forthcoming. "Using Covariance Structure Analysis to Detect Correlates and Predictors of Individual Change Over Time." *Psychological Bulletin.*

Wohlwill, J. F. 1970. "Methodology and Research Strategy in the Study of Developmental Change." In *Lifespan Developmental Psychology: Research and Theory.* Ed. L. R. Goulet and P. B. Baltes. New York: Academic.

Wolf, M. 1992. *A Trice-Told Tale: Feminism, Postmodernism, and Ethnographic Responsibility.* Stanford, Calif.: Stanford University Press.

5   Culture, Development, Disability

R. P. MCDERMOTT AND HERVÉ VARENNE

What I liked about anthropology was its inexhaustible faculty for negation, its relentless definition of man, as though he were no better than God, in terms of what he is not.

Samuel Beckett, *Molloy* (1955)

It is always easier to see misfortune rather than injustice in the afflictions of other people. Only the victims occasionally do not share the inclination.

Judith Shklar, *The Faces of Injustice* (1990)

Cultural Contexts for Disability

In the eighteenth and nineteenth centuries, people on Martha's Vineyard, a small island off Cape Cod, suffered, or, we might say, were privileged by a high rate of genetically inherited deafness, approximately one person in every 155. It is easy to use the word *suffered* to evoke sympathy for the plight of the "deaf." It is a physical difference that can count, and it is not unusual for deaf people to suffer terribly for the way it is made to count in various social settings. Interestingly, the people of Martha's Vineyard did not share the horror with which most Americans approach deafness. The Vineyard deaf could not hear, but the community there turned not hearing into something everyone could easily work with, occasionally work around, and sometimes turn into a strength. In Nora Groce's *Everyone Here Spoke Sign Language* (1986), we are given a picture of deaf persons thoroughly integrated into the Vineyard community and the hearing thoroughly integrated into the communicational intricacies of sign. When surviving older members of the community were asked to remember their deaf neighbors, they could not always remember who among them had been deaf, for everyone there spoke sign language, sometimes even the hearing people with other hearing people.

The case of the Vineyard deaf, and it is not the only such case (Kakumasu 1968), raises interesting questions about the nature of disability, questions that go beyond etiology to function and circumstance: When does a physical difference count, under what conditions, and in what ways, and for what reasons? When, how, and why: these are deeply cultural issues, and, depending on how a physical difference is noticed, identified, and made consequential, the lives of those unable to do something can be either enabled or disabled by those around them. From Martha's Vineyard, there is good news: it is possible to organize a culture in which deafness does not have to isolate a person from a full round in the life of a community; not being able to hear can cut off behavioral possibilities that can be taken care of in other ways, and, by everyone speaking sign, other possibilities can be explored. There is also bad news: Martha's Vineyard was not an island unto itself, but a peripheral area in a larger social field within which deafness was treated as an appalling affliction.

The easy use of the term *suffer* often carries an invidious comparison of the "disabled" with those seemingly "enabled" by the conventions of a culture. A more principled account of life inside a labeled/disabled community would show, for example, that the abjection with which normals approach the problems of labeled/disabled people is one-sided and distorting. A recent advance in cochlea implants, for example, has deaf children hearing, a seeming advance to researchers, but the source of unrest in the deaf community. Outsiders to the deaf experience are surprised to find that being able to hear is not as important as being a member of the deaf community. Similarly, sighted persons are surprised that lifelong blind persons surgically given the "gift" of sight in their adult years are usually overwhelmed by the drabness of the seen world; "suffering" blindness is minimal compared to "suffering" the depression that follows the recovery of vision (Gregory and Wallace 1963). We must not confuse our ignorance of life with a physical difference for an account of that life; nor should we forget that the particulars of our own ignorance are likely a more crucial determinant of the disabilities manifest in some lives than any differences in the physical makeup of the people.

On Martha's Vineyard in the nineteenth century, people had jobs to do, and they did them. That one person could do them faster or better than another was likely less important than that the jobs got done. In such a world, it was not important to sort out the deaf institutionally from the hearing. By important social measures—rates of marriage and propinquity, economic success, and mastery of a trade—deaf persons were indistinguishable from hearing persons on Martha's Vineyard. There is record of an unbalanced deaf person in the community, but the order to have him committed to an institution did not emphasize his deafness as part of his problem and was, in fact, signed by a deaf person. It is possible to organize a culture in which the deaf play an equal and unremarkable role in most parts of life. On Martha's Vineyard, when it was time to institutionalize a troubled person, a deaf person could be asked to play either side of the culturally constructed divide between the unbalanced and the incarcerator, but not either side of the culturally irrelevant divide between hearing and deaf.

Unfortunately, deaf persons on Martha's Vineyard were not treated well by outsiders who could not sign, and the fortunes of the deaf declined as the island opened up to extensive tourism. That they could not hear was made worse by outsiders who pitied them, wrote them up in Boston newspapers, explained their origin in scientific tracts (one popular claim was that their deafness was a result of a melancholy suffered by their mothers), called for a remedy of their situation, and suggested a eugenics program for their erasure. An irony can be found in the fact that perhaps the people best able on Martha's Vineyard to read such reports were deaf. Although most Vineyarders went to school for only five years, in the late eighteenth century, by mandate of the state educational system, deaf children were supported through ten years of school, and, when faced with a difficult reading and writing task, the hearing would often go to a deaf person for help. This is particularly difficult for participants in contemporary American culture to imagine, as it is now the case that the most difficult task of deaf educators is to get their students past the basic levels of reading and writing.

If the case of the Vineyard deaf suggests that we might want to rethink our understanding of the role of culture in the diagnosis and remediation of developmental disorders, a case study from New York City in the late 1980s can make more specific how that rethinking might develop. First, we can look at the case study of a deaf child at home and school. Then we can take up its implications for how we should think about the very notions of culture, disability, development, and the relations between them.

In a dissertation with the appropriate title "Arrangements for the Display of Deafness," Linda Rosa-Lugo (1989) studied a six-year-old deaf girl at school, where she seemed to be having a difficult time, and at home, where she seemed to be having an easy and highly communicative life. Fortunately, she was born into a fantastic family, albeit with the twin difficulty that she and her older brother were both deaf and their parents were native Spanish speakers in an English-speaking world. A third and middle child could hear. Together, the five members of the family give us a glimpse of a small version of what Martha's Vineyard might have been like for deaf children, namely, a place where people communicated with each other whatever the difficulties, a place where inclusion in family and community were more important than exclusion. In their study of deaf culture in America, Padden and Humphries, themselves deaf, state the basic case: "being able or unable to hear does not emerge as significant in itself; instead it takes on significance in the context of other sets of meaning to which the child has been exposed" (1988:22). Rosa-Lugo looks at four scenes, or sets of meaning: two at school, where the performance of a communication was understood and evaluated primarily as a pedagogical success or failure; and two at home, where tasks seemingly identical to those tackled at school were woven as a part of a different relational fabric and understood primarily as fun.

The school settings involved the six-year-old Raquel, her mother, a teacher, and an assistant teacher. The three adults worked hard to get Raquel to identify, at different times, in American Sign Language (ASL), in English, or in Spanish, various objects or actions, for example, juice, napkin, cup, and to pour. Mostly, Raquel refused, and when she did reply, she sometimes did so incorrectly. The adults were relentless and pushed Raquel to perform just the right word, in just the right code, at just the right time. In her own turn, Raquel mixed together crying, running to her mother, and answering rightly and wrongly on occasion, all apparently in just the right order to get the teachers confused about what questions were being answered or even asked at any given time. In desperation, to organize her attention (or theirs), the teachers would withhold rewards from Raquel until she voiced particular words. The overall tone of the events is unpleasant and perhaps painful to all.

The scene at home is quite different. The naming tasks given to Raquel, even when school related, are attached to quite different social activities. All members of the family use three codes, spoken English, spoken Spanish, and sign, to get done the jobs that come before them. When the mother organizes an activity around Raquel identifying various objects and their colors, her older brother becomes a full participant, holding objects in the air, repeating questions, urging and evaluating answers. Raquel gets some things right and some things wrong, but never stops participating. The confrontation that marked some of the interactions at school never developed. Unlike the school scene in which the teachers insist that answers be spoken, deafness seems not to have been the issue. The answers were accepted for their content, rather than their code. Sometimes Raquel spoke, and sometimes she signed, just like the others in her house, just like what might have happened on Martha's Vineyard.

It is important to note that Rosa-Lugo does not claim to have distinguished all cases of school from all cases of home by producing only two examples from each, and she encourages the reader to imagine how deafness, under the right conditions, could be a strength in school just as it could become a maximum problem in a home where parents did not manage a smooth transition from one code to another. The analysis even produces evidence to the point; note, for example, that Raquel's mother is on the scene at both school and home. The key question concerns the identification of just what kind of thing deafness is in any given interaction. At home, there is evidence that deafness is usually a workable deficit and can even be a plus. The extraordinary event on Rosa-Lugo's tape comes with a display of a fourth communicative code, namely, spoken deafness. While the mother and older brother are working with Raquel on her naming tasks, the middle and hearing child is apparently feeling quite left out of the interaction. She calls her mother often, announces an emergency or two, calls out the answers to some of the questions put to Raquel, and, when all this fails to distract the home lesson, she starts to scream in a good imitation of the way a deaf child pronounces and intones spoken English. She is attended to immediately. On Martha's Vineyard, hearing people sometimes found it easier or more efficient to use sign than to speak, for example, for land-boat communication, for passing secrets around tourists, for intimate conversations in public places like hospitals. In Raquel's house, not only sign, but the high-pitched spoken English of the deaf sometimes had its moment.

Martha's Vineyard and Raquel's family together show how even a difference as definite as not being able to hear in a social world built for the hearing does not have to be a problem. It is one kind of problem to have a behavioral range different from social expectations, and it is another kind of problem to be in a cultural nexus in which that difference is used by others to make one look bad. The argument of this chapter is that the second problem is often the more serious.

THREE WAYS OF THINKING ABOUT CULTURE AND DISABILITY

At the very moment in which this object, "madness," took shape, there was also constructed the subject judged capable of understanding madness. To the construction of the object madness, there corresponded a rational subject who "knew" about madness and who understood it. . . . I tried to understand this kind of collective, plural experience which was defined between the sixteenth and nineteenth centuries and which was marked by the interac-

tion between the birth of "rational" man who recognizes and "knows" madness, and madness itself as an object susceptible of being understood and determined.
                                    Michel Foucault, *Remarks on Marx* (1991)

There are numerous ways to think about the nature of culture, and the terms *disability* and *development* have been defined and debated ad nauseam. Within the variety, there is enough order to show that there are three approaches to using the terms *culture, development,* and *disability* and that they differ along a continuum of assumptions about the world, its people, and the ways they learn. In the present section, we contrast the three approaches to highlight the range of assumptions and biases that come with using the terms.[1] The three approaches are discussed in the same order that they developed across the past thirty-five years; the second approach represents an advance over the first, and the third approach, in turn, not only extends the first two but takes them into account as data.

The sequence represents not only a theoretical advance, but ideally an increase in the resources available to the moral order. We are aware, as Judith Shklar has argued, that "the outraged jeremiad is the mark of a moralistic rather than a moral society" (1979:24), and so it is that in calling for a defense of all against all others, a defense of each of us against our own culture, we run the risk of whining more than actually fixing. We envision no great society where the problems of people being labeled and disabled are forever cured; it is the human situation to create such problems and every generation's responsibility to confront them in their particulars. Many cultures have been harder on its citizens than the United States, but many have been gentler. In pointing to how the very term *disability* has been used to make things harder rather than gentler, and this despite great efforts on the part of our very kindest citizens, we hope to help stem the tide.

The *cultural deprivation* approach takes up the possibility that people in various groups develop differently enough that their members can be shown to be measurably distinct on presumed developmental milestones. This approach is founded analytically on the assumption of a stable set of tasks that can be used to record varying performances across persons and cultures. Low-level performances by members of a group are taken as examples of what the people of the group have not yet developed (for example, certain versions of abstraction, syllogistic reasoning, metacontextual accounts of linguistic behavior, and so on). A crude version of this argument has it, "We have culture, and you don't"; or a little more carefully put, "We seem to have more culture than you do." To unpack the assumptions underlying the argument, consider the following state of the world, its problems, and their consequences:

> The world consists of a set of tasks, some of which are difficult. Development refers to progress up preordained steps to well-defined competencies in handling important tasks. The contrast between the enabled and the disabled can be found in the work people do that shows that some are able to do the most important tasks and that others cannot keep up. The fate of the disabled rests in the easy attitude that institutions can work with those who lag behind, but basically they are out of the running for the rewards that come with a full cultural competence.

By method and style of argument, this approach has been based mostly on psychology and has attracted the intuitive wrath of many anthropologists, who have argued that all cultures, and all languages, however interesting their differences, are essentially equivalent; this has not stopped anthropologists, particularly those working with minorities in their own cultures, from falling for the rhetorical attraction of the deprivation stand and once again finding a "they" who are less than our "we."

The *cultural difference* approach takes up the possibility that people in different groups develop in ways equivalently well tuned to the demands of their culture and that different cultures, though various, offer equivalent roads to complete human development. This approach relies less on predefined tasks and focuses instead on the tasks performed by ordinary people, well beyond the reach of the laboratory, as a matter of course in different cultures. If it is possible to describe the task structure of varying cultures, then it is possible to discern what abilities and disabilities cultures might develop (for example, quantity-estimation skills among Kpelle farmers and Baltimore milk-truck dispatchers, calculation skills among Vai tailors, mnemonic strategies among navigators using the skies for direction). A crude version has it that, "We have culture, and you have a different one." To unpack the assumptions underlying the argument, consider a world similar to the one considered above, but with different problems and consequences:

> The world consists of a wide range of tasks, all of them situated, all of them emerging within a cultural context. Development refers to progress along many roads to task competence, each with its own pace, each with its own price, but all interesting. The contrast between the enabled and the different can be found in the work people do that shows, for any given task, that some achieve full competence, others focus on only parts, and a few seem unable to develop any mastery, all a case of different skills for different wills. The fate of the different as disabled rests in the liberal lament that human variation is wonderful, but those who cannot display required skills in the correct format at the right time are out of the running for the rewards of their culture.

This approach is favored among ethnographically oriented psychologists and anthropologists, particularly those working on school problems among minority populations.

The third approach, the *culture as disability* stand, takes up the possibility that all cultures both socialize and sort and that, indeed, in teaching its members what to aspire to and hope for, every culture also teaches how to notice, handle, mistreat, and remediate those who fall short. As a pattern of institutions, a culture produces a wealth of positions for human beings to inhabit. Each position requires that the person inhabiting it must possess, and must be *known as possessing,* particular qualities that symbolize, and thereby constitute, the reality of their position *to others.* The people in any position may be unable to perform what people in other positions can perform, but the limits on learning what others do is socially not as primary as Americans like to believe. People are only incidentally born or early enculturated into being different. It is more important to understand how they are put into positions for being treated differently. Notice that by this approach, subcultures or otherwise labeled groups do not stand alone, nor even in a simple relation to more dominant other groups, but always in relation to the wider system of which all groups, dominant and minority, are a part.

This approach starts with the question of why any culture, or more likely, any elite group within a culture, would develop an assumed stable set of tasks and a theory of cognition and development against which people of various kinds might be distinguished, measured, documented, remediated, and pushed aside. On what grounds could experts have assumed that the complex worlds of individuals in multiple relationships with each other would stand still enough to be characterized by simplified accounts of either their culture, their cognition, or the ties between whatever culture and cognition are taken to be? One version of the grounds for simplicity is that such theorizing and the methodological assumptions that go with them are part of wider-scale institutional and political agendas, in particular, that it has been handy for modern, ideologically rationalistic, class-divided, industrial- and information-based states to isolate individuals as units of analysis and to record the intimacies of their minds for public scrutiny and control. The contemporary nation state is above all a recordkeeper, much more than it is a container of culture or an organizer of learning (Thomas, Meyer, Ramirez, and Boli 1988). A crude version of this approach has it thus:

> We have a culture, or at least we think we do, and, uh, so do you, well, most likely; but it is difficult to tell the difference between

when we are analyzing our culture and when we are living it, and, despite the fact that you people seem to be less than we are, or different enough that you might just as well be less than we are, we are unsure that we have available either the analytic categories or the political awareness to know whether it is we or you who are being most disabled by our situation together.

To unpack the assumptions underlying the argument, consider a variation on the worlds considered above, this time with a third set of problems and consequences:

> The world may or may not be a set of well-defined tasks, but it has definitely been shaped by modern societies into a set of measurable tasks of varying difficulty, and task competencies can be impossible to develop or show off at the right time. Development refers to the institutional arrangements by which individual behavior is measured, and individuals made responsible for, progress up the road to task competence, generally without theoretical, methodological, or political attention to the possibility that both the tasks and occasions for their use are conventions at best and political fabrications at worst. The contrast between the enabled and the oppressed can be found in the work people do to show that some display task competence, some hide away at task relevant moments, some isolated from task performance mill about the bottom of the social structure complaining, some only a few task moves better than those on the bottom claim themselves to be lord of all, and only a few disparage the task competencies others have built. The fate of the oppressed as disabled rests on the cynical assumption that, with a severity depending on the conditions of economic and political growth, whatever solutions can be momentarily developed, new kinds of tasks and new kinds of disability can take their place.

Being acquired by a position in a culture is difficult and unending work for all involved—for those being acquired, children, for example, and for those doing the acquiring, their teachers and employers. Every culture invites a delineation and specification not just of what has to be done and who can do it, but of what is difficult, in what ways for whom, and under what circumstances. In fact, even things that do not have to get done on simply functional grounds can be enshrined as the most important measure of the people in a culture. *Cultures are not only occasions for disabilities, they actively organize ways for persons to be disabled.*

By this last approach, culture refers to how we organize our hopes and dreams of how the world should be. The same people, using the same materials and in ways systematically related to our hopes and dreams, also give us our problems. Without a culture we would not know what our problems are; culture, or better, the people around us in culture, help to define the situation-specific, emotionally demanding, and sensuous problems that we must work on today with only the tools we have available here and now. We might just as well say that culture fashions problems for us and, from the same source materials, expects us to construct solutions. It is from life inside this trap that we often get the feeling that working on problems can make things worse.

There is a significant sense in which, or, at the very least, there is much analytic leverage to be gained by thinking as if: without a money system, there is no debt; without a kinship system, no orphans; without a class system, no deprivation; without schools, no learning disabilities; without a working concept of truth, no liars; without eloquence, no inarticulateness. The problems that exist in one culture do not have to exist in another culture, or at least not with the same interpretations and consequences, and the same is true in the same culture at different points of its history or at different levels of its hierarchy. Even a sure physical condition, for example, severe mental retardation, as constraining as it is on any individual's development, is an amazingly different phenomenon in different cultures (Edgerton 1970), across the last century of our own culture (Sarason and Doris 1979), or within different households on the same block of our here and now (Mannoni 1972). For the parents of a retarded child, the situation is culturally complex. Parents are supposed to give birth to fully healthy children who can live out the cultural agenda, and anything less brings two problems to the child's situation: the child must not only suffer from not being able to engage in certain activities, but from being mistreated by those who can. Cultures define what should be the case. They are often explicit, and often unfair, about what mothers should think about their own children and what the rest of us should think about both the children and their mothers; were it not for melancholy, remember, Martha's Vineyard would not have had so many deaf. If being deaf can go unnoticed in one culture and be a point of torture in another, so it is for being a bastard, a twin, an intersexed person, or even, so simply in a sexist society, a girl.

If cultures define their own problems, can we figure out how they define the ones they claim to have? If a disability corresponds to a situation, just what is our situation that we would have these particular disabilities? From what cultural materials are these problems put together, and from within what institutional and political nexus? And where can we get the tools to confront the system that has given us the problems we have?

IF CULTURES ARE DISABLING, HOW CAN WE RESEARCH
AND CONFRONT OUR SITUATION?

> The search for method becomes one of the most important prob-
> lems of the entire enterprise of understanding the uniquely human
> forms of psychological activity. . . . the method is simultaneously
> prerequisite and product, the tool and the result of the study.
> Lev Vygotsky, *Mind in Society* (1978)

> A curious analogy could be based on the fact that even the hugest
> telescope has to have an eye-piece no larger than the eye.
> Ludwig Wittgenstein, *Culture and Value* (1931)

The three approaches to culture, development, and disability have enormous consequences for how one proceeds methodically to research and
confront our present situation. A brief account of the differences can focus
on the role of context in the organization and subsequent analysis of behavior (see Goodwin and Duranti 1992; Kendon 1990; McDermott 1993).
The deprivation approach ignores context as much as possible; the difference approach plays up the importance of context as if the contexts were
preestablished sites for people to display their competencies; and the culture as disability approach tries to understand context as a product of the
work people do in the course of making sense with each other and the
preconstructed materials of their culture, materials filled with the biases
and inequalities of their social structure. The approach to context is crucial, because it defines one's unit of analysis and sets limits on the conclusions that can be reached. Without a strong sense of context, research uses
the individual for a unit of analysis, and kinds of individuals—the deaf,
the learning disabled, the illiterate—are the referents for conclusions.
With a dynamic sense of context, the units are usually not individual persons, but their activities as they reach backward and forward in behavioral
time; the conclusions then are about the structure of the activities.

These are complex issues, and this section offers only a brief summary
of the methodological commitments and habits of each approach.

The deprivation approach places great trust in received and institutionally established categories. The reliance is that we know how to identify
tasks in the world and that we can measure the performances of individuals on such tasks. For any hypothesis about how culture figures in the
distribution of successful and failing performances, it is equally important
that analysts have ways to identify the stable social identity of any group
member.

The assumption that there are stable tasks, stable persons with stable
social identities, and stable descriptions of stable tasks performed by sta-

ble persons with stable and always relevant social identities is not well grounded. The systematic study of persons performing predefined tasks can perhaps tell us a great deal about predefined tasks and the biases of their makers, but it is difficult to show that they have anything to say about what people do when they are not acting within such tasks. There is an old and quite sturdy argument about the danger of operationalizing one's procedures without regard for contextualizing one's results: the argument is that the conditions that operationally define a given object for analysis are only analytically useful while the conditions apply; once the conditions are removed, for example, once a banana is removed from the chemical solution that reacts in a defining way to bananas, then the banana, for analytic purposes, is no longer a banana. There is sometimes reason to abandon this argument, but it must be done carefully and with a forfeit of certainty of conclusion (Bateson 1972; Cole, Hood, and McDermott 1978).

Some argue that performances on tasks predefined by psychologists overlap with stable patterns in the shifting terms of social identity. This should raise questions of believability, despite the fact that we all make such correlations in our daily language; we all assume, for example, that the deaf cannot hear and that is what constitutes their place in the world as deaf persons. The mechanisms that might allow for such a match in reality have not been well explicated, and the correlations that do exist have been claimed by some to be nothing more than a manifestation of how various biases, class and color racist categories, for example, infiltrate, and make relevant, the kinds of tasks developed by schools and developmental psychologists for purposes of measurement. To display what someone knows is analytically difficult, and to display what someone does not know or cannot do, if only because they may be trying to do something else, if only because they may be operating on aspects of the task not well understood by the task definer, may be impossible. Such difficulties and impossibilities have not stopped psychometric and experimental cognitive psychology from becoming the institutional language of schooling and its problems.

The difference approach in principle accepts no categories for analysis, whether of tasks or of persons, until they can be shown to be in use in the behavior of the persons under analysis. Where can we get the categories we need to describe the world in which people live? If we ask the people directly what we would like to know, we will ask them our questions, fully loaded with our assumptions. We need their categories to ask even elementary questions of them. We need, in fact, the questions they ask of each other, or, as phrased three decades ago by Charles Frake (1964), we need notes on their queries, not so much to learn how they talk about each other, but how they actually talk with each other, in their very processing of each other. If every culture has its own categories, its own skills, and its own modes of interpretation, then a description of the people in a culture relies on long-term participation that allows the analyst to derive categories people themselves use to handle their lives with each other. One must look and listen as methodically as possible to discern the sensitivities people use to get around making something of nothing and nothing of something in culturally prescribed ways.

There is a simple epistemology behind this work. The world is likely not available on only your terms and may be more difficult to see and hear than you had thought, but the categories needed to describe the lives of the people you are studying are available upon extended looking and listening. The world is a good place; if you are careful enough, you can understand a part of it; if you are sensitive enough, as the people of Martha's Vineyard were sensitive enough to find the strengths of deaf persons, you can even make the world a better place.

Methodologically, studies based on the possibility that all people make sense and develop fully, albeit in accord with the particulars of the situation, albeit in accord with what David Plath (1980) has called the "idiom of their heritage," have been dedicated to more careful data analyses than insisted on by most anthropologists and to more careful accounts of the contexts with which behavior is organized than is allowed by experimental psychology. At their best, such studies have insisted on both rigor and respect, on both precision and context sensitivity. At their worst, such studies threaten to fail where traditional anthropology failed, in the practical but naive assumption that native categories are simple and stable, that they form uniquely real patterns, and that the best metaphor for the flow of human history is the mosaic, solid and well-bounded bits of color and shape intelligible only to natives. The alternative to this assumption is a focus on culture as an ongoing achievement filled with tensions, disputes, borders, resistances, neuroses, compromises, and repairs (Drummond 1980). Culture, says David Plath (1980), is a "parliament of prodigals," and its every seemingly stable pattern is the product of compromise by all involved.

The culture as disability approach commits us to a constant confrontation with received categories. The categories we need to study our lives are not available for the asking, nor are they available to those who would simply look and listen, no matter how sensitively. The categories we need are not only difficult to come by, they are systematically unavailable; we might just as well say that they are hidden. As Karl Marx once noted (in the third volume of *Capital*), and as Lev Vygotsky (1978; 1986) liked to cite, if the surface of appearances coincided with reality, we would not need science. There is nothing inherently wrong in describing deaf persons as deaf, learning-disabled persons as LD, or people who cannot read as illiterate, but in a social order that is anxious to use disability as a way to stratify and degrade, the categories are in need of constant revision.

This is bad news for more than just the scientist, for it suggests we are all in need of new categories to reorganize our lives. If everyone in a culture thinks that situation X is a problem, it is likely the case that (1) the problem that must be confronted lies elsewhere, and (2) the formulation that situation X is the problem, by keeping the focus on situation X, is in fact part of the problem. By this way of thinking, if deafness appears to be a problem in a community, it is likely the case that the deaf, whom we know from Martha's Vineyard can be complete members of any culture, are put upon by tensions from other sectors of their society. By this way of thinking, if developmental disabilities of various kinds appear to people in the schools to be our problem, then our easy acceptance of their arguments should be one of our first topics of consideration for gaining an understanding of the institutional and cultural contexts of the problem and its consequences.

How then can we get the categories we need to gain a new perspective and to solve our problems? There is no one answer to this, of course, but one place to start is to construct environments that play to people's strengths rather than their weaknesses. We need to create conditions that would make the most rather than the least of disabled persons, of those already disabled by the environments we have available and of those who will meet that fate later in life. We need most of all to construct a world in which the disabled do not have to spend their time arranging to avoid degradation by those around them. Such work will take more than just asking our questions and tallying the answers, and it will take more than figuring out their questions and how they are tied to answers, no matter how sensitive our approach. In addition to figuring out how the members of a disabled minority make sense, there are the even more difficult tasks of showing how they could have been made to look so bad in the eyes of the community and, more importantly, how to change the world enough for them to look sometimes wonderful and sometimes not, just like everyone else. Work on any of these levels can produce categories and research that could make a difference.

THE ACQUISITION OF PERSONS BY CULTURALLY WELL-FORMULATED DISABILITIES

Research on the psychological essence of childhood presupposes an examination of its social ethos, its internal link with the social

demands that are made with respect to the shaping of a person as a main unit of the productive forces.
V. V. Davydov, *Problems of Developmental Teaching* (1988)

Examples of culture as disability may be ubiquitous, but descriptions of disabilities from enough perspectives to allow for a contrast of our three approaches to culture in relation to disability are still rare. The following discussion offers only two examples, the learning-disabled child and the illiterate adult, to complement our introductory example from Martha's Vineyard.

Learning Disabilities (LD)

Deprivation. The school is a set of tasks, and people from the LD subculture, because there is something wrong with them, cannot perform the tasks as quickly or as well as others.

Difference. The school is a set of quite arbitrary tasks not necessarily well tied to the demands of everyday life (consider, for example, phonics, words out of context, digit-span memory), and people from the LD subculture are restricted in various institutional circumstances to operating on tasks in ways that reveal their weaknesses. The performance of LD people on other kinds of tasks, or even the apparent same tasks in other circumstances, can reveal their strengths.

Culture as disability. The world is not a set of tasks, at least not of the type learned, or systematically not learned, at school, but made to look that way as part of political arrangements that keep people documenting each other as failures. Over the past forty years, school performance has become integral to established political arrangements, and, by pitting all against all in the race for measured academic achievement on arbitrary tasks, school has become a primary site for the reproduction of inequality in access to various resources. The use of the term *LD* to describe, explain, and remediate children caught in the system of everyone having to do better than everyone else is a good case in point. Even if used sensitively by good people trying to do the right thing for children apparently disabled, the term has a political life that involves millions of people operating on little information about the social consequences of their work.[2]

The Case of Adam, Adam, Adam, and Adam. A group of us (Michael Cole, Lois Hood, Ray McDermott, and Kenneth Traupmann) worked with Adam and his third- and fourth-grade classmates across a range of settings for over a year (Cole and Traupmann 1981; Hood, McDermott, and Cole 1980; McDermott 1993). The settings included an oral test on experimental and psychometric tasks, classroom lessons, more relaxed after-school clubs, and one-on-one trips around New York City. We knew Adam well enough to notice elaborate differences in his behavior across the four settings that seemed to make up a continuum of competence, arbitrariness, and visibility:

Everyday life   After-school clubs   Classroom work groups   One-to-one tests
————————→   ————————————→   ——————————————→   ——————————→

The continuum is arranged from left to right and can be conceived as an increase of either (1) task difficulty and cognitive competence (from mastery in everyday life events, at one end, to minimal performance on test materials, on the other); (2) the arbitrariness of the task and the resources the child is allowed to use in the task performance (from everyday life, where tasks are well embedded in ongoing relations among persons and environments and one can use whatever means available to get the job done, at one end, to tasks ripped from their usual contexts and isolated specifically to measure what a child can do with them unaided by anything other than his or her mind); or (3) the social visibility, and often measurability, of the task performance (from invisible as a problem of any kind in everyday life settings to painfully and documentably noticeable on tests). How are we to understand the four Adams who show up in the different contexts? Our three approaches to culture, development, and disability offer a framework for articulating Adam's situation.

By the deprivation approach, Adam is part of a group of people, who display particular symptoms in the face of reading and other language-specific tasks. These are persons grouped together by having been diagnosed LD. Adam is often described, by both diagnostic tests and school personnel, as having trouble paying attention and remembering words out of context. His symptoms are easily recognized, and his life in school is one of overcoming his disability. Life in school is particularly difficult, because he is often embarrassed by what he cannot do that other children find comparatively automatic.

By the difference stand, Adam can be understood in terms of what he cannot do only if he is also appreciated for what he can do. One way to understand the continuum of scenes along which his behavior varies is that it moves from unusually arbitrary in its demands on the child to completely open to local circumstance. At the test end of the continuum, one must face each question armed with only what is in one's head; if Adam has to remember a string of digits, he cannot ask for help, look up the information, or even take time to write it down. At the other end of the continuum, in everyday life, whatever one needs to do to get a job done is allowable; if Adam has to remember a telephone number, he is unconstrained in how he can proceed. In focusing on what Adam can do, we can see that he is fine in most of his life, and it is only in response to the arbitrary demands of the school culture that he is shown to be disabled. A careful examination of how he proceeds through life indicates he has a culture in need of respect from those better acculturated to the arbitrary demands of school.

By the culture as disability approach, Adam must be seen in terms of the people with whom he interacts and the ways in which they structure their activities together. Such an approach delivers an account not so much of Adam, but of the people most immediately involved in the production of moments for him to be recognized as a learning problem. It turns out that everyone in his class—the teachers, of course, but all the other children as well—are involved at various times in recognizing, identifying, displaying, mitigating, and even hiding what Adam is unable to do; if we include his tutors, the school psychologists, the local school of education where he goes for extra help (and his teachers for their degrees), and the social scientists who show up to study him and the government agencies that finance them, the number of people found contributing to Adam being highlighted as LD grows large. If we add on all the children who do well at school because Adam and others like him fail on standardized tests, then most of the country is involved in Adam being LD. We use the term *culture* for the arrangements that allow so many people to be involved in Adam's being LD, for this allows us to emphasize that, whatever problems Adam may have in his head, whether due originally to genetic or early socialization oddities, these would have had a different impact on his relationships with others if the culture he inhabits did not focus so relentlessly on individual success and failure. The culture that promises equality of opportunity while institutionalizing opportunities for less than half of the people is a culture that invites a category LD and its systematic application within the educational system. Adam is a display board for the weaknesses of the system.

The Illiterate

Deprivation. The world is a text, and some people know how to read better than others. The illiterate are missing what they need to get around the world, and, as a culture and an economy, we are being weighed down with unproductive workers who cannot read. That a high percentage of illiterate persons are in minority groups with a wide range of other problems shows what happens to people who cannot read and write in the modern world.

Difference. Literacy is a complex term covering a wide range of activities that differ from one context or culture to another. Its role in different societies, indeed, even in our society, can vary quite remarkably, and it is not at all clear that it has positive or even uniform effects on a people, their ways of thinking, or their modes of production (Scribner and Cole 1981; Street 1984).

Culture as disability. Illiteracy is a recent term in our lives; it was introduced in England about a century ago and has been gathering increasing attention since that time, to the point where now just about any shift in the definition can leave different portions of the population outside its attributive powers—for example, the computer or mathematically illiterate. The circumstances of the application of the term *illiteracy* to persons then and now have been intensely political more than pedagogical or remedial (Donald 1985; Smith 1986; Varenne and McDermott 1986). The fundamental and powerful assumptions of our culture are that: literacy is inherently good for the individual; mass literacy is good for society; literacy is difficult to acquire; literacy should be transmitted to illiterates through classrooms tasks. There is little comparative evidence to support any of these positions. Worse, and this is the crux of the matter, these positions may be least true in societies in which people believe them: the more people believe that literacy is difficult to acquire, the more they find reasons to explain why some read better than others and, correspondingly, why some do better than others in the economic and political ups and downs of the society; the more people believe that literacy is cognitively and culturally transformative, the more they can find reasons to degrade those without such powers; and the more people believe that literacy is best achieved in classrooms, the more they ignore the various other sources of literacy in the culture, and the more they insist on bringing back into school the persons who have already "failed" to develop literacy in school. The truth does not always beareth away the spoils. Even against the facts that literacy can help transform a social and information-processing system and can well be taught in classrooms, the very insistence on the truth of the facts can arrange conditions by which neither is possible.

The Case of Exterminating Literacy. With the help of a union local in New York City, a few of us (Shirley Edwards, David Harman, and Ray McDermott) ran a literacy program for the pest exterminators who service the city's housing projects. Half the exterminators were not fully licensed, and they faced lower pay and job insecurity until they could pass a written exam. The exam was written on an eleventh-grade level, and it would have been easy to find the men simply not knowing enough to work through the materials. If we had simply followed the deprivation approach, there was much at hand to guide our way. Standardized tests were in place, and experts could be hired to handle the many levels of reading ability or spoken-English competence to which the curriculum might be addressed. As lower-level city workers, the exterminators could be understood as missing many of the skills they would need to get through the test; coming from a "culturally deprived culture"—yes, we have culture, but they don't—one could only wonder how they could get through the day.

In our organization of the literacy program, we instead took a difference approach, which, by the counterexample of the exterminators' success in the program, gradually grew into a culture as disability stand. We assumed that the exterminators were not culturally deprived as much as they might be different from those with more education and that such differences were made most manifest on standardized tests. There was some evidence we were right, for the men had been working as exterminators for many years; if nothing else, we reasoned, they must know a great deal about exterminating. If we could appreciate what they could do, we might find a way to focus their skills in ways that could show up even on a difficult paper and pencil test. To maximize their participation and to make best use of their pest-control subculture, we hired exterminators who had passed the tests to teach those who had not. Yes, we have a culture, and so do they. The best way for them to operate in our culture, the reasoning goes, is on their own terms.

After weeks in the exterminator classrooms we had more evidence that the men knew much more than anyone might have imagined, and, even better, they were using it to help each other prepare for the exam. How could we have assumed otherwise? How could we have believed that they did not know? What is it about our culture that would have us systematically believing that we knew better than they did; what is it about our culture that would have us in effect disabled when it came to seeing the knowledge base of the exterminators? One answer to this question is in what happened in the classrooms that enabled the exterminators to become book learners. They already knew exterminating, but they had to organize their knowledge by its test relevance. One practice test opened with the question, "Fumigants do not burn the skin. True or false?" Half the men answered true and the other half, false. A quick look around the room indicated they all knew the answer; they all used fumigants in the field, and they had been careful not to have burned their hands off. Knowing that fumigants burn the skin is not the same has knowing the answer to a test question about whether fumigants burn the skin. The teacher understood their problem and addressed it directly: "Let me help you out with this one. Every time you get a question, true or false, if the question is false, the answer, automatic, is false. Why? Because fumigants burn the skin." His intervention is met with a chorus of affirmation. What is being taught here is an approach to the test, not knowledge about the world.

After answering incorrectly a question about the amount of pesticide in a particular application, "five percent to forty-five percent, true or false," a student was told, "You gonna go by the book, give or take five or ten percent. Don't go by your own ideas." On the job, their ideas rarely had to be within five or ten percent. Tests went by a different and, in terms of exterminator practice, a quite arbitrary standard of precision.

In the union classes, the men used "their" culture to run the classrooms, and they had a way of talking to each other that outsiders might not have managed well. They mobilized their community both in the classroom and beyond. Teachers and students who did not find it easy to operate in a classroom were found helping each other on lunchhours and weekends. Perhaps most exciting, the shop steward often reminded them it was not possible to fail at exterminating literacy forever. One could fail a big test, but one could take it over again and again. Every night they were told that the union would stick with them until they passed. By breaking through the constant threat of failure, they were reorganizing their access to school knowledge, and simultaneously they were showing us how much we were the other half of their failure. As they became more visible as knowing people, our own surprise made more visible to us how much we had invested in not seeing them as knowing people, and this even though we had organized the program to honor what they knew. Yes, culture can be disabling, not just to those labeled, but to those doing the labeling.

By the dictates of the culture, in American education, everyone must do better than everyone else. Of course, this is both logically and social-structurally impossible. Failure is a constant possibility in American schools, and, by the dictates of the normal curve, it absorbs about half the students along the way. Failure is always ready to acquire someone. Our exterminators had for the most part been acquired by school failure. We in turn had been acquired by school success in exact proportion to the difficulties of those designated as failures: we above the norms and they below. It is not easy to get the threat of failure out of the classroom. It keeps some mobilized and some hiding in the corner, but either way, it is difficult to avoid. For a moment, the exterminators were not acquired by failure, and they forced us to see how much we had managed to not see their literacy all along. Of course they could read and write, and they could handle whatever literacy chores came their way in the daily round. Everyday literacy acquires its readers, and this includes the bug exterminators of New York City. Test literacy, on the contrary, is designed to acquire failures, that is, to identify and document illiterates, and this can include the very same bug exterminators. For a brief moment, their union had made it possible for the exterminators to confront their tests and to move beyond. The system will have to make the next test harder if it is to maintain the balance established by the previous test. American education will have its failures. American culture will have its disabilities.

SUMMARY AND CONCLUSION

> Men make their own history, but they do not make it just as they please; they do not make it under circumstances chosen by themselves, but under circumstances directly encountered, given and transmitted from the past. The tradition of all the dead generations weighs like a nightmare on the brain of the living.
>
> Karl Marx, *The Eighteenth Brumaire of Louis Bonaparte* (1852)

> Unless we move expeditiously and imaginatively in the direction of a systematic response to the needs and rights of the handicapped, it is we, as a nation, as a people, and as individuals, who shall in the eyes of subsequent history be judged as morally handicapped.
>
> John J. McDermott, *Streams of Experience* (1986)

The terms *culture* and *development* have shared a long history in referring to botanical growth, and it has been easy for analysts to write as if culture were simply a controlled environment, as if a petri dish, for the development of children (see Williams 1977, 1984, for both a history of the terms and a critique of their use). By the logic of the botanical approach, the ethnographic study of development would deliver accounts of how life in different cultures would vary the timing and quality of developmental stages, and the distribution of developmental disabilities across cultures would be one point of focus. This essay has instead pointed to the ethnographic study of disabilities as a resource for rethinking the role of the terms *culture* and *development* in our own lives. The point has been that life in any culture is precarious enough that well-defined identifications of what persons should be, and of how they should develop, are irremediable distortions of the complex persons forced to live inside the limits of the identifications. An analysis of the cultural construction of institutional occasions for the creation and display of various disabilities—deafness, learning disabilities, and illiteracy—reveals not broken persons but inadequate identifications neatly tuned to the workings of institutions serving political and economic rather than educational ends (McDermott 1988).

The term *culture* allows us to talk about patterns in the work people do in organizing their lives together. The term *development* allows us to talk about milestones in the acquisition of individuals by cultural patterns. If in their collective life people find it necessary to arrange differential access to material resources, individuals will be acquired differentially into main-stream cultural identifications. It is a mistake to make believe that any such identifications should be taken as developmental standards. Instead, careful work with those locked out of mainstream identifications, by the ingenuity of the ways they resist being constrained, by the ways they resist being made into less than they could be, or less than they are, helps to reveal our part in the pattern of their development. In the ethnographic study of disability, the subject shifts from them to us, from what is wrong with them to what is wrong with the culture we have organized for them, from what is wrong with them to what is right with them that they can tell us so well about the world we share. They know that "the tradition of all the dead generations weighs like a nightmare," and they know that we risk being "judged as morally handicapped" if we cannot allow a proper social life for those who could be left out, dropped out, and locked out of current arrangements.

In organizing a science of development it may be necessary to begin with the recognition that life in any culture gives us much to fall short of and that we are all disabled often, or at least eventually, in precisely the ways organized by those around us following the dictates of a culturally grounded common sense (Murphy 1987). It is a telling practice that, in the community of physically disabled persons, those who can get around the world of curbs, stairs, and other conveniences built without regard for those who cannot use them are called TABs—the Temporarily Able-Bodied (Halpern 1988). There is an unfortunate certainty in this promise. Age, for sure, can bring on the impossibility of going up stairs or opening food packages. But we do not have to change to become disabled, for the world can do that for us. Just as we can focus on how those not yet labeled are only temporarily, and with the cooperation of others, in command of their situation, so we can focus on the potential strengths in any disability. We end with a case in point.

The young Irish poet Christopher Nolan was born unable to move or even to speak, and until his family discovered that he could communicate by typing messages with an apparatus tied to his head and connected to a keyboard, he was locked away from the wonders of sharing language with others. From such a difficult first fourteen years he emerged with a way of looking to what was possible and a way to express it that was not possible before the English language had spent years unspoken and alone inside his head:

Century upon century saw crass crippled man dashed, branded and treated as dross in a world offended by their appearance, and cracked asunder in their belittlement by having to resemble venial human specimens offering nothing and pondering less in their life of mindless normality. So [he] mulled universal moods as he grimly looked back on the past, but *reasons never curb but rather create new gleeful designs.* (Nolan 1987:15; emphasis added)

In all cultures, there may be reasons to identify disabilities and reasons to curb what some are asked to do. But there are no good reasons, whatever the cultural particulars, to inhibit the creation of "new gleeful designs," no good reasons for anyone to be less than they could be, anything less than they are.

Acknowledgment

Eric Bredo, Robbie Case, Paula Fleisher, Laura Kerr, D. C. Phillips, Joseph Reimer, and George Spindler offered helpful corrections on versions of this chapter. Mark Breimhorst offered a particularly powerful critique that will take us years to digest.

Notes

1. To this end, we rely on: Bakhtin 1981, Becker 1971, Garfinkel 1967, Goffman 1963, Pollner 1978, Scheflen 1973, Selby 1976, Wieder 1974, and Williams 1977; and from the study of development and learning: Bateson 1972; Church 1961; Cole 1992; Erickson and Shultz 1982; Frankel, Leary, and Kilman 1987; Goodwin 1990; Lave 1988; Lewin 1951; Mehan 1986; and Vygotsky 1986. Although a diverse group, they all share a point of entry with George Herbert Mead: "In the process of communication, the individual is an other before he is a self. It is in addressing himself in the role of another that his self arises in experience" (1932:168). One cannot be disabled alone; it takes a culture to make the most of our potential for suffering (see Henry 1963 and Spindler 1974 for accounts of schooling as disability; see Cipolla 1979 and Shiller 1992 for epidemics).

2. See Coles 1988 for a social history of the category of learning disability and its demographics; see the work of Mehan (1986, 1993; and Mehan, Meihls, and Hertweck 1986) for a nicely detailed and theoretically sophisticated account of how children are labeled.

References

Bakhtin, M. 1981. *The Dialogic Imagination.* Austin: University of Texas Press.
Bateson, G. 1972. *Steps to an Ecology of Mind.* New York: Ballantine.
Becker, H. S. 1971. *Outsiders.* 2d ed. New York: Free Press.
Beckett, S. 1955. *Molloy, Malone Dies, The Unnamable.* New York: Grove Press.

Breimhorst, M. 1992. "A Disability Interpretation of Shakespeare's Tragic Characters." Humanities Honors Essay, Stanford University.

Church, J. 1961. *Language and the Discovery of Reality.* New York: Random House.

Cipolla, C. M. 1979. *Faith, Reason, and the Plague: A Tuscon Story of the Seventeenth Century.* Sussex: The Harvester Press.

Cole, M. 1992. "Culture in Development." In *Developmental Psychology: An Advanced Textbook.* Ed. M. Bornstein and M. Lamb, 731–89. Hillsdale, N.J.: Erlbaum.

Cole, M., L. Hood, and R. P. McDermott. 1978. "Ecological Niche Picking: Ecological Invalidity as an Axiom of Experimental Cognitive Psychology." Working Paper no. 14, Laboratory of Comparative Human Cognition, Rockefeller University.

Cole, M., and K. Traupmann. 1981. "Comparative Cognitive Research: Learning from a Learning Disabled Child." In *Aspects of the Development of Competence.* Ed. W. A. Collins, 125–54. Minnesota Symposium on Child Psychology, vol. 14. Hillsdale: Erlbaum.

Coles, G. 1987. *The Learning Mystique.* New York: Pantheon.

Davydov, V. V. 1988. "Problems of Developmental Teaching." *Soviet Education* 30: 6–97.

Dexter, L. A. 1964. "On the Politics and Sociology of Stupidity in Our Society." In *The Other Side.* Ed. H. S. Becker, 37–50. New York: Free Press.

Donald, J. 1985. "How Illiteracy Became a Problem." *Journal of Education* 165: 35–51.

Drummond, L. 1980. "The Cultural Continuum." *Man* 15: 352–74.

Edgerton, R. 1970. "Mental Retardation in Non-Western Societies." In *Sociocultural Aspects of Mental Retardation.* Ed. H. C. Haywood, 523–59. New York: Appleton-Century-Crofts.

Erickson, F., and J. Shultz. 1982. *The Counselor as Gatekeeper.* New York: Academic Press.

Foucault, M. 1991. *Remarks on Marx: Conversations with Duccio Trambadori.* New York: Semiotext(e).

Frake, C. O. 1964. "Notes on Queries in Ethnography." *American Anthropologist* 66: 132–45.

Frankel, R., M. Leary, and B. Kilman. 1987. "Building Social Skills through Pragmatic Analysis." In *Handbook of Autism and Pervasive Developmental Disorders.* Ed. D. Cohen and A. Donnellan, 333–59. New York: Wiley.

Garfinkel, H. 1967. *Studies in Ethnomethodology.* Englewood Cliffs, N.J.: Prentice-Hall.

Goffman, E. 1963. *Stigma.* Englewood Cliffs, N.J.: Prentice-Hall.

Goodwin, C., and A. Duranti. 1992. *Rethinking Context.* New York: Cambridge University Press.

Goodwin, M. 1990. *He-Said-She-Said.* Bloomington: Indiana University Press.

Gregory, R. L., and J. Wallace. 1963. *Recovery from Early Blindness: A Case Study.* Monographs of the *Quarterly Journal of Experimental Psychology,* supp. 2.

Groce, N. 1985. *Everyone Here Spoke Sign Language.* Cambridge, Mass.: Harvard University Press.

Halpern, S. M. 1988. "Portrait of the Artist." *New York Times Book Review,* 30 June, 3–5.

Henry, J. 1963. *Culture Against Man.* New York: Vintage.

Hood, L., R. P. McDermott, and M. Cole. 1980. "'Let's try to make it a good day"—Some Not So Simple Ways." *Discourse Processes* 3:155–68.

Kakumasu, J. 1968. "Urubu Sign Language." *International Journal of American Linguistics* 34: 275–81.

Kendon, A. 1990. *Conducting Interaction.* New York: Cambridge University Press.

Lave, J. 1988. *Cognition in Practice.* New York: Cambridge University Press.

Lewin, K. 1951 [1935]. *Dynamic Theory of Personality.* New York: McGraw-Hill.

Mannoni, M. 1972. *The Backward Child and His Mother.* New York: Basic Books.

Marx, K. 1963 [1852]. *The Eighteenth Brumaire of Louis Bonaparte.* New York: International Publishers.

McDermott, J. J. 1986. *Streams of Experience: Reflections on the History and Philosophy of American Culture.* Amherst: University of Massachusetts Press.

McDermott, R. P. 1988. "Inarticulateness." In *Linguistics in Context.* Ed. D. Tannen, 37–68. Norwood, N.J.: Ablex.

———. 1993. "The Acquisition of a Child by a Learning Disability." In *Understanding Practice.* Ed. S. Chaiklin and J. Lave, 269–305. New York: Cambridge University Press.

Mead, G. H. 1932. *The Philosophy of the Present.* Chicago: University of Chicago Press.

Mehan, H. 1986. "The Role of Language and the Language of Role in Institutional Decision Making." In *Discourse and Institutional Authority.* Ed. S. Fisher and A. Todd, 140–63. Norwood, N.J.: Ablex.

———. 1993. "Beneath the Skin and Between the Ears." In *Understanding Practice.* Ed. S. Chaiklin and J. Lave, 241–69. New York: Cambridge University Press.

Mehan, H., L. Meihls, and A. Hertweck. 1986. *Handicapping the Handicapped.* Stanford: Stanford University Press.

Murphy, R. F. 1987. *Body Silent.* New York: Holt.

Nolan, C. 1987. *Under the Eye of a Clock.* New York: Doubleday.

Padden, C., and T. Humphries. 1988. *Deaf in America: Voices from a Culture.* Cambridge, Mass.: Harvard University Press.

Plath, D. 1980. *Long Engagements.* Stanford: Stanford University Press.

Pollner, M. 1978. "Constitutive and Mundane Versions of Labeling Theory." *Human Studies* 1: 269–88.

Rosa-Lugo, L. 1989. "Arrangements for the Display of Deafness." Ph.D. diss., Columbia University.

Sarason, S., and J. Doris. 1979. *Educational Handicap, Public Policy, and Social Change.* New York: Free Press.

Scheflen, A. E. 1973. *Communicational Structure.* Bloomington: Indiana University Press.

Selby, H. 1976. *Zapotec Deviance.* Austin: University of Texas Press.

Scribner, S., and M. Cole. 1981. *Psychology of Literacy.* Cambridge, Mass.: Harvard University Press.

Shiller, N. 1992. "What's Wrong with This Picture? The Hegemonic Construction of Culture in AIDS Research in the United States." *Medical Anthropology Quarterly* 6: 237–54.

Shklar, J. 1979. "Let's Not Be Hypocritical." *Daedalus* 108: 1–25.

———. 1990. *The Faces of Injustice.* New Haven, Conn.: Yale University Press.

Street, B. 1984. *Literacy in Theory and Practice.* New York: Cambridge University Press.

Smith, D. 1986. "The Anthropology of Literacy Acquisition." In *The Acquisition of Literacy: Ethnographic Perspectives.* Ed. B. Schieffelin and P. Gilmore, 261–75. Norwood: Ablex.

Spindler, G. D. 1974. "Beth Anne." In *Education and Cultural Process.* Ed. Spindler, 139–53. New York: Holt, Rinehart, and Winston.

Thomas, G., J. Meyer, F. Ramirez, and J. Boli. 1988. *Institutional Structure: Constituting State, Society, and the Individual.* Beverly Hills, Calif.: Sage.

Varenne, H., and R. P. McDermott. 1986. "'Why' Sheila Can Read." In *The Acquisition of Literacy.* Ed. B. Schieffelin and P. Gilmore, 188–210. Norwood: Ablex.

Vygotsky, L. 1978. *Mind in Society.* Cambridge, Mass.: Harvard University Press.

———. 1986 [1934]. *Thought and Language.* Cambridge, Mass.: MIT Press.

Wieder, D. L. 1974. *Language and Social Reality.* The Hague: Mouton.

Williams, R. 1977. *Marxism and Literature.* New York: Academic Press.

Williams, R. 1984. *Keywords: A Vocabulary of Culture and Society.* 2d ed. New York: Oxford University Press.

Wittgenstein, L. 1980. *Culture and Value.* Chicago: University of Chicago Press.

6 The Epistemological Crisis in the Human Disciplines: Letting the Old Do the Work of the New

NORMAN K. DENZIN

A double crisis of representation and legitimation confronts the human disciplines. Embedded in the discourses of post-structuralism and post-modernism (Lather 1991, 1993; Richardson 1991, 1992, 1993), these two crises are, as Lather (1993) notes, coded in multiple terms, variously called and associated with the "interpretive, linguistic, and rhetorical turns" in social theory. This linguistic turn makes problematic two key assumptions of social theory and interpretive research. The first assumption presumes that theorists and researchers can no longer directly capture lived experience; such experience, it is argued, is created in the social text written by the researcher. This is the representational crisis. It confronts the inescapable problem of representation, but does so within a framework that makes the direct link between experience and text problematic (Denzin 1991a).

The second assumption makes the traditional criteria for evaluating interpretive theory and research problematic. This is the legitimation crisis. It involves a serious rethinking of such terms as *validity, generalizability,* and *reliability,* terms already retheorized in postpositivist, constructionist-naturalistic (Lincoln and Guba 1985:36), feminist (Fonow and Cook 1991:1–13; Smith 1992), and interpretive (Hammersley 1992; Lather 1993) discourses. This crisis asks, How are interpretive, ethnographic studies to be evaluated in the post-structural moment? Clearly these two crises blur together.

These two crises are pernicious. Their effects, like viruses moving in two directions at the same time, spread across the human disciplines. On the one hand they undermine from within long-standing canonical beliefs in the positivist and postpositivist epistemological project. Connected to what is now called postmodern doubt (Richardson 1993), these crises, as

Shweder, Becker, Campbell, and Mishler note elsewhere in this volume, challenge old ways of knowing and doing ethnographic, interpretive science. This is the epistemological virus.

Second, these crises threaten interdisciplinary projects like human development. They not only raise doubts about how the scholars in this field know their subject matter, but at a deeper level they raise ontological issues about this being called human. Campbell asks, Can another mind ever be known? And we can ask, Does the other know their own mind? Is the other a fiction of the knower's ideological biases? Can we know ourselves except through our constructions of the other? Are we the other? How do race, class, gender, and ethnicity shape our understandings of the other? Are the discourses which define the field of human development ideological constructions which, in the words of Ray McDermott, confuse culture and disability in ways that impose epistemological and cultural biases on our subject matter? This is the ontological virus.

This conference intersects with each of these issues. Each of its major moments, from epistemological issues to methods and social problems, carries important implications for how the qualitative, ethnographic approach will be fitted to the study of adolescent development among youth in high-risk settings. Mishler suggests that a paradigm shift is occurring in the human disciplines, a shift moving closer and closer to a case-based, narrative approach to human experience. Shweder argues for a new way of configuring human experience within the shifting mosaics of culture. These are major paradigmatic shifts. The ways this conference charts multiple paths into them become extremely critical, and even more so as resolutions to the above crises are suggested.

My intentions in the present essay are fourfold. First, to define the sprawling, interdisciplinary field called qualitative research. Second, to examine these interrelated crises and to locate them within the history of ethnographic, qualitative research in the United States (for other histories both in the United States and in Europe, see Wolcott 1992; Spindler and Spindler 1992). Third, to interrogate the resolutions and pictures of these crises, as given by Shweder, Becker, Mishler, McDermott, and Campbell. Fourth, I conclude with a brief discussion of possible new directions for ethnographic approaches to the study of human development. Here I will elaborate a cultural studies approach (Nelson, Treichler, and Grossberg 1992) to the study of youth in high-risk situations.

The Field of Qualitative Research and Its History

Qualitative research operates in a complex historical field that crosscuts five historical moments. (I discuss these moments in detail below.) These five moments simultaneously operate in the present. I define them as the traditional (1900–50), the modernist, or golden age (1950–70), blurred genres (1970–86), the crisis of representation (1986–90), and postmodern, or present moment (1990 to the present). The present moment is defined, Laurel Richardson argues, by a new sensibility, the core of which "is *doubt* that any discourse has a privileged place, any method or theory a universal and general claim to authoritative knowledge" (199:11:73).

Successive waves of epistemological theorizing move across these five moments. The traditional period is associated with the positivist paradigm. The modernist or golden age and blurred genres moments are connected to the appearance of postpositivist arguments. At the same time, a variety of new interpretive, qualitative perspectives made their presence felt, including hermeneutics, structuralism, semiotics, phenomenology, cultural studies, and feminism. In the blurred genres phase the humanities became central resources for critical, interpretive theory and the qualitative research project broadly conceived. The blurred genres phase produced the next stage, the crisis of representation. Here researchers struggled with how to locate themselves and their subjects in reflexive texts. The postmodern moment is characterized by a new sensibility which doubts all previous paradigms.

Any definition of qualitative research must work within this complex historical field. Qualitative research means different things in each of these moments. Nonetheless, an initial, generic definition can be offered.

Qualitative research is multimethod in focus, involving an interpretive, naturalistic approach to its subject matter. This means qualitative researchers study things in their natural settings, attempting to make sense of or interpret these things in terms of the meanings people bring to them. Qualitative research involves the studied use and collection of case-study, personal experience, introspective, life-story, interview, observational, historical, interactional, and visual texts which describe routine and problematic moments and meanings in individual lives. Accordingly, qualitative researchers deploy a wide range of interconnected interpretive methods, hoping always to get a better fix on the subject matter at hand.

The Qualitative Researcher as Bricoleur

The multiple methodologies of qualitative research may be viewed as a bricolage, and the researcher, a bricoleur. Nelson, Treichler, and Grossberg (1992:2), Claude Lévi-Strauss (1966:17), and Weinstein and Weinstein (1991:161) clarify the meaning of these two terms.[1] A bricoleur is a "Jack of all trades or a kind of professional do-it-yourself person" (Lévi-Strauss 1966:17). The bricoleur produces a bricolage; that is, a pieced-together, finely knitted set of practices that provide solutions to a problem in a concrete situation. "The solution (bricolage) which is the result of the *bricoleur's* method is an [emergent] construction" (Weinstein and Weinstein 1991:161) which changes and takes new forms as different tools, methods, and techniques are added to the puzzle. Nelson, Treichler, and Grossberg describe the methodology of cultural studies "as a bricolage. Its choice of practice, that is, is pragmatic, strategic and self-reflexive" (1992:2). This understanding can be directly applied to qualitative research.

The qualitative researcher as bricoleur uses the tools of his or her methodological trade, deploying whatever strategies, methods, or empirical materials are at hand (Becker 1989). If new tools have to be invented, or pieced together, then the researcher will do this. The choice of which tools to use, which research practices to employ, is not set in advance. The "choice of research practices depends upon the questions that are asked, and the questions depend on their context" (Nelson, Treichler, and Grossberg 1992:2), what is available in the context, and what the researcher can do in that setting. The product of the bricoleur's labor is a bricolage, a complex, dense, reflexive, collagelike creation that represents the researcher's images, understandings, and interpretations of the world or phenomenon under analysis.

Qualitative Research as a Site of Multiple Methodologies and Research Practices

Qualitative research, as a set of interpretive practices, privileges no single methodology over another. It has no theory or paradigm that is distinctly its own. Multiple theoretical paradigms claim use of qualitative research methods and strategies, from constructivism to cultural studies, feminism, Marxism, and ethnic models of study. Qualitative research does not belong to a single discipline.

These separate and multiple uses and meanings of the methods of qualitative research make it difficult to agree on any essential definition of the field, for it is never just one thing. Still, a definition must be made. I borrow from and paraphrase Nelson, Treichler, and Grossberg's attempt to define cultural studies (1992:4):

> Qualitative research is an interdisciplinary, transdisciplinary, and sometimes counterdisciplinary field. It cross-cuts the humanities, the social and the physical sciences. Qualitative research is many things at the same time. It is multi-paradigmatic in focus. Its prac-

titioners are sensitive to the value of the multi-method approach. They are committed to the naturalistic perspective; and to the interpretive understanding of human experience. At the same time the field is inherently political and shaped by multiple ethical and political positions.

Qualitative research embraces two tensions at the same time. On the one hand it is drawn to a broad, interpretive, postmodern, feminist and critical sensibility. On the other hand it is drawn to more narrowly defined positivist, postpositivist, humanistic and naturalistic conceptions of human experience and its analysis.

This rather awkward statement means that qualitative research, as a set of practices, embraces within its own multiple disciplinary histories, constant tensions and contradictions over the project itself, including its methods, and the forms its findings and interpretations take.

Resistances to Qualitative Studies

The academic and disciplinary resistances to qualitative research further illustrate the politics embedded in this field of discourse. The challenges to qualitative research are many. Qualitative researchers are called journalists, or soft scientists. Their work is termed unscientific, or only exploratory, or entirely personal and full of bias. It is called criticism and not theory, or it is interpreted politically, as a disguised version of Marxism or humanism.

These resistances reflect an uneasy awareness that its traditions commit one to a critique of the positivist project. But the positivist resistance to qualitative research goes beyond the "ever-present desire to maintain a distinction between hard science and soft scholarship" (Carey 1989:99). The positive sciences (physics, economics, and psychology) are often seen as the crowning achievements of Western civilization, and in their practices it is assumed that truth can transcend opinion and personal bias (99). Qualitative research is seen as an assault on this tradition, whose adherents often retreat into a "value-free objectivist science" (104) model to defend their position. They seldom attempt to make explicit and critique the "moral and political commitments in their own contingent work" (104).

The opposition to positive science by the postpositivists and the poststructuralists is seen, then, as an attack on reason and truth. At the same time, the positive science attack on qualitative research is regarded as an attempt to legislate one version of truth over another.

The Representational Crisis

A single but complex issue defines the representational crisis. It involves the assumption that much if not all social science and ethnographic writing is a narrative production, structured by a logic that "separates writer, text, and subject matter" (Denzin 1991a:278). Any social text can, accordingly, be analyzed in terms of its treatment of four paired terms: the "real" and its representation in the text; the text and the author; lived experience and its textual representations; and the subject and his or her intentional meanings. The text presumes a world out there (the real), that can be captured by a "knowing" author through the careful transcription (and analysis) of field materials (interviews, notes, and so on). The author becomes the mirror to the world under analysis. This reflected world then re-presents the subject's experiences through a complex textual apparatus which typically mingles and mixes multiple versions of the subject (Denzin 1994a,b). The subject is always a textual construction, for the "real" flesh-and-blood person is always translated into either an analytic subject as a social type or a textual subject who speaks from the author's pages. In no case does the "real" subject come to life on the author's page.

Ethnographers have historically assumed that their methods probe and reveal lived experience. They have also assumed that the subject's word is always final, and that talk directly reflects subjective or lived experience. The literal translation of talk thus equals lived experience and its representation.

Post-structuralism challenges these assumptions. Language and speech do not mirror experience, they create it and in the process constantly transform and defer that which is being described. The meanings of a subject's statements are, therefore, always in motion. There can never be a final, accurate representation of what was meant or said, only different textual representations of different experiences. As Lather observes, these arguments do not put an end to representation, they signal instead the end of pure presence (Lather 1993:3). The task at hand is to understand what textually constructed presence means, since there is only ever the text, as Derrida reminds us. This leads to the question of a text's authority.

The Legitimation Crisis

A post-structural interpretive social science challenges postpositivist arguments concerning the text and its validity. It interprets validity as a text's call to authority and truth, and calls this version of validity *epistemological.* That is, a text's authority is established through recourse to a set of rules concerning knowledge, its production, and representation. These rules, as Scheurich (1992:1) notes, if properly followed, establish validity. Without validity there is no truth, and without truth there can be no trust in a text's claims to validity (Lincoln and Guba 1985). With validity comes power (Cherryholmes 1988), and validity becomes a boundary line "which divides good research from bad, separates acceptable (to a particular research community) research from unacceptable research. . . . it is the name for inclusion and exclusion" (Scheurich 1992:5).

Post-structuralism reads the discussions of logical, construct, internal, ethnographic, and external validity, text-based data, triangulation, trustworthiness, credibility, grounding, naturalistic indicators, fit, coherence, comprehensiveness (Eisenhart and How 1992:657–69), plausibility, truth, relevance (Atkinson 1992:68–72), as attempts to reauthorize a text's authority in the postpositivist moment. Such moves still hold (all constructionist disclaimers aside) to the conception of a "world out there" that is truthfully and accurately captured by the researcher's methods and written text.

These words, and the methodological strategies that lie behind them, represent attempts to thicken and contextualize a work's grounding in the external empirical world. They represent efforts to develop a set of transcendent rules and procedures that lie outside any specific research project. These rules, if successfully followed, allow a text to bear witness to its own validity. Hence a text is valid if it is sufficiently grounded, triangulated, based on naturalistic indicators, carefully fitted to a theory (and its concepts), comprehensive in scope, credible in terms of member checks, logical, and truthful in terms of its reflection of the phenomenon in question. The text's author then announces these validity claims to the reader. Such claims now become the text's warrant to its own authoritative representation of the experience and the social world under inspection. A fertile obsession, validity is the researcher's mask of authority (Lather 1993:5) which allows a particular regime of truth within a particular text (and community of scholars) to work its way on the world and the reader.

The Five Moments of Qualitative Research

As indicated above, the history of qualitative research in this century may be divided into five phases.[2] The first moment is the traditional period. It begins in the early 1900s and continues until World War II. During this period, qualitative researchers wrote "objective," colonializing accounts of field experiences. They were concerned with offering valid, reliable, and objective interpretations in their writings. The other who was studied was alien, foreign, and strange.

The fieldworker during this period was lionized, made into a larger-than-life figure who went into and then returned from the field with stories about strange people. Rosaldo describes this as the period of the Lone Ethnographer, the story of the man-scientist who went off in search of his native in a distant land. There this figure "encountered the object of his quest [and] underwent his rite of passage by enduring the ultimate ordeal of 'fieldwork'" (Rosaldo 1989:30). Returning home with his data, the Lone Ethnographer wrote up an objective account of the culture that was studied. These accounts were structured by the norms of classical ethnography. This sacred bundle of terms (31) organized ethnographic texts in terms of four beliefs and commitments: a commitment to objectivism, a complicity with imperialism, a belief in monumentalism (the ethnography would create a museumlike picture of the culture studied), and a belief in timelessness (what was studied never changed). This model of the researcher, who could also write complex, dense theories about what was studied, holds to the present day.

The commitment to objectivism is now in doubt. The complicity with imperialism is openly challenged today, and the belief in monumentalism is a thing of the past.

The modernist phase, the second moment, builds on the canonical works from the traditional period. Social realism, naturalism, and slice-of-life ethnographies are still valued. It extended through the postwar years to the 1970s and is still present in the work of many (Wolcott 1992). In this period many texts attempted to formalize qualitative methods (for example, Glaser and Strauss 1967).[3] The modernist ethnographer and sociological participant observer attempted rigorous, qualitative studies of important social processes, including deviance, and social control in the classroom and society.

This was the golden age of rigorous qualitative analysis, bracketed in sociology by *Boys in White* (Becker et al. 1961) at one end and *The Discovery of Grounded Theory* (Glaser and Strauss 1967) on the other. In education, qualitative research in this period was defined by the Spindlers, Jules Henry, Harry Wolcott, and John Singleton. This form of qualitative research is still present in the work of such persons as Strauss and Corbin (1990), and Miles and Huberman (1993).

By the beginning of the third stage (1970–86), "blurred genres," qualitative researchers had a full complement of paradigms, methods, and strategies to employ in their research. Geertz's two books, *The Interpretation of Culture* (1973) and *Local Knowledge* (1983), defined the beginning and end of this moment. In these two works he argued that the old functional, positivist, behavioral, totalizing approaches to the human disciplines was giving way to a more pluralistic, interpretive, open-ended perspective. This new perspective took cultural representations and their meanings as its point of departure. Calling for "thick descriptions" of particular events, rituals, and customs, Geertz suggested that all anthropological writings were interpretations of interpretations. The observer had no privileged voice in the interpretations that were written. The central task of theory was to make sense out of a local situation.

A profound rupture occurred in the mid–1980s. What I call the fourth moment, or the crisis of representation, appeared with *Anthropology as Cultural Critique* (Marcus and Fischer 1986), *The Anthropology of Experience* (Turner and Bruner 1986), *Writing Culture* (Clifford and Marcus 1986), *Words and Lives* (Geertz 1988), and *The Predicament of Culture* (Clifford 1988). These works made research and writing more reflexive, and called into question the issues of gender, class, and race. They articulated the consequences of Geertz's "blurred genres" interpretation of the field in the early 1980s.

The fifth moment is the present. The two crises just sketched out define the contours of the future. Theories are now read in narrative terms, as tales from the field (Van Maanen 1988). Preoccupations with the representation of the other remain. New epistemologies from previously silenced groups emerge to offer solutions to this problem. The concept of the aloof researcher has been abandoned. More action, activist-oriented research is on the horizon, as are more social criticism and social critique. The search for grand narratives will be replaced by more local, small-scale theories fitted to specific problems and specific situations (Lincoln and Denzin 1994).

Reading History

Four conclusions can be drawn from this brief history. Each of the earlier historical moments still operates in the present, either as legacy or as a set of practices that researchers continue to follow or argue against. The multiple and fractured histories of qualitative research now make it possible for any given researcher to attach a project to a canonical text from any of the previous historical moments. Multiple criteria of evaluation now compete for attention in this field. Second, an embarrassment of choices now characterizes the field of qualitative research. There have never been so many paradigms, strategies of inquiry, or methods of analysis to draw upon and utilize. Third, we are in a moment of discovery and rediscovery, as new ways of looking, interpreting, arguing, and writing are debated and discussed. Fourth, the qualitative research act can no longer be viewed from within a neutral or objective perspective. Class, race, gender, and ethnicity shape the process of inquiry, making research a multicultural process.

Epistemological Issues and the Ethnographic Project

Richard Shweder creates a plurality of spaces for the ethnographic project which he defines as a commitment to study cultural practices. Culture becomes those "everyday realities lit up by morally enforceable schemes institutionalized as routine, practice." As Becker (1986) might argue, culture is what people do together, and what they do together is always normative, shaped by structures of power, ideology, and truth. A normative cultural-studies project is necessarily political and historically situated. Such a project seeks, perhaps, a plurality of norms for health and human development which are uniformly desirable for a given time and place. This is the traditional liberal project, with the state lending its helping hand when needed, and using, as needed, the findings from social science. In another framework this is called applied action research (Reason 1994).

Howard Becker keeps things simple. Aligned with the traditional and modernist project of Robert Park and the Chicago school of sociology, he advocates a multimethod approach to ethnography and its practices, an approach equally at home with qualitative and quantitative methodologies. Etic and emic approaches merge in his perspective, cases rest on general laws, and general laws imply specific cases. Thus there are really very few differences between the quantitative and qualitative approaches.

His kind of ecumenicism has been thwarted by the negative discourses of epistemology, a project which concerns itself with "oughts" rather than "is's." Shunning this discourse, he offers a set of recipes for producing credible, believable results, results produced by those older traditions, not the newer, trendy versions (like the hermeneutic reading of texts). Not wanting to waste energy haggling over philosophical issues, he looks at what qualitative and quantitative researchers actually do, arguing that there are few real differences. Each tradition simply asks different types of questions. The bottom line is clear; each tradition offers answers to the same set of questions: How does society work? How is this particular strip of social reality organized? and so on.

But of course qualitative research does have an epistemology, a set of practices which place importance in securing the actor's point of view, embedding action in the everyday world of experience, and offering detailed descriptions of that world. Invoking Blumer and Park he shows how their methodological strategies allows the researcher to secure credible, believable results. Practitioners of qualitative and quantitative research really, then, just work in different situations and ask different questions. But underneath they share a commitment to an empirical science which tells causal stories about the world out there.

Of course, this is a comfortable story. It says that all the messy, trendy stuff that has been going on from the 1970s forward is really irrelevant. The older tradition is working just fine. There is no need to be concerned about crises of representation and legitimation. If the traditional field-worker does what he or she is supposed to do, then accurate interpretations and descriptions of what people do can be produced.

This is an instance of an earlier historical moment continuing to operate in the present, both as legacy and as a set of practices that researchers may still follow. Becker enacts a long and hallowed tradition in qualitative research, a tradition that has produced and continues to produce canonical texts from its moment. So his project must be situated within its moment, and it remains for future practitioners to decide if this is the moment they wish to continue into the present. To the extent that multiple criteria of evaluation now compete for attention in this field, Becker's framework may well be read as one which has value for the production of only a certain kind of text. It connects itself, that is, to texts which display at least three of the four beliefs Rosaldo connects to the traditional period: objectivism, monumentalism, and timelessness.

Elliot Mishler seeks to recover those missing persons who have been ignored by those positivist scientists working in the traditional and modern phases of inquiry. Desiring to recuperate the new narrative, case-based turn in developmental research, he seeks an approach that retains individuals and their experiences as the unit of analysis. Intrigued by Abbott's (1992) optimal matching models for analyzing historical processes, he examines how the structures of life-history narratives might be combined with Abbott's method. Optimal matching sequences are then fitted to recurrent, recursive features of work-history narratives.

This is an admirable project which has great promise. It too must be situated in its historical moment. The recent social science narrative turn has moved in three directions at the same time, directions set first by a shifting postpositivist agenda and then modified by more radical post-structural, feminist, and postmodern sensibilities.

Postpositivist arguments from Abbott (1992) to Griffin (1993) accept narratives as interpretive materials. However, postpositivists regard narratives as antecedents to real, thoroughgoing causal work. Narrative materials are flawed because they compress and confuse underlying causal structures. These underlying structures that narrative masks are better understood with methods like event-structure analysis. Thus a new set of rhetorical, narrative devices are used to justify this new narrative turn.

In contrast, radical post-structuralists and postmodernists wholly embrace this narrative turn and seek a form of writing and interpretation that challenges these traditional and newer models of causal analysis. Rejecting grand narrative interpretive schemes, these scholars work within local narratives that help them make sense of specific cases. Midway between these two extremes are those scholars who call for more narrative analysis (Maines 1993) while outlining, as Mishler does, a more agency-based approach to the study of temporally ordered sequences which are given narrative form by everyday actors.

A single inadequacy unites these three interpretive positions toward narrative. Each offers a formal analytic approach to narrative, while refusing to align itself with a content-based perspective that would permit the reading of narrative through the lenses of a larger interpretive framework. This framework understands that there lurks out there in the everyday world a set of master narratives which the cultural machines continually commodify and insert between human consciousness and lived, existential experience. We need to learn how to study these cultural machines and the stories they tell, for these stories then become the stuff of the stories that contemporary craftspersons, and others like them, tell themselves and one another.

Raymond McDermott outlines three approaches to the study of culture: as a set of stable tasks which crosscut persons and cultures; as the things everyday people do outside the laboratory; and as the understandings any culture develops and then selectively applies to certain classes and groups of individuals. He contrasts these three moral approaches as they pertain to the study of disabilities. The first two stress deficiencies anchored in the individual, while the third places the blame on the culture and its categories.

Any developmental model can be fitted into one of these three approaches, but the third takes precedence. How do cultures assemble the texts and documents that allow them to define some people as disabled and others as normal? Cultures can be organized in many different ways. Those deaf people on Martha's Vineyard did not think they had a disability. Where do we get the tools to stop this form of reproduction and domination? Theory, method, and goal all merge into one in this situation. In the end everything is ideological, normal, deviant, disabled. We want a liberating ethnographic, cultural project that respects pluralistic differences, while promoting the health and welfare of everyone.

Donald Campbell's conference presentation takes on increased relevance in this context. Caught midway between the postpositivists and the so-called postmodern nihilists, he wants to retain a modified cultural relativism based on the principles of charity, which allows us to achieve valid knowledge about the other. Unwilling to forsake knowledge of the other, his postpositivist epistemology takes the more old-fashioned approach. He wants to reduce the bias which comes from his method, while keeping the goal of understanding the other.

His is a modernist text which revises the traditional canon. The classic psychophysicists' are rewritten. Their findings were based on pseudo-differences due to failures of comprehension. The principle of charity was not operating. Two simple points were not understood: the other is sort of like us; he or she sees the world sort of like we do, and he or she deploys a version of rationality in the perception process. So the other's mind can be known, if we ask the right questions.

Thus Campbell saves the postpositivist project. The radical relativists are no longer a threat. Their project does not endanger ours. Like Becker, Campbell takes a sophisticated, commonsense approach to the problems at hand. If we study the lessons from the past, we can make our way through the current so-called crises that confront the human disciplines. This is an example of "moving an old idea into a new context and discovering that it can do the work of a new idea" (Grimes 1993:B1). This principle works with great success in popular culture. There is no reason to believe it will not also work in scientific culture.

Back to the Beginning: Getting There from Here

Reflections first. As bricoleurs, each author wants to use many different tools to get the job at hand accomplished. Campbell and Becker use tools which have always worked, giving them slightly new meanings and uses. Mishler, McDermott, and Shweder seek to invent new methods and ways of doing what needs to be done. These texts move, then, across and between the modernist and contemporary moments of interpretive ethnographic inquiry. Each author sees the crises of representation and legitimation on the horizon, and each seeks to fit their conceptions of persons, culture, ethnography, epistemology, science, and human development somewhere within, outside, or against the postpositivist, relativist, doubting discourses of postmodernism. Becker and Campbell rework the old to fit the new. Shweder, Mishler, and McDermott are more radical, doubting that the old formulations will do the work that is now needed.

These authors articulate the two extremes which now define the field of qualitative research. Becker and Campbell embrace the more narrowly defined version of this project, sustaining in their arguments the postpositivist and naturalistic conceptions of this enterprise. Mishler, McDermott, and Shweder are drawn to the more broadly interpretive, critical sensibilities that define the other position in this discursive field.

Finally, each author engages and reformulates the resistances that have historically defined qualitative research. Becker and Campbell keep the postpositivist tradition alive, resisting the radical relativists, while Shweder, Mishler, and McDermott embrace them, with varying degrees of comfort. All five authors retreat from a value-free, objective science position, yet there is a sense in which Becker and Campbell still hunger after generalizations and laws that transcend observers and their moments. Yet everyone seeks a more humane science. How to get there is the issue, and on this point there are considerable differences between the four positions. Can we get to where we want to go from where we are now? Can we continue to allow the old to do the work of the new?

Enter Cultural Studies

Here is where that multidisciplinary, fragmented project called cultural studies enters the picture (Frow and Morris 1993; Blundell, Shepherd, and Taylor 1993; Chow 1993; Agger 1992). There are multiple cultural studies projects, including those connected to the Birmingham school, and the work of Stuart Hall and his associates (Grossberg 1989, 1993; Johnson 1986–87; Budd, Entman, and Steinman 1990); the American cultural sociology project of Alexander and associates, which draws on the work of Bourdieu and Parsons (Sherwood, Smith, and Alexander 1993); the Latin American model that elaborates and then departs from the Birmingham approach (O'Connor 1991); the Australian and Canadian models which de-Anglicize the British model while focusing on policy and public culture (Frow and Morris 1993; Blundell, Shepherd, and Taylor 1993); a black feminist cultural criticism (Wallace 1993); an American-based, ethnographic, critical cultural studies model centered on a resistance to postmodernism (Kincheloe and McLaren 1993; Agger 1992); and more recently a transnational cultural studies focused on the critical ethnographic study of public culture and the flow of cultural forms and cultural representations from one site to another, particularly in the journal *Public Culture.*

Like qualitative research, "cultural studies is an interdisciplinary, transdisciplinary, and sometimes counterdisciplinary field that operates in the tensions that embrace both a broad anthropological and a more narrowly humanistic conception of culture" (Nelson, Treichler, and Grossberg 1993:4). Cultural studies is political. It believes that its interpretive practices can make a difference in the social world. Scholars in this tradition examine those cultural texts and cultural practices that reproduce and articulate class, race, and gender stereotypes. Viewing human experience as a text, cultural studies attempts to deconstruct and unravel the ideological meanings that are coded into the taken-for-granted meanings that circulate in everyday life (Carey 1989:60). Culture in its meaning-making forms becomes a site of political struggle. A central problem becomes the examination of how interacting individuals connect their lived experiences to the cultural representations of those experiences (Denzin 1992). This is called the study of lived textuality.

Cultural Studies and Youth in High-Risk Settings

In cultural studies there is a long tradition of studying youth in high-risk settings (Nelson, Treichler, and Grossberg 1992:8). Gender, race, ethnicity, and class are central to this research tradition. Indeed, the cultural category "youth in high-risk settings" contains social meanings that are intimately connected to gender, race, and class, and of course youth in such settings are frequently nonwhite and from the lower classes. Racial matters are at the heart of the problem.

While internal colonial, social-adaptation, constructionist, and resistance models of interpretation structure contemporary studies of youth, race, and ethnicity (Pedraza 1993:4), the more traditional assimilationist approach appears to operate in the area of human development. This framework argues that the members of racial and ethnic group pass through a race relations cycle (contact, conflict, acculturation), culminating in cultural and structural assimilation into the mainstream of American society. This now-rejected model has organized much of the previous research on youth at risk. Rebellious youth, those who cause trouble, are defined as cultural members who refuse to assimilate to the dominant values of American society.

This normative reading ignores the processes that have colonized youthful, racial, and ethnic minorities in American society. Trapped in internal ghettos, youth are subjected to the surveillance structures of police, state, and school. Inside these colonies (housing projects, schools), radical and normative racial and ethnic identities are socially constructed, often against the larger cultural readings of the group in question (Nagel 1993). Adolescents display cultural rebellion by endorsing and embodying styles of work, leisure, intimacy, appearance, and musical taste that are at odds with the adult cultural mainstream. The youthful ethnic minority group member becomes a cultural other whose negative values, experiences, and identities are interpreted in terms of long-standing cultural stereotypes.

Cultural Diaspora and American Youth

Recent cultural studies scholars (Chow 1993) have challenged the assimilationist model by articulating the concept of diaspora. (The term *diaspora* is taken from the dispersion of the Jews after the Babylonian exile.) A cultural studies model of diaspora references the displacement and dispersal of youthful racial and ethnic identities across multiple boundaries, markers, and territories. Diaspora refuses any firm and certain set of essential, homogeneous, or monolithic meanings brought to a racial or ethnic group (Rosaldo 1989; Stanfield 1993:19–25). Thus the identities of a male or female adolescent African Americans wander across multiple borders and boundaries, including those specific to childhood, manhood, femininity, women, sexuality, mothers, fathers, siblings, family, education, residence, the drug culture, AIDS, MTV, cinema, the police, peer groups, gangs, music, professional sports (especially basketball), race, and ethnicity.

The diaspora framework understands that there are constant social pressures brought to bear on youthful minority group members whose identities are socially constructed by the media, cinema, popular music, and the larger society. These pressures encourage assimilation, the relinquishing of one's personal and cultural identity to an essentializing, homogenous identity constructed and endorsed by the white community. A process of colonization occurs; a cultural politics is at work. This process labels, oppresses, and victimizes the youthful cultural other.

Accordingly, an oppositional discourse is required if the lived realities of problematic youth are to be understood. The concept of diaspora suggests a new way to read and interpret the experiences of minority youth who find themselves in trouble.

Reading Youth Against the Cultural Text

The core emotional experiences of the contemporary (postmodern) historical moment revolve around the meanings brought to race, class, and gender. Popular (and scientific) cultural texts, including films aimed at male (and female) American youth (*White Men Can't Jump, Boyz N the Hood, Colors, Bound by Honor, Breakin', Beat Street, New Jack City, Menace II Society, Jungle Fever*) are political productions. In the stories they tell, in their sights and sounds, complexly gendered ideological messages and meanings are carried and articulated (Denzin 1994c).

These meanings, as utopian political fantasies, mythic narratives, and allegories (Jameson 1992:3) effectively erase the corrosive consequences of an oppressive racial and gender stratification system in the United States. The kernels of utopian fantasy contained in them "constitute the fulfillment of what is desired [yet] absent within the status quo" (Stam 1989:224); that is, an emotionally harmonious gender system that has successfully integrated racial and ethnic differences into the core emotional elements of the contemporary self. Popular cinematic texts (*White Men Can't Jump*) co-opt black postmodernist practices (bebop music, rap, the hustling culture, the aesthetic execution of black sports, especially basketball) into their filmic world, contending that white men have a rightful place in African-American culture (West 1988:278–83).

The postmodern sensibility defines a logic of ironic nihilism or authentic inauthenticity toward the structures of meaning that organize everyday life (Grossberg 1992:224). Under this logic all meanings, styles, and desires become possible poses, or masks that one can wear. All that matters is affect, an emotional investment in the mask one has just put on. Cornell West describes one of these poses. He has observed that in black culture the athlete is an artist of great importance. He argues:

> The black player tries to *style* reality so that he becomes spectacle and performance, always projecting a sense of self . . . smooth, clever, rhythmic, syncopated. . . . A lot of time and energy and discipline goes into it but usually with a certain *investment of self* that does not express the work ethic alone . . . whereas his white counterpart tends toward the productivistic and mechanistic.

Popular films neutralize and displace the racial and gender crises that now permeate America. The white adolescent male seeks the deep, emotionally rich self of the gifted black athletic male. White youth culture "symbolically appropriates aspects of black culture through style and music" and sports (Tucker 1993:206; see also Gaines 1991 and Hebdige 1984). Barthes (1972) elaborates, suggesting that the dominant culture operates by "appropriation: it abstracts the specific signs of social groups into mere signifiers that are then recoded as general cultural myths" (Foster 1988:264).

Much of youth-oriented contemporary cinema and television colonizes the specific signs, symbols, and myths of African-American male and female culture and recodes these myths in terms of a white man's or white woman's story, for example, the film *Passion Fish.* As a consequence, black postmodernist practices end up "highly packaged, regulated, distributed, circulated, and consumed" (West 1988:279, 281) by those in American white male (and female) culture. In the process, the original aesthetic and cultural practices of the disadvantaged group are stripped of their radical meanings. They have been co-opted by the dominant, gendered, white culture.

Basketball *is* community for the African-American community. It is public life as spectacle. In it the deeply radical and practical elements of the hustling culture, which turns on survival, are enacted (West 1988:282). One hustles on the court as one hustles on the street, and for many of the same reasons. Moreover, on the basketball courts the community comes alive in a cacophonous bricolage of street music. Everywhere the music and sounds of Jimi Hendrix, Aretha Franklin, James Brown, Ray Charles,

Boyz II Men, College Boyz, Boo-Yaa Tribe, Bebe and Cece Winans, Cypress Hill, the O'Jay's, and Queen Latifah can be heard. It is as if this music, with its sensuous melodic polyrhythms and high technical virtuosity, had been choreographed to fit and structure the performances of the finely sculpted black male athletic bodies, whose balletlike actions flow in and through the sounds that blast from the omnipresent boomboxes that sit courtside in the sun.

This street culture embodies diaspora. It recognizes the performance art of the preacher, the musician, and the black athlete (West 1988:281–83). Each of these artists aesthetically articulates the subversive energies, hopes, dreams, and promises of an oppressed culture that has been forced to fit itself to the racism and repressive political lethargy of American society (West 1988:281). Pageantry and spectacle are at the center of this culture. In its carnivals the dystopian realities of black life are recreated by performers who enact a collective, deep, expressive, ritual self that speaks for the community at large.

This collective postmodern self flows through the three structures of religion, black music, and basketball. It synthesizes these three structures of affective meaning into a collective and individual self whose meanings are given in a commitment to family and community. This self is invested in performance art (dress, music, dance, verbal wit [sounding and the dozens], basketball, and singing). These performances deify the collective self of the group. In them is produced the expressive postmodern African-American self.

This self finds itself embroiled in a network of contradictory cultural practices that pull in several different directions at the same time. The politics of assimilation urge the suppression of ethnic identity, while the African-American street culture celebrates cultural difference from and conflict with the white majority.

The Rituals of Resistance

Understandings of these processes are supplemented by British research on working-class culture, or youth subcultures. This tradition has examined how the media and the educational structures of a society produce consensus on issues of race, class, gender, violence, and deviance. These studies (Willis 1977, 1990; Cagle 1989) have been preoccupied with the passive and aggressive forms of rebellion that characterize youth in such situations, noting the following. This rebellion reproduces itself in self-destructive ways, including delinquency, drug and alcohol abuse, violence and crime. At the same time, youth subcultures make their presence in society known by rebelling in dramatic, often shocking ways. These forms of expression, often drawn from the mass media, "create empowering forces in the lives of youth, providing both personal and collective identities" (Cagle 1989:303). This flaunting of style creates a desired wedge between youth and the larger adult society. Yet it works back against itself, for such youth soon find themselves in the life situations they are rebelling against. The resistance is symbolic, theatrical, not political.

Style thus provides a symbolic mechanism which mediates a complex relationship with the larger political and economic world. The forbidden, violent identities of youth mark a nihilistic relationship to the larger world, which provides neither hope nor the means for escape. Thus do youth in high-risk situations create the circumstances of their own self-destruction. But this destruction is a mediated production. It is caught in a vicious loop that connects the youth subcultures to the mass media and the political economies of everyday life.

Applied to the topic at hand, the several cultural studies traditions suggest a multifocused, interpretive, interventionist, and narrative approach to human development. This approach, with its emphasis on "writing diaspora" (Chow 1993) would work outward from youth subcultures to the surrounding cultural structures that define violence, disability, deviance, and normality. It would move inward to these worlds, ascertaining the meanings and styles of resistance that operate therein. At the same time, it would study how the mass media turns youth into news, and examine those cultural texts that valorize and denigrate them. Finally, it would study the gendered, ethnic, and racially self-conscious personal experience and self-stories the members in this social group tell one another. This narrative approach would connect these stories to the cultural myths and fables that given meaning to this social group.

Youth, like social scientists, are bricoleurs. Our challenge is to find the tools that will allow us and our youth to better work together. The old tools aren't working.

In the End

In 1800 Friedrich Schlegel, the early German romantic student of language and history, contended "that modern literature lacked a centre, such as mythology was for the ancients." He went on to predict the emergence of a new mythology which "would be less a radical act of creation than a 'collaboration' between old and new." He continued, "'Why should not what has already been emerge anew, and why not in a newer and finer, greater manner?'" This is how we can read *Ulysses,* Eliot's *The Wasteland,* and Picasso's *Guernica;* new mythologies, finer and grander mergers of the new with the old (Kiberd 1992:4).

Today, human development, interpretive theory, and ethnographic inquiry lack a center. We confront Schlegel's situation anew. We seemingly no longer know who the subject is, let alone how to write his or her experiences. We have no agreed upon method, no new text which points the way forward, no unassailed theory. We have lost our myths, those larger-than-life paradigms we did battle with during our earlier historical moments. We seek today a new mythology, perhaps not a radical collaboration with the old myths, but a redoing of the old in light of where we have traveled.

Perhaps we need to invent a new language, a new form of writing that goes beyond auto-ethnography, "teletheory," and "mystories" (Ulmer 1989). This must be the language of a new sensibility, a new reflexivity, a language that refuses the old categories, a language that reflexively and parasitically, in a rhizomatic manner (Deleuze and Guattari 1987:chap. 1), charts its own course against history's repressive structures of economy, religion, race, class, and gender. This new language, post-structural to the core, will be personal, emotional, biographically specific, minimalist in its use of theoretical terms. It will allow ordinary people to speak out, and to articulate the interpretive theories that they use to make sense of their lives. This new language will express the personal struggles of each writer as he or she breaks free of the bonds that connect to the past. This language will be visual, cinematic, kaleidoscopic, rhizomatic, rich, and thick in its own descriptive detail, always interactive as it moves back and forth between lived experience and the cultural texts that shape and write that experience (Denzin 1994b).

We move forward by moving inward. Finding our lost center in ourselves, we seek to create new forms of verisimilitude and new forms of truth; a truth from experience. We seek forms of writing that shamelessly transgress the personal while making public that which modernism kept hidden and repressed. Writing our way out of *Writing Culture,* qualitative research and human development in the fifth moment discover what has been known always. We are our own subjects, and how our subjectivity becomes entangled in the lives of others is and has always been our topic.

This is the lesson this conference teaches us.

Acknowledgment

This chapter is based on my reading of the original, not the revised, conference presentations of Shweder, Becker, Mishler, McDermott, and Donald Campbell's "Can We Overcome Worldview Incommensurability/ Relativity in Trying to Understand the Other?" Campbell's manuscript provides an important backdrop to my comments.

Notes

1. "The meaning of *bricoleur* in French popular speech is "someone who works with his (or her) hands and uses devious means compared to those of the crafts-man. . . . the *bricoleur* is practical and gets the job done" (Weinstein and Weinstein 1991:161). These authors provide a history of this term, connecting it to the works of the German sociologist and social theorist Georg Simmel, and by implication, Baudelaire.

2. This history is not a pleasant one. It has always been colonializing and politi-cal, from the ethnographies of the Native American, Asian, African, and Euro-pean other in the seventeenth, eighteenth, and nineteenth centuries, to the twentieth-century community studies of American immigrants, and the studies of ethnicity and assimilation in American cities from midcentury to the present. In each of these moments ethnographers were and have been influenced by their po-litical hopes and ideologies, discovering findings which confirmed prior theories and beliefs. Early ethnographers, as Lyman and Vidich (1993) note, confirmed the racial and cultural diversity of peoples throughout the world and attempted to fit this diversity into a theory about the origin of history, the races, and civilizations. Colonial ethnographers, before the professionalization of ethnography in the twen-tieth century, fostered a colonial pluralism that left natives on their own as long as their leaders could be co-opted by the colonial administration. European eth-nographers studied third-world peoples of color. Early American ethnographers studied the American Indian, using this life-world as a window into the prehistoric past. Qualitative community studies of the ethnic other proliferated from the early 1900s to the 1960s, and included the work of E. Franklin Frazier, Robert Park, and Robert Redfield and their students. The post–1960 ethnicity studies challenged the "melting pot" hypothesis of Park and his followers. It corresponded to the emergence of ethnic studies programs which saw Native Americans, Chicanos, Asian Americans, and African Americans attempting to take control of the study of their own people.

3. See Lincoln and Guba (1985) for an extension and elaboration of this tradi-tion in the mid–1980s.

References

Abbott, Andrew. 1992. "From Causes to Events: Notes on Narrative Positivism." *Sociological Research and Methods* 20:428–55.

Agger, Ben. 1992. *Cultural Studies as Critical Theory.* London: Falmer Press.

Atkinson, Paul. 1992. *The Ethnographic Imagination.* London: Routledge.

Barthes, Roland. 1972. *Mythologies.* New York: Hill and Wang.

Becker, Howard S. 1966. Introduction to *The Jack-Roller.* Ed. Clifford R. Shaw, v–xviii. Chicago: University of Chicago Press.

———. 1986. *Doing Things Together.* Evanston, Ill.: Northwestern University Press.

———. 1989. "Tricks of the Trade." *Studies in Symbolic Interaction* 10: 481–90.

Becker, Howard S. et al. 1961. *Boys in White.* Chicago: University of Chicago Press.

Blundell, Valda, John Shepherd, and Ian Taylor, eds. 1993. *Relocating Cultural Studies: Developments in Theory and Research.* New York: Routledge.

Budd, Mike, Robert Entman, and Clay Steinman. 1990. "The Affirmative Character of U.S. Cultural Studies." *Critical Studies in Mass Communication* 7: 169–83.

Cagle, Van M. 1989. "The Language of Cultural Studies: An Analysis of British Subculture Theory." *Studies in Symbolic Interaction* 10: 301–13.

Carey, James W. 1989. *Culture as Communication.* Boston: Unwin Hyman.

Cherryholmes, Celo H. 1988. *Power and Criticism: Poststructural Investigations in Education.* New York: Teacher's College Press.

Chow, Rey. 1993. *Writing Diaspora: Tactics of Intervention in Contemporary Cultural Studies.* Bloomington: Indiana University Press.

Clifford, James. 1988. *The Cultural Predicament.* Cambridge, Mass.: Harvard University Press.

Clifford, James, and George E. Marcus, eds. 1986. *Writing Culture.* Berkeley: University of California Press.

Clough, Patricia Ticineto. 1992. *The End(s) of Ethnography.* Newbury Park, Calif.: Sage.

Deleuze, Gilles, and Felix Guattari. 1987. *A Thousand Plateaus.* Minneapolis: University of Minnesota Press.

Denzin, Norman K. 1989. *Interpretive Interactionism.* Newbury Park, Calif.: Sage.

———. 1991a. "Back to Harold and Agnes." *Sociological Theory* 9: 278–85.

———. 1991b. *Images of Postmodern Society: Social Theory and Contemporary Cinema.* London: Sage.

———. 1991c. "Representing Lived Experiences in Ethnographic Texts." *Studies in Symbolic Interaction.* 12:59–70.

———. 1992. *Symbolic Interactionism and Cultural Studies: The Politics of Interpretation.* Cambridge, Mass.: Blackwell.

———. 1995. "The Lessons James Joyce Teaches Us." *Qualitative Studies in Education* 7:295–308.

———. Forthcoming. "On Hearing the Voices of Qualitative Research: Review Essay." *Curriculum Inquiry.*

———. 1995. "White Men Can't Jump? The Politics of Postmodern Emotionality." *Social Perspectives on Emotion* 3:33–54.

Denzin, Norman K., and Yvonna S. Lincoln. 1994. Introduction to *Handbook of Qualitative Research.* Ed. Denzin and Lincoln, 1–17. Newbury Park, Calif.: Sage.

Derrida, Jacques. 1976. *Of Grammatology.* Baltimore: Johns Hopkins University Press.

Eisenhart, Margaret A., and Kenneth R. Howe. 1992. "Validity in Educational Research." In *The Handbook of Qualitative Research in Education.* Ed. Margaret D. LeCompte, Wendy L. Millroy, and Judith Preissel, 643–80. New York: Academic Press.

Ellis, Carolyn, and Michael G. Flaherty, eds. 1992. *Investigating Subjectivity: Research on Lived Experience.* Newbury Park, Calif.: Sage.

Fonow, Mary Margaret, and Judith A. Cook. 1991. "Back to the Future: A Look at the Second Wave of Feminist Epistemology and Methodology." In *Beyond Methodology: Feminist Scholarship as Lived Research.* Ed. Fonow and Cook, 1–15. Bloomington: Indiana University Press.

Foster, Hal. 1988. "Wild Signs." In *Universal Abandon? The Politics of Postmodernism.* Ed. Andrew Ross, 251–68. Minneapolis: University of Minnesota Press.

Frow, John, and Meaghan Morris, eds. 1993. *Australian Cultural Studies: A Reader.* Urbana: University of Illinois Press.

Gaines, Donna. 1991. *Teenage Wasteland: Suburbia's Dead End Kids.* New York: Pantheon.

Geertz, Clifford. 1973. *The Interpretation of Culture.* New York: Basic Books.

———. 1988. *Words and Lives.* Stanford: Stanford University Press.

Giroux, Henry. 1992. *Border Crossings: Cultural Workers and the Politics of Education.* New York: Routledge.

Glaser, Barney, and Anselm Strauss. 1967. *The Discovery of Grounded Theory.* Chicago: Aldine.

Griffin, Larry J. 1993. "Narrative, Event-Structure Analysis, and Causal Interpretation in Historical Sociology." *American Journal of Sociology* 98: 1094–1133.

Grimes, William. 1993. "In Pop Culture, a Revival of the Fittest." *New York Times,* 24 May, B1, B4.

Grossberg, Lawrence. 1988. "Putting the Pop Back into Postmodernism." *Universal Abandon? The Politics of Postmodernism.* Ed. Andrew Ross, 167–90. Minneapolis: University of Minnesota Press.

———. 1989. "The Circulation of Cultural Studies." *Critical Studies of Mass Communication* 6: 413–21.

———. 1992. *We Gotta Get Out of This Place: Popular Conservatism and Postmodern Culture.* London: Routledge.

———. 1993. "An American in Birmingham." In *Relocating Cultural Studies: Developments in Theory and Research.* Ed. Valda Blundell, John Shepherd, and Ian Taylor, 21–66. New York: Routledge.

Guba, Egon G. 1990. "The Alternative Paradigm Dialog." In *The Paradigm Dialog.* Ed. Guba, 17–30. Newbury Park, Calif.: Sage.

Guba, Egon G., and Yvonna S. Lincoln. 1989. *Fourth Generation Evaluation.* Newbury Park, Calif.: Sage.

Hall, Stuart. 1986. "On Postmodernism and Articulation: An Interview with Stuart Hall." Ed. Lawrence Grossberg. *Journal of Communication Inquiry.* 10:45–60.

Hammersley, Martyn. 1992. *What's Wrong with Ethnography?* London: Routledge.

Hebdige, Dick. 1984. *Subculture: The Meaning of Style.* London: Routledge.

Jameson, Fredric. 1992. *The Geopolitical Aesthetic: Cinema and Space in the World System.* Bloomington: Indiana University Press.

Johnson, Richard. 1986–87. "What Is Cultural Studies Anyway?" *Social Text* 16:38–80.

Kiberd, Declan. 1992. "Bloom the Liberator." *Times Literary Supplement.* 3 Jan., 3–6.

Kincheloe, Joe L., and Peter L. McLaren. 1994. "Rethinking Critical Theory and Qualitative Research." In *Handbook of Qualitative Research.* Ed. Norman K. Denzin and Yvonna S. Lincoln, 138–57. Thousand Oaks, Calif.: Sage.

Lather, Patti. 1986. "Issues of Validity in Openly Ideological Research: Between a Rock and a Soft Place." *Interchange* 17: 63–84.

———. 1991. *Getting Smart.* New York: Routledge.

———. 1993. "Fertile Obsession: Validity After Poststructuralism." *Sociological Quarterly* 35: 673–93.

Lévi-Strauss, Claude. 1962 [1966]. *The Savage Mind.* Chicago: University of Chicago Press.

Lincoln, Yvonna S., and Egon G. Guba. 1985. *Naturalistic Inquiry.* Beverly Hills, Calif.: Sage. 1981.

Lincoln, Yvonna S., and Norman K. Denzin. 1994. "The Fifth Moment." In *Handbook of Qualitative Research.* Ed. Denzin and Lincoln, 575–86. Newbury Park, Calif.: Sage.

Lyman, Stanford, and Arthur Vidich. 1994. "The History of Qualitative Research in North America." In *The Handbook of Qualitative Research in the Social Sciences.* Ed. Norman K. Denzin and Yvonna S. Lincoln, 23–59. Newbury Park, Calif.: Sage.

Maines, David R. 1993. "Narrative's Moment and Sociology's Phenomena: Toward a Narrative Sociology." *Sociological Quarterly* 34: 17–38.

Marcus, George, and Michael Fischer. 1986. *Anthropology as Cultural Critique.* Chicago: University of Chicago Press.

Miles, Matthew B., and A. Michael Huberman. 1994. *Qualitative Data Analysis.* 2d. ed. Thousand Oaks, Calif.: Sage.

Mishler, Elliot G. 1990. "Validation in Inquiry-Guided Research: The Role of Exemplars in Narrative Studies." *Harvard Educational Review* 60: 415–41.

Nagel, Joane. 1993. "Constructing Ethnicity: Creating and Recreating Ethnic Identity and Culture." *Social Problems* 41: 152–76.

Nelson, Cary, Paula A. Treichler, and Lawrence Grossberg. 1992. "Cultural Studies." In *Cultural Studies.* Ed. Lawrence Grossberg, Cary Nelson, and Paula A. Treichler, 1–16. New York: Routledge.

O'Connor, Alan. 1989. "The Problem of American Cultural Studies." *Critical Studies of Mass Communication* 6: 405–13.

Pedraza, Silvia. 1993. "The Sociology of Immigration, Race and Ethnicity in America." *Social Problems* 41: 1–8.

Public Culture. 1988. "Editor's Comments." 1:1–5.

Reason, Peter. "Applied Action Research." In *The Handbook of Qualitative Research.* Ed. Norman K. Denzin and Yvonna S. Lincoln, 324–39.

Richardson, Laurel. 1991. "Postmodern Social Theory." *Sociological Theory* 9: 173–79.

———. 1992. "The Consequences of Poetic Representation: Writing the Other, Rewriting the Self." In *Investigating Subjectivity: Research on Lived Experience.* Ed. Carolyn Ellis and Michael G. Flaherty, 125–37. Newbury Park, Calif.: Sage.

———. 1993. "Writing as a Method of Inquiry." In *The Handbook of Qualitative Research in the Social Sciences.* Ed. Norman K. Denzin and Yvonna S. Lincoln, 516–29. Newbury Park, Calif.: Sage.

Rosaldo, Renato. 1989. *Culture and Truth.* Boston: Beacon.

Scheurich, James Joseph. 1992. "The Paradigmatic Transgressions of Validity." Unpublished.

Sherwood, Steven Jay, Philip Smith, and Jeffrey C. Alexander. 1993. "Review of Lawrence Grossberg, Cary Nelson, and Paul A. Treichler, *Cultural Studies*." *Contemporary Sociology* 22: 370–75.

Smith, Dorothy. 1992. "Sociology from Women's Perspective: A Reaffirmation." *Sociological Theory* 10: 88–97.

Spindler, George, and Louise Spindler. 1992. "Cultural Process and Ethnography: An Anthropological Perspective." In *The Handbook of Qualitative Research in Education.* Ed. Margaret D. LeCompte, Wendy L. Millroy, and Judy Preissle, 53–92. New York: Academic Press.

Stam, Robert. 1989. *Subversive Pleasures: Bakhtin, Cultural Criticism and Film.* Baltimore: Johns Hopkins University Press.

Stanfield, John H., II. 1993. "Epistemological Considerations." In *Race and Ethnicity in Research Methods.* Ed. Stanfield and Rutledge M. Dennis, 16–36. Newbury Park, Calif.: Sage.

Strauss, Anselm. 1987. *Qualitative Analysis for Social Scientists.* New York: Cambridge.

Strauss, Anselm, and Juliet Corbin. 1990. *Basics of Qualitative Research.* Newbury Park, Calif.: Sage.

Tucker, Kenneth H., Jr. 1993. "Aesthetics, Play and Cultural Memory: Giddens and Habermas on the Postmodern Challenge." *Sociological Theory* 11: 194–211.

Turner, Victor, and Edward Bruner, eds. 1986. *The Anthropology of Experience.* Urbana: University of Illinois Press.

Ulmer, Gregory. 1989. *Teletheory.* New York: Routledge.

Van Maanen, John. *Tales of the Field.* Chicago: University of Chicago Press.

Wallace, Michele. 1993. "Negative Images: Towards a Black Feminist Cultural Criticism." In *Cultural Studies.* Ed. Lawrence Grossberg, Cary Nelson, and Paula A. Treichler, 854–64. New York: Routledge.

Weinstein, Deena, and Michael A. Weinstein. 1991. "Georg Simmel: Sociological Flaneur Bricoleur." *Theory, Culture, and Society* 8:151–68.

Willis, Paul. 1977. *Learning to Labour.* Westmean: Saxon House.

———. 1990. *Common Culture.* Milton Keynes: Open University Press.

Wolcott, Harry F. 1992. "Posturing in Qualitative Research." In *The Handbook of Qualitative Research in Education.* Ed. Margaret D. LeCompte, Wendy L. Millroy, and Judy Preissle, 3–52. New York: Academic Press.

West, Cornell. 1988. Interviewed by Anders Stephanson. In *Universal Abandon? The Politics of Postmodernism.* Ed. Andrew Ross, 269–86. Minneapolis: University of Minnesota Press.

7

Can We Overcome Worldview Incommensurability/Relativity in Trying to Understand the Other?

DONALD T. CAMPBELL

Postpositivist, post-structuralist, and postmodern epistemologies make understanding "the other" problematic. Four "others" potentially relevant to this volume are other scholarly paradigms (as in paradigm incommensurability), other cultures (as in cultural relativism), other social classes (as in Mannheim's [1949] sociology of knowledge), and other historical periods (differing zeitgeists as in Collingwood's [1946] historical relativism, Foucault's [1973] epistemes, or more specifically in Ariès, *Centuries of Childhood* [1962], and its successor literature).

In each case there has been a linked critique of a "centrism," as in ethnocentrism for cultural relativism, naive "presentism" or whig history for the past, and so on. In each case, we ingroup observers are criticized for overlooking the very possibility of different worldviews, mistaking our own views as reality itself, and therefore interpreting the other as incompetent or immoral (immature, primitive, inferior, and so forth). Positivism is rightly criticized for this, for assuming the "immaculate perception" of untheory-laden "facts" available in the same way to every observer. In contrast, the critics of centrisms validly emphasize the worldview embeddedness of all observations.

Contemporary social epistemologists and methodologists seem to me to split into two camps at this point. Those I will stereotype as "ontological nihilists" seem to me to argue a relativity of paradigms (cultural frameworks, worldviews) which precludes knowing the other. They seem to recommend giving up on the effort to do so. Under some versions of modern hermeneutics, they may regard the concept of truth as incoherent, and celebrate a multiplicity of novel interpretations while disparaging any efforts to choose the most valid among them. Under the banners of deconstructionism, post-structuralism, and postmodernism, they sometimes seem to deny to language any degree of competent reference to a nonlinguistic world. In the flourishing "sociology of scientific knowledge," leading social constructionists seem to regard the obvious truism that scientific beliefs are socially constructed as implying the total absence of competent reference to a mind- and language-independent world. For example, in a summary of a vigorous decade of such studies, Collins concludes they have shown that "the natural world has a small or non-existent role in the construction of scientific knowledge" (1981:3). (Within this volume, Denzin's chapter most nearly exemplifies this view.)

My use of the term *ontological nihilism* may exaggerate the degree to which these movements represent total skepticism about the possibility of discriminating different degrees of validity among competing beliefs (Sassower 1991). Perhaps I characterize an ideal type (or straw man). Certainly I want to recognize that many of the ablest of young social scientists are attracted to such views, an attraction which often seems to result from an exceptional scrupulosity in avoiding self-deception or in believing without full warrant. While these ontologically nihilistic movements reject mainstream Anglo-American epistemology and philosophy of science, note that the latter also produces a generalized skepticism.

Even if those I classify as ontological nihilists really recommend relinquishing efforts to know, their analyses can be of value to those of us who still so strive. Knowing the other requires giving up a naive implicit assumption that how we see things is the way "nature is," available for all competent and well-intentioned humans to directly perceive as we do. The very able arguments of the ontological nihilists should jolt us out of this complacent and misleading certainty, and this is prerequisite to a more self-critical effort. Furthermore, the arguments of the ontological nihilists may focus on very specific unconscious assumptions that need challenging and changing in an improved search for validity. Finally, if these new epistemologies have produced exemplars of how postmodern social science should be done, we should study these exemplars to see if they impress us both as being worth doing and as different from our current practice. What I recommend we reject is any message (if such be present) that we should give up the effort to know, and the dialog of mutual criticism as to the comparative validity of such efforts.

In contrast to the ontological nihilists, most of the critics of unconscious centrisms in knowing the other have made these criticisms in the context of trying to improve the validity of social science. Before getting to them, and to methodological cultural relativism in particular, I want to make some comments on postpositivist epistemology in mainstream Anglo-American analytic philosophy.

The overthrow of logical positivism came from within the Anglo-

American academic philosophical establishment. One conspicuous, originally sympathetic early critic was Nelson Goodman, who generated several damning paradoxes of induction. He ended up an ontological nihilist, in my judgment, with his *Ways of Worldmaking* (1978). But the overwhelming majority have continued to try to explicate how we establish "knowledge" as opposed to mere opinion. Quine is a case in point. His "Two Dogmas of Empiricism" (1951) was the first conspicuous attack on logical positivism. It was full of skeptical content. It emphasized that no observations can unequivocally confirm any theory, that any belief in the truth of a theory is underdetermined, never proven, and that all of our beliefs, including logic, must be open for revision. In *Word and Object* (1960) he set forth the problem of radical translation (an anthropologist in a strange language community with no interpreter), and concluded that "reference is inscrutable," that the ostensions used in language learning are ambiguous, and as to translation, "there is no truth of the matter." He has found indeterminacies at every stage, including both in the establishment of fact and in the choice of theory (Quine 1990).

In the great bulk of postpositivist epistemologies, there is awareness that the skeptics have not been answered, and this includes traditional skepticism about visual perception as well as about linguistically communicated belief. Even those who are centrally concerned with "knowledge as justified true belief" emphasize or concede that "justification" does not produce certainty, but rather depends upon the employment of usually reliable sources of belief, or a choice of the best of available rival explanations of perceptual input. Almost all are anti-foundational. Among the most traditional heirs of the analytic tradition, Pollock (1974) and Lehrer (1989) would now revise the traditional recipe to read "knowledge is undefeated justified true belief," conceding that the best of justified belief is still defeasible. One of Kuhn's (1962) crucial contributions to the demise of logical positivism was to demonstrate with historical examples the great dependence of science on unproven assumptions, most of which the practitioners were unaware of until these assumptions were challenged by the new paradigm.

Rather than reacting to these skeptical realizations with ontological nihilism, mainstream epistemology and philosophy of science has gone ahead trying to explicate how we achieve the improvements in the competence of belief that we believe to be exemplified in the best of science. New beliefs are to be justified by improved *coherence* among the bulk of our beliefs (rather than by foundational perceptions and entailing logic). We start out the search for improved belief with a vast store of beliefs already on hand. We are to trust the great bulk of these while we revise a small subset (but all beliefs are to be open to revision). This omnifallibilist trust

(Cook and Campbell 1986) is sometimes given the misleading label of "holism."

For the "radical translation" situation Quine (1960) recommends a "principle of charity." We are advised to assume that the speaker of the unknown language is like ourselves in the perceptual reification of middle-sized objects and in quasi-logical inference patterns. The ostensions (the pointing to objects) involved are both essential and fundamentally ambiguous rather than definitional, as both Quine (1969:30–32) and Wittgenstein (1953:13–14) have noted. One can never be sure that one has translated perfectly, but one can do well enough to make an approximate learning of the other's language worthwhile. After all, our children share the same epistemological predicament. Thus mainstream analytic philosophy has arrived at a position quite similar to that of validity-seeking hermeneutics (Campbell 1991). I include Habermas (1971, 1983) and Geertz (1973, 1983) as exponents of validity-seeking hermeneutics, along with the founders, Schleiermacher, Dilthey, and Weber. Both antifoundationalism and omnifallibilist trust is shown in the task of deciphering ancient manuscripts, in which a hermeneutic community is capable of deciding that a particular contested passage represents an early copyist's error.

This postpositivist, post-Kuhnian consensus in philosophy of science is a part of the methodological perspective I recommend for knowing the other. But it must be supplemented. The "principle of charity" can be used to deny cultural differences in cognitive frameworks, as Davidson (1984) has explicitly done (see also Popper 1976). It must be modified or extended.

The older critiques were all made in the service of an *improved* validity, rather than giving up the goal of validity. This is clear in Mannheim (1949) and in his translators, Louis Wirth and Edward Shils, in their introduction to the English edition. It is clear in Collingwood (1946). Foucault (1973) is less clear, but he made the case for differing historical epistemes plausible by telling us what they were like. It is especially clear in the "cultural relativism" of the Boas anthropological tradition, for example, as presented by Herskovits (1948, 1972). Most relevant is what Herskovits has called *methodological* cultural relativism, which is based upon two empirical generalizations *about the ethnographer,* the scholar from our own society who studies an exotic culture. In Herskovits's essays, cultural relativism is always copresented with an assertion of the unconscious ethnocentrism of the anthropologist, an ethnocentrism which is an obstacle to validly understanding the other. Methodological cultural relativism is designed to minimize this obstacle. Ethnographers (just as the exotics they study) experience the world through biological and cultural filters. What is perceived is in fact a joint product of the referent and the cultural-biological lenses through which it is seen. But the perceptions and cognitions that result do not give evidence of their cultural-biological roots. Instead, the perceptions *seem* to be wholly "objective," wholly determined by the referent. We have called this phenomenal absolutism (Segall, Campbell, and Herskovits 1966, chap. 1), but this is not an ideal term. "Experiential pseudo-objectivity" and "naive realism" are other possibilities. Durkheim (cf. Bourdieu, Chamboredon, and Passeron 1991) spoke of "the illusion of immediate knowledge" or "the illusion of transparency."

A second empirical generalization about ethnographers is that thorough knowledge of the exotic language and extended residence produce a conversion experience, in which the ethnographer comes to participate in the exotics' worldview, and to find their beliefs rational. In the process, ethnographers come to realize that many of their understandings were biased by their own original ethnocentric enculturation. Most anthropologists intend to be methodological cultural relativists in this sense. Geertz (1983, 1984) makes this explicit.

Methodological cultural relativism does not preclude finding human universals in moral norms, personality types, or life-cycle crises. But it warns ethnographers that their own ethnocentric enculturation will lead to an exaggeration of the extent to which such universals are the same as what is found in their own culture, a warning that most philosophers have failed to heed (Krausz 1989; Krausz and Meiland 1982; Dascal 1991; Rorty, in Krausz 1989, is an exception). Thus the "principle of charity" must be extended to acknowledge the powerful effects of culture on cognition. It must include the recognition that, "Had I been reared in this culture and ecology, I would see things as they do, believe as they do, and be equally unaware of the effects of my enculturation on these cognitions." Analogously, the hermeneutic decoder of an ancient script must speculate about the different cultural framework and physical ecology of the original scribe, and use this empathy—revised in each hermeneutic recycling—in achieving the tentative translation.

Shared linguistic representation is so problematic, and so essential in knowing the other, that a review of the extent to which it can be achieved, and how, is in order. The "scandal of representation," or the "crisis of representation," are among the ontologically nihilistic themes in the post-structuralist, deconstructionist, and postmodernist epistemologies. The epistemology advocated here recommends that shared representation and reference always be regarded as problematic, inevitably imperfect, but plausibly achieved to a useful degree in many settings.

Shared representation is problematic in first-language learning. If one takes an exaggerated version of the Cassirer-Whorf hypothesis, in which the entification of the perceptual world into objects and acts is caused by the categories provided by language, then shared reference is impossible. The ostensions (useful, but not definitional) required in the child's learning the language would not be available until after the language was learned (Campbell 1989). The slogan, "One can't teach a language by telephone," captures the problem. More plausible is the view that infants (and some animals) already share panhuman perceptual reification tendencies which guide or dominate their guesses as to word meanings for objects pointed to. Shared reference is still problematic and imperfect, as children's early "rational errors" in word meanings show, but for middle-sized objects in the shared visual field, their reification of entities is so similar to that of their adult mentors that errors rarely persist (Campbell 1973, 1988b).

In learning the language of the other, the ethnographer has the clues to guessing available to the others' children, but is handicapped by the ethnographer's own first-language learning. The shared perceptual reifications are for middle-sized objects (and clear-cut, simple, universal, purposive acts). Horton (1982) emphasizes both this limitation and its availability as an entrée to second-language learning. Bulmer's "Why the Cassowary Is Not a Bird" (1967) has been cited to emphasize the cultural arbitrariness of categorization (for example, Barnes 1983). Note, however, that Bulmer and his local others had no difficulty in achieving shared reference for *cassowary,* a category that included adult males and females plus infants.

In this model, the more abstract and generic vocabulary is learned by indirect quasi-ostensions employing words from the primary simple object-and-act vocabulary. These quasi-ostensions are much more equivocal than are the ostensions of the primary vocabulary. It is for this secondary vocabulary that semantic and cognitive "accents" from the ethnographer's first culture most strongly intrude. It is at this level that shared reference becomes truly problematic in second-language learning (and also, to a lesser degree, within the first-language community). If this theory is correct, ideally the ethnographer should use an interpreter only for the primary language vocabulary, and then learn the rest of the vocabulary by quasi-ostensions provided by the local others in their own language. This converges on the methods recommended by the "ethnoscience," "folk vocabulary," "componential analysis" schools of anthropological linguistics (for example, Werner and Schoepfle 1987).

Integrating This View with Other Chapters

Shweder's "True Ethnography" is a brilliant essay full of concrete exemplars. It seems to me to present a viewpoint which amplifies and is fully consistent with methodological cultural relativism. It is particularly important because it comes from one who has shown in other essays that he is fully cognizant of those current intellectual enthusiasms which I have crudely lumped as ontologically nihilistic, such as postmodernism, post-structuralism, deconstructionism, and more recent imports from the cafés of Paris (Shweder 1989).

The "solipsism" which Shweder asserts that postmodernism can produce (and which he rejects) is a species of what I have called ontological nihilism. He not only rejects it, but in affirming the goals of "true ethnography" and knowledge of "other minds," he has chosen a dialectical dramatization of the contrast, flaunting the epistemological modesty of which skepticism is an exaggeration. He recognizes the obstacles to knowing the other that come from our own ethnocentric enculturation, recommending that we ethnographers "suspend our disbeliefs," and "transcend our own habitual modes of moral judgment and emotional reaction." With Evans-Pritchard's help, he recommends an initial role-playing at believing as the other does, or at least a vigorous bracketing of the "truth" and "rightness" of the ethnographer's own culture's beliefs and evaluations and those of the other.

Shweder links his posit of "original multiplicity" of worldviews to a universal humanness. We have ended up with different worldviews, he says, but (as in the principle of charity) each of us could have ended up with that of the other. This "original multiplicity" remains as a latent cognitive capacity for ethnographers, enabling them to come to understand the worldview of the other. (It no doubt also helps the readers of their ethnographies to feel convinced that such a worldview is humanly possible.) Methodological cultural relativism is similarly based upon the assumption that all cognitive and behavioral cultural differences are learned, not innate, and hence it, too, assumes panhuman unity in the biological equipment for knowing and acting.

Shweder's view is that our knowledge of the other is to be achieved by a trial-and-error of hypothetical models of their worldview. These are to be mental models with behavioral implications. In this extended trial-and-error substitution of one mental model by another, the observations of the others' practice, their own articulations to the ethnographer, their discourse among themselves, their response to novel puzzles presented by the ethnographer, and their response to "superficial" methods such as rating scales and questionnaires, all are to be used, but none treated as foundational. In this latter sense the mental model finally chosen may disagree with any of the data sources, including the others' own articulations of their worldview.

All this I am happy to endorse. I also applaud the inspirational affirmation that knowing *other minds* and *true ethnography* can be done, even though I feel the need to put a fallibilist gloss on these terms, a gloss with which I feel Shweder would agree. These terms of his represent *goals* that will never be achieved to perfection. The iterative trial-and-error of revised models will never perfectly asymptote, even though coherence/plausibility may affirm each successor model as probably an improvement. In addition, just as the ethnographers end up speaking the others' languages with phonetic, grammatic, and semantic "accents," so too there will be residual cultural "accents." The "nominalist" versus "natural kind" contrast which he says he deliberately "compromises" for the concept of culture has a parallel in a nominalist-realist duality for the models of other minds. The closest to describing reality that a fallibilist-realist can come is through a winnowed subset of nominalist categorizations. Thus the charge of nominalism or conventionalism for a well-winnowed model of the others' mental experience does *not* imply an arbitrariness equal to that of any random nominalist construction. (Indeed, the best "knowledge" of any kind remains a nominalist construction, plausibly well-selected by presumed symptoms of the referent and in interaction with the referent.)

In Shweder's examples, the iterative replacement of trial models has gone on within the problem-solving fieldwork of one ethnographer in critical dialogue within his local research team. In science and validity-seeking humanistic scholarship, this dialectic usually goes on within a larger community of independent scholars. But in understaffed and underfunded anthropology it is rare that there exists such a community focused on the same attributes of a single ethnic group.

Ethnographic searches for valid knowledge of other minds are jeopardized by other sources of bias than the ethnographer's first culture. As will be belabored in the final section of this essay, failures of communication with the other have the same type of symptoms as do cognitive differences. Ambiguities in inferring causation from observed concomitancies have led anthropologists to attempt total abstention, but they find it hard to live up to this vow, and sometimes mistake the direction of causation or overlook causation by unnoted background variables. At various times in my career I have assembled lists of scholarly interpretative biases, beginning with Francis Bacon's lists of "idols" or false images. Several of these lists are reprinted in Campbell (1988a:72–93, 263–65, 464–82). For example, unrepresentative striking events early in fieldwork often overdominate interpretive models. Initial oversimplification is an essential strategy in knowing (Campbell 1988a:467–71; 1987), but is also a source of bias. Thus in one of the few cases of multiple ethnographies and focused disagreement, Ruth Benedict's early dramatic portrait of the Hopi mind has probably been invalidated (Bennett 1946). In the search for improved validity, improved competence of reference will never achieve absolute proof (even in ordinary visual perception or the best of physical science). Critical dialogue (including a dialogue of persuasive demonstrations or experiments) is essential. What is particularly to be rejected from the ontological nihilists is any recommendation that we give up this dialectical search for what Shweder calls true ethnography.

Howard Becker's chapter seems to me quite compatible with both Shweder's views and my own as presented here. This latter compatibility is no accident. He and I cotaught and shared dissertation supervision at Northwestern University in the years 1960 to 1979, with Becker being the major director on at least two psychology dissertations. In our joint teaching, I generally played the role of quantitative and experimental methodologist, and although we both recognized the joint relevance of quantitative and qualitative data, he has been a major influence on my two essays (Campbell 1975, 1978) acknowledging this. Because he has used Campbell and Stanley's (1963) list of threats to validity in a seminal paper on photography as a mode of data collection and research reporting in a militantly nonquantitative article (Becker 1979), I claim an influence on him as well. In his chapter here he reaffirms a joint relevance to the same goals for qualitative and quantitative data, and this is asserted in Shweder's chapter as well.

While Becker affirms joint relevance, he nonetheless makes important critiques of standard quantitative social science research. These criticisms strike me as both valid and as extremely important. He stresses that those whose scientific evidence is mean differences and correlations on quantified questionnaire items go on to interpret them in terms of the meanings and actions of respondents. Not only are these interpretations very often wrong, they could have been made right by participant observation. Quantitative data often represents low-cost, mass-produced research and is often wrong. The others' meanings as inferred from questionnaire averages are overly determined by the ethnocentric subjectivity of the researcher. Fieldwork, says Becker, is both more difficult and more accurate than quantitative questionnairing. (Herskovits [1962] has similarly claimed a superior validity for anthropology practiced as a humanity.)

Becker's reminder that we should regard official statistics as the persuasive communications of administrators and not as unbiased reflections of reality is also important. Our Northwestern colleagues, Kitsuse and Cicourel (1963) documented this truism and it has become a regular emphasis of my own (Campbell 1988a:269–70, 306–7; 1994). This emphasis on the interest-laden social construction of measures is compatible with poststructuralist, social-constructivist epistemologies. We should also keep this perspective in mind with regard to our informants' and questionnaire respondents' manipulative interests. Becker's particular critique of social science customs of interviewing in private (where the social context is dominated by the researcher, not the respondent's usual associates) and anonymous questionnaires seems to me quite correct where our goal is to know and understand normal social meanings and behavior. (This must be qualified depending on the goal, as I will discuss below.)

Researchers often approach fieldwork with strong expectations, but Becker has convinced me that his kind of fieldwork regularly leads researchers to change these expectations, and in a direction of increased validity. It also enables them to learn about important issues they had not anticipated. In contrast, questionnaires, fixed interviews, and experimental designs limit the dimensions of inquiry in advance. Often this precludes learning information that would have discredited the validity of the quantitative results and the hypotheses that guided the research.

An illustration of the value of Becker's approach can be found in the Northwestern University dissertation of Louise Kidder. Prior to going to India (where she had spent a year in a Peace Corps-like activity some years earlier), she planned a quasi-experimental design to measure the impact of Indian culture on newcomers from England and the United States. She had taken Becker's fieldwork methods course, and he was on her Ph.D. committee, and thus she was prepared not only to study the details of the local contexts, but also to be alert to take note of the unexpected. This saved her dissertation. She was able to go beyond the prepared-in-advance interview schedules to learn that the primary adaptation of the newcomers was to the local culture of expatriates like themselves, and not directly to Indian culture. While in her methodological writings (for example, Kidder 1981 and subsequent revisions) she has loyally presented both types, her major identification has remained with Becker's methods.

Aspects of McDermott's stimulating and perspective-enlarging chapter can be translated to support the perspective I am advocating here. Deafness is not intrinsically a social problem. If we see it so, that is because of the unconscious presuppositions we have inherited from our culture or from our scientific paradigm. There could be, indeed there have been, cultures in which it was not a problem. Our culture (and our test-constructing psychologists) tends to create problem disabilities on every dimension flattering to elites and relevant for our competitive status-seeking. In the name of a higher objectivity (and an emancipatory social science) we should not take these culturally imposed category systems for granted, but seek a methodology that can avoid reifying them as a part of nature.

In citing Frake, McDermott calls attention to a well-developed system of inquiry within anthropology that scrupulously tries to avoid a form of questioning that imposes our categories upon the other (that avoids asking, What is your word for aunt?). For the purposes of this volume, these methods deserve great attention. (For an up-to-date report on such "folk classification" or "ethnoscience" methods, see Werner and Schoepfle 1987.) In agreement with Shweder and the methodological cultural relativism tradition, McDermott emphasizes both the long time often required and its reliance on the panhuman capacity for understanding the worldview of the other. In his third perspective, culture as disability, he calls our attention to the difficulty of noticing, and methodologically avoiding, cultural categories that both the investigator and the other share. But while I feel our views are fully compatible, my comments are tangential to his overall orientation.

McDermott cites Bakhtin and in other ways identifies himself with post-structuralist and postmodern epistemologies, but I interpret this as part of a search for greater validity, not as a justification for abandoning that search. As I interpret him, "the social constructions of reality" (for example, Berger and Luckmann 1966) are a society's historical constructions, and are Durkheimian "real social facts." Far from being the social constructions of the social scientist (although such are not ruled out), they are "real" in that any competent social scientist (well trained in epistemological cultural relativism) should be able to cross-validate them to a very considerable degree.

McDermott's commitment to knowing other minds has involved creative methodological explorations beyond those reported in his chapter that are relevant to the goals of the volume. In the conference discussions, he reported on taking lessons in Stanislavsky method acting to improve his empathy, and in rehearsing an asthmatic retarded child's "mee-ee" to better learn how she felt.

In this volume and conference aimed at introducing fixed-dimensional measurers to ethnographic methods, attention should be called to Elliot Mishler's classic *Research Interviewing: Context and Narrative* (1986). No text is more effective in teaching already well-trained survey research methodologists what they have been missing in investigator-driven interrogation and questionnairing, and what can be gained by respondent-empowering interviews, and in general by a more receptive listening-and-observing approach. Studying that text would ideally be a prerequisite to reading his chapter, and, indeed, this whole book.

Mishler's chapter persuasively reports that both observational narratives of children's narratives to their mothers and life history career narratives of adults have the great advantage of being respondent driven and expressed in the respondent's categories and dimensions. Statistical averages on fixed-dimensional messages methodologically (iatrogenically) preclude all but one developmental pattern, and that one is very indirectly inferred. Consistent with Becker's exhortation that the researcher not guess at what can be more directly inferred, the methods Mishler recommends to us in his chapter make possible the discovery of multiple developmental paths, and reduce greatly the inference gap in interpreting them.

The search for a useful methodology and epistemology for "knowing the other" is far from complete. In extending our methodology, if we are to avoid being paralyzed by skepticism, we must learn from what Kuhn (1962) calls exemplars. For the social sciences, these exemplars should be examples from social science (not physics) that we find impressive (even though, for sure, none will have answered the skeptics). Such exemplars should play a role comparable to the ostensions employed in first-language learning. They are *illustrations,* not definitions or logical nodes in a deductive system. Each exemplar is to some degree ambiguous or equivocal, yet essential to the process. (I have called them quasi-ostensions [1988b: 461–97].)

As exemplars of successfully knowing the other, the substantive chapters that make up the bulk of this volume should, ideally, be examined to learn how it was done, and thus build a general methodology from these successes. While this has not been done, a few illustrative observations can be made. (These come as much from the oral discussions at the conference as from the written papers.)

The socially realistic methodologies that all in this volume have recommended will no longer allow the pretense of the ethnographer as but an inconspicuous fly on the wall, or write-ups in the "third-person omniscient." The ethnographer is inevitably a part of the social reality being described, and should be so represented in the research report. The local population's perception of the researcher's social role is crucial to the kind of data produced. These perceptions will not be fully under his or her control. In his chapter for this volume, William Corsaro describes creating a not previously existing role as a sort of childlike older brother, "Big Bill Manchild," which was very effective until the children he was studying decided he was really a teacher.

Several of the other chapters describe training local participants to be researchers. In the early University of Chicago symbolic-interactionist studies, graduate students would pass unannounced as factory workers, and such disguise is available for any social situation in which strangers are often present, although the ethics of informed consent presents problems.

Becker recommends studying people when they are under their normal social constraints, in their usual social settings. In contrast to this in both method and research goal are those studies taking advantage of the role of transient stranger, as Georg Simmel and Arnold Rose have separately argued. Margaret Lock's chapter provides an example. In her ethnography, she has the goal of "thick description." She feels that, on some topics at least, it increased the richness of her interviews with Japanese men that she was neither Japanese nor male, nor likely to remain a part of their social environment. She finds that many Japanese (both men and women) feel it easier to be critical of their own society, and also to disclose some of their own inner thoughts, to a stranger. Regarding the research described in her chapter, Linda Burton believes black women were better interviewers of black men for the purposes of her study than would have been a black man, who would have activated the macho stereotyped responses shared among males.

Knowing the Other Is Problematic: Mistaking Failures of Communication for Cultural Differences

I would like to close this essay with a focus on the most ubiquitous source of error in efforts to know the other. This is to interpret as a cultural difference what is in reality a failure of communication. The epistemology offered here is double-edged. On the one hand, it emphasizes legitimate sources of doubt, the lack of foundations and proof, the necessity of employing unproven assumptions, and so on. On the other hand, it argues that to a practically useful degree we not only overcome these in our everyday, ingroup life, but can also do so in knowing the other. However, we will do so most validly if we are aware of the pitfalls.

I personally am convinced that many of the cultural differences reported by psychologists and others using questionnaires or tests come from failures of communication misreported as differences. I remember a study by a British sociologist around 1960 that reported social-class differences in child-rearing values which at the time I thought were instead almost certainly the product of failures to communicate. A questionnaire was used, in university-educated vocabulary. For many items, the "obviously correct" value choice was at one extreme in a fixed list of alternatives. The middle- to upper-class respondents uniformly chose this answer. Among the less well educated, failures to understand the question, or alienated, perfunctory answers on a boring or humiliating task would lead to chance, haphazard responding which, on average, would differ from the "obviously correct" answer in a systematic direction, and could thus generate social-class differences mistaken as being differences in values.

Since the focus of this volume is on qualitative methods, note that if the information had been collected in open-ended interviews, the interviewer would probably have been aware of misunderstandings and failures to comprehend. Self-administered questionnaires are the worst for hiding failures in communication from the researcher. Whether free-response or fixed-response interviewing is done, pilot testing for comprehensibility should be done. A useful technique is to ask respondents to paraphrase the question in their own words.

When we come to research on others who speak a different language, a process of translation is involved. Anthropological linguist Oswald Werner and I long ago distinguished between the "ethnocentric" translations of research instruments and "decentered" translations (Werner and Campbell 1970). In an ethnocentric translation, the English version of a questionnaire, personality, or ability test is translated literally into the other's language. What was idiomatic, colloquial, popular vocabulary in the English version becomes awkward and difficult, using unusual vocabulary, and misunderstood in the other's-language version. The resulting differences in response are misinterpreted as personality, attitude, or ability differences. For example, ethnocentered translation seems to me the only plausible explanation of a 1966 finding that male-female differences in interests were much smaller in Turkey and Italy than in the United States (Gough 1966).

The technique of back-translation provides both a confirmation of effective translation (available even to a monolingual researcher) and a route to a decentered translation. In this technique, there is a translation from language A to language B by one translator, then the language B version is translated back to language A by another translator. My wife, Barbara Frankel, relays this anecdote from early efforts at machine translation between English and Russian: the original English message reads, "The spirit is willing, but the flesh is weak." The back-translated English returns, "The vodka is good, but the meat is rotten." Back-translation using the locally available bilinguals is usually a disappointing experience, and is too rarely done. Nor should it be assumed that translation is possible on all topics. In my brief research experience under Robert LeVine's tutelage among the Gusii of Kenya, we found that *brave* usually came back as "fierce" or "cruel" (Campbell and LeVine 1970).

To avoid the bias of ethnocentered translation, we (Werner and Campbell 1970) set up the ideal of collecting new data in English on an English version that has been produced by an iterative series of back-translations, with monolingual judges approving the equivalence of the versions at each stage. These decentered English and others'-language versions will be banal and will avoid ambiguous reference by repeating nouns rather than using indirect reference, for example. To start out with two English versions, each a paraphrase of the other with as few repeated words as possible (a translation from English to English as it were) should also help.

I would like to end this critique on a more optimistic note, akin to

Shweder's chapter, emphasizing that in spite of all it can be done. In spite of the most extreme epistemological quicksand, it *is* possible to know that the other perceives differently than we do (and in what way and to what degree), but only when such differences are small.

W. H. R. Rivers, in papers published between 1901 and 1905, reported that the peoples of the Torres Straits and the Todas of India were less susceptible to the Muller-Lyer illusion than were the English. In the Muller-Lyer illusion, one compares the length of two horizontal lines, to one of which diagonal distractor lines have been added, making an arrow-headed pattern. To the other have been added distractor diagonals extending out beyond the comparison line, suggesting the feathers on an arrow. The illusion is that the feathered line is seen as longer when in fact the comparison lines are equal. In Rivers' work and in the scattered studies that followed, there were many possibilities for misunderstandings that might have produced pseudo-differences. We set out to replicate and extend these studies with techniques intended to maximize competent communication (Segall, Campbell, and Herskovits 1966; Campbell 1964). In contrast to earlier studies, there was a gap between the lines to be compared and the distractor lines. (Those not the cultural heirs of Euclid might lack a concept of line that terminated where the lines bent or split.) The lines to be compared were printed in red, the distractors in black. There were twelve separate pages of Muller-Lyer figures, on which the percentage by which the illusion-supported (feathered) figure exceeded the arrow-headed figure ranged from 48 percent to –8 percent. The items were presented in a haphazard order, and the feathered figure was to the right half of the time. For each page, the respondent was asked, "Which of these red lines is longer?"

The test items were preceded by four comprehension checks, three of which had two red lines of substantially different lengths. It dramatizes the epistemological problem to note that the final comprehension check was in the form of a Muller-Lyer item. If on this item, the respondent answered differently than would the anthropologist administering the test, a failure of communication was assumed. But on the test items, such a difference was interpreted as a difference in perception.

In spite of this foundationless quicksand, we believe that we demonstrated that persons from different cultures (or visual ecologies) differed in their perceptions. In addition, we specified the direction of difference and estimated its magnitude. For example, we found representative adults of Evanston, Illinois, to have an average illusion of 19 percent; white South Africans, 13 percent; Ankole, 7 percent; Zulus, 5 percent; Ijaw, 3 percent; South African bushmen, 1 percent. But we could only achieve this because the differences were relatively small. Had the differences been very large, we could not have confirmed that we were communicating (nor could the other's language have been learned).

The four "comprehension checks" were only interpretable as such under the assumption that the perceptual differences were small. On these four items the longer of the comparison lines exceeded the shorter by 336 percent, 218 percent, 182 percent, and, for the Muller-Lyer figure, 587 percent. In using the "principle of charity" we interpreted those who did not respond as we would as having failed to understand the task.

In the data analysis, we received another confirmation of conjoint fellow humanness and successful communication. In choosing the values for the test items, we had used previous research to attempt to bracket the full anticipated range of illusion susceptibility. Insofar as we succeeded in this, we expected an ogive-shaped distribution of responses in each group when the response percentages were plotted with the test items rearranged in magnitude of discrepancy. That is, the frequency of choosing the "illusion supported" feathered line should go from near 100 percent for the –8 percent and –2 percent items, and drop to near zero for the 45 percent and 48 percent items. This ogive-shaped distribution was found for all samples (14 adult samples, 13 child samples). While with the raw data the range was from 87 percent to 100 percent (rather than all 100 percent) at the low end, to 0 percent to 13 percent (rather than all 0 percent) at the high end, in each case the distribution was smooth enough to justify picking a "point of subjective equality" where the ogive value was 50 percent. (There was a minimum of forty-three persons in each adult sample.)

In spite of this overall orderliness in all of the data sets, there were some inconsistent individual response patterns that could not plausibly be regarded as measuring a degree of illusion susceptibility. When such persons were removed (over half of the sample for the Zulu), the ogives all reached 0 percent at the high end. (Thus we could have used the 48 percent item as one more comprehension check.) At the low end, all were 94 percent or higher. The points of subjective equality computed for these purified samples correlated (over N groups) 0.98 with those obtained for the unpurified sample. (For the Zulus, and for most groups, the values were identical.)

It should not be denied that efforts to make sure that there is competent communication may well introduce a bias in the direction of selecting respondents who are somewhat more like ourselves than the average member of their groups. This is a bias we can never completely overcome. It is the price we must pay to avoid mistaking failures of communication for cultural differences. Where the anthropologist's selection of informants is concerned, it has often been noted that the informants will be persons who share the anthropologist's interests. They may, for that reason, be more exposed to several cultures. They are often marginal to their own cultures (see Paul 1953 for an early observation on this, and Campbell 1955).

Summary

Those who make knowing the other problematic are correct. Those who regard it as impossible to any degree are wrong. We need an epistemology and methodology which explains how, and to what degree, knowing the other is possible, as well as the common errors made in the attempt. Mainstream postpositivist philosophy of science points the way both in its holistic coherence-based strategy for belief revision, and in its principle of charity for the radical translation problem. What we find here is a convergence with the older validity-seeking hermeneutics. To the principle of charity must be added principles from methodological cultural relativism which call attention to the cultural contributions to cognition operating unconsciously to bias both the ethnographer's and the other's perception of what is objectively real. There is also an unavoidable equivocality in distinguishing between failures of communication and cultural differences in cognition, but these can plausibly be distinguished in some cases.

References

Ariès, P. 1962. *Centuries of Childhood: A Social History of Family Life.* New York: Knopf.

Barnes, B. 1983. "On the Conventional Character of Knowledge and Cognition." In *Science Observed: Perspectives on the Social Study of Science.* Ed. K. D. Knorr-Cetina and M. Mulkay, 19–51. London: Sage Publications.

Becker, H. S. 1979. "Do Photographs Tell the Truth?" In *Qualitative and Quantitative Methods in Evaluation Research.* Ed. T. D. Cook and C. S. Reichardt, 99–117. Beverly Hills, Calif.: Sage Publications.

Bennett, J. W. 1946. "The Interpretation of Pueblo Culture." *Southwestern Journal of Anthropology* 2: 361–74.

Berger, P. L., and Luckmann, T. 1966. *The Social Construction of Reality.* New York: Doubleday.

Bourdieu, P., J.-C. Chamboredon, and J.-C. Passeron. 1991. *The Craft of Sociology: Epistemological Preliminaries.* New York: de Gruyter.

Bulmer, R. 1967. "Why Is the Cassowary Not a Bird? A Problem of Zoological Taxonomy among the Karam of the New Guinea Highlands." *Man* 2: 5–25.

Campbell, D. T. 1955. "The Informant in Quantitative Research." *American Journal of Sociology* 60:339–42.

———. 1964. "Distinguishing Differences of Perception from Failures of Communication in Cross-Cultural Studies." In *Cross-cultural Understanding: Epistemology in Anthropology.* Ed. F. S. C. Northrop and H. H. Livingston, 308–36. New York: Harper and Row.

———. 1972. "Herskovits, Cultural Relativism, and Metascience." In *Cultural Relativism: Perspectives in Cultural Pluralism.* Ed. M. J. Herskovits, v–xxiii. New York: Random House.

———. 1973. "Ostensive Instances and Entitativity in Language Learning." In *Unity through Diversity,* part 2. Ed. W. Gray and N. D. Rizzo, 1043–57. New York: Gordon and Breach.

———. 1975. "'Degrees of Freedom' and the Case Study." *Comparative Political Studies* 8: 178–93. Rpt. in Campbell 1988a:377–88.

———. 1978. "Qualitative Knowing in Action Research." In *The Social Contexts of Method.* Ed. M. Brenner, P. Marsh, and M. Brenner, 184–209. London: Croom Helm. Rpt. in Campbell 1988:360–76.

———. 1987. "Neurological Embodiments of Belief and the Gaps in the Fit of Phenomena to Noumena." In *Naturalistic Epistemology.* Ed. A. Shimony and D. Nails, 165–92. Dordrecht and Boston: D. Reidel.

———. 1988a. *Methodology and Epistemology for Social Science.* Ed. E. S. Overman. Chicago: University of Chicago Press.

———. 1988b. "Quasi-Ostension, Exemplars, and Gestalt Shifts." In Campbell 1988a:461–64.

———. 1989. "Models of Language Learning and Their Implications for Social-Constructionist Analyses of Scientific Belief." In *the Cognitive Turn: Sociological and Psychological Perspectives on Science.* Ed. S. Fuller, M. DeMey, T. Shinn, and S. Woolgar, 153–58. Dordrecht and Boston: Kluwer.

———. 1991. "Coherentist Empiricism, Hermeneutics, and the Commensurability of Paradigms." *International Journal of Educational Research* 15: 587–97.

———. 1993. "Plausible Coselection of Belief by Referent: All the 'Objectivity' That Is Possible." *Perspectives on Science: Historical, Philosophical, Social* 1: 85–105.

———. 1994. "How Individual and Face-to-Face-Group Selection Undermine Firm Selection in Organizational Evolution." In *Evolutionary Dynamics of Organizations.* Ed. J. A. C. Baum and J. V. Singh, 23–38. New York: Oxford University Press.

Campbell, D. T., and R. A. LeVine. 1970. "Field Manual Anthropology." In *A Handbook of Method in Cultural Anthropology.* Ed. R. Naroll and R. Cohen, 366–87. New York: Natural History Press/Doubleday.

Campbell, D. T., and J. C. Stanley. 1963. "Experimental and Quasi-Experimental Designs for Research on Teaching." In *Handbook of Research on Teaching.* Ed. N. L. Gage, 171–246. Chicago: Rand McNally. Rpt. as *Experimental and Quasi-Experimental Designs for Research.* Chicago: Rand McNally, 1966.

Collingwood, R. G. 1946. *The Idea of History.* Oxford: Oxford University Press.

Collins, H. M. 1981. "Stages in the Empirical Programme of Relativism." *Social Studies of Science* 11: 3–10.

Cook, T. D., and D. T. Campbell. 1986. "The Causal Assumptions of Quasi-Experimental Practice." *Synthese* 68: 141–80.

Dascal, M., ed. 1991. *Cultural Relativism and Philosophy: North and Latin American Perspectives.* Leiden, The Netherlands: E. J. Brill.

Davidson, D. 1984. *Inquiries into Truth and Interpretation.* Oxford: Clarendon Press.

Foucault, M. 1973. *The Order of Things: An Archaeology of the Human Sciences.* New York: Vintage Books.

Geertz, C. 1973. "Thick Description: Toward an Interpretive Theory of Culture." In Geertz, *The Interpretation of Cultures.* New York: Basic Books, 3–30.

———. 1983. *Local Knowledge: Further Essays in Interpretive Anthropology.* New York: Basic Books.

———. 1984. "Anti Anti-relativism." *American Anthropologist* 86: 263–78.

Goodman, N. 1978. *Ways of Worldmaking.* Indianapolis: Hackett.

Gough, H. G. 1966. "A Cross-Cultural Analysis of the CPI Feminity Scale." *Journal of Consulting Psychology* 30: 136–41.

Habermas, J. 1971. *Knowledge and Human Interests.* Boston: Beacon Press.

———. 1983. "Interpretive Social Science versus Hermeneuticism." In *Social Science as Moral Inquiry.* Ed. N. Haan, R. N. Bellah, P. Rabinow, and W. M. Sullivan. New York: Columbia University Press.

Herskovits, M. J. 1948. *Man and His Works.* New York: Knopf.

———. 1962. "The Humanism in Anthropological Science." *Actes du VI Congrès International des Sciences Anthropologiques et Ethnologiques* 1: 89–93. Rpt. in Herskovits 1972:242–61.

———. 1972. *Cultural Relativism.* Ed. Francis Herskovits. New York: Random House.

Horton, R. 1982. "Tradition and Modernity Revisited." In *Rationality and Relativism.* Ed. M. Hollis and S. Lukes, 201–60. Cambridge, Mass.: MIT Press.

Kidder, L. H. 1981. *Research Methods in Social Relations.* 4th ed. New York: Holt, Rinehart, and Winston.

Kitsuse, J. I., and A. V. Cicourel. 1963. "A Note on the Uses of Official Statistics." *Social Problems* 11:131–39.

Krausz, M., ed. 1989). *Relativism: Interpretation and Confrontation.* Notre Dame, Ind.: University of Notre Dame Press.

Krausz, M., and J. W. Meiland, eds. 1982. *Relativism: Cognitive and Moral.* Notre Dame, Ind.: University of Notre Dame Press.

Kuhn, T. S. 1962. *The Structure of Scientific Revolutions.* Chicago: University of Chicago Press.

Lehrer, K. 1989. "Knowledge Reconsidered." In *Knowledge and Skepticism.* Ed. M. Clay and Lehrer, 131–54. Boulder, Colo.: Westview.

Mannheim, K. 1949. *Ideology and Utopia: An Introduction to the Sociology of Knowledge.* London: Routledge and Kegan Paul.

Mishler, E. 1986. *Research Interviewing: Context and Narrative.* Cambridge, Mass.: Harvard University Press.

Paul, B. D. 1953. "Interview Techniques and Field Relationships." In *Anthropology Today.* Ed. A. L. Kroeber, 443–44. Chicago: University of Chicago Press.

Pollock, J. 1974. *Knowledge and Justification.* Princeton, N.J.: Princeton University Press.

Popper, K. 1976. "The Myth of the Framework." In *The Abdication of Philosophy: Philosophy and the Public Good; Essays in Honor of Paul Arthur Schilpp.* Ed. E. Freeman, 23–48. LaSalle, Ill.: Open Court.

Quine, W. V. 1951. "Two Dogmas of Empiricism." *Philosophical Review* 60: 20–46.

———. 1960. *Word and Object.* New York: Wiley.

———. 1969. *Ontological Relativity and Other Essays.* New York: Columbia University Press.

———. 1990. *Pursuit of Truth.* Cambridge, Mass.: Harvard University Press.

Sassower, R. 1991. "Postmodernism and Philosophy of Science: A Critical Engagement." *Philosophy of the Social Sciences* 23: 426–45.

Segall, M. H., D. T. Campbell, and M. J. Herskovits. 1966. *The Influence of Culture on Visual Perception.* Indianapolis: Bobbs-Merrill.

Shweder, R. A. 1989. "In Paris: Miniskirts of the Mind." *New York Times Book Review,* 8 Jan., 1, 28–31.

Werner, O., and D. T. Campbell. 1970. "Translating, Working Through Interpreters, and the Problem of Decentering." In *A Handbook of Method in Cultural Anthropology.* Ed. R. Naroll and R. Cohen, 398–420. Garden City, N.Y.: Natural History Press.

Werner, O., and G. M. Schoepfle. 1987. *Systematic Fieldwork.* 2 vols. Newbury Park, Calif.: Sage Publications.

Wittgenstein, L. 1953. *Philosophical Investigations.* Oxford: Oxford University Press.

PART 2

Ethnography as Method

8

Quanta and *Qualia:* What Is the "Object" of Ethnographic Method?

RICHARD A. SHWEDER

No doubt the distinction between quantitative and qualitative research has something to do with methodology—with real differences between intellectual operations such as pointing, sampling, counting, measuring, calculating, and abstracting, on the one hand, and intellectual operations such as empathizing, imagining, interpreting, narrating, contextualizing and exemplifying, on the other. Nevertheless, if that was all the distinction amounted to (a difference in intellectual operations) one would be hard pressed to make sense of the persisting tension in social research between quantitative and qualitative approaches. As everyone knows, in science, as in life, two hands (measuring and interpreting, abstracting and exemplifying) are usually better than one. And yet the tension persists. Why?

In this brief introduction to this section on ethnography as method I want to suggest that one way to understand the appeal of ethnography (to those for whom it has appeal) is to view it as a species of qualitative research, and one way to understand the appeal of qualitative research is to appreciate the difference between *quanta* and *qualia* as intellectual "objects." Hence, I want to propose that the separation (and persistence of a tension) between quantitative and qualitative (including ethnographic) research turns less on methodological issues and more on one's answer to ontological questions about *quanta* and *qualia.* What are *quanta* and *qualia,* how are they interrelated, and what is their respective (causal) roles (if any) in making the social world go round? In other words, ironic as it may seem, one of the best ways to think about the methodological side of ethnography may be to put our metaphysical cards on the table (our assumptions about the underlying nature of social reality), thereby revealing what we think ethnography is really all about.

An alternative formulation of those ontological questions can be derived from Thomas Nagel's discussion of the body/mind problem and the opposition between objective and subjective points of view. He writes, "There is a tendency to seek an objective account of everything before admitting its reality. But often what appears to a more subjective point of view cannot be accounted for in this way. So either the objective conception of the world is incomplete [the ontological premise of qualitative research], or the subjective involves illusions that should be rejected [the ontological premise of quantitative research]" (1979:196).[1]

I recognize, of course, that the perceived distinction between quantitative and qualitative research is not always thought of in ontological terms. Indeed, the contrast is so stereotypically associated with methodological or procedural issues, and is so time worn, that it is easy to lose sight of the type of metaphysical difference ("quanta" versus "qualia") I have in mind. One all-too-familiar and beguiling interpretation of the quantitative/qualitative distinction holds that the difference is about whether or not one counts and measures the things one studies. (Other interpretations assimilate the contrast to the distinction between magnitude and kind, or to the difference between nominal and interval scales). That methodological interpretation may be commonplace but unfortunately it is not very helpful for making sense of the tensions on the current empirical research scene. Setting radical, chic, skeptical, "nonsense" arguments to the side, almost everyone these days is prepared to acknowledge that to understand is to compare and that, in some sense or another, to observe is to count. The real and tantalizing clash between quantitative and qualitative approaches lies elsewhere, and I suspect it has something more to do with the ontology of science than with intellectual procedures.

I recognize, too, that the received distinction between quantitative and qualitative research is not always thought of as a "clash," and that there are prominent scholars who find it difficult to understand why the distinction should be framed as an opposition or should be controversial at all. Indeed, these days increasing numbers of sanguine voices can be heard asking, What is the problem? Why not just combine numbers and narratives, measurements and meanings, calculations and interpretations, magnitudes and qualities, and get on with doing better and more complete research? Such optimism is not surprising (although, ontologically speaking, it may be a bit delusive). For if one focuses only on the epistemological side of science (on method and reasoning), thereby overlooking the question of the metaphysical status of the objects of scientific inquiry, the demarcation between quantitative and qualitative research must seem either cut and dry (obviously not all intellectual operations are the same—numbers are not narratives, measurements are not meanings; so what?), or threadbare (certainly anyone concerned with the prevalence or distribution of a meaning, interpretation, or narrative is sooner or later going to have to count, and, as Richard Jessor notes in his introduction to the section of this book on ethnography as epistemology, in the social sciences at least, numerical results are open to interpretation), or invidious (for isn't there an underlying logic of causal inference that applies to all scientific research, whether qualitative or quantitative?; see, for example, D'Andrade 1984; King, Keohane, and Verba 1994). Thus, it must seem quite natural, in the light of the received methodological or procedural interpretation of the quantitative/qualitative contrast, to conclude that the tension between the two approaches has been overblown.

With due respect for such views I want tentatively to suggest that the distinction between quantitative and qualitative research is neither superficial, obvious, nor invidious. I want to suggest that the tension between the two approaches is real and significant, and that to understand the separation, one must begin with an analysis of the difference between *quanta* and *qualia* as intellectual objects.

This is a necessary exercise because the basic difference (and true friction) between quantitative research and qualitative research (of which ethnography is a species) resides primarily in the nature of the objects they study and their subject matter, *quanta* and *qualia,* respectively. And while there may be merit in the claim that there are connections between the ontology of a discipline (its intellectual objects) and the epistemology of a discipline (its ways of gaining knowledge of, and representing, the objects of its study; its intellectual "texture"; see Converse 1986; D'Andrade 1986), I actually think the well-publicized tension between quantitative and qualitative approaches has a greater ring of truth when formulated as a problem in ontology rather than as a problem in method (or epistemology). I believe that one way to appreciate the intellectual temper of some of the essays in this book it to view the contrast between quantitative and qualitative research in this less familiar, or at least less misleading, light.

Ontologically speaking, quantitative research (with its methodological emphasis on pointing, sampling, counting, measuring, calculating, and abstracting) is premised on the notion that the subjective involves illusions that should be rejected. The basic idea is that it is only when all subjectivity has been subtracted from the world that the really real world remains. And what remains that is really real is the world of *quanta.* Think of *quanta* as all the things that are what they are (retain their true identity) from, as Thomas Nagel puts it, no point of view. Mathematical and logical truths (for example, if p is true, then p or q is true) are *quanta.* So are the objects, events, and processes of an idealized physical or biological science, such as black holes or neurological nets. Such objects, events, processes, and truths are what they are and produce their effects objectively, regardless of our (subjective) acknowledgement(s) of them. That is what makes them *quanta*.[2]

In contrast, qualitative research (with its procedural emphasis on empathy, interpretation, thematization/enplotment, narration, contextualization, and exemplification/concreteness/substance) is premised on the notion that the objective conception of the real world is partial or incomplete. The basic idea is that one of the very important things left out of the real world by the objective conception are *qualia*. Think of *qualia* as things that can only be understood by reference to what they mean, signify, or imply (not in and of themselves and regardless of point of view but rather) to us (or to me) in this or that time and place and/or by reference to what it is like for us (or for me) to experience them. When it comes to *qualia* it is fair to say (again paraphrasing Thomas Nagel and borrowing his argot) that not everything that is really real is something (retains its true identity) from no point of view, for anything real whose identity has a trace of either history, place, or "us" in it, has its real identity by virtue of some subjective point of view.

The difference between the premise of qualitative research and the premise of quantitative research is ontological or metaphysical. Ernest Nagel (not to be confused with Thomas Nagel) gives clear expression to that metaphysical contrast in his account of the difference between science and common sense. Scientific notions, he suggests, must be "unusually abstract" and distant from "experience." Scientific explanations, he argues,

> can be constructed only if the familiar qualities and relations of things, in terms of which objects and events are usually identified and differentiated can be shown to depend for their occurrence on the presence of certain other pervasive relational or structural properties that characterize in various ways an extensive class of objects and processes. Accordingly, to achieve generality of explanations for qualitatively diverse things, those structural properties must be formulated without reference to, and in abstraction from, the individualizing qualities and relations of familiar experience. It is for the sake of achieving such generality, that, for example, the temperature of bodies is defined in physics not in terms of directly felt differences in warmth [*qualia*], but in terms of certain abstractly formulated relations characterizing an extensive class of reversible thermal cycles [*quanta*]. (1961:11)

If I am right about the basic ontological premises of quantitative versus qualitative research, then it would seem to follow that, ontologically speaking, if you truly are a quantitative researcher, you ought to believe that the only things that are really real, that have determinate causal force, that are proper objects for an explanatory science are those things that exist and have identity (and power) independent of our experience and awareness of them. Such things are *quanta*.

It is not too hard to imagine how this ontology of *quanta* spawns its own epistemology and ideals for measurement. Thomas Nagel (not to be confused with Ernest Nagel) has this to say about scientific measurement:

> If there is a way things really are, which explains their diverse appearances to differently constituted and situated observers, then it is most accurately apprehended by methods not specific to particular types of observers. That is why scientific measurement interposes between us and the world instruments whose inter-actions with the world are of a kind that could be detected by a creature not sharing the human senses. Objectivity requires not only a departure from one's individual viewpoint, but also, so far as possible, departure from a specifically human or even mamma-lian viewpoint. The idea is that if one can still maintain some view when one relies less and less on what is specific to one's position or form, it will be truer to reality. (1979:209)

It is with this type of ontological issue in mind that I want to suggest that to point or not to point, to count or not to count, to measure or not to measure, to sample or not to sample, are not the kinds of questions that deeply separate quantitative from qualitative approaches. The true difference between the approaches is not over whether to count and mea-sure but rather over what to count and measure, and over what one actu-ally discovers by doing so. The true difference is over the question whether *qualia* are really real versus really illusory as objects of science. The true difference is over the question of whether the specificity and particularity of our "position or form" (our historically and culturally contingent per-spective on things) obscures our perception of reality or (alternatively) actually makes it possible for us to truly see. The true difference is over the question, how much more is there to the understanding of reality than the procedures for studying *quanta* (pointing, counting, measuring, sam-pling, calculating) can supply?

Qualitative research exists because (again using Thomas Nagel's argot, in paraphrase) not everything really real is something from no point of view. The real things studied by qualitative researchers must always be identified (and ultimately explained) at least in part by reference to the unobservable subjective experiences (for example, sensations or feelings) and the nondeducible meanings that are on-line in the mental life of par-ticular (types of) situated observers (that is to say, by reference to some "native point of view"). This is so because the kinds of properties studied in qualitative research are the properties associated with "consciousness."

Those properties derive from the (perhaps inherently "mysterious") capacity of "qualitative" beings to symbolize, to form concepts, to be aware, to have experiences, to want, to value, to choose—in other words, to have a mental life (on the notion that consciousness is a mystery, see McGinn 1991). In a sense the aim of ethnography (and of all qualitative research) is to elucidate the way *qualia* are underspecified and/or underdetermined by *quanta.* The aim is to show how something suprasensible and non-deducible (a value, a meaning, a purpose, a rationale) has been historically or culturally added to the world of *quanta* to make the real world more complete. In the world of *quanta,* the world of objectivity, all things can be directly grasped and measured and there is nothing more to a thing beyond what calculation can provide. In a world of *qualia,* measurement and calculation (and even research design) are fine as far as they can go, but they can go only just so far. That is one reason why the real things studied by qualitative researchers (including our own accounts of those things, which being "accounts" are also *qualia*) must be historicized and contextualized if they are to be understood.

It is important to recognize that, ontologically speaking, there is an asymmetry between quantitative and qualitative research. The ontological premise of quantitative research implies that *qualia* (feelings, beliefs, goals, desires, meanings, values) are not only illusory (or "epiphenomenal"; perhaps "epinoumenal" would be the more accurate term for something that is supposed to be unreal) but can play no part in an objective account of the causes of human behavior. If you are faithful to the ontology of *quanta* you know that the phrase "quantitative researcher" is not simply a synonym for a person who is a counter, a measurer, a sampler, or an experimental designer. True quantitative researchers are not agnostic or indifferent about the kinds of "things" that they count, measure, sample, or experimentally manipulate. If you are truly a quantitative researcher then, you are committed to the view that *quanta* must replace *qualia* in any "scientific" account of reality.

Conversely, if you engage in the kind of research that is now routine in the social sciences wherein you try to count, measure, sample, or experimentally manipulate *qualia*—beliefs, desires, feelings, concepts, attitudes symbolically expressed in language—then you are not studying *quanta* at all. Ontologically speaking, you remain a qualitative researcher, even though you try to count, measure, sample, and experimentally manipulate the things you study. And if that is all you ever did (or thought you did) when you studied *qualia*—count, measure, sample, manipulate "variables"—you would remain vulnerable to the criticism that there is some kind of incommensurability or lack of fit between your intellectual procedures and the objects of your investigation. You would be open to the critique that all the real work in understanding the things you study (*qualia*) must be going on informally, before, after, or outside the formal application of any *quantitative* procedures. You would be asked to be more self-conscious about what is really involved in "grasping" the objects of your study. This is one source of the persisting tension between "scientists" and "interpretivists" in the area of social research.

In contrast, the ontological premise of qualitative research is far less imperialistic. The premise of qualitative research does not imply that *qualia* must replace *quanta* in any interpretive account of reality. The premise does not imply that *quanta* have no part to play in the causal structure of the really real world.[3] The premise of qualitative research also does not imply that counting, sampling, measurement, and experimental design must be totally superseded by other intellectual operations. What it does assert is that the objective conception of the really real is partial and incomplete and must be supplemented with other procedures. Ontologically speaking, all the essays in this section on ethnography as method are investigations of qualitative realities in search of other procedures for better comprehending their intellectual objects.

Notes

1. By an "objective" account Nagel means an account of the nature of a thing as it exists independent of our particular awareness-experience-evaluation of it; as it exists without regard to our situated and hence contingent reaction to it. By a "subjective" point of view Nagel means the way a thing appears or feels to us, to me, from here, right now; he means the way the thing is understood, experienced or reacted to by us, by me, with this or that contingent sensory apparatus, in this or that parochial state of mind.

2. The case of mathematical and logical truths is fascinating because it suggests that there are *quanta* in the normative as well as the empirical sciences and that even suprasensible things can have a standing in an objective world. It is but a short step to the claim that all abstract forms, "Platonic essences," or definitional truths—for example, the formal definition of the normative ideal of "justice" as "treat like cases alike and different cases differently"—are *quanta*, too, for their claims hold true regardless of the contingencies of time, place or point of view.

3. For example, any interpretive account of the *qualia* of justice would have to presuppose, and thereby take account of, the abstract form or *quanta* of justice— "treat like cases alike and different cases differently." Indeed such an interpretive investigation might make use of the *quanta* of justice to discover the historically or culturally situated *qualia* of justice. That would be done by documenting and explaining why in such and such place at such and such time for such and such people such and such particular likenesses and such and such particular differences were believed to be relevant in the pursuit of any just cause.

References

Converse, P. 1986. "Generalization and the Social Psychology of 'Other Worlds.'" In *Metatheory in Social Science: Pluralisms and Subjectivities.* Ed. D. W. Fiske and R. A. Shweder, 42–60. Chicago: University of Chicago Press.

D'Andrade, R. 1984. "Cultural Memory Systems." In *Culture Theory: Essays on Mind, Self, and Emotion.* Ed. R. A. Shweder and R. A. LeVine, 88–122. New York: Cambridge University Press.

———. 1986. "Three Scientific World Views and the Covering Law Model." In *Metatheory in Social Science: Pluralisms and Subjectivities.* Ed. D. W. Fiske and R. A. Shweder, 19–41. Chicago: University of Chicago Press.

King, G., R. O. Keohane, and S. Verba. 1994. *Designing Social Inquiry: Scientific Inference in Qualitative Research.* Princeton, N.J.: Princeton University Press.

McGinn, C. 1991. *The Problem of Consciousness.* Oxford: Blackwell.

Nagel, E. 1961. *The Structure of Science: Problems in the Logic of Scientific Explanation.* New York: Harcourt, Brace, and World.

Nagel, T. 1979. "Subjective and Objective." In *Mortal Questions.* Ed. T. Nagel, 196–213. New York: Cambridge University Press.

9

Instantiating Culture through Discourse Practices: Some Personal Reflections on Socialization and How to Study It

PEGGY J. MILLER

All children grow up to be cultural beings. This characteristic is unique to our species and helps to account for the prolonged period of human immaturity (Bruner 1972). Child development is thus inextricably bound to the process of orienting oneself within systems of meaning, a process known variously as "socialization," "acquisition of culture," "enculturation," and "development-in-cultural-context." The very diversity of terms attests to the variety of social sciences that have a stake in understanding how children become members of cultures (Gaskins, Miller, and Corsaro 1992). This problem is also intimately related to problems of perennial interest to particular disciplines. In anthropology, for example, it has long been recognized that unique insights into the nature of culture can be gained by studying how children acquire culture (for example, Sapir 1934). In psychology, proposals for studying psychological functioning as an outgrowth of cultural life have recurred throughout its history (Cahan and White 1992; Jahoda 1989), dating back to its origins as a scientific discipline and continuing vigorously in the present (Bruner 1990; Shweder 1990; Wertsch 1991).

And yet none of the social sciences has claimed socialization fully as its own. Because of the way in which human action has been partitioned for study, development-in-cultural-context has remained marginal to the intellectual agenda of each. As a result, it has been extraordinarily difficult to devise an adequate conceptualization, one that slights neither culture nor development.

In recent years several powerful theoretical currents—Vygotsky's theory of mediated action (Wertsch 1985, 1991), practice and performance approaches to language and verbal art (Bauman 1986; Hanks 1990; Ochs 1988), practice theories of social life (Bourdieu 1977, 1990)—have revitalized thinking about this problem. Taken together, these theories converge on the view that social actors maintain, change, and reproduce the societies in which they live by participating in culturally organized routine practices. They also imply a particular view of language, the preeminent tool of meaning construction. Language is seen as a form of situated action. It is not just a representational system but a set of practices that are organized beyond the sentence level into genres, types of discourse, and multichanneled performances. Language, or more precisely, talk, is recognized to be not only reflective of meaning but constitutive of meaning, with the implication that an adequate model of socialization must incorporate talk in a principled way.

Such a model confers several important advantages. First, the actual processes of socialization are rendered accessible through analysis of the forms and functions of everyday discourse. Second, in keeping with a basic insight of modern developmental psychology, an active role is accorded to the child through a focus on child and caregivers' mutual, negotiated participation in discourse practices (Rogoff 1990). Third, because language practices systematically index social statuses and ideologies (Ochs 1988, 1990), a discourse practices model helps to explain the variety of affective stances—eager acceptance, resistance, playfulness—that children assume as they attempt to invest cultural resources with meaning. Both the nonneutral, ideologically charged nature of the socializing environment and the necessarily evaluative responses of the child-in-context are taken into account (Goodnow 1990).

Yet another advantage of a practice-centered approach to socialization is that it invites reflection on the researcher's own practice (Bourdieu 1977, 1990). This theoretical position thus resonates strongly with the self-reflexive turn that has become so prominent in discussions of ethnographic inquiry (for example, C. L. Briggs 1986; Clifford and Marcus 1986; Eisner and Peshkin 1990). In this chapter I reflect on my own practice as a researcher who has tried to understand development and culture as intertwined processes. I will begin by identifying some of my basic commitments, as they are instantiated in my past and present experiences of doing interpretive research. I will then address an aspect of my practice that has changed over the years. I will describe how my stance as an ethnographer evolved from "nonparticipant" to "participant" observer and from invisible to visible in accounts of my findings. I will focus here on my current work on personal storytelling in Chinese and American families to show how analysis of the researchers' participation in the families' narrative practices can deepen our understanding of the processes of socialization. Finally, I will conclude with some reflections on issues that arise in constructing and evaluating ethnographic texts when cultural boundaries are crossed.

Continuities in Practice

In the introduction to their recent book on qualitative inquiry in education, Eisner and Peshkin (1990) say that many of the contributors to the volume "evolved as qualitative researchers by taste rather than by socialization" (8). In some ways this is true for me as well. My Ph.D. is in developmental psychology. Although most of my research has been interpretive, I have never taken a course in qualitative or ethnographic methods; yet I was socialized to do interpretive work. My apprenticeship as a researcher was done in Lois Bloom's child language lab several years after she had published her landmark study of children's early grammatical development (Bloom 1970). In that study she devised a method for inferring the compositional meanings of children's first sentences by examining the distribution of words in relation to the nonverbal contexts in which they were uttered. In other words, she found a way to rigorously interpret what two-year-olds meant.

Although my own work has moved from semantic-syntactic analysis to pragmatic and discourse analysis and from interpretation of meaning in relation to the immediate context to interpretation of meaning in relation to multiple embedded contexts, much of the discipline of my "craft" is carryover from my mentor's practice. This is apparent, for example, in my comparative study of narrative practices in Chinese and American families. In this project my students and I have been studying early socialization through the prism of personal storytelling, a type of conversational discourse in which participants recreate past experiences from their own lives. We want to understand how caregivers wittingly or unwittingly structure children's participation in narrative activities and how children come to find paths through these narrative labyrinths. Our approach is to observe young children talking, listening, and doing with others in the course of everyday domestic life. We observe them and their families for extended periods of time, returning again and again to see how they change during the preschool years. We record our observations on audio and video tapes from which we extract events of narration. Using standardized transcription conventions, we reconstruct in writing what the focal child says and does in relation to what other people say and do, preserving the temporal sequence of the interactive flow. We check and recheck for accuracy.

We then work from these transcripts to analyze and interpret the narrative practices that we see. We began with the expectation, derived from earlier work, that young children would assume a variety of participant roles, such as conarrator, listener, ratified participant, and copresent other (Miller and Moore 1989; Miller et al. 1990). We also had a strong hunch from pilot work conducted by Heidi Fung that the Chinese families would be more didactic than American families in their personal storytelling practices. With these ideas in mind, and with intuitions that developed in the course of the study, we scan and rescan the transcripts. The "final" set of categories will emerge as the outcome of repeated passes through the transcripts, repeated revisions of tentative categories (Bloom 1974). At some point we will feel satisfied that we have "captured" some regularities in the meanings that children and caregivers constructed. Or rather, we will feel satisfied that we have captured our vision of what those regularities are. This feeling will be short-lived, giving way rapidly to the next analysis and, hopefully, to a deeper interpretation.

This is by no means the whole of what I do as a researcher. My practice has evolved in many ways over the years, just as my theoretical framework has changed, but what I have just outlined remains a core practice around which others have grown. I believe that we cannot hope to understand development-in-cultural-context without watching and listening to children create meanings with others in the course of their everyday lives. This is especially important with respect to early development because young children's construction of the moral and social world is intuitive, not reflective (Dunn 1988; Much and Shweder 1978). It is meaning-in-action, or more precisely, meaning-in-interpersonal-action. From the standpoint of practice theory, young children create meaning by participating with others in culturally organized routine practices. To understand this process requires careful documentation of how children and caregivers negotiate meanings moment by moment and how their mutual participation changes over time. Thus, from my current vantage point, a practice theory of socialization is appealing because it provides an updated and more powerful rationale for a methodological approach that has become second nature to me.

But before I abandon the narrative that began in Lois Bloom's lab, I want to discuss briefly another experience that was crucially important in strengthening my commitment to this core practice of observation and description. After my apprenticeship, I went to South Baltimore, a working-class community of Irish, Italian, German, Polish, and Appalachian descent, to study early language development and socialization in low-income families. At the time, the view that poor and minority children suffered from a language deficit caused by linguistically impoverished home environments was still prevalent in psychology and education. Invoked in support of this position was a large body of research that showed that less privileged children lagged behind their middle-class counterparts on standardized tests of verbal ability. I will not take the space to review the devastating critiques of this literature (see, for example, Baratz 1973; Blake 1984; Labov 1972; Cole and Bruner 1971; Leacock 1972; Miller 1982). But I do want to note that this literature provides an excellent example of what can happen when the heuristic, Don't make up what you can find out (Becker, this volume), is violated. The language-deprivation position flourished in the virtual absence of family- and community-based inquiry into the verbal experiences of poor children.

My study in South Baltimore was designed to address this gap. What I witnessed was quite different: two-year-olds whose language was developing with normal rapidity amidst verbal environments that were rich and varied and mothers who had sound reasons for raising their children as they did and whose understanding of how to support their children's development was informed by their own experience of growing up in a tough urban environment (Miller 1982, 1986; Miller and Sperry 1987).

These findings, along with many others (for example, Blake 1984; Mitchell-Kernan and Kernan 1977; Tizard and Hughes 1984; Sperry 1991; Stockman and Vaughn-Cooke 1982; Ward 1971), including the pathbreaking work of Heath (1983; this volume) and Burton, Obeidallah, and Allison (this volume), suggest that a major shortcoming of the earlier research was that it was comparative in the wrong way: when less privileged children are compared only with their more privileged counterparts and never on their own terms, comparison is inherently invidious and simply affirms the status quo (Bernstein 1972; Miller 1982). What is needed is a broadly comparative framework that goes beyond the vantage point of the privileged sector of our society to represent human plurality more fully. Thus I came to another basic commitment: research that aims to be both developmental and cultural must be informed by comparisons within and among cultural groups, each of which has been described in its own terms.

But how does one go about describing children's worlds in their own terms? For example, what do we make of the fact that two-year-old girls in South Baltimore were already quite skilled at speaking up and fighting back? I came to realize that an answer to this question required a more deeply contextualized approach than was characteristic of child language studies. I could not make sense of the children's worlds without knowing more about the worlds of their caregivers. Why did the mothers routinely tease their daughters? Why did they talk about violent death, wife beatings, and child abuse in front of their children? As supplement to the observations of how youngsters and caregivers talked and interacted with one another, I interviewed mothers about their life histories and beliefs and values concerning childrearing, listened to their stories of personal experience, and recorded their interpretations as they viewed videotapes of their own interactions. By juxtaposing these various sources of evidence, along with the observations of family-child interaction and information about macro contexts (for example, the history and identity of South Baltimore as a working-class community), it was possible to identify convergences and divergences among them and use each to contextualize the others. Listening to caregivers interpret their life experiences thus emerged as still another basic practice for me.

In sum, as I reflect back on how my practice has evolved over the years, I trace several enduring commitments that continue to ground my practice of studying early childhood socialization. I privilege disciplined long-term observation of young children and their families as they engage in the meaning-making practices of everyday life. I listen as caregivers interpret their worlds to one another, to their children, and to me. I try to contextualize these various sources of evidence in relation to one another and to macro contexts. I privilege derived or emic description because my goal is to understand socialization from the perspectives of the children and caregivers themselves. And, accepting the premise of "original multiplicity" (Shweder, this volume), I bring a broad case-based comparative framework to bear in trying to understand particular worlds in relation to other particular worlds. If there are universals to be found, I want concrete universals—those that are arrived at by comparing specific cultural cases that have been studied in great detail (Erickson 1986).

A Change in Practice

Although each of these basic commitments deserves further scrutiny, I want to examine instead an aspect of my practice that has changed over the years, namely, the nature of my presence in the field and in reports of my findings. This issue will lead us into the study of Chinese and American storytelling introduced earlier, by way of another backward glance at South Baltimore.

I was aware in my earlier work of the interpersonal dimensions of entering a community and recruiting families for the study. I spent a great deal of time getting to know people and lots more time getting to know the focal children and their families. I considered the latter to be the rapport-building phase of the study, preliminary to the videotaped observations. I justified this phase of the study by arguing that it would minimize the effects of my presence on the family, thereby yielding less "distorted" observations of their behavior (Miller 1982). During the actual observations I tried to hide behind the camera as much as possible. The reports of my findings echoed my stance in the field: I was visible in the text only insofar as necessary to convince readers that I had been invisible in the field. What was at stake was the ecological validity of my findings.

However, I was not able practically or ethically to sustain a stance of detached observer over the course of an intensive long-term study. There are many ways in which my relationship with the families changed, but the one that I was slowest to recognize was their impact on me. For example, I was astonished to discover, long after the study ended, that the videotapes contained a record of my own recruitment into teasing. The children were not the only ones who got socialized into the families' discourse practices.

Thus in designing my current study of personal storytelling, I began with the premise that the researchers would assume a participatory role as they tried to determine how personal storytelling was actually practiced in Chinese and American families. But how should they participate so as to achieve this goal? The answer has been far from obvious. Ideally, one would be guided by prior child- and family-focused ethnographies of speaking. Since these were not available for the communities under study, we used a variety of other strategies. We assigned researchers to communities that were culturally similar to their own. The researcher who worked with the middle-class European-American families in Chicago had grown up in similar communities in the United States; the researcher who worked with the middle-class Chinese families in Taipei was born and raised in Taipei. The rationale was that the researchers would be able to make use of their native intuitions in custom designing their participation. We also adopted the following general guideline: try to participate as a family friend who has stopped by for a casual visit; at the same time, don't "push" narrative talk. Within these parameters, the ethnographers were left to their own ingenuity in negotiating a role with the families.

As it turned out, the two ethnographers negotiated roles that contrasted in some important ways. The American researcher came to be treated as a family friend who was addressed by her first name by parents and children. The Chinese researcher was granted fictive kin status. She was introduced to the families' relatives and was frequently invited to family events such as dinners or picnics. Children were encouraged to address her as "Aunty." In addition, the Chinese ethnographer was much more likely than the American researcher to be invoked as audience to the child's past transgressions. This almost never happened in the American families, a point which I will develop further below. The American families seemed to go to great lengths to cast their children's past actions in a positive light when child and researcher were both present. When minor misdemeanors occurred during the taping, American parents responded with negative feedback but if a more serious transgression occurred—as when a two-

and-a-half-year-old slapped his mother in the face—the child was taken out of the room to be disciplined. This did not happen in the Chinese families. The point is that the researchers were treated in systematically different ways in the two communities. How should these differences be taken into account in interpreting cultural differences in narrative practices?

Ethnographers' Participation as an Object of Comparative Study

The approach that we have taken is to make the ethnographers' participation in the families' narrative practices an object of comparative study in its own right. In taking this approach we are following in a tradition of ethnographic research that differs from more typical social-scientific studies of human development in that it acknowledges and turns to advantage the inevitable social positioning of researchers. Within this tradition, systematic documentation of the ethnographer's activities and changing role, expressed in daily fieldnotes, is a hallmark of the disciplined conduct of participant observation. Corsaro's work (1985, this volume) provides an excellent example, showing how his negotiated position as a funny kind of big kid enabled him to gain access to peer culture on its own terms. A notable early example is J. L. Briggs's classic study (1970) of Inuit socialization, which anticipated by nearly two decades the current trend toward self-reflexiveness in ethnographic description. These and other studies provide precedent for treating the ethnographers' interactions with the children and caregivers as another source of evidence about similarities and differences in Chinese and American storytelling.

In this section I provide a brief review of some of our findings (see Miller, Fung, and Mintz, in press, for a more extensive report of the study), but first it is necessary to provide some further details about the design of the study. The Chinese data were collected in Taipei, Taiwan; the American data in Longwood, a middle-class European-American community in Chicago. The Chinese and American families were similar in that they were two-parent families who were economically secure. Parents owned their own homes and most were college educated. Each researcher spent at least two years in the community, conducting fieldwork and making audio and video recordings of naturally occurring talk in at least fourteen families. Both cross-sectional and longitudinal data were collected, encompassing the period from two and a half to five years of age. The choice of the lower age limit reflects recent findings that children are able to recount past experiences in conversation by two and a half years (Eisenberg 1985; Fivush and Fromhoff 1988; Heath 1983; Miller and Sperry 1988; Miller et al. 1992; Sperry 1991; Peterson and McCabe 1983).

In this chapter I refer only to findings from the two-and-a-half-year-olds, each of whom was observed for at least four hours.

Similar Access to Personal Storytelling

We found that in both Chinese and American families, stories of personal experience were told *with* young children as conarrators. The child collaborated with family members in constructing stories about his or her own past experiences, contributing at least two substantive utterances to the conarration (Miller et al. 1992). The researchers assumed a variety of communicative roles ranging from silent witness to conarrator. For example, a Chinese child coconstructed a story with his mother and older sister about an event in which he cried and made a scene at his older sister's music lesson, causing his mother to lose face. During the first twenty-five turns of this lengthy conarration,[1] the researcher watched and listened, laughing occasionally. Later the child addressed the researcher, drawing her in as a conarrator.

In addition, stories of children's personal experiences were told *about* them in their presence in both Chinese and American families. A parent or older sibling appropriated the child's past experience and recounted it to another person, often the researcher, with or without treating the child as a ratified participant. As narrator, rather than conarrator, the parent or older sibling claimed the right to author the young child's past experience, thereby indexing the child's lower status (Miller et al. 1990). Instead of prompting, editing, and responding to the child's contributions, as they did in conarrations, caregivers exercised more extensive control over the story and provided a fuller interpretation of the child's past experience.

Both telling stories with children and telling stories about children in their presence occurred several times per hour in Chinese and American families. These findings thus suggest an important similarity in the narrative experiences of two-and-a-half-year-olds in the two cultures, namely, that both had ready and varied access to personal storytelling.

Different Frameworks for Interpreting Children's Experience

However, we also found a striking contrast at another level of analysis. Chinese families were much more likely than their American counterparts to invoke rules and rule violations in narrating the child's past experiences, and they were more likely to structure their narrations so as to establish the child's transgressions as the point of the story. For example, one of the longest conarrations (fifty turns) in the Chinese corpus began with the caregiver prompting the child to confess a misdeed to the researcher,

"Have you told Aunty why I spanked you yesterday? Have you? Tell her why I had to spank you." Through a series of queries and responses from the child, the following story unfolds: the child interrupted a church meeting, the caregiver spanked her, she cried, and the other adults who were presented "saved" her by allowing her to distribute snacks to them. The story ends with an exchange in which the caregiver asked, "Do you still want to go there again?" and the child replied, "I next time [*nods*] dare not do that again," shaking her head. The conarration is thus bounded at the beginning by the caregiver's prompt to the child to confess her misdeed to the researcher and at the end by the child's explicit commitment not to transgress in the future.

There is nothing comparable to this in the American stories. Rule violations were seldom invoked and those that were did not contribute to the point of the story. For example, an American child initiated a story about the tooth fairy's visit by saying to the researcher, "I went to the dentist and he pulled it out." As the conarration unfolded, the child elaborated on what happened (for example, "He [the tooth fairy] gave me, um, two dollars.") and the researcher responded with questions and comments ("Wow—that's a lot. You get a lot for teeth these days."). A transgression was mentioned only once. In the final contribution to the conarration, an older sibling said, "She was eating bad food so she had to go to the dentist and he had to pull the tooth out." Both the placement of this response and the fact that it was not elaborated render the rule violation peripheral to the main action of the story.

In parallel with conarrated stories, American stories about the child were less likely to invoke rule violations or to be structured so as to establish the child's transgression as the point of the story. Instead, caregivers selected benign or entertaining events that illustrated how cute or smart or odd the child was. The following example is one of a chain of stories that an American mother told about her young daughter's language errors:

Example 1
Child and her older sister are playing a board game nearby.
Mother to Researcher: You'll get a big kick out of this one. Friday
    night, we were just sitting around. Jim took Friday off, I
    don't know what we did but we were just sitting here at night.
    Jim and I were sitting on the ground and Jack was [inaud-
    ible]. She puts her hand on me and says, "Me happy." And
    I'm, like, "That's good, Mollie. You happy."
Researcher: I love it, it sounds so cute.
Mother: I said, "I don't think I ever heard anyone say that," and

> Jim says, "I know *I* never heard anyone come up with [in-
> audible]."
> *Researcher:* Me happy.

There are two notable features of this narration. First, the story is structured around the child's funny pronoun usage, rendered in direct quota-
tion, and the parents' response, which is quoted, recycled, and elaborated.
The narrator thereby conveys the surprising and endearing quality of the
child's expression. What is reportable is not only the unusual usage but
the sentiment that is expressed and the novel, unprecedented nature of the
error. The child's act is represented in a manner that is consistent with the
parents' view, articulated in other interactions, that this is their goofy
child, the one who is "touched." Second, the researcher has a definite role
to play as audience for and participant in this narration. The mother introduces the story with a comment about the story's anticipated impact
on the researcher—"You'll get a big kick out of this one."—and the
researcher obligingly replies, "I love it, it sounds so cute."

This type of story about the child was common in the American families
as was the researcher's response of joining with the caregiver in appreciating the child's antics, accomplishments, and enjoyable experiences. Some
of the Chinese stories were similar in that the researcher participated with
family members in appreciating or affirming the child's benign or decidedly positive experience, for example, a feat of memory or quick-
wittedness. However, the Chinese stories about young children, like the
conarrated stories, were much more likely to be organized around the
child's transgression.

Thus the Chinese researcher often found herself in a somewhat delicate
position. As party to accounts in which the caregiver assumed the voice
of authority toward the child's past misdeeds, she could side either with
the caregiver or with the child. Most of the time the researcher affirmed
the caregiver's stance in relation to the child. For example, after a caregiver
told a story about how the child had made a false accusation that could
have created dissension in the family, the researcher said to the child,
"You're young but tricky, aren't you?" At other times, however, the researcher took the child's perspective on the event, thereby mitigating the
caregiver's interpretation of the child's wrongdoing. For example, when
the same caregiver told a story illustrating the child's greediness, the researcher said, "But I think she [the child] knows [that there are limits on
what she can have]."

In sum, these analyses suggest that personal storytelling was readily
available to two-year-olds in the two cultural cases but that it instantiated

contrasting interpretive frameworks. In the Chinese families, the primacy of an explicitly didactic, overtly self-critical framework was evident both in conarrated storytelling and in stories told about the child. This framework was jointly maintained by the coordinated efforts of the several participants. It was maintained by caregivers as they invoked rules explicitly, structured stories so as to establish the child's transgression as the point of the story, and recruited the researcher's support against the errant child. It was maintained by older siblings as they aligned themselves with the caregiver, speaking in the voice of authority. It was maintained by the children themselves as they confessed to misdeeds, kept silent, laughed, or expressed feelings of shame—"I want to faint away." And it was maintained by the ethnographer as she alternately aligned herself with the caregiver and with the child.

In the American case, a different interpretive framework was at work in personal storytelling practices, one that we might call implicitly evaluative and overtly self-affirming. Our sense is that the narrative practice of portraying the child protagonist in a favorable light is part of a wider network of practices that caregivers use to protect their children's self-esteem—handling discipline in the here and now without dwelling on the child's past misdeeds, conducting serious disciplining in private, putting the best face on the child's shortcomings or even recasting shortcomings as strengths. As with the Chinese, this framework was maintained through the active collusion of the several participants, including the researcher.

In identifying contrasting interpretive frameworks in the two cultural cases I do not mean to imply that these frameworks are the only interpretive frameworks that are instantiated in narrative practices (Miller et al. 1992), nor do I mean to imply that these particular frameworks are dichotomous. Chinese families find ways to portray their children favorably and American families find ways to enforce moral and social rules. Also, within each cultural group families differ among themselves in the extent and manner in which they instantiate these interpretive frameworks. These are the paths of inquiry that we are currently pursuing. In addition, we are attempting to contextualize these analyses more fully in terms of key indigenous concepts. Shame is one such concept that leaps out in the Chinese materials, not only in the families' narrative practices but in their disciplinary practices and in interviews with caregivers (Fung 1994). Thus the findings reviewed here are partial and will require a great deal more analysis and contextualization before we will be satisfied with our interpretations.

However, we have learned a few things about the process of socialization by studying narrative practices. We were able to expose both the dynamics and the cross-cutting redundancies of narrative practices as a socializing activity. Each story that the child conarrates, each story that someone tells about the child, provides her with yet another opportunity to interpret her past experiences and to hear how other people interpret them—which of her acts were appreciated, if and how she transgressed, whether a transgression was serious or funny. Each telling instantiates these frameworks somewhat differently, for no two tellings are ever identical. Even when the "same" story is retold, it is recontextualized in terms of the particular circumstances of the telling as they become relevant within the ongoing negotiation of meaning by child and other participants (Miller et al. 1993).

The term *recontextualized* is critically important here, for it points to a more dynamic and processual view of context than is commonly assumed. Richard Bauman, whose work on oral narrative has contributed to a reconceptualization of context in linguistic anthropology, describes how understandings of context have changed:

> we are seeing a shift away from context, understood as the conventional, normative anchoring of an item or form within institutional structures, event structures, or general patterns of cultural or psychological meaning, and toward the active process of contextualization in which individuals situate what they do in networks of interrelationship and association in the act of production. (1992:128)

When stories of personal experience are treated as situated practices, it becomes possible to see that the relationship between text and context is not a given but rather something to be accomplished. Context is not dictated by the physical and social environment, but emerges in negotiations among the several participants (Bauman and Briggs 1990).

This active, agent-centered conception of context is compatible with developmental psychologists' premise that children play an active role in their own development. At the same time it takes issue with the idea that child and context can be studied apart from one another, as independent variables; rather child and context are seen as mutually constituting (Corsaro and Miller 1992). When children participate in routine narrative practices, they repeatedly operate with and upon interpretive frameworks for the creation of contexts. This repeated and varied engagement of frameworks, beginning in early childhood and continuing day by day, helps to explain how cultural frameworks come to be grasped by children and how they come to be "naturalized" or taken for granted.

It also helps to explain how interpretive frameworks become personally meaningful and self-defining. These frameworks are not empty or distant abstractions; they are repeatedly instantiated in terms of the child's own experiences. In a recent paper on socialization among the Inuit of the Canadian Arctic, Jean Briggs offers a conceptualization of the meaning-making process that resonates strongly with our findings. She argues that personal instantiation of cultural premises invites children's emotional involvement and motivates them to pay attention to any clues that might help them to understand their experiences: "Meanings will cumulate, and in this way, little by little, children will create for themselves worlds that contain variants of the plots of their parents worlds" (1992:44). My work on personal storytelling from within a practice model suggests that this process of personalization lies at the heart of socialization—this is how persons and cultures create each other. A major methodological point of this chapter is that further access to this process can be gained by studying how ethnographers participate as persons in the cultural practices that they seek to understand.

Problems in Writing and Evaluating Ethnographic Accounts
When Cultural Boundaries are Crossed

Leaving ethnographers in the data implies leaving them in the text as well. Does this mean that ethnographic writing is necessarily a first-person genre? Does it mean that an ethnographic account that fails to document how the researcher negotiated his or her role vis-à-vis the group is an inadequate ethnography? Curiously, these kinds of questions received little discussion at the conference for which the chapters in this volume were prepared, despite the fact that Shweder (this volume), in his opening address, invited such discussion by staking out a territory between superficialism and solipsism as the proper place for the study of plural norms. Indeed, the larger issue of how to write ethnography, identified as a critical issue by Denzin (this volume), and raised several times during the discussion, never took off as a topic of debate. Again, this is curious because ethnographers have written extensively about this problem. As I listened to the papers I heard many guidelines for "doing" ethnography—how to's of fieldwork, of handling data, even of drawing interpretations, but very little about the writing of ethnography. On the final day of the meeting, Margaret Lock referred to this omission as "baffling," given the fervor with which the issue of writing is being debated in cultural anthropology.

In my view, it is a mistake for those of us who study human development from an ethnographic perspective to skirt the issue of how we construct ethnographic texts, for this issue is tied very closely to the fundamental problem of how to evaluate ethnographic accounts. Within the wider community of scholars who study human development, the problem of evaluation can seem confusing if not intractable. Part of the confusion stems from differences in deep assumptions about what it means to "write up" a study within the genre constraints of an ethnographic description, on the one hand, and a research report, on the other. To trace out the implications of these genre differences is a very large task. In this final section, I want to raise a much more limited and seemingly mundane problem of text construction that arises in research on language socialization, namely, how to incorporate discourse "data" into the text so that readers can judge for themselves whether the ethnographer's interpretation is valid. These afterthoughts, stimulated by the conference and raising more questions than answers, are offered in the hope of encouraging future discussion.

A solution to the problem of public scrutiny that is widely favored is to present meticulously detailed transcripts of talk as supplement to "standard" narrative ethnography. Although I endorse this as a necessary step in establishing "trustworthy" interpretations (Mishler 1990), it does not eliminate the difficulties involved in "reading" transcribed talk across cultural or socioeconomic boundaries. Those difficulties, in turn, can make it very difficult to evaluate the trustworthiness of ethnographic accounts.

Consider, for example, the case of teasing in South Baltimore. The families whom I studied there regularly engaged their young daughters in teasing interactions such as the following.

Example 2
Amy, a nineteen-month-old girl, has been drinking soda from her mother's cup. When she reaches out again for the cup, her mother jabs her fist into Amy's belly and pushes her away, saying in a provocative tone of voice, "You're gonna get punched right in the gut." Amy smiles and raises her fist at her mother, who replies loudly, "Ya wanna fight?" Amy strikes a fighting pose. Smiling, her mother continues to goad her until Amy swats at her and kicks the sofa.

In interviews, mothers offered nuanced rationales for why they engaged in this practice:

Example 3
That's why a lot of times when we used to play little games together, I'd take my fist and like punch her in the chest. You know, not hard enough to hurt her, but, you know, to knock her down. She'd get back up. She'd think it was funny, right? Or I'd take my fist and I'd hit her in the arm and then she'd hit me back and I'd pretend it hurt and I'd [say], "Oh," you know, but it toughened her up. When she got out there to where somebody really meant it, then she realized, you know, "Hey, this is it, they're really pickin' on me." And she just, you know, punch back. So, I think that helps, too, if you sit down and try to tell your kid, you know,

"Hey," you know, "they're gonna punch you, you punch them." And by acting this out with them. By pushing them down and lettin' them feel theirself hit the floor, whatever. I think it toughens them up. And I think that's good for a girl nowadays, anyway, because with everything that's goin' on, even a girl has to defend herself. And, yeah, I think that's good. (Miller 1986:205)

My interpretation of teasing as a complex form of verbal play and an important means by which mothers prepared young girls for the realities of life was based on these and other types of evidence: discourse analyses of the structure of teasing sequences, microlevel analysis of the subtle metacommunicative cues that framed the sequences as nonliteral, analysis of the comments that mothers made while watching videotapes of their own teasing practices. In making these analyses available for public scrutiny, I included line-by-line transcriptions of teasing interactions (see Miller 1986:202 for a line-by-line transcription of example 2) and extended quotes from the mothers.

What I discovered was that transcripts of teasing sequences were not necessarily comprehensible to audiences from more privileged backgrounds. The problem was one of translation—confronted with texts in a language they knew but from a sociocultural world with which they were unfamiliar, readers knew too little about that world to be able to make sense of the texts. The burden was on me, the ethnographer, to provide enough background information, enough contextualization, so that readers were in a position to make an informed interpretation. Often, however, constraints of length precluded the necessary contextualization, especially when it was also essential to present lengthy transcript material.

But the problem goes deeper than this: transcriptions of talk, even when accompanied by video recordings and prefaced by ample background information, are never transparent (Mishler 1991). There is always room for alternative interpretations of discourse. At the same time, interpretations are not free to vary infinitely. For example, the evidence from my study does not support the interpretation that teases were framed as literal disputes or that the children (except at the earlier ages) misconstrued them as such. Nor does it support the interpretation that the mothers teased recklessly, unaware of the potential to humiliate or undermine their children; indeed, they spoke of the dangers of going too far with teasing. These interpretations—which amount to "misreadings," from my perspective—are not hypothetical but came up repeatedly.

The implication is that making fuller, richer, more detailed materials available for public scrutiny does not necessarily enable readers to make defensible interpretations across marked cultural boundaries. But in saying this, haven't I backed myself into a position of privileging the ethnographer's interpretation over other interpretations, thereby violating the very commitment with which I began, namely, that the discourse materials on which interpretations are based must be available to public scrutiny? After all, *my* interpretation may be a "misreading." This is the dilemma that lies at the heart of the problem of how to evaluate ethnographic accounts when there is a perilous cultural divide between the community under study and the audience to the account, with the ethnographer commuting uneasily between the two. Who gets to do the arbitrating? Isn't that the role of the scholarly community, acknowledging the possibility that some interpretations will remain contested? My concern about this solution is that the families under study are not necessarily represented in that community.

The problems I encountered in constructing intelligible accounts of teasing in South Baltimore have taken on renewed importance for me in the context of my current research, described earlier. The challenge this time is to make Chinese practices intelligible to American audiences and American practices intelligible to Chinese audiences.

Consider the following example. The child, Angu, is two years, nine months old. She is a precocious child, verbally skilled for her age, and highly expressive. Angu has a close relationship with her aunt, who is her primary caregiver, and our recordings contain ample evidence of the aunt's care and affection for her niece. In this story, the aunt shames Angu for a recent transgression. As narrated from the aunt's perspective, the story actually involved two transgressions: first, Angu wrote on the wall, and then she tried to evade responsibility for her misdeed by calling her mother on the telephone and implying that her aunt had mistreated her. The episode begins as a conarration, initiated by the aunt, in which the aunt tries to draw a confession from the child. Notice that it is the more serious transgression—complaining about the aunt—that the aunt forefronts.

Example 4

Aunt: After you scribbled on my wall, how did you tell your
    mother? [*Pause*] Tell me! [*Pause*] Tell me! [*Child is silent, tries
    to get on sofa rest, gazes at aunt. Louder.*] Tell me!
Child: Hmm.
Aunt: You tell Aunty [the researcher], how did you "accuse" me?
    [*Pause; louder.*] Hmm?
[*Child maintains silence through twelve turns*]
Aunt: You won't say, right? Good, we're leaving. Goodbye.
    [*Pretends to move away from the sofa*] We're leaving.
Researcher: Goodbye.

> [*Six more turns*]
> *Aunt:* How did you tell Teaching Mother [referring to child's mother]?
> *Child:* [*Lowers her head, sad facial expression*] "Mama [referring to Aunt], I'm not going to come back to your home [*whining*]. I'm, I'm going to go to Teaching Mother's home" [*whines, looks at aunt, and enacts sobbing*].

Although Angu provides a partial confession, her aunt continues to try to elicit from her a more detailed account of how she complained to her mother after writing on the wall. The aunt shames the child through seventy-five turns, occasionally invoking the researcher's support against the child and repeatedly expressing her displeasure. The child continues to respond with silence and confession, saying at times, "I faint." However, the serious keying of this interaction is sometimes alleviated by laughter from the child and the researcher. Eventually, the aunt turns to the researcher and renarrates the story to her, with the child looking on as audience.

This kind of example strikes a nerve when presented to audiences who have grown up in the United States and have not had extensive experience in Taiwan. Empathizing with the child, many people feel that to shame a child in this way is wrong. It is self-evident that the child's mental health and self-esteem are being compromised. When I say "self-evident" I mean that a certain kind of interpretation comes to mind ready-made. As a parent of like cultural background, I operate with a similar interpretive framework. At the same time, I am convinced that these childrearing practices have a different meaning in Chinese culture, where shame is positively valued, than they do in my own. The first challenge is to discover concretely what that meaning is. The second challenge is to make it intelligible to audiences who are unable to fill in for themselves the wider set of Chinese beliefs and values and who carry with them compelling alternative frameworks. Sometimes the second challenge seems as daunting as the first.

Acknowledgment

This essay was supported by a grant from the Spencer Foundation. I am grateful to the families who participated in the studies described in this essay. I thank Lisa Burger and Heidi Fung for many stimulating discussions of the findings presented here.

Notes

1. The terms *turn* and *turn at talk* refer to the basic unit that is used to characterize how talk is distributed among speakers in a conversation. A turn consists of the entire stretch of talk by a given speaker before he or she relinquishes the floor to the other speaker. A turn may consist of several sentences, a single word, or even a nonverbal action or gesture such as a nod.

References

Baratz, J. C. 1973. "Language Abilities of Black Americans." In *Comparative Studies of Blacks and Whites in the United States.* Ed. K. S. Miller and R. M. Dreger. New York: Seminar Press.

Bauman, R. 1986. *Story, Performance, and Event.* New York: Cambridge University Press.

———. 1992. "Contextualization, Tradition, and the Dialogue of Genres: Icelandic Legends of the *Kraftaskald.*" In *Rethinking Context: Language as an Interactive Phenomenon.* Ed. A. Duranti and C. Goodwin, 125–45. New York: Cambridge University Press.

Bauman, R., and C. L. Briggs. 1990. "Poetics and Performance as Critical Perspectives on Language and Social Life." *Annual Review of Anthropology* 19: 59–88.

Bernstein, B. 1972. "A Critique of the Concept of Compensatory Education." In *Functions of Language in the Classroom.* Ed. C. B. Cazden, V. P. John, and D. Hymes, 135–51. New York: Teachers College Press.

Blake, I. J. K. 1984. "Language Development in Working-Class Black Children: An Examination of Form, Content, and Use." Ph.D. diss., Columbia University.

Bloom, L. 1970. *Language Development: Form and Function in Emerging Grammars.* Cambridge, Mass.: MIT Press.

———. 1974. "The Accountability of Evidence in Studies of Child Language." Comment on *Everyday Preschool Interpersonal Speech Usage: Methodological, Developmental, and Sociolinguistic Studies.* Ed. F. F. Schacter, K. Kirshner, B. Klips, M. Friedricks, and K. Sanders. Monographs of the Society for Research in Child Development 39, no. 156.

Bourdieu, P. 1977. *Outline of a Theory of Practice.* New York: Cambridge University Press.

———. 1990. *The Logic of Practice.* Stanford: Stanford University Press.

Briggs, C. L. 1986. *Learning How to Ask: A Sociolinguistic Appraisal of the Role of the Interview in Social Science Research.* Cambridge: Cambridge University Press.

Briggs, J. L. 1970. *Never in Anger: Portrait of an Eskimo Family.* Cambridge, Mass.: Harvard University Press.

———. 1992. "Mazes of Meaning: How a Child and a Culture Create Each Other." In *Interpretive Approaches to Children's Socialization.* Ed. W. A. Corsaro and P. J. Miller, 25–49. New Directions for Child Development, no. 58. San Francisco: Jossey-Bass.

Bruner, J. 1972. "Nature and Uses of Immaturity." *American Psychologist* 27: 687–708.

———. 1990. *Acts of Meaning.* Cambridge, Mass.: Harvard University Press.

Cahan, E. D., and S. H. White. 1992. "Proposals for a Second Psychology." *American Psychologist* 47: 224–35.

Clifford, J., and G. E. Marcus, eds. 1986. *Writing Culture: The Poetics and Politics of Ethnography.* Berkeley: University of California Press.

Cole, M., and J. S. Bruner. 1971. "Cultural Differences and Inferences about Psychological Processes." *American Psychologist* 26: 867–76.

Corsaro, W. A. 1985. *Friendship and Peer Culture in the Early Years.* Norwood, N.J.: Ablex.

Corsaro, W. A., and P. J. Miller, eds. 1992. *Interpretive Approaches to Children's Socialization.* New Directions for Child Development, no. 58. San Francisco: Jossey-Bass.

Dunn, J. 1988. *The Beginnings of Social Understanding.* Cambridge, Mass.: Harvard University Press.

Eisenberg, A. R. 1985. "Learning to Describe past Experiences in Conversation." *Discourse Processes* 8: 177–204.

Eisner, E. W., and A. Peshkin. 1990. *Qualitative Inquiry in Education.* New York: Teachers College Press.

Erickson, F. 1986. "Qualitative Methods in Research on Teaching." In *Handbook of Research on Teaching.* Ed. M. C. Wittrock, 119–61. 3d ed. New York: MacMillan.

Fivush, R., and F. A. Fromhoff. 1988. "Style and Structure in Mother-Child Conversations about the Past." *Discourse Processes* 11: 337–55.

Fung, H. 1994. "The Socialization of Shame in Young Chinese Children." Ph.D. diss., University of Chicago.

Gaskins, S., P. J. Miller, and W. A. Corsaro. 1992. "Theoretical and Methodological Perspectives in the Interpretive Study of Children." In *Interpretive Approaches to Children's Socialization.* Ed. W. A. Corsaro and P. J. Miller, 5–23. New Directions for Child Development, no. 58. San Francisco: Jossey-Bass.

Goodnow, J. J. 1990. "Using Sociology to Extend Psychological Accounts of Cognitive Development." *Human Development* 33: 81–107.

Hanks, W. 1990. *Referential Practice: Language and Living Space among the Maya.* Chicago: University of Chicago Press.

Heath, S. B. 1983. *Ways with Words: Language, Life and Work in Communities and Classrooms.* Cambridge: Cambridge University Press.

Jahoda, G. 1989. *Our Forgotten Ancestors. In Cross-Cultural Perspectives.* Nebraska Symposium on Motivation, no. 36. Lincoln: University of Nebraska Press.

Labov, W. 1972. *Language in the Inner City: Studies in the Black English Vernacular.* Philadelphia: University of Pennsylvania Press.

Leacock, E. B. 1972. "Abstract versus Concrete Speech: A False Dichotomy." In *Functions of Language in the Classroom.* Ed. C. B. Cazden, V. P. John, and D. Hymes, 111–34. New York: Teachers College Press.

Miller, P. J. 1982. *Amy, Wendy, and Beth: Learning Language in South Baltimore.* Austin: University of Texas Press.

———. 1986. "Teasing as Language Socialization and Verbal Play in a White, Working-Class Community." In *Language Socialization Across Cultures.* Ed. B. B. Schieffelin and E. Ochs, 199–212. New York: Cambridge University Press.

Miller, P. J., H. Fung, and J. Mintz. In press. "Self-Construction through Narrative Practices: A Chinese and American Comparison of Early Socialization." *Ethos.*

Miller, P. J., L. Hoogstra, J. Mintz, H. Fung, and K. Williams. 1993. "Troubles in the Garden and How They Get Resolved: A Young Child's Transformation of His Favorite Story." In *Memory and Affect in Development.* Ed. C. A. Nelson, 87–114. Minnesota Symposium on Child Psychology, no. 26. Hillsdale, N.J.: Erlbaum.

Miller, P. J., J. Mintz, L. Hoogstra, H. Fung, and R. Potts. 1992. "The Narrated Self: Young Children's Construction of Self in Relation to Others in Conversational Stories of Personal Experience." *Merrill-Palmer Quarterly* 38: 45–67.

Miller, P. J., and B. B. Moore. 1989. "Narrative Conjunctions of Caregiver and Child: A Comparative Perspective on Socialization Through Stories." *Ethos* 17: 428–49.

Miller, P. J., R. Potts, H. Fung, L. Hoogstra, and J. Mintz. 1990. "Narrative Practices and the Social Construction of Self in Childhood." *American Ethnologist* 17: 292–311.

Miller, P. J., and L. L. Sperry. 1987. "The Socialization of Anger and Aggression." *Merrill-Palmer Quarterly* 33: 1–31.

———. 1988. "Early Talk about the Past: The Origins of Conversational Stories of Personal Experience." *Journal of Child Language* 15: 293–315.

Mishler, E. G. 1990. "Validation in Inquiry-Guided Research: The Role of Exemplars in Narrative Studies." *Harvard Educational Review* 60: 415–42.

———. 1991. "Representing Discourse: The Rhetoric of Transcription." *Journal of Narrative and Life History* 1: 255–80.

Mitchell-Kernan, C., and K. T. Kernan. 1977. "Pragmatics of Directive Choices among Children." In *Child Discourse.* Ed. S. Ervin-Tripp and C. Mitchell-Kernan, 189–208. New York: Academic Press.

Much, N., and R. A. Shweder. 1978. "Speaking of Rules: The Analysis of Culture in the Breach." In *Moral Development.* Ed. W. Damon, 19–39. New Directions for Child Development, no. 2. San Francisco: Jossey-Bass.

Ochs, E. 1988. *Culture and Language Development.* New York: Cambridge University Press.

———. 1990. "Indexicality and Socialization." In *Cultural Psychology: Essays on Comparative Human Development.* Ed. J. W. Stigler, R. A. Shweder, and G. Herdt, 287–308. New York: Cambridge University Press.

Peterson, C., and A. McCabe. 1983. *Developmental Psycholinguistics: Three Ways of Looking at a Child's Narrative.* New York: Plenum Press.

Rogoff, B. 1990. *Apprenticeship in Thinking.* New York: Oxford University Press.

Sapir, E. 1934. "The Emergence of the Concept of Personality in a Study of Cultures." *Social Psychology* 5: 408–15.

Shweder, R. A. 1990. "Cultural Psychology: What Is It?" In *Cultural Psychology: Essays on Comparative Human Development.* Ed. J. W. Stigler, R. A. Shweder, and G. Herdt, 1–43. New York: Cambridge University Press.

Sperry, L. L. 1991. "The Emergence and Development of Narrative Competence among African-American Toddlers in a Rural Alabama Community." Ph.D. diss., University of Chicago.

Stockman, I., and F. Vaughn-Cooke. 1982. "Semantic Categories in the Language of Working-Class Black Children." In *Proceedings from the Second International Congress for the Study of Child Language* 1: 312–27.

Tizard, B., and M. Hughes. 1984. *Young Children Learning: Talking and Thinking at Home and School.* London: Fontana Press.

Ward, M. C. 1971. *Them Children.* New York: Holt, Rinehart, and Winston.

Wertsch, J. V. 1985. *Vygotsky and the Social Formation of Mind.* Cambridge, Mass.: Harvard University Press.

———. 1991. *Voices of the Mind.* Cambridge, Mass.: Harvard University Press.

10 Neighborhood Social Organization: A Forgotten Object of Ethnographic Study?

MERCER L. SULLIVAN

The decline of community has been a staple topic in social science since the nineteenth century, subject to cycles of neglect and rediscovery. In U.S. social science in the latter half of the twentieth century, the ethnographic methods appropriate to the study of the social organization of local communities have often been treated as marginal tools, sources of qualitative embellishment for quantitative studies that often and wrongly ascribe to themselves alone the attribute of being "empirical." The ethnographic study of the social organization of communities has been and still is thought of by many social scientists as the collection of impressionistic data about ill-defined and insignificant units of analysis. This essay discusses the substantive and methodological contributions of community studies and their relevance to the study of human development, with particular attention to issues raised in recent debates about the existence of an underclass in the inner cities of the United States.

The Underclass Debate

One of the most discussed, cited, and controversial works of recent social science, William Julius Wilson's *The Truly Disadvantaged: The Inner City, the Underclass, and Public Policy* (1987), treats the social organization of inner-city neighborhoods as a central topic. Wilson's ambitious theory cuts across many levels of analysis, ranging from the macrostructural to the social psychological.

At its core, however, are a set of assertions about the social organization of relatively small geographical areas, urban neighborhoods. Economic restructuring at the national level is said to translate into high rates of social deviance concentrated in poor, urban neighborhoods. Wilson claims that economic restructuring is mediated through local environments in its effects on individual attitudes and behavior. Concentration of poverty leads in this way to an amplification of deviance, particularly through the impairment of the socialization of children. Community-level change is thus linked directly to changes in patterns of human development.

This is a powerful and complex theory. It has stimulated a great deal of renewed attention to neighborhoods as important units of analysis. Yet the great bulk of research on Wilson's hypothesized "neighborhood effects" has not dealt with data bearing directly on the internal social organization of neighborhoods. Both Wilson himself and the great majority of his legions of critics and commentators have relied on indirect indicators of neighborhood social organization, primarily census tract data on factors such as family composition, employment patterns, and school participation (Ricketts and Sawhill 1988).

Meanwhile, other researchers—anthropologists, a few maverick sociologists, and some sympathetic members of other disciplines willing to employ nontraditional methods—have continued to do ethnographic research in urban neighborhoods. Much recent ethnographic research, however, has not attempted to situate the phenomena of interest carefully in the context of local social organization. The ends of recent ethnographic work have more often been either grandly theoretical but confined to interpretation of texts or, conversely, narrowly pragmatic and applied, removed from engagement in a larger, comparative enterprise of understanding the transformation of local communities.

As a result, the ethnographic enterprise and the underclass debate have largely failed to connect, despite the fact that comparative ethnographic data appear to be essential for addressing the questions that have been raised about the transformation of inner-city neighborhoods and the consequences of that transformation for understanding and addressing poverty and the problems associated with poverty, particularly those concerned with human development.

This chapter traces some of the currents that have led to this situation, examines some of the methodological problems that stand in the way of moving beyond this impasse, and discusses examples from my own work and that of others of attempts to do this.

The Community Studies Tradition

Ferdinand Toennies opposition of "community" and "society," first published in 1887, is one of the founding texts of social science, and a source of recurrent interest. The notion of an underclass is but the latest incarnation of the notion that community has disappeared, dissolved in impersonal and hostile mass society. Yet community has continually been rediscovered, in such forms as "street-corner society" (Whyte 1943) and "urban villages" (Gans 1962).

It might seem, in light of these cycles of neglect and revival, that the notion of community itself is hopelessly fuzzy and not amenable to systematic research. Yet the tradition of community studies offers a number of methodological lessons on how to produce useful and cumulative research that reflects various and changing forms of community. A brief review of this tradition highlights some of these methodological issues as a prelude to a more sustained discussion of current concerns about inner-city neighborhoods and how to study processes of human development within these and other environments.

The best community studies have linked structure to process and provided models of community structure that are not merely idiosyncratic but rather represent modes of human settlement widely repeated within certain limits of time and space (Bell and Newby 1972; Arensberg and Kimball 1965).

The two most often cited criticisms of community studies are that they are atheoretical and noncumulative, but that does not have to be nor has it always been the case, as is evident from two seminal streams of research on forms of community in the United States. The first is the Chicago school itself, revolving around the great organizing theories of Park and Burgess. The second, related tradition grows from the work of W. Lloyd Warner and his efforts to apply the methods of social anthropology to the study of American communities.

Concern with crime and deviance links the theoretical tradition of the Chicago school's conception of community to the current underclass debates. Shaw and McKay's (1931) application of Park and Burgess's (1925) conception of urban form to the problem of juvenile delinquency prefigures many elements of current concerns. It combines the elements of class, space, race/ethnicity, and deviance into a unified theory, much as Wilson has done in a different way for a different era.

The strengths of Shaw and McKay's work were amply demonstrated in replications of their findings by themselves and others over the years in various cities (Shaw and McKay 1942; Bordua 1958–59; Chilton 1964). The major shortcoming of their work was the same as that of Park and Burgess's theories more generally, namely, the overemphasis on physical ecology as a causal factor in and of itself.

The community studies tradition launched by Warner (Warner and Lunt 1941) also combined elements of class, race/ethnicity, and space, but delved more deeply into local-level social organization. It looked not just at deviance but at a wide realm of political and associational life. While the achievements of this school also rank among the classic works of American social science (Davis, Gardner, and Gardner 1941; Hollingshead 1949), they also reveal a number of other problems with community studies that remain relevant to current concerns. Along with the Park and Burgess tradition, the Warner tradition has been criticized for presenting a static portrait of community organization, one that does not allow for the analysis of social change (Thernstrom 1964).

A turning point in the history of American community studies was Julian Steward's sharp critique of their lack of cumulativeness and his admonition to concentrate on closely controlled comparisons within carefully bounded culture areas as the only feasible avenue for avoiding unwarranted generalizations (1950).

Steward's position, however, was more honored in his own studies of Puerto Rico (1956) than in subsequent mainland studies. In the era inaugurated by W. F. Whyte's *Street Corner Society* (1943), studies began to focus on "partial communities," neighborhoods within larger metropolitan areas. In Arensberg's strict definition of the term *community* (Arensberg and Kimball 1965), the metropolitan area had become the actual community, in the sense of a unit of human settlement containing all the interactive roles comprising the culture. The focus on the whole metropolis of the Park and Burgess tradition or on self-contained small towns and cities of the Warner tradition gave way to the study of neighborhoods.

These neighborhood studies, both of suburbs (Seeley, Sim, and Loosely 1956; W. H. Whyte 1957) and of "urban villages" (Gans 1962), have made their own substantial contribution. Though they have left questions about representativeness and cumulativeness unanswered in many ways, our understanding of local-level social organization rests in large measure on these studies to this day.

The last period of great vitality in community studies occurred in the 1960s and early 1970s with landmark studies of urban ghettos (Hannerz 1969; Aschenbrenner 1975; Rainwater 1970; Ladner 1971; Stack 1974; Suttles 1968; Valentine 1978), many of them inspired by the debate over the culture of poverty that still echoes throughout the underclass debate. These studies showed, effectively and in considerable detail, that the behavior of the urban poor is driven not by self-perpetuating deviant values but by survival strategies that have their own logic, at least in the unavoidable short term, as adaptations to their environments. These studies portray the environments, the individual strategies, and the relationships between the two.

The emphasis of this last group of studies on survival strategies was driven strongly by a reaction to the notion of a "culture of poverty," itself the product of ethnographic work (Lewis 1966). The specter of the culture-of-poverty debate continues to haunt ethnographic work on the urban poor. By focusing on processes internal to a poor community, the researcher continually runs the risk of ascribing the causes of problems within the community entirely to its own members and neglecting processes of disinvestment, exploitation, and exclusion emanating from powerful interests and institutions outside the community.

Recent theoretical work has criticized these studies for failing to connect survival strategies at the local level to the larger forces of political economy that powerfully shape environments and available choices from the top down (Mullings 1987). These critiques have come primarily from within anthropology, including Fox's 1977 charge that ghetto studies have treated ghettos like self-contained islands at a time when we have come to understand that even islands in the South Pacific are not self-contained; Ortner's 1984 observation that ethnographers seemed to have forgotten about political economy during the 1970s; and Sanjek's 1990 review of urban anthropology in the 1980s that notes the new prominence of themes of homelessness and dislocation and their challenge to any easy assumption of tidy urban villages.

Another important critique of the importance of community studies is to be found in the notion that localities have receded in importance as organizing units of social life. Theory and research organized around the concept of social networks have suggested that, under modern systems of transportation and communication, people's primary interactions are less likely to be with their residential neighbors. A related notion is that urbanization makes possible specialized subcultures on an unprecedented scale, so that common interests shared through networks, rather than physical proximity, become the glue of social life (Fischer 1982; Wellman 1979). This social network research reinforces Arensberg's emphasis on the metropolitan area as the community and neighborhoods as "partial communities." Nonetheless, questions remain concerning the extent to which primary relationships are still locality based and whether locality-based relationships are more prominent for some groups of people, such as the poor.

If one tries to characterize the progression of theoretical and methodological assumptions underlying American community studies from the 1930s to the present, an oversimplified but perhaps useful generalization would be that researchers in the early period tried to grasp communities whole while those in subsequent periods have recoiled from the enormity of that task in progressively finer-grained attempts to do justice to smaller pieces of the whole, at the substantial cost of losing the ability to situate those pieces within the larger whole.

The tradition of community studies is undeniably messy, but nonetheless valuable. Community studies have not been demonstrably uncumulative even if we have not done very well at explaining how they do accumulate. Their documentation of American cities during their great era of expansion, of the development of suburbs, of "urban villages," and of poverty-stricken ghettos constitutes an invaluable record of the progression of community forms throughout the century.

These reflections on the community studies tradition point to a number of methodological requirements that need to be met in order for ethnographic data to address the important questions about the social organization of inner-city neighborhoods that have arisen in the underclass debates. Wilson claims that the inner cities became not just poorer during the 1970s but also suffered a breakdown of local institutions. He points to a sharp gap in the continuity of socialization of children and youth resulting from changes in family structure, institutional structure, and neighborhood environment. Effective research on such issues requires data on collective phenomena, not just the primarily individual-level data provided by the census and social surveys.

In order for community studies to provide cumulative knowledge about these kinds of issues, they must: analyze the internal social organization of neighborhoods; account for how much of a particular phenomenon of interest—such as participation in voluntary associations or supervision and education of children—is organized spatially and how much through nonlocality-based networks; provide comparable data on different neighborhoods that allow for systematic comparison; and connect the neighborhoods to the larger metropolitan area, society, and world economic and social systems in which they are embedded.

These criteria are used below to discuss some recent ethnographic work taking neighborhoods and local communities as primary units of analysis.

Recent Neighborhood Ethnographies Bearing on the Underclass Debate

Recent neighborhood ethnographies amply demonstrate the power of community studies to portray contexts of child and adolescent development and dimensions along which these contexts differ. The studies discussed below are primarily those that deal with phenomena emphasized in the underclass debates, particularly crime and early, out-of-wedlock childbearing. Three groups of studies in which I have had some involvement are discussed in particular: my studies of crime and of teenage pregnancy in Brooklyn (1989a,b; 1991; 1993) and two groups of studies organized under the auspices of the Social Science Research Council (SSRC), one of the ecology of crime and drugs in seven neighborhoods (Fagan

1992) in four regions of the country and the other of nine poor, Latino neighborhoods (Moore and Pinderhughes 1993).

After examining the ways in which neighborhood ethnographies capture and portray variations in neighborhood context, the next section takes a closer look at the implications of this kind of information on variation in neighborhood context for the study of human development.

The recent ethnographic record of crime, delinquency, and drug use and markets has been extensive. Besides my studies and those of the SSRC group directed by Fagan, notable examples include the work of Bourgois (1993), Taylor (1989), Vigil (1988), Hagedorn (1988), Williams (1989), Padilla (1992), and Moore (1978; 1991).

My work on youth crime (1989a) provides comparable ethnographic data on three groups of about a dozen young males in three separate neighborhoods of Brooklyn, supported by census and police data confirming the patterns revealed in the ethnographic data. The book's major contribution is its portrayal of age-related patterns of criminal involvement in conjunction with a systematic comparison of the local contexts in which these patterns unfold. The ethnographic data are consistent with quantitative studies showing age-related patterns of criminal involvement. These quantitative studies confirm the concentration of criminal involvement among young males and the sharp drop of such involvements during the midtwenties (Hirschi and Gottfredson 1983; Greenberg 1977, 1985). What the ethnographic data show that the quantitative studies ignore is how young males become involved in crime in different places and how the social organization of their neighborhoods presents distinctive incentives and sanctions for their continued involvement.

This approach to the study of crime and delinquency both illuminates patterns found in quantitative studies and also offers a different way of thinking about delinquency and development from the narrow emphasis on social psychology that dominated most delinquency research in the 1970s and 1980s (Akers 1973; Hirschi 1969; Elliot, Huizinga, and Ageton 1985). The social psychological issues have not become unimportant, but the ethnographic portrayal of actual social contexts raises quite different theoretical and policy questions from those involved in the increasingly rarefied and arcane debates over strain, labeling, social control, attachment, social learning, and the like. Attention is directed away from an exclusive focus on individuals and families toward the environments that constrain and shape the opportunities and stresses that people experience.

The analyst of youth crime begins to go beyond the usual and important questions about family and school relationships, and begins asking contextual questions about the extent to which local adults or gangs recruit youthful criminal operatives and about the presence of and incentives for adult males to sanction delinquent acts of burglary and car theft so often committed close to the delinquent's residence. One begins to ask who is buying drugs, when, and under what circumstances youthful drug-sellers sell to their neighbors, to nonneighborhood residents who are attracted by a local area's reputation as a drug market, or to buyers in citywide markets located outside the seller's own neighborhood.

Such locality-based patterns can be quite distinctive. For example, systematic comparison of the group of studies by Jeffrey Fagan (1992) shows how very different the phenomena referred under the rubric of "gang behavior" can be from one place to the next. Things called gangs differ significantly in the extent to which they are hierarchically organized; directly tied to adult organized crime groups; marked by ritual name, dress, or ceremony; dedicated to instrumental or expressive purposes; or composed primarily of minors (Sullivan 1992).

The presence of gangs in a neighborhood can be a significant feature in the socialization of young people growing up in that environment. The presence of gangs, however, is not a unitary phenomenon, nor is it an individual-level phenomenon. It is a collective phenomenon that varies from place to place along certain dimensions that are not that difficult to identify and assess, if the trouble is taken to do this. Such identification and assessment, however, require comparative ethnographic work. Collective phenomena of this sort are easily and routinely neglected in other types of research.

Besides portraying the internal organization of gangs and their articulation with other aspects of the social organization of their neighborhoods, this group of studies also provides information on other aspects of neighborhood life that makes it possible to test some of Wilson's assertions about neighborhood social organization, even though more precise quantitative work on some questions could be usefully undertaken. Some parts of Wilson's theory, particularly his emphasis on the effects of economic restructuring during the 1970s, receive strong support. Others aspects of the theory come into question. For example, this group of studies suggests strongly that the disruption of a formerly integrated class structure and consequent breakdown of local institutions given such strong emphasis by Wilson are factors in some places but not others. In addition, these studies point to Wilson's conspicuous lack of attention to patterns of immigration, residential segregation, institutional racism, and political fragmentation in shaping the environments of poor, urban neighborhoods (Sullivan 1992).

My work on teenage pregnancy has similarly portrayed variations in family formation related to local context that are consistent with patterns found in quantitative research (Danziger 1987; Sullivan 1989a, 1993a,b; Testa et al. 1989; Haskins et al. 1985). In this case the collective phenomena identified have to do with different patterns of abortion, early marriage, common-law marriage, household composition, and ways of caring for the children of young parents who cannot care for and support children on their own.

Comparisons with the work of Burton further extend the ethnographic record on these issues. For example, my comparative work on teenage pregnancy in three Brooklyn neighborhoods shows differences in marriage and abortion patterns between working-class whites, poor African Americans, and poor Puerto Ricans. In contrast to my finding of high rates of abortion among young African Americans in Brooklyn, Burton's work shows much lower rates of abortion among African Americans in other kinds of neighborhoods, both urban and semirural. Burton also emphasizes the diverse ways in which local environments shape behavior, citing the "unique, context-specific set of co-occurring economic, social, and psychological factors" that can differentiate poor neighborhoods from one another as well as from more affluent areas (Burton 1990; Sullivan 1993a,b).

In both the crime and teenage pregnancy studies, I devote considerable attention both to the effects of labor market opportunities and to the local, collective, and diverse responses to the presence or absence of such opportunities. The ethnographic data reveal the local neighborhoods to be significant but not wholly determining influences on individual behavior. Comparisons across neighborhoods reveal similarities and differences, pointing to both the salience and permeability of neighborhood boundaries in determining contexts and processes of socialization.

A final set of recent studies of the social organization of poor neighborhoods is the product of the SSRC working group organized by Moore and Pinderhughes (1993). These studies pose a similar set of questions, based on Wilson's assertions about underclass formation, to a wide range of poor Latino communities. Again, Wilson's emphasis on the impact of economic restructuring on the social organization of neighborhoods receives strong support. Other aspects of his theory, however, are shown to be quite varied in their applicability, particularly his emphasis on the co-occurrence of high rates of crime; early, out-of-wedlock childbearing; withdrawal from the labor market; and breakdown of local institutions. Family and institutional structure appear to be quite resilient in a number of poor, urban, Latino communities.

Studying Human Development in Community Context

Despite the rich history of community studies and the apparent need to connect research on community context to research on human development in order to begin to answer questions posed in the underclass debate, a large gap currently exists between these two types of research. Differing theoretical and methodological assumptions and goals appear to inhibit the potentially rich cross-fertilization of inquiries into community structure with those into processes of human development. Closer examination of the differences between these two types of research reveals some of the barriers to integrating them.

The gap between studies of community and studies of human development is somewhat surprising, since both fields have long acknowledged, in theory, their interdependence. A number of classic community studies have been directly concerned with questions of individual development, particularly youth development and the etiology of deviant behavior. Shaw and McKay (1931) and Thrasher (1927), for example, made explicit connections between urban spatial form and delinquency. Shaw and McKay proposed social disorganization theory as the mediating link between the two (Shaw and McKay 1931, 1942). Both Whyte (1943) and Hollingshead (1949) provided detailed portraits of youth development in community context, and Cloward and Ohlin (1960) wove together a highly influential theory of "blocked opportunities" at the community level as the driving force behind delinquent development, relying primarily on accumulated threads spun by ethnographic research.

Developmental studies, for their part, have formally acknowledged the importance of context and environment, from the early field theory of Lewin (1951) through recent theories of interactional psychology (Magnusson 1988) and problem-behavior theory (Jessor and Jessor 1977; Jessor, Donovan, and Costa 1991). "Environment" for psychologists, however, has rarely been operationalized at the level of community and neighborhood.

Comparison of studies in these two traditions, however, rather quickly reveals a primary source of the gap between them. Community studies have provided rich descriptions of context but paid relatively little attention to individual variations in development within those contexts, while developmental studies have looked closely at patterns of individual variation while incorporating as markers of context a sketchy set of social indicators that fall far short of the richness of ethnographic data. As a result, developmentalists reading ethnographic studies tend to be uncomfortable because of two types of unanswered questions. One set of questions concerns methods of selection and representativeness of research subjects that might allow for generalizations to a broader population. A second set of questions concerns variations in patterns of development among individuals in similar environments. Similarly, ethnographers reading developmental studies tend to be dissatisfied with the lack of information about community context. Neither group discounts the other's perspective, but the demands of the two research traditions are quite different even when they share the goal of understanding how environments shape human development.

In order to take a closer look at some of these problems, I reexamine some of my comparative ethnographic findings on the development of delinquent and criminal behavior here and compare them with findings from quantitative research by psychologists and criminologists on the same phenomena. Similarities and differences in these findings are then assessed in light of the differing methods employed for data collection and analysis.

In the book *Getting Paid: Youth Crime and Work in the Inner City,* I compare patterns of development from the early teens through the early twenties of three groups of about a dozen youths each from three separate neighborhoods in Brooklyn, New York. The neighborhoods varied in income and race/ethnicity: the predominantly white neighborhood was one of the poorest nonminority neighborhoods in New York City, but levels of household poverty and female-headedness there were much lower than the over-forty-percent levels characteristic of the other two neighborhoods, which were predominantly African-American and Puerto Rican, respectively.

Research based on extended ethnographic contacts when the youths studied were in their middle and late teens and retrospective life-history interviews showed similar levels of delinquency in the early teens. Development from the middle teens onward, however, showed a number of distinctive patterns. For purposes of this discussion, some of these patterns can be characterized as follows: illegal activities became more frequent and serious in all three groups during the middle and late teens; escalation of offending to more frequent, more risky, and more violent crimes was more prevalent among the two minority groups; as the youths reached their early twenties, most members of all three groups tended to discontinue or deintensify their criminal activities, shifting towards less frequent, risky, and violent acts if they did continue; within each delinquent peer group, a small number of individuals were especially committed to crime, committed a large number of offenses, and did not cease or deintensify their activities over time in the same manner as their peers.

These findings resonate with findings in the developmental and criminological literatures in a number of ways. First of all, they are generally consistent with a number of well-established findings from quantitative studies. The age-graded nature of involvement in crime and delinquency is one such finding (Hirschi and Gottfredson 1983; Greenberg 1985; Blumstein et al. 1986). As shown by various measures, criminal offending rises to a sharp peak from the middle teens through the early twenties and then decreases sharply thereafter.

The similarity between ethnographic and quantitative findings on this point is striking because of the nonrandom manner in which the ethnographic samples were recruited. Both the neighborhoods and the individuals studied in *Getting Paid* were recruited precisely because they had reputations for delinquency. Although the young males studied certainly had higher rates of delinquent and criminal involvement than the general population, it is striking that, even among delinquent peer groups, the age-graded patterns of illegal activity found in more representative samples of the general population are also apparent.

The finding that, even within these delinquent peer groups, a small minority (two or three out of about a dozen in each group) were especially high-rate offenders is also entirely congruent with quantitative studies, which indicate that a small proportion of active offenders appear to commit over half of all known crimes (Wolfgang, Figlio, and Sellin 1972).

While the age-graded patterns across neighborhood groups and patterns of individual variation within groups in the ethnographic data are largely consistent with quantitative studies, the findings of sharply patterned differences between groups differentiated by race, class, and neighborhood of residence do not find unproblematic reinforcement in quantitative studies in the developmental and criminological literatures. While it is beyond the scope of this article to provide an exhaustive review of these topics, some of the main outlines of relevant controversies can be traced.

The main axis of controversy concerns the issue of social versus individual-level causation. For several decades—beginning with the pioneering work of Shaw and McKay (1931), continuing through the classic studies of W. F. Whyte (1943) and Cohen (1955), and culminating in the work of Cloward and Ohlin (1960)—social causation of delinquency was assumed to be primary. Ethnographic studies, along with analyses of spatial distributions of arrests, were major sources of data, and neighborhood of residence was assumed to be a primary factor. With the advent of self-report studies of delinquency (Short and Nye 1958), the emphasis shifted toward individual causation. This trend culminated in the influential work of Wilson and Herrnstein (1985) that advanced a wholesale repudiation of social causation, arguing that "constitutional" differences between individuals, present from early childhood, account for individual differences in involvement in crime and delinquency across the life course, without recourse to social explanation. Subsequently, Gottfredson and Hirschi (1990) have also offered a comprehensive theory of crime, emphasizing personality formation during early childhood as the major criminogenic factor.

There is also considerable convergence of the criminological and developmental literatures on the finding of stability of antisocial behavior across the life course (Sampson and Laub 1993; Moffitt 1993). It is clearly true that individuals who are destined to experience a wide range of behavioral problems continuing into adulthood are overwhelmingly likely to exhibit problem behaviors at early ages. High rates of criminality and other antisocial behaviors that begin in adulthood are rare.

At this point in the argument it might appear that the battle lines between different methodological traditions on the question of social versus individual-level causation are clearly drawn. Both *Getting Paid* and the older tradition of ecological and ethnographic studies attribute primary importance to social context as defined by race, class, and neighborhood in generating crime and delinquency. Recent quantitative research based on sampling methods allowing for greater generalizability of findings appears to support the conclusion that it is individuals who start out and remain deviant, regardless of social context.

A closer examination of the state of theory and research in criminology and human development, however, belies the notion that quantitative research in these traditions decisively rejects the importance of social causation. While it is true that quantitative, longitudinal studies have heightened our awareness of the early childhood roots of much antisocial behavior, the question of the relative roles of social and individual-level causation is currently a matter of lively debate.

Recent work by Sampson and Laub (1993) has brought both empirical reexamination and theoretical reformulation to bear on these questions. In reanalyzing the original data used in the seminal, longitudinal studies conducted by Sheldon and Eleanor Glueck (1950, 1968), Sampson and Laub have provided convincing evidence that the later careers of delinquents are characterized by change as well as stability. In particular, they show that both cohesive marriage and attachment to the labor force in adulthood lead to reduced criminality. They conclude that "whether one views the glass of stability as half empty or half full stems at least as much from theoretical predilections as from empirical reality" (1993a:11). They explicitly attribute changes in the later careers of delinquents to social causation, relying on the notion of "social capital" (Coleman 1990) to explain these changes.

The purpose here is not to resolve these issues but rather to explore sources of tension and overlap between ethnographic studies of community context and studies of human development. From this perspective, the considerable overlap between some of the main findings of *Getting Paid* and the findings of quantitative, longitudinal studies has already been noted. The recent theoretical and empirical work of Sampson and Laub also recapitulates many of the themes of *Getting Paid.* The theoretical explanations in the two bodies of work are congruent, as is evident from a closer examination of the data on social context provided by the comparative ethnographic work.

Much of the explanation of differences between neighborhood groups documented in *Getting Paid* rests on analysis of neighborhood-based social networks, a salient example of "social capital." The youths in the white, working-class neighborhood appeared to become less involved in systematic, high-risk crime than their minority peers because of two features of their neighborhood context: networks providing access to desirable sectors of the labor market and household networks containing stably employed adult males who exercise informal social control in the local area. Sampson and Laub note that such "ecological constancy" can account for stability of behavior patterns just as well as innate differences in constitution and temperament: "In other words, behavioral stability does not necessarily imply causal forces operating solely at the level of the individual" (1993:308).

Other developmental studies make this same point. For example, Jessor, Donovan, and Costa's longitudinal research on multiproblem behavior, while continuing to support the notion of remarkable career stability in problem behavior, also admonishes that psychosocial change is "as much an outcome of the person's embeddedness in a socially organized and structured context . . . as it is of internal dispositions and intentions" (1991:160). This theoretical notion of embeddedness is dealt with explicitly in *Getting Paid* in terms derived from economic anthropology. The notion of nonmarket economic processes of reciprocity and redistribution (Polanyi 1957) is introduced in order to differentiate between economic transactions that can be accounted for easily in terms of rational choices made by impersonal actors and other transactions that are inextricably embedded in personal relationships between residents of poor neighborhoods and political relationships between them and agencies of social control outside the neighborhood.

Besides dealing with the embeddedness of rational choices in social context (in this case the context of neighborhood), *Getting Paid* goes farther and considers changes in the contexts themselves. The neighborhoods are described not just in terms of the activities and careers of delinquent peer groups within them, but in terms of the processes of political economy that are transforming the environments themselves.

In this way, *Getting Paid* attempts to deal directly with the large and complex questions raised in the underclass debate about the relationship of economic restructuring at the national level to the transformation of local neighborhood environments and the effects of these contextual transformations on processes of child and youth development. Sustained patterns of criminality are explained not in terms of abstract cultural processes of the breakdown of values but rather in terms of local-level social organization: who is around to monitor local youths, and the social networks into the labor market that provide more opportunities for legitimate employment in some environments than in others.

Getting Paid describes both group differences in developmental patterns and the social contexts that shape these neighborhood-specific developmental patterns. While exploratory criminal activities during the early teens were essentially similar across the three neighborhoods, the youths in the two poorer minority neighborhoods were far more likely to become involved in sustained criminal activities in pursuit of income than their working-class white peers. Lack of both social controls and social networks connecting young people to the labor market in the poor minority neighborhoods both contributed to these higher levels of criminality. Sustained involvement in highly risky criminal activities led in turn to major disruptions of schooling and labor market entry, sometimes involving sustained periods of incarceration. While some individuals in all three environments were considered psychologically disturbed even by their own peers, the significant differences across groups in evolving patterns of criminality during the later teens and early twenties appear to be clearly attributable to differences in their environments.

From the vantage point of recent developments in debates about the underclass and research and theory dealing both with political economy and with human development, there are many criticisms and gaps that can be found in *Getting Paid,* but the book anticipates many of these issues and raises questions at different levels of analysis in an inductive manner based on systematically collective ethnographic data. The purpose of this essay is to suggest that more of this kind of work can be of great value in advancing knowledge of these issues.

The experience of putting together *Getting Paid* demonstrated both the difficulties as well as the potential payoffs of the comparative ethnographic approach for the study of human development. The tendency to slight individual variation in the effort to produce a community profile, for example, was highlighted by the comments of one of the study's subjects who read early drafts of the material. Commenting on the portrayal of the youths in the Latino neighborhood, for example, one of the youths described in the book told me, "You got a lot of it right, Mercer, but you made it seem too much like all the same guy." Both that comment and reflections provoked by the publication of Wilson and Herrnstein's *Crime and Human Nature* prompted a renewed examination of within-group variation at the end of the book.

This process of reanalysis led to more emphasis on the phenomenon of the small minority within each delinquent peer group who continued to commit frequent, high-risk crimes even when their peers had begun to desist. In reexamining the relationships and attitudes within the peer groups, it became clear that these individuals were considered irrational and unreliable, even by their own delinquent peers. The white youths spoke incredulously about one of their number who repeatedly ingested amounts of drugs and then smashed jewelry store windows in broad daylight, leading inevitably to arrest. The African-American youths spoke similarly of one of their number who kept fighting back against police who had their weapons drawn. They talked about how irrational that behavior was and indicated that they themselves knew when to stop. The Latino youths had similar attitudes toward one of their number whose careless behavior leading to arrest seemed to indicate that he wanted to get caught. Even at the level of their own analysis of their behavior then, these youths clearly differentiated between criminal behavior that was "rational," in the sense of offering a reasonable possibility of concrete rewards, and behavior that was, in their words, "crazy," in the sense of leading almost inevitably to undesirable outcomes.

Similarly, the effort to portray the neighborhoods as changing contexts proved difficult and seems not entirely satisfactory in retrospect. More work on patterns of housing development and processes of labor market transformation could have enriched this effort. Similarly, the issues raised by Wilson about the importance of local institutions—schools, stores, churches, social service agencies, political organization—for promoting neighborhood stability and positive child socialization could have been developed further.

Despite these shortcomings, *Getting Paid* does show that questions about individual development and questions about context can be posed simultaneously, and that some answers can emerge when this happens. The enterprise is not easy. Very different epistemological frames guide these different kinds of inquiry. Anthropologist William Roseberry has contrasted the search for "transhistorical laws" with the study of "culture as historical product, shaped and shaping, socially constituting and socially constitutive" (1989:53). The study of human development has usually started from the former pole, the study of human communities, from the latter. Yet individuals and communities both exhibit continuity and change. At some point, these epistemological frames must converge, particularly if we are to arrive at a satisfactory understanding of the patterns of crime and other forms of destructive behavior that have become pandemic in the inner cities of the United States.

References

Akers, R. L. (1973) *Deviant Behavior: A Social Learning Approach.* Belmont, Calif.: Wadsworth.

Arensberg, C. M., and S. T. Kimball. 1965. *Culture and Community.* New York: Harcourt, Brace, and World.

Aschenbrenner, J. 1975. *Lifelines: Black Families in Chicago.* New York: Holt, Rinehart, and Winston.

Becker, H. S. 1963 [1973]. *The Outsiders: Studies in the Sociology of Deviance.* New York: The Free Press.

Bell, C., and H. Newby. 1972. *Community Studies: An Introduction to the Sociology of the Local Community.* New York: Praeger.

Blumstein, A., J. Cohen, J. A. Roth, and C. A. Vishers, eds. 1986. *Criminal Careers and "Career Criminals."* Vol. 1. Washington, D. C., National Academy Press.

Bordua, D. J. 1958–59. "Juvenile Delinquency and Anomie: An Attempt at Replication." *Social Problems* 6:230–38.

Bourgois, P. 1993. *In Search of Respect: Selling Crack in Spanish Harlem.* New York: Cambridge University Press.

Burton, L. M. 1990. "Teenage Childbearing as an Alternative Life-Course Strategy in Multigenerational Black Families." *Human Nature* 1: 123–43.

Burton, L. M., K. Allison, and D. Obeidallah. 1994. "Social Context and Adolescence: Perspectives on Development Among Inner-city African-American Teens." Unpublished.

Cohen, A. K. 1955. *Delinquent Boys.* New York: Free Press.

Danziger, S. K. 1987. "Father Involvement in Adolescent Welfare Mother Families." Paper presented to the Association for Public Policy and Analysis, Ninth Annual Research Conference, Bethesda, Md., 30 Oct.

Davis, A., B. B. Gardner, and M. R. Gardner. 1941. *Deep South.* Chicago: University of Chicago Press.

Chilton, R. J. 1964. "Continuity in Delinquency Area Research: A Comparison of Studies for Baltimore, Detroit, and Indianapolis." *American Sociological Review* 28: 71–83.

Cloward, R. A., and L. Ohlin. 1960. *Delinquency and Opportunity: A Theory of Delinquent Gangs.* New York: Free Press.

Coleman, J. S. 1990. *Foundations of Social Theory.* Cambridge, Mass.: Harvard University Press.

Elliott, D., D. Huizinga, and S. Ageton. 1985. *Explaining Delinquency and Drug Use.* Beverly Hills, Calif.: Russell Sage.

Fagan, J. 1992. *The Ecology of Crime and Drugs in American Cities.* Social Science Research Council. Unpublished.

Fischer, C. S. 1982. *To Dwell among Friends: Personal Networks in Town and City.* Chicago: University of Chicago Press.

Fox, R. G. 1977. *Urban Anthropology: Cities in Their Cultural Settings.* Englewood Cliffs, N.J.: Prentice-Hall.

Gans, H. J. 1962. *The Urban Villagers: Group and Class in the Life of Italian-Americans.* New York: Free Press.

Glueck, S., and E. Glueck. 1950. *Unravelling Juvenile Delinquency.* New York: Commonwealth Fund.

———. 1968. *Delinquents and Nondelinquents in Perspective.* Cambridge, Mass.: Harvard University Press.

Gottfredson, M. R., and T. Hirschi. 1990. *A General Theory of Crime.* Stanford, Calif.: Stanford University Press.

Greenberg, D. F. 1977. "Delinquency and the Age Structure of Society." *Contemporary Crises* 1: 189–223.

———. 1985. "Age, Crime, and Social Explanation." *American Journal of Sociology* 91: 1–21.

Hagedorn, J. M. 1988. *People and Folks: Gangs and Crime in a Rustbelt City.* Chicago: Lakeview Press.

Hannerz, U. 1969. *Soulside: Inquiries into Ghetto Culture and Community.* New York: Columbia University Press.

Haskins, R., A. W. Dobelstein, J. S. Akin, and J. B. Schwartz. 1985. *Estimates of National Child Support Collections Potential and Income Security of Female-Headed Households.* Final Report to the Office of Child Support Administration, Social Security Administration, Bush Institute for Child and Family Policy, Frank Porter Graham Child Development Center. Chapel Hill: University of North Carolina.

Hirschi, T. 1969. *Causes of Delinquency.* Berkeley: University of California Press.

Hirschi, T., and M. R. Gottfredson. 1983. "Age and the Explanation of Crime." *American Journal of Sociology* 89: 552–84.

Hollingshead, A. 1949. *Elmstown's Youth: The Impact of Social Classes on Adolescents.* New York: Wiley.

Jencks, C. 1991a. "Is the American Underclass Growing?" In *The Urban Underclass.* Ed. C. Jencks and P. E. Peterson. Washington, D.C.: The Brookings Institution.

———. 1991b. "Is Violent Crime Increasing?" *The American Prospect,* no. 4: 98–109.

Jessor, R., J. E. Donovan, and F. M. Costa. 1991. *Beyond Adolescence: Problem Behavior and Young Adult Development.* Cambridge: Cambridge University Press.

Jessor, R., and S. Jessor. 1977. *Problem Behavior and Psychosocial Development: A Longitudinal Study of Youth.* New York: Academic Press.

Ladner, J. A. 1971. *Tomorrow's Tomorrow: The Black Woman.* New York: Anchor Books.

Lewin, K. 1951. *Field Theory in Social Science.* New York: Harper and Brothers.

Lewis, O. 1966. *La Vida: A Puerto Rican Family in the Culture of Poverty.* New York: Random House.

Magnusson, D. 1988. *Individual Development from an Interactional Perspective: A Longitudinal Study.* Hillsdale, N.J.: Lawrence Erlbaum.

Massey, D., and M. L. Eggers. 1989. "The Ecology of Inequality: Minorities and the Concentration of Poverty 1970–1980." Chicago: National Opinion Research Center/University of Chicago.

Moffit, T. E. 1993. "Adolescence-Limited and Life-Course-Persistent Antisocial Behavior: A Developmental Taxonomy." *Psychological Review* 100: 674–701.

Moore, J. W. 1978. *Homeboys.* Philadelphia: Temple University Press.

———. 1991. *Going Down to the Barrio: Homeboys and Homegirls in Change.* Philadelphia: Temple University Press.

Moore, J., and R. Pinderhughes. 1993. *In the Barrios: Latinos and the Underclass Debate.* New York: Russell Sage.

Mullings, L. 1987. Introduction to *Cities of the United States: Studies in Urban Anthropology.* Ed. Mullings. New York: Columbia University Press.

Ortner, S. B. 1984. "Theory in Anthropology Since the Sixties." *Comparative Studies in Society and History* 26: 126–66.

Padilla, F. M. 1992. *The Gang as an American Enterprise.* New Brunswick, N.J.: Rutgers University Press.

Park, R. E., and E. W. Burgess. 1925. *The City.* Chicago: University of Chicago Press.

Polanyi, K. 1957. "The Economy as Instituted Process." In *Trade and Market in Early Empires.* Ed. Polanyi, C. M. Arensberg, and H. W. Pearson. Glencoe, Ill.: Free Press.

Rainwater, L. 1970. *Behind Ghetto Walls: Black Families in a Federal Slum.* Chicago: Aldine.

Roseberry, W. 1989. *Anthropologies and Histories: Essays in Culture, History, and Political Economy.* New Brunswick, N.J.: Rutgers University Press.

Ricketts, E. R., and I. V. Sawhill. 1988. "Defining and Measuring the Underclass." *Journal of Policy Analysis and Management* 7: 316–25.

Sampson, R. J. 1986. "Neighborhood Family Structure and the Risk of Personal Victimization." In *The Social Ecology of Crime.* Ed. J. M. Byrne and Sampson. New York: Springer-Verlag.

Sampson, R. J., and J. H. Laub. 1993. *Crime in the Making: Pathways and Turning Points through Life.* Cambridge, Mass.: Harvard University Press.

Sanjek, R. 1990. "Urban Anthropology in the 1980s: A World View." *Annual Reviews in Anthropology* 19: 151–86.

Seeley, J. R., R. A. Sim, and E. W. Loosely. 1956. *Crestwood Heights: A Study of the Culture of Suburban Life.* New York: Basic Books.

Shaw, C. R., and H. D. McKay. 1931. *Social Factors in Juvenile Delinquency.* Report of the National Commission of Law Observance and Enforcement (Wickersham Commission), vol 2, no. 13. Washington, D.C.: U.S. Government Printing Office.

———. 1942. *Juvenile Delinquency and Urban Areas.* Chicago: University of Chicago Press.

Short, J. F., Jr., and I. Nye. 1958. "Extent of Unrecorded Delinquency: Tentative Conclusions." *Journal of Criminal Law, Criminology, and Police Science* 49: 296–302.

Stack, C. B. 1974. *All Our Kin: Strategies for Survival in a Black Community.* New York: Harper and Row.

Steward, J. H. 1950. *Area Research.* Bulletin no. 63. New York: Social Science Research Council.

———. 1956. *The People of Puerto Rico.* Urbana: University of Illinois Press.

Sullivan, M. L. 1989a. "Absent Fathers in the Inner City." *Annals of the American Academy of Political and Social Science* 501: 48–58.

———. 1989b. *Getting Paid: Youth Crime and Work in the Inner City.* Ithaca, N.Y.: Cornell University Press.

———. 1991. "Crime and the Social Fabric." In *Dual City: Restructuring New York.* Ed. J. H. Mollenkopf and M. Castells, 225–44. New York: Russell Sage Foundation.

———. 1992. "The Ecology of Crime and Drugs: Reflections from American Community Studies." Paper presented to the Social Science Research Council, Committee for Research on the Urban Underclass, Research Synthesis Conference, Ann Arbor, Mich.

———. 1993a. Culture and Class as Determinants of Out-of Wedlock Childbearing. *Journal of Research on Adolescence,* 3, 295–316.

———. 1993b. "Young Fathers and Parenting in Two Inner-City Neighborhoods." In *Young Unwed Fathers: Changing Roles and Emerging Policies.* Ed. R. I. Lerman and T. J. Ooms. Philadelphia: Temple University Press.

Suttles, Gerald. 1968. *The Social Order of the Slum: Ethnicity and Territoriality in the Inner City.* Chicago: University of Chicago Press.

———. 1972. *The Social Construction of Communities.* Chicago: University of Chicago Press.

Taylor, Carl S. 1989. *Dangerous Society.* East Lansing: Michigan State University Press.

Testa, M., N. M. Astone, M. Krogh, and K. M. Neckerman. 1989. "Employment and Marriage among Inner-City Fathers." *Annals of the American Academy of political and Social Science* 501: 79–91.

Thernstrom, S. 1964. *Poverty and Progress: Social Mobility in a Nineteenth-Century City.* Cambridge, Mass.: Harvard University Press.

Thrasher, F. M. 1927. *The Gang.* Chicago: University of Chicago Press.

Toennies, F. 1887 [1957]. *Community and Society: Gemeinschaft and Gesellschaft.* New York: Harper Torchbooks.

Valentine, B. L. 1978. *Hustling and Other Hard Work: Life Styles of the Ghetto.* New York: Free Press.

Vigil, Diego. 1988. *Barrio Gangs.* Austin: University of Texas Press.

Warner, W. L., and P. S. Lunt. 1941. *The Social Life of a Modern Community.* New Haven, Conn.: Yale University Press.

Wellman, B. 1979. "The Community Question: The Intimate Networks of East Yorkers." *American Journal of Sociology* 84: 1201–31.

West, D. J., and D. P. Farrington. 1977. *The Delinquent Way of Life.* London: Heinemann.

Whyte, W. F. 1943. *Street Corner Society: The Social Structure of an Italian-American Slum.* Chicago: University of Chicago Press.

Whyte, W. H. 1957. *The Organization Man.* New York: Simon and Schuster.

Williams, T. 1989. *The Cocaine Kids: The Inside Story of a Teenage Drug Ring.* Reading, Mass.: Addison-Wesley.

Wilson, J. Q., and R. J. Herrnstein. 1985. *Crime and Human Nature.* New York: Simon and Schuster.

Wilson, W. J. 1987. *The Truly Disadvantaged: The Inner City, the Underclass, and Public Policy.* Chicago: University of Chicago Press.

Wolfgang, M. E., R. M. Figlio, and T. Sellin. 1972. *Delinquency in a Birth Cohort.* Chicago: University of Chicago Press.

11 Ruling Places: Adaptation in Development by Inner-City Youth

Anthropologists studying development across societies of the world have always been curious about the fact that psychologists center their studies of development almost exclusively on the first few years of an individual's life and spotlight children engaged in settings and tasks created by adults. Though many developmental psychologists point out the importance of their work with young children to adolescent development and sometimes to adult learning as well, infants and preschool children in dyadic interactions with adults continue to receive the bulk of attention from psychologists.

Anthropologists, on the other hand (perhaps because of the publicity surrounding Margaret Mead's early work on adolescents in the Pacific), tend to pay far less attention to young children than to societal members beyond early youth.[1] Much of this work has asked in one way or another how youth prepare for adulthood, generally in the socializing settings adults create for them. Rites of passage (Van Gennep 1960), as celebrations of transitions, especially those surrounding puberty, have particularly drawn the attention of anthropologists eager to describe their rule systems and psychodynamic effects. These studies follow a socialization model that sets out adults, their goals, and their rules for children, as given and often by implication as "good" for the young and entirely consistent with the continued beneficial existence of the society. Those anthropologists (and sociologists) who study nonadult-governed worlds created by youth use terms such as *subcultures* and *resistance* to characterize how the young set themselves apart, break adult rules, and become "deviant." Resulting analyses, often of groups within urban settings of complex societies, often characterize youth by descriptors that either medicalize or criminalize them (Griffin 1993, esp. chaps. 4, 5). From such research we gain little understanding of adaptive strategies of the young or ways they question and negotiate the rules of what they see as imperfect institutions and situations created by adults.

This chapter considers a situation in which youth verbally illustrate such adaptive strategies. Described here is a group of inner-city males, ages twelve to eighteen, primarily African-American, who are members of a community-based basketball team, as they learn, reshape, test, and adapt rules for their work as a team. Highlighted here is a time of crisis, when their coach, apparently in the interest of winning, breaks rules on which he and team players have agreed. He and they have talked of the team as parallel in norms and demands to jobs, "the real world," and higher-education institutions, and the group has agreed that the rules they set for themselves prepare them for expectations of what will be "out there" ahead of them. Their talk and expressions of belief circulate around the view that what happens now in the place they create for themselves on the team will set them up for what happens later in the distant places of work, further schooling, and adulthood. In the situation of focus in this chapter, the youth come up against the realization that leaders, rules, and expectations work in give-and-take relationships. The chapter closes with some surmises about the contributions to developmental studies that could result from research on ways the young adapt to breaches of rules by adults. Researchers speak far too consistently about the regularities that make it possible for people to communicate and connect through their systems of meaning; we need to talk much more about the irregularities. Close observations of how the young negotiate contradictions between what adults say and what they do give us a good start in this direction.

Ethnography in the Inner City

One reason neither anthropologists nor psychologists have described ways that young people adapt to inconsistent or nongeneralizable behaviors of adults derives from the fact that access to such data is not easy. Only long-term immersion within a group of young people and collaborative research with the young can provide such data. Collection of materials used in this chapter began in 1987 and has now been ongoing for nearly a decade among young people participating in youth-based organizations in inner cities of three major metropolitan centers of the United States. Some background on the context of the specific data of this chapter, as well as an overview of predominant public views about inner-city youth and African-American males in particular, will orient the reader to the data and discussion that follow.[2]

In 1987, Milbrey McLaughlin, a public policy analyst, and I began fieldwork in three major metropolitan areas (one in the Northeast, one in the Midwest, and another in the Southwest) to identify organizations urban youth believed effective for them and to learn what happened in these institutions. All metropolitan areas had strong traditions of ethnic identity and separation, and each had also pursued efforts since the 1960s to relieve ethnic tensions and to create improved education for their young. Yet political and philanthropic leaders in all sites despaired over the increased substance abuse, violence, and sexual activity of their young and the seemingly immovable socioeconomic barriers being constructed around their inner cities. These leaders declared repeatedly in public their intention to "do something." Some of these efforts, as well as those of grass-roots groups, resulted in organizations such as basketball, baseball, and softball teams, community centers for youth, performing arts groups, tumbling teams, expanded boys and girls clubs, and gang intervention programs by groups such as the YMCA.

We began our work by soliciting from community leaders, foundation officers, juvenile justice officials, and educators their lists of exemplary local organizations that attracted youth after school, on weekends, and during the summers. We simultaneously found ways to ask the same questions of youth on the streets, in parks, and on subways. After a year or so of both being on the streets talking with youth and meeting with local civic leaders, we gained entry into over sixty organizations through whose doors approximately 24,000 young people passed during our first five years of fieldwork.[3] These organizations were those judged by the youth (and sometimes by civic leaders) to be effective, and their judgments were confirmed by oversubscriptions, waiting lists, and high positive visibility within their neighborhoods. Only sometimes were the organizations judged by the youth as effective similarly evaluated by local officials; extent of resources, facilities, and local reputation at city hall did not bear a direct relationship to estimations of effectiveness by the young people themselves. But what made these institutions "effective" or "safe places to be" in the eyes of the youth who found their way there?

We set out to answer this question by immersing ourselves, along with two full-time trained fieldworkers in their twenties, in the everyday happenings of the organizations. We four adults followed traditional field methods of ethnographers, recording fieldnotes, talking with the youth to ask their versions of events, and tape-recording language in as many settings as possible. The two full-time fieldworkers observed and participated, to the extent possible, in the activities of the youth within their youth organizations and worked to bring these "unstable, complex, and disorderly" (Flax 1987:643) recordings of life into patterns for analysis. Anchoring these analyses were segments of time, space, and action,

brought together at the microlevel of minute-to-minute linguistic interactions (on the basketball court, in drama rehearsal, or in the van) with
descriptions of individuals and their roles under different situations provided by the youth-based organizations. These roles included not only
those expected within athletic and artistic pursuits of these organizations—pitcher, stagehand, forward, van driver—but also "jobs" within
the organizations' daily life, such as receptionist, travel coordinator, or
person assigned to telephone absent players. All groups we studied managed to bring youth into the daily operations of the organization itself,
thus providing multiple opportunities for oral performances to outsiders
and recordkeeping that required map-reading, numeracy, and literacy
skills. Fieldworkers' analysis of patterns of behavior at the microlevel were
then coordinated with patterns of organizational structure and governing
rules, as well as stated and unstated goals, purposes, and philosophies of
adults (including coaches, parents, secretaries, and boardmembers).

Aiding the two full-time fieldworkers were approximately twenty junior
ethnographers, young people from the inner-city organizations who were
asked to join our research team after the first year or so. These young
ethnographers tape-recorded and transcribed language data and sat in
on sessions with adult ethnographers for analysis of their transcripts.
Charged to collect data to help the older fieldworkers understand all the
ways that life *within* their youth-based organizations slipped into beliefs
and experiences *outside* these settings, the junior ethnographers were given
strict guidelines on the ethics of recording. They were to record only when
everyone present knew the recording was taking place and only under
circumstances that related to activities of the youth-based organizations:
travel to and from games and events in vans, informal get-togethers after
school, and overnight stays in distant cities when the team or troupe participated in regional or national competitions.

In attempting to link microlevel behaviors with macro-organizational
features of these youth groups, we relied heavily on language data supplemented by fieldnotes. All materials which were recorded were transcribed,
often by two different transcribers, into a data base exceeding a million
words. Through a concordance program and extensive eye-scanning, with
close analysis of selected portions of the transcripts, we could capture both
statistically, and through discourse analysis, patterns of the linguistic webs
of behavioral interactions. Following anthropological tradition, we seg-
mented the "seasons" of youth organizations into major activity phases
moving toward "harvest" or final performance: planning, preparation,
practice, performance, and evaluation. Phases of each season corresponded also to the extent of socialization of new members into the culture
of the group. Fieldnotes portrayed in detail where and when these seasonal
phases occurred, who spoke (adult or young person, newcomer or old-

timer) and in coordination with which kinds of events, and how repeats and reruns of earlier aspects worked themselves into later phases. Especially critical for this study was the extent to which macro-organizational structures and norms enabled or inhibited communication by the youngsters among themselves and in different kinds of roles.

Over the course of single sessions, as well as within different phases of each season, our concordance program allowed us to look not only at the relative frequency of specific linguistic items (such as negatives, modals, and if-then constructions), but also at patterns of turn-taking and length of utterances for adults and specific youngsters over the course of single sessions, as well as within different phases of the season. Discourse analysis of randomly selected transcripts of youth organizations committed to different types of activities (drama, basketball, Girl Scouts, gang intervention, and others) revealed both specific patterns and those common across organizations within certain phases. For example, within all groups, youngsters heard within the planning phase a high proportion of hypotheticals and sociodramatic bids directed to the group and not the adults present—"Okay, it's the week before the play, and the guy playing the lead gets sick; what happens then?" Analysis of specific linguistic features, such as hedges ("Maybe we could think about"), inclusive plural pronouns (such as *we* and *us*), and teasing strategies revealed patterns we could compare with self-reports by youth and with expressed organizational goals. For example, if we found minimal talk from adults in the midst of drama practices, we sought evidence that youngsters were conscious of adults "taking a backseat" during these times to let the youth director lead the group. Similarly, we checked interviews with adult leaders, public performances (such as awards banquets), and printed promotional materials for compatible goals, such as youth participation in leadership roles. In other words, we looked across various types of data to identify mutual or dissenting perceptions of links between ideology and behavior.

Youngsters quickly make and break relationships through their choice of words. Hence we traced growing cohesiveness of the group, as well as ways of handling breakdowns in relationships, by noting relative frequencies of features such as successful completion of each other's utterances, interruptions that resulted in break-off of the first speaker's speech, and repetitions of phrases, themes, and overtly expressed credit for positive/ negative behavior and ideas from one youth member to another. The methods of data collection and analysis of this study were designed to show how microlevel communication strategies linked with macro-organizational structures and norms and how the youngsters made meaning of these connections.

Actual physical settings of youth-based organizations in which we worked included everything from empty lots where young people gathered in the afternoons to meet their coaches to complexes of buildings that served as community centers. Youngsters within these organizations ranged in age from eight to twenty-eight, since in many organizations youngsters above the age of fourteen served as counselors, coaches, teachers, receptionists, and support backup for younger members of the groups. Participants in the youth organizations included those who came from tightly knit families whose parents had urged their child's participation in the organization, as well as those active in street life and living independently with little parental contact. Some bore major financial and caregiving responsibilities for younger siblings and sometimes for parents who were either ill or addicted to drugs or alcohol.

The youth unanimously saw themselves as heavily criminalized by media coverage and given little credit for positive contributions they made to their families, communities, and peer groups. African-American males, in particular, expressed resentment about excessive media attention to criminal activities in certain neighborhoods (see also Burton, Obeidallah, and Allison, this volume). They also frequently talked about their ambivalence over media portrayals that suggested African-American males could "make it" only through sports, especially basketball. Coaches and other adults of youth-based organizations pushed hard the message that sports builds skills and habits useful for getting another kind of job; they discouraged youngsters from seeing sports *as a job* or as a free and easy ticket to higher education. Coaches also talked openly about the need to excel in sports in order to attract attention from representatives of other institutions, and thereby to increase opportunities for study, work, and travel.

Within youth-based organizations, the youth reported that they found "something to belong to" and "a group to hang with." The youngsters highly valued the travel—whether across town or across the country—the youth-based organizations offered from time to time. Some saw their youth organizations as substitutes for either family or gang membership, and adult leaders within these groups sometimes promoted these metaphors, often terming the group "one big family" or "*this* gang." Youth-based organizations incorporated positive aspects of an ideology of "family" and "gang" or "youth affiliation," stressing the value of belonging, being loyal and responsible, and relying on teamwork in their athletic and artistic teams (Irby and McLaughlin 1990; Heath and McLaughlin 1991, 1993; Vigil 1993).

Creating a Sense of Place

For even those groups that had no consistent physical space for meeting, youth organizations created a sense of *place* by emphasizing an ongoing management and planning approach to life within the group. Rules created by the youth with help from adults framed their interactions with each other. Ways of handling conflict, facing disappointments, and managing newcomers, marginals, and sometime goof-offs dotted conversations between adults and the youth. Within theater groups of young people, over 50 percent of the utterances in the first few weeks of working together centered on rules, structures, frames, limits, boundaries, divisions, barriers, and the like within society and also within the organization. Invariably, talk about talk and its role in strengthening, breaking, or reshaping relationships raised debate. Why people said what they did and the way they did could hold young people in conversation for well into the night, as they debated back and forth intent, fairness, right and wrong, and implications or outcomes from "bad talk"—meaning words that brought pain.

The nature and occasions for such talk emerged out of larger structural arrangements of the youth organizations. Plenty of time to talk resulted from not only highly specific occasions within a group's particular activity focus (for example, improvisation planning sessions of theater groups), but also from adult encouragement of talk of particular types: planning, problem solving, checking up, and "cooling down." Talk provided the glue for the predictability and stability upon which youngsters relied in their youth organizations. Each group set rules at two levels. The first set of rules, highly visible and immediately offered in response to the query, "What are the rules of this place?," secured *safety* for the group (no drugs, gang symbols, weapons, or, this is a place where nobody is supposed to get hurt). Through these rules, known to all members and intensely pressed on newcomers, youngsters broke up arguments, identified troublemakers among novices, and paid close attention to symbols in dress and hand signals likely to be known only by other youth and not adults.

The second level of rules, in contrast to the first, seemed never to be seen as actual "rules," though these governed much of daily organizational life. Central to interactions within the actual production of the work of the group, these rules came sometimes from the literature of national headquarters (for example, Little League rules about good sportsmanship). But more often they emerged from the philosophy of local adult leaders about youth, mainstream institutions of education and employment, and ways for youngsters to "stay outta trouble and get somewhere." Most leaders viewed their operations as groundwork for successful entry by the youngsters into mainstream institutions of formal education and employment. They often spoke of the mainstream world "out there" as filled with prejudice, unfair rules, and authorities who had "wrongheaded ideas about kids." Again and again, when youngsters complained about school, for example, youth leaders listened, assessed teachers and administrators in harsh terms, and then told the youngsters to "hang in there, because you can't let 'em get you down; you gotta show 'em what you can do."

Criticisms of mainstream institutions took place alongside second-level rules that pushed youth toward institutional values, often characterized as middle-class and aimed toward advancement academically, socially, and economically. For example, if a drama group insisted that everyone learn to play at least three roles, and that everyone take part in all aspects of support for productions (costuming, scenery design, acting), adults justified these rules in statements such as, "In life, you can't always do just what you think you do best." Added to such statements were the inevitable calls to improvement and its rewards: "Besides, the more things you try, the more you'll know about what you can do well, and that's how you get ahead—match your talents to what you have to do."

Adults told youngsters that their jobs would surely ask them to do just what the youth organization wanted them to do: show up on time, respect property, be neat and clean, follow the rules of the group, know how to speak clearly and correctly, and be able to ask for something "in the right way." Basketball or baseball teams closely linked to academic improvement for players insisted that players keep their grades up, do a certain number of hours of homework before practice, stay in school in order to remain on the team, and perform some kind of community service. These expectations were justified on the grounds that following them showed discipline, commitment, and connection—qualities employers and school personnel would reward.

Long-term youth members and adult leaders, especially sports and drama coaches, set out for newcomers and old-timers alike both first- and second-level rules during the first phase of each seasonal cycle. First-level rules rarely were invoked or restated again unless an infraction occurred, and often infractions were obvious enough that neither they nor repercussions for the offenders needed re-expression in language. Everyone "just knew" what happened and why. On the other hand, second-level rules moved in and out of language in quite different ways within the organizations. Adults and old-timers among the youth often invoked them, especially in the planning and practice phases at the beginning of each day and also during episodes where the possibility existed that one of these rules was broken or was being questioned by a newcomer. Such occasions gave opportunity to restate principles of operation or the "philosophy" of the youth group as well: "Don't forget this is not a job, but it is about getting and holding a job."

Structural arrangements that enable such talk within the effective youth organizations we studied include the following.

1. Organizations center their activities around athletics or artistic performance and productions, often with a strong component of academic and vocational preparation. The pervasive philosophy behind these activities is that *youth can do:* they are resources and not problems.

2. Organizations run on few first-level or highly visible rules, often developed by the youth and created to offer safety and security for members. Negotiation of meanings of rules is encouraged, though obvious infractions are rapidly and rigidly punished—usually by temporary suspension from high-status activities or by expulsion from the organization. These rules are not arbitrary or controlling for control's sake, and they are seen as fair—applied to everyone.

3. Activities and practices surrounding these are seen as preparation for life. The rules behind these are invisible as specific codes, but they permeate events and interactions. Adults give these out as philosophy and then members, young and old, negotiate their meanings. Youth and leaders work together to make many decisions affecting the ongoing life of the organization. Youth across ages work together, with each individual being aware that anything they learn in practice, they will probably have to teach to a younger player or member at some point as teacher, tutor, or assistant coach, and they will then have opportunities to express and enforce their own philosophy or second-level rules. Each individual thereby experiences what it is like to be expert or model as well as learner.

4. Youth activities move through seasonal cycles in which members take part in a long-term project or production that runs from planning and practice through performance and evaluation. Youngsters see projects and performances through, with a clear sense of knowing what involvement over the long term can offer. High challenges of performance are accepted as given or "normal" for youngsters. No practice, game, rehearsal, or planning session is accepted as ordinary; all seem motivated by the group's conviction they can and will have to work hard and probably "harder than ever before."

5. Youth have opportunities to work toward increasing levels of responsibility and employment within the institutions, carrying out a variety of paid and volunteer roles from assistant coach to receptionist to youth counselor. The path of progress is clear and the payoffs predictable and straightforward.

6. The guiding metaphor of these organizations is "family" and the need to stick together in spite of difficult times. An aura of "being there for you" permeates the organizations, along with acceptance that members of the group may be experiencing events in their lives "outside" that could affect their mood, performance, and attitude "inside" the group.

Representing Symbols

Symbols of communication other than those that are verbal also reinforce a sense of belonging and of owning the rules that hold the group together in their tasks. Youth organizations ensure that their members are protected not only within the group, but also through specific symbols that mark their membership outside the group. Young people have to *learn*— to *develop* in their sense of being a member and of using symbols appropriately to handle such membership. Development in this context means not only carrying out with some consistency skills necessary to any activity (for example, pitching, running, drumming, calling out cues), but also being able to strategize and step back to explain what is going on. As young people assume different roles in the organizations and set their own goals for moving up in the group, they see more of each of these steps as evidence that they are following an expected program of development. Adults often speak of youngsters as metaphorically "coming along" or "moving up the line" on some course of linear development. Thus though adults stress that each person can and will develop along a path consistent with his or her special talents, key metaphors of the organization reflect a general trajectory or path of development through the stages of either a single season or performance and across a span of several seasons.

Once young people become members of a youth organization, they take on identity as a member of the "family" to which they now belong. They become "one of Al's boys," or a player for the Redhots. The calling up of their special name operates as a form of protection because it suggests a network of defenders as well as a stable institution. Gym bags, T-shirts, shoestrings, caps, jackets, and other markings on large mobile pieces of property (such as vans or pieces of stage sets) carry this identity with them both within and outside the organization. On the street in gang-controlled territory, a young member of a youth organization is encased in a bubble of being a special kind of homeboy or homegirl and therefore within the safety of a support group. This status parallels that which underlies long-term dependence of group formation on "home" associations—through families linked by kinship, marriage, and residential proximity.

Within the organization, photographs, trophies, and awards line the walls of the club or the office of the director in those cases where the group has no space of its own other than the temporary office of the coach or the director. On the shelves of directors' offices are notebooks that contain past accounts, often scattered and incomplete, of the group. Newspaper clippings and photos fill albums that line office walls, and award ceremonies include not only brief case histories of "family" members, but also distribution of smaller versions of the club's history in memory books or albums.

"The Dynamos"—Practice and Potential

Our power to predict what others will do enables us to exist as members of any group. Most of what we learn therefore must be shared and socially agreed upon. But preparing to know what to do in all possible situations that may arise, and especially for those that break from predictable patterns, becomes increasingly necessary as one gets older. This preparation often comes for youth through recognizing that adults who make rules also break them, and that adults may break these rules for purposes they find difficult, if not impossible, to explicate. Such breaches of rules offer, perhaps ironically, opportunity to draw up other rules or a store of strategies, behaviors, and attitudes to prepare youth to go forward in the immediate situation of the rule-breaking and also to think about future similar events.

Used here to illustrate these points is a midwestern basketball group of thirty to forty males between the ages of twelve and eighteen coached by an African-American male and divided into a senior and a junior team. Victor Cage, called Cage by team members, is the coach and also a vice principal and middle-school science teacher. A grass-roots group started by Victor nearly a decade before our research began in order to give African-American males an alternative to the streets and some substantive help with their homework, the Dynamos depend primarily on the energy of Victor to raise funds, find and sustain volunteers, and keep the group going. Several nights each week the boys invited to join the team at one of the two levels come together for tutoring sessions in which volunteers work in one-on-one relationships with each youth to go over schoolwork and to prepare for taking examinations related to college entry. After their time of study, the youth practice basketball, and on weekends they usually congregate both for practice and at the local community multipurpose center (where Victor has a small office) to help him file receipts, maintain the team's archives, and plan fundraising and future trips for tournaments. Both the senior and junior teams participate in local, regional, and national tournaments, showing off their excellence before college scouts and hoping for financial support to help members go to college.

Second-level rules for the Dynamos reflect Victor's philosophy that young men can use basketball and their ways of playing as a metaphor for their lives: "work hard, do your best, and be a good member of a team." Victor has no intention that the young men go on in careers of professional basketball; on the contrary, he insists that they see basketball as a way to get through the institutional barriers that might otherwise keep them from going to college. They can use basketball to get into colleges and to get financial help, and they can use the discipline, practice, and hard work they demonstrate in their winning form to show off their abilities in these highly prized "mainstream" behaviors and attitudes. He minces no words in making clear to the young men that there are institutional racist barriers they must cross and will continue to face, but he also tries to help them avoid racist attitudes that generalize the behavior of individuals to groups.

Second-level rules flow out of Victor's philosophy that academic achievement and continuity will help ensure (though not guarantee) a way both to survive in their neighborhoods and to know choices exist beyond these streets and their peers who are rapidly disappearing into jails or mortuaries. Staying busy and having something to do and a group to hang with will help keep the young men away from drugs, car theft, and other hazards of inner-city street life. A key second-level rule is that no player who drops out of school can play on the team. Staying on the team depends on being in school and keeping grades up.

When the boys join the team's study sessions, their questions center around immediate tasks. "We gonna go over there now?" "Did I get that problem right?" Questions of this type account for more than 80 percent of those asked by the boys. Victor's talk, on the other hand, is filled with hypotheticals, asking the boys to develop strategies and to understand the functional significance of planning in advance *and* adapting strategies. Believing that "too much planning ahead can be a bad thing—I don't want these boys packing their bags for college yet," Victor often sets up sociocultural dramas for the boys, in which he asks them what they would do if certain events occurred. For example, within a few years after Victor began the team, it had acquired a strong regional reputation, and the team had many invitations to travel. Often this travel was to all-white areas, where the opposing team and all the spectators would be white. Victor chose to engage the boys in a number of "what if" scenarios to test their planning before such trips each year. Similarly, on a practice-to-practice basis, he did the same—stressing strategies, asking for plans to be verbalized, and pushing the boys to articulate what they meant in better ways. He wanted their descriptions of plans to be as specific as possible; he often gave them tasks, such as filing expense receipts, planning budgets, and calling airlines for travel reservations, for which he prepared them ahead by asking them to think aloud about what they were going to do "before you get on that telephone."

By the middle of the season, the percentage of questions of the simple and direct sort by the boys dropped to 12 percent, while those that indicated planning (including hypotheticals and brief sociodramatic bids) among the boys and in interaction with Victor climbed to 72 percent. In addition, whereas in the early weeks of the season only 18 percent of the boys' utterances included mental state verbs (like *think, believe, plan*), by the final weeks of practice before tournament time, 32 percent of the boy's utterances in debriefing sessions after practice included such verbs.

The study of planning, remembering, and feeling can be facilitated by such "active" evidence as talk (Rogoff, Baker-Sennett, and Matusov 1995). Over the relatively brief span of several weeks, the Dynamos came to exhibit stronger and more frequent evidence of their knowing that they had the knowledge and the ability to plan. These team members not only had to maintain steady work on academic subjects and improve their basketball game, but they also had to become active in exploring possibilities, attempting solutions, and learning to articulate these within the appropriate time frame—not too far ahead and, certainly, not too late (Rogoff 1982).

Planning under Crisis

The following episode, tape-recorded when Victor was not present, illustrates the extent to which the boys used their own conversations to assess what went on around them in terms of team philosophy and second-level rules. Team members are on a tournament trip to the West Coast, and they have gathered back in the hotel room just after they have lost an early game in the tournament. Their discussion includes the assistant coach, a young man who is a relative newcomer to the group and not yet considered a "real" member of the team. Several of the boys are seniors and had been hoping to go farther in the tournament in order to enhance their visibility to college scouts. The recording was made by a junior ethnographer and includes discussions that cover their second-level rules—those that regulate general treatment of other players and dictate who plays and when and how certain strategic rules on the court work. The transcript portions below illustrate an example of each of these rules under negotiation among the team members.[4]

> Episode 1: When Howie, an older player who acts as junior coach on the team, enters the room, he comments on its state of disarray and the way clothes are scattered about. He teases the boys about whether or not they are packed and how they like the soap supplied by the hotel. A series of exchanges follows about who among the members is the messiest and who cleans up the mess others make.

Player 1: Dwayne buy a damn toenail clipper, be, you know, it
         come in a package, he take the damn thing out and there, it
         on the floor
Player 3 (Dwayne): is it down there? Naw
Player 1: =then he start pickin' at them big-ass toes=
Player 3: =when I got through I picked it up, punk, /be quiet.
Howie: /did you let Terrance use it? He was lookin' for a toenail
         clipper.
Player 3: I ain't lettin' him use nothin'.
Howie: Aw, don't wanna help your teammate, huh?
Player 3: That brother better go downstairs like I did, I needed
         one, and I went downstairs and bought one.
Howie: You just being selfish, man.
Player 1: Yeah, that's all /that is
Howie: /You guys are selfish.

This is the first of three tries that Howie makes to introduce Terrance
and the game of the previous evening into the conversation with references
to such behavior as helping out a teammate. Terrance, younger than most
of the other players, had played much of the game, made many mistakes,
and was not called out of the game and replaced. He had hogged the
ball and made some bad shots, leaving out possible assists from his team
members that might have been more productive than his one-man show.
The boys do not immediately take up Howie's veiled invitation to open
discussion on the game, but they announce indirectly their understanding
of the rules of the team: pick up after yourself, help your brother out, and
be self-sufficient. Note that the boys do not latch onto Howie's utterances
as they do each other's. His utterances hang in the air separated by brief
junctures of silence, while the boys banter rapidly with quick rebuttals to
any challenge offered. Howie also interrupts twice in this episode, but each
time, the boy he interrupts just keeps talking.

Episode 2: Within a few minutes after the episode above, the boys
move into a discussion of the game and the infractions of rules as
they see them. They denounce the coach for breaking team rules,
and they point out that someone else—college recruiters—will, if
they pursue him, soon discover that Terrance has been kicked out
of school.

Player 1: Bill say Terrance get the ball and don't look to pass the
         mother [the ball].
Howie: That motherfucker be—why, that motherfucker, we down

six points and a one-on-one move, he want to do a three-sixty in the lane [*laughter*].

Player 3: The last jumpshot he shot was a airball, he pull up like he money=

Player 1: =Cage don't never say shit about him, /he don't. . . .

Howie: /He the one should've stole them damn balls, he was gettin' on your [*nodding to player 3*] case about, that motherfucker back there, how I'm 'ona make a fuckin' pass from over here all the way over here all the way over to the other side, and he standing' right there in the middle.

Player 3: He just a sophomore.

Howie: Huh?

Player 3: He a sensation, sweepin' the nation, everybody askin' about him, cuz he a freshman.

Player 2: Wait till them motherfuckers find out he don't go to school, kicked out=

Player 1: =[*Slams fist into open hand*].

In this episode, the knowledge the players have that Terrance did not attend classes the last month of school comes out in their anger over his playing the entire game and the coach overlooking his mistakes. Howie, the junior coach, does not indicate whether he knew Terrance's situation, and he seems surprised to learn Terrance is only a sophomore now. How the coach handled the matter of who played and for how long, who broke team rules regarding assists, and when timeouts and penalties were called becomes the next topic of conversation, led by Howie. The team players and Sam, a team manager, show reluctance to condemn the coach and keep pushing against Howie's points to debate what happened. Behind this scenario is the fact that since the tournaments are places where the seniors can show off and be seen by college recruiters, they, rather than younger players, are usually allowed to play for the greater part of the game.

Episode 3

Howie: I told Sam [one of the team managers] what the problem is, we gettin' outcoached.

Player 3: Who?

Howie: We are.

Player 3: Wait a minute. /Why?

Howie: /We don't, we refuse to press the ball, man, that don't make no sense.

Player 2: All he [Cage] say is get back, get back. It's like when we

do get back, we will stop it, and we'll go down and shoot a
shot, they'll just run, they beat us, even if we do score, they
beat us right back up the court.

Sam: Y'all know, what, if Cage smart and he want y'all to use that
rule that he gave, if it's a call in the back court, you can grab
the ball and just throw it in, he'll keep remindin' y'all, y'all
don't be thinkin' 'bout that.

Howie: That's true.

Player 1: That *is* true.

Howie: Cuz, cuz we so use to givin' the ball to the ref.

Raoul (2d manager): Cuz, cuz that black team, he be like, let's go,
let's go, let's go, get the ball.

Player 3: Now, now, why did he tell Peter to call a timeout when it
was a two-on-one fastbreak, and didn't call a timeout when
they just now went on a 6–0 run and got it back up to like 11
or 12?

The boys continue to debate specific points of the game and disagree
about whether they were outcoached or whether they just made some mistakes. One or two players suggest that the previous night, Cage seemed to
pull individual players aside to correct their game rather than talking to
the group as a whole. They go on to recite other incidents of favoritism
toward Terrance, such as the time they saw Cage compliment him after a
game in which they felt they too had played well. They end the conversation in a dispirited slump about whether they can get the coach to listen
to their grievances, but they decide to talk to him as a group the next day.
At that time, the coach listens, talks about Terrance's situation, admits he
was not thinking clearly, and asks the team how they can help get Terrance
back on the right track, since what Victor saw as his efforts to do so did
not work well for the team or for Terrance.

Their talk in the hotel room makes clear the rules of play and of social
interaction around which the team moves, and their awareness of one of
the key motivations for their hard work on the team—keeping their grades
up and winning scholarships to college. Throughout their talk, echoes of
the coach's own words, as well as ways of talking, shape their language
and provide chunks of specific discourse. Like their coach, they use an
abundance of hypotheticals (if-then constructions), latch their speech in
cohesive ways from one statement to the other, with members completing
each other's sentences, and recite rules for specific playing situations. They
illustrate their understanding about the game of basketball in the past
decade (heavily influenced by the style of Magic Johnson's playing): assist,
assist, assist, and don't try to be a lone star on the court. Throughout their

conversation, they announce Terrance's violation of this rule. "He a star." "Yeah, he a star."

Distressed about their sense of team letdown and disappointed by their loss, the boys nevertheless remain within the discourse model and rule-governing frame of their coach and the youth organization.[5] Here the effects of modeling—of both linguistic and mental strategies for problem solving—show up. Their team membership has enabled them to develop a framework within which to operate as they work out ways both to take care of immediate rule infractions (even by the highest-ranking authority of the group—the coach and Terrance, someone they all admit is indeed a good player) and to move beyond the situation to some resolution for benefit to the group. Though they realize they cannot recoup their opportunity to win more games in this particular tournament, they want to resolve the issue because of their expectation of clarity and consistency in rules.

The norms of behavior and talk that team members have learned since they joined the Dynamos give them the sufficient self-confidence, self-efficacy, *and* appropriate discourse to handle such situations. The redundancy of displays of problem solving through and with language within a framework of rules builds a sense of moral code as well as sets of rules that should not be broken by members of the community. Like their older neighbors in years past who kept an eye out for youngsters who broke neighborhood rules, these team members now watch out for rule breakers and call them up short. Their respect for that code and for Victor's role in incorporating them into it does not diminish their expectations of respect: know the rules and play by them.

Finding Discipline in Rules and Models

Many of these young men reported that playing with the Dynamos had meant the difference for them between dropping out of school to enter gang and criminal activity and having some hope for a future. Few had within their own families adult males with whom they engaged in frequent and sustained activities that also included extensive talk about rules, norms, values, and future consequences. Most had been either mediocre or marginal within school performance before joining the team, and they saw a direct correlation between their life on the team and being with Victor and their continuation and improvement in school.

The players' complaints about Victor in the episodes reported above do not contradict their assurance that Victor is out to help them in the codes and rules of their comembership. On many occasions, players talked of Victor as their father and chief supporter. They spoke of him most consistently as the one who saw to it that they knew what was right and wrong and "stayed right." The following excerpts from several conversations the boys had with each other and with our fieldworkers indicate their overall view of Victor and of their relationship with him.

> J: Yeah, he do a lot for us to try to get us to go out of town [to play in tournaments].
> K: It's hard for him. He's a vice principal, too.
> M: He gets somethin' too. He like get around, you know, he like helps people=
> J: =He, I think he figure that if, I think he figure that if he helps us, it'll help *us.* Cuz, he, if he help us, it'll help us. See, like, if he wasn't here, you [*turning to another player*] probably wouldn't—I mean, it'd be bad. I think I'd be bad
> M: Yeah, but sometime you don't do things, but somethin' goes wrong, and then one, it's like you do somethin' wrong, it make him feel bad, cuz he figure he put all this time and effort into helpin' us and=
> J: =and this what we givin' him back.

The boys sometimes talk about what they've learned from Victor besides basketball:

> J: Communicate. He tells us to go and talk to our teachers. "You're a man, do it yourself."
> G: Mainly he just, Cage he jus', he just stay on your case. Like, see, like, what, you were on the honor roll last markin' period. I was on the honor roll last markin' period. One of you all [*looking around at other players*].
> M: Fred.
> J: Fred, you were on the honor roll. Was you on it third? See, and I wasn't on it third. Now he on our case. He on our case tough.
> J: Every time Cage he /gotta make a little remark
> G: /Gotta make a little joke. See, he so mad that you just gotta prove to him that you gotta go get these, get back these good grades, see?
> M: It works.
> J: Oh, it worked. As much as he talk about it, you would go to class everyday. Even on the half of a day, you'll be ready to go to them classes.

The boys go on to recount all the ways that Victor finds to surprise and reward them. At banquets, he'll announce grade-point averages and give out awards for grades as well as for basketball achievements. He will challenge the older guys to help the younger team members get money by selling candy to help them go out of town on a trip.

> *J:* Is' one big team, but we just=
> *G:* =It's like just, really one big family. We help each other out, you know, it's just different teams.
> *M:* Cage help a lot that way. I mean, uh=
> *J:* =He'll stay up all night to write a letter of proposal to somebody, to get us some money to go out of town and do some things. And then they'll send us some money and then=
> *J:* =And then we'll be on our way.

The boys elaborate on how Victor works with them in ways that differ from the help their school coaches offer.

> *J:* He [Victor] makes sure that, he tries to make sure that my grades are accurate, he does more, he keeps in touch with my family and he just helps more.
> *M:* He told me where you could have fun and be smart at the same time, you know?
> *G:* If we needed help with our homework or something, we could bring it in and he'll help us out.

To this last point, another adds, "Right, and you know what? He'll try to find something for us to help us out." Another offers a specific: "Yeah, he'll send you to basketball camp for four days. . . . he like a older brother or uncle, that he keep in touch with the family, like I said, and he keep in touch with xxx and make sure our grades are up."

Elaborations of this dual theme of "being there for you" and "knowing what you're up to" permeate the boys' talk about Victor, characterizing him as coach, father, mother, brother, sister.

> *R:* He makes sure we don't fall into the wrong hands and=
> *D:* And when we *were* goin' the wrong way, he put us back to the *right* way, told us what we should be doin', what we should get, what we should—where everything needs to be.
> *P:* He would talk to us, he would talk to us, he would know when something ain't right, and he would individually talk to us, team talk to us, however he you know felt like doin' it.

One interchange indicates how Victor gets the boys to do "what's right":

> *F:* And I mean, he didn't—he didn't try to force us to do anything—

> *J:* =He would just ask=
> *F:* =He'll just say it in such a way that it sounded right, you
>   couldn't do nothin' but what he said, cuz=
> *J:* =It was the right thing=
> *F:* =It was the right way, you know?
> *C:* He was always checkin' up on us cuz as soon as we got on=
> *G:* =He would call us all the time.

These views of the team members about their sense of family and the role of rules in giving them a sense of place and of having predictable structures in which to move echo those expressed by Victor himself.

A man who never had any black teachers until he went to college, Victor decided early in his life to become a teacher. The creativity of teaching attracted him and the possibility of having extended contact with young people led him to expand his teaching day into the afternoons, evenings, and weekends by coaching a neighborhood-based team. Reluctant to talk about anything other than game strategies and ways he tries to link the boys with college teams, Victor opens up rarely about his reasons for forming the team and his role with the young men. When he does so, he explains:

> I think they think of the team as a family, or a gang. I really do, because they really are close knit. I think gangs and our team are both the same. A gang is like a surrogate family, for the family involved in it. But the only reason why I say gangs is because that's what they're used to. I mean, they more closely relate to a gang than most of 'em do to a family. I mean, let's face it. So it's like a "nice" gang. You know what I mean: it's like the Boy Scouts or something. And they stick together. We had a really raunchy incident out of town in Phoenix where some racial slurs were thrown and caught 'em off guard. And they surprised me. They reacted real well, because I thought they were gonna fall apart. I think they'd never had that happen to 'em. . . . And it was good for 'em. But I mean, they learned a lot.

Victor once said of his own style of interacting with the boys, "I set some rules they have to meet. We only have two rules—you know: go to school and stay outta trouble." These overarching rules beyond those of the game or immediate task at hand center the key function of the team—maintaining group cohesion within a working/learning environment that will help them earn their way into college. Though no one can mandate or govern by hard and fast rules the achievement of group bonding, youth organizations such as those headed by Victor make developing into a responsible member of a group involved in performance and production of the highest quality the youngsters' reason for being. They do so by creating an atmosphere in which they make clear that members of the group will not differentiate themselves through competition in highly specifiable skills (for example, playing forward). Instead, members will focus their differentiations within the framework of team accomplishment and planning and through communication strategies that uphold the team's rules, goals, and ideals of achievement.

Development in Contradictions

Victor and the Dynamos, like other effective youth organizations, as well as gangs, have created a family context and a community of strong moral rules and norms of behaving in the void of family and neighborhood as traditionally conceived. Their immersion in first- and second-level rules—and their ability to handle adult contradictions of these—ensure both their critical take on the organizations and leaders around them and a sustained sense of self. A breach of rule by a beloved coach enables them to step back, albeit reluctantly, take stock of who they are as a group, and plan what they must do to go forward as a team. Self-efficacy in a range of discourse situations, as well as their experiences of success as a respected and winning team in their region, allow them to develop beyond the immediacy of contradictory behavior by adult leaders.

We have talked here of a male-only team. What of youth organizations that include only females? Though far fewer of these exist in inner cities (Hansot 1993), they show similar patterns of enabling development of youngsters' short-term planning horizons (Heath and McLaughlin 1994). A major difference, however, lies in the content of talk between adults and youth in planning, preparing, and practicing phases. All-female groups, except those that are exclusively athletic (such as softball teams), tend to slip far more often than coed or all-male groups into details related to gender-specific roles and interests. Topics range from ways to handle unwanted sexual advances from males to details of clothing and scheduling of social life and home responsibilities. Long-term planning talk within all-female youth organizations centers almost exclusively on these topics or celebrations of the group involving food and social entertainment.

Male groups and coed youth organizations talk about an array of short-term planning needs, as well as abstract nongendered topics such as filling out a job application, handling an interview, finding the best price for the team on airline travel, or planning the team budget for an upcoming trip. All-female organizations involve less travel and have fewer citywide associations with groups such as employment services and GED programs.

Hence the topics that adult leaders address center primarily in the here and now or on tasks and problems associated with traditional female roles as caregivers for children and managers of households.

A Look Forward

This essay has looked at organizational structures, adult philosophies of activities and planning, and language development for inner-city youth organizations and one all-male African-American basketball team. This little universe uses symbol systems—particularly oral and written language—to socialize youth to a sense of place with a keen notion of the role of rules and ways of planning and talking about relations between rule setting and rule breaking. This close look at the Dynamos' language, especially around the matter of rules, illustrates how important symbolic creations of place ("knowing where to stand") can be to young people. Theirs is not a learned helplessness, as the derivative culture-of-poverty case studies of individuals would have us believe, but learned *helpfulness* for themselves and the groups they form in their adaptation of old and familiar structures.[6]

The macrostructural features of effective youth organizations of the inner city allow youth to recreate there a framework that emulates their idea of intimate stable productive families. These youth organizations are "natural experiments" that allow the individuals who self-select into membership to internalize "executive control" in a social setting (Brown and Reeve 1987). Appropriate discourse to use this control surrounds activities that lead the boys to question, elaborate, offer premises and supporting evidence, and revise arguments in their path toward identifying and solving problems. Blaming, reacting impulsively, ignoring history and current context, and turning disappointment to destructive ends do not exhibit the self-regulation and group allegiance Victor has modeled and explicated. Moreover, the young men have had ample opportunity to practice such executive control before several types of audiences and within a variety of circumstances, both local and distant.[7]

Since the organizations involve the youngsters for many hours each week (and our audiotapes and fieldnotes captured the youngsters during most of these hours), it is highly unlikely that the youngsters came into the organizations habituated into the linguistic and planning skills they began to exhibit usually by the third week of practice. Certainly, they had the basic syntactic structures within their grammars, and they knew the appropriate vocabulary. Missing were habits of articulating short-term planning horizons and a sense of how the metacognitive and metalinguistic challenges from Victor and older members would transform their own self-regulation and their ability to express plans and problem-solving processes within the group. Their roles in academic study, basketball practice and tournaments, and participation in managing the team and its affairs put them in the center of *doing* and *thinking* for themselves and the group. Within the frame of team goals, their talk in the crisis of rules broken by their coach illustrates their ability to transfer their developed sense of place and responsibility from a leader-dominated situation to one created and controlled by them.

Understanding youth development—and particularly the elusive matter of the locus of control for an individual and a group—requires a mixture of methods and continued efforts to talk across methods, discipline borders, and settings. Those who would understand human development stand to gain much from moving away from individuals as units of analysis to consider group contexts and task environments that depend on carrying distributed knowledge, shared skills, and discourse patterns through a project over a period of time. Needed is more attention to youth in settings they choose and their patterns of microinteractions in concert with certain governing organizational structures.[8]

Within inner cities, as well as in many societies around the world, children and young people move, more often than not, in units separate from those that society considers ideal or age appropriate. Many young people not only care for their siblings as surrogate parents, but they also bear their own children earlier than in past decades. They often cannot wait for adults to give them jobs; they must go out and make or find their own jobs, often in the illicit worlds of prostitution, drugs, or theft. Reasons for early sexual, drug-related, and criminal experiences became evident in the 1980s, when groups such as the Children's Defense Fund and epidemiological studies from the National Institute of Mental Health documented the extent of drug addiction and AIDS infection among *parents* in their twenties and thirties. Economists reported both the increase in single-parent families and those in which both parents worked. School officials complained that students increasingly reported that they were absent because they had to care for younger siblings left to their charge when parents were either working or incapable of caring for them. On the streets and in public gathering places for the young, older siblings frequently were shadowed by their younger counterparts.

Both strategically and substantively, scholars of inner-city life for youth need to move away from individual case studies and research that focuses only on ways that families do or do not nurture and socialize their children. Instead, children and youth within peer contexts merit close scrutiny of the ways they achieve a sense of place for themselves in particular situations and with certain kinds of planning. Despite the violence, drugs, crime, alcohol, disease, poverty, and lack of local resources there, the inner city is their *home* and young people do find ways to adapt or to find adaptive niches in which they gain experience with mainstream organizations' structures and norms. To remove young people—either psychologically or physically—from environments that may not be "good" for their development is not possible except on a case-by-case basis. What effective youth organizations in these settings have managed to do is to provide micro and macro contexts for the development of adaptive strategies by individuals engaged in a long-term task in a familylike group. Here youth practice and talk about the social, linguistic, and mental habits they need to bridge their different worlds. Here they find *place*—both mentally and physically—to prepare them for adaptation.

Notes

1. Beatrice and John Whiting, beginning with their study of children in six cultures published in 1963 and continuing with both in-depth analyses in Kenyan societies and periodic returns to their comparative data (1975; Whiting and Edwards 1988), have been a major exception among anthropologists in their careful attention to young children and the worlds they create for themselves. Other ethnographers consider children in relation to themes not directly related to childhood but to contexts and tasks created by adults. For example, Wylie (1957), describing life in a French village, devotes separate chapters to infancy, school, and adolescence, as well as to early adulthood. More recent anthropologists look at development of older children with regard to particular roles in reciprocal exchanges and caregiving (Schieffelin 1990), family adaptation in refugee camps (Long 1993), as caregivers and economic resources (Scheper-Hughes, 1992), and as independent groups taking up a social life outside that of their biological families (Wulff 1988). Hundreds of studies in the anthropology of education describe learning processes and environments of children, with an eye to information and skills transmitted by formal schooling. The most sustained work in the final decades of the twentieth century focused on ethnographic studies of children has come from the Norwegian Centre for Child Research (Berentzen 1989).

2. Data come from studies carried out between 1988 and 1993 by Heath and McLaughlin among youth in community-based organizations of inner cities. Yet many of the general points made here with reference to youth development apply also to late-twentieth-century youth in other contexts, ranging from rural areas to midsized towns (populations 20–100,000). Research in these latter settings, begun in 1994 by Heath and McLaughlin to complement our earlier work in urban areas, points to several similarities in the patterns of adaptation and development described here for inner-city youth.

3. McLaughlin, Irby, and Langman (1994) detail work in these organizations and give voice to the youth there. For nearly three of the first five years in these sites, senior ethnographers Merita Irby and Juliet Langman participated, ob-

served, audiotaped, and interacted intensely on a regular basis with two dozen youth-based organizations. McLaughlin and Heath also attended performances and meetings, observed daily activities, and generally "hung out" around the organizations from time to time (Heath and McLaughlin 1993). The research was funded by the Spencer Foundation through a grant to Heath and McLaughlin. In 1993, additional funding from the Spencer Foundation provided the opportunity to extend contact with the youngsters in a selection of the inner-city communities, following the youth as they moved from the youth organizations into early adulthood and the search for regular employment.

4. Certain transcription conventions indicate linkages between utterances. Slashes mark the point at which the current talk is overlapped by other talk. The second speaker can sometimes cut off the prior speaker, but with the Dynamos, both speakers simply kept talking. Thus only overlaps, not interruptions, occurred. The equal sign signals a latching of talk where the second speaker immediately picks up, without hesitation, from the first speaker and continues talking. Sections of the recorded data that cannot be understood are marked by a series of x's. Italics indicate a portion of the utterance given special emphasis.

5. Heath and Langman (1993) analyze the register of coaching and elaborate the syntactic, lexical, and discursive features that keep the team positive, cooperative, and strongly oriented to analysis of hypothetical situations in which rules of play will apply.

6. Literature documenting strategies and personality types viewed as adaptive within African-American working-class communities include persistence, assertive problem solving, and patient planning in human relations. Authoritative—firm but supportive—human bondings receive high praise as "tough love" (Moses 1985; Spencer, Brookin, and Allen 1985).

7. The internalization of regulation by others has been a major focus of developmental psychologists studying mother-child dyads within a Vygotskian tradition (Wertsch 1991). But psychologists working with older individuals have also studied this transition from other-regulation to self-regulation. Dashiell (1935), for example, described six group activities that could lead an individual to internalize some form of executive control as part of personal cognition: (1) a difficulty motivating a sense of need, (2) a stepping back for analysis, (3) hypothesizing a possible solution, (4) projecting into the future implications and consequences, (5) launching a "trial balloon," and (6) accepting or denying feasibility of the launched proposal. Bales (1950) follows much the same pattern but within a discourse frame that overtly explicates the types of talk that might accompany each phase: asking for and giving information, clarifying ideas, describing, hypothesizing, comparing, proposing, and evaluating.

8. The assertion of this need is by no means a new one but one that has come with increasing frequency from psychologists themselves since the mid-1980s. Statements such as the following appear, however, far more often in edited volumes than in the mainline journals of the fields of developmental psychology, child development, and adolescent development: "We believe a main agenda for development psychologists is to expand their theories to account for environments in

which learning and development occur. As developmental psychologists, if we can come to understand: (a) self-directed learning, (b) sensitive methods of assessing readiness for change, (c) the dynamics of social situations that are successful in inducing change, and (d) supportive experimental contexts, we will have gone a long way in unraveling the complex interactions of learning and development" (Brown and Reeve 1987:216–17).

References

Baker-Sennett, J., E. Matusov, and B. Rogoff. 1993. "Planning as Developmental Process." In *Advances in Child Development and Behavior.* Vol. 24. Ed. H. W. Reese, 253–81. New York: Academic Press.

Bales, R. F. 1950. *Interaction Process Analysis: A Method for The Study of Small Groups.* Cambridge, Mass.: Addison-Wesley.

Berentzen, S., ed. 1989. *Ethnographic Approaches to Children's Worlds and Peer Cultures.* Trondheim, Norway: Norwegian Centre for Child Research.

Brown, A. L., and R. A. Reeve. 1987. "Bandwidths of Competence: The Role of Supportive Contexts in Learning and Development." In *Development and Learning: Conflict or Congruence?* Ed. L. S. Liben, 173–223. Hillsdale, N.J.: Lawrence Erlbaum Associates.

Dashiell, J. R. 1935. "Experimental Studies of the Influence of Social Situations on the Behavior of Individual Human Adults." In *Handbook of Social Psychology.* Vol. 2. Ed. C. Murchison, 1097–1158. Worcester, Mass.: Clark University Press.

Flax, J. 1987. "Postmodernism and Gender Relations in Feminist Theory." *Signs* 12: 621–43.

Griffin, C. 1993. *Representation of Youth: The Study of Youth and Adolescence in Britain and America.* Cambridge: Polity Press.

Hansot, E. 1993. "Misperceptions of Gender and Youth." In *Identity and Inner-City Youth: Beyond Ethnicity and Gender.* Ed. S. B. Heath and M. W. McLaughlin, 196–209. New York: Teachers College Press.

Heath, S. B., and J. Langman. 1994. "Shared Thinking and the Register of Coaching." In *Sociolinguistic Perspectives on Register.* Ed. D. Biber and E. Finegan, 82–105. Oxford: Oxford University Press.

Heath, S. B., and M. W. McLaughlin. 1991. "Community Organizations as Family." *Phi Delta Kappan,* 623–27.

———, eds. 1993. *Identity and Inner-City Youth: Beyond Ethnicity and Gender.* New York: Teachers College Press.

———. 1994. "Learning for Anything Everyday." *Journal of Curriculum Studies* 26: 471–89.

Irby, M. A., M. W. McLaughlin. 1990. "When Is a Gang Not a Gang? When It's a Tumbling Team." *Future Choices: Toward a National Youth Policy* 2: 31–40.

Long, L. D. 1993. *Ban Vinai: The Refugee Camp.* New York: Columbia University Press.

McLaughlin, M. W., M. A. Irby, and J. Langman. 1994. *Urban Sanctuaries: Neigh-*

borhood Organizations in the Lives and Futures of Inner-City Youth. San Francisco: Jossey-Bass.

Moses, E. G. 1985. "Advantages of Being Disadvantaged: A Paradox." *Journal of Negro Education* 54: 333–43.

Rogoff, B. 1982. "Integrating Context and Cognitive Development." In *Advances in Developmental Psychology.* Vol. 2. Ed. M. E. Lamb and A. L. Brown, 125–70. Hillsdale, N.J.: Erlbaum.

Rogoff, B., J. Baker-Sennett, and E. Matusov. 1995. "Considering the Concept of Planning." In *Future-Oriented Processes.* Ed. M. Haith, J. Benson, B. Pennington, and R. Roberts, 353–73. Chicago: University of Chicago Press.

Scheper-Hughes, N. 1992. *Death without Weeping: The Violence of Everyday Life in Brazil.* Berkeley: University of California Press.

Schieffelin, B. B. 1990. *The Give and Take of Everyday Life: Language Socialization of Kaluli Children.* Cambridge: Cambridge University Press.

Spencer, M., G. Brookin, and W. Allen, eds. 1985. *The Social and Affective Development of Black Children.* Hillsdale, N.J.: Lawrence Erlbaum.

Spindler, G. D. 1974. *Education and Cultural Process: Toward an Anthropology of Education.* New York: Holt, Rinehart, and Winston.

———. 1982. *Doing the Ethnography of Schooling: Educational Anthropology in Action.* New York: Holt, Rinehart, and Winston.

Van Gennep, A. 1960. *The Rites of Passage.* Chicago: University of Chicago Press.

Vigil, D. 1993. "Gangs, Social Control, and Ethnicity: Ways to Redirect." In *Identity and Inner-City Youth.* Ed. S. B. Heath and M. W. McLaughlin, 94–119. New York: Teachers College Press.

Wertsch, J. V. 1991. *Voices of the Mind: A Sociocultural Approach to Mediated Action.* Cambridge, Mass.: Harvard University Press.

Whiting, B. B., ed. 1963. *Six Cultures: Studies of Child Rearing.* New York: Wiley.

Whiting, B. B., and C. P. Edwards. 1988. *Children of Different Worlds: The Formation of Social Behavior.* Cambridge, Mass.: Harvard University Press.

Whiting, B. B., and J. W. M. Whiting. 1975. *Children of Six Cultures: A Psychocultural Analysis.* Cambridge, Mass.: Harvard University Press.

Wulff, H. 1988. *Twenty Girls: Growing Up, Ethnicity and Excitement in a South London Microculture.* Stockholm, Sweden: Stockholm Studies in Social Anthropology.

Wylie, L. 1957. *Village in the Vaucluse: An Account of Life in a French Village.* New York: Harper Colophon.

12 Role-Relationship Models: A Person-Schematic Method for Inferring Beliefs about Identity and Social Action

MARDI J. HOROWITZ, CHARLES STINSON, AND CONSTANCE MILBRATH

Ethnographic methods in anthropology are sometimes said to be based upon a core concept of culture as enduring through knowledge structures. This concept is also core to clinical studies of personality configurations in terms of meanings about self and relationships with others. Person schemas theory and related methods, such as formulation of role relationship models, are pertinent across the psychological and social disciplines.

From a psychological, psychiatric, and psychoanalytic perspective the issues central to this domain concern how individual character preserves socially transmitted and learned meaning structures in relation to motivations and emotional states. Methods have been evolved that can describe enduring conflicts about self, identity, and affiliational meaning structures such as those in various types of attachments in a relationship and bonds to institutions. These methods have addressed the complexity of layers of intentionality and conflicts between the meanings and goals of various layers. For this reason, some methods for study of character in psychology and psychiatry may be useful additions to ethnographic methodology.

The theoretical construct of person schemas has recently become important in anthropology as well as in psychology and psychiatry (D'Andrade 1991). Cognitive anthropologists have proposed a theory which focuses upon understanding how shared schemas of roles and practices are passed on to individuals of succeeding generations by verbal and nonverbal, explicit and implicit communications within social groups. These schemas are important whether or not they are consciously accessible because they inform the individual about how to behave and how to evaluate the behaviors of others (D'Andrade 1991).

In this chapter we will use *schemas* as the modern plural of *schema* rather than the classical *schemata.* Person schemas theory, shared across disciplines and grounded in a common language derived from modern cognitive and developmental psychological sciences, can contain issues of culture conflict and personal identity conflicts in ways that solve problems recognized when earlier psychoanalytic id and ego psychological theories were used as the source of terms and constructs in some areas of anthropological investigation.

Role and Status

Status-oriented relationships within an ethnic group are schematized within that group or within its wider social context. Status structures of role provide a rank ordering of the relative power positions of each role in a group structure. Friction and trouble are reduced to the extent that these meanings are shared by individuals and rules are followed in expectable ways. Pride of adherence to rules and stigmatization of people or subgroups who break rules is a prepared ground because the meaning structure, a kind of person schematization, endures.

Another aspect of status is the prepared ground of how value judgements will be made in an ethnic group (Ridgeway and Walker 1995). Value priorities are also schematized, and the relative weights assigned to items in a hierarchy of values will also effect social and individual choices. The stories, practices, roads, buildings, and transactive memories of an ethnic group preserve the relative prestige within value schemas and also continue both social role structure and some conflicts in cultures. The meaning structure within such forms will, in the context of perception of the forms, activate complementary meaning structures within the minds of individuals (Wegner 1987). We can, as scientists, compare the schemas of persons in a cultural matrix with the schemas of persons in the mind of individuals. We can also examine the degree of sharing and conflict, as well as address the big question of intraperson-extraperson transmissions of defined role and identity. Intrapersonal motives probably affect ethnic roles and ethnic roles guide intrapersonal motives.

Conflict can mar the harmonious surface of some states of ethnic group functioning. The conflict is between contradictory views of role structure and relative values of roles (Bales 1950; D'Andrade 1991; Shweder 1991). In cognitive-psychodynamic clinical investigative methods we have focused particularly on how to clarify such conflicts (Horowitz 1988b, 1991). The aim is to clarify contradictions and discrepancies rather than to reduce meaning to a single, dominant personality attribute of personal role, value, or intention. The methods evolved for formulating dilemmas of identity and social affiliation may be especially useful in ethnographic situations where there is disharmony in what belief structures about persons are shared across group members. A graphic format may be necessary for clarifying the complexity of conflicting roles and values about social practices and individual motives. While it would be easier to look for a unifying main theme and to regard contradictory meanings as "noise" in the research methodology, the result would be too reductionistic.

The Evidence Studied

The starting points of looking for information are stories, narratives, and observations of behavior. The talk can be transcribed for repeated review, and the interactions videotaped. The videotaped records can be sampled for content analyses of nonverbal patterns and used to inform scientists about how to reinterpret what was said. This is the basis for the kind of clinically derived methodology to be described in this chapter.

Such records are voluminous but they can be reduced to salient portions by clearly defining the meaningful categories in order to sift out other important but overwhelming complexities of information. A theory of schemas concerning the linkages of roles between self and other provides the most relevant categories for this task. This will be discussed in terms of models of role relationships in what follows.

As a first example of what is meant, let us consider an ethnic group that emphasizes socially the importance of self-sacrificing mothers. What happens in the transmission of valuing such a role as societal person schemas are transmitted to a mother, and a mother teaches a child by precept and example?

A child will tend to identify with the mothering figure as well as learn its own reciprocal role. Learning roles through identification might include learning to value altruism, restraint of self-centered greed, and how to improve the well-being of others and gain pride in caretaking. Reciprocal role learning might also occur and lead toward values which appear opposite to those of the mother. The child might learn to bank on the mother's self-sacrifice and may learn to feel very special, entitled, and grand. Practices of imperiously demanding power, "love," and possessions may become habitual and automatic rather than chosen as appropriate to situations.

Any child of a self-sacrificing mother in the usual American context may learn both how to be self-sacrificing and self-demanding of attention. Which polarity of this set of roles is more likely to organize a state of behavior depends on many codetermining factors. One of these is the mother's states of mind. Is she always self-sacrificing, or does she have state cycles of sacrifice followed by demands of concern for her suffering self-deprivations? If it's the latter, is that regarded as a normal payback and power shift or a culturally repulsive form of masochism and guilt provocation? Is there a culture-based temporal or life-cycle change in roles so that one puts in a decade of self-sacrifice and then can rightly expect to get a decade of being entitled to being cared for (as described for some aspects of Japanese culture by Margaret Lock in this volume)? What if ethnic "rules" shift by the time of that second decade? Will the self-sacrificing mother feel cheated by the child, or society? Perhaps she will then develop symptomatic psychosomatic responses as in a case reported by Lock (an example to be examined in more detail as an example of the role relationship models method, later in this chapter).

The attitudes of mother, child, surrounding family, extended family, and friends, as well as secondary institutions such as schools and tertiary institutions such as governments, will all influence the mood and well-being of the child as the child becomes a parent and the various identificatory and reciprocal roles are enacted. This is an aspect of ethnic character structure that may be mapped in terms of self and other schemas by using methods derived from clinical character analyses. These methods will be described after a consideration of relevant background theory and research.

Background: Research in Psychotherapy Contexts

Psychotherapy has as one of its tasks the identification of individual personal meaning within various contexts, such as different social settings, interpersonal situations, and cognitive reflections upon self. The psychotherapist assumes a double role of participant and observer, participating in the therapeutic process but also assuming ethnographer-like roles in gathering and understanding information about personal meanings in social contexts. More recently, psychotherapy researchers have developed more robust methods for gathering, organizing, structurally representing, and communicating this information about personal meaning (Luborsky 1977; Horowitz 1979, 1991). In addition to growing importance in empirical clinical science, these theoretical and methodological tools have potential for other domains; they are important to understanding individuals who, for whatever reasons, have maladaptive patterns in exchanges with others and/or who have contradictory role concepts within their own sense of personal identity.

The individual subject in psychotherapy expects to frankly disclose personal information to the therapist, to examine this information with the aid of the therapist's interpretations, and to change some problems of the self or the world as a result. The therapist is an active participant in the endeavor of therapy, with the expectation of effecting changes in the personal meaning structures of the subject. How this actually takes place may not be entirely known to either party, but study of change processes, where meanings are sometimes not consciously explicit, is a frontier of clinical research (Horowitz 1989; Horowitz, Weinshel, and Kernberg 1993). Recorded therapies, reliable inferences, and formulation methods are essential to such research efforts (Horowitz, Stinson et al. 1993; Stinson and Horowitz 1993). Central variables include formulations about enduring, but not necessarily accurate, views of self and others.

In the process of subjectively and objectively understanding the existing meaning structures of the subject, the therapist and patient construct a dyadic microworld of self and other. Tenets of psychodynamic theory hold that interpersonal processes of this microworld mirror important features of the intra- and interpersonal macroworld of the patient's life: through transference the client/patient tends to automatically attribute to the therapist, rightly or wrongly, features from relationships with significant others. The therapist observes and may comment on how these attributions affect their dyadic relationship. Similarly, the therapist observes his or her own countertransference feelings elicited in working with the client/patient and assesses how such emotional responses may affect other individuals who interact with the client/patient.

Most importantly, the therapist does not report observations to external observers, but selectively reports back to the patient—sometimes in a manner that seeks confirmation of interpretations, but often in a manner that is expected to challenge or test beliefs and to bring about change. In the process, the therapist attempts to cause the patient to develop new ways of thinking and acting; often times these changes in ways of thinking are expected to become self-sustaining (for example, the assumption of an increasingly mature self-analytic stance and the learning of new integrations of schemas of self and social relationships).

The interview and intervention practices of psychotherapy are designed to draw forth and understand as fully as possible the beliefs, feelings, and behavioral practices of the individual. Making sense of the information gathered is challenging. Recent psychotherapy research, especially work bridging psychodynamic theory with schema theory of cognitive science (Horowitz 1988, 1991; Singer and Salovey 1991) allows description of individual's beliefs and interaction patterns (including manifestations in transference and countertransference) as schemas, or active structures of knowledge and information (Knapp 1991; Luborsky 1991).

This area of theoretical work has also led to promising methods for systematic detection and reporting of these information structures. We outline in this work methods for describing person schemas, interactions of person schemas in role-relationship models (RRMs), and interactions of multiple schemas in the form of role-relationship model configurations

(RRMCs). Such methods promise empirical reliability and validity in the examination of personal meaning in psychotherapy research, and will likely be useful as well for formatting beliefs about role relationships in groups in the context of ethnographic research.

Background: The Person-Schema Construct in Understanding Personality

Schema theory asserts that an individual's knowledge is organized in knowledge structures called schemas (Bartlett 1932). Thus, although "knowledge" in schemas may include facts used in discursive thought and language ("The capital of Texas is Austin"), schemas are also thought to organize information in all aspects of mentally mediated processes including perception, thought, emotion, and practiced complex motor behaviors (Mandler 1984). Typically, schemas are defined as hierarchically organized general knowledge structures that are abstracted from past experiences and that guide current processing of information (Singer and Salovey 1991). There are clear adaptive advantages to this type of information processing in terms of efficiency and speed of information processing and recall.

New information can be quickly processed by assimilation into existing schematized frameworks. Missing information or gaps can be filled in from partial information because activating parts of a schema makes the whole accessible (Mandler 1984). Responses are also part of a schema. For example, affective responses to meeting a new individual who fits a social stereotype is organized as part of that stereotypic schema (Fiske 1982).

There is a price for such rapid information processing as accelerated by schemas. Overlearned habits can interfere with learning new ones (Hayes-Roth 1977) and selective attention, encoding, representation, and retrieval of information can result in information loss or distortions as new information is assimilated into existing schemas (Fiske and Linville 1980). There is also a strong bias toward ignoring or defending against disconfirming information (Langer and Abelson 1972; Markus 1977).

Examining such consequences of schema processing has led to proposals that self and relationship schemas can organize our states of mind (Horowitz 1989, 1991) and the availability and accessibility of our thought content (Fiske and Linville 1980; Higgins and Bargh 1987; Segal 1988). Schemas of persons, including schemas of self, enable recognition of individuals over time and prediction of expected behavioral actions. They also organize an individual's response patterns in interpersonal behavior. Person schemas thus organize key aspects of personality (Horowitz 1991).

Developmentally, each person forms person schemas as kinds of cognitive maps of social relations. An individual's schemas, therefore, are profoundly influenced by exact developmental experiences, by temperament, and by the personal historical context of the moment. Similar to Erikson's concept (1952) that development of identity involves evolution of various views of self, person-schema theory also holds that grown individuals have multiple person schemas of one's self as well as of other people, constituting a repertoire of multiple selves and role-relational interaction patterns with others (Horowitz 1979, 1988; Markus and Wurf 1986). Symbolic derivatives of these views in conscious representation function as "self-concepts" important in conscious attitudes, self-knowledge, and action plans involving the self. Any given social situation can activate different schema-organized states of mind, depending in part on which internal schemas have the best fit with the features of the social situation (Fiske 1982; Linville 1982).

An individual's various schemas of self and others may nest into a hierarchical structure that involves supraordinate and subordinate forms (Allport 1977; Piaget 1970; Horowitz and Zilberg 1983). Not all schemas are consistent or complete, and the overall assembly may contain contradictions. Discrepant representations may exist, such as differences in perception of one's body in different states of mind. Learning in the course of a person's development is theoretically viewed as both adding new conceptual meaning elements and also developing an integrated hierarchical structure by establishing linkages among subordinate, supraordinate, and other associated meaning elements. The result may be different kinds of subjective meaning systems and different complex emotional responses in different contexts and in different states of mind within a single individual (Horowitz, Fridhandler, and Stinson 1991).

Just as activation of a single schema functions in perceptual identity recognition, combinations of schemas are presumed to function dynamically as mental models for understanding and acting in socially complex situations. Knowledge of interpersonal behavior, for example, is thought to be represented in two or more person schemas and in scriptlike sequences of the expected flows of each person's actions (Horowitz 1989). These scripts for transactions include timing and quality of emotional expressions, physical actions, communications, and also critical evaluations (what is right, wrong, good, bad, pride-rewarded, shame-punished).

All these person schema features can be organized schematically into models of relationship roles. We call these role-relationship models. Any individual possesses multiple RRMs; some may be explicitly known, as with familiar interactions, and others may exist in potential, as in predictable interaction patterns with an individual or type of person one has heard a lot about but never actually met.

At any given time, one schema will be activated and dominant, perhaps a self-schema, a schema of other, or a supraordinate schema in the form of an RRM (including subordinate schemas both of self and of other). This dominant schema serves as an overall organizer of a given state of mind. Thus an individual has a repertoire of schemas for different states of mind, and these constitute aspects of his or her personality (Horowitz 1991).

Supraordinate schemas can subsume, and therefore contain, previously unresolved contradictions and conflicts among meaning elements (Horowitz and Zilberg 1983). One aspect of change in psychotherapy is development of such containment in a healthy ambivalence—softening forms of meaning. For example, the same act may have opposite valuations, sometimes viewed as good (safe and pleasurable) and at other times bad (dangerous and painful). A supraordinate schema may construct such views as "both good and bad" or "either good or bad." More complex knowledge structures capable of resolving conflicts and avoiding extreme position-taking are important in forming resilient social interactions and in flexibly adapting to stressor life events.

Person-schema theory predicts problematic deflections or perturbations in development of schemas of self and other in disorders of personality and in certain other forms of psychopathology. Problematic sequelae to traumas, found in some stress-response syndromes for example, include failure to establish schemas appropriate to changed situations (Horowitz 1990). Some personality disorders following childhood traumas involve dissociative isolation of identities or subschemas that would more adaptively be integrated into supraordinate schemas. Other disorders involve formation of schemas that avoid activities that lead to threat, but that actively interfere with activities to achieve objectively more adaptive goals (Horowitz 1992). The personality disorders as specified (still poorly and not necessarily validly) in the psychiatry nomenclature (DSM III and IV) include typologies based upon schemas that lead to disturbed interpersonal relationship patterns, dissociations, confusions, fragmentations, and resistances to identity development, and upon deficiencies in learning identity and attachment schemas during development.

Although clinicians make use of this sort of knowledge about an individual's patterns (whether or not explicitly using person-schema theory), there still remained a need for a means to infer, organize, and describe this role and identity information from recurrent statements in narrative and themes of observed action. Also needed in psychiatry was a means to structurally configure concepts of conflict, contradiction, or discrepancy among roles and transactions.

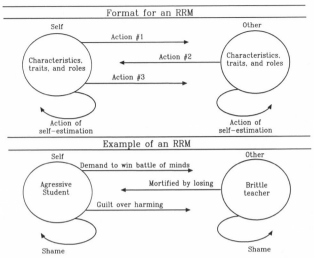

Figure 1.   A role-relationship model (Horowitz 1991).

Person Schemas, Role-Relationship Models, and Role-Relationship Model Configurations

Varied identities in different states of mind have been described by Federn (1952). Berne (1961) developed a generalized transactional schema for clinical case formulations, and Luborsky (1977) described a core conflictual relationship-theme method for inferring systematic conflicts in psychotherapy patients. Amplifying on such approaches, Horowitz developed a systematic format for describing role and transaction patterns in RRMs and applied it in descriptive longitudinal case studies (Horowitz et al. 1984; Horowitz 1987, 1988, 1989) to formulate interpersonal interactions of meaning, motivation, emotion, and defensive states. Indices of convergent validity (Horowitz 1989; Horowitz, Luborsky, and Popp 1991; Horowitz et al. 1994) and reliability (Eells et al.; Horowitz and Eells 1993) have been obtained. A specific RRM may contain various schematic elements such as those in figure 1.

The single RRM with the best fit to the social situation becomes activated, dominating other alternate, and perhaps contradictory, RRM schemas and consequently organizes perception, conceptualization, emotion, modeling current social transactions, and planning action. Both parties in a social transaction have such internal repertoires of meaning, and may not have the same working model of what is happening between them (fig. 2).

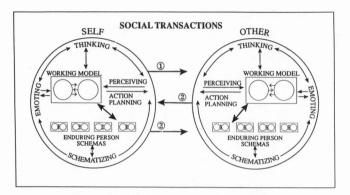

Figure 2.   Social transactions modeled within the mind (Horowitz 1991).

When roles conflict, defensive compromises may activate alternative identities and scripts of transactions. These alternative activation patterns may act to ward off dreaded emotional states or strife-ridden interpersonal transactions.

A general motive is to integrate diverse roles into a unified sense of personal identity, but reaching this goal is an ideal that even a healthy person can approximate only in some states of mind. Many people have internal conflicts about a significant relationship, such as that with a spouse, boss, or work subordinate. The systematic repetitive aspects of one such conflict can be inferred as multiple RRMs. Multiple RRMs can be systematically organized into a configuration, called an RRMC, as illustrated in figure 3.

An RRMC is organized as a set of quadrants around a central circle representing the overall self-organization. Within the central circle, multiple self-schemas are depicted with their roles, characteristics, traits, or attributes. Each of these self-concepts is an element of one or more related RRMs. The roles, characteristics, and attributes of others are depicted in the circles outside the overall self-organization.

The quadrant organization allows inference of motivational structure. The desired RRM, in the lower-right quadrant of the configuration, may relate to feared consequences of the initial desired acts of the self, and so lead to threat rather than pleasure. This dreaded RRM is in the lower-left quadrant. Thus the lower half of an RRMC often contains a wish-fear dilemma—the emotionally charged desired and dreaded RRMs around a given theme, such as a relationship or set of practices.

The top half of the RRMC contains RRMs that may be activated in order to ward off the dreaded consequences in a wish-fear dilemma, as embodied in the dreaded RRM. In other words, RRMs shown in the up-

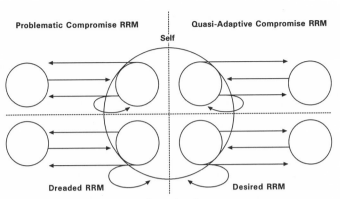

Figure 3.   Role-relationship models configuration format.

per half of the RRMC may be activated in order to form states of mind that ward off too dangerous, intensely negative, and out-of-control states of mind.

Despite a desire for a stable, continuing sense of a satisfactory identity and self-esteem, each individual is prone to certain problematic states of mind. These are represented in the upper-left quadrant of the RRMC in terms of maladaptive compromises. Since problems are often recognized first in a case, this is the "first read" position in the form of an RRMC. Quasi-adaptive compromises, represented in the upper-right quadrant, have less negative affect and symptomatology. Although quasi-adaptive in that these RRM are associated with states of lessened distress because the schemas serve to ward off dreaded anticipated consequences and because they may provide some satisfaction, the state organized by these person schemas is still a defensive compromise because it does not satisfy the individual's deeply desired goal.

Cycles of States

An RRMC can represent cycles of states as a person in a type of situation activates different RRM of the configuration. The RRMC provides a way of looking at contradictory behavior patterns based on cycles of activation of several organizing schemas of self and other role-taking. The RRMC structure represents state cycles in which the individual may shift identities as felt consciously as well as roles as perceived by others socially.

By engaging "too much" in pleasures, one might ignore important tasks, be unaware of major hazards, receive envy and disdain of others, or act in a sinful, socially condemned manner. Guilt, shame, and other circumstances wherein one's self-concept is endangered or diminished could result. If the person then shifts from a desired state to a state organized emotionally by dreaded roles, then he or she may cycle further into the role of the maladaptive compromise as the best available solution to reducing distress under the circumstances. This maladaptive compromise has untoward effects, which prompt the person, as he or she can manage it, to shift into the role for self of the quasi-adaptive compromise. This relatively comfortable state that often compromises the desired goals may be stable for some time. Eventually, however, the person desires to achieve deeper goals and may cycle back into activities that lead into the desired state. This shift begins the state cycle again, and again the person follows a repetitive, seemingly obligatory, and potentially maladaptive script.

Social Contexts

Social contexts offer an individual varied and even antithetical roles. Shift in social contexts can trigger shifts in state cycles of individuals. Pluralistic, urbanized societies are more likely to provide, even stimulate, conflicting roles. Cyclical state-shifting patterns may be more likely in such societies, especially in times of social flux.

For example, a woman could be criticized by feminist companions for behaving within homemaker roles praised by earlier generational cohorts in her family. Such identity conflicts, as enduring in subjective meaning structures, can be combined within RRMC formats. Configuration of role-relationship models, RRMC, depicts the association of even contradictory self-concepts and so can be used to specify conflicts and dilemmas. These discrepant views of self may be both intrapersonal and interpersonal. Specific self-concepts may contradict a personal ideal, a socially expected role, and personal values may conflict with social group expectations.

Method

RRMs and RRMCs may be derived from any of several types of observations, either live or recorded in various media (live interview, observation of session/interview/storytelling, videotapes, audiotapes, transcripts, session notes). Clinicians may find it useful to sketch perceived RRMs and RRMCs in understanding recent session material or to construct such models mentally during sessions. Such informal models are useful in communicating case material to consultants, colleagues, or trainees. More formally derived RRMs and RRMCs have better empirical utility in research, however, and may need to be derived with some mechanisms for achieving consensus or some metric of agreement and reliability. Horowitz and Eells (1993), for example, have described a reliability study in which independent and "blind" clinician judges successfully matched correct RRMCs to psychotherapy sessions of the patients for whom the RRMCs were formulated, as compared with matched appropriate control RRMCs. Likewise, Eells et al. (1995) described a reliability study in which two independent teams reliably formed similar RRMCs from the same transcripts of psychotherapy discourse. Horowitz et al. (1995) reported on RRMC validity: RRMCs from early sessions predicted process patterns more than a year later.

The general procedure involved selectively sifting through data to designate information pertinent to these categories of information: (1) attributes, roles, traits, and characteristics of the self; (2) attributes, roles, traits, and characteristics of others (sorted by the identities of these individuals or groups of others); (3) actions of self toward others or others toward self, noting especially (*a*) which actions initiate a transaction, (*b*) which actions are responses and reactions to preceding actions, (*c*) which actions and emotions are actually expressed and which are suppressed, stifled, or imagined; (4) real, expected, or imagined critical evaluations leading to important feelings or attitudes such as pride or shame, and such as evaluations of the self by the self (self-appraisals), of others by themselves, of the self by others, and of others by the self.

For each particular person (self or other) descriptors are then aggregated into subsets of similar meaning. Contradictory elements are sorted into different subsets. Description of some person as kind and generous will be in a different subset from a description of the same person as shrewd, malicious, and conniving. Investigators then select a synonymous word or phrase to label each relatively homogenous subset. That word or phrase is placed into the appropriate space in an RRM (that is, it becomes the descriptive label for the particular schema of a specific self or other object). In a like manner, similar actions and transactions are summarized in prototypic sequences between specific self and other objects, thereby completing the descriptions of one or more RRMs. Unless the source material is extremely limited, there are usually several RRMs, including some that seem contradictory.

These RRMs are then assembled into one or more RRMCs, sorting the transactions represented by each RRM into the one most appropriate quadrant, as shown in figure 3: desired, dreaded, problematic compromise, or quasi-adaptive compromise. The desired-quadrant RRMs are those with strongly positive emotionality; the dreaded-quadrant RRMs have highly undesired emotionality; the problematic-compromise-quadrant RRMs have mild or moderately undesired emotionality, and the quasi-adaptive-compromise-quadrant RRMs have moderately desired emotionality and only mildly undesired emotionality. Contradictions are thus represented by different RRMs within an RRMC.

Again, RRMs and RRMCs can be derived from several sources; one is transcribed discourse.

Derivation of RRMs and RRMCs from Psychotherapy Transcripts

Discourse describing interactions with the self and other are identified in the transcript; these may be narratives about specific events and interactions, or enactions of events within the interpersonal context of the session itself (for example, the subject may act with anticipation that the interviewer will be critical, or may indicate he or she found a neutral comment by the interviewer as condemning). The specific views of self and another are identified by highlighting or annotating sections of transcripts. Transaction sequences are then identified and may involve a reordering of spoken sequences. Imagined elements are designated as such to differentiate them from features found in stories about what really happened in the past.

It may help to use a mapping sentence: "subject" does toward "object," "object" does toward "subject." The sentence used for paraphrasing can be amplified for roles: "I, who am like this and that, did thus and so, to my husband, who is like this and that, and he responded by doing thus and so, and I then felt like this." One can take discourse and paraphrase it by such formats in order to clarify the key descriptions. This locates repetitions which are then summarized in RRMs. The RRMs that are repeated and related to specific relationship or type of attachment or role are then assembled into configurations of role relationship models using RRMC formats.

Here is an example of using a mapping sentence to paraphrase what is said. Suppose a person says this is about a new intimate relationship of the type they had with a now deceased husband, James:

> I went for a weekend with Sidney and it started out to be happy and exciting for me. Just when I wanted to enjoy how good I looked for the first time in a long time and what a fine man he really is, I suddenly thought of James. I felt, I don't know why, it seems so irrational, very, very badly. Like I was a cheater.

The paraphrase begins with the "I, who am," format like this: "I who am a cheater, felt bad about James." By implication, one might add that she views James as accusing her of cheating. The paraphrase also has: "I, who am a good-looking woman, was happy and excited with Sidney, who is a fine man."

The latter can go into a *desired* RRM, the former ("cheater") into a *dreaded* RRM. An approach-avoidance dilemma results in the cycle or sequence. It could be paraphrased as: "(Whenever) I, who am a good-looking woman, wanted to feel happy and excited with Sidney, who is a fine man, I, who was a wife to James, felt badly that I am cheating on James (who is in my mind yet alive although I know he is dead)."

As a result of activating this role relationship model of loving Sidney and so (as she imagines) hurting James, she enters a guilty-feeling state of mind. The roles of Sidney and James in this kind of dilemma are also reversible. She feels guilty toward Sidney if she retains her identity as faithful with and intimate to only James as in the following discourse. In reading the material below, the reader is invited to form a paraphrase and so a role relationship model as already illustrated above.

> For some reason I was thinking yesterday about what, how I would feel, I mean, if I could bring him [James] back, if I could go back and somehow turn back the clock and just back two years [before the death] and start over. But in order to do that would mean of course erasing Sidney and I mean honestly, I felt, yeah, I would still go back. I would still rather have that life than this life, and that, that didn't make me very happy either. I mean a little part of me felt relieved that I felt that way, but then I thought that's not very fair to Sidney. . . . But I still feel a little guilty that I, that I would go back if I could. . . . And maybe it's just that there's more time invested in that than what I have now. I don't know that I honestly loved James anymore than I love Sidney. I love Sidney a great deal. But you know James was, I don't know, James was a life, you know, James was everything to me. And I don't know Sidney and I are new enough, I guess that I could. That I would go back if I could. But in a way I guess I'm glad that it's a choice I don't have to make. It would be incredibly difficult to hurt Sidney, to leave him would be hard on everyone.

A paraphrase might simplify and select words, as follows: (1) "I, who was James's wife, would remain married to James and give up Sidney, a new man, who would be hurt, and then (2) I would feel guilty toward Sidney." This case example from Patricia (all names are fictitious) will be put into an RRMC later in this chapter, after more information on Patricia is presented.

In a similar manner RRMs and RRMCs may be derived directly from observation of video or audiotape. Observers note RRM elements and then proceed as above. Alternatively, testing procedures can be used to gather RRM and RRMC information by asking an individual to provide descriptors of various views of self and specific important others. An interviewer might use a structured technique to gather RRM and RRMC information. Issues related to various states or situations could be explored, asking, for example, "Can you describe the worst situations when you did things others felt were breaking important rules?" This approach can get information on extreme states that occur only rarely and may otherwise not be reported.

A structured format of asking for descriptors of self and others is useful in group studies. Various systems are used to ask each subject to first describe important relationships and then to give descriptors of role of each person. Several authors describe such methods in detail in a book edited by the first author. Benjamin and Friedrich (1991) and Horowitz (1991) described a coding system for social transactions (one that can be placed in RRM formats), and Kihlstrom and Cunningham (1991) describe a computer-assisted way of obtaining role descriptors.

Clinical Illustration of RRMC Use

This illustration was drawn from a combination of videotape and transcripts of case material involving Patricia, the young widow already mentioned who was on the brink of a new intimacy. What is appropriate mourning and what is appropriate regarding new relationships when recently widowed were important value questions that she wrestled with during her mourning process as she reschematized her beliefs about herself and others. Her social group's attitudes about widows were not exactly the same as her attitudes. During the course of therapy, it became apparent that she had several important self-concepts that seemed desired, dreaded, and alternative defensive compromises.

As illustrated in figure 4, she could feel good as a vibrant woman living a pleasurable and exciting life or she could be subject to remorse with a view of herself as a wife cheating on her deceased husband through a new relationship. She could view her doubt about whether to proceed into new intimacy as a kind of incompetency, or she could view herself as a very competent worker and caretaker who was now beyond sexual romance because of her widow status in society (an emotion-reducing compromise). These self-concepts gain more emotional-relational salience and the individual's motivations become more clear on assembling an RRMC format, as shown in figure 5.

Still more understanding of the complex personal meanings is obtained by observing when defensive control processes seem to be used and by noting what emotions these seem to stifle.

Convergent evidence supporting RRM and RRMC structures can be obtained by using formal content analyses of narratives, including both

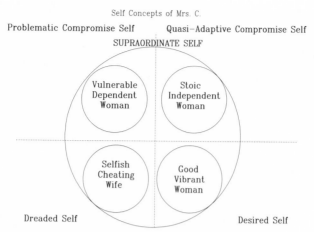

Figure 4.   Self-concepts of Patricia in the RRMC format.

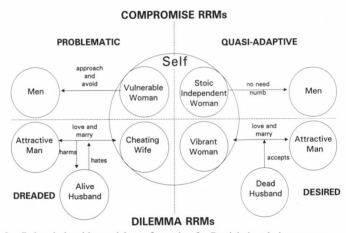

Figure 5.   Role-relationship models configuration for Patricia in relation to men.

judged ratings and computer text analyses (Horowitz, Milbrath et al. 1994; Horowitz, Stinson et al. 1993; Milbrath et al. 1995; Stinson, Horowitz, and Milbrath forthcoming; Stinson and Horowitz 1993).

Possible Application to Anthropology

Although RRMs and RRMCs are descriptive tools originally designed for use in psychotherapy research and practice and based on theoretical models that bridge psychodynamic theory and cognitive science, RRMs and RRMCs also hold promise for use in ethnography. Schematized organization of interpersonal and social knowledge can be inferred from witnessing behavioral patterns and from interviews in the field (Fiske 1982). RRM and RRMC formats can be used to depict desired and dreaded or "defensively safe" roles and repeated practices within a social group. RRM and RRMC formulations of a representative individual interacting with expected "Everyman-others" in specific socially expected roles and transactions could provide illuminating descriptions of persons who are in harmony or in conflict with beliefs of their ethnic peers (Agar 1986). An individual rejecting a social role of unquestioning obeisance to a parent, for example, might expect criticism from all others in the social group, even if there are others who also do not hold that belief. Conceivably, a particular social schema may actually exist in its pure form in none of the social group's members, but only in a collective and idealized sense. Similarly, these schemas may exist in forms superseding schemas of persons: these knowledge structures may be about different forms of deities, spirits, pluralities of "I" or "we" (Boddy 1989; Shweder 1991). All of these forms of social schemas can strengthen or weaken an individual's conscious sense of identity and can actuate different elements in that individual's repertoire of multiple possible selves. In this way frequent identity conflict in an ethnic group could be systematically described.

As a further example of applying RRMs and RRMCs to organize and understand nonpsychiatric material, we examined the transcript excerpts of an interview with a woman about her experiences within her family reproduced below in chapter 16. In that chapter, Lock describes this as a representative Japanese woman who is coping with a dilemma of competing roles: her potential for feeling like an unsatisfied, oppressed woman versus being a quiet, satisfied caretaker. The desired RRM of this woman, shown in figure 6, is that she would feel good about being a quiet caretaker working hard for a loving family who admire her now and who will gradually elevate her status in the future. She has to do what she can to maintain this desired RRM of working hard and feeling admired by her family because she dreads the consequences of stopping work. In that dreaded RRM, shown in figure 6, she would be seen as a selfish woman deserving shame.

However, she also has concerns about experiencing herself as an oppressed woman in relation to an unappreciative family, represented in the problematic quadrant in figure 6. She suppresses socially unacceptable angry feelings that her hard work is not appreciated enough, and instead somatizes and develops headaches. It is acceptable for her to complain about these headaches; she may be exempted from some work because of

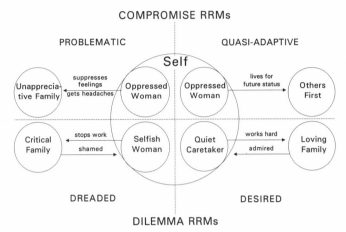

Figure 6.   Role-relationship modes configuration for the Japanese woman reported by Lock.

them, and may also receive more personal attention. In her more adaptive compromise, also in figure 6, she endures feelings of oppression because in the future she will achieve high status as an older woman who has been through the decades of hard work as a quiet caretaker.

Conclusion

Role-relationship models and configurations are part of a person-schematic method used in psychotherapy research. It is hoped that this theory and method will have some utility in ethnography. With these approaches, investigators can formulate organized personal knowledge structures that an individual holds about herself or himself, about other people, and about actual and possible interpersonal interactions. These models involve emotion, and help represent, explain, and predict state-related behavior changes, sequences, and cycles. Conflict and contradiction can be graphically represented in RRMs and RRMCs.

The key constructs that are "psychodynamic" in this method are (1) any individual may have a range of self-identities based on a repertoire of multiple—and even contradictory—self-concepts, (2) that these self-identities are embedded in schemas of relationship with others, and (3) that there may be defensive layering of enduring but possibly contradictory person schemas. It will be for anthropological investigators to determine the degree to which polarities of identity, contradictory role-relationship models, and habitual defensive styles of inhibiting one type of affiliation by activating an alternative are ethnically based, and if such concepts help clarify the more complex areas of how societies inform individuals how to behave and how to feel about their behavior.

References

Agar, M. H. 1986. *Speaking of Ethnography.* Beverly Hills, Calif.: Sage.

Allport, D. A. 1977. "On Knowing the Meaning of Words We Are Unable to Report: The Effects of Visual Masking." In *Attention and Performance.* Vol. 6. Ed. S. Dornie. London: Academic Press.

Bales, R. 1950. *Interaction Process Analysis.* Cambridge, Mass.: Addison-Wesley.

Bartlett, F. C. 1932. *Remembering: A study in Experimental and Social Psychology.* Cambridge: Cambridge University Press.

Benjamin, L. S., and F. J. Friedrich. 1991. "Contributions of Structural Analysis of Social Behavior (SASB) to the Bridge between Cognitive Science and a Science of Object Relations." In *Person Schemas and Maladaptive Interpersonal Patterns.* Ed. M. J. Horowitz, 379–412. Chicago: University of Chicago Press.

Berne, E. 1961. *Transactional Analysis in Psychotherapy.* New York: Grove Press.

Boddy, J. 1989. *Wombs and Alien Spirits.* Madison: University of Wisconsin Press.

D'Andrade, R. 1991. "The Identification of Schemas in Naturalistic Data." In *Person Schemas and Maladaptive Interpersonal Patterns.* Ed. M. J. Horowitz, 279–302. Chicago: University of Chicago Press.

Eells, T., M. J. Horowitz, J. Singer, P. Salovey, and D. Daigle. 1995. "The Role-Relationship Models Method: A Comparison of Independently Derived Case Formulations." *Psychotherapy Research* 5: 161–75.

Erikson, E. H. 1952. *Childhood and Society.* New York: Norton.

Federn, P. 1952. *Ego Psychology and the Psychoses.* New York: Basic Books.

Fiske, S. T. 1982. "Schema-Triggered Affect: Applications to Social Perception." In *Affect and Cognition: The Seventeenth Annual Carnegie Symposium on Cognition.* Ed. M. S. Clark and Fiske, 79–109. Hillsdale, N.J.: Erlbaum.

Fiske, S. T., and P. W. Linville. 1980. "What Does the Schema Concept Buy Us?" *Personality and Social Psychology Bulletin* 48: 839–52.

Hayes-Roth, B. 1977. "Evolution of Cognitive Structures and Processes." *Psychological Review* 84: 260–78.

Higgins, E. T., and J. A. Bargh. 1987. "Social Perception and Social Cognition." *Annual Review of Psychology* 38: 369–425.

Horowitz, M. J. 1979. *States of Mind: Configurational Analysis of Individual Psychology.* New York: Plenum Press.

———. 1987. *States of Mind: Configurational Analysis of Individual Psychology.* 2d ed. New York: Plenum Press.

———. 1988a. *Introduction to Psychodynamics: a New Synthesis.* New York: Basic Books.

———, ed. 1988b. *Psychodynamics and Cognition.* Chicago: University of Chicago Press.

———. 1989. "Relationship Schema Formulation: Role-Relationship Models and Intrapsychic Conflict." *Psychiatry* 52: 260–74.

————. 1990. "A Model of Mourning: Change in Schemas of Self and Others." *American Psychoanalytic Association* 38: 297–324.

————, ed. 1991. *Person Schemas and Maladaptive Interpersonal Patterns.* Chicago: University of Chicago Press.

————, ed. 1992. *Hysterical Personality Style and the Histrionic Personality Disorder.* Hillsdale, N.J.: Aronson.

Horowitz, M. J., and T. Eells. 1993. "Case Formulations Using Role-Relationship Model Configurations: A Reliability Study." *Psychotherapy Research* 3: 57–68.

Horowitz, M. J., T. Eells, J. L. Singer, and P. Salovey. 1995. "Role-Relationship Models for Case Formulation." *Archives General Psychiatry* 52: 625–56.

Horowitz, M. J., B. Fridhandler, and C. H. Stinson. 1991. "Person Schemas and Emotion." *Journal of the American Psychoanalytical Association* 39: 173–208.

Horowitz, M. J., L. Luborsky, and C. Popp. 1991. "A Comparison of the Role-Relationship Models Configuration and the Core Conflictual Relationship Theme." In *Person Schemas and Maladaptive Interpersonal Patterns.* Ed. M. J. Horowitz. Chicago: University of Chicago Press.

Horowitz, M. J., C. Marmar, J. Krupnick, N. Wilner, N. Kaltreider, and R. Wallerstein. 1984. *Personality Styles and Brief Psychotherapy.* New York: Basic Books.

Horowitz, M. J., C. Milbrath, D. Jordan, C. H. Stinson, M. Ewert, D. J. Redington, B. Fridhandler, S. P. Reidbord, and D. Hartley. 1994. "Expressive and Defensive Behavior During Discourse on Unresolved Topics: A Single Case Study. *Journal of Personality* 4: 527–63.

Horowitz, M. J., C. H. Stinson, D. Curtis, M. Ewert, D. Redington, J. L. Singer, W. Bucci, E. Mergenthaler, C. Milbrath, and D. Hartley. 1993. "Topics and Signs: Defensive Control of Emotional Expression." *Journal of Consulting and Clinical Psychology* 61: 421–30.

Horowitz, M. J., E. M. Weinshel, and O. F. Kernberg. 1993. *Psychic Structure and Psychic Change.* New York: International University Press.

Horowitz, M. J., and N. Zilberg. 1983. "Regressive Alterations in the Self-Concept." *American Journal of Psychiatry* 140: 284–89.

Kihlstrom, J., and R. L. Cunningham. 1991. "Mapping Interpersonal Space." In *Person Schemas and Maladaptive Interpersonal Patterns.* Ed. M. J. Horowitz, 311–38. Chicago: University of Chicago Press.

Knapp, P. H. 1991. "Self-Other Schemas: Core Organizers of Human Experience." In *Person Schemas and Maladaptive Interpersonal Patterns.* Ed. M. J. Horowitz. Chicago: University of Chicago Press.

Langer, E. J., and R. P. Abelson. 1972. "The Semantics for Asking a Favor: How to Succeed in Getting Help without Really Dying." *Journal of Personality and Social Psychology* 24: 26–32.

Linville, P. W. 1982. "Affective Consequence of Complexity Regarding the Self and Others." In *Affect and Cognition: Seventeenth Annual Carnegie Symposium on Cognition.* Ed. M. S. Clark and S. T. Fiske. Hillsdale, N. J.: Erlbaum.

Luborsky, L. 1977. "Measuring a Pervasive Psychic Structure in Psychotherapy: The Core Conflictual Relationship Theme." In *Communicative Structures and*

Psychic Structures. Ed. N. Freedman and S. S. Grand. New York: Plenum Press.
————. 1991. "Freud's Concept of a Transference Template: Hypotheses and Evidence." In *Person Schemas and Maladaptive Interpersonal Patterns.* Ed. M. J. Horowitz. Chicago: University of Chicago Press.

Mandler, G. 1984. *Mind and Body: Psychology of Emotion and Stress.* New York: Norton.

Markus, H. 1977. "Self-Schemata and Processing Information about the Self." *Journal of Personality and Social Psychology* 42: 38–50.

Markus, H., and E. Wurf. 1986. "The Dynamic Self-Concept: A Social Psychological Perspective." *Annual Review of Psychology* 38: 299–337.

McClelland, J. L., and D. E. Rumelhart. 1985. "Distributed Memory and the Representation of General and Specific Information." *Journal of Experimental Psychology* 114: 159–88.

Milbrath, C., R. Bauknight, and M. J. Horowitz. 1995. "Topic Sequences." *Psychotherapy Research* 5: 199–217.

Piaget, J. 1970. *Structuralism.* New York: Basic Books.

Ridgeway, C., and H. A. Walker. 1995. "Status, Structures." In *Social Perspectives on Social Psychology.* Ed. K. Cook, G. Fine, and S. Hauser, 281–309.

Rumelhart, D. E., and J. L. McClelland, eds. 1986. *Parallel Distributed Processing: Exploration in the Microstructures of Cognition.* Vols. 1 and 2. Cambridge, Mass.: MIT Press.

Segal, Z. 1988. "Appraisal of the Self-Schema Construct in Cognitive Models of Depression." *Psychological Bulletin* 102: 147–62.

Shweder, R. A. 1991. *Thinking through Cultures.* Cambridge, Mass.: Harvard University Press.

Singer, J. L., and P. Salovey. 1991. "Organized Knowledge Structures and Personality: Person Schemas, Self-Schemas, Prototypes and Scripts." In *Person Schemas and Maladaptive Interpersonal Patterns.* Ed. M. J. Horowitz, 33–80. Chicago: University of Chicago Press.

Stinson, C. H., and M. J. Horowitz. 1993. "PSYCLOPS: An Exploratory Graphical System for Clinical Research and Education." *Psychiatry* 56: 375–89.

Stinson, C. H., M. J. Horowitz, and C. Milbrath. Forthcoming. "Dysfluency and Topic Orientation in Bereaved Individuals: Bridging Individual and Group Studies." *Journal of Consulting and Clinical Psychology.*

Wegner, D. M. 1987. "Transactive Memory: A Contemporary Analysis of the Group Mind." *Theories of Group Behavior.* Ed. B. Mullen and G. Goethals, 185–208. New York: Springer-Verlag.

13 Studying Cognitive Development in Sociocultural Context: The Development of a Practice-Based Approach

GEOFFREY B. SAXE

In the late 1970s, Michael Cole and his colleagues at the Laboratory of Comparative Human Cognition published two critical review papers, one intended for psychologists (LCHC 1979) and the other for anthropologists (LCHC 1978). Reflecting on the state of the art at that time, Cole and his associates concluded that psychology had offered only a superficial treatment of culture in cognitive functioning and that anthropology had lacked systematic empirical approaches to hard questions of culture-cognition relations.

The fields are changing. Increasingly investigators are using models in which constructivist views of cognition and development are wedded with social or cultural analyses (Corsaro and Miller, both in this volume). A general thrust in the new wave of work is to understand culture and cognition as intrinsically related, constituting one another in people's daily activities.

The active scholarly interest in culture-cognition relations has led to the development and/or reemergence of a wide range of constructs like *cultural psychology* (Cole 1990, 1991; Shweder and Sullivan forthcoming), *situated cognition* (Brown, Collins, and Duguid 1989), *distributed intelligence* (Hutchins 1991; Pea 1994), and the *zone of proximal development* (Campione, Brown, Ferrara, and Bryant 1984; Rogoff 1990; Vygotsky 1978, 1986; Wertsch 1984). While in these efforts there is movement toward richer interpretations of culture in cognitive development, to date the conceptual work is only beginning to seriously inform empirical analyses. In this chapter, I review the development of a heuristic method for the study of culture-cognition relations, focusing specifically on relations between frameworks and empirical techniques over the course of its development.

An Organizational Note on Method: Frameworks and Techniques

Discussions of method can take two forms. One is *technique-based*. Its purpose is to abstract classes of procedures, whether particular coding systems, like ones to represent social interaction, or particular data-gathering techniques, like time sampling, or more general ethnographic approaches to participant observation and informant interview. Technique-based reviews point the reader to contexts in which particular procedures have borne fruit and review the threats to validity and reliability to which they may be subject. The second approach is *framework-based*. With this approach, an effort is made to outline methodological approaches linked to general epistemological and/or psychological assumptions. The framework-based review provides a means of framing questions about a general class of phenomena.

Both approaches have their weaknesses. The technique-based approach suffers from its positivistic roots (Pepper 1942). In large measure, the value of a particular technique should be gauged by how usefully it extends an interpretive framework into a field of study not (solely) by how precisely and reliably the technique serves as a measurement instrument. At the same time, the framework-based approach may lack specificity, falling short on discussions of how conceptual approaches can be translated into particular techniques.

In the following pages, I make an effort to coordinate both approaches to review, focusing on the productive tensions between methodological frameworks and empirical techniques. To this end, I sketch four quite different empirical projects with which I have been engaged over the course of a twenty-year period, projects that mirror some of the shifting values about what should be taken as core cultural phenomena in cognitive developmental research. I trace two developments over this body of work. First, I use the projects to explain the protracted development of a research framework that is geared for addressing core empirical and conceptual issues in current thinking about culture-cognition relations. Second, I use the projects to illustrate the shifting data-gathering techniques that have extended the framework into empirical analyses and that have, in turn, led to its shifting form.

Culture in Cross-Cultural Studies of Moral Development: Early Discontents with Method

In 1969 as an undergraduate I spent a summer living in a small Eskimo village in sub-Arctic Alaska. One purpose of my stay was to extend Kohlberg's framework for the study of moral reasoning (Kohlberg 1969) to cultures that were dissimilar from our own. I had adapted Kohlberg's moral dilemmas into versions that I thought would be relevant to village life and I interviewed village children and adults. As an interested and concerned twenty-one-year-old, I returned from the field with a wealth of feelings about the community, ones that were not well reflected in my documentation of only the first three of Kohlberg's six stages. My efforts to reconcile my experience of village life with the representation of development yielded by the interview techniques were disconcerting and the tension that emerged foreshadowed a methodological concern that became a major theme in my later work.

I had two principal reactions to the three-stage results. First, I saw the reduction as one that reflected the wisdom of thoughtful scholars. Indeed, I was (and continue to be) fascinated by the elegance and insight that structural-developmental treatments of cognition can offer (Langer 1969; Kohlberg 1969; Piaget 1970). The representation of development as a form-building process through commerce with an environment that individuals are structuring was both elegant and in tune with an epistemology that I was growing to deeply appreciate.

Second, I was uneasy. While perhaps strong as an epigenetic treatment of ethics, Kohlberg's six-stage model seemed weak as a means of elucidating complex relations between culture and the ethical thinking of individuals. The concern to document universal stages hid the complex strands of relations between the moral life as lived by these people, the social structure of the community, and the historical circumstances that were shaping social change in this part of the world.

The methods that I used in Alaska reflected a prominent paradigm of the times: a researcher, seeking to garner supportive evidence that a framework-based stage sequence was universal, sampled divergent communities using a more or less standard set of interview tasks developed in research with Western children (for example, conservation, classification, moral dilemmas) and coded the interviews with preestablished schemes. The results of such investigations were often similar to those I had produced in Alaska: researchers reported confirmation of behaviors that indexed the existence of a posited set of stages and lack of documentation of behaviors that indexed the highest of those stages. I came to believe that not only did my own work fail to represent well some critical dynamics of culture-cognition interactions, but the same critique could be made more generally of cognitive developmental research.

The dilemma for me was how to preserve the strong developmentalist orientation to cognition while creating techniques that allowed for greater insight into culture-cognition relations. It seemed that the very focus on universal stages precluded the analysis of cultural specificity in development.

Another concern that grew out of this early work was related to the status of ethnography in studies of the cognitive development of individuals. On the one hand, I was a participant observer in the Eskimo community (naive of his ethnographic task)—bathing with elders, attending ceremonies, and developing friendships. On the other hand, I was conducting a confirmatory study of moral development stages in which I scheduled interviews with residents, much like the norm in cross-cultural research in developmental psychology at the time. In my mind, and very much in tune with the psychological research literature of the times, these two activities were not aspects of the same research enterprise. Context was to serve only as a backdrop for the confirmatory social scientific enterprise with which I was engaged. I ended with a reduction of moral development of villagers into three age-related stages.

Representing Culture in Practice: Mathematics in the Oksapmin of Papua New Guinea

Methodological frameworks for representing culture in cognitive development remained limited in the 1970s. Indeed, the thrust of developmental research concerned age-related shifts in universal structures of intelligence. My graduate training was very much in tune with such conceptual and methodological frameworks, most notably Piaget's genetic epistemology.

In 1978 and again in 1980, I experienced the tensions between the representation of culture and the representation of the cognitions of individuals that had emerged in my early venture into cross-cultural research in Alaska. The occasion was an opportunity to extend my dissertation research on the early development of numerical cognition in a series of studies with a remote cultural group in Papua New Guinea, the Oksapmin. Now, the tension foregrounded rather than emerged from the fieldwork.

I entered the Oksapmin community with a loosely structured plan that reflected extant methodological frameworks. I was to begin with a study of the more traditional confirmatory variety that extended my dissertation research on number development in Western populations, focusing on relations between the development of children's use of counting and the formation of Piagetian concepts of number conservation. I reasoned that, like my early experience in Alaska, techniques associated with confirmatory efforts depended minimally upon on-site efforts to design tasks; therefore, if I had preformulated tasks and general questions that bore on issues of universality, I would have "insurance" that the visit to these groups would satisfy productivity commitments to funding sources, allowing me some opportunity to devote efforts to my second, more challenging concern.

It was the second part of the plan that was more ambitious, breaking from the mold of research paradigms of the times. I had followed the writings and thinking of various authors who had pointed to cultural practices as a fruitful context for study of culture-cognition relations. For instance, early in this century, Franz Boas (1911) argued that people generate intellectual skills in the context of the practices with which they are engaged. In his work with Native Americans, he pointed out that cultural practices vary in complexity both within and across groups, and the character of people's knowledge varies accordingly. In the 1960s and 1970s, the focus on cognition and practices reemerged in the work of psychologists. In Piagetian studies, researchers had documented that in certain practices like economic exchange (Posner 1982) or pottery making (Price-Williams, Gordon, and Ramirez 1967) children develop Piagetian cognitive structures at an age younger than children from the same communities not engaged in such practices. In work that reflected more contextual frameworks for understanding cognition, researchers had shown how practices created important contexts for culture-specific intellectual growth (Cole et al. 1971; Cole and Scribner 1974; Gay and Cole 1965; Lave 1977). For instance, in studies with Kpelle rice farmers, Cole et al. pointed to culture-specific measurement practices in which rice farmers displayed marked proficiency. As a whole, the empirical work associated with Piagetian and contextual frameworks was quite consistent with Boas's early observations. People's intellectual adaptations were related to the cultural practices in which they were participants.

For me, the focus on practices had promise, though that promise was far from being fully realized as a method of study. The existing research studies did not reveal much of the dynamics of cognitive work that was accomplished in practices nor how that work created context for novel cognitive developments. Indeed, the Piagetian developmental research largely was concerned with documenting either universals in cognitive structures or relative retardation or acceleration of these structures across practices and/or cultures. While the contextually oriented research seemed more revealing about culture-cognition relations (Cole and Scribner 1974), the approach did not satisfy my own commitments toward elevating culture more centrally in structural-developmental analyses of cognition.

I went to Papua New Guinea with two commitments as a part of the second part of my plan: a commitment to a developmental perspective and a commitment to using cultural practices as a focus for framing questions about culture and cognitive development. I went with few tools. Like the comparative methods in cognitive development at the time, the techniques that I had used in my own prior research were based on interviews organized around tasks designed to provide insight into general cognitive developmental structures, not to reveal the dynamics of culture-cognition interactions, nor the cultural specificity of cognitive developments.

Some Preliminaries

My research on mathematics in Oksapmin was aided by two linguistic anthropologists, Tom Moylan and Virginia Guilford, who were engaged in their dissertation research. It was through their established friendships with people and progress in learning the Oksapmin language that I was afforded access to important informants and gained knowledge of the community. In addition to help from Tom and Virginia, I had the benefit of support from the Indigenous Mathematics Project of the Papua New Guinea Ministry of Education, an affiliation that provided me access to the government bush school and helped in establishing rapport with teachers. The ministry affiliation also gave me an entry into talking with adults about number.

Oksapmin and Number, Part 1: Confirmatory Studies

I first learned about the Oksapmin number system through Tom and Virginia. Later, I apprenticed myself to others (Oksapmin adults and children) and through my additional confirmatory studies on counting/conservation relations in Oksapmin children (Saxe 1983), I had an opportunity to learn much about how the system was used by children.

The standard Oksapmin system is based upon body parts. To count as Oksapmin do, one begins with the thumb on one hand and enumerates twenty-seven places around the upper periphery of the body, ending on the little finger of the opposite hand. If one needs to count further, one can continue back up to the wrist of the second hand and progress back upward on the body (fig. 1). In discussions and observations with others, I learned various functions for the system in everyday activities. For example, aside from using the system to count (pigs, currency, and so on), people also use it to denote the ordinal position of an element in a series of elements (the ordinal position of a hamlet in a series of hamlets on a path), or in basic measurement operations (as a means of measuring and representing the length of string bags, a common cultural artifact). Procedures for computation are not used in traditional life; however, there are some analogs of a computational process. For instance, in traditional eco-

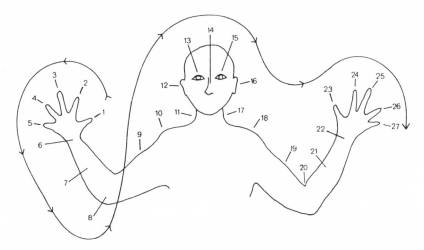

Figure 1.   Oksapmin body-part counting system.

nomic exchanges, Oksapmin traded goods directly in one-for-one or one-for-many exchanges (bows for leaves of salt, axes for bows). In general, such analogs lack a representational solution procedure in which an answer can be determined in the absence of the objects.

In my first set of studies, I focused on age-related shifts in children's counting and its relation to children's understanding of a Piagetian construct, number conservation (Saxe 1981, 1983). Some of these studies served to support my dissertation findings concerning the developmental relation between counting and conservation and revealed the increasingly common finding that people in remote groups develop understandings of conservation, but at later ages than their Western counterparts. Others provided insight into the way the organization of a numeration system leads children to different conceptual hurdles in its acquisition (Saxe 1981).

The second part of my plan for the Oksapmin work took form as I learned more about practices with which individuals were engaged. I focused my attention on the way number was used in two selected practices in an effort to better understand how culture is interwoven with cognitive development.

Oksapmin and Number, Part 2: Elevating Culture More Centrally in Cognitive Developmental Analyses

The timing of my two stays in the Oksapmin area (1978 and 1980) was quite favorable for a study of cultural practices and cognitive development.

The Oksapmin people were just experiencing contact with Westerners in the 1960s and 1970s, resulting in the emergence of novel practices that involved number. Two practices—economic exchange with currency and Western-style schooling in arithmetic—became central targets of my work. However, it took some time for me to identify and then realize that these were ripe contexts for analyses in which I might be able to integrate cultural and developmental analyses in a study of cognition in these practices, and some time to understand how I might begin to proceed.

Economic exchange. Western currency had entered the Oksapmin community through a number of routes. Some Oksapmin men earned about 200 kina (the equivalent, at the time, of about $300 in purchasing value) from two-year stints of labor on copra and tea plantations. These men typically returned to the Oksapmin community; some built tiny trade stores, having brought with them bags of rice and tinned fish to sell to people in their hamlets. Many of the other plantation returnees were principal customers at the trade stores.

I saw the new practice of economic exchange as one in which people were accomplishing problems that were novel in their own social history. I needed a framework and techniques from which to ask questions about cognitive development linked to the practice. I saw little utility in the kind of information that Piagetian practice-based study or a contextual study would provide.

Seeds for a framework came from two formative books in my own development, one by Luria (1978) and the other by Werner and Kaplan (1962). In structuring a study on cognitive developments linked to the practice of economic exchange, I drew on these works, finding that both could be adapted and reformulated to capture what emerged as remarkable developments occurring in the Oksapmin community.

Luria's study. In his seminal study conducted in the early 1930s in a remote part of postrevolutionary Russia, Luria was concerned with documenting a shift in the organization of thinking that he argued would be related to dramatic changes in the organization of people's daily practices, changes from feudal to collectivist forms of social and economic organization. Luria argued that what characterized the shift in groups was the emergence of "new motives for action and also new forms of access to a technological culture and mastery of mechanisms such as literacy and other new forms of knowledge. The transition to a socialist economy brought along new forms of social relations and, with them, new life principles" (1978:15). Following Vygotsky, Luria argued that with the new motives, people would be shifting from "graphically oriented" or unmediated forms of thinking toward mediated forms of thinking. To this end, Luria sampled individuals from five groups that reflected the societal movement.

At one extreme were Ichakari women who were illiterate and not involved in any modern social activities; at the other extreme were women students admitted to a teachers' school. To document the expected shifts in thinking, Luria engaged villagers in conversation and gradually introduced standard tasks that contained problems involving perception, generalization and abstraction, deduction and inference, reasoning and problem solving, imagination, and self-analysis.

In Luria's sampling method—choosing population groups that reflected a projected shift in forms of social organization—I found a valuable technique, applicable to issues of economic exchange in Oksapmin. Indeed, I could use an analogous procedure by sampling individuals with varying levels of participation in the money economy and then study the nature of their arithmetical problem solving.

I was less inspired by Luria's methods for studying cognition. The tasks used to assess categories of knowledge were divorced from the targeted practices that Luria was studying. Like the Piagetian analyses of cognitive development, I found problematic the reduction of knowledge into pre-formulated categories that bore little relation to targeted practices and little in the way of an epigenetic analysis of how one form of knowledge might be generated from another in practice.

Werner and Kaplan's treatment of symbol formation. Where Luria's analysis was weak, I saw strength in Werner and Kaplan's form-function analysis of symbol formation. Though Werner and Kaplan created their treatment in analyses of early language development, I saw their treatment as potentially applicable to an analysis of cognitive development that more richly represented cultural processes.

In their analysis, Werner and Kaplan considered the effect that an emerging linguistic function, such as denotative reference, had on the children's generation of novel linguistic forms (syntactic, pragmatic, and morphological). Werner and Kaplan argued that during infancy, gestural and intonational forms—early reaching, cooing, and babbling—have prelinguistic functions (for example, grasping and affective expression). With the emerging function of denotation in early childhood, children attempt to adapt their already acquired gestural and intonational forms (reaching and cooing) as means to accomplish goals associated with the new function (for example, reaching while vocalizing to indicate that a parent should attend to a particular object). Such prior forms are clearly limited in their ability to serve the purpose of the newly emerging denotative function, and children gradually structures novel forms of a function-specific character. The process of construction passes through various transitional phases, such as the generation of onomatopoeic forms (as in "choo-choo" for train) and, later, the generation of more clearly specialized syntactic and morphological forms (as in such expressions as, "Look at the train"). Children's generation of new forms reciprocally creates conditions for the emergence of new functions and novel goals.

Unlike the analyses of cognition provided in Luria's work and more generally in the cross-cultural Piagetian tradition, the form-function analysis had promise as a means of understanding intrinsic relations between culture and cognition in development, particularly if coupled with a strong treatment of cultural practices. Cognitive forms are often initially cultural forms, like the Oksapmin number system; further, the cognitive functions that forms serve are interwoven with the practices with which individuals are engaged.

Arithmetic and economic exchange. My efforts to bring forward Luria's and Werner and Kaplan's prior work were first realized in a study on economic exchange. Following Luria, I sampled adults who had different levels of experience with the money economy (Saxe 1982). I interviewed about eighty individuals from four population groups that had varying levels of participation with the new practice of economic exchange with currency. These groups included trade store owners, men who had returned from a period of work at a plantation, and groups of younger adults who had never left the area but who had acquired minimal currency and older adults who had little experience with economic exchange that involved currency.

Interview tasks were created that would allow for analyses of arithmetical reasoning. In a typical addition task, a subject was told, "You have nine coins and are given seven more. How many do you have altogether?" The results of the interviews revealed some dramatic differences among the four groups in the way Oksapmin used their body system to solve the tasks, differences that could be made intelligible in a developmental framework using the form-function model. Consider four approaches to the solution of nine-plus-seven coins that emerged with increasing participation in the money economy depicted in figure 2.

Those Oksapmin people with only minimal participation in the money economy first attempted to extend the body-counting cognitive form as it is used to serve enumerative functions in traditional activities to accomplish arithmetical tasks that emerge in economic transactions. This direct extension, however, was not adequate to accomplish arithmetical solutions, and it was not even clear that Oksapmin with little experience treated the task as one that involved the cognitive function of arithmetic. In these preliminary efforts, Oksapmin attempted to count the sum with a prior counting strategy linked to the body system. Figure 2a illustrates this "global enumeration strategy." In this strategy, an individual began with the first term (7) of the problem—thumb (1) to forearm (7)—and then

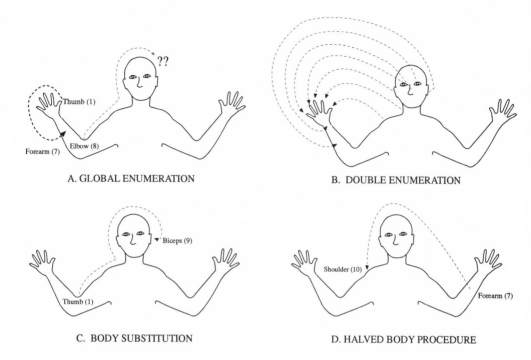

Figure 2.   Oksapmin arithmetical strategies.

continued to count the second term (9) from the elbow (8). Since the problem of nine coins plus seven coins seemed to be understood as an enumeration rather than an addition, individuals did not recognize the need to keep track of the addition of the second term to the first term, and they typically produced an incorrect sum.

Oksapmin with greater experience in the money economy made a clumsy and labored effort to restructure their prior global counting strategy in such a way that one term is added on to the other (the double-numeration strategy). In one example of this strategic form (fig. 2b), individuals again enumerate the first term—thumb (1) to forearm (7)—but now, as they enumerate the second, they make efforts to keep track of their enumeration. Thus, the elbow (8) is paired with the thumb (1), the biceps (9) is paired with the index finger (2), and so on, until the ear on the other side (16) is paired with the biceps (9), yielding the answer. Thus in this initial extension of the body system to accomplish the arithmetical problem, the body parts begin to take on a new function of keeping track of the addition of one term to another.

With higher levels in the sequence, we see the body-part counting form progressively specialized into more sophisticated cognitive forms that serve distinctly arithmetical functions. Now, individuals, rather than establishing physical correspondences between body parts as they did previously, efficiently use the name of one body part to refer to another in a "body-substitution strategy" (fig. 2c). To solve seven plus nine, the elbow (8) is called the thumb (1), the biceps (9) is called the index finger (2), and so on, until the ear on the other side (16) is called the biceps (9). The result is a more rapid computational process, one in which body-part names are differentiated from the names of body parts themselves.

Cognitive forms that are distinctively specialized to serve arithmetical and not enumerative functions were more frequently displayed by trade store owners who have the most experience with problems of arithmetic that emerge in economic transactions with currency. In their strategies, some trade store owners incorporated a base-ten system linked to the currency as an aid in computation. With this strategic form (fig. 2d), individuals use the shoulder as a privileged value. In their computation of nine plus seven, they may represent nine on one side of the body as biceps (9) and seven on the other side of the body as forearm (7). To accomplish the problem, a trade store owner might simply "remove" the forearm from the second side (the seventh body part of 7) and transfer it to the first side where it becomes the shoulder (the tenth). He then "reads" the answer as ten plus six, or sixteen.

By incorporating elements of both Luria's and Werner and Kaplan's analytic frames, I was able to reveal some practice-specific developmental processes occurring in the Oksapmin community. In their efforts to accomplish goals that emerge in economic practices, Oksapmin appropriate practice-linked cognitive forms initially specialized to serve earlier emerging cognitive functions (enumeration) for new uses—in this case, arithmetic. In the process of this appropriation and specialization, the function of the body system shifts and the original form used to accomplish enumerative functions undergoes a progressive development. In this process, Oksapmin were creating, over time, progressively more specialized and sophisticated uses of the indigenous number system, a process of specialization that is deeply interwoven with both developmental and cultural processes.

In an effort to further explore the cognitive developments as they emerged in individuals' participation in practices, I turned next to the analysis of Oksapmin children's mathematics learning in a new Western-style bush school. The study was one that required the development of a new data-gathering technique—a systematic, though limited, observational coding scheme. It was also an occasion to push the form-function framework to see whether it would be useful applied to a different practice in Oksapmin.

Arithmetic linked to schooling. At school, Oksapmin children participate in a wide range of activities—from formal school lessons to the building and maintenance of the school grounds. Children come to school with knowledge of the body system, speaking only the Oksapmin language. They are taught to use Western numeration and arithmetical procedures in English. I suspected that like adults engaged in economic practices, children might be appropriating the indigenous body system in an effort to make sense of their school math, and in a developmental process, show similar form-function shifts as the adults. I used two types of techniques to analyze the development of arithmetical problem solving in the context of school.

My first concern was to document whether children spontaneously used the body system during arithmetical problem solving. To this end, I collaborated with teachers in structuring an arithmetic test to be used at three grade levels that would be administered during class time, a context in which we would be able to observe children solving mathematical problems in the course of an everyday classroom math routine. The observations revealed that many children used the conventional body-part system during the test; though the frequency with which children overtly used their bodies to solve the tasks declined over grade level.

Having documented children's use of the indigenous system in school, my second concern was to analyze developmental shifts in children's arithmetical understandings. To this end, children were interviewed individually about a variety of arithmetic problems. In addition, a group of nonschooled adolescents was interviewed to determine whether these inventions were attributable to the school experience or merely developed in the course of everyday activities.

Similar to the adults who had little experience with exchange involving currency, I found that grade 2 children used strategies similar to the global enumeration procedure, using body parts to accomplish strictly enumerative functions. In contrast, grade 4 and grade 6 children tended to use strategies that resembled those of the adults who had experience with currency. The nonschooled contrast group of age-matched grade 6 children used strategies similar to the grade 2 children. Thus the form-function shifts documented in these Oksapmin children were linked to participation to school-based practices.

A Critique of the Research in Oksapmin

The Oksapmin studies of arithmetic in trade and in school illustrate well the way form-function analyses can represent the interplay between culture and cognitive development in the study of practice. In practices, individuals make use of cultural forms, tailoring them to serve particular, practice-linked cognitive functions. With use and specialization of these forms, individuals often create new functions for which there is again a process of specialization. The dialectic between form and function is thus a process whereby history (as enduring cultural forms) and cognition become interwoven with one another in the developing understandings of the individual.[1]

While the focus on form-function relations satisfied some of my early concerns about the representation of culture in analyses of cognitive development, I saw that I could have pushed harder in the Oksapmin work. Missing was a critical treatment of how environments emerged in the practices of economic exchange in the trade store and in the school. While in the Oksapmin fieldwork I had spent time observing social interactions in which arithmetical problems were generated and resolved in the trade store, I had not attempted systematic social interactional analyses. Lack of such analyses seemed, in hindsight, a critical omission for two reasons. First, emergent environments in practices themselves reflect socially and culturally organized cognitive work. *In situ* analyses of the environments would offer a window into the ways in which cultural and cognitive processes are constituting one another in the daily dynamics of people's activities. Second, the form-function model is based on the assumption that individuals are constructing goals and means to accomplish them in practices. Goals are not set by the structure of an activity; rather, they emerge as individuals motives and understandings are realized in practices.

Documenting Emergent Goals through Social Interactional Analyses: A Fine-Grained Study of Practices

In subsequent work with colleagues in the United States (Saxe, Gearhart, and Guberman 1984; Saxe, Guberman, and Gearhart 1987), I turned my attention back to young Western children's understanding of number—a focus of my dissertation research conducted five or six years earlier. In the new work on young children's numerical understanding, I brought forward the focus on practices, the form-function framework, and now a focus on social interactions.

In the research literature on number development, various researchers had revealed that children at a young age show considerable knowledge (Fuson 1978; Gelman and Gallistel 1978; Saxe 1977, 1979); however, little attention had been addressed to the enculturating processes that supported children's number development. Were young children, like the Oksapmin, participating in everyday numerical practices in which they were constructing and accomplishing numerical goals linked to social and cultural processes? If so, could children's developments be understood in terms of shifting relations between cognitive forms and functions?

The research was set in a neighborhood in Brooklyn, New York. The neighborhood was largely Caucasian and contained families that were both working and middle class (as defined by standard indices). We sampled families that contained either two-and-a-half-year-olds or four-year-olds from each socioeconomic group.

Form-function analyses. Drawing upon prior work on early numerical understandings, my colleagues and I identified four principal functions for number words in young children's development, functions that had implications for children's construction of numerical goals (Saxe, Guberman, and Gearhart 1987). These functions included nominal reference (using number words in naming activities), cardinal/ordinal representations of single sets, comparing and reproducing sets, and arithmetical transformations of numerical values. We also identified a range of the strategic forms that children used to realize these functions, like strategies to achieve an accurate count, to represent cardinal values of a single set, or various strategies to compare or reproduce sets.

To document the way these forms and functions were realized in children's activities, we developed interview techniques that were used to elicit from mothers rich descriptions of the numerical practices with which her child was engaged with or without her direct support. We also elicited from mothers their retrospections and projections of prior and possible future practices. These descriptions were then analyzed with schemes that coded both the content (games of mothers' and children's own invention, store-bought games, and so on), and, more importantly, their goal-structure complexity of the activities based upon our prior analysis of the cognitive functions involved in the activities. For instance, based on the form-function analysis, we identified activities in which goals were principally ones of nominal reference (for example, identifying and pushing numbered elevator buttons; level 1), representation of cardinal values (counting coins to determine their amount; level 2), comparing the numerical values of two collections (comparing two collections of pennies; level 3), and arithmetical (adding and subtracting checkers to find their sum; level 4).

Our interviews with mothers revealed that, across our age and social-class groups, children regularly participated in practices involving number, practices that had goal structures of varying levels of complexity. We found age differences in the goal structure complexity of home activities, differences that mirrored our developmental analyses of children's achievements: younger children tended to be engaged with activities of level 1 and 2 goal structures; older children, children who showed competence reflecting higher-level goals, tended to be engaged with activities with higher-level goal structures. Working-class four-year-olds tended to be engaged with social activities of less complex goal structure than were their middle-class peers, again reflecting social-class differences in children's numerical achievements. Thus these analyses provided a window into children's numerical practices and the way form-function shifts in children's numerical cognition is interwoven with their practice participation.

Our next step was to ask how numerical goals emerged for children during play with their mothers and whether these emergent goals differed for younger and older children. To this end, we videotaped mother-child pairs during their engagement in two prototypical activities. One containing a goal structure that required a cardinal representation (level 2) and the other involving an activity with a numerical reproduction goal structure (level 3). We also videotaped children accomplishing the activity in solitary play.

We found that in our analyses of mother-child videotaped interactions, the goal structures took form and shifted over the course of activities regardless of children's age. Further, goal structures could best be understood as a product of mothers' and children's adjustments to one another. In the number reproduction activity, for instance, children were presented with a board containing pictures of either three or nine Cookie Monsters (a model set) and a cup. The child had to get just the same number of pennies from a collection about five feet away as there were Cookie Monsters in the picture (fig. 3). We found that the mothers of the children who were older (and who performed at higher levels in their unassisted performances) attempted to structure the task at more superordinate level goals and the mothers of two-and-a-half-year-olds (and who demonstrated less ability in their unassisted performances) attempted to provide directives that supported children's construction of less complex goals. Further, it was possible to document the dynamics that led to different goal structures emerging for children. When mothers provided goal directives that the child was not successful in accomplishing, mothers tended to shift to a less complex numerical goal directive; in contrast, when children successfully accomplished a goal directive, mothers tended to shift to a more superordinate numerical goal directive. Reciprocally, children were also adjusting their own activities to their mothers. For instance, children who did not appropriately count one or both sets when unassisted (an important strategic component in the solution of the task) were likely to count with their mothers' assistance. Further, children who did not successfully complete the task on their own were likely to do so with their mothers.

The analyses of videotaped interactions provided a remarkable window

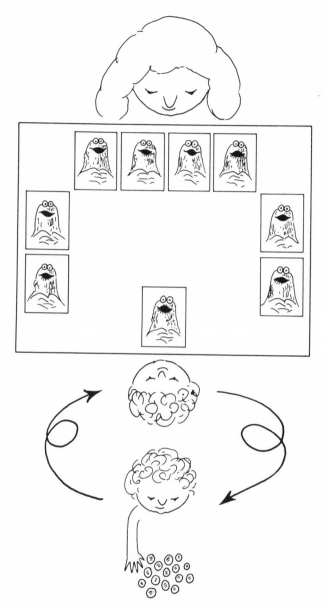

Figure 3.   Number-reproduction activity.

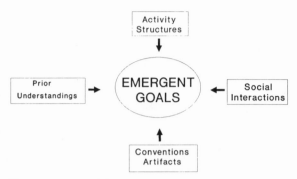

Figure 4.   Four-parameter model.

into the emergence of goals in practices: mothers were adjusting their goal-related directives to their children's understandings and task-related accomplishments and that children were adjusting their goal-directed activities to their mothers' efforts to organize the task. Further, as children's ability to produce numerical goals of different complexity levels changed with development, they were afforded new opportunities for creating more complex numerical environments.

A Practice-Based Research Framework

New efforts and ambitions to better represent the interplay between cultural practices and cognitive development led me to systematize a general research approach. The systematization took the form of a three-component research framework.

Component 1: Emergent Goals

Central to my prior work in Oksapmin and Brooklyn was the thesis that children create cognitive developments in their efforts to accomplish numerical goals, goals that emerge in practices. The first component of the framework is geared for understanding the dynamics of goal formation in practices (fig. 4). The focus is on the way artifacts (currency, for example), social interactions (a mother's efforts to assist her child in face-to-face discourse), activity structures (the routine activities to make a purchase at a trade store), and an individual's own prior understandings (of arithmetic, counting) are interwoven with the goals that children construct.

Component 2: Form-Function Shifts

The second component brings forward an analysis of the interplay between form and function in analyses of cognitive development. The analyses of cognitive development in Oksapmin and Brooklyn demonstrated the utility of asking questions about cognitive development in terms of form-function relations: what cultural forms has the child appropriated and specialized to accomplish emergent goals in practices and what cognitive functions are these forms serving? The focus on form-function analyses became central in systematizing data gathering and analytic techniques to understanding development in practices.

Component 3: The interplay between cognitive developments across practices. In their daily activities individuals are engaged in multiple practices in which mathematical goals may emerge. The third component is concerned with questions of the interplay across practices: in what way do cognitive forms elaborated in one practice become appropriated and specialized to accomplish new functions in others?

The Practice-Based Approach Applied to Candy Selling

The three components served to coordinate a wide ranging set of analyses concerned with culture and cognition in relation to a single but pivotal construct to the analysis of development—emergent goals. To illustrate the framework, I draw on research conducted in Brazil's northeast.

At the invitation of Terezinha Nunes, Analucia Schliemann, and David Carraher at the Federal University of Pernambuco, I had taken a sabbatical leave and taken up residence in Recife, Brazil. I went with a Fullbright fellowship for teaching that put me in touch with graduate students at the Federal University and with a grant from the National Science Foundation to support research on the interplay between culture and cognitive development in urban and rural practices with which children were engaged. My search for practices to target for study was guided by five principal concerns, several of which had proved useful for organizing empirical studies in my prior work: (1) targeted practices were to be ones that appeared to support the development of complex mathematical cognitions in children; (2) children of various ages were participants (to allow for a study of age-related shifts in children's understandings); (3) children of considerable numbers had to be involved to insure that trends observed in children's mathematics were reliable; (4) a large number of participants in targeted practices should have little or no schooling—this would allow me to study mathematical understandings children construct without the benefit of schooling; (5) a large number of participants in the targeted practices should be attending school to enable a study of the interplay between math learning at school and math learning in the streets.

Guided by these general constraints, I spent time with faculty colleagues and graduate students discussing and visiting various communities in the process of selecting sites for study. Two emerged that satisfied most criteria: candy selling in urban children and straw weaving in rural children. Below I draw on research with candy sellers to explain the three component framework.

The candy selling practice (see Saxe 1991) is set in the context of a major urban center in Brazil's northeast in which there is a large informal sector. Due to a long history of an inflating economy, sellers must deal with very large numerical values in everyday transactions; many of these sellers have little or no schooling.

Component 1: Emergent goals. To document the arithmetical goals with which sellers were engaged, I organized analyses of sellers' practice with reference to each of the four parameters of the first component. Below I point to the way these parameters are implicated in analyses of sellers' goals.

Activity structures. Activity structures consist of the general tasks that must be accomplished in a practice and the general motives for practice participation. In the case of candy selling, the activity structure is an economic one (the inner rectangle in figure 1). To accomplish their practice, sellers must purchase their boxes from wholesale stores during a *purchase phase,* price their candy for sale in a *prepare-to-sell phase,* sell their candy in the street in a *sell phase,* and then select new wholesale boxes for purchase in a *prepare-to-purchase phase.* The cycle then repeats back to the purchase phase. In selling candy, children generate mathematical goals that are linked to this cyclical activity structure to accomplish economic ends. For instance, in the prepare-to-sell phase, one type of mathematical goal that typically emerges is the markup from wholesale to retail price.

Social interactions. The social interactions that emerge in a practice, the second parameter, may simplify some goals and complicate others. During each phase in the practice, sellers typically interact with other people. For instance, in the purchase phase, sellers buy their boxes from wholesale store clerks. In these transactions, clerks may offer varied forms of assistance in helping children mark up their boxes for retail sale. Sometimes this assistance may be merely in the form of telling children how much the box costs if sellers cannot read posted prices. Other times, clerks may accomplish the markup for children by telling them what an appropriate markup would be to sell on the streets. Regardless, an inherent property of these interactions is that practice-linked numerical goals emerge and

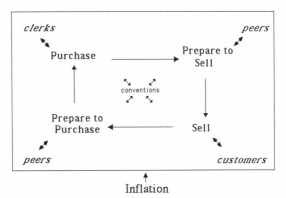

Figure 5.   Schematic of the candy-selling practice.

are modified in social interactions. Often children who are less capable construct and accomplish less complex numerical goals, the more complex ones being structured and accomplished by the store clerk.

Cultural artifacts. The third parameter consists of the artifacts that are interwoven with the practice. Consider a pricing convention that has emerged over the history of the practice. In selling their candy, sellers price their candy using a price-ratio form. Children might offer their candy to customers for two prices, three packages for five hundred cruzeiros or five for Cr$1000. While this convention may reduce the complexity of arithmetical computations in making change, it may complicate others. For instance, a seller must mark up a multi-unit wholesale box price in terms of a retail price ratio. The final selling ratio (the retail price) should reflect the wholesale box price plus a profit margin. Thus the price ratio convention is interwoven with the mathematical goals that emerge as sellers address problems of markup.

Prior understandings. The prior understandings that sellers bring to bear on the practice—the fourth parameter—are fundamental to the kinds of goals that emerge in a practice. For instance, a seller who does not understand the relation between wholesale price and retail price does not generate markup goals—or at least, if he does, the mathematical goals in his computation will be of a quite different sort from the seller who does.

An eclectic set of techniques were used to gather information on sellers' mathematical goals in the practice. These included *in situ* observation and interview of principal participants in the candy-selling practice (six- to fifteen-year-old candy sellers, store clerks, cashiers, and customers in the streets and on buses). Further, we recruited wholesale store clerks to keep records of their transactions with their child customers (the candy sellers) and asked them to note if they provided the sellers any assistance, and if so, what form. We also conducted systematic analyses of the exchanges that took place in wholesale stores. We analyzed the particular mathematical goals that sellers formed in their practice and the way children's goals shifted with sellers' ages.

Component 2: Form-function shifts in development. We used observation and informal interview procedures to collect information on the development of sellers' mathematical understandings. We accompanied some sellers as they plied their trade, asking about their activities at opportune moments. We noted various ways in which children were making use of cultural forms to accomplish cognitive functions in sellers' practice and the shifting relations between cognitive forms and functions that occurred over age.

Consider one strand in shifting relations between form and function in sellers' mathematics. All sellers made use of a price-ratio convention (a cultural form) to offer goods to customers. Sellers, for instance, would sell candy for a specific number of units for Cr$1000, but would make use of the price ratio in different ways in their computations. For the six-year-old seller, the price ratio served the cognitive function of mediating exchanges of candy for currency in seller-customer transactions: the child-seller exchanges, for instance, one C$1000 bill for three candy bars. For the young seller, issues of price markup are taken care of by others.

As sellers took on more responsibility, we saw a shift in the cognitive functions the price ratio served. Rather than being solely used in the context of seller-customer transactions, sellers began to use the price ratio as a means to organize their markup computations. They began to use the ratio to determine a potential gross price for their boxes were they to use a particular ratio for a retail price ("what if" computations). For instance, sellers would empty their boxes, replacing their candy in groups (for example, three by three, or two by two), counting Cr$1000 with each placement. Once they replaced all of their candy, they would have determined the gross value of the box if it were sold at the specified grouping ratio.

To collect systematic information on form-function shifts in sellers' mathematics, interview tasks were designed in the areas of markup, number representation, and arithmetic. We interviewed sellers, and, for comparison purposes, age-matched urban and rural nonsellers; we paid children for the time they spent as interviewees.

Most sellers appeared rarely if ever to make use of our standard orthography for number. For instance, when sellers would enter wholesale stores to purchase boxes of candy rather than reading posted prices, they would often ask store clerks the price of boxes. Other times, sellers already knew the price of a box of a type of candy in a store from word of mouth provided by other sellers. Rarely were sellers observed using paper and

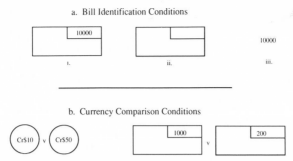

Figure 6. Currency identification and comparison tasks.

pencil to accomplish arithmetical computations. I suspected that many sellers were using currency itself (a cultural form) as a means of identifying numerical values in transactions with customers. Bills were printed with different colors, and children seemed to be identifying the numerical value of bills not by the printed numerals on them but by the figurative characteristics of bills. Further, with knowledge of ordinal and multiplicative relations between currency values, children could use a representational system for number in their computations.

To investigate children's number representations, I developed tasks to determine sellers' abilities. For a standard orthography task, sellers were asked to read and compare twenty multidigit numerical values, values that were within the range that they addressed in their practice. To determine sellers' ability to use currency as an alternative system for large-number representation, I constructed two types of additional tasks. First, in bill-identification tasks, children were presented with twelve bills (or printed-bill values) in each of three conditions (fig. 6a): standard bills, bills with their numbers occluded by tape, and photocopies of cutouts of the numbers. In each condition, children were required to identify the values of the bills or numbers. Second, in the currency comparison tasks, children were presented with fourteen pairs of currency units and asked to tell which was the larger of the two (for example, bills of Cr$200 and Cr$1000) as well as the multiplicative relations between units—how many of the smaller units were equivalent to the larger unit (fig. 6b)? I reasoned that if sellers could identify currency units and compare them numerically, they have the basis for a representational system to manipulate large numerical values, a system that would serve them well in their everyday computations.

Analyses of the interviews revealed that sellers' develop a mathematics that differs from the mathematics that we have learned in school, and one that their nonselling peers do not construct. Further, the character of their

mathematics becomes more powerful with age, displaying a shifting relation between the culturally linked forms that sellers appropriate in their
solutions (for example, currency and the price-ratio selling convention)
and the functions that these forms serve.

Component 3: The Interplay between Cognitive Developments Across Practices

The third component is concerned with questions of the interplay across
practices: in what way do cognitive forms elaborated in one practice become appropriated and specialized to accomplish new functions in others?

In the candy-selling work I focused on the interplay between sellers'
street mathematics and the mathematics that some of these children were
learning at school, an issue that resonates well with current concerns of
mathematics educators in the United States (NCTM 1989). I analyzed
whether learning math at school was appropriated by sellers as they structured and accomplished emergent goals in the street; I also analyzed
whether sellers in school made use of their street mathematics to accomplish computational problems in class.

To determine whether children's schooling in math led to differences in
how they approached problems that emerged in the candy-selling practice,
I contrasted the mathematical understandings (as revealed by the tasks
noted above) of twelve-to fifteen-year-old sellers who had differing levels
of school experience.[2] The groups included children who had none or little
schooling (no schooling to second grade), children who had completed
the third or fourth grade, and children who had completed the fifth, sixth,
or seventh grade. These findings revealed some notable differences and
some notable similarities. With schooling, sellers increasingly were able
to read the standard orthography, whereas sellers without schooling performed poorly on the orthography tasks. Further, there was an occasional
schoolchild in observations in the street that made use of paper and pencil
in markup calculations and in strategies to accomplish some of the arithmetic tasks. However, there were no differences linked to schooling in sellers' accurate solutions of the mathematically more complex currency
arithmetic, ratio comparison, and inflation tasks.

To study whether sellers used their street mathematics to help them
understand math at school, I used school-type computation problems,
administering them in individual interviews to sellers and nonsellers in
second- and third-grade classrooms. The findings revealed that sellers did
make use of their practice-linked mathematics in solving school problems:
at second grade, sellers achieved accurate solutions to greater numbers of
problems than nonsellers; further, sellers strategies appeared to be adap-

tations of the currency-linked computation procedures that were manifest in sellers arithmetical problem solving in their practice. At third grade, while sellers still performed with greater accuracy than nonsellers, the differences were attenuated.

Subsequent Research on Practices and Children's Mathematics

In subsequent work, I have made efforts to elaborate and systematize the research framework in studies on cultural practices and cognitive development, one on urban children's play of an educational game (Saxe 1992; Saxe and Bermudez 1992; Saxe and Guberman 1993), and in collaborative research in progress, on reform-minded and traditional fifth-grade mathematics classrooms. The studies have spawned new and more eclectic techniques as colleagues and I try to represent emergent mathematical environments in classroom settings and the kinds of knowledge that participants (teachers and students) are creating in their practices.

Concluding Remark

In their efforts to understand, researchers make use of frameworks to guide the identification and reduction of phenomena into interpretable categories. Increasingly, in studies of cognition and development, we find efforts to create frameworks in which culture and cognition are conceived as intrinsically related to one another, and to create and adapt empirical techniques that accordingly reveal cultural dimensions of cognitive development.

My own struggles to mitigate the tension between cultural and developmental analyses of cognition have been protracted. They provide one case study of the productive relation between framework and technique in a body of developmental research. I began with limited empirical techniques that served essentially no more than confirmatory functions in research on moral development in an Eskimo community. Confronted with the schism between the culturally textured qualities of peoples' everyday lives and the confirmatory methods for studying universal developmental stages, I moved toward the three-component framework. The shift brought with it new framework-linked research goals for documenting cognitive developments specific to cultural practices. To accomplish these research goals, I adapted prior techniques to serve new functions, and these techniques became specialized as my research goals became more differentiated. Thus in Oksapmin I created interviews that were geared for eliciting strategies for solving arithmetical problems in the context of a new practice of economic exchange using indigenous numeration. In Brooklyn I created means of assessing young children's numerical understandings and their links to their everyday number activities. And in Brazil I created observational and interview techniques for documenting the character of mathematical problems that emerged in practices and assessment techniques informed by the observational studies. Now, confronted with new challenges of comparative studies of traditional and reform-minded mathematics classrooms, colleagues and I are viewing classroom practice as cultural practice. In this endeavor, we are again adapting techniques to represent the emergent environments in classrooms and the form-function shifts in teachers and students as they engage with the new challenges of educational reform.

Acknowledgments

Thanks to Maryl Gearhart for comments on an earlier draft of this chapter. Support from the Spencer Foundation (grant no. M890224) and the National Science Foundation (grant no. MDR-8855643) during the preparation of the manuscript is gratefully acknowledged. The opinions expressed in this chapter are my own, and not necessarily those of the funding agencies.

Notes

1. This analytic concern is similar to Vygotsky's target of study in his "method of double stimulation" (Vygotsky 1978). Vygotsky, however, focused principally on the construct of "internalization" in his analysis of shifting relations between artifacts and cognition. Further, Vygotsky's research was lab based, with the principal exception of the study he supervised with Luria reviewed above.

2. It is common in poor communities in northeastern Brazil for children to drop out of school at a young age or to never attend school. Thus, unlike in the United States, in Recife it was possible to contrast children of the same age who had differing levels of school experience.

References

Boas, F. 1911. *The Mind of Primitive Man.* New York: Macmillan.
Brown, J. S., A. Collins, and P. Duguid. 1989. "Situated Cognition and the Culture of Learning." *Educational Researcher* 18: 32–41.
Campione, J. C., A. L. Brown, R. Ferrara, and N. R. Bryant. 1984. "The Zone of Proximal Development: Implications for Individual Differences and Learning." In *Children's Learning in the Zone of Proximal Development.* Ed. B. Rogoff and J. V. Wertsch, 45–63. San Francisco: Jossey-Bass.
Cole, M. 1990. "Cultural Psychology: A Once and Future Discipline?" In

Nebraska Symposium on Motivation 1989: Cross-Cultural Perspectives, no. 37. Ed. J. J. Berman. Lincoln, Nebr.: University of Nebraska Press.

―――. 1991. Conclusion to *Perspectives on Socially Shared Cognition.* Ed. L. B. Resnick, J. M. Levine, and S. D. Teasley, 398–417. Washington, D.C.: American Psychological Association.

Cole, M., and S. Scribner. 1974. *Culture and Thought: A Psychological Introduction.* New York: Wiley.

Cole, M., J. Gay, J. A. Glick, and D. W. Sharp. 1971. *The Cultural Context of Learning and Thinking: An Exploration in Experimental Anthropology.* New York: Basic Books.

Dasen, P. R. 1975. "Concrete Operational Development in Three Cultures." *Journal of Cross-Cultural Psychology* 6: 156–72.

Fuson, K. 1988. *Children's Counting and Concepts of Number.* New York: Springer-Verlag.

Gay, J., and M. Cole. 1965. *The New Mathematics in an Old Culture: A Study of Learning among the Kpelle of Liberia.* New York: Holt, Rinehart, and Winston.

Gearhart, M., G. B. Saxe, and D. Stipek. 1991. "Portfolios in Practice." Unpublished.

Gelman, R., and R. Gallistel. 1978. *The Child's Understanding of Number.* Cambridge, Mass.: Harvard University Press.

Hutchins, E. 1991. "The Social Organization of Distributed Cognition." In *Perspectives on Socially Shared Cognition.* Ed. L. B. Resnick, J. M. Levine, and S. D. Teasley, 283–307. Washington, D.C.: American Psychological Association.

Kohlberg, L. 1969. "Stage and Sequence: The Cognitive-Developmental Approach to Socialization." In *Handbook of Socialization Theory and Research.* Ed. D. A. Goslin. Chicago: Rand-McNally.

Laboratory of Comparative Human Cognition (LCHC). 1978. "Cognition as a Residual Category in Anthropology." *Annual Review of Anthropology* 7: 51–69.

―――. 1979. "What's Cultural about Cross-Cultural Cognitive Psychology?" *Annual Review of Psychology* 30: 145–72.

Langer, J. 1969. *Theories of Development.* New York: Holt, Rinehart, and Winston.

―――. 1986. *The Origins of Logic: One to Two Years.* New York: Academic Press.

Lave, J. 1977. "Tailor-Made Experiments and Evaluating the Intellectual Consequences of Apprenticeship Training." *Quarterly Newsletter of the Institute for Comparative Human Development* 1: 1–3.

―――. 1990. *Cognition in Practice.* New York: Cambridge University Press.

Luria, A. R. 1976. *Cognitive Development: Its Cultural and Social Foundations.* Cambridge, Mass.: Harvard University Press.

National Council of Teachers of Mathematics (NCTM). 1989. *Curriculum and Evaluation Standards for School Mathematics.* Reston, Va.: NCTM.

Pea, R. D. 1994. "Practices of Distributed Intelligence and Designs for Education." In *Distributed Cognitions: Psychological and Educational Considerations.* Ed. G. Salomon, 47–87. New York: Cambridge University Press.

Pepper, S. 1942. *World Hypotheses.* Berkeley: University of California Press.

Piaget, J. 1966. "Need and Significance of Cross-Cultural Studies in Genetic Psychology." *International Journal of Psychology* 1: 3–13.

———. 1970. "Piaget's Theory." In *Carmichael's Manual of Child Psychology.* Ed. P. Mussen. New York: Wiley.

Posner, J. 1982. "The Development of Mathematical Knowledge in Two West African Societies." *Child Development* 53: 200–208.

Price-Williams, D., W. Gordon, and M. Ramirez. 1967. "Manipulation and Conservation: A Study of Children from Pottery-Making Families in Mexico." *Memorias del XI Congreso Interamericao de la psicologia.* Mexico City, 106–21.

Rogoff, B. 1990. *Apprenticeship in Thinking: Cognitive Development in Social Context.* New York: Oxford University Press.

Saxe, G. B. 1977. "A Developmental Analysis of Notational Counting." *Child Development* 48: 1512–20.

———. 1979. "Developmental Relations Between Notational Counting and Number Conservation." *Child Development* 50: 180–87.

———. 1981. "Body Parts as Numerals: A Developmental Analysis of Numeration among a Village Population in Papua New Guinea." *Child Development* 52: 306–16.

———. 1982. "Developing Forms of Arithmetic Operations among the Oksapmin of Papua New Guinea." *Developmental Psychology* 18: 583–94.

———. 1983. "Culture, Counting, and Number Conservation." *International Journal of Psychology* 18: 313–18.

———. 1985. "The Effects of Schooling on Arithmetical Understandings: Studies with Oksapmin Children in Papua New Guinea." *Journal of Educational Psychology* 77: 503–13.

———. 1988a. "Candy Selling and Math Learning." *Educational Researcher* 17: 14–21.

———. 1988b. "The Mathematics of Child Street Vendors." *Child Development* 59: 1415–25.

———. 1991. *Culture and Cognitive Development: Studies in Mathematical Understanding.* Hillsdale, N.J.: Erlbaum.

———. 1992. "Studying Children's Learning in Context: Problems and Prospects." *Journal of the Learning Sciences* 2: 215–34.

Saxe, G. B., and T. Bermudez. 1992. "Emergent Mathematical Environments in Children's Games." Paper presented at the 1992 meetings of the International Congress of Mathematics Education, Quebec City.

Saxe, G. B., and M. Gearhart. 1990. "The Development of Topological Concepts in Unschooled Straw Weavers." *British Journal of Developmental Psychology* 8: 251–58.

Saxe, G. B., M. Gearhart, and S. Guberman. 1984. "The Social Organization of Early Number Development." In *Children's Learning in the Zone of Proximal Development.* Ed. B. Rogoff and J. V. Wertsch. New Directions for Child Development, no. 23. San Francisco: Jossey-Bass.

Saxe, G. B., and S. R. Guberman. 1993. "Emergent Goals in the Context of Distributed Problem Solving." Paper presented at the meeting of the Society for Research in Child Development, New Orleans.

Saxe, G. B., and T. Moylan. 1982. "The Development of Measurement Operations among the Oksapmin of Papua Guinea." *Child Development* 53: 1242–48.

Saxe, G. B., M. Gearhart, M. Note, and P. Paduano, P. Forthcoming. "Peer Interaction and the Development of Mathematical Understandings: A New Framework for Research and Educational Practice." In *Charting the Agenda: Vygotskian Perspectives.* Ed. H. Daniels. London: Routledge.

Saxe, G. B., S. R. Guberman, and M. Gearhart. 1987. *Social Processes in Early
Number Development.* Monographs of the Society for Research in Child Development, no. 52. With reviews by B. Rogoff, R. Gelman, and C. Massey.

Shweder, R. A., and M. A. Sullivan. Forthcoming. "Cultural Psychology: Who
Needs It?" *Annual Review of Psychology* 44.

Vygotsky, L. S. 1978. *Mind in Society.* Cambridge, Mass.: Harvard University
Press.

———. 1986. In *Thought and Language.* Ed. A. Kozulin. Cambridge, Mass.: MIT
Press.

Werner, H., and B. Kaplan. 1962. *Symbol Formation.* New York: Wiley.

Wertsch, J. V. 1984. "The Zone of Proximal Development: Some Conceptual
Issues." In *Children's Learning in the "Zone of Proximal Development."* Ed. B.
Rogoff and Wertsch. New Directions for Child Development, no. 23. San
Francisco: Jossey-Bass.

———. 1991. *Voices of the Mind: A Sociocultural Approach to Mediated Action.*
Cambridge, Mass.: Harvard University Press.

14 Why Ethnography Should Be the Most Important Method in the Study of Human Development

THOMAS S. WEISNER

Ethnography Brings Cultural Places Around the World into the Study of Human Development

I have asked various groups of students and colleagues, "If you could do one thing to influence a child's development, and could pick something that would be the single most important influence, what would it be?" Another version of this thought experiment is, "Imagine a newborn baby, neurologically sound and healthy. What is the single most important influence that you would point to influencing the life of that baby?" The responses are quite predictable: touch and hold the child close for attachment and bonding; provide it with nutrition, physical security, and good medical care; talk with it responsively and often; provide it with a quality education, both formal and informal; find playmates for it; give it a sense of self-esteem; make sure its parents are wealthy (Weisner 1993). What comes to mind are qualities of the dyadic interactional system in which a child develops, or the physical needs of the developing organism, or the need for stimulation to encourage cognitive and social competencies, or the importance of a kind of self, deemed important in contemporary North American economy and society.

Although every one of these responses undeniably is important in the development of a child, in my view none of these is the most important—the most important is to give the child a specific culture in which to mature and develop. Almost never does anyone spontaneously mention the cultural place where the child is going to grow up. By a "cultural place" I mean the cultural beliefs, practices, meanings, and ecological setting characteristic of members of that community. The most important thing you could do would be to place the child within some cultural community on earth. Ethnography is the most important method in the study of human development because it ensures that the cultural place will be incorporated into understanding development.

Place the child in a community of Tamil Hindus, Muslims, and Sinhala Buddhists in Sri Lanka (McGilvray 1988); or among Brahmans in the temple city of Bhubaneswar, Orissa, India (Shweder, Mahapatra, and Miller 1990); or among the Balinese of Indonesia (H. Geertz 1961; Mead 1955; Mead and Macgregor 1951; Wikan 1990); or among families living in a kibbutz in Israel in the 1950s (Spiro and Spiro 1975); or among the FulBe or RiimaayBe communities of the Fulani of Burkina Faso (Riesman 1992); or among the horticultural and migratory wage earning Abaluyia in Western Kenya (Weisner 1979); or among Gusii mothers and wives in Western Kenya (LeVine and LeVine 1979; LeVine et al. 1994); or among the !Kung foragers and hunters of Botswana and Namibia (Draper 1976; Shostak 1981); or in a squatter settlement in contemporary Cape Town, South Africa (Reynolds 1989); or among the horticulturalist and small-animal hunting Sambia of the New Guinea Highlands (Herdt 1987); or among the Mehinaku, a small Brazilian fishing and mixed-subsistence Indian village community in the Amazon basin (Gregor 1977); or in a Sioux Indian community in South Dakota in 1969 (Dorris 1989); or among Navajo of the Southwest in the 1970s (Chisholm, 1983); or among Inuit (Eskimo) communities of the Canadian Arctic (Briggs 1970; Condon 1988); or in a Samoan village (Ochs 1988); or in Tahiti (Levy 1973); or in a native Hawaiian community in Honolulu (Gallimore, Boggs, and Jordan 1974); or in a poor neighborhood in Mexico City in the 1950s (Lewis 1961); or in an impoverished neighborhood in a town in contemporary northeast Brazil (Scheper-Hughes 1992).

In all of these studies, the sense of childhood being lived in another cultural place, with their different cultural careers (Goldschmidt 1990), stands out. If you went to these or a hundred other cultural places, you would discover the startling, disturbing, wonderful variety of what it means to be a child or parent and the variety of forms development can take. Children there would surprise you with the remarkable cultural abilities they have acquired and which they clearly are developmentally prepared for cultures to discover. The theories, findings, and developmental concerns of the authors of these cross-cultural studies vary enormously, but that is another matter.

The cultural place, it is fair to say, is not a routinely thought-about part of the accepted cognitive schema for thinking about human development in most of the developmental sciences, which is why ethnography should be among the most important methods in those fields. Yet why doesn't the cultural place, which is everywhere recognized as important once it is mentioned, leap to mind immediately and forcefully as crucially important? It should, because culture offers us the tools for the mind which make development possible.

Of course, recognition of the cultural place as a powerfully important influence in development immediately suggests that there is no "one" important thing, and that development is multiply determined in cultural context. All of the influences which usually come to mind are important in every cultural place. Developmentally sensitive and appropriate interactions are indeed crucial, for example, but the existence of those dyadic interactions is due to the everyday cultural routine of life and to shared understandings which surround and scaffold them. Self-understanding and esteem are important as well, but culturally provided settings and their meanings make these possible. Attachment and trust are important, but how do infants and children experience strangers and learn whom to trust?

Ethnography brings the importance of the cultural place to the center of attention, transforming it from ground to figure. An important goal of ethnographic research is to describe and understand the cultural place and its influence on the everyday lives of its members. Whatever one's opinions are about epistemological issues and methodological concerns regarding ethnographically derived knowledge (and there surely are such concerns, as for all methods), the remarkable *findings* from ethnographic work regarding the varying cultural tools children use to develop in cultural places throughout the world alone provide sufficient reason for ethnography's deep incorporation into developmental work.

The chapters in this section offer interesting findings and their own models for how to integrate ethnography into developmental research. My comments on the chapters take advantage of their work to develop some general points about fieldwork and ethnography. First and foremost, ethnography and fieldwork get the researcher out into the cultural place of children and families. Once there, many ways of doing ethnography are possible and are illustrated in these chapters. Second, "methodocentrism"—the exclusive use of one method and fear of others—should be resisted, as these chapters illustrate. It is not plausible that any important question in developmental studies can be answered with a single method. Ethnography can and should be complementary with other methods. I suggest a way to talk about research methods differen than the iconic qualitative/quantitative contrast, which seems to encourage polarizing discourse and is in any case not very useful or accurate. Third, ethnography is not limited only to early exploratory stages of research and to description of local meanings. It can and should be question driven; it provides valid evidence to test against our models of the world; and it produces findings, as these chapters demonstrate. Next, I suggest that ethnography is to the developmental sciences as siblings or cousins are to one another—a part of the same broad lineage in the naturalistic traditions of the social sciences. John Modell imagines ethnography and development as two fascinated and mutually dangerous lovers. Both metaphors are probably appropriate at times. Finally, I suggest that a number of salutary things would happen if fieldwork in another cultural place, like learning statistics, was a normal, expected part of every developmentalist's training.

Varieties of Ethnographic Methods

When I went to East Africa to study family change and child rearing, I had a plan. I chose the Abaluyia, a patrilineal, patrilocal, horticultural group of communities in Western Kenya to work with. I was going to study Abaluyia families living in rural and urban settings, adapting to cultural, political, and economic change. I planned on using ethnography, systematic observations of children and caregivers, informal interviews, questionnaires, and child and parental assessments of varying kinds (Weisner 1976, 1979, 1987, 1989; Weisner and Abbott 1977). I went as a participant in a systematic cross-cultural research program in human development (Whiting and Whiting 1975; Whiting and Edwards 1988). It took months of confusion and stubbornness on my part, and constant involvement with and interviewing of families (not to mention struggles with languages, my role in the community, my health, and so on) before it gradually dawned on me that the cultural place did not always fit my design or prior expectation.

For one thing, children were being taken care of by other children much of the time, not by their mothers or fathers, and even when mothers were present, they were not directly involved in care, but rather managed, coordinated, and struggled with the tasks of domestic life in a way I did not grasp. The cultural system of caretaking—that is, the rules of discipline, talking with children, evaluations of child competence, beliefs about gender—or the principles used in maintaining domestic life, were complicated; I didn't understand these. Mothers and fathers talked with me about parenting not primarily in terms of dyadic interaction and stimulation with their children but in terms of inheritance, generations, pride, obligation and obedience, and family-adaptive tasks. Mothers were more concerned with the complex adult relationships in their large households than they were with childrearing as a specialized activity. Modernization, mother-child stimulation, and stress may have been themes in North American developmental work at the time (and still are), but there was a lot more going on in the families I was observing.

Not only that, my "urban" and "rural" samples did not stay put. After I had worked with my urban sample for three months, 40 percent of them were gone. They kept commuting back and forth between city and country locations or to other parts of the country altogether. My sample members left their assigned groups even while I was trying to identify or relocate them. I had to scrap that design and try to find a way to study family change using a sample and cultural categories which were socially and culturally meaningful to Abaluyia. I had to completely change my sample to a rural-urban family-matched network because that represented the shifting social world children lived in. I had to come up with a matched, family-pair design, since that was the only way to embed my study into their cultural place, as children experienced it.

I had to figure out the system of sibling caretaking, or socially distributed nurturance. Changes in the sibling group due to complex patterns of migration turned out to have a lot to do with changing child social behaviors, more so than changes in mothers' caretaking. The older and younger children were separated in the city, leading to many ramifying changes in children's social behavior and mother's adaptations in the city. I had to change some of my ways of measuring child competence, since parents' own criteria for recognizing competence (social and task competence being highly elaborated, not individual cognitive or verbal expression) made a huge difference in children's abilities and the ways necessary to elicit them. Everything I anticipated doing did not have to be scrapped. I still could use many of the methods I originally had planned, and the comparative enterprise in which I participated has made lasting contributions to the systematic study of children and families. But the topics I studied got modified, the samples and designs were changed, the questions were sometimes quite different. I was learning from my fieldwork.

Ethnography gets us out there in the midst of some cultural place and in the midst of cultural practices and it gets at the meanings and experiences and moral significances of those cultural activities to the participants themselves. Ethnography, among other uses, assists in what Geertz (1988:147) proposed as a "next necessary thing to do" in anthropology and, I would suggest, in human development as well:

> It is to enlarge the possibility of intelligible discourse between people quite different from one another in interest, outlook, wealth, and power, and yet contained in a world where, tumbled as they are into endless connection, it is increasingly difficult to get out of each other's way.

The possibilities are enhanced for better understanding of development in these cultural places after reading most of these chapters. Through Saxe's work, I could at least start trying to count things with the Oksapmin in

Papua New Guinea, or sell things with Brazilian street sellers. I could have lunch with a couple who had "fallen from grace" (Newman 1988), or meet their children in my classes and have a sense of empathy I would not have had before. I could see a Chinese-American family scold their young child, participate in their family activities, and begin to grasp through Miller's work the reasons why. Sullivan's work expands the debate about those "truly disadvantaged," through grasping the meaning of the notion of wanting to "get paid," as a local cultural model. I could appreciate through Heath and her junior ethnographers the fierce loyalties inner-city youths attach to their local sports clubs and church organizations as they seek to achieve a sense of place within their communities and display often intense achievement striving.

Ethnographic methods in human development typically include direct observation and interviewing of families in naturalistic settings in homes and communities over long periods of time. Fieldnotes and qualitative information are central. But ethnography is not limited to informal participant observations, informal interviews, and notes, as even a casual perusal of standard texts and references in the field with varying points of view about fieldwork will confirm (Agar 1980; Bernard 1988; Edgerton and Langness 1974; Levine et al. 1980; Lofland and Lofland 1984; Narroll and Cohen 1970; Pelto and Pelto 1978; Spradley 1979, 1980; Werner and Schoepfle 1987a,b). Most of the studies in this book used varied ethnographic methods and used methods in addition to ethnographic ones. Nothing in ethnographic methods, theory, or epistemology precludes this, and much encourages multiple methods.

As with any serious method, there are conventional (and hotly debated) ways available to assess the validity, reliability, and bias in qualitative ethnographic data (Miles and Huberman 1984, 1994). Although overtly out of fashion nowadays (but nonetheless still very often sought after for field use), there are standard topical lists and domains around which to orient general ethnographic inquiry in fieldwork (Johnson and Johnson 1990; Murdock et al. 1961). There also are lists focused more specifically on childhood and human development (Hilger 1966, 1992; Gallimore et al. 1993; Weisner 1984; Whiting and Edwards 1988; Whiting and Whiting 1975).

Every particular cultural place will require that alterations be made to the standard topics presented in these kinds of comparative summaries, sometimes profound alterations. But the overwhelming evidence is that we will not need to completely start over each time we go out in order to understand human development in another cultural place, because there are enduring adaptive problems and developmental concerns that will appear always or very often, and because there are ecocultural features that appear to influence child development everywhere. Ethnography, in complement with other methods, provides much of the basic data for the understanding of cultural and human universals (Brown 1991), as well as differences. It includes systematic comparative developmental research using ethnographic techniques and findings in complement with others (Cole et al. 1971; Edgerton 1971; Hewlett 1992; Munroe and Munroe 1994a; Whiting and Whiting 1975; Whiting and Edwards 1988; Wozniak 1993).

Ethnographic work often involves a sustained, long-term commitment to research, with intense personal involvement by the researcher. Ethnographers typically are engaged with *participants* in their research, rather than assessing subjects, clients, or patients. This often places the ethnographer as a participant in events and openly an active constructor of the data being collected. The implicit choices made in other methods are seen more explicitly in ethnographic work. The buzzing confusion and complexity of everyday events comes to the fore; neat analytical categories are tested by this intense exposure to real activities, multiply shaped. The meaning and interpretation of events is an immediate and continuing problem to the researcher. Ethnography is not a unilateral process whereby a naive and "open-minded" fieldworker is shaped by the circumstances of the field situation. It is, rather, the process of matching the prior, evolving schema in the mind of the ethnographer against the changing and evolving materials gained from the field experience.

Is this why ethnographic and qualitative methods frequently seem to evoke ruminations by fieldworkers, including several of the authors in this book, about their personal biographies, why they chose these topics and cultural places (Saxe), or whether they were accepted by preschoolers and had good rapport and language skills (Corsaro)? Some of Miller's research findings *are* the reflexive processes her ethnographers experienced in the discourse practices they went to the field to study. Experiments, social surveys, or questionnaires do not seem to bring forth such personal disclosures, perhaps because of their standardization and because they offer an illusion of distance and objectivity.

The studies in this group made highly *selective* use of the various components of the ethnographic method. No one did a full ethnography or even a partial holistic study. Each study utilized a piece of the broader ethnographic method. These methods included field behavioral observations, interviews, and structured arithmetic tasks for Saxe; sociolinguistic transcriptions and observations for Miller; and clinical interviews for Horowitz and colleagues. Heath entered into collaborative ventures with a group of twenty "junior ethnographers" who were themselves from the inner-city organizations Heath and her colleagues wanted to study. These "research-apprentice-participants" tape-recorded and transcribed language data and context. Sullivan and his colleagues used local expert informants to understand delinquent peer groups. Taken together, these various methods constitute many of the tools of a full ethnography.

Nor did any of the studies involve full participant observation, or a comprehensive attempt to provide a full cultural account of a community. Each instead carved out a particular activity setting (teen sports and community organizations for Heath, street selling of candy for Saxe, family sociolinguistic events for Miller) to concentrate on. These pieces of ethnographic method can stand alone, even without a full ethnography of the families and communities—although a full account is the ideal.

Ethnography has too many uses right across the research process and takes too many forms to be compartmentalized as a method only used for exploration but not useful for verification; or useful mainly for the study of subjective meanings but not for analyzing behavior patterns or child outcomes. The authors in this volume followed the practice of using their "ethnographic imagination" even before going to the field to think about the cultural context and conceptualize their study. They used ethnography once in the field, or while interviewing, to explore—talk, participate, observe, listen closely, or work with co-ethnographers. They then discovered relationships between events, new terms and categories, possible new explanations for patterns of family life and childhood. Some then used ethnographic methods to assist in the work of verifying what they thought they had discovered—along with complementary methods, such as more structured interviews or surveys, analyses of videotapes, school records, tests, and so forth.

In spite of these varied and productive uses of ethnography, there are heightened anxieties, ironies, and concerns over ethnography today. Ethnographic research and writing is vigorously debated and worriedly critiqued (Geertz 1988; Clifford and Marcus 1986; Sanjek 1990). Critical and feminist theories alike question the historical bases of gender, power, or control from which ethnographies and ethnographers come (di Leonardo 1991; Marcus and Fischer 1986). All the epistemological and philosophical concerns raised by the ancient philosophers and present in the social sciences since their emergence, such as problems of reflexivity and knowing another, not surprisingly continue to remain at issue. So has developmental research "found" ethnography at the very moment when the ethnographic enterprise is lost in a cloud of criticism, doubt, and confusion?

Quite to the contrary, an enduring ethnographic project remains. To write and speak about others in as clear and plain a style as possible. To assemble a scholarly, high-quality, enduring ethnographic record of family life and human development around the world for systematic comparative research (Whiting and Whiting 1970; Ember and Levinson 1991; Munroe and Munroe 1994b). To get the news out, as Margery Wolf puts it, citing Watson (1987:36), in order to try to understand why people around the world do what they do (Wolf 1992:1). To retain the core ethnographic commitments to empathy, scrupulousness, concreteness, fair-mindedness, and hopefully "revelatory" discovery and understanding (Fernandez 1993:183, citing Feeley-Harnik 1991).

Ethnography Has a Complementary Relationship to Other Methods; "Methodocentrism" Should Be Resisted

I and my colleagues watched a mother watch her child being assessed in the Strange Situation Procedure (SSP) many years ago. When the mother left the room and the child was left with a stranger (part of the experimental procedure), the child did not fuss or howl, but played alone. When the stranger also left and then the mother returned, the child fussed but did not require its mother for comforting. The SSP scoring for this pattern of behavior was that the child was not "securely" attached to the mother. The child was "avoidant" in this scoring scheme compared with a child who would cry upon the mother's departure and then be comforted not by the stranger but by the mother's return to the experimental room.

The mothers could watch portions of this experimental drama unfold through a one-way window while they were out of the room. This particular mother watched her child acting in a way attributed to "avoidant attachment"—and proudly commented to the researchers standing there, "This is what I have been working for by having him be with other kids and families while I am working. Look how independent he is! See how he can play by himself?" This mother was a single parent by choice. She had told us about her cultural goals for independence for herself and her child, her commitment to feminism, her struggles to sustain work and parenting, and many other values. Her construction of her child's behavior came from this framework of beliefs and practices. In this ethnographic moment in which the mother and I were observing the administration of the SSP, the tension between the intimacy and interdependence of the ethnographic researcher with what he or she researches, on the one hand, and the distance and "independence" presumably present in the formal SSP itself, on the other hand, was revealed. Our longitudinal research suggests thus far that the cultural goals mattered for long-term child outcomes, while SSP scores do not (Weisner et al. 1991; Weisner and Garnier 1992).

Understanding trust and attachment in its cultural context requires fieldwork and ethnography. Harwood, Miller, and Irizarry (1995), LeVine and Miller (1990), Reed and Leiderman (1981), Takahashi (1990), and many others have commented on the wide variations around the world in how children are exposed to strangers, who takes care of them and in what manner, and the consequences of these variations in trust, sociality, and emotional expression for understanding attachment. The SSP method depends on processes of intimacy and basic trust which may be culturally conditioned; it depends on the cultural practices around infant care and parent-child experience to give it meaning. There may well be lasting differences in the dispositional tendencies in children presumably measured in the SSP, and it will matter in children's development to understand those tendencies. Although I am dubious that the SSP is the gold standard against which to assess that dispositional tendency, it is one among several methods worth trying. But first I would make "attachment" itself a subject of ethnographic study.

This moment also stands as a positive experience regarding my greatest fear about methods: that the methods chosen will not bring me close enough to what it is I am trying to understand. Yet that is not the concern, fear, or anxiety about methods one hears very often. The concerns are almost always regarding possible biases, sample size, validity, reliability, veridicality, verifiability, replicability, efficiency of a method, its cost, and so forth. All worthy and important concerns—and all concerns in fact that ethnography, used in complement with other methods, can help us deal with.

Several methods are required to get us closer to understanding attachment or other developmental topics. Resistance to or denigration of other serious methods, which might be called methodocentrism in the study of human development, should be resisted. Methodocentrism, like ethnocentrism, may be inevitable and be understandable in certain circumstances, but generally both should be avoided. Methodocentrism can lead to invidious ranking of methods, and to imperialistic tendencies where one discipline or method tries to overshadow another. It can lead to a confusion of a measure of something with what is being measured.

The chapters in this volume share the view that other methods should play a complementary role with ethnography. Peggy Miller uses the personal experience of field observers, but also engages in intensive analysis of tapes and transcripts using standard analytical methods in sociolinguistics, to understand messages to children regarding self-esteem or autonomy. Horowitz argues for moving from laboratory to field situations in comparing ethnic groups' stereotypes. Corsaro administered questionnaires to his Italian teachers and tested the children, as well as hunkering down on the preschool floor. He argues that quantitative and longitudinal data are better for assessing reliability and generalizability of studies in his field.

Many of these researchers intervened in their field settings. For instance, Saxe asks the candy wholesalers to track retailers' buying when they come in to restock. He intervenes on the street or in kids' math tasks in order to try to understand cognitive and memory processes "in flight." Saxe argues for the complementary use of specific structured techniques and sampling frames because of their precision and the history of our experience with them.

Newman and Saxe both develop the argument that careful sampling also can be crucial for ethnographic work. Newman samples particular groups of families for generational identity differences, and Saxe compares Brazilian street sellers who are adept and others who are novices in folk math tasks. Newman combines knowledge of the recent trends in employment from survey research and economic analysis, and argues for using longitudinal family samples as complementary to ethnographic data, even if there are only quantitative data available for some of those samples. Lock used large-scale social-survey data from Japan. Sullivan struggles with the tension between survey and "neighborhood" or census-tract data and the findings of participant observation in such neighborhoods. Heath, Miller, and Corsaro all use the interconnections between sociolinguistics and ethnography in their studies to generate their research findings. Miller uses information on reciprocal influences between her home observers and the participants as a type of sociolinguistic data. Corsaro uses differences in children's and teachers' perception of him and his Italian language abilities as indicators of their folk beliefs and the relational qualities among children and teachers. Heath combines intensive transcript-based sociolinguistic analysis along with her ethnographic work.

The prevailing discourse elsewhere in the social sciences regarding methods does not make the complementary nature of ethnographic work clear, as Don Campbell saw long ago. Nor does the prevailing academic discourse and the terms it uses help in debating the matter. Qualitative research, in the current model, is typically opposed to its presumed opposite, quantitative research. Naturalistic research is paired with its presumed opposite—experimental research. Cultural or comparative research is contrasted with its assumed opposite of monocultural work, which is somehow magically culture-free. It is apparent that the cultural categories and terms of discourse often used to define ethnographic as contrasted to other methods are part of the difficulty in placing ethnographic and qualitative cultural research within the family of methods in the social sciences. These conventional methodological dichotomies, however common they are in everyday parlance, are neither accurate nor useful. Let's revise them.

Saxe's work on mathematics illustrates that the opposite of qualitative or holistic research is certainly not quantitative research, but rather *particularistic* or specifically focused research. Quantitative is not the opposite of qualitative, but rather has to do with the level of measurement available or appropriate for a study. Quantitative levels of measurement could be contrasted with *nominal* or categorical levels. Naturalistic studies contrast with research that is in some way *contrived* by the researcher or others. Experimental work, which attempts to infer cause, is usefully contrasted with *correlational* studies attempting to discover relationships and patterns. Comparative studies have no opposite, it seems to me. All studies have an implicit comparative frame of reference of some sort—a meaning in a context relevant to some cultural place, whether for the purpose of cultural comparison or not. In this sense, all studies have an "ethnographic" component embedded in them, even if ethnography was not done. If authors in this volume had been asked the standard-discourse question—Did you use quantitative or qualitative methods?—they collectively might have answered, We did contrived as well as naturalistic studies, using nominal and interval levels of measurement, sometimes highly particularistic as well as holistic, for the purpose of discovering both relationships and cause, in several cultural places.

Ethnographic Work Is Question Driven and Produces Findings

What did these studies discover; what findings did ethnography produce? Heath wants to understand how inner-city youth achieve a sense of place, a process involving a kind of familism and sharing among a trusted group; shared rules that matter; predictable structures (social, physical, emotional) in which to move; and a common value placed on achievement and hope for the future. More fundamentally, Heath searches for the mechanisms producing a "symbolic creation of place" and finds some of these in the language of rules shared in the youth organizations she studied. It seems to me that every one of these processes occurs in *all* cultures and communities adapting reasonably successfully; their absence is a sign of maladaptation in a cultural place (Edgerton 1992). So a more general question generated by these findings is, How can interventions at individual, family, and neighborhood levels assist in the developmental achievement of a meaningful sense of cultural place?

Corsaro asks whether children negotiate with adults, and thereby assist or resist the reproduction of their sociocultural circumstances, or whether they primarily "internalize" features of adult culture presented to them.

He finds negotiation common in everyday life in the preschool. He asks, To what extent are important cultural routines in which children participate over time a key set of activities driving child socialization? Recognizing the predictability and redundancy of such routines over time is crucial in understanding their force in his Italian preschool, as in most cultural situations. Longitudinal ethnography is probably the preeminent method for understanding this patterned activity, and Corsaro thus sets out to find these expectations and cultural routines. The Italian teachers he studied are valorized in their roles, and do not seem to need to, or be expected to, engage in "therapeutic" interactions vis-à-vis Italian parents. Nor are teachers asked by parents to demonstrate that they are treating each child as a unique individual whom they personally like, as some North American parents seem to expect (Tobin, Wu, and Davidson 1989). What is it about Italian life that produces such a preschool cultural world?

Miller argues for the importance of language as a "preeminent tool of meaning construction," in which "talk is recognized to be not only reflective of meaning but constitutive of meaning." Intensive ethnographic work involves describing language development and cultural practices each "in its own terms." This leads to emergent questions based on sometimes troubling and painful experiences discovered in doing her fieldwork: "Why did [middle-class Chinese mothers in Taipei] routinely tease their daughters? Why did they talk about violent death, wife beatings, and child abuse in front of their children?" She also asks ethical and moral questions: Does ethnography require a certain kind of nonevaluative empathy and analysis of the reflexive relationships of ethnographer and participant?, Miller asks. If we want insiders to interpret their own practices for the researcher, does this thereby legitimate, justify, rationalize, the practices?

Miller provides insight into the parents' meanings and reasons for these practices, but does not move out into the wider cultural analysis of these families necessary to address such questions. Further, as Miller certainly recognizes, Taipei is not the only cultural place in which children learn that the same kin community who cares for you and protects you can also tease, dominate, and exploit you. This is a widespread kind of socialization experience across cultures. Hence, although the mechanisms of talk in this cultural socialization process are beautifully set out in Miller's work, other levels of analysis and complementary data (such as measures of self-esteem or identity, or ethnographic work on mothers' and fathers' cultural values and socialization goals) are also needed.

Saxe integrates findings regarding cognitive developmental abilities in math and the ethnographic context in which they are developed and exercised. He asks, What are the emergent goals for activities and actors in mathematics use? How do form-function patterns in math practices shift over time in individuals as well as in *communities of use?* Saxe was into his third cross-cultural study by the time he arrived in Brazil to study child street sellers. His work among Alaskan Inuit (Eskimo) and then Oksapmin in Papua New Guinea persuaded him that communities of use and local apprenticeship knowledge were central in math practices. He asks about the interconnections of developmental abilities *across* different practices (for example, school arithmetic, street selling of candy, and negotiations with wholesalers). The striking situational competence of these children is matched against other views of street children as dangerous, failed, disabled, or wild. The social and family circumstances which provide a wider context for these Brazilian street sellers would have further enriched Saxe's account. I think the evidence suggests that most of these children *do* in fact face serious developmental problems and threats to their survival.

Sullivan explicitly frames his work around the underclass debate regarding inner-city youth, much as Heath does. The ethnographic enterprise and the underclass debate have largely *failed* to connect in his view. He found that in groups of youths followed through their teens, two or three out of a dozen persisted in delinquent and criminal activities, while most others seemed to begin a process of "maturing out" of some of these activities. Sullivan's groups and individuals *within* his neighborhood show that causal inferences regarding "inner-city neighborhood" effects require knowledge of individual developmental trajectories, peer-group developmental processes, and family influence, as well as of the larger social forces refracted into the neighborhood.

Horowitz, Stinson, and Milbrath's goal is laudable: to search for role-relationship models (RRM) and scripts, to relate these to different social situations individuals might face, and to search then for the multiple selves and identities these authors postulate are constitutive of the self. Although this cognition-to-social-situation matching is accessible to ethnography, and the transcripts of their subjects are susceptible to cultural analysis, I barely discern ethnographic work in this particular chapter. The question of the relationship of these RRMs to behavior in everyday cultural activities remains to be explored.

Ethnography Should Be to the Developmental Sciences as Siblings Are to One Another

John Modell (in this volume) describes the relationships between developmental researchers and ethnography as that between "fascinated and mutually dangerous lovers." There is that delicious excitement and tension, and there are no doubt some unresolvable and unexamined conflicts, as Modell's metaphor implies and his comments point out. But the sibling relationship metaphor is a useful alternative; it certainly seems to fit the chapters in this volume better, both their methods and their developmental findings.

We tend not to think of siblings as representing our culturally ideal relationship model, but many cultural places do (Marshall 1983; Weisner 1987, 1993). Certain kinds of cousins are also often classified as siblings— and marriage is sometimes encouraged between the appropriate cousins while being completely prohibited between others. I won't belabor the so-roral/fraternal metaphor, but consider this: ethnography and human development share a common social science tradition, a common intellectual ancestry. We can appreciate this if we stand back from our local, sibling rivalries and consider the developmentalist ancestors who so often studied cases and their own children first (Sigmund Freud and Jean Piaget, for example), and our ethnographic ancestors, many of whom emerged from the natural sciences and psychology to do cultural comparison or to provide cultural interpretations of human variation in the face of the racist and Social Darwinist alternatives of the times (W. H. R. Rivers, Alfred Kroeber, Franz Boas, Margaret Mead). The rise of the social sciences as an autonomous set of disciplines in the twentieth century benefited developmentalists and ethnographers alike. Anthropology and developmental studies also share many cousins in the biological, psychological, and archaeological/historical fields, as well as in life history and biography. If we share the study of families, children, aging, and other topics, we often compete for the same sources of research funds. We certainly compete for resources within universities and research institutes. This competition could be valuable for ethnographers and developmentalists alike; exogamy with selective-cousin marriage may help insure continued innovation and vitality. But, like siblings, we should recognize our mutual interdependence.

Doing Fieldwork in Another Cultural Place Should Be an Expectable Part of Developmental Training

This interdependence should be institutionalized in training and our routine research practice. Imagine if every developmentalist (whether psychologist of one of the various persuasions, sociologist, pediatrician, anthropologist, or member of yet another discipline) had to have done fieldwork in another cultural place in order to receive a degree. Imagine that this was a routine, institutionalized, self-evident part of developmental training, a core requirement like statistics. Ideally, such fieldwork would be an apprenticeship experienced with members of that cultural place as well as with mentors and fellow students. This training would involve firsthand ethnographic experience, not just readings as part of a course on the subject. Developmentalists from other countries would be coming to North America, because they would be engaged in the same training regimen in their countries, and important exchanges would occur with them in North America as well. Every nonconforming developmentalist would have to explain why he or she had not for some reason done fieldwork in another cultural place, or had not tested his or her findings from one place to another. How had they been able to (shamefully) "petition out" of such an obviously important research training experience? Those without such training would be at a disadvantage in the job market. To be sure, preferences for or against ethnographic work in another cultural place would not go away. Some would never do ethnography again; some (like the authors in this volume) would use it as one among many useful methods; some would embrace it fully.

If such an ethnographic requirement became widespread, methodocentrism would decline. Useful conventions would emerge for methods descriptions, along with frequent citations of cross-cultural material. The exploratory and discovery phases of research would become better reported, more valorized. A common body of cross-cultural experience would be brought to bear on important developmental problems. Communication across cultures and ethnic communities would benefit, and developmental researchers would be in a much better position to engage in that discourse in an increasingly tumbled world that so many see is upon us. Recognition of the influence of the cultural place in development, and of the power of ethnographic methods to study that influence, would come much more systematically, easily, and in a more useful, experience-rich form, to the developmental sciences.

Acknowledgments

The National Institute of Mental Health, the National Institute for Child Health and Development, the Carnegie Corporation of New York, the W. T. Grant Foundation, the Child Development Research Unit of Kenyatta University College, Nairobi, the Academic Senate research grant program of UCLA, and the Department of Psychiatry and Biobehavioral Sciences of UCLA have all provided research support for the Kenya and family research mentioned. Dennis McGilvray made valuable suggestions on an earlier draft after hosting a 1993 conference at the University of Colorado, Boulder, called "Redesigning Ethnography: Responses to Postmodernist, Feminist, and Other Critiques."

References

Agar, M. 1980. *The Professional Stranger.* New York: Academic Press.

Bernard, R. H. 1988. *Research Methods in Cultural Anthropology.* Newbury Park, Calif.: Sage.

Briggs, J. L. 1970. *Never in Anger. Portrait of an Eskimo Family.* Cambridge, Mass.: Harvard University Press.

Brown, D. E. 1991. *Human Universals.* New York: McGraw Hill.

Chisholm, J. S. 1983. *Navajo Infancy: An Ethological Study of Child Development.* New York: Aldine.

Clifford, J., and G. E. Marcus, eds. 1986. *Writing Culture: The Poetics and Politics of Ethnography.* Berkeley: University of California Press.

Cole, M., J. Gay, J. A. Glick, and D. W. Sharp. 1971. *The Cultural Context of Learning and Thinking: An Exploration in Experimental Anthropology.* New York: Basic Books.

Condon, R. G. 1988. *Inuit Youth: Growth and Change in the Canadian Arctic.* New Brunswick, N.J.: Rutgers University Press.

di Leonardo, Micaela, ed. 1991. *Gender at the Crossroads of Knowledge: Feminist Anthropology in the Postmodern Era.* Berkeley: University of California Press.

Draper, P. 1976. "Social and Economic Constraints on Child Life among the !Kung." In *Kalahari Hunter-Gatherers: Studies of the !Kung San and Their Neighbors.* Ed. R. B. Lee and I. DeVore, 119–207. Cambridge, Mass.: Harvard University Press

Dorris, M. 1989. *The Broken Cord.* New York: HarperCollins.

Edgerton, R. B. 1971. *The Individual in Cultural Adaptation: A Study of Four East African Peoples.* Berkeley: University of California Press.

———. 1992. *Sick Societies: Challenging the Myth of Primitive Harmony.* New York: Free Press.

Edgerton, R., and L. Langness. 1974. *Methods and Styles in the Study of Culture.* San Francisco: Chandler and Sharp.

Ember, C., and D. Levinson. 1991. "The Substantive Contributions of Worldwide Cross-Cultural Studies Using Secondary Data." *Behavior Science Research* 25: 79–140.

Feeley-Harnik, G. 1991. *A Green Estate: Restoring Independence in Madagascar.* Washington, D.C.: Smithsonian Institution Press.

Fernandez, J. W. 1993. "A Guide to the Perplexed Ethnographer in an Age of Sound Bites." *American Ethnologist* 20: 179–84.

Gallimore, R., J. W. Boggs, and C. Jordan. 1974. *Culture, Behavior and Education: A Study of Hawaiian-Americans.* Beverly Hills, Calif.: Sage.

Gallimore, R., T. S. Weisner, D. Guthrie, L. Bernheimer, and K. Nihira. 1993. "Family Response to Young Children with Developmental Delays: Accommodation Activity in Ecological and Cultural Context." *American Journal of Mental Retardation* 98: 185–206.

Geertz, C. 1988. *Works and Lives: The Anthropologist as Author.* Stanford, Calif.: Stanford University Press.

Geertz, H. 1961. *The Javanese Family: A Study of Kinship and Socialization.* New York: Free Press.

Goldschmidt, W. 1990. *The Human Career.* London: Routledge and Kegan Paul.

Gregor, T. 1977. *The Mehinaku: The Drama of Daily Life in a Brazilian Indian Village.* Chicago: University of Chicago Press.

Harwood, R. L., J. G. Miller, and N. L. Irizarry, eds. 1995. *Culture and Attachment: Perceptions of the Child in Context.* New York: Guilford Press.

Herdt, G. 1987. *The Sambia: Ritual and Gender in New Guinea.* New York: Holt, Rinehart, and Winston.

Hewlett, B., ed. 1992. *Father-Child Relations.* New York: Aldine de Greyter.

Hilger, M. I. 1966. *Field Guide to the Ethnological Study of Child Life.* New Haven, Conn.: Human Relations Area Files.

———. 1992. *Chippewa Child Life and Its Cultural Background.* St. Paul: Minnesota Historical Society Press.

Johnson, A., and O. R. Johnson. 1990. "Quality into Quantity: On the Measurement Potential of Ethnographic Fieldnotes." In *Fieldnotes: The Makings of Anthropology.* Ed. R. Sanjek, 161–86. Ithaca, N.Y.: Cornell University Press.

Levine, H. G., R. Gallimore, T. Weisner, and J. Turner. 1980. "Teaching Participant-Observation Research Methods: A Skills-Building Approach." Anthropology and Education Quarterly 11: 38–54.

LeVine, R., S. Dixon, S. LeVine, A. Richman, P. M. Leiderman, C. H. Keefer, and T. B. Brazelton. 1994. *Child Care and Culture. Lessons from Africa.* New York: Cambridge University Press.

LeVine, R., and P. Miller. 1990. Commentary. *Human Development* 33: 73–80.

LeVine, S., and R. LeVine. 1979. *Mothers and Wives: Gusii Women of East Africa.* Chicago: University of Chicago Press.

Levy, R. I. 1973. *Tahitians: Mind and Experience in the Society Islands.* Chicago: University of Chicago Press.

Lewis, O. 1961. *The Children of Sanchez: Autobiography of a Mexican Family.* New York: Vintage Books.

Lofland, J., and L. M. Lofland. 1984. *Analyzing Social Settings: A Guide to Qualitative Observation and Analysis.* 2d ed. Belmont, Calif.: Wadsworth.

Marcus, G. E., and M. M. J. Fischer. 1986. *Anthropology as Cultural Critique: An Experimental Moment in the Human Sciences.* Chicago: University of Chicago Press.

Marshall, M., ed. 1983. *Siblingship in Oceania: Studies in the Meaning of Kin Relations.* ASAO Monograph no. 8. Lanham, Md.: University Press of America.

McGilvray, D. 1988. "Sex, Repression, and Sanskritization in Sri Lanka?" *Ethos* 16: 99–127.

Mead, M., and F. C. Macgregor. 1951. *Growth and Culture: A Photographic Study of Balinese Childhood.* New York: Putnam.

Mead, M. 1955. "Children and Ritual in Bali." In *Childhood in Contemporary Cultures.* Ed. M. Mead and M. Wolfenstein, 40–51. Chicago: University of Chicago Press.

Miles, M., and A. M. Huberman. 1984. "Drawing Valid Meaning from Qualitative Data: Toward a Shared Craft." *Educational Researcher* May: 20–30.

———. 1994. *Qualitative Data Analysis: An Expanded Sourcebook.* 2d ed. Thousand Oaks, Calif.: Sage.

Munroe, R. L., and R. H. Munroe. 1994a. "Behavior Across Cultures: Results from Observational Studies." In *Psychology and Culture.* Ed. W. J. Lonner and R. Malpass, 107–11. Boston: Allyn and Bacon.

———. 1994b. *Cross-Cultural Human Development.* Prospect Heights, Ill.: Waveland Press.

Murdock, G. P., C. S. Ford, A. E. Hudson, R. Kennedy, L. W. Simmons, and J. W. M. Whiting. 1961. *Outline of Cultural Materials.* 4th ed. New Haven, Conn.: HRAF Press.

Naroll, R., and R. Cohen, eds. 1970. *A Handbook of Method in Cultural Anthropology.* New York: Columbia University Press.

Newman, K. 1988. *Falling from Grace: The Experience of Downward Mobility in the American Middle Class.* New York: Free Press.

Ochs, E. 1988. *Culture and Language Development: Language Acquisition and Language Socialization in a Samoan Village.* New York: Cambridge University Press.

Pelto, P., and G. Pelto. 1978. *Anthropological Research: The Structure of Inquiry.* 2d ed. Cambridge: Cambridge University Press.

Reed, G., and H. P. Leiderman. 1981. "Age-Related Changes in Attachment Behavior in Polymatrically Reared Infants: The Kenyan Gusii." In *Culture and Early Interactions.* Ed. T. M. Field, A. M. Sostek, P. Vietze, and P. H. Leiderman, 215–34. Hillsdale, N.J.: Lawrence Erlbaum Associates.

Reynolds, P. 1989. *Childhood in Crossroads Cognition and Society in South Africa.* Grand Rapids, Mich.: Wm. Eerdmans.

Riesman, P. 1992. *First Find Your Child a Good Mother: The Construction of Self in Two African Communities.* New Brunswick, N.J.: Rutgers University Press.

Sanjek, R., ed. 1990. *Fieldnotes: The Makings of Anthropology.* Ithaca, N.Y.: Cornell University Press.

Scheper-Hughes, N. 1992. *Death without Weeping: The Violence of Everyday Life in Brazil.* Berkeley: University of California Press.

Shostak, M. 1981. *Nisa: The Life and Words of a !Kung Woman.* Cambridge, Mass.: Harvard University Press.

Shweder, R. A., M. Mahapatra, and J. G. Miller. 1990. "Culture and Moral Development." In *Cultural Psychology: Essays on Comparative Human Development.* Ed. J. W. Stigler, R. A. Shweder, and G. Herdt, 130–204. Cambridge: Cambridge University Press.

Spradley, J. P. 1979. *The Ethnographic Interview.* New York: Holt, Rinehart, and Winston.

———. 1980. *Participant Observation.* New York: Holt, Rinehart, and Winston.

Spiro, M. E., and A. G. Spiro. 1975. *Children of the Kibbutz: A Study in Child Training and Personality.* Cambridge, Mass.: Harvard University Press.

Takahashi, K. 1990. "Are the Key Assumptions of the 'Strange Situation' Procedure Universal? A View from Japanese Research." *Human Development* 33: 23–30.

Tobin, J., D. Wu, and D. Davidson. 1989. *Preschool in Three Cultures. Japan, China, and the United States.* New Haven, Conn.: Yale University Press.

Watson, G. 1987. "Make Me Reflexive—But Not Yet: Strategies for Managing Essential Reflexivity in Ethnographic Discourse." *Journal of Anthropological Research* 43: 29–41.

Weisner, T. S. 1976. "Urban-Rural Differences in African Children's Performance on Cognitive and Memory Tasks." *Ethos* 4: 223–50.

———. 1979. "Urban-Rural Differences in Sociable and Disruptive Behavior of Kenya Children." *Ethnology* 18: 153–72.

———. 1984. "Ecocultural Niches of Middle Childhood: A Cross-Cultural Perspective." In *Development During Middle Childhood: The Years from Six to Twelve.* Ed. W. A. Collins, 335–69. Washington, D.C.: National Academy of Sciences Press.

———. 1987. "Socialization for Parenthood in Sibling Caretaking Societies." In *Parenting Across the Life Span.* Ed. J. Lancaster, A. Rossi, J. Altmann, and L. Sherrod, 237–70. New York, Aldine Press.

———. 1989. "Social Support for Children Among the Abaluyia of Kenya." In *Children's Social Networks and Social Supports.* Ed. D. Belle, 70–90. New York: Wiley.

———. 1993. "Siblings in Cultural Place: Ethnographic and Ecocultural Perspectives on Siblings of Developmentally Delayed Children." In *Siblings of Individuals with Mental Retardation, Physical Disabilities, and Chronic Illness.* Ed. Z. Stoneman and P. Berman, 51–83. Baltimore: Brooks.

Weisner, T. S., and S. Abbott. 1977. "Women, Modernity and Stress: Three Contrasting Contexts for Change in East Africa." *Journal of Anthropological Research* 33: 421–51.

Weisner, T. S., M. Bernstein, H. Garnier, C. Hamilton, and J. Rosenthal. 1991. "Why Does Attachment Classification at Age One Not Predict Subsequent Child Outcomes?: A Seventeen-Year Longitudinal Study." Poster presented at International Conference on Infant Studies, Miami, May.

Weisner, T. S., and H. Garnier. 1992. "Nonconventional Family Lifestyles and School Achievement: A Twelve-Year Longitudinal Study." *American Educational Research Journal* 29: 605–32.

Werner, O., and G. Schoepfle. 1987a. *Systematic Fieldwork: Foundations of Ethnography and Interviewing.* Vol. 1. Newbury Park, Calif.: Sage.

———. 1987b. *Systematic Fieldwork: Ethnographic Analysis and Data Management.* Vol. 2. Newbury Park, Calif.: Sage.

Whiting, B., and C. Edwards. 1988. *Children of Different Worlds: The Formation of Social Behavior.* Cambridge, Mass.: Harvard University Press.

Whiting, J., and B. Whiting. 1970. "Methods for Observing and Recording Behavior." In *Handbook of Methods in Cultural Anthropology.* Ed. R. Naroll and R. Cohen, 282–315. Garden City, N.Y.: Natural History Press.

———. 1975. *Children of Six Cultures: A Psychocultural Analysis.* Cambridge, Mass.: Harvard University Press.

Wikan, U. 1990. *Managing Turbulent Hearts: A Balinese Formula for Living.* Chicago: University of Chicago Press.

Wolf, M. 1992. *A Thrice-Told Tale: Feminism, Postmodernism and Ethnographic Responsibility.* Stanford, Calif.: Stanford University Press.

Wozniak, R. H. 1993. *Worlds of Childhood.* New York: HarperCollins.

PART THREE

Ethnography and the Context of Development

15 The Multiple Contexts of Human Development

ANNE COLBY

Each of the chapters in part 3 of this book addresses the problem of how to understand human development in a manner that does justice to its many varieties and to the particular shapes it takes as it is played out in diverse contexts. Of course, this is one of the main organizing themes of the book as a whole, and many of the chapters in the first two sections also address this problem. Even within the four chapters and commentary collected in this section, however, we see a very wide array of perspectives on development in context and a wealth of provocative issues concerning development at different points across the life span and the multilayered and interpenetrating cultural, historical, biological, and ideological contexts of that development. Each of the chapters that we have assembled together in this section of the book provides a unique perspective on the common endeavor.

The chapter by Margaret Lock focuses on the cultural construction of the female life course in Japan, its relationship to social ideology and policy goals of the state, and some dramatic differences in the experience of menopause in Japanese and American women. Lock uses ethnographic and survey data from Japan and the United States to explicate the ways in which the meaning of the life course in particular settings is influenced by myths promulgated by the state or other institutions, such as the medical establishment, in pursuit of policy-related goals. In particular, she describes a shift in postwar Japan away from the extended family structure toward a nuclear family and the current pressure to return to an extended family in order to care for the country's rapidly growing elderly population. This pressure is bolstered by widespread popular conceptions of "woman's nature" that emphasize the primary importance of nurturance of others, and movement through the female adult life cycle is experienced largely in terms of how one's relations with others, especially family members, changes over time. This emphasis means that it is not in the interest of the state for older women to focus on declining health or strength, so it is not surprising that little weight is given to the biological changes of aging. In line with this lack of emphasis on physical aging, menopause is not experienced as an important biological or medical event, as it is in the United States. It is accompanied by few physical symptoms and those that are reported are entirely different from symptoms reported by American women. Lock concludes that both biology and culture should be seen as contingent and that we should not assume that there is a universal base of biological development onto which is layered a culturally constructed experience of the life cycle. Although the question of biomedical aspects of the life course and their relationship to culture is not dealt with in other chapters in this book, it is an area of growing research interest and a critical part of a full picture of life-course development in cultural perspective. Lock's investigation of the relationships among historical change, culturally constructed life-course changes, and the biology of aging provides an excellent example of the potential benefits of coming together across disciplines to create a more complete picture of development, in which the individual is embedded in multiple contexts among and within which we can identify a multiplicity of dynamic relationships. Lock's chapter is also unique in raising the issue of resistance to cultural prescriptions, in this case by feminist analyses arising from within Japan. Of course, as Lock points out, in order to be successful, ideological discourse must be actively embraced and translated into everyday life. But cultural norms, even though supported by sanctions from the moral community as Shweder has described, can also be subjected to social criticism from within the society, potentially leading to social change.

Katherine Newman's essay deals with the historical contextualization of life-course development by laying out the ways in which individuals who have experienced especially salient social change at crucial points in their development build a sense of identification with their generations into their core sense of who they are. In doing so, she reminds us that social change is as important a feature of the context of human development as cultural setting. She argues that, in effect, people who identify strongly with different generations constitute distinct subcultures, with distinctive expectations, values, norms, and "symbolic dialects" or ways of symbolizing and expressing their shared experiences. In distinguishing between the concepts of *cohort* and *generation,* Newman reminds us of the importance of understanding the *meaning* for the individual of being in a particular generation. Not all birth cohorts share strong generational identities, and individuals who lived through the same historical events differ in the extent to which their participation in these events forms an important part of their personal identities. Whereas survey research can chart the impact of being a member of a particular birth cohort, we need ethnographic, interpretive methods to get at the meaning of generational identity.

In her treatment of the intersection of personal biography and cultural history, Newman suggests a mechanism, identity formation, through which macrolevel forces reflecting political, economic, and cultural circumstances are incorporated into the experience of individuals. It is critical to note that multiple contexts come into play simultaneously in this process, and the meaning of a historical event or set of economic conditions will vary with race, gender, regional location, and other crosscutting dimensions. Again, it is only through qualitative, interpretive methods that we can get at what the distinctive histories of particular racial, ethnic, or other groups mean in the present-day lives of people from these different cultural groups.

The Burton, Obeidallah, and Allison chapter documents vividly the experience of adolescence for economically disadvantaged African-American teenagers, portraying a life stage that looks quite different from the white middle-class adolescence that has been taken for granted as normative. The authors describe overlapping worlds of teens and their parents in which differentiation between generations is much less clear than in middle-class families and "age-condensed" families, in which the typical age difference between generations is thirteen to seventeen years, a pattern resulting from consistent teenage childbearing across several generations. These family patterns result in inconsistencies between chronological and generational positions, blurred developmental role boundaries, diminished parental authority, and distinctive perceptions of age-appropriate behavior. An environment with so few economic and social resources, and in which teenagers must take on economic and family-management demands not expected of middle-class teens, has a major impact in reshaping the developmental tasks of adolescence and may lead to a foreshortening of this developmental stage. In the Burton, Obeidallah, and Allison account we can see that indicators marking the transition from adolescence to adulthood in middle-class American teens do not apply in this low-income setting, and that efforts to adapt to this very challenging context lead to distinct ideologies, values, and conceptions of what constitutes a successful outcome. This research clearly shows how important it is to create ethnographic accounts of developmental trajectories and adaptations within particular racial/ethnic and economic groups. Without filling in these pictures, we are left with developmental theories that are insensitive and inappropriate to the experiences of these important segments of our population, and schools and other programs that are unable to meet their needs.

William Corsaro's essay provides a very clear statement of what he, as an ethnographic researcher, means by "development" or "socialization" and what he means by "context." Both of these concepts are informed and shaped by the cross-cultural, longitudinal ethnographies he has created in a number of quite different settings. Corsaro conceives of *socialization,* a term which he uses synonymously with *development,* not as individual internalization of adult culture but rather as a collective process of participation in cultural routines or communal events that are the basis of shared culture. Development conceived in this way *must* be studied ethnographically since it consists of the participation in practices through which culture is constituted and maintained, with children becoming a part of adult culture through their negotiations with adults and their creative production of a series of peer cultures with other children. Although many features of these peer cultures reflect particular aspects of the specific adult culture in which they are embedded, Corsaro also outlines some suggestions for what appear to be universal features of young children's peer cultures. He provides a wealth of detail on his methods in order to show how the particular ethnographic techniques he uses allow him to identify both universal and culturally specific aspects of children's peer-group interactions.

Context, for Corsaro, is also dynamic, with cultural context seen not as a variable or static environmental niche that affects the developing child but rather as "continually constituted in routine practices collectively produced at various levels of organization." In describing socialization in the particular cultural contexts of an Italian preschool and an American Head Start program, Corsaro takes seriously the idea that the context can be changing and evolving simultaneous with, and in part because of, the development of the participants in that social context.

As we see in the other chapters in this section, adaptation within the peer cultures that Corsaro describes is context dependent, so what works well in one setting may not work well in another. Corsaro's attention to transitions from one context to another documents what does and does not facilitate adaptive movement from one context to another.

William Damon's commentary on this section begins with an analysis of the shortcomings of developmental psychology that prevent it from capturing development as it is played out in multiple contexts. These include various ethnocentric biases that have led developmentalists to assume, for example, that ontogenetic trends established in studies of Western children reveal universal capacities against which children from other cultures can be measured. In addition, Damon points out developmental psychologists' tendency to represent variation in social context as a "factor" exerting external impact on essentially nonsocial individuals rather than as a dynamic set of practices in which the individual actively participates. According to Damon, ethnographic approaches have the potential to correct these "blind spots" by revealing widely varied forms of human adaptation and providing more interactive accounts of social contexts.

In order to realize its full potential to illuminate human development in cultural context, however, Damon argues that the ethnographic tradition will need to incorporate a number of insights from developmental psychology. He makes the rather provocative claim that ethnographic studies will need to return to some consideration of the individual as the unit of analysis if they are to help us understand what people learn or carry with them as they move from one context or setting to the next. He also argues that a developmental analysis must confront explicitly the question of developmental direction, so that what constitutes developmental progress within a domain is specified, though recognizing that better adaptation or greater competence within one set of circumstances or cultural setting might not represent better adaptation in another setting.

Although for heuristic purposes we have separated the chapters of this book into sections addressing epistemological, methodological, and developmental issues, in reality all of the issues cut across all three sections, and many chapters could have been placed almost equally well in at least two of the three sections. There are a number of chapters from the other sections dealing with key developmental questions that the reader ought to consider in conjunction with the four chapters in this section. I will mention some of these only briefly here.

Clearly, one of the key goals in the integration of ethnographic and developmental approaches is to provide rich accounts of development as it occurs in different cultural settings, to explicate the variety of developmental patterns yielded by adaptation to particular circumstances. We see three further examples of this kind of explication in the chapters by Miller, Sullivan, and Saxe. Miller documents fundamental differences between the narrative practices that constitute important avenues of socialization in Chinese and American families, Sullivan draws our attention to the sometimes adaptive aspects of criminal behavior in some economically disadvantaged settings, and Saxe provides a detailed description of the development of numeracy in the practices of Brazilian street children who sell candy for a living.

Not surprisingly, Geoffrey Saxe, as a developmental psychologist, confronts more explicitly than do the other authors the issue of the directionality of development that Damon raises in his commentary. It is clear in Saxe's work on the candy sellers, though, and especially in reviewing his

chronicle of the changes in his work over time, that specifying directionality, in this case increasing mathematical competence, need not involve
placing a Western template on the development of children from other
cultures.

A third issue taken up by several chapters in the section on ethnography
as method is the critical question of how to characterize context. This is,
of course, a primary concern of Sullivan's chapter on neighborhood social
organization. In Heath we see essentially the same population that Burton
and her colleagues have described. Burton's description of what it is like
to grow up in an American inner city under conditions of severe economic
hardship is complemented by Heath's account of programs that seem to
be effective in supporting the positive development of these youth. Heath's
treatment of adolescent development in this population provides a detailed description of one very specific kind of context with which some
of the teens engage and recognizes the dynamic and social nature of the
context. This dynamic and processual view of context is central to Peggy
Miller's understanding of socialization as well. By reading Corsaro's and
Miller's chapters together one can see how the same conception of the
relationship of developing individual and cultural context is played out
using two quite different kinds of data—observations of children's peer
cultures and narrative practices of mothers and their children.

This volume brings together a very wide variety of approaches to the
questions of development in context and the context of development, using different methods, focusing on different populations, and addressing
different substantive questions. Clearly, ethnographic and developmental
approaches are already being combined to yield original insights about
important theoretical issues and social problems. By reading these chapters together, one comes away with a sense of exciting momentum in this
emerging multidisciplinary field.

Having given this overview of the section to come, I would now like to
change roles and briefly suggest a few points as a conference participant
rather than as an editor and conference organizer. I make these comments
from the perspective of a developmental psychologist whose work in the
field of moral development has led me to be especially concerned with
issues of developmental direction, prescriptivity, and ethical relativism. In
particular, I want to address three themes that came up in the chapters in
this section and other parts of the book: the concept of development and
the issue of directionality, the question of developmental domains, and the
issue of moral prescriptivity.

Whenever scholars from several disciplines and traditions work together, they encounter the task of creating a common language and sorting

out the subtle, or not so subtle, differences in the ways that they use the same terms. In the spirit of this ongoing task I would like to point here to two different ways of using the terms *development* and *developmental* that sometimes lead to confusion if they are not clearly distinguished from each other. What many developmental psychologists and some developmentalists from other disciplines mean by "development" is strongly tied to a notion of developmental direction, increasing maturity, adequacy, sophistication, and the like. We see this use of the term explicitly in Shweder, Saxe, and Damon in this volume and implicitly in many others, including Mishler, Campbell, Miller, and Corsaro. Developmental sequences or trajectories are seen to have an internal logic such that the organization of the capacity in question is moving from simple to differentiated, from less to more functionally adaptive, and so on. This need not mean that they are *universally* more adaptive, however. In fact, in recent theoretical work and empirical research, there has been a movement away from defining these sequences in universal terms, abstracted from the particular practices within which children develop, toward the identification of various kinds of expertise that are locally defined within the terms of a particular cultural context, and the charting of developmental progress in relation to these locally defined goals, end points, or types of expertise (Rogoff 1990). This kind of shift is elaborated in detail in the chapter by Geoffrey Saxe. It is important that development is clearly differentiated from age in both the older and more contemporary versions of this concept of development. In this view, changes that occur with age (such as increased vocabulary) need not be *developmental* shifts, which represent a qualitative change in organization rather than a quantitative increment.

A contrasting use of the term links development more closely with age, such that development refers to typical age-normative patterns that can be observed within a particular context. Often these descriptions of age-normative patterns are specified at a rather global level, referring to the way that, for example, adolescence, the transition to adulthood, or midlife are typically played out. Many life-course sociologists use the phrase "development across the life course" to refer to this kind of descriptive account of age-related life patterns. Although some people who describe life patterns in this way may suggest or be misinterpreted as suggesting that these patterns are universal or characterized by developmental necessity or intrinsic directionality, generally these patterns are recognized to be culturally contingent and to apply only to the particular cultural, class, historical period, and gender intersection from which the descriptions were derived.

The important issue for communication across traditions is to understand that scholars using *development* in the former sense would not apply the notions of directionality, sequentiality, and internal logic to the kinds of normative patterns that are termed *developmental* in the latter view. Thus a developmental psychologist, for example, would not be in the least taken aback by the data presented by Shweder and Lock indicating that female midlife in India and Japan look quite different from each other and from female midlife in the United States. This kind of "life-course development" is assumed by developmentalists of the first sort to be culturally contingent, so a recognition that "stage markers" in this sense are "entirely socially or culturally constructed" does not at all "threaten to put developmentalists out of business," as John Modell suggests in his closing commentary.

Related to this issue is the problem of domain specificity. In considering developmental trajectories leading toward end points that represent full-fledged expertise, it is important to note that these sequences or trajectories are defined not on a global life-stage level but rather within well-defined, coherent domains such as numeracy, language acquisition, or an aspect of social cognition like conceptions of friendship or distributive justice. Development in some domains may be interrelated, but in many cases the domains are largely independent of each other. Because development is specified within domains and because domains are generally not highly related, it is appropriate to represent movement across the life course as a pattern of ongoing, simultaneous gains and losses. (Gains within some domains or on some dimensions, losses in others.) Of course, in order to sort out what constitutes gains versus losses, one must go back to empirical accounts of developmental shifts within the particular domain in question toward a level of greater maturity or expertise, keeping in mind, as I said earlier, that these sequences need to be defined in context-specific ways. What constitutes a developmental gain or greater adaptation within one context might not be a gain at all within another setting or context.

In my view, these strategies of working within domains and specifying gains and losses across a number of domains is an important part of what it means to apply a developmental analysis to an ethnographic account. Let me provide a concrete example of what I mean by this. Many ethnographic sociologists and anthropologists are centrally concerned with describing particular cultural settings that can be assumed to powerfully affect young people who engage with those settings. Unless the ethnographer undertakes a developmental analysis of the sort that I am suggesting here, however, the precise ways in which individuals are changed (or socialized) by participating in the context or setting remains vague. In *The Cocaine Kids*, for example, Terry Williams defines the aims of the ethnography in the preface as in part to document the sense in which the young people working in the drug trade are simply teenagers aspiring to make good in a world that offers them limited options. He argues that to "get behind the scale" or to rise in the organization of cocaine sales is like "landing a top sales job in a major corporation, or being named a partner after a long apprenticeship, in a brokerage firm with a seat on the Stock Exchange" (1989:x). The book provides a rich and fascinating description of the world of young people who are involved in the sale of cocaine in an American inner city. There is no doubt that this is a powerful experience for those young people. The book does not, however, provide a detailed developmental analysis of the multifaceted impact of the experience on participants. The authors seem to imply that the responsibilities of running what amounts to a small business require and result in some valuable mathematical, organizational, and managerial skills that indicate an unappreciated level of competence and sophistication that could perhaps be harnessed in the pursuit of less risky endeavors.

The parallel with the work on Brazilian candy sellers reported in Geoff Saxe's chapter in this book is evident, and Saxe's work makes clear the missed opportunity of *The Cocaine Kids* to delineate precisely the developmental impact of this kind of experience. In addition to looking at just what skills are developed through selling cocaine, the work also provides the opportunity to look at the less benign impact of participation in this violent and mutually exploitative world on young people's social and moral development—the ways they think about and treat others, their values and goals, their view of and relation to social institutions such as the legal system, and the like. I believe that an explicitly developmental analysis of these questions would enrich this kind of ethnography and help it to illuminate more clearly the impact of this complex experience on the teenagers who take part in it.

The *Cocaine Kids* example, like the chapter by Burton, Obeidallah, and Allison in this book, raises the issue of moral prescriptivity in developmental analyses of moral values, goals, and behaviors. Within nonmoral domains, such as mathematical reasoning, directionality does not imply prescriptivity in the sense that one "ought" to operate at the higher levels in a noncontingent sense. That is, one ought to operate at the most sophisticated levels of mathematical ability if one wants to be equipped with the most powerful tools for solving mathematical problems, but in this use of the word *ought,* no moral prescriptivity is implied. Thus those of Saxe's candy sellers who were able to understand price ratios mathematically could use the ratios to organize their markup computations rather than depending on older children to take care of the markup from wholesale to retail prices. The greater numerical sophistication is more adaptive, but one would not say that in a morally prescriptive sense one *ought* to be more numerically sophisticated. In contrast, within the moral domain, one ought to behave in the more morally adequate way in a sense that is *not* contingent on one's goals. One ought to do it, because it is morally right.

Damon suggests in his commentary on this section of the book that "defining developmental directions is *not,* in any sense, an empirical endeavor." I expect that he would mean this to apply especially in the moral domain. He and Shweder would agree that what people want and what they *should* want can be two quite different things. Thus Damon raises the question in regard to Burton et al.'s portrayal of inner-city adolescents of whether the alternative developmental outcomes that Burton describes are all equally successful outcomes from the moral point of view—outcomes which include the achievement of economic independence through crime, through having a child and enrolling in Aid to Families with Dependent Children (AFDC), or through employment; or the outcomes of amassing expensive possessions through crime, amassing possessions through legal means, or developing spiritual harmony and integrity, expressing creativity through the arts, or becoming involved in activities that assist family members and other members of the community.

Of course, the problem with making the kinds of distinctions that Damon urges us to make is the question of whose perspective is taken as authoritative in making this kind of evaluation. Shweder, Campbell, McDermott, and others remind us of the myriad dangers of ethnocentrism and the range of abuses that have resulted from judgments made about one group by another. On the other hand, a position of moral relativism has its own dangers. Many contemporary social scientists and social critics (Bellah et al. 1985; Gardner 1991; Etzioni 1988; Mansbridge 1990; Wilson 1993; and Wuthnow 1991) have written about the urgent need to move beyond a morally relativistic worldview, a worldview that is perhaps itself a product of our own individualistic culture, and that leaves us with no basis for any enduring commitment beyond the self.

Richard Shweder's position of "universalism without uniformity" provides us a way out of this dilemma. According to Shweder, there are many fundamentally different ways of defining ideals of the good, but these involve different ways of combining and setting priorities among a finite set of universal moral goods. In this view there are many different ways to be moral, but not all ways of being qualify as moral; there are multiple paths of successful development, but not all paths are successful. Thus, in order for Burton et al. to respond to Damon's call to distinguish among the various alternative developmental outcomes they have observed, they will need to complete a "true ethnography" which will specify the "sanctionable behaviors" within the relevant moral community. In doing so, according to Shweder, they will need to keep in mind that not all members of a moral community are equally qualified to speak on this issue, since "not all members of a moral community are experts about their own way of life" and what people say they want and what they *should* want are not necessarily the same thing. What one is after here is an ethnographically authentic account of the moral community's ideals of the good. Then Burton et al.'s adolescents' values, goals, and behavior can be evaluated as gains and losses relative to their own culture's ideals. Of course, one must be careful, as Donald Campbell so persuasively reminds us, not to confuse miscommunications with assumptions of cultural difference. In looking at a different subculture within one's own society, as in looking at a culture outside one's own, a misattribution of fundamental differences in values, goals, and ideals is at least as likely a mistake as the reverse. The more information we have, the fuller the ethnography, the more likely it is that we will be able to differentiate between real and apparent differences.

Despite the appeal of Shweder's pluralistic yet not relativistic approach, it leaves some questions unanswered when applied to specific cases. One wonders, for example, how to define the boundaries of a moral community—could a violent youth gang or a group of teenagers involved in the drug trade as in *The Cocaine Kids* constitute a moral community? What is the appropriate unit of analysis for this kind of ethnography? And what about contexts in which moral communities seem to be breaking down, as in the inner-city environment described as "the street" by Eli Anderson (1990) in *Streetwise?* We will also have to address the question not only of what is adaptive within a culture but also what is adaptive when moving between subcultures. For disadvantaged groups, this raises political and ideological issues about one's stance in relation to the dominant culture.

The issues raised in this section of the volume, as in the other sections, are provocative, at times contentious, and in many cases unresolved. The authors have confronted the questions of how and according to what criteria we can recognize developmental progress, how to take seriously a dynamic conception of the individual in continual interaction with a dynamic context, how to understand the interrelations among many levels of analysis from the political/ideological to the historical to the biological, the critical and inescapable analysis of the *meaning* of individuals' experiences, and the role of ethnographic methods in allowing us to understand these meanings and their place within multiple layers of context.

References

Anderson, E. 1990. *Streetwise: Race, Class, and Change in an Urban Community.* Chicago: University of Chicago Press.
Bellah, R., R. Madsen, W. Sullivan, A. Swidler, and S. Tipton. 1985. *Habits of*

the Heart: Individualism and Commitment in American Life. New York: Harper and Row.

Etzioni, A. 1993. *The Spirit of Community.* New York: Crown.

Gardner, J. 1991. *Building Community.* Washington, D.C.: Independent Sector.

Mansbridge, J. 1990. *Beyond Self-Interest.* Chicago: University of Chicago Press.

Rogoff, B. 1990. *Apprenticeship in Thinking: Cognitive Development in Social Context.* New York: Oxford University Press.

Williams, T. 1989. *The Cocaine Kids.* New York: Addison-Wesley.

Wilson, J. Q. 1993. *The Moral Sense.* New York: Free Press.

Wuthnow, R. 1991. *Acts of Compassion.* Princeton, N.J.: Princeton University Press.

16 Ideology and Subjectivity: Midlife and Menopause in Japan and North America

Margaret Lock

Among the many consequences of the formation of the state, wherever its geographical location, has been the subjection of the family and the individuals which constitute it to surveillance and normalization (Foucault 1979; Armstrong 1983; Hewitt 1991). As part of this transformation, the course of life itself, from birth to death, and in particular female life-cycle transitions, have become the subject of debate and policymaking, although the form that this takes is dependent upon local knowledge, history, and culture.

The experience of maturation is simultaneously a social and a biological process, but in northern Europe and North America, commencing at approximately the beginning of the last century, life-course transitions became subject to increasing medicalization (Freidson 1970; Zola 1978). The focus of attention was gradually confined ever more intently to the body physical, with the result that, with respect to adult women, for example, both the subjective experience of reproduction and maturation and related changes in human relationships have been rendered largely inconsequential in medical discourse. This progressive fragmentation of knowledge, although initially a product of the medical world, is by no means confined to it, since there exists today a widely shared (but nevertheless contested) belief among the public that an approach to female reproduction and aging which confines itself almost exclusively to biological change is the most rational and appropriate for contemporary times; a biological focus facilitates, it is believed, not only professional but also individual control over reproduction and aging.

In Japan, although the medical profession has shown an interest in the management of the life course since the early part of the twentieth century, clinical gynecology (with the exception of surgery) has yet to achieve the status and power that it is accorded in Europe and North America. Medicalization of the female life course, especially its latter phases, has not taken root to anything like the same extent as in the West. This difference cannot be fully accounted for by examining the structure and power of the respective medical professions, but poses a larger and, to my mind, more interesting problem.

Inseparable from the process of modernization is the development, institutionalization, and expansion of scientific knowledge, one component of which is biomedicine, which, it has been assumed until recently, is essentially a universal endeavor, at least in terms of knowledge production. A rapidly expanding body of social science research has demonstrated, however, that biomedical knowledge and practice is shot through with assumptions and values and it is now recognized that we should, to be accurate, talk of biomedicines in the plural (Lock and Gordon 1988; Wright and Treacher 1982). Gynecological knowledge, for example, is infused with cultural assumptions about the "nature" of women and their place in society, assumptions which in contemporary life are disguised as scientific facts, with the result that culture influences the way the female body is "seen" and "managed" in medical settings (Jordanova 1989; Lock 1993; Martin 1987). Reciprocally, the state frequently draws on medical knowledge to legitimize its position with respect to the position assigned to women in contemporary society, in particular the importance attributed to their participation in reproduction and nurturance of the family; this knowledge then forms the basis for normative conceptualizations about passage through the female life course (Farquhar 1991; Leys Stepan 1986; Lock 1993).

The female body, therefore, being a potent and malleable signifier, is a forum for the delineation of sex and gender relations, notably at this historical moment to what extent women should be granted equity in social life (in reality and not only in name), together with autonomy over their own bodies. The extent to which medicalization of the life cycle takes place is not simply the product of changing medical knowledge and practice, nor is it merely a manifestation of the power of the medical profession, but also the result of potent, never settled, partially disguised political contests intimately linked to surveillance and normalization of the family in late modern and postmodern societies. In contemporary North America the "menopausal woman" has become a synecdoche for female middle age—individual and social maturation are eclipsed by the emphasis given to what is assumed to be universal biological change. As we will see, in Japan, by contrast, social maturation, including responsibility for the nurturance of others, takes precedence over individual aging and biological change.

I will devote this chapter primarily to Japan, and provide an interpretation which highlights the relationship among several sets of data: themes which appear in the subjective accounts of individual women about the end of menstruation and middle age in general; the results of a survey questionnaire distributed to over 1,300 Japanese women aged forty-five to fifty-five inclusively; historical transformations in connection with the family and with medical discourse, and thematic analysis of contemporary government, medical, and feminist representations about this stage of the life cycle. These distinct forms of representation provide interrelated and complementary lenses for understanding the experience of female middle age in Japan today. However, they cannot be subsumed into one another to produce a tidy package; on the contrary, the degree of disjunction between dominant ideologies, as they are created in professional and policy-related literature and the everyday worlds of individual women, highlights contradictions and sites of contestation. One question which is inevitably raised, and briefly discussed, is the extent to which women actively embrace, resist, or ignore dominant ideologies. The Japanese and North American situation will be compared, albeit superficially, in order to decen ter received wisdom about female midlife, in particular about that which is assumed to be biologically universal. Emphasis will be given to the way in which historical change, generational change, culturally constructed life-course changes, and the biology of aging are inevitably interdependent and context dependent. In conclusion I will consider the importance of a research approach which makes use of multiple methods.

Toward the New Extended Household

The three-generation household, the *ie,* was for three-quarters of a century, from the formation of the early modern Japanese state at the Meiji Restoration until the end of the Second World War, recognized as the official family unit in Japan. In this household are enshrined the ancestors, representatives of moral order and spiritual values. Whereas feudal Japan exhibited an acute sensitivity to class and occupational differences, with the creation of the unifying state, difference was obliterated, and Japanese women were appealed to for the first time as one body in terms of gendered social roles to be carried out within the confines of the household (Nolte and Hastings 1991). Modeled on the samurai system of feudal times, and laced with a little late nineteenth-century European sentiment, the "good wife and wise mother" was educated to discipline herself for her role in the family.

Although Japanese women are described in feudal times as "borrowed wombs," it is evident that historically their economic contribution to the household was of primary importance. Obviously, reproduction was important, and the bearing of a son particularly so, but the Japanese have through the years been remarkably flexible about the formal adoption into their families of not only children but also adults, should the necessity arise. From the beginning of the nineteenth century onward, however, the dominant image associated with women shifted from that of a contributing member of the workforce to one of nurturer of other household members, a quality with which all females were assumed to be "naturally" endowed (Mitsuda 1985). In this group-oriented society, ideological emphasis was, and still is, given to dedication to a lifelong gendered role, in which actual reproduction is rendered secondary to nurturance of others. Japanese feminists have coined the term *boseishugi* (the doctrine of motherhood) to capture the essence of this ideology.

As part of the *ie,* a woman reached the prime of life in her fifties and, in theory, enjoyed the acme of her responsibility, which, although it gradually waned, was never extinguished unless she succumbed to severe senility or some other catastrophe. Although the *ie* has been abolished for nearly fifty years, a good number of Japanese women (more than 20 percent) still live in an extended residence, and their days are filled with monitoring the household economy, care and education of grandchildren, and care and nursing of dependent in-laws, added to which many work part-time. As we will see, life in the extended family does not always bring the rewards or prestige that the ideology suggests are associated with such an arrangement.

A widely shared sentiment exists in Japan today to the effect that although the "economic health" of the country is excellent (until very recently, that is), health does not extend to the state of the nation itself, nor to the spiritual condition of its peoples (Mochida 1980). The conservative Liberal Democratic Party, which maintained until recently an unbroken postwar rule in Japan, together with like-minded intellectuals, laments what they describe as a loss of traditional values, in particular the "thinning" of family relationships and the decline of the extended family, leading, it is asserted, to an undue emphasis on the "Western" value of individualism. There has been an official call for a return of "warmth" to the family which appears to be driven in part by a concern about the decline of tradition, but also by an accelerating disquiet produced by the rapidly proliferating "aging" society with its ever increasing nonproductive and dependent population (*Ōhira sōri no seisaku* 1980).

It is calculated that, if present trends continue (that is, fertility remains low and mortality continues to decline), by the year 2025, people aged sixty-five and over will make up a remarkable 24 percent of the Japanese population. Among the elderly, more than 53 percent will be over seventy-five years old, and it is projected that the most dramatic demographic changes will occur when the postwar baby boomers reach old age, during the first quarter of the next century. This transformation will not only produce a rapidly aging labor force and a major increase in expenditures of all kinds for the elderly, but, it is also widely agreed, it will be accompanied by a decline in economic growth (Ogawa 1988). Naohira Ogawa points out that (again, if present trends continue), there will be more than two and a quarter million Japanese suffering from senile dementia by 2025, of whom 66 percent will be women, and more than two million people will be bedridden, of whom 62 percent will be women. Ogawa voices a major government concern when he questions where the "manpower" will come from to take care of this decrepit population (1988:274) known euphemistically as the "silver" generation. Other Japanese writers, ranging from feminists (Higuchi 1985) to healthcare professionals (Hosoya 1987), have expressed similar concerns.

Since the 1970s, when the aging society began to seriously capture the attention of Japanese policymakers, succeeding conservative governments have commented on the dangers of the "English disease," with reference to the pre-Thatcher social welfare system of the United Kingdom, which is thought to have been excessive. The Liberal Democratic party set out to create instead what has come to be known as the "Japanese Welfare Society," in which individuals and their families are made responsible to some extent for taking care of and financing their own health and welfare needs. Not even the most conservative of policymakers has resorted to the prewar term for the household (the *ie*) to describe the kind of family which is being promoted, no doubt because of its oppressive symbolic associations, but their intention nevertheless is clear. The "new residence system" (*atarashii jūtaku shisutemu*) goes under the less inflammatory tag of "living together in three-generation households" (*san sedai dōkyo*) (*Ōhira sōri no seisaku* 1980:189) and clearly the government has in mind an extended family as the ideal.

Together with an emphasis on extended family life it is now accepted policy that, as far as possible, the elderly should not be placed for any length of time in hospitals or even nursing homes, despite the fact that more of these institutions are being constructed. Although funds have been set aside for care of the elderly, including the training of home helpers, public health nurses, and nurses who make home visits, the task of these personnel is above all to *assist* middle-aged and older women in the care of ailing relatives. It is emphasized that "the quality of life" of the elderly will only be achieved if there is cooperation on the part of families in keeping the elderly at home, that is, the "good" quality of life associated with an extended family (Kōsei Hakusho 1989).

A white paper authored by feminists has highlighted the gap between government policy and the realities of family life. Despite government plans, the lack of professional or even volunteer assistance for women who are nursing elderly relatives remains acute; the maximum time most people receive help is half a day per week, which in any case has to be paid for. Short stays in nursing homes and other facilities are limited to seven days, and can be lengthened only under extenuating circumstances. The report concludes that the burden of care for the elderly is simply dropped into the laps of younger (that is, middle-aged) women (Nihon Fujin Dantai-Rengōtai 1989) and social critic Keiko Higuchi has asserted that "hidden behind the superficial glamour [of the modern household] the pre-war family system lives grimly on" (1985:57).

A government document put out on the proposed "enrichment" of the Japanese family explicitly discusses the role of middle-aged women as a vital force inside the family. After stressing the importance of cultivating their own psychological and physical welfare through hobbies, sports, cultural activities, and further education, it is stated that women should take a positive attitude toward work, and, with their newly found freedom from childrearing demands, they should take up suitable part-time employment, or alternatively, should consider volunteer work such as assisting other women in the care of the mentally ill or the infirm (Ōhira sōri no seisaku 1980). At the government's suggestion, female middle age, as every Japanese woman well knows, is simply being turned into a training period for the time when they are expected to take on complete responsibility for the care of parents-in-law, together sometimes with that of their own parents, and eventually that of their husbands in the final years of their own lives before, it is assumed, daughters-in-law take over the cycle of nurturance.

The Pathology of Modernity

In contrast to the "warm" extended family, the nuclear household, in which approximately 60 percent of Japanese live these days, lacking both enshrined ancestors and the elders, is thought by many commentators to be a fragile "pathological" conglomeration. Particularly so because the juridical powers of the male household head were stripped away at the end of the war leaving a vacuum devoid of both an authoritative and moral voice (Mochida 1980; Eto 1979). Kelly has pointed out that the New Middle Class (to which over 90 percent of Japanese when surveyed claim to belong) is a "folk sociology" (1986). This core institution of postwar mass society, synonymous in the minds of most with a nuclear family, is generally assumed by those in power to be symbolic of the privatization of life (*shiseikatsushugi*), the fragmentation of a state-controlled value system, and the incursion of personal and family concerns into the running of the country. Visualized as a four-person household composed of working husband, full-time housewife/mother, and two studious children (1.32 according to the latest statistics), it is this "normalized" family targeted in government ideology as not being in the best interests of the nation.

A plethora of newly "discovered" syndromes and neuroses said to be of recent origin and intimately associated with a loss of traditional values and the embrace of individualism are thought to abound in the urban centers of modern Japan. Glossed as "diseases of modernization" (*gendaibyō*) or "civilization" (*bunmeibyō*) (Kyūtoku 1979; Murakami, Shunpei, and Seizaburō 1979), they are portrayed as a nuclear family plague. Men, women, and children are all vulnerable to these diseases which have arresting names: apartment neurosis, moving-day depression, childrearing neurosis, the kitchen syndrome, school-refusal syndrome, adolescent frustration syndrome, video-generation lethargy, salary-man depression, maladjustment-to-the-job syndrome, fear of going to work, and the latest and most unnerving of all these problems, death from overwork. The incidence of this wave of distress is accounted for in government, medical, and in many popular accounts, by means of a moralistic rhetoric in which a close relationship is postulated between health and well-being, both physical and mental, and individual behavior. It is frequently suggested that rapid postwar changes in both values and the structure of social relationships, in particular the family, are directly implicated in producing transformations in individual behavioral styles which are not conducive to good health (Imazu, Hamaguchi, and Sakuta 1979; Monbushō 1983). The painful and sometimes fatal symptoms from which victims of *gendaibyō* suffer are often dismissed out of hand by those in power as, in effect, signs of indolence or willful nonconformity (Lock 1988, 1991). Alternatively, patients are medicated and monitored by the medical and psychological professions—thus individual narratives of distress are transformed into a medicalized discourse about the sick body, although recently victims and their families have been fighting back in certain instances (*Karōshi Bengo Dan* 1990).

Among the diseases of modernization is "menopausal syndrome," an ailment associated by both physicians and the public alike with the professional housewife (as she is known), living in an urban nuclear family. The life of the hypothetical modern housewife has been subject to ridicule as a result in part of the mechanization and commoditization of housework. Housewives have sardonically had their day described as *san shoku hiru ne tsuki* (three meals provided, with a nap thrown in) and the rhetoric associated with them implies that, in contrast to all other Japanese, many are selfish, idle, and just play around, unsurpassed consumers with endless time to fill, living a life of luxury and ease unknown in Japanese society until this time (Eto 1979; Kyūtoku 1979). Alternatively, housewives have been accused of becoming excessively fastidious, withdrawn and nervous, overly concerned with tidiness and order. In both scenarios the middle-class housewife has departed from the fully occupied, balanced, and correctly disciplined life of the "good wife and wise mother" of the traditional extended household. In a society driven by the work ethic, this anomalous woman, once she becomes middle aged, is highly vulnerable it is believed to a distressful time at the end of menstruation, and is singled out as a potential victim of "menopausal syndrome." It is this kind of woman whom policymakers have uppermost in mind when they call for a return to three-generation households and incite women to undertake voluntary work, for it is clearly she who is liable to abandon her in-laws and turn them over as so much garbage (*kuzu*) to the care of the state.

When asked what kind of woman is most likely to have trouble at *kōnenki* (menopause) a Kobe gynecologist had the following to say:

> Let me see. I guess those who are relatively well-off, who have few children and lots of free time, and those whose families don't have much "communication" with one another. Also, those who are introverted. Women who go out a lot, or who have lots of hobbies and friends don't have so many symptoms. The ones who have trouble tend to concentrate on their own bodies.

An Osaka gynecologist, when asked if he thought that all women experience trouble at *kōnenki,* answered, "Not necessarily. Women who are busy, who don't have much leisure, don't have many complaints. *Kōnenki shōgai* is a sort of 'luxury disease' [*zeitakubyō*], it's 'high-class.' Women with lots of free time on their hands are the ones who say its so bad."

A Tokyo physician responded:

> These women have no *ikigai* [purpose in life]. They have free time but can't think of anything to do, so they get a psychosomatic reaction; they can't complain openly so they use "organ language" [said in English]. They find that there is no reward today for all their sacrifice and suppression, and they're lonely. Working women have fewer symptoms and in any case don't notice them; housewives can't control and master their symptoms like they used to.

A physician who specializes in the practice of traditional herbal medicine focused on family dynamics in addition to individual shortcomings:

Being in a nuclear family affects women very much. There's no one to teach life's wisdom to the children and everything falls onto the shoulders of the housewife. She often becomes neurotic, obsessed with trying to create a good child. Her husband doesn't talk to her. Also women have changed, they used to *gaman* [persevere, endure], but they've lost all that since women's lib. They have low self-control now.

These excerpts from physician narratives[1] reveal the extent to which the symptoms associated with *kōnenki* are tagged with a moral discourse, one which centers on a metaphorical association between lack of work and physical distress; thus the selfish and ailing housewife becomes one piece of an allegorical myth about the supposed waning of solidarity in the late modern Japanese family and society.

The irony of this rhetoric, a rhetoric abundant in popular literature written for women, does not pass unnoticed by feminist commentators (Higuchi 1985). In theory the "homebody" is idealized; she is the standard by which all modern women are measured, and women have systematically been deprived of full participation in the work force in postwar Japan. However, it is estimated that less than 30 percent of Japanese women are "professional housewives" since by far the majority are employed, the majority as "temporary" blue- or pink-collar workers, classified as part-time, who labor for long hours with no benefits, and are subject to hiring and firing as the economy waxes and wanes. Aside from the "helping" professions, married women are rarely found in white-collar and professional jobs because of the enormous social pressure placed on them to resign once they become pregnant. Being rehired at a later date in a responsible job is virtually impossible, even though most women express a wish to work. Nevertheless, once their children are raised, housewives are subject to stigmatization because while the rest of the nation, with the exception only of some of the elderly, is worked to exhaustion, middle-aged housewives pass their time by playing tennis and making plastic flowers.

It is against this discursive background, in particular a sense of urgency about the pressures the aging society is starting to place on the economy, and an ongoing concern about a loss of traditional values, that individual Japanese women are maturing, ending their reproductive years, and becoming middle aged.

Contradictory Consciousness: Rhetoric and Reality

Because it is taken as exemplary, the finding that the actual tally of ideal nuclear families centered around a genuinely full-time housewife is relatively small, is clearly of significance. Even more important is the question of the relationship of the everyday lives of Japanese citizens to state ideology about this normalized modern family. A long-standing intellectual tradition in Japan demonstrates a keen awareness of ideology which is perceived, in Gluck's words, as "two worlds in interaction with one another: the state . . . with its dominant ideology, and society, or the people, with ideologies actively opposed or privately detached" (Gluck 1990:284). It is now well recognized that political dissent has been and remains common and effective in, at the very least, keeping those in power on their toes. When it comes, however, to the largely unarticulated values and practices of daily life, it is much harder for participating "natives" to articulate resistance (and here Japan is no different from other societies (Bourdieu 1977; de Certeau 1984)). That which is taken to be "natural" in connection with techniques of socialization, gendered behavior, family relationships, the relationship of individuals to society, ideas about "human nature," and so on—everyday practices which "civilize" the body and penetrate to the very core of subjectivity—are only dimly grasped for what they are: fables which make society tick.

The dominant Meiji ideology (or its present-day reconstruction, at least), is one in which the body is visualized as immersed in the cycling planetary cosmos, the rhythms of the seasons, continuity of generations, and the daily round of communal labor and harmonious living. From the beginning of the Meiji era, segments of this ideology began to be legitimized as scientific knowledge, thus making it all the more powerful. The "scientific" concept of "human nature" (*jinsei*) was invented at this time, and became part of official dogma (*shisō*); so too did the idea of a mothering "instinct" (*bosei honno*) on the basis of which women were understood as biologically destined to nurture others and therefore best suited to domestic life. Although this ideology has been increasingly subjected to criticism in recent years by Japanese feminists and others, it nevertheless survives as a reinvented tradition around which politicians and certain intellectuals can spin very effective webs of nostalgia in which the "warm" extended family is contrasted to the "thin" relationships taken to be characteristic of the nuclear family (Harootunian 1989).

Ideological discourse does not exist in a vacuum, however, but to be successful it must be actively embraced and reproduced in everyday life. By drawing on over one hundred interviews conducted in 1984 in the households of women who were then aged between forty-five and fifty-five inclusively,[2] I will briefly discuss the reception and reproduction of ideologies among Japanese women themselves about the contradiction between modern leisured women and their true destiny to nurture others. Middle-aged women, perhaps more than anyone else in Japan today, embody a contradictory consciousness. They sit on the cusp, Janus-faced, between early and late modernity, between an integrated traditional society characterized by the extended family, and its evaporation into one fragmented and driven, it is so often claimed, by consumption. This was the last generation of women explicitly raised to be "good wives and wise mothers," disciplined for a life of devotion to the extended family. When they reflect on the past, a certain ambivalence is evident: grateful that they do not have to endure the incredible hardships which they believe dogged their mothers, and happy that the poverty of their wartime childhood is long behind them, they are nevertheless concerned that, *because* their lot is relatively easy, they do not perhaps have the endurance or will power of Japanese women who have gone before them. A factory worker agreed that her life had been tough, but immediately added, "it was nothing like as hard as my mother's. She really suffered for us. Thanks to her strict childrearing, though, I can take anything."

A Nagano farmer was explicit that it is appropriate for a woman to suppress her feelings, in particular inside the family:

> I try to suppress my feelings like my mother, although I don't always succeed like she did. If I were always blowing up about things, that would cause fights with my husband, which would be unpleasant for the children. But as long as I just keep quiet and endure, then it's easily forgotten. It doesn't make much difference no matter what I say, so in that case we might as well keep things pleasant.

Statements such as these reveal the extent to which women take pride in self-control and endurance, qualities which are highly valued. The majority of women interviewed took a similar position but then went on to elaborate, as the gynecologists had done, in more abstract terms about women in general:

> I think that if a woman keeps herself occupied every day and intellectually active, then she might be able to avoid *kōnenki*. Its a disease of housewives who are financially secure and have a lot of spare time and nothing much to worry about. I think they could avoid it by keeping their eyes open to the outside world, and do some volunteer work such as becoming home helpers or helping with people who are mentally ill—by contributing to society instead of being so selfish. Around here we always encourage each other, and someone who might have a difficult *kōnenki* is usually asked to become the leader of our local women's group to keep her mentally active.

A textile factory worker articulated a similar message about people who do not apparently contribute to society: "I've heard from one or two housewives that they have severe headaches [at *kōnenki*]—so much so that they can't keep their heads up. I told them it's because they have so much free time. I think they should get out and do some work, even if their husband's complain about it."

A few women at first sight appear to accept the ideology of leisured life as applicable to themselves, as did this Kobe housewife:

> My mother had seven children, and the way it was in those days, she had no freedom, in fact she had no self (*jibun ga nai*); she was always suppressing herself and not letting anything show on the surface. I can't do that, I'm a spoiled type and I had trouble at *kōnenki*. Women who work or have hard lives don't suffer with *kōnenki*.

However, her ensuing narrative about married life with a drunken husband clearly revealed that she did not take her own platitudes seriously; her statement was rhetorical, a pro forma response (*tatemae*) with which it was assumed, correctly, that her listening friends would heartily disagree.

As with any other myth, when its authenticity is prodded and poked a little, rents and tears are readily apparent. When talking about themselves women may flirt self-consciously with negative images, but this is most often deliberate dissembling. Usually any distress which they or their friends have at *kōnenki* (which most in any case do not experience) is accounted for in terms of a faulty biological system, philandering husbands, stress at work, or other social problems; an ideology of indolence is simply not entertained, or else rejected outright. It is usually only when talking about people whom they do not know that women launch into critical sermonizing. Only as pure rhetoric do the majority agree with a luxury induced illness as an authentic account of a distressful *kōnenki*.

Thus the myth of the leisured housewife is contested in personal life, but nevertheless survives in the abstract largely untrammeled, fueled mostly by the media and popular medicine; a divisive and pernicious narrative, grist for the mill of nostalgia for a traditional moral order. When I have produced statistical data to show that housewives report fewer symptoms than do working women at *kōnenki,* this information is inevitably greeted with audible gasps in Japan; I found only a very few women who actively dispute the mythology in toto, among them a gynecologist who would like to see this part of female life stripped of its "superstitions" and treated in a more scientific fashion (Sasaki 1985).

Satisfaction, Resignation, and Reform: Vicissitudes of Middle Age

The lives of the women whom I interviewed are, not surprisingly, extremely varied. The majority report that they are happy and fortunate (*shiawase*), but a large number, working or otherwise, are decidedly not content, and many keep up a barrage of "low-profile" (Scott 1990) resistance against the perceived perpetrators of their unhappiness, usually their husbands. Blue-collar working women at times expressed a good deal of hostility about working conditions and in particular, when relevant, about a permanent lack of job security. When asked to talk about care of the elders, however, although everyone agreed that it was hard work which often demanded considerable sacrifice on the part of many women, nevertheless, there was almost no argument that female relatives should be primarily responsible. Those women already living with the older generation and those in line to do so, whatever their occupation, assumed usually without hesitation that their lives should be restructured and, if necessary, their financial contribution to the household curtailed to take on this task, in spite of the fact that few women today when they in turn become infirm, expect to be looked after by their daughters-in-law.

Provided that one's parents-in-law do not become incapacitated, and above all senile, then caring for the elderly can be a satisfying and rewarding task. I found many women who had worked out an amicable and even loving relationship with their in-laws over the years, and who did not feel particularly oppressed by their extended family situation. On the contrary, a good number are proud of their achievements on the domestic front. Rather than endure the punishing routines associated with white-collar work in Japan, many middle-class women actively embrace and reinforce the ideology of their worth as a "homebody," particularly so because care of the family is publicly recognized as a crucial and valued activity. Conflicts usually occur, however, when there is a major health problem in the family (and sometimes it is the middle-aged woman herself who is sick in addition to an elderly relative), or when the woman has to give up work from which she derives satisfaction or financial security, or, alternatively, when the usual caregiver, the wife of the eldest son, does not step forward to fulfill her designated task. Today, geography compounds the problem because urban residents are more often than not completely removed from their elders who remain in the countryside. Situations such as these are by no means unusual, as the following narratives reveal.

Shiba-san, fifty-two at the time of the interview, worked for nearly thirty years in the farm cooperative in the village where she lives, keeping the account books. Two years previously she had resigned from this job in order to take care of both her parents-in-law. Until she became ill, Shiba-san's mother-in-law had done all the housework and cooking while Shiba-san put in a full day at the coop, and her husband worked their land in addition to doing a part-time office job in the nearby town. Two months after resigning from her job, her mother-in-law died, but Shiba-san could not take up outside employment again because her father-in-law was not able to take care of himself.

Her son, married to a nurse and with two small children aged two years and eight months, intimated that now that Shiba-san was at home all day she probably felt rather lonely, and went on to suggest that perhaps his family should move into the "big house." Shiba-san's husband encouraged his son with the result that for six months prior to the interview the family had been living with four generations under one roof.

"What's your day like?"

"Well, I get up at 6:30 and make breakfast for everyone. My daughter-in-law helps sometimes, but because she's a nurse she often works at nights so I pretty much do everything. After everyone leaves for work I do the cleaning and the washing. The washing has increased enormously with all these people in the house. My daughter-in-law does some of the children's things, but I help with the diapers and so on."

"How does it feel to be a housewife after working full-time most of your life?"

"Well, the best part about the work was getting out of the house each day. I really enjoyed it, and I had a lot of friends. I was giving some psychological counseling, too, and I particularly liked that. Now, as a hobby, I manage to do Japanese classical dancing once a week. It's good exercise and I feel really fit afterward. But unfortunately I can't do any practice at home because my father-in-law is here and it would disturb him."

"Do you find it constraining to live in an extended family? What was it like when you were first married?"

"When I came here my mother-in-law was only about forty-six years old. She was a very independent woman and at first it was hard. I was working in the co-op already, but I had to start looking after this huge family as well—my parents-in-law, my husband and his four brothers.

"It's never been my intention that my daughter-in-law should experience the same kind of hardships that I had. My husband knows it's a bit hard on me at present, but he says that if we are to keep the peace in this family, then everything depends on me. So I must stay quiet and try to fit in with the young people's needs. On Sundays, when my daughter-in-law is at home, in order to let her sleep in, I try to stay in bed as long as possible although I really want to get up. In the past, if a mother-in-law got up earlier than her daughter-in-law and fixed breakfast than the daughter-in-law wouldn't be able to swallow the food from shame. But now young people don't take things that way any more."

"Will you live together for a long time?"

"Well, we have some land. We could build a house on one of

the rice fields, but somehow I don't think that will happen for a long time."

"How do you feel about taking care of the grandchildren?"

"They go to a day-care center for a few hours each day so that helps." Here Shiba-san paused, clearly wondering whether she should go on or not. She looked down, sighed, and then continued in one long rush:

"My daughter-in-law has a good, steady job, and she may be an exception, but in general I think that a mother should stay at home for a while and raise her own children, otherwise everyone suffers. Of course, if she stopped her work as a nurse she would probably never find a decent job again. I think the children are much too small to go into day care all day, and anyway there're no facilities around here for full time care. So its very hard on me, but I'm still young and so I'm helping her. Sometimes I feel upset, I don't really agree with how things are working out, but I keep that to myself."

"Do you find it hard to do that?"

"Yes, but I was trained to suppress my feelings, and I've had plenty of practice living with mother-in-law for so long. When I get older I'll be able to say what I want—but not yet."

Shiba-san assumes that when she is infirm her daughter-in-law will probably not relinquish her work in order to look after her. When pushed she admits that she feels caught between the generations, since she expects little recompense for a life devoted to the care of others (Lebra 1984:266). In common with virtually all women of her age, she believes that raising children is a woman's vocation. Men are usually characterized as helpless and passive onlookers at home, and Shiba-san has no expectations that her husband can ease her present burden, nor does she call on her son to give even the minimum of assistance with his children. Shiba-san does not mention this, but her family may well have suffered considerable economic hardship when she gave up her job. In addition to being the pillar of the family, the majority of middle-aged women today *must* work to meet the basic necessities of life.

Ishida Atsuko has, in contrast to Shiba-san, spent all her married life in a nuclear family and is, therefore, a candidate for the proverbial selfish housewife. She sat in her cramped high-rise apartment and recounted the highlights of her life for me:

"I don't think my husband and I ever had a very good marriage, but when my mother-in-law moved in, things started to get worse. She was widowed, and because my husband is the oldest son, she decided that she wanted to come here and live with us; my daughter was living here, too, then, in this small apartment. *Obāsan* [mother-in-law] had the front room. As you know, I teach the tea ceremony to students here at home and that front room has the special *tatami* mat that can be taken up easily so that the tea kettle can be heated up in there. It wasn't easy after *obāsan* came because there was always some tension about having to ask her to stay out of her room for a few hours once a week while I met the students. My husband and I slept in the room next to her, with just the sliding doors separating us from her—that was very difficult, too. My daughter was in the little single room at the back where I sleep now."

"It must have been very crowded for you all."

"When she first came it wasn't so bad, although she was quite bossy, and tried to make me do everything her way. I changed a lot of my habits about cooking and so on just to keep the peace. But she went out a lot and was involved with various social activities. Then, all of a sudden it seemed, she started to decline quite rapidly and about three years after she'd been living with us. I noticed that she was becoming forgetful and doing strange things, like hiding food in the closets. Then she had a mild stroke and she was in hospital for a good number of months. After she came out, things were never the same again. She was taking medication, but she had become really senile, and she was incontinent, too. I did all the nursing myself, and of course the worst part was changing the diapers. She was bedridden and wouldn't do anything for herself."

"Did your husband help at all?"

"No! You know what Japanese men are like. It was my job, naturally, to look after *obāsan* and he barely talked to her even when he was here. Toward the end she would call him in when he came home at nights and tell him that I was trying to poison her by giving her rotten food. All he did was to tell me to try harder to be nicer to her. I really didn't go out much for about eleven years except to do the shopping. I always had to be here looking after her."

"Couldn't you get any outside help? No social services or anything?"

"Well, the doctor came twice a week, and he was always very kind, but of course there was nothing to be done. He said if things got really bad I could ask to have a volunteer come round sometimes, but I didn't feel comfortable about that, and *obāsan* wouldn't tolerate the idea for an instant. In fact, we tried a volunteer one time and *obāsan* was so awful to her I didn't dare ask anyone in again. When my daughter got older she was very helpful though, and sometimes, after she came home from school, I could go out for a while"

"How did you endure it?"

"You know, Japanese women still think they are supposed to

endure everything and put everyone else first. I decided that I would see the job through until she died. Fortunately, it happened almost at the same time as my daughter left home and entered college. I wasn't angry with *obāsan*—she was pitiful—but I decided that I couldn't live with my husband any longer. I asked him to leave. I own this apartment so I just drove him out. He'd been having an affair for some time anyway, so I just said that he had to go. It was then that I started to look back over my early life and felt some regrets. Not that it could have been any other way I suppose—well, maybe it *could* have been different. My mother died when I was thirteen, and I had four young brothers. My father decided to take me out of school and make me into a kind of maid at home. I had to do all the housework for all those men. I think he probably could have afforded a caretaker quite easily, but he didn't want to ask a stranger into the house."

"Didn't he ever marry again?"

"No. So what I really regret now is not having had a proper education. All my brothers went to university, but I didn't even go to high school."

"That must have been really hard on you when you had to find a job after your separation."

"Well, not too bad, considering, because I'd done a lot of reading all those years I was looking after *obāsan,* and I'd started to get interested in interior design as well, so my mind wasn't dead. Anyway, for most ordinary jobs they expect to have to train you more or less from scratch, so they weren't too hesitant, even though I'm getting a bit long in the tooth. I have an exam next week, and I'm rather nervous about that."

"So you didn't have to look around a long time to find a job?"

"No, not really, because I don't want to work full-time. I can manage if I work two or three days a week. They weren't looking for a young, full-time woman, but for someone older like me so that they don't have to pay any benefits. It works out well because I go to study two mornings a week, I work two and a half days a week, and I still have time to teach the tea classes on Saturday afternoons."

"Do you feel happy in your new life?"

"So far it's fine, I'm fairly healthy, and I don't mind commuting too much. I've made some friends at work, but I'm a bit lonely sometimes, especially because my daughter lives in Tokyo now."

"Do you see your brothers and their families?"

"Not very often, about once a year."

In every interview the expectations of and unequivocal demands made by family members on middle-aged women were clearly evident. One woman, for example, had been bullied by her brothers and their wives into giving up her lifelong employment with a printing company in order to look after their parents. This woman, the youngest child in the family and therefore not normally expected to care for elderly parents, never married, and therefore having no "real" responsibilities was expected by the rest of the family to take on the task. She is now at serious risk of becoming impoverished as she grows older.

Miyata-san is a self-employed Tokyo architect, who chose her present life in order to avoid the discrimination she experienced in the company which formally hired her. While working at home she keeps an eye on her reasonably active mother-in-law who lives with the family. Miyata-san's husband is supportive of her work, helped convince his mother when it was needed that she must allow her daughter-in-law to work uninterrupted, but plays no part in the running of the household except to do a little cooking on Sundays. Miyata-san is hoping that she can persuade her sisters-in-law to help with their mother in the future, because if the full burden of nursing falls entirely into her hands she will have to give up her work entirely.

At forty-nine Inagaki-san looks frail and tired. She lives on a Nagano farm which she used to work almost single-handedly, and is at present nursing her mother-in-law. When interviewed she was recovering from major surgery for breast cancer. During her stay in hospital Inagaki-san's mother-in-law had also been hospitalized but, at her insistence, was discharged the same day as Inagaki-san, who resumed full care of her right away with only a little assistance from her husband and father-in-law. Inagaki-san's incision did not heal well—she had an allergic reaction to the chemotherapy—and she received no psychological counseling of any kind. She struggles on surrounded by the sad remains of the largely untended farm, with some occasional help with the housework from her husband and mature children. She is still unable to look at her body in a mirror, and is terrified each time she visits the doctor that she will hear that the disease has returned. Inagaki-san made every effort to retain her composure throughout the interview, but several times was reduced to tears as she recounted her story.

Given the realities of daily life, clearly government preaching about "warm" families is out of place, and to suggest that women should take up more hobbies or do volunteer service is obviously gratuitous. The stereotypical image of the indolent middle-class woman taken as representative of middle-aged females in Japan today is not tenable, although there are, of course, a good number who are not "productively" occupied, at least for small portions of their life cycle. Among those women whose lives are given over in service to the family, outright resistance is rare; on the contrary, many are genuinely content, especially when they compare their situation with that of their own mothers. Others however, unhappy with their lot, adjust and work toward gaining small changes on the domestic front. Only a very few women are actively engaged in combating the government rhetoric. When it comes to nursing sick elderly, since there are very few realistic alternatives, it would take a remarkable combination of indifference to the suffering of family members combined with the surmounting of numerous social pressures to resist what is naturalized as appropriate behavior for middle-aged females.

Perhaps it was after all the extended family through which the ideology of service to a household was largely perpetrated, until recently, as a Nagano woman suggested when she reflected on her past life with her mother-in-law:

> At first when I came to live with this family, because I didn't know anything, it was very hard. That's natural, it takes a long time to master the customs of a particular household. It took me about nine or ten years. After that it was easy. *Obāsan* was very smart, and she was a hard taskmaster, but she was never unreasonable. Because she was so strict I learned things really well. My husband pretended not to notice any conflict between us. He always said that my troubles were nothing compared to what he had as a soldier. At first I was never confident enough to say what I thought about anything, but after about ten years I got some confidence and began to speak up a bit. Once *obāsan* started to be nicer to me I began to feel that I wanted to take good care of her when she got older.
>
> I lived with her for twenty-eight years. She was bedridden for her last two months; before that she would sometimes do things for herself, but I always had to help her dress once she got old. I had two sets of *futon* for her, one was always hanging out because there were quite a lot of accidents. It was just like having a baby in the house. She could eat by herself, but I had to carry her on my back to take her outdoors for some fresh air. It was like that for many years until she died last year. She was eighty-eight.

Without the authority of the traditional extended household and its disciplinary rigors, perhaps both the government and middle-aged women are right to worry about the predicament of Japanese elders of the future.

The Japanese Life Course, Maturation, and *Kōnenki*

Despite a concern about the "greying" of the nation, individual aging is not thought of as an anomaly; on the contrary, Japan is a society exquisitely sensitive to the passing of time, and positively wallows, on occasion, in the ephemeral nature of human life. Life-cycle transitions of both men and women were formally marked and celebrated as social events; continuity with past generations, and the presence of the ancestors reinforce even now in many households the notion that each individual is part of a larger, cosmically ordained order (Smith 1974); women who are at present aged fifty were immersed in this ideology as children, and the majority still embrace it (Lebra 1984; Lock 1993). As we have seen from the above narratives, movement through the life cycle is subjectively experienced largely in terms of how one's relationships with other people shift through time, and particularly for women, life is expected to become meaningful as a result of what they accomplish for others (Plath 1980:139) regardless of their private aspirations. Under these circumstances biological aging and the end of menstruation are not very potent symbols. While there is some mourning for lost sexual attractiveness and mixed feelings on the part of a few women, emphasis is given by most to what is described as the inevitable process of aging itself: to greying hair, changing eyesight, lapses in short-term memory, and so on (Lock 1986). Furthermore, these signs of aging, while they obviously represent irretrievable youth, are primarily signifiers for the future, for what may be in store in terms of an enfeebled body, and hence an inability to contribute to the family once old age sets in. Some women apparently do not associate the end of menstruation with the idea of *kōnenki* (menopause) at all. In a survey which I conducted with over 1,300 women aged forty-five to fifty-five, 24 percent of the subsample who had ceased menstruating for more than one year reported that they had no sign of *kōnenki* (Lock 1986:30).[3]

In both the survey research and follow up interviews, I devoted a good deal of effort to establishing what meaning *kōnenki* holds for Japanese women, and which symptoms, if any, they associate with this event. Nearly 80 percent of the interview responses were along the following lines:

> I've had no problems at all, no headaches or anything like that. I've heard from other people that their heads felt so heavy that they couldn't get up. A few of my friends complain that they don't exactly have pain, but that they just feel generally bad.

> I started to have trouble sleeping when I was about fifty; that was *kōnenki*. I think. Some people have dizziness, headaches, stiff shoulders and aching joints.

> In my case my eyesight became weak. Some people get sensitive and have headaches.

My shoulders feel as if they are pulled and I get tired easily.

The most common disorders that I've heard about are headaches, shoulder stiffness, and aching joints. Some women get irritable, too.

A small number of women, twelve out of the sample of more than one hundred, made statements such as the following: "The most noticeable thing was that I would suddenly feel hot; it happened every day, three times or so. I didn't go to the doctor or take any medication. I wasn't embarrassed and I didn't feel strange, I just thought that it was my age."

A long, culturally appropriate symptom list of fifty-seven items was included in the questionnaire, not all of which were necessarily associated with *kōnenki,* and women were asked if they had experienced any of these symptoms in the previous two weeks. Overall reporting was low among Japanese women, and significantly different from comparable North American samples (Lock 1993). Most frequently reported symptoms were, in descending order of frequency: shoulder stiffness, headaches, lumbago, constipation, chilliness, irritability, insomnia, aches and pains in the joints, frequent colds, sore throat, feelings of numbness; and then, reported equally, loss of memory and hot flashes (only 10 percent of the sample as opposed to 31 percent and 35 percent in the Manitoba and Massachusetts samples, respectively). These were followed closely by "heavy head" (*atama ga omoi*), ringing in the ears, and eventually, almost at the bottom of the list, night sweats (only 4 percent of the sample as opposed to 20 percent in Manitoba and 12 percent in Massachusetts). The "classical" symptoms of menopause—hot flashes and night sweats—are not, therefore, reported to anything like the same extent as in comparable North American samples (Lock 1993).

Over 40 percent of Japanese women interviewed agreed with this statement, made by a Kyoto factory worker: "*Kōnenki* starts at different ages depending on the person. Some start in their late thirties and some never have any symptoms; they don't have *kōnenki* at all." The term *shōgai* (ill effects) has to be added to *kōnenki* (literally, "change of life") before most women start to think in terms of symptoms that could be thought of as distressing.

The end of menstruation has been recognized for many hundreds of years in traditional Sino-Japanese medicine as the "seventh" stage in a woman's life, when a quality known as *tenki,* intimately associated with the female reproductive cycle, goes into decline. When this decline is too abrupt it is thought to cause numerous nonspecific symptoms which may last for a few years, including dizziness, palpitations, headaches, chilliness, stiff shoulders, a dry mouth, and so on (Yasui and Hirauma 1991), but no specific word was reserved for this time of life, or for the physical distress sometimes associated with it.

Toward the end of the nineteenth century the concept *kōnenki* was explicitly created to convey the European idea of the "climacterium" (Nishimura 1981). The term *climacteric* had been used for many centuries in Europe to describe the dangers associated with several critical transitions associated with the life cycle, regardless of age or gender. However, by the late nineteenth century, this concept was confined to the female life cycle, and indicated a time span of several years during which, among other changes, menstruation ceased. At the same time the notion of menopause was formulated for the first time in the gynecological literature to indicate the specific event of the end of menstruation. Although a few Japanese medical professionals were aware of the changes in nomenclature taking place in Europe, nevertheless *kōnenki* has continued to be used in both medical and popular literature to signify a gradual transition in female midlife of anything from ten to twenty years duration. To this day no widely used term exists in colloquial Japanese which expresses the specific event of the end of menstruation, although healthcare professionals use the technical term (*heikei*), much as *menopause* was a technical term in English until as recently as forty years ago, and used little in daily parlance. Moreover, no specific word exists in Japanese to convey the experience of a hot flash.

Although a focus on the end of menstruation did not make intuitive sense to turn-of-the-century Japanese physicians as being of medical significance, the newly discovered "autonomic nervous system" was of much more interest to them. This idea, when it was first clearly articulated in Germany in 1898 caused a stir in medical circles everywhere, and in Japan it "fitted" with the holistic, physiological approach characteristic of Sino-Japanese medicine (Lock 1980). Later, in the 1930s when a close association was postulated between the endocrine system and the autonomic nervous system (Sheehan 1936), Japanese physicians comfortably adopted this idea and made a link between *kōnenki* and disturbances in the autonomic nervous system, an association which the majority of Japanese women and Japanese physicians (but not their North American counterparts) still accept today (Lock 1986).

Stiff shoulders, headaches, ringing in the ears, tingling sensations, dizziness, and so on, all associated with an unbalanced autonomic nervous system, are the symptoms which form the core of the *kōnenki* discourse. This discourse is, in part I believe, contingent upon "local" biology (which *may* be associated with diet) in which neither hot flashes nor sudden sweats are very evident. The survey research showed that the experience of distress at *kōnenki* is not limited to the leisured middle-class housewife (Lock 1993), but it is widely accepted that she is the one likely to complain and "fuss" about symptoms, and to seek out medical care rather than simply maintaining the correct mental attitude which would allow her to "ride over" (*norikoeru*) the event.

Japanese physicians keep abreast of the medical literature published in the West, and so one might expect that in a country which is actively dedicated to preventive medicine there would be considerable pressure to prescribe hormone-replacement therapy on a long-term basis to middle-aged women as a prophylactic against heart disease and osteoporosis, as is currently the case in North America. This approach to female aging is grounded in the assumption that lowered estrogen levels place women at an increased risk for major disease in later life. Once again, local biology plays a part, because mortality from coronary heart disease for Japanese women is about one-quarter that of American women (World Health Statistics 1991), and, although the figures are not very reliable, it is estimated that, even though Japanese women become osteoporotic twice as often as do Japanese men, the rate is half as frequent as among North American women (Ross et al. 1991). These figures, combined with a mortality rate from breast cancer which is about one-quarter that of North America, has meant that there has been relatively little pressure for Japanese gynecologists to enter into the international arena of debate about the pros and cons of the long-term use of hormone-replacement therapy, something about which many of them are, in any case, decidedly uncomfortable because of a concern about iatrogenesis. The usual medication for those relatively few women who report symptoms at menopause is herbal medicine, if anything is used at all, together with the promotion of good dietary practices and exercise habits (Lock 1993). Recently, under pressure from drug company promotions, and a fear of appearing "backward" and "unscientific" in the eyes of the West, this pattern has started to change toward more widespread use of hormones.

In summary, neither doctors nor women in Japan have found the end of menstruation to be a particularly potent signifier, especially because the concept of reproduction implies much more than a clearly demarcated biological process. Replication of the household is first and foremost what reproduction is all about, and assurance of continuity of this process usually transcends concerns about the biology of individual women. *Kōnenki* is regarded above all as a natural part of the aging process, and until recently it was assumed that, with the exception of a minute number of pathological cases, women would simply "ride over" any physical distress which might occur at this stage of the life cycle. I well recall one Japanese gynecologist asking me, with more than a touch of jingoism, I thought, "Why do Western women make such a fuss about menopause?"

The assumption about middle-aged women in Japan, shared by many women themselves, therefore, although increasingly disputed today, is that they should be available as unpaid caregivers and nurses—the linchpin of the family into which they marry, a stable force, fully responsible for the health and well-being of others. This rhetoric gives little weight to the biological changes of aging, to chronological age, the closing of the reproductive years, the end of menstruation, or to possible declining health in midlife (although this too is currently changing), all of which are central to the current North American discourse on female aging, which I want to introduce briefly by way of contrast to the Japanese case.

Female Middle Age as Augury for Decrepitude

The aging society is currently of great concern in North America, too; however, because the discourse starts out not with the family as the basic unit, as it does in Japan, but takes off instead from the individual, the argument about what middle-aged women should "do" for society is developed in an entirely different way. In North America, despite the fact that many middle-aged women put a good deal of resources and energy into care of their aged family members (although not usually by actually living with them), this goes largely unacknowledged except in some of the gerontological literature (Harrington, Newcomer, and Estes 1985). Government promotion of extended households is simply not "thinkable," and it is generally assumed that old people should within reason remain essentially independent and responsible for the provision of their own welfare, which in the United States, at least, is highly commodified.

The focus of attention with respect to middle-aged women is not as caregivers, but it is the health of their aging bodies which is at the present time a target of national concern. Of course, the theme of health promotion is highly visible in Japan, too, but middle-aged women are expected above all to look after their bodies for the sake of the family, since physical labor is required of them as caretakers. In North America the ideology is constructed in quite a different way, namely, out of predictions about the encapsulated life cycle of individual women, and little or no heed is paid to the way in which their life course is inevitably enmeshed with those of other people. Both the American and Canadian governments have recently become very alert to the projected burden which the so-called post-menopausal woman is likely to place on society; it is the very process of individual physical aging, therefore, which is considered to be the greatest threat to the economy.

In complete contrast to Japan, the end of menstruation has in North America been described in recent gynecological discourse as a deficiency disease, and is likened to diabetes or thyroid deficiency disease (Van Keep, Greenblatt, and Albeaux-Fernet 1976; Sarrel 1988). This interpretation is due in part to the attention which has been given in European and North American gynecology from the middle of the last century onward to the effects of the "aging" ovary on the entire body (Oudshoorn 1990). This complex story set in motion a pathological discourse in which emphasis was and continues to be given to the "deterioration," "decline," "decay," and "the inevitable demise" of the ovary at menopause (Haspels and Van Keep 1979).

When this negative assessment of female aging is linked, as it so often is, even in medical literature (Dewhurst 1981), to the mistaken assumption that because the *average* life expectancy was approximately fifty years until the beginning of this century, women never lived past the end of their reproductive years, a picture emerges which suggests that something contrary to nature's purpose has happened with increasing frequency over the past one hundred years. The fact that until recently life expectancy was low due to high infant and maternal mortality, and the elderly have always been among us (although their numbers are indeed increasing today) is effectively ignored. Instead, emphasis is given to the way in which society is being left with an ever growing superfluity of anomalous postreproductive women whose very longevity is considered a liability because their bodies are subject to inevitable decay as a result of depleted estrogen levels, in turn the product of "decayed" ovaries. In the past twenty years this metaphor of pathology has increasingly been accepted as fact so that menopause is now not merely *likened* to a deficiency disease but is usually assumed to be one (Lock 1993).

The implications of such a discourse for an aging society are enormous. The medical literature repeatedly alerts it readers as follows: "More than 40 million American women are menopausal; another 3.5 million will be reaching the climacteric age each year for the next 12 years. These women will have a life expectancy of 30 years after menopause" (Sarrel 1988). But it is not simply the numbers of postmenopausal woman who are of concern, it is the projected cost of their illness and deaths from the so-called killer diseases which are the real target for reform. In recent years, since declining estrogen levels have been linked in the epidemiological literature to an increased risk for osteoporosis and, of even more significance, to heart disease in later life, it is recommended that *all* middle-aged women take hormone-replacement therapy for the remainder of their life. These findings are hotly contested and by no means established as fact—research results are confusing and contradictory, and in any case based on probability samples from which extrapolations cannot be made to individuals and, moreover, hormone-replacement therapy has been linked to an increased risk of cancer. Nevertheless, powerful interest groups (drug companies, researchers, certain physicians) recommend lifelong medication.

The governments of America and Canada are interested in the possibility of saving healthcare expenditure in connection with the elderly, as is the Japanese government, but the path they have chosen to follow is to promote a massive drugging of middle-aged women. In contrast to Japan, therefore, where the question of the elderly and the contribution middle-aged women are expected to play in their care has become politicized, in North America it is primarily the rapidly declining "estrogen-deficient" bodies of women which are politicized, subject to enumeration and repeated epidemiological evaluation, and endless debates in professional and popular literature.

Representing the Life Course

Life-cycle transitions have usually been understood as socially and culturally constructed transformations layered over a universal biological base. The above findings from Japan indicate, I believe, that we should conceptualize *both* biology and culture as contingent—as being in an ongoing dialectic throughout the life course. Local biologies profoundly influence but do not, of course, determine either the experience or the construction of a discourse about aging. What confounds the issue is that scientific discourse assumes a universality derived from the Western body, but this account often comes to rest in local settings in an uneasy relationship to both professional knowledge and subjectivity.

Carefully designed, culturally sensitive survey research provides important data on variation in connection with symptom reporting and subjective experiences in connection with the life course of any given population. The survey research discussed in this essay (and described fully in Lock 1993), was undertaken with the experience of more than fifteen years of research in Japan as a foundation, and with the cooperation of several native speakers and one fully bilingual research assistant. The questionnaire was based on one already used in Manitoba and Massachusetts, but adapted in light of cultural knowledge about Japan and preliminary interviewing with twenty women and five medical professionals. Questions about family structure, physician and medication use, traditional medicine, religion, and so on had to be modified, as did the symptom list. The preliminary interviews revealed, as I had hypothesized on the basis of prior knowledge about Japan, that the concept of *kōnenki* cannot be equated with menopause. These interviews also revealed that symptoms associated with *kōnenki* are not the same as those thought of as menopausal; it was immediately apparent that many symptoms would have to be added to the list and, moreover, that there was no single term for the hot flash. Furthermore, I was already aware from previous research that the concept of depression could not be expressed by a single word.

In short, instruments for use in survey research designed in one cultural context cannot be made use of in another without modification on the basis of knowledge about the second culture, and a thorough acquaintance with the language in question. Even after modification, the results of questionnaires applied cross-culturally are not *directly* comparable. Findings must initially be interpreted in the context of local history and culture; generalizations can only be asserted very cautiously and provisionally, and even then are subject to never ending revision in the ongoing melée of political change, revised scientific knowledge, and transformations in everyday life. Failure to take these precautions means that one is in constant danger of imposing an external value system on the entire endeavor. Ideally, questionnaire research should always be accompanied by independent ethnographic research, allowing for a movement back and forth between narratives and numbers—from a culturally informed ethnographic account grounded in local analogies and tropes to survey findings.

One distinct advantage of survey research is that the results may contradict, as is the case in the above example of Japanese middle age, narrated local beliefs and stereotypes about aging. Quantitative research can therefore facilitate a prying apart of received wisdom. By contrast, quantitative research is inevitably constrained by the types of questions posed, and is, moreover, in constant danger of misuse when results are taken out of context and reduced to abstractions. Survey research frequently provides, for example, rich pickings for the promotion of dominant ideologies. Without an accompanying ethnography, my own findings could potentially be made use of in Japan to support the idea that middle-aged women exhibit little physical distress and therefore must be leisured and ideally suited as caregivers for the elderly. It is only when survey research is fully supplemented by narrative accounts that the relationship of normative rhetoric, both political and medical, often detrimental and incompatible with the lives of individuals, is exposed.

Notes

1. Open-ended interviews were conducted with thirty-five Japanese physicians, including four who specialize in traditional medicine.

2. Interviews lasting between one and one-half and two hours were conducted in their homes with 105 women. Approximately one-third were Kobe housewives, one-third were factory workers in south Kyoto, and one-third lived and were occupied in farming villages in southern Nagano, a fishing village in Shikoku, and a forestry village in Shiga. Names appearing in the text are fictitious. Interviews with physicians reported above (see note 1) were conducted in 1984 and 1986.

3. In a 1984 survey that I conducted with over 1,300 women aged 45 to 55 inclusively, three occupational groups were included: farming women, factory workers, and full-time housewives.

The middle-class urban sample was selected from the register of names and addresses available at many city halls in Japan. The register used is classified according to residential areas. Two areas regarded as representative of middle income families were selected and every woman between ages 45 and 55 (= 525) was noted and mailed a questionnaire. This was followed up by a reminder postcard and then a second mailing of the questionnaire to those who had not responded. After the first mailing, 191 usable questionnaires were returned; after the postcard, 68 more; and after the second questionnaire, another 75 were returned, giving a total of 324 usable responses. The usual response rate to Japanese mail questionnaires is between 10 and 15 percent.

The factory workers were selected by first making contact with the director of the Kyoto Industrial Health Association who facilitated the distribution of 405 questionnaires to 15 factory managers who then passed out all of the questionnaires to women of the appropriate age. Replies were sent back by mail directly to the researchers. A second group of 145 women working in small silk-weaving factories were contacted by personal distribution of the questionnaire to factory managers after receiving the support of the local union in the form of a letter of introduction. Three hundred and seventy-seven usable responses were obtained from this sample.

The final sample of 650 farm workers were mostly selected through the support of the public health department of a large country hospital. The questionnaires were distributed by traveling public-health workers to the women's organizations of 45 villages; responses were mailed directly back to the researchers and yielded 434 usable responses. A second, smaller sample of 176 usable responses was obtained through the cooperation of the local head of the department of public health, who introduced the researchers directly to the local women's organizations.

This survey was designed to be comparable with one conducted in Massachusetts using 8,000 women and another in Manitoba with 2,500 women aged 45–55 inclusively.

References

Armstrong, David. 1983. *Political Anatomy of the Body: Medical Knowledge in Britain in the Twentieth Century.* Cambridge: Cambridge University Press.

Bourdieu, Pierre. 1977. *Outline of a Theory of Practice.* Cambridge: Cambridge University Press.

de Certeau, Michel. 1984. *The Practice of Everyday Life.* Berkeley: University of California Press.

Dewhurst, John. 1981. *Integrated Obstetrics and Gynecology for Postgraduates.* Oxford: Blackwell Scientific Publications.

Eto, Jun. 1979. "The Breakdown of Motherhood is Wrecking our Children." *Japan Echo* 6: 102–9.

Farquhar, Judith. 1991. "Objects, Processes, and Female Infertility in Chinese Medicine." *Medical Anthropology Quarterly* 5: 370–99.

Foucault, Michel. 1979. *Discipline and Punish: The Birth of the Prison.* New York: Vintage.

Freidson, E. 1970. *The Profession of Medicine.* New York: Dodd, Mead.

Gluck, Carol. 1990. "The Meaning of Ideology in Modern Japan." In *Rethinking Japan.* Ed. A. Boscaro, F. Gatti, and M. Raveri, 283–97. Folkestone: Japan Library, Ltd.

Harootunian, H. D. 1989. "Visible Discourses/Invisible Ideologies." In *Postmodernism and Japan.* Ed. M. Miyoshi and H. D. Harootunian, 63–92. Durham: Duke University Press.

Harrington, C., et al. 1985. *Long- Term Care of the Elderly.* Beverly Hills, Calif.: Sage.

Haspels A. A., and P. A. Van Keep. 1979. "Endocrinology and Management of the Peri-Menopause." In *Psychosomatics in Peri-Menopause.* Ed. A. A. Haspels and H. Musaph, 57–71. Baltimore: University Park Press.

Hewitt, Martin. 1991. "Bio-politics and Social Policy: Foucaults Account of Welfare." In *The Body: Social Process and Culture Theory.* Ed. M. Featherstone, M. Hepworth, and B. S. Turner, 225–55. London: Sage Publications.

Higuchi, Keiko. 1985. "Women at Home." *Japan Echo* 12: 51–57.

Hosoya, Tsugiko. 1987. "Rōjin kango no tsuma no sutoresu" (The Stress of Wives Nursing their Old Folks). In *Gendai no Espuri.* Tokyo: Shibundo, 151–62.

Imazu, Kōjino, Esyun Hamaguchi, and Keiichi Sakuta. 1979. "Shakai Kankyō no Henyō to Kodomo no Hattatsu to Kyōiku" (Strategic Points in the Social Environment and the Development of Children). In *Kodomo no Hattatsu to Kyōiku I* (Child Development and Education, vol. 1). Tokyo: Iwanami Shoten, 42–94.

Jordanova, Ludmilla. 1989. *Sexual Visions: Images of Gender in Science and Medicine Between the Eighteenth and Twentieth Centuries.* Madison: University of Wisconsin Press.

Karōshi bengo dan zenkoku renraku kaigihen. 1990. Karōshi (Death from Overwork). Tokyo: Mado-sha.

Kelly, William. 1986. "Rationalization and Nostalgia: Cultural Dynamics of New Middle-Class Japan." *American Ethnologist* 13: 603–18.

Kōsei Hakusho. 1989. "Arata na kōreishazō to katsuryoku aru chōju fukushi shakai o mezashite" (Toward a New Image of the Aged and a Vigorous, Long-Lived Society with Good Welfare). Tokyo: Kōseishō.

Kyūtoku, Shigemori. 1979. *Bogenbyō* (Illnesses Caused by Mother). Tokyo: Sanmaku Shuppan.

Lebra, Takie. 1984. *Japanese Women: Constraint and Fulfillment.* Honolulu: University of Hawaii Press.

Leys Stepan, Nancy. 1986. "Race and Gender: The Role of Analogy in Science." *Isis* 77: 261–77.

Lock, Margaret. 1980. *East Asian Medicine in Urban Japan: Varieties of Medical Experience.* Berkeley: University of California Press.

———. 1985. "Models and Practice in Medicine: Menopause as Syndrome or Life Transition?" In *Physicians of Western Medicine.* Ed. R. A. Hahn and A. D. Gaines, 115–39. Dortrecht: D. Reidel.

———. 1986. "Ambiguities of Aging: Japanese Experience and Perceptions of Menopause." In *Culture, Medicine, and Psychiatry.* Ed. A. Klainman, 23–46. Dordrecht: D. Reidel.

———. 1988. "A Nation at Risk: Interpretations of School Refusal in Japan." In *Biomedicine Examined.* Ed. M. Lock and D. R. Gordon, 391–414. Dordrecht: Kluwer Academic Publishers.

———. 1991. "Flawed Jewels and National Dis/Order: Narratives on Adolescent Dissent in Japan." *Journal of Psychohistory* 18: 507–31.

———. 1993. *Encounters with Aging: Mythologies of Menopause in Japan and North America.* Berkeley: University of California Press.

Lock, Margaret, and Deborah Gordon, eds. 1988. *Biomedicine Examined.* Dordrecht: Kluwer Academic Publishers.

Martin, Emily. 1987. *The Woman in the Body: A Cultural Analysis of Reproduction.* Boston: Beacon Press.

Mitsuda, Kyōko. 1985. "Kindaiteki Boseikan no Juyō to Kenkei: Kyōiku Suru Hahaoya Kara Ryōsai Kenbo e" (The Importance and Transformation of the Condition of Modern Motherhood: From Education Mother to Good Wife and Wise Mother). In *Bosei o tou* (What is Motherhood?). Ed. H. Wakita, 100–129. Kyoto: Jinbunshoin.

Mochida, Takeshi. 1980. "Focus on the Family." *Japan Echo* 3: 75–76.

Monbushō. 1983. *Tōkōkyohi mondai o chūshin ni: chūgakko, kōtōgakko ron* (A Discussion of Junior and Senior High Schools: Focus on School Refusal). Tokyo: Ministry of Education.

Murakami, Yasusuke, Shunpei Kumon, and Seizaburō Sato. 1979. *Bunmei to Shite no ie shakai* (Household Society as Civilization). Tokyo: Chūō Kōron Sha.

Nihon Fujin Dantai-Rengōkai, eds. 1989. *Kōrei sha fukushi* (Welfare in the Aging Society). Tokyo: Horupu Shuppan.

Nishimura, Hideo. 1981. *Josei to Kanpō* (Women and Herbal Medicine). Osaka: Sōgensha.

Nolte, Sharon, and Sally Ann Hastings. 1991. "The Meiji State's Policy." In *Recreating Japanese Women, 1600–1945.* Ed. Gail Lee Bernstein, 151–74.

Ogawa, Naohiro. 1988. "Population Aging and Medical Demand: The Case of Japan." In *Economic and Social Implications of Population Aging.* Proceedings of the International Symposium on Population Structure and Development, Tokyo, 254–75. New York: United Nations.

Ohira sōri no seisaku kenkyūkai hōkokusho #3 (Reports of the Policy Research

Bureau of the Ohira Cabinet #3). 1980. *Katei no kiban no jūjitsu* (Enrichment of the Japanese Family Base). Tokyo: Ōkurasho Insatsu Kyoku.

Oudshoorn, Nelly. 1990. "On the Making of Sex Hormones: Research Materials and the Production of Knowledge." *Social Studies of Science* 20: 5–33.

Plath, David. 1980. *Long Engagements.* Stanford, Calif.: Stanford University Press.

Ross, Philip D., Hiromichi Norimatsu, James W. Davis, Katsuhiko Yano, Richard D. Wasnick, Saeko Fukiwara, Yutaka Hosoda, and L. Hoseph Melton. 1991. "A Comparison of Hip Fracture Incidence among Native Japanese, Japanese Americans, and American Caucasians." *American Journal of Epidemiology* 133: 801–9.

Sarrel, P. M. 1988. "Estrogen Replacement Therapy." *Obstetrics and Gynecology* 72 (supp.): 2S–5S.

Sasaki, Shizuko. 1985. "Kōnenki o Minaosu" (Another Look at Kōnenki). In *Kōnenki o Ikiru* (Living through *Kōnenki*). Ed. Y. Komano, T. Biyneru, and M. Tawara, 113–31. Tokyo: Gakujo Shobō.

Scott, James. 1990. *Domination and the Arts of Resistance: Hidden Transcripts.* New Haven, Conn.: Yale University Press.

Sheehan, Donald. 1936. "Discovery of the Autonomic Nervous System." *AMA Archives of Neurology and Psychiatry* 35: 1081–1115.

Smith, Robert. 1974. *Ancestor Worship in Contemporary Japan.* Stanford, Calif.: Stanford University Press.

Van Keep, P. A., P. B. Greenblatt, and M. Albeaux-Fernet, eds. 1976. *Consensus on Menopause Research.* Lancaster, England: MTP Press.

World Health Statistics. 1991. *World Health Statistics: 1990.* Geneva: World Health Organization.

Wright, Peter W. G., and Andrew Treacher, eds. 1982. *The Problem of Medical Knowledge: Examining the Social Construction of Medicine.* Edinburgh: University of Edinburgh Press.

Yasui, Hiromichi, and Naokichi Hirauma. 1991. "Kanpo dekangaeru kōnenki shogai to wa donna mono deshoka" (What Are *Kōnenki* Disorders from the Point of View of Traditional Herbal Medicine?). *Fujin Gaho* (Sept.): 370–79.

Zola, I. K. 1978. "Medicine as an Institution of Social Control." *Sociological Review* 20: 487–504.

17 Ethnography, Biography, and Cultural History: Generational Paradigms in Human Development

KATHERINE NEWMAN

> A historical generation is not defined by its chronological limits
> or its borders. It is not a zone of dates; nor is it an army of con-
> temporaries making its way across a territory of time. It is more
> like a magnetic field at the center of which lies an experience or
> series of experiences.
>
> Robert Wohl, *The Generation of 1914* (1979: 210)

Robert Wohl's moving study of the men who returned from the nightmare
of World War I provides the intellectual departure for this chapter: an
excursion into the importance of generation as a theoretical concept for
the study of human development. The idea of generation, as a source of
social orientation and personal identity, is hardly original. For apart from
the many studies of particular generations, there is an important theoretical literature on the topic, approached from the vantage point of survey
research. The pioneering work of Glen Elder Jr. comes to mind here: *Children of the Great Depression* is but one of his many contributions to the
exploration of generational experience, a landmark book which explores
how the economic catastrophe of the 1930s shaped the lives of the children
who grew up in its shadow. And before Elder came other, less empirical
thinkers, including Karl Mannheim, who asked some profound questions
about how generations should be defined, how their boundaries should
be established.

This rich literature forms an important backdrop to the present chapter.
Yet it provides only the barest beginnings for scholars of human development who wish to pursue the importance of the ethnographic methods in
particular and cultural analysis more generally. For the existing literature
on generational identity is drawn either from the study of literary texts
or from survey-oriented social psychological research. While these ap-

proaches are perfectly compatible with an ethnographic orientation, their purpose is different: the literary approach seeks to define the orienting themes of a generation's experience as it is crystallized in the lives of public intellectuals, especially writers. The social psychologist focuses on ordinary people, utilizing attitudinal questionnaires to gather quantifiable data on developmental milestones, comparing generations in their relative successes and failures in marriage, childrearing, occupational trajectories, and overall degrees of satisfaction or efficacy.

Both approaches leave gaps in our understanding of generational culture. We have no way of knowing how iconic intellectuals compare to the man or woman in the street where generational culture is concerned. Ernest Hemingway and Eldridge Cleaver may capture something of the ethos of their time, but it is hard to know how their experiences or perspectives map onto the identities of ordinary folk. Survey research has the distinct advantage of representativeness and there is a clear place for it in studies of generational culture—for example, in verifying the findings of ethnographic or interview-based inquiry on larger samples. However, questions of interpretation and meaning, cultural elaboration and historical experience, cannot be answered to anyone's satisfaction using fixed-choice surveys. At the very least, the two approaches must be considered complementary, with ethnographic inquiry serving as a primary tool for the exploration of generational nuances and issues of meaning, and large-scale surveys providing the opportunity to explore their differential salience in segments of the population.

Hence, in advocating the use of generational paradigms in ethnographically oriented research on human development, I mean to encourage at least two new frontiers: one methodological and the other substantive. From a methodological perspective, I argue that ethnographers would do well to select the subjects of developmental studies with reference to generational differences. Life histories, one of the major tools of the ethnographic method, can be scoured for representations of generational culture if "informants" are culled from distinct cohorts and their life stories are examined for generational nuances. Moreover, a focused life history can be structured so as to encourage reflection upon the watershed events of an individual's life. Looking across these kinds of life histories, the ethnographer is able to understand the salience (or lack of importance) of generational culture for any given cohort.[1]

From a theoretical or substantive perspective, a generational approach brings two important phenomena into sharp relief, namely, the interplay of historical experience and personal identity and the contrastive symbolic "dialects" which are generated by divergent historical experiences.

Scholars of human development have long been interested in the ways individuals develop identities, particularly as they move from one life stage to the next. The approach suggested here focuses on the ways in which the process of identity formation is historically situated and shaped, rather than invariantly organized into developmental stages. This is not to deny that people move, for example, from childhood to adolescence in a patterned fashion. It is simply to note that the circumstances—political, economic, and cultural—under which this transition occurs play an important role in defining its meaning.

During the Great Depression, ordinary childhood came to an abrupt end for millions of young people who were suddenly forced to focus on family survival. Today we see adolescence elongating as a weak economy sends an unprecedented number of boomerang children back home to their parents' nests (Newman 1993:54). The timing of independence and the importance we invest it with alters with the vagaries of the market. So too do our normative conceptions of adolescence.[2] Hence an ethnographic approach that fuses history and biography provides an opportunity to examine one of the most important contextual features of human development in complex societies: social change. But it does so not simply by pointing to statistical patterns—the residential choices of adolescents—but by examining the meanings attached to these phenomena and the language we use to express them.

As powerful as generational identity may be, it clearly exists on a competitive plain with other forms of self-definition. One may construct a social character with reference to generational experience, but consciously identify with fellow members of a racial, ethnic, gender, or class-based group as well. One critical theoretical task, then, involves the articulation of these competing categories, understanding when they produce "hybrid" selves that easily blend different dimensions of an individual's biography, when they foster dichotomous or situational selves, and when they set up contested forms of identity. All of these possibilities exist "on the ground," and if a generational approach to human development is to capture cultural experience accurately it must provide for theoretical approaches that can account for these possibilities, among others.

An emphasis on symbolic dialects provides an opportunity to consider a new perspective on social change as well (Newman 1986). Social scientists often speak of change as a societal phenomenon which is all encompassing, even as it may impact in variable forms. The generational analysis I am advocating here would have us focus more attention on the disjunctures in any complex society caused by generational differences.

At any given moment, a complex society is crosscut by generations which represent very different forms, for example, of American culture. Side by side sit generations with divergent values, expectations, beliefs, and socially constructed meanings. The disjuncture results from the differential impact of social change, the ways in which economic events or political upheavals catch people at different points in the life cycle. For example, wars may exert the most profound impact on the life course of young men, leaving others largely untouched. Models of social organization need to incorporate the fact that history slices through a society, carving us into generational cultures which may only intersect on the surface, even though we occupy the same social and chronological space. These forms of difference may be as important as race, gender, ethnicity, and class—the dominant variables in sociological studies of social difference. Generational identity becomes a form of subculture, and society itself becomes a patchwork quilt of groups defined by the formative events that shaped their lives as young adults.

The Meaning of Generational Identity

The term *generation* has widespread lay currency. Most people, including those any social scientist is likely to subject to a life-history interview, have a definite notion of what it means, even when they do not feel a strong identification with a particular generation. For most people, a generation is a group of people who lived through a time period together, developing a shared culture around its iconic screen heroes, social movements, political figures, musical innovations, and cataclysmic events. They understand, as Wohl himself understood, that an intense generational identity shapes and defines the individuals who fall within its boundaries and separates them from others who have no claim on its immediacy. As Wohl put the matter, "What is essential to the formation of a generational consciousness is some common frame of reference that provides a sense of rupture with the past and that will later distinguish the members of the generation from those who follow them in time" (Wohl 1979:210). Generational identity then is both a source of social bonding, drawing members into a cocoon of shared assumptions and moral vocabularies, as well as a source of division, for the intensity of the integration is paralleled by a feeling of separation from other generations. It is produced by common experience which provides the stuff of a symbolic culture, the raw material which leads disparate individuals to feel bonded to one another. The bond, in turn, is expressed on occasion through collective behavior, but more often through the integration of social experience into personal identity. Individuals come to define themselves in a fundamental fashion as members of a social generation, to elevate this aspect of their myriad backgrounds in such a way as to see themselves first and foremost as survivors of particular historical experiences.

For the young men who fought in World War I—and Wohl studied the war generation in several European nations—the rupture was so great that they were unable to reintegrate into civilian society when the guns fell silent. The unprecedented and relentless brutality of the Great War pushed its survivors into an enduring isolation from civilian society. The feeling that their generation had been "used" as human pawns, dragged through the trenches, and forced to run hopeless gauntlets, induced a deep cynicism.[3] Never again were these young men and women able to feel themselves a part of their national culture. For the rest of their lives they identified with their own generation, whether in bitterness or romantic nostalgia. The depth of their attachments to one another was paralleled by the gulf between them and the rest of their society.

Defining generations in terms of this kind of extraordinary social bonding has had a surprisingly modest effect on those who study the life course. For these developmental scholars, generations are best understood as birth cohorts who move through time together. From this perspective, everyone is a member of a group tied together by the common historical circumstances that attend their movement along the developmental path. Historical context is reduced mainly to the economic circumstances that generate differences in the ways in which different cohorts weather developmental milestones.

Children of the Great Depression examines the ways in which middle-class and working-class children born in the early 1920s and cresting into the labor market in the mid-1930s were forever influenced by the hard times they experienced (for good and ill).[4] Elder examines how economic deprivation influenced the timing of major events in their life course, particularly marriage and childbearing, the way it shaped their occupational trajectories or influenced the duration of their marriages. From this work we learn a great deal about how crossing the developmental threshold into young adulthood was shaped by catastrophic levels of unemployment during the Depression. We can see in the statistical patterns, how a stumbling entry into the labor market doomed young men to a lifetime of underachievement, their occupational biographies forever tainted by having gotten off to a poor start.

What the life-course approach does *not* do, however, is capture the *meaning* of generational experience. It cannot, for example, address crucial questions of representation, of the ways in which the culture of a generation forms around these iconic experiences. This data cannot tell us whether or to what extent the Depression generation recognized themselves (then or now) as kindred spirits, forever bound together by the experience of extreme adversity.

An ethnographic approach sheds light on the ways in which these representational processes develop and examines the way they impact upon the formation of individual identities. To use an overworked phrase, strong generations develop a "discourse" or dialect, a way of speaking about themselves that represents their experience to outsiders and simultaneously reinforces among insiders the importance of belonging. This discourse is likely to be recognized by others, understood as a special code which demarks insiders, but cannot be convincingly shared by those who fall outside the generational boundaries, vague as they may be.

A focus on meaning and interpretation solves some problems, and opens up many others. How do we locate the boundaries of a generation? How do we decide who really belongs, whose experience or interpretative framework represents the heart of a generation? If we are to speak of meaning, whose meanings "count"? How are these meanings refracted and altered according to class or gender? How are generational boundaries or identities reflected in behavior? Applying these questions, for example, to Wohl's work, we find major differences between groups of people whose lives intersected World War I at different points in the life cycle. Men who were old enough to have established themselves in careers, only to have them interrupted by the war, defined the experience quite differently from those who were torn from their youth and thrust into the horror of the trenches. These people, in turn, saw the war from a very different vantage point than those whose lives were turned inside out by the transformation of civilian society, but who were too young to enlist or be drafted. This last group grew up, as it were, in the shadow of the war, without ever having the chance to participate directly. Ironically, Wohl explains, they always carried with them the sense of missed opportunities for adventure and heroism and remembered the war for the material deprivations it brought to bear on civilian life.

Which of these groups constitutes the "generation of 1914"? All of them were alive at the time, all of them were affected by the trauma of war, but each has a different vantage point. Glen Elder put the matter in more abstract terms when he noted that "the impact of a historical event on the life course of a cohort reflects the stage at which the change was experienced. The implications of mass unemployment or military conscription obviously vary among individuals of different ages, from children to the middle-aged" (Elder 1985:25). In Elder's later work on the generation that fought in World War II, we see that in addition to cohort-based variation, an emphasis on gender is required. Women who "stayed behind" think of the war in very different terms than the men who enlisted. The home front and the battlefield were two distinct vantage points, both of which created disjunctures from normal experience. These examples point to the importance of analyzing generational experience from a multicultural and cross-gender perspective if we are to understand the full range of meanings that are bound up in a generation's symbolic culture.

If we broaden his point beyond the question of "impact" toward the question of meaning we see that here, too, the salience of a historical event or set of economic conditions, for example, will vary as well with the age (or race, gender, ethnicity, and regional location) of any given individual. None of these observations solve the problem posed above: whose experience constitutes the defining for a generation's "symbolic dialect"?

There is no single answer to this question, for all "takes" on a particular event or era are of some importance. But for the purposes of discussion, I would argue that generational identity is best conceived of as what mathematicians call a "fuzzy set," where membership is less an all-or-nothing proposition and more a matter of degree. As I put the matter elsewhere,

> Imagine a core at the middle of people who are unambiguously identified with a particular generational experience, and then wrap concentric circles around the core that express a less tightly integrated identification with, for example, the Depression generation. The farther one moves out from the core, the "fuzzier" the sense of identification becomes. (Newman 1993:247–48)

The fuzzy-set approach speaks to the meaning of generational identity in one sense: it tells us that membership does not mean the same thing to everyone who was in a position to experience the events or conditions that give rise to a generational culture, that people vary in the degree to which their identity is shaped with generation in mind.

But what constitutes the content of the center—or whether there is a center for any given era—not to mention how different individuals come to occupy the circles that radiate out from the core? How does a cohort, a group of people born at a particular point in time, become a subculture, a meaningful group that draws boundaries around itself? I would argue that it takes more—much more—than the accident of birth timing to forge a generation. First and foremost, as Wohl reminds us, it takes the stuff of collective memory, most particularly the experience of genuinely cataclysmic events to bind otherwise unrelated individuals together. Wars, revolutions, natural disasters, and massive economic upheavals are most likely to generate the sense of rupture that is required to demark a generation.[5] This is not only because events of this magnitude catch people's attention, jolting them out of the sense most of us have of ordinary or mundane lives. It is because these upheavals force dramatic departures from the normative course of daily life and the life course itself. Uprooted in time and space, we see ourselves as specially bound to others who have similarly been knocked free of the expected pathways of life.

The Depression is an obvious example here. Young people who might have expected to pursue an ordinary pathway through life, a pathway dominated by the completion of their education, movement into adulthood via the labor market, independent households, marriage, and childbearing, found the entire trajectory derailed. Young men discovered they could not afford to leave home and set up their own households. Young women often found themselves pressed into obligations at home that they would otherwise have been exempted from. The impact of these departures from the status quo were long in duration, lasting a lifetime for many people who never did recover their footing in the job market, who "missed" the opportunity to marry, remaining instead in their natal homes, helping to pick up the pieces of domestic lives torn apart by persistent unemployment. A case can be made that these young people, essentially those who were teenagers and young twenty-year-olds in the early 1930s, form the heart of the Depression generation.

This is not to suggest that others were unaffected or were somehow bystanders to the experience. Older people who suffered the brunt of unemployment, particularly fathers and men in general, and little children who watched the adults around them sink into despair, were also part of the Depression experience. Yet they might be placed in various concentric circles around a core composed of those people whose trajectories in life were so powerfully and permanently affected. For the older generations alive in the 1930s already had identities, careers, places in society which, while powerfully affected, competed with the new, shaken identity created by the shattering power of the Depression. Little children were clearly affected in myriad ways (Komarovsky 1940; Jahoda, Lazarsfeld, and Zeiel 1933), but the twists and turns of their personal and occupational lives were powerfully affected by the end of the Depression, the onset of World War II, and the sustained economic boom that followed. Hence, though they were products of the Depression in one sense, the core of their generational identity involves both hardship and affluence.

Glen Elder's recent research on the experience of Chinese youth "sent down" to the countryside in the course of the Cultural Revolution in China is another case in point of a wrenching event that bound a generation together. Uprooted from their homes in urban China, the sons and daughters of the country's intelligentsia, political class, and artistic community were sent out to peasant villages to be reeducated in the image of Chairman Mao's proletarian revolution. The Cultural Revolution threw the established order of the People's Republic into complete chaos and forever transformed the social experience of millions of people. But it had a particularly profound generational impact upon those who were in their late teens and early twenties when the great experiment took them from their families and sent them to places where they were so unwelcome and their heritage so despised that they never quite recovered their footing. Twenty-five years later, as Elder is now discovering, the youth on the receiving end of the Cultural Revolution, recognize themselves as a group bonded together by the experience of being ostracized.[6]

These examples would suggest that the core of a generational culture is likely to be formed during the developmental period which might loosely be called coming of age, the period during which youth are (or "should be," according to their normative ideals) in the process of striking out on their own, separating from their families and setting the course of their adult futures. It is therefore a special concern for researchers who work on the developmental tasks of adolescents and young adults. But it is not simply a task undertaken at a particular point in the life course and then forever fixed. Generational identity is subject to reformulation, nostalgic elaboration, even rejection as subsequent experience modifies the meaning and centrality of this special bond. Indeed, for many people, the most powerful aspects of generational culture are those which emerge in the process of collective retrospection. Living through a war, a depression, a collective nightmare of any kind absorbs the energies of its "victims" in the practical problems of survival. Hence an important developmental task of later adulthood may well involve coming to terms with the rupture and the collective meaning it has for those who were at the center of the experience.

If cataclysmic events that impact upon the life course are the orienting center of generational cultures, how are they likely to be marked or represented in the language, memory, and "morality"[7] of those who carry them? Here I believe at least two domains of representation must be considered.

Performance and cultural elaboration. Events like World War I or the Depression are likely to achieve a degree of cultural embroidery—in the form of popular music, film, street culture, and other forms of performance—that become part of the fabric of a generational center. Forms of performance alone are not powerful enough to create generational solidarity, but when they occur in the company of, or even more in response to, major social upheaval, popular culture and political icons become the stuff of collective memory, the aspects of experience most likely to be recalled in qualitative life-history interviews. They will be most salient and powerful for those people whose life trajectories are permanently altered by rupturing events, for through performance and culturally elaborated memory, they are codified and symbolized. Vera Lynne forever connotes World War II in Britain, just as the Grateful Dead will always signify the popular essence of the 1960s in the United States. Merely hearing their tunes evokes a visceral experience of the past, an intense nostalgia that is more powerful in the generations that suffered the ruptures of these epochs than anyone else.

Moral architecture. Generational representation also involves a set of morality tales, or principles by which one should live that evolve out of the retrospective process of codifying generational experience. When the Depression generation considers the importance of this experience for their sense of self, it is thoroughly intertwined with the virtues of frugality, of the near-sacred importance of living *below* one's means. Extravagance, even when technically affordable, is regarded as a sin or source of shame. Conspicuous consumption is a source of moral condemnation and an indication of character flaws.

In Wohl's telling, the center of cultural gravity for the generation of 1914 was an existential antimorality, laced with a foreboding emphasis on the fleeting nature of life, the insanity of focusing on the long-term and the durable. Live for today, for there may not be a tomorrow; disengage from society's institutions, for political life is a sham. These are the dominant morality tales of the generation that survived the Great War; they catalyzed much of the modernist literature and art of the postwar period in Europe.

For the generation marked by the social upheavals of the 1960s (discussed at some length below), the moral tale is somewhat reminiscent of Wohl's war-weary generation, but is even more transformative in its rejection of the mainstream. If the generation of 1914 remembers itself as disillusioned by society and desirous of constructing life for the moment, the generation of the 1960s casts itself as an agent of change, dedicated to the overhaul of private and public life. The morality plays that dominate the latter's cultural core reflect this insistence that a "good life" cannot be one that is disengaged from the social world, even if the forms of involvement are countercultural.

In speaking of this moral architecture I do not mean to imply that generational culture is entirely successful at shaping behavior according to these maxims or that condemnation rains down upon those who fail to exemplify these values. Nor do I mean to suggest that these moral dialects are necessarily orthogonal to the "mainstream," unrecognized by members of other generations, or even wholly different societies.[8] I am suggesting that these are values or moral orientations that have a special meaning for those who embrace them as a central aspect of their generational identity and that they too are likely to be the subject of literary or performative elaboration. A moral architecture of this kind must be elaborated publicly, through memoirs, theater, popular performance, protest, film, music, and other communicative modalities that codify personal experience into a recognizable set of moral messages.

Forms of performance and morality plays are often creatures of the moment—expressions of generational identity that emerge during periods of cataclysmic transition, forever identified with the epoch in which they were produced. Yet we must also note that the symbolic dialects of generations are often retrospective constructions, tapestries of meaning that are woven after the fact, after the era. The process of looking back to understand the real significance of a generational experience can produce new understandings of an era, meanings which are important to ordinary people who take that experience as central to their own identities. Indeed, moral maxims may only be clarified in the decades that follow the events that generate the ruptures that transform cohorts into generations. During wars and depressions, people are often caught up in the pragmatics of survival. Only later do they have the luxury of reflecting upon the meaning of the upheaval, and the process of reflection itself begins to generate the bonds that tie their age mates together.

Retrospection can go on for a very long time and meanings can shift as cultural critics and writers step in to cast the past in varying lights. Hence the 1950s may be regarded as a period of quietude, of resurgent traditionalism. With the publication of David Halberstam's 1993 best-seller, *The 1950s,* we see a new definition of the epoch, as one in which the seeds of rebellions yet to come were germinating, where racial barriers in baseball and music were beginning to crumble, and where critiques of men in gray flannel suits were heard on the fringes of polite society. Whether these redefinitions of an epoch take, whether they seep into the souls of the members of a generation (as opposed to the intellectual community who are the primary consumers of cultural critique), is another matter. New perspectives may or may not resonate with the carriers of generational ideals and values. However, they are illustrative of a more general and more important process: the retrospective construction of the generational core.

In closing this section on the meaning of generation, I must comment finally on the strength of this form of subculture. For it would be a mistake to assume, as some developmental theorists might, that everyone belongs to a generation as I have used the term here. All members of the human community belong to cohorts, but not everyone takes generational culture or morality as central to personal identity. There are many periods in our history in which social change is slow, incremental, and relatively imperceptible. Without belaboring the tendency to identify generations with decades, the interwar years, the post–Korean War 1950s, and the 1980s were all periods where it would be hard to pinpoint the kind of dramatic social or economic change that catalyzes a strong generational sensibility. This is not to suggest that these periods are devoid of films, music, politicians, and myriad small disasters. It is to suggest that the kind of ruptures that Wohl speaks of, the events that jar a vulnerable group of people (especially young adults just "coming of age") are noticeably absent during those eras.

These periods of "normality" tend *not* to generate a sense of generational solidarity. Personal, community-based, local identities survive and flourish at such times, but the strong cohesion that characterizes the generation of 1914 does not. Hence when we look across our society, or any other, for that matter, we see an array of strong generations interspersed among cohorts, birth groups that do not conceptualize themselves as groups at all, much as they may display recognizable demographic trends or watch the same movies.

Strong generations will, of course, be crosscut in complex ways by competing forms of solidarity and identity, including race, class, and gender, with divergent aspects of the symbolic forms at the cultural core capturing their imaginations. African Americans who served in World War II carried home different memories and divergent meanings, some none too pleasant reminders of how they were never fully accepted as American boys out to win a war. But the war itself was an equally defining generational experience for them, as was the war in Vietnam for others. The social upheavals of the 1960s may be remembered by many baby-boom whites for the flower-power motif and the politics of the antiwar movement; the Black Panthers and the Attica prison rebellion may stand out to a greater degree for African Americans who anchor their own sense of self in this "revolutionary" era. I do not pretend to solve this complex problem here, but merely wish to signal the importance of exploring the refracted nature of the generational core. For alongside quantitative comparisons of well-being, adjustment, or the timing of marriage between ethnic groups in the same generations, we also want to be attuned to the ways in which these competing forms of identity shape divergent forms of collective memory.

One must also recognize that generational identity, even when powerful as a source of orientation, does not necessarily capture everyone who might be considered "eligible" or likely to embrace it. For many men who served in World War II, the experience of battle was a zenith never to be repeated. Never again did they feel the heightened sense of importance, the feeling of making a difference in history. They continued to define their war years as the most important aspect of their identity and express this attachment through periodic reunions, participation in veterans organizations, and other celebrations of those watershed events. Yet for others, wartime service was a nightmare of regimentation, a firsthand encounter with mindless rules, an experience to be repressed. These are the onetime soldiers who want nothing to do with reunions or the trappings of military celebration. In both instances, military service is a critical, defining moment, shared by millions of age mates. Yet its meaning is multifaceted. Generational culture, as this example shows, is not the seamless web of meanings that one might imagine. But it does partake of central, orienting events and experiences that exert a power over imagination and identity, whichever particular meanings are most compelling to the individual.[9]

Gathering the Collective Memory

Applying this representational perspective requires the use of research methods that fall in between the systematic, longitudinal survey approach that Elder and others draw upon and the thematic, textual, but entirely nonsystematic approach embodied in the work of Wohl or Halbwachs. Ethnographic methods, particularly intensive life histories drawn from systematic samples of distinctive generations, balance the demands of representativeness and the need for greater insight and texture.

Several methodological examples may serve to illustrate the approach recommended here. In the mid-1980s I began to collect life-history data from divorced mothers who had been pushed into downward mobility by virtue of their financial obligations for their children, their weak position in the labor market, and the virtual abandonment of their children by ex-husbands (Newman 1988: chap. 7). This was part of a broader study of middle-class disarray, most of which focused on the symbolic and material significance of unemployment. For women, particularly older women, the loss of a job is less of a blow than the disintegration of a marriage where material well-being is concerned. The reasons are simple: most women face formidable barriers to the high-paying end of the labor market, hence their access to a middle-class standard of living depended largely upon their husbands' support.[10] Divorce sent them into a tailspin of economic loss from which they were largely unable to recover.

These distressing accounts of mangled identity and material deprivation did not begin as a generational story. Yet the life history texts—some forty of them in all—bifurcated sharply by generation. Women who were born during the Depression and married during the boom years of the postwar period were invested in different versions of American culture than those who were raised amidst the plenty of the 1950s and 1960s only to undergo downward mobility in the 1980s. The older women were steeped in a culture of scarcity as children and had lasting, almost visceral, memories of economic insecurity. They knew all too well what it meant to watch one's standard of living collapse through the floorboards. Prior experience of hardship made these women resilient in some ways—able to scrimp and cut corners—but it catalyzed a gnawing, inescapable fear as well. This generational investment in traditional gender roles, expressed as a dependence of women upon their husbands for security, led the women of the Depression generation to feel terrified in the face of responsibilities that were now theirs alone.

The second group of women in this study were born in the midst of plenty and raised to expect more of the same. Baby boomers to the core, they were products of the postwar expansion and the modern middle class. They were also bystanders to the feminist movement among other forms of cultural renewal in the 1960s. Their prescriptions for a moral life differed sharply from those of the Depression-era women. They were traditional enough to have married and had children (a trajectory not everyone followed in those heady days), but they did not embrace the same models of male-female relations. The combination of their affluent upbringing and less traditional gender roles left them with a very different, but equally strong set of generationally based motifs with which they confronted divorce-induced downward mobility. Scarcity was not part of their vocabulary and they felt wholly unprepared to confront it. As one daughter of a prosperous lawyer put the matter, "'I grew up in very comfortable surroundings. . . . My background really affects me now. I was never prepared for how to deal with the situation I find myself in now: a low income and raising three kids. My parents just didn't prepare me for reality. I got cheated out of that training'" (Newman 1988:215). While this view was characteristic of many (relatively) young divorced women in my study, it was balanced by a desire for independence from men, by the value of self-reliance and autonomy. Where the older, divorced mothers were anxious to be rescued, and imagined their rescuer to be a traditional man, the sixties generation divorcees imagined themselves as the source of recovery and were skittish about becoming intimately involved with men again. Indeed, they repeatedly emphasized the importance of transmitting this fear of dependence and desire for self-determination to their own children. As the same woman quoted above put it, "'I don't want my kids to ever have to be dependent on anyone, especially my daughter. . . . I don't want her to go through what I went through. [This] is a very important experience. My kids will all be better off for what they've had to go through.'"

The life-history data collected for this study was intended originally to be nothing more than a portrait of the most important source of downward mobility for women: divorce and its aftermath. Upon further analysis, however, it became an opportunity to explore generational consciousness, to understand how divergent expectations, values, norms, and experiences had carved out different kinds of American women. For even when they had undergone much the same event—divorce, income loss, labor market reentry, and near total responsibility for the support of their children—their responses were as alike as night and day. It became clear that the source of their views was a fairly tightly woven and self-conscious generational culture, or symbolic dialect, as I termed it there, which was the grid through which this new and unwelcome experience of economic displacement was filtered.

In a more recent study I undertook a more deliberate examination of generational cultures (Newman 1993). My focus in this research was on the sharp differences in economic prospects between post–World War II parents and their baby-boom offspring. But of equal concern was the largely unrecognized divide in the political cultures of two separate generations within the boomer cohort.

The methodology of this study involved life-history interviews with two cohorts of graduates from a single high school in a suburban community in northern New Jersey (as well as their parents). Oldest among them was the high school graduating class of 1970, while the second group finished up in 1980. The ten-year span that separates these two groups of boomers marked a profound shift in the economic and political fortunes of the United States, leaving one group with a strong generational culture and the other with a minimal sense of generational identity.

Pleasanton,[11] the community where my informants grew up, was little more than a country outpost until the construction of the George Washington Bridge (by the Public Works Administration, in the 1930s) began to bring the area into the orbit of New York City. Growth accelerated sharply in the 1950s, when the Palisades Parkway made it possible for commuters to reach the city easily. The oldest cohort in my study grew up in the fifties and sixties, when Pleasanton was a multiclass community populated by skilled craftsmen, retail clerks, teachers, physicians in training, and sales managers. Working-class families often needed to draw upon mothers' labor to support their households, but for the most part the families of Pleasanton could live a comfortable existence on the strength of a single income. It was a time of employment stability and security for the emerging suburban middle class, the heyday of "Leave It to Beaver."

As the oldest boomers matured into the town's only high school, the social transformations of the 1960s began to seep into their consciousness. Local struggles against school dress codes and more cosmopolitan marches against the war in Vietnam are among the more vivid memories of this generation. But the formative events of their generational culture were the deep ruptures that surfaced in the early 1970s. Pleasanton's older boomers left the cloistered community and the private world of their natal households and found themselves in the midst of turbulent college campuses throughout the Northeast.

Much has been written about this period of America's modern history in an attempt to define the experience of the 1960s, but these accounts are largely in the tradition discussed earlier: memoirs of national activists from Bobby Seale to Mario Savio. How did a generational consciousness form in the minds of those who sat on the sidelines, absorbing the messages of change and rebellion? And, more importantly for present purposes, how did this generational identity persist over the decades that followed the events which gave birth to it in the first place?

In life-history interviews collected between 1989 and 1991, retrospective accounts of the sixties reveal something more than an affection for the politics of liberation. They suggest a more durable attachment to the value of rebellion. Kathy Hayes,[12] now forty, remembers the "wake-up call" of the late sixties, the way she and her age mates suddenly discovered how cosseted they had been:

> We felt really rebellious against the feeling that we had grown up in a vacuum. We had this contrast [before us] of New York City. Pleasanton was like a sterile, Republican sort of unreal society, where everybody had everything that they needed. . . . the summer of my junior year was Woodstock. Suddenly we were all dressing differently. . . . we thought, 'Hey, what have we been doing here? We've been cheerleaders [for the high school and for the country], saying America, America, rah, rah, rah!' [We suddenly realized] we'd been such stupid conformists here in our little sheltered world. . . . It was as if we suddenly woke up to see that . . . the country wasn't all so rosy and safe; there were a lot of people out there with problems we were blind to in Pleasanton. We were ashamed of our ignorance and wanted to make a lot of changes. (Newman 1993:176–77)

Terry Morrison, a high school classmate of Kathy's, echoed the same view—even though the two barely knew each other in school and have not seen each other in twenty years:

> "I was always raised not to question authority. But the saying during the sixties was the opposite: question everything. I thought it was important to develop a social conscience. I grew up in a community where there were no blacks, but I thought desegregation was very important. Marches on Washington, the bombing of Cambodia. These events made a very big impression on me. The period . . . was absolutely the essence of life. It made me see that if everybody shared some kind of concern then maybe something important could happen, things could change." (Newman 1993:180)

Paul Cornell, who knew neither of these women, though they were all schoolmates, echoes much the same vision of this formative period of his youth:

> "We finally had people who cared about something other than their football uniform. This gave us a tremendous sense of freedom, casting off the past like some old oppressive shroud that had just hung over everything. Everything in the past seemed like some bizarre nightmare: the fifties, the cars, the fashions, the way everyone was expected to behave. It seemed like such a horrible tyranny. The sixties offered an alternative." (Newman 1993:182)

Today Paul is a creative writing teacher in New Mexico, where he continues to define not only his own character, but his mission as a teacher, by the values of his generation. He sees himself in opposition to younger Americans who do not share his political culture:

> "These eighteen-year-olds, just trying to get them to believe that just because our side did it doesn't make it right! Oliver North is not a hero because he has a uniform on. Ronald Reagan was not a great president because he made it seem like we were back in the old days. . . . You can't go back in time to the sixties, but we have to hold on to what was good about it. . . . We have to stop thinking so damn much about what movie we're going to rent tonight." (Newman 1993:207)

Paul's symbolic dialect, constructed in the process of remembering the past and selecting from it those moral principles that define his own identity, is shared by most of his age mates in Pleasanton. For he is part of a strong generation, and this has had an enduring impact on the way he understands his own life, the moral architecture of his experience.

If we look at Pleasanton youth who were exactly ten years younger, we see striking differences in educational and occupational pathways, not to mention politics and values. By the time this younger cohort graduated from Pleasanton High School (in the spring of 1980), the United States was cresting toward double-digit unemployment, the oil shock of the mid-1970s had long since set in, the social movements of the sixties were dead, and the political culture of the country had lurched to the right. Pleasanton's younger boomers emerged from high school a frightened crew, in no mood to experiment. They eagerly sought the safety of pragmatic careers—accounting, white-collar management, and the like—more concerned with security and stability than fulfillment or experimentation. For these younger boomers, the economic landscape was full of sink holes, and for many this precarious state of existence has continued to plague them into the 1990s.

One might imagine that the widespread impact of these unstable conditions—economic and political—would leave a mark in the form of a strong generational culture for the younger boomers. Not so. The trends that have shaped their options in life did not add up to a sharp break in the flow of history that is prerequisite to a strong generational culture. Thus although one can easily point to a commonality of outlook, similarities in experience, expectations, values and fears, one can look high and low for a conceptualization of this package as a generational consciousness—it is not there. Oran MacDowell, a thirty-year-old who grew up in Pleasanton, finds it nearly impossible to identify himself with any generation:

> "I can see my friends from high school, but a larger group is tough for me to see. The sixties/seventies generation had all this action that labeled them, but we didn't have anything to get us to that point. In essence, we were born in the sixties, grew up in the seventies, and matured in the eighties. So which generation do we belong to? There just wasn't any binding point." (Newman 1993:203)

Joe Cornblum, a classmate of Oran's, echoes the same sentiment in describing his cohort as a nongeneration:

> "I grew up after the sixties and after the Vietnam War. It was a noneventful period. . . . America was trying to get its shit back together after the crisis of the sixties. My [older] brother's friends were involved in a lot of group activities—huge parties, marches. We were just sort of there and had a disco. But there weren't any major problems going on that we were aware of." (Newman 1993:204)

Memories can be dredged up from this cohort, of course. In the distant recesses of their minds lies the Watergate scandal and the resignation of Richard Nixon. But because these events never catalyzed social movements, never caused the dramatic rupture that would make them feel bound together as fellow travelers, they do not possess a generational culture in the sense I have used the term here.

This does not mean that Pleasanton's younger boomers lack identities; that would be an absurd claim. It does mean that their identities are grounded in local and individual experience to a greater degree.[13] They define themselves as part of a social network of friends and family, not as members of some broad solidarity of age mates across the nation.[14]

Generational Identity and the Inner City

The examples offered here are drawn from studies of middle-class communities, largely white or white ethnics of one variety or another. A full appreciation of the meaning of generational culture cannot stop at this class-ethnic boundary. It is imperative that studies of this kind expand to consider other populations, particularly minority communities whose own political and economic milestones (for good or ill) have caused the same kinds of ruptures of historical experience as those discussed above.

William Julius Wilson's landmark book, *The Truly Disadvantaged,* portrays an economic breakdown in the central cities of the United States that is not unlike the Great Depression in the magnitude of its devastation.[15] He catalogs the relentless cascade of downward trends that have reshaped economic prospects (for the worse), shattered employment possibilities (particularly for young men), and imposed tremendous hardship on families. One could add to his before/after economic portrait, one drawn from political culture. The epoch of the civil rights movement was followed by various nationalist movements, and the emergence of mainstream African-American and Latino political leaders. These transformations have reshaped the political culture of many inner-city communities. Have the economic trends and/or the political movements that have swept the inner city made a difference where generational identity is concerned?

We need far more studies of generational culture among contemporary minority communities than we have today. This is not to suggest that we lack studies of political movements or of historical periods. It is to argue that we need to know a great deal more about what those histories mean in the present-day lives of African Americans, Latinos, Asians, and others. How have the experiences of these distinctive pasts translated into divergent generational cultures within U.S. ethnic groups? In what ways does the generation that was youthful at the height of the civil rights movement, who witnessed the dramatic battles for desegregation, differ from those who came before or after?[16] What about the experience of the Vietnam War from the perspective of the thousands of black men who were on its front lines? Is generational identity salient for some cohorts within these ethnic communities and unimportant for others? Elijah Anderson's work on gentrification and underclass development (1991) shows that at least one African-American community clearly displays a generational cleavage, with the older order of respected elders and obedient youngsters having been replaced by street-oriented chaos. This change is conceptualized in the accounts of people living in the community he studied and understood as a matter of generational change. But this is just the beginning of what must become a broader inquiry into the nature of generational identity in minority communities. These are questions that need to be explored if we are to have a more complete portrait of generational cultures in the United States.

This is important not only because we need a multicultural appreciation of generational culture, but because the competing bases of personal identity must be better understood. Race, class, gender, and other sociological categories of social status intersect in powerful ways with identities drawn from generational culture. But the integration can be more or less complete; it can draw individuals into conflicts between divergent sources of identification, conflicts that may be resolved in a situational fashion or never resolved at all. African Americans confronted by rejection may see themselves as a group defined by a racial identity. Yet the cleavages that have developed lately between older generations steeped in the culture of the civil rights movement or the church and young people attracted to rap music and separatist politics reveal the competing influence of generation internal to the black community.

Ethnography, Biography, and Cultural History

In this chapter, I have suggested that one important way in which ethnographic methods can illuminate the study of human development is to focus on the intersection between personal biographies and cultural histories. Through the pioneering work of people like Elder, Wohl, Halbwachs, and others interested in the impact of major historical events on generational trajectories, we have already seen how powerful this form of social solidarity can be in carving personal identities. Elder's work, in particular, has demonstrated convincingly that the life course is dramatically affected by the economic experience and social history of generations: patterns of marriage and family formation, occupational success, and more subjective questions of adjustment and well-being fall out into distinctive patterns depending upon generationally based experience (as well as crosscutting factors such as class and gender).

What we know less about is the texture, the meaning, the cultural significance of historical contexts. Learning how these "irregular" features of historical epochs influence the construction of personal identity is a long-term task worthy of ethnographic investigation and developmental attention. Life histories, longitudinal fieldwork, and participant observation in commemorative settings, are all methods which can help in capturing the symbolic dialects of generations. Human development is more than a series of invariant hurdles. It is a cultural project which is evaluated and in a sense redefined by generations constructing their particular vision of the trajectory. Scholars working in this field can utilize these ethnographic methods to learn more about context and meaning, about the ways in which the hurdles of development are shaped by economic and political change that is made personal and interior through generational identity.

Notes

1. Fieldwork is also an important source of data on the social construction of generations. In the United States in particular, tremendous energy is poured into the commemoration of generational experience through reunions, especially of high school graduating classes. The act of remembrance becomes a collective endeavor on these occasions and can be captured through participant observation at these events.

2. Note the difference between this view and the more common perspective of social anthropologists interested in life-course studies. Robert Levine's insightful life-course analysis of Gusii and nineteenth-century Essex County, Massachusetts, Americans note that collective definitions of the life span are integral to both societies. "The individual's subjective representation of his life course includes his version of the collective standards and the conclusions he has drawn from retrospection and contemporaneous monitoring, concerning his place vis-à-vis those standards" (Levine 1978:278–79). The perspective advocated here is one which emphasizes the discontinuous and potentially conflictual nature of those standards. I suggest that they are often generationally bounded rather than collectively embraced.

3. The Australian film *Gallipoli* captured (and nurtured) the same cynicism in its portrait of the "colonial" soldier's exploitation at the hands of the British. The film tells the story of regiments from Down Under thrown into suicidal battles in order to protect the lives of more valued English soldiers during World War I.

4. Elder divided the study into class-based subgroups of children, half were defined as deprived and half as nondeprived, based upon the income losses their families sustained during the Depression.

5. This is not to deny that less disruptive events do not leave a generational mark. The roaring twenties, for example, cultivated a youth culture that clearly had an impact upon those who experienced the era as a breakaway decade of cultural experimentation. Further research will be needed to understand how and to what extent "noncataclysmic" periods encourage the formation of generational identities.

6. Biographical accounts of the Cultural Revolution are beginning to come out in the English-language press which provide the insider's view of this cataclysm. Those written by veterans of the experience of being sent down clearly reflect the common generational consciousness generated by the upheaval (Chang 1991). Elder's current research will tell us much more about the lasting impact of the upheaval in the later lives of these youth.

7. I use this term here to connote the maxims of behavior and belief that gain particular moral force in a generational culture. The idea is elaborated below.

8. The issue of the relationship between generational values and mainstream values is too complex to take up here, but is a crucial subject for anyone interested in subcultural identity.

9. There are avenues of escape from generational identity, of course. In the years that followed World War II, economic expansion was rapid in the United States, a trajectory that brought unprecedented levels of upward mobility to Americans. Those that leaped the boundary between working-class childhoods and a new middle-class adulthood were often able to transcend the orienting power of the war itself and claim a new identity as overriding. Several colleagues who heard this as a paper in the original conference in which it was presented talked about how they deliberately walked away from their war service as an orienting event and "adopted" their identities as postwar professors as more meaningful. They are reluctant indeed to attend reunions of their World War II mates, largely because they do not want this identity to intrude upon their postwar sense of self. Class mobility enables them to "escape" the war, where their less mobile age mates cleave to it.

10. One would like to think that times have changed, and indeed they have, to an extent. But it remains the case that women with small children lose far more in the aftermath of divorce than men do, largely because so many become sole providers for kids, and the fact that women still earn about seventy cents for every dollar men earn. Awareness of this fact holds many a marriage together, even in the face of considerable pressures to fission (Hochschild 1989).

11. A pseudonym for the actual community, which is located about a half-hour's drive from Manhattan.

12. A pseudonym, as are all other personal names in this essay.

13. If the fiscal crisis in the United States continues into the mid-1990s, we may begin to see a solidification of generational identity among those who followed the boomers. "Generation X" may rally around the idea that they are the cohort left out of the expansive eighties, left to bear the burden of the federal deficit, unable to find a place in the labor market. For the moment these trends are too continuous and incremental to force the kind of bonding that is needed for a "strong generation."

14. This view was exemplified in a recent essay appearing in a student publication at Columbia University. Matthew Dallek argues that "the forty million Americans who were born during the 1960s, reared in the 1970s, and who reached political consciousness in the 1980s will enter middle age without a generational tag line. Despite countless articles, books, movies, marketing strategies, and television series, today's young are still without a name" (Dallek 1993).

15. Katz (1993) has argued that many of the trends Wilson describes were not new in the 1970s, but had been gathering force for some time.

16. More traditional approaches to the study of human development, like those of the life-course theorists, could no doubt benefit from a greater emphasis on the ways different racial and ethnic groups refract events like wars and depressions.

References

Anderson, E. 1990. *Streetwise.* Chicago: University of Chicago Press.

Chang, J. 1991. *Wild Swans: Three Daughters of China.* New York: HarperCollins.

Dallek, M. 1993. "A New Guard?" *Helvedius* 4: 37–40.

Elder, G. Jr. 1974. *Children of the Great Depression: Social Change in Life Experience.* Chicago: University of Chicago Press.

———. 1985. "Perspectives on the Life Course." In *Life Course Dynamics: Trajectories and Transitions, 1968–1980.* Ed. Elder Jr., 23–49. Ithaca, N.Y.: Cornell University Press.

Halberstam, D. 1993. *The 1950s.* New York: Random House.

Halbwachs, M. 1980. *The Collective Memory.* New York: Harper and Row.

Hochschild, A. 1989. *The Second Shift.* New York: Vintage.

Jahoda, M., P. Lazarsfeld, and H. Zeiel. 1933 [1971]. *Marienthal: The Sociography of an Unemployed Community.* New York: Aldine-Atherton.

Katz, M. *The Underclass Debate: Views from History.* Princeton, N.J.: Princeton University Press.

Komarovsky, M. 1940. *The Unemployed Man and His Family.* New York: Dryden Press.

Levine, R. 1978. *Transitions: The Family and the Life Course in Historical Perspective.* New York: Academic Press.

Newman, K. 1986. "Symbolic Dialects and Generations of Women: Variations in the Meaning of Post-Divorce Downward Mobility." *American Ethnologist* 13: 230–52.

———. 1988. *Falling From Grace: The Experience of Downward Mobility in the American Middle Class.* New York: Free Press.

———. 1993. *Declining Fortunes: The Withering of the American Dream.* New York: Basic Books.

Wilson, W. J. 1987. *The Truly Disadvantaged: The Inner City, the Underclass, and Public Policy.* Chicago: University of Chicago Press.

Wohl, R. 1979. *The Generation of 1914.* Cambridge, Mass.: Harvard University Press.

18 Ethnographic Insights on Social Context and Adolescent Development among Inner-City African-American Teens

LINDA M. BURTON, DAWN A. OBEIDALLAH, AND KEVIN ALLISON

Exploring the relationship between adolescent development and social context has been of interest to social scientists for nearly a century (Coleman 1961; Hall 1904; Hollingshead 1949; Gillis 1974; Linton 1942; Mead 1928; Modell 1989). Traditionally these explorations have focused on the adolescent experience in non-Western cultures (Mead 1928; Savin-Williams 1987) and among white middle-class Americans (Adelson 1986; Feldman and Elliott 1990; Petersen 1988). However, spawned by recent popular, political, and scholarly discourse on risks and resilience, and the social vulnerabilities of urban adolescents, there has been a growing interest in the study of social context and the developmental experiences of ethnic/racial minority and economically disadvantaged teens (Jessor 1993; Masten 1988). Of particular interest has been the influence of social context on the developmental outcomes of poor inner-city African-American adolescents (Duncan, Brooks-Gunn, and Aber, forthcoming; Anderson 1990).

With the growing focus on social context and development among urban African-American adolescents, social scientists have become increasingly aware that traditional theories of normative development are not necessarily the appropriate conceptual frameworks for studying the lives of inner-city African-American teens (Dilworth-Anderson, Burton, and Boulin-Johnson 1993; Edelman and Ladner 1991; Bell-Scott and Taylor 1989; Gibbs 1989; Spencer and Dornbusch 1990; McLoyd 1990; Ogbu 1981). Ecological and life-course perspectives, as well as historical accounts of the lives of urban African-American families suggests that the developmental pathways of inner-city African-American adolescents may be quite different from those of mainstream teens (Bronfenbrenner 1979; Elder, Modell, and Parke 1993; Ladner 1971; Ogbu 1974; Stack 1974).

African-American adolescents, particularly those who grow up in some economically deprived, high-risk neighborhoods, may follow developmental paths that are based on ideologies, role expectations, behavioral practices, and "rites of passage" that are contextually distinct from those reported in studies of white suburban middle-class teens (Silbereisen, Eyferth, and Rudlinger 1986; Spencer 1995). As such, traditional developmental frameworks which are often used in the study of mainstream adolescents may have limited applicability in the study of inner-city African-American teens.

Although traditional developmental frameworks have limited utility for studying some populations of inner-city, economically disadvantaged African-American adolescents, the use of a relatively untapped resource—ethnographic accounts of the lives of urban African-American families—can provide valuable insights to social scientists on the developmental pathways of some inner-city teens. Illustrated most recently in the work of Jarrett (1990, 1995) and Burton and Jarrett (1991), existing ethnographic accounts of urban African-American families provide thick, descriptive roadmaps of contextual forces and developmental processes that shape the lives of adolescents. For example, a number of existing ethnographies of urban African-American life have provided insights on the contextual meaning of adolescence (Burton, Allison, and Obeidallah 1995), definitions of successful and problematic developmental outcomes (Jeffers 1967; Ladner 1971; Newman 1992; Rosenfeld 1971; Sullivan 1988; MacLeod 1987), and behavioral expectations for inner-city adolescents of neighborhood, school, and family environments (Jarrett 1990; Stack 1974; Valentine 1978; Aschenbrenner 1975; Burton, Price-Spratlen, and Spencer, forthcoming).

Using several existing ethnographic accounts of the lives of urban African-American families, this chapter outlines three issues that are important to consider in developing appropriate conceptual frameworks for the study of social context and adolescence among economically disadvantaged inner-city African-American teens. The first issue concerns contextual variations in the meaning of adolescence and successful developmental outcomes (Allison and Takei 1993). The second focuses on inconsistencies in role expectations for adolescents within families and across social contexts (Linton 1942). The third examines the implications of an "accelerated life course" on the developmental pathways of inner-city African-American teens (Burton 1991; Hogan 1978).

Contextual Variation and the Social Meaning of Adolescence among Urban African-American Teens

Adolescence in contemporary American society is traditionally defined as a transition period, marking the change from childhood to adulthood. Occurring between the ages of eleven to twenty, normative adolescent development is characterized by qualitative biological, social, and cognitive changes for the individual (Feldman and Elliott 1990). The onset of puberty is the biological marker that signals the beginning of adolescence as a life-course phase (Brooks-Gunn and Reiter 1990). At the cognitive level, it is believed that adolescents, through the development of abstract reasoning, begin to acquire a more complex and integrated notion of self, the ability to be self-reflective, and the capacity to make social comparisons and entertain thoughts about future expectations (Graber and Petersen 1991; Keating 1990). At the social level, adolescence is characterized as a life period when individuals develop stronger ties with peers at the same time they develop increasing autonomy with respect to their relationships with their parents and family (Steinberg 1990; Youniss and Smollar1985).

In mainstream contexts, social institutions and families provide specific guidelines concerning the role expectations and behaviors of adolescents. Schools, for example, plan developmentally appropriate curriculum and activities for teens. Parents offer directives to adolescents concerning their place in families and society. Under these directives, adolescents are often reminded that they are no longer children but are not yet adults. While the activities adolescents engage in are designed to prepare them for adulthood, in most cases adolescents are not allowed to fully assume adult roles, such as parenthood, or legitimately engage in the domains of the adult world until their post-teenage years.

Increasingly, social scientists have argued that the role expectations and behaviors of adolescents are, in fact, culturally and contextually circumscribed and thus may reflect variable patterns as a function of distinct populations of youth growing up in particular societies during certain historical periods (Elder 1974; Kett 1977; Gillis 1974; Modell 1989). Dannefer (1984:108) states that

> "adolescence" is generally accepted in modern Western societies as "objectively real," a "normal" age-linked stage with specific developmental tasks. The social basis of this "reality" has been documented by research showing that the meaning and experience of these years has been markedly different in other cultures . . . and in earlier North American and European society.

As such, some teens, particularly those who are currently growing up in socially and economically deprived contexts, may have perspectives concerning adolescence as a life stage that differ from traditional views of what comprises the "normative teenage years" (Burton 1991; Ogbu 1985; Spencer and Dornbusch 1990).

A guiding assumption of this chapter is that teens, particularly those developing in economically disadvantaged contexts, may attach different meanings to adolescent roles and behaviors than do their mainstream counterparts. In fact we argue, as have others, that in some inner-city neighborhoods, directives concerning appropriate adolescent roles and behavior may be quite ambiguous (Burton, Allison, and Obeidallah 1995). Bush and Simmons (1987) and Hamburg (1974) have suggested that, in these neighborhoods, adolescence may not be clearly defined as a distinctive life-course stage that occurs between childhood and adulthood. For example, ethnographic accounts of the lives of economically disadvantaged African-American teens living in inner-city "ghettos" suggest that by adapting certain skills to survive in their environments, and by assuming adult responsibilities such as primary caretakers of siblings, many teens move from childhood to adulthood without distinctly experiencing the intermediate stage of adolescence (Hippler 1971; Jarrett 1990; Jeffers 1967; Kotlowitz 1991; Ladner 1971; MacLeod 1987; Silverstein and Krate 1975; Sullivan 1989; Williams 1978; Williams and Kornblum 1985). Robert Coles in his ethnographic description of the life course of an African-American male underscores this point with this question: "Is a sixteen-year-old [African-American] boy who has lived in stark, unremitting poverty, worked since eight, earned a living since fourteen, married at 15, and soon to be a father, a child?" (1964:319).

Not only may teens in some urban contexts attach different meanings to the distinctiveness of adolescence as a life-course stage, they may also define issues of risk and resilience within this life stage in different ways. Indeed, Masten, Best, and Garmezy (1990) highlight the importance of considering the specific characteristics of contexts when identifying resilient behavior. They define resiliency as effectively coping within the demands of one's environment. As such, a positive coping skill in one context could potentially be a risk factor in another context (Cunningham 1993; Spencer et al. 1993). For example, Burton (1991) in her ethnographic study of childcare strategies in high-risk neighborhoods reports that at very young ages some children are required because of family circumstances, to assume parental responsibility for the care of younger siblings. A behavior also noted in studies of economically disadvantaged white youth (Elder 1974; Elder and Conger 1994; Weisner and Gallimore 1977), the children in Burton's study developed adultlike "take-charge attitudes" which were manifest in their styles of communication with adults and other children. The comments of Tameka, an eight-year-old sibling caregiver who participated in the study, illustrates this point: "I take care of my brothers and sisters all the time. I boss them around. I tell them what to do. And they better mind me or I whip their butt. If they don't mind me they could get hurt. . . . like running in the street and getting hit by a car or something. I am the boss. Sometimes I have to scream at them too, but that is what you do when you are the boss." While Tameka's take-charge attitude benefits her in the role of sibling-caregiver, it creates problems for her in school. Tameka's second grade teacher commented, "She is a very difficult child. She always *tells* me what she will do and what she won't do, *whenever* she's in school. I can't handle this little girl or, should I say grown woman in a girl's body" (Burton 1991:34).

Another source of contextual variation in the meaning of adolescence for African-American teens concerns the assessment of successful developmental outcomes. In assessing outcomes for inner-city African-American adolescents, survey researchers have tended to focus on traditional indicators of developmental successes and failures used in studies of white, middle-class teens. These indicators include the completion of high school, the presence or absence of a premarital teen pregnancy, and the attainment of stable legitimate employment (Allison and Takei 1993; Entwisle, Alexander, and Olson 1994). While clearly these are important developmental markers, they do not exhaust the potential range of successful outcomes that inner-city African-American teens experience (Ogbu 1981). For example, in their ethnographic studies of African-American families in four communities, Stack and Burton (1993) noted that a teen's commitment to care for a frail elderly relative was considered a successful developmental outcome by community residents. This outcome runs counter to mainstream perspectives on adolescent development which suggest that adolescence involves a process of individuation and separation from family and thus less involvement in family caregiving activities (Powers, Hauser, and Kilner 1989).

Ethnographic accounts of family life for inner-city African Americans also indicate that an important parameter for assessing successful outcomes among teens concerns their access to mainstream opportunities (Ogbu 1981; MacLeod 1985). For example, African-American teens involved in Burton, Allison, and Obeidallah's (1995) ethnographic study of urban neighborhoods and multigenerational family development indicated that they had limited access to paths of success as defined by mainstream society. The adolescents who participated in the study noted that they had few educational opportunities and employment options. Thus many of these teens did not achieve traditional adolescent developmental successes, such as completing high school. Rather, data from this study suggested that the teens, as well as some of their parents and community residents, had alternative perspectives about what merited a successful developmental outcome for individuals in their environment. The outcomes reported by those who participated in the study were categorized into three groups—outcomes which reflect cultural and situational success; outcomes which represent the realities of survival in the community; and outcomes which suggest new possibilities for success.

Cultural and Situational Outcomes

Burton, Allison, and Obeidallah (1995) have reported that three types of alternative outcomes emerged in the cultural and situational category— the "revised American dream"; the achievement of adult status; and the development of cultural and gender role identities. Each outcome implicitly emphasized present well-being of the adolescent as opposed to long-term success. The adolescents' focus on immediate and readily apparent symbols of success underlies the fact that legitimate avenues to success were severely restricted in their environment. The restriction relates to systematic racism and classism found in the contexts in which the adolescents lived (Spencer and Dornbusch 1990; Ogbu 1981).

The "revised American dream" concerned the adolescent's ability to own material goods (for example, clothing and jewelry) as indicators of success. This external manifestation of success was not relevant just for the individual teen, but had implications for the level of success reported by the teen's parents as well. Many of the teens and their families took pride in being able to dress well. For example, Roger, a sixteen-year-old tenth grader remarked, "We don't have much money, but at least I always look good in my clothes. That's important to me. It makes me feel good, like I'm doing something I can be proud of when I dress fine."

The second outcome, achievement of adult status, can be considered a ubiquitous indicator of a positive outcome. The pathway to adult status became transformed in the context of neighborhoods explored in the study. Adult status, self-sufficiency, and autonomy was manifest among the teens in their ability to be economically independent whether it was financed through traditional employment, through federal aid (for example, Aid to Families with Dependent Children), or through illegal means. In the study, achievement of adult status was also reflected in teens' ability to father or give birth to a child. Regardless of the source of achieving "adult status," a number of the respondents in the study suggested that becoming an adult as soon as possible in the teen years was a positive life-course outcome.

The final category of cultural and situational outcomes noted in the Burton, Allison, and Obeidallah study concerned the teens' ability to be comfortable with their cultural and gender role identities. This aspect was exemplified in the comments of one mother in the study who stated, "As long as my son Alan knows that he is a man and he can be proud of being a black man, that's all right with me. That's how I know he is a success right now. And no one can tell me any different."

Community Realities

The harsh community realities that many African-American teens face daily were clearly intertwined with the indicators of successful developmental outcomes among the teens involved in the Burton, Allison, and Obeidallah study. Among many urban male youth in high-risk environments, participation in sports has served as a chosen pathway or trajectory to financial success. However, the odds against achieving success through these routes are high. Alternatively, participation in the drug industry has provided risky although highly profitable employment opportunities for a number of youth with good odds for financial success. The high-risk nature of this option, and the associated community violence, however, has made the simple physical survival of an African-American male in many urban communities difficult. As many of the teens who participated in the study reported, one of the only relevant indicators of a successful adolescent outcome was physical survival. Stephon, a fourteen-year-old eighth grader noted, "I know I'm successful because I know how to survive on the streets. I bet them rich white kids couldn't do what I do."

The pride associated with surviving "on the streets" was paralleled only by the positive feelings associated with the ability to make it out of one's community of origin. Leaving one's community, even if this meant transferring and surviving in a school outside the school district, was considered a success. For example, Cherise, a seventeen-year-old eleventh grader commented, "All my homies think I'm something because I go to school across the river now. Me and my momma worked a thing to get me in school over there. And I'm making it, too."

New Possibilities

The last category of outcomes noted in the Burton, Allison, and Obeidallah study represents developmental successes for which adolescents, particularly African-American, are rarely given credit. The first outcome reflects success in terms of spiritual development and involvement in religious activities. While traditionally conceptualized in the research literature as a coping strategy, many people in the African-American community consider spiritual integrity and harmony to be the most important indicator of positive adjustment. The importance of spiritual development was further supported by several accounts present in the study. For example, Tanya, a fifteen-year-old ninth grader noted, "I've been in the church since I was five. My grandmother is proud of me for that. She always says that the best gift I could have ever given her is me being saved. I am of the Lord and for the Lord."

The second outcome concerns fostering the development of one's creative talents. In the study, the expression of creativity in contextually relevant modes, such as rapping, voguing, dancing, and "doing hair and nails well," were acknowledged as viable successful outcomes. Shantée, an eighteen-year-old indicated, "I've been braiding hair for six years. They call me the master around here. I do it faster and better than anyone. My braids also stay in long. I get much props for what I do."

The third outcome involves the range of roles provided for teens within specific family and community contexts. Within families and communities, teens may serve important roles as facilitators of familial cohesion, as interpreters and negotiators of social institutions for elderly family and community members, and as peacemakers and contributors to cohesion in communities. For instance, one community leader who participated in the study described Anthony, a nineteen-year-old high school dropout: "Anthony may not have finished high school, and he may not have a job, but he is the treasure of our community. He helps the young mothers around the neighborhood with their kids. He does the grocery shopping for some of the old folks around here who can't get out. And he keeps the peace between rival street gangs in the community."

Role Expectations and Adolescence: Inconsistencies within Families and across Contexts

As the preceding discussion indicates, there is notable variability in the social meaning, role expectations, and behaviors attached to adolescence across diverse contexts and cultures. One of the most pervasive issues that emerges in the ethnographic literature on inner-city African-American families and teens concerns the degree of consistency in role expectations that adolescents experience within families and across the range of these social contexts and cultures. This issue is reflected in three themes within the ethnographic literature: inconsistent role expectations between parents and social institutions, age-condensed families and the blurring of intergenerational boundaries and developmental stages, and the overlapping worlds of teens and their parents.

Inconsistent Adolescent Role Expectations across Families and Social Institutions

A relatively common finding in the ethnographic literature on inner-city African-American teens concerns inconsistent expectations between parents and social institutions regarding the social roles of teenagers. While inconsistent role expectations in adolescents' experiences across different social settings is also present among mainstream populations (Phalen, Davidson, and Cao 1991), contextual influences such as economic deprivation and racial inequality may increase the presence and exacerbate the magnitude of these inconsistences among inner-city teens (Davis and Dollard 1964; Lerner 1986; Simmons and Zhou 1994). Youth may confront difficulties in satisfying the competing demands of different social domains, such as expectations between school and family realms (Phelan, Davidson, and Cao 1991). Negotiating the role expectations of "multiple worlds" may place youth at risk for experiencing a "mismatch" between their individual characteristics and the demands of their social contexts.

Lerner and Lerner (1983) categorize youth whose individual characteristics satisfy the expectations of their social context as experiencing a "good fit," which is indicative of successful adaptation. Eccles et al. (1988, 1993) have applied the goodness-of-fit model to the study of youth in both the school environment and the family context, noting that despite differences between school and family settings, both environments should optimally encourage similar expectations for positive development. However, a common occurrence noted in the ethnographic literature involves divergent role expectations of teens in their school life and home life (Clark 1983).

A pattern identified in a number of ethnographies is that school systems generally expect adolescents to adhere to mainstream educational aspirations, adult-monitored activities, and academic protocols (Ogbu 1981). Within the context of the school setting, adolescents are often treated like "older children" who require assisted learning. At home, however, some inner-city adolescents are treated like "grown folks," often saddled with adult responsibilities that are in direct conflict with the "older child" treatment and adult monitoring they receive in school (Burton and Jarrett 1991). For example, an adolescent Mexican male from a migrant or illegally immigrated family may work a full-time job to support his extended family while simultaneously being expected to adhere to a subordinate "teenager" role in school (Allison and Takei 1993).

MacLeod recounts the school/family conflict experienced by an inner-city African-American male teen: "I got seven brothers. . . . My brother Joe had to quit school when he was sixteen years old, just because my father was an alcoholic. He had to go out and get a job. . . . But Joe was out gettin' a job at sixteen to support all the kids. . . . He's our father. That's what he really is. He's our father. . . . Every penny that my brother got he threw right into the house. Cuz my mother can't work. She almost died three times" (1987:51).

Williams and Kornblum further illustrate the point in the comments of a young African-American adolescent living in Harlem: "I went to work in a restaurant in the back of a bar. I was 11 years old at the time. My schedule was one that most grown people would never had survived. I woke each morning, went to school, and when school was out I went directly to work. I got off work at 1:00 A.M. each night, no earlier, but sometimes later. I went home, did whatever I had to do, went to sleep and to school in the morning" (1985:19).

Some youth expressed frustration over their competing roles and conflicting responsibilities. For example, Slick, an urban teenager, discusses problems balancing the demands of the school setting with those of home responsibilities: "[Teachers] don't know how it's like to hafta come to school late. 'Why'd you come to school late?' 'I had to make sure my brother was in school. I had to make sure certain things—I had to make sure that there was breakfast" (MacLeod 1987:108–9). Shorty, another inner-city youth, defends Slick's position: "Responsibilities. See, that's what I mean. Now, the teachers will not understand. He [Slick] ain't got no father, right? The father ain't living there, just like me. He's the oldest kid now. And he has big responsibilities at home because his brothers are growing up and his sister—he's got to keep an eye on 'em. Now you gotta do all that, and you got teachers giving you a hard . . . time?" (MacLeod 1987:109).

Experiences of inconsistent role expectations for adolescents are also exemplified in Burton, Allison, and Obeidallah's (1995) ethnographic account of inner-city African-American families. Interviews revealed that most of the teenagers involved in the study were expected to behave as adults in their families. However, they were often treated, as one respondents states, "as stupid, irresponsible, incompetent white teenagers" in school. It was not uncommon for teenagers in this study to assume dual roles: the role of primary caretaker of the household as well as the role of student. Adolescents' recognition of these mixed roles is represented by this fifteen-year-old respondent: "Sometimes I just don't believe how this school operates and thinks about us. Here I am a grown man. I take care of my mother and have raised my sisters. Then I come here and this know-nothing teacher treat me like I'm some dumb kid with no responsibilities. I am so frustrated. They are trying to make me something that I am not. Don't they understand I'm a man and I been a man longer than they been a woman?"

Additionally, the experiences of Candyce, a thirteen-year-old mother involved in the Burton, Allison, and Obeidallah study, illustrates the confusion that youth may experience when confronted with behavioral expectations that are inconsistent across various domains. Shortly after the birth of her child, Candyce experienced what appeared to be an episode of depression. Out of concern for her, the researchers approached the school counselor about the possibility that Candyce may have been experiencing postpartum depression. The school counselor indicated the following: "There is no way a teenager can have postpartum depression. She's just a kid who is lazy and doesn't want to do work. You know how teenagers are." Juxtaposed with Candyce's view of her own situation, the contrast between the school counselor's perception of Candyce is striking. Candyce noted, "I am a grown woman. Why these people keep treating me like a kid? I don't even know what being a kid is like."

Further evidence of the frustrations experienced by youth confronted with inconsistent expectations is summarized by Tony, a fifteen-year-old male involved in the study: "Do this, do that. School says one thing. Momma says another. Am I a young man, grown man, or a child? You tell me!"

These examples suggest that the "adult" expectations of families, and the "older child" behavior expected in school contexts, send adolescents mixed messages concerning appropriate adolescent role behavior. These mixed messages may result in adolescence being considered an abridged or ambiguous developmental stage among teens who are struggling to survive in challenging environments. The implications of mixed messages and the ambiguity of adolescence as a developmental stage are far-reaching in terms of how teens may interpret their own behaviors. As noted earlier, while "older child" behavior is rewarded in one context, it may be a liability in another. Thus teens may be forced to choose one behavioral style over the other. For many inner-city teens who confront economic deprivation and racial inequality, that choice results in behaviors which trigger a premature transition to adulthood.

Age Condensed Families, Developmental Stages, and Blurred Intergenerational Boundaries

A second source of inconsistency in the role expectations of teens concerns age condensed families (Bengtson, Rosenthal, and Burton 1990). Age condensed families are characterized by a relatively narrow age distance between generations, typically thirteen to seventeen years. The age-condensed structure is prevalent in families where teenage childbearing has occurred consistently across generations (Burton 1990; Burton and Dilworth-Anderson 1991).

Previous research has highlighted the importance of examining the impact of age-condensed family structures on family members (Burton and Dilworth-Anderson 1991; Burton, in press). In age-condensed families, developmental boundaries and roles of family members are often blurred. Blurring of intergenerational boundaries has implications for the influence of parental authority and adolescents' perceptions of age-appropriate behavior. As the entire family structure is affected by age-condensed families, adolescents' perception of distinct patterns of behavior expected of them when they become adults may be unclear.

Consider, for example the description of a four-generation age-condensed family identified in Burton's (1995) ethnographic study of multigeneration, teenage childbearing families. In this family, the child generation included both a young mother (age fifteen) and her child (age one), a young-adult generation, which is comprised of a twenty-nine-year-old grandmother, and a middle-age generation, which includes a forty-three-year-old great-grandmother. As a result of the closeness in generational ages, chronological and developmental challenges often become inconsistent with generational positions. This is evident by the fact that the adolescent mother, as a function of giving birth, is launched into the young-adult role status; however, she remains legally and developmentally a member of the child generation. Similarly, the young-adult female has moved to the status of grandmother, a stage typically embodied by middle-aged or older women. Further, the middle-aged woman has been propelled to the status of great-grandmother, a role usually occupied by women in their later years (Burton and Bengtson 1985).

Families interviewed in the Burton, Allison, and Obeidallah (1995) study provide further evidence of age-condensed families and the consequent blurred developmental role boundaries. In their study, the average age distance between generations was only fourteen years. The daughters and mothers in several of the families behaved like siblings toward each other rather than like parents and adolescent children. This created some dissonance with respect to how the parents and the teens thought about themselves developmentally. For example, one sixteen-year-old female remarked: "My mom and me seem to be going through the same things at the same time. Like dealing with that relationship stuff. So what does that make me, a woman or a kid?"

Comparable statements were made by the young men in the study with respect to their fathers. For instance, Darrell, a fifteen-year-old, reported on his relationship with his thirty-three-year-old father: "I don't really know what my place is. I don't seem like a teenager because I hang with my old man. We is buds! We're no different from each other. I guess we both just men."

Associated with the age-condensed family structure is the weakening of parental authority over developing children. The nature of the generational proximity between parents and their teenage offspring encouraged these family members to behave in ways consistent with sibling roles, rather than roles characterized by parental hierarchy. The result is that parents often confronted difficulties in disciplining their children.

The lack of clarity in role expectations and developmental boundaries thus can also contribute to the ambiguity of families identifying adolescence as a distinct life-course stage. The ambiguity of role expectations and developmental stages in age-condensed families is even further exacerbated by the overlapping of social worlds that parents and children in age-condensed families often experience.

The Overlapping Worlds of Teens and Their Parents

A third source of inconsistencies in the expectations of adolescent roles involves the overlapping worlds of teens and their parents. Bronfenbrenner (1986) suggests that parents are involved in certain life contexts which have limited access for their children. These contexts include the work worlds and peer networks of parents. The child's limited access to these worlds may in some ways help to differentiate the developmental status of parents and their offspring and thus provide youth with distinct ideas about socially expected role behaviors.

However, within some African-American inner-city communities and families, the distinction between the world of adults and that of children is often blurred. As a number of ethnographies indicate, overlaps between social roles and relationships occur across multiple levels for teens and their parents (Kotlowitz 1988; Silverstein and Krate 1975; Stack 1974). The lack of mutually exclusive developmental stages may contribute to intrafamilial conflict and thus have additional implications for adolescent development. The overlapping worlds of teens and their parents are particularly evident in the relationships between mothers and daughters in age-condensed families (Hembry 1988). Ladner describes the lack of mutually exclusive developmental stages among family members in a description of the behaviors of a young mother and her fifth-grade daughter, Kim: "Kim's behavior was similar to that of her mother's and her 16-year-old sister. She cursed and occasionally imitated sex with her 12-year-old boyfriend. Frequently, she also had to baby-sit with the two-year-olds while their parents were away, help her mother prepare meals, clean house and face the bill collectors when her mother was in hiding because she didn't have the money" (1971:56).

A similar example of overlap is found in Kotlowitz's *There Are No Children Here.* In his depiction of the survival of a young family in a Chicago ghetto, he describes a situation where a young mother, La Joe, has just learned that her federal aid has been cut off. She immediately turned to her 12-year old son, Lafeyette, for emotional support: "He was the only person she felt she could talk to about it. It was as if he were as much a husband as he was a son. He was her confidant" (1991:97). She recognized this overlap and stated, "the things I should have been taking to Paul (her husband) about I was talking to Lafie. I put him in a bad place. But I didn't have anyone to talk to. Lafie became a twelve-year-old man that day" (101–2).

Other ethnographic accounts further illustrate the notion of overlapping worlds of several generations. In the Burton, Allison, and Obeidallah (1995) study, the high unemployment rate among African-American males in the community created competition for the same jobs between teenage sons and their adult fathers. For example, James, a sixteen-year-old respondent, commented, "It's hard for a man to get a job here. Sometimes me and my friends go to apply for a job, and our fathers and grandfathers are trying for the same jobs, too! It's not fair."

For females, the overlapping worlds of teenagers and their parents, who participated in the Burton, Allison, and Obeidallah study, had implications for adolescent girls' relationships with their mothers. Previous work has shown that this relationship may be associated with psychosocial development of adolescent girls (Youniss and Smollar 1985; Obeidallah, McHale, and Silbereisen 1995). For instance, given the limited number of marriageable African-American males in the communities studied by Burton, Allison, and Obeidallah, mothers and their teen daughters often competed for the same male partners. Under such circumstances, it is difficult to differentiate developmental stages of parents and adolescence. Joann, an eighteen-year-old female in the study, stated, "It's hard to have ever thought about myself as a teenager when I've had boyfriends as old as my mom's boyfriends since I was fourteen."

One implication of the lack of mutually exclusive developmental stages for adolescents is that youth such as Joann may have a less clear notion of behavioral expectations regarding their roles as teenagers. In turn, this lack of clarity may have implications for teens' sense of self and role placement in the larger social order.

The Accelerated Life Course

The third issue that emerges in the ethnographic literature concerning the impact of social context on development among economically disadvantaged African-American teens concerns the notion of an "accelerated life course" (Burton 1990; Hamburg 1986; Hogan and Kitagawa 1985; Ladner 1971). The accelerated life course is based on an individual's view that he or she has a foreshortened life expectancy. Previous work has shown that in comparison to white adolescents, African-American males "almost always . . . enter adolescence early by demonstrating . . . more reported conflict with parents, less high GPA [grade point average], more dating behavior, more interest in the opposite sex, more positive body images and attitudes toward their own gender, and less positive attitudes to their new junior high schools" (Simmons and Zhou 1990:171). Perceptions of an accelerated life course may have further implications for adolescents' willingness and likelihood of engaging in certain behaviors.

An accelerated and truncated view of the length of one's life course reflects the realities of life expectancy and mortality rates in African-American populations. The life expectancies at birth are 63.7 years for black males and 72.3 for black females, compared with 70.7 years and 78.1 years for white males and females, respectively. In addition, the mortality rates of black men aged 25 to 44 are notably higher than the rates of their white counterparts. In 1984, the mortality rate of black men in this age range was two to two and a half times higher than that of white men (Farley and Allen 1987). Although precise estimates by socioeconomic status are not available, mortality rates have been suggested to be even higher at younger ages for poor blacks (Jackson 1988). High death rates are related to the consequences of poverty, including limited access to quality medical care, deficient diets, and substandard living environments (Burton 1990; Gibbs 1989). Further evidence of the profound realities of life expectancy among African-American populations was identified in the Burton, Allison, and Obeidallah (1995) study. In each of the families interviewed at least one male relative under age twenty-one was either incarcerated or killed during the course of the study. As such, a significant number of the teen males interviewed did not expect to live past the age of twenty-one.

Given the realities of lower life expectancies, it is plausible that some African-American teens may envision survival to a ripe old age as an unlikely prospect. When asked to reflect on the developmental stage of adolescence as part of their life course, most of the young men in the Burton, Allison, and Obeidallah study replied as did Sam, a seventeen-year-old high school senior: "Me, a teenager? Be for real, lady. Who's got time for that? I'm a man. I'd better be one before I lose my life out on these streets."

Comparably, MacLeod reports the comments of three youths responding to the question what will you be doing in twenty years:

> *Stoney:* Hard to say. I could be dead tomorrow. Around here, you gotta take life day by day.

> *Boo-Boo:* I dunno. I don't want to think about it. I'll think about it when it comes.

> *Frankie:* I don't know. Twenty years. I may be dead. I live a day at a time. I'll probably be in the pen. (1987:61)

This view of the accelerated life course was also shared by females in the Burton, Allison, and Obeidallah study. The mothers, sisters, and girlfriends of the young men involved in the study expressed sentiments comparable to those voiced by sixteen-year-old Tara: "I don't expect James [her boyfriend] to be around too long. He lives fast. He has to. Most of his friends are dead or in jail. I expect the same will happen to him."

The impact of an accelerated life course emerges in the trajectories of friendships as well. Liebow discusses this aspect of friendships in *Tally's Corner:*

> As if in anticipation of the frailty of personal relationships, to get as much as he can from them while they last and perhaps hopefully to prolong them, the man hurries each relationship toward a maximum intensity, quickly upgrading casual acquaintances to friends, and friends to best friends and lovers. This rush to upgage personal relationships, to hurry them on to increasingly intense levels of association, may itself contribute to a foreshortening of their life span, prematurely loading the incumbents with expectations and obligations which their hastily constructed relationships simply cannot support. (1967:217)

Perceptions of a foreshortened life course have important implications for the adolescent development experience. If young children, such as those portrayed in Kotlowitz's *There Are No Children Here,* perceive that they have a limited life expectancy, they may attempt to move from childhood to adulthood without taking the time to be "adolescents." This trajectory may be most pervasive in what Garbarino, Kostelny, and Dubrow (1991:376) describe as "war zones and inner-city neighborhoods plagued by violence and crime" (1991:376). In these environments children witness, on a fairly regular basis, the loss of life among the very young. Under these circumstances it is quite tenable to believe that children as well as adults accelerate their developmental transitions.

Discussion and Conclusions

Drawing on the rich, descriptive data of several existing ethnographic accounts of urban African-American family life, this chapter highlights three conceptual issues that are relevant to the study of social context and development among economically disadvantaged inner-city African-American teens: contextual variation in the meaning of adolescence and successful developmental outcomes, inconsistencies in role expectations for adolescents within families and across various social contexts; and the impact of an "accelerated life course" on developmental trajectories. Although the issues outlined here were based on a small body of ethnographic literature, they nonetheless raise a number of important conceptual questions. These questions at best, may challenge social scientists to evaluate the applicability of traditional developmental perspectives to the lives of ethnic/racial minority youth and to value the utility of ethnographic research in providing insights to the contextual meaning of developmental pathways for adolescents in urban areas.

First, the issues outlined in this chapter raise questions concerning the conceptual starting points of studies of development among African-American adolescents. In particular, the discussion of the ambiguity of adolescence as a developmental life stage among some inner-city teens suggests that before social scientists superimpose traditional developmental models on the study of teens in diverse environments, they must first determine whether adolescence is a distinctly defined stage of the life course within that environment (Dilworth-Anderson, Burton, and Turner 1994). As cross-cultural studies indicate, adolescence may not be a universal life-course experience (Adelson 1986; Jessor 1993). Consequently, when mainstream perspectives on adolescent development are applied in contexts where they do not fit, researchers may be generating inaccurate and uninterpretable profiles of the development of many teens.

Second, the present discussion raises questions concerning the prevalence of adolescence as an ambiguously defined life stage among economically disadvantaged and ethnic/minority teens. As noted previously, the ideas presented here draw upon a sparse ethnographic literature which have examined the lives of a small number of African-American families. As such, the developmental issues outlined are not necessarily representative of patterns in the broader ethnic/minority population of adolescents. Currently, however, there are no existing large-scale studies that examine the nature of development among economically and racially diverse subpopulations of teens. Do teens in diverse contexts experience inconsistencies in how their families and schools define their roles? What impact does the age structure of families have on delineating developmental boundaries between teenagers and adults? Is the prevalence of assuming adult responsibilities early in the life course more prevalent for economically disadvantaged African-American, Hispanic, Native-American, Asian-American, and white adolescents? What implications does adhering to an "accelerated" perspective of the life course have on the choices teenagers make? Clearly, large-scale studies which examine both within-group and across-group variability in these experiences are needed to address these questions.

Finally, the ideas highlighted in this article present intervention researchers with a challenge to identify what constitutes normal development in certain contexts and how that definition of normalcy is reflected in contextual perspectives of successful adolescent outcomes. Current interventions are often designed using a mainstream template and thus promote as desirable outcomes for adolescents those outcomes that are traditionally defined as successful (for example, completion of high school). Within these intervention programs, teens are not necessarily recognized for the successful outcomes they achieve which are culturally and contextually relevant (for example, taking care of an elderly relative). Ogbu eloquently speaks to this issue noting that the "competencies" or successful developmental outcomes individuals achieve are a unique function of group experiences dealing with "the demands of physical social, political, economic, and supernatural environments" (1981:419). Thus adolescents who struggle each day at the level of survival and who have difficulty garnering resources to meet their basic needs may experience greater challenges in thriving and coping in their environments than adolescents who do not have comparable experiences (Seidman 1991). Consequently, what constitutes a successful developmental outcome for each group may differ. What is the range of contextually defined successful developmental outcomes for teens? What impact does the lack of recognition for contextually defined successful outcomes have for adolescents achieving traditional outcomes? What are the long-term developmental implications for adolescents who embrace only contextually defined successes? These questions are yet to be systematically addressed in existing intervention research.

The ideas presented here are arguably preliminary but they nonetheless have implications for future research and interventions for inner-city and economically disadvantaged minority teens. This discussion is not meant to imply that all inner-city African-American teenagers have the same experience. Clearly there is tremendous heterogeneity in the experiences of African-American adolescents (Jones 1989). Our objective here, however, was to provide additional ways to think about adolescence as a developmental experience among teens who grow up in contexts that are not white, middle class, nor identified as mainstream.

This chapter raises more questions than it answers. However, the ways of thinking about development among inner-city African-American teens presented here prod us to reexamine the paradigms that guide current research and intervention strategies directed toward economically and racially disadvantaged adolescents. We encourage social scientists to join us in moving beyond the exercise of examining adolescents within a traditional developmental perspective. We ask fellow researchers to draw upon the realities of social life experienced by many youth today—realities that are often carefully described in ethnographic research. Our hope is that research which incorporates nontraditional conceptual frameworks of development will increasingly yield more accurate assessments of the relationship between social context and the developmental pathways of ethnic/minority and economically disadvantaged teens.

Acknowledgments

The research reported in this chapter was supported by grants to Linda Burton from the William T. Grant Foundation, Social Science Research Council, and a FIRST Award from the National Institute of Mental Health (no. R29 MH46057-01) and by a supplemental grant from the William T. Grant Foundation to Kevin Allison. We extend our thanks to Jeanne Brooks-Gunn, Greg Duncan, Glen Elder Jr., and Warren Critchlow for their helpful comments on earlier drafts of this essay.

References

Adelson, J. 1986. *Inventing Adolescence.* New Brunswick, N.J.: Transaction.

Allison, K., and Y. Takei 1993. "Diversity: The Cultural Contexts of Adolescents and Their Families." In *Early Adolescence: Perspectives on Research, Policy, and Intervention.* Ed. R. M. Lerner, 516–69. Hillsdale, N.J.: Erlbaum.

Anderson, E. 1990. *Streetwise: Race, Class, and Change in an Urban Community.* Chicago: University of Chicago Press.

Ashenbrenner, J. 1975. *Lifelines: Black Families in Chicago.* New York: Holt, Rinehart, and Winston.

Bell-Scott, P., and R. Taylor 1989. "The Multiple Ecologies of Black Adolescent Development." *Journal of Adolescent Research* 4: 119–24.

Bengston, V. L., C. Rosenthal, and L. M. Burton. 1990. "Families and Aging." In *Handbook of Aging and the Social Sciences.* Ed. R. Binstock and L. George, 263–87. New York: Academic Press.

Bronfenbrenner, U. 1979. *The Ecology of Human Development.* Cambridge, Mass.: Harvard University Press.

———. 1986. "Ecology of the Family as a Context for Human Development: Research Perspectives." *Developmental Psychology* 22:723–742.

Brooks-Gunn, J., and E. O. Reiter. 1990. "The Role of Pubertal Processes in the Early Adolescent Transition." In *At the Threshold: The Developing Adolescent.* Ed. S. S. Feldman and G. R. Elliott, 8–29. Cambridge, Mass.: Harvard University Press.

Burton, L. M. 1990. "Teenage Childbearing as an Alternative Life-Course Strategy in Multigeneration Black Families." *Human Nature* 1:123–43.

———. 1991. "Caring for Children: Drug Shifts and Their Impact on Families." *The American Enterprise* (May–June):34–37.

———. 1995. "Intergenerational Family Structure and the Provision of Care in African-American Families with Teenage Childbearers." In *Intergenerational Issues in Aging.* Ed. K. W. Schaie, V. L. Bengston, and L. M. Burton, 79–96. New York: Springer.

———. In press. "The Timing of Childbearing, Family Structure, and the Role Responsibilities of Aging Black Women." In *Stress and Coping in Children and Families.* Ed. E. Mavis Heatherington and E. Blechman. Hillsdale, N.J.: Erlbaum.

Burton, L. M., K. Allison, and D. Obeidallah. 1995. "Social Context and Adolescence: Perspectives on Development among Inner-City African-American Teens." In *Pathways through Adolescence: Individual Development in Relation to Social Context.* Ed. L. Crockett and A. C. Crouter, 119–38. Hillsdale, N.J.: Erlbaum.

Burton, L. M., and P. Dilworth-Anderson. 1991. "The Intergenerational Family Roles of Aged Black Americans." *Marriage and Family Review* 16: 311–30.

Burton, L. M., and R. L. Jarrett. 1991 "Studying African-American Family Structure and Process in Underclass Neighborhoods." Paper presented at the annual meeting of the American Sociological Association, Cincinnati, August.

Burton, L. M., T. Price-Spratlen, and M. B. Spencer. Forthcoming. "On Ways of Thinking about and Measuring Neighborhoods: Implications for Studying Context and Developmental Outcomes for Children." In *Neighborhood Poverty: Context and Consequences for Development.* Ed. G. Duncan, J. Brooks-Gunn, and L. Aber. New York: Russell Sage.

Bush, D. M., and R. G. Simmons. 1987. "Gender and Coping with the Entry into Early Adolescence." In *Gender and Stress.* Ed. R. C. Barnett, L. Brener, and G. K. Baruch, 129–50. New York: Free Press.

Clark, R. M. 1983. *Family Life and School Achievement: Why Poor Black Children Succeed or Fail.* Chicago: University of Chicago Press.

Coleman, J. S. 1961. *The Adolescent Society: The Social Life of the Teenager and Its Impact on Education.* New York: Free Press.

Coles, R. B. 1967. *Children of Crisis: A Study of Courage and Fear.* Boston: Little, Brown.

Conger, R. D., and G. H. Elder, Jr. 1994. *Families in Troubled Times: Adapting to Change in Rural America.* New York: Aldine de Gruyter.

Conger, R. D., K. J. Conger, G. H. Elder, and F. D. Lorenz. 1993. "Family Economic Stress and Adjustment of Early Adolescent Girls." *Developmental Psychology* 29: 3206–19.

Conger, R. D., G. H. Elder, F. Lorenz, R. Simons, and L. Whitbeck. 1992. "A Family Process Model of Economic Hardship and Adjustment of Early Adolescent Boys." *Child Development* 63: 526–41.

Cunningham, M. 1993. "Sex Role Influences on African Americans: A Literature Review." *Journal of African-American Male Studies* 1: 30–37.

Dannefer, D. 1984. "Adult Development and Social Theory: A Paradigmatic Reappraisal." *American Sociological Review* 49: 100–116.

Davis, A., and J. Dollard. 1964. *Children of Bondage: The Personality Development of Negro Youth in the Urban South.* New York: Harper and Row.

Dilworth-Anderson, P., L. M. Burton, and L. Boulin-Johnson. 1993. "Reframing Theories for Understanding Race, Ethnicity, and Family." In *Sourcebook of Family Theories and Methods: A Contextual Approach.* Ed. P. Boss, W. Doherty, R. Larossa, W. Schumm, and S. Teinmetz, 627–46. New York: Plenum.

Dilworth-Anderson, P., L. M. Burton, and W. Turner, W. 1993. "The Importance of Values in the Study of Culturally Diverse Families." *Family Relations* 42: 238–42.

Duncan, G., J. Brooks-Gunn, and L. Aber, eds. Forthcoming. *Neighborhood Poverty: Context and Consequences for Children.* New York: Russell Sage.

Eccles, J. S., C. Midgley, A. Wigfield, C. M. Buchanan, D. Reuman, C. Flanagan, and D. MacIver. 1993. "Development during Adolescence: The Impact of Stage-Environment Fit on Young Adolescents' Experiences in Schools and Families." *American Psychologist* 48: 90–101.

Eccles, J. S., C. Midgley, H. Feldlaufer, D. Reuman, A. Wigfield, and D. MacIver. 1988. "Developmental Mismatch and the Junior High School Transition." Paper presented at the biannual meeting of the Society for Research on Adolescence, Alexandria, Va., March.

Edelman, P., and J. Ladner. 1991. *Adolescence and Poverty.* Washington, D.C.: Center for National Policy Press.

Elder, G. H., Jr. 1974. *Children of the Great Depression.* Chicago: University of Chicago Press.

Elder, G. H., Jr., J. Modell, R. D. Parke, eds. 1993. *Children in Time and Place.* New York: Cambridge University Press.

Entwisle, D. R., K. L. Alexander, and L. S. Olson. 1994. "The Gender Gap in Math: Possible Origins in Neighborhood Effects." *American Sociological Review* 59(6): 822–838.

Farley, R., and W. R. Allen, W. R. 1987. *The Color Line and the Quality of Life in America.* New York: Russell Sage.

Feldman, S. S., and G. R. Elliott, eds. 1990. *At the Threshold: The Developing Adolescent.* Cambridge, Mass.: Harvard University Press.

Garbarino, J., K. Kostelny, and N. Dubrow. 1991. "What Children Can Tell Us about Living in Danger." *American Psychologist* 46: 376–83.

Gibbs, J. T. 1985. "Black Adolescents and Youth: An Endangered Species." *American Journal of Orthopsychiatry* 54: 6–21.

———. 1989. "Black Adolescents and Youth: An Update on an Endangered Species." In *Black Adolescents.* Ed. R. L. Jones, 3–27. Berkeley, Calif.: Cobb and Henry.

Gillis, J. R. 1974. *Youth and History.* New York: Academic Press.

Graber, J. H., and A. C. Petersen. 1991. "Cognitive Changes at Adolescence: Biological Perspectives." In *Brain Maturation and Cognitive Development: Comparative Cross-Cultural Perspectives.* Ed. K. R. Gibson and Petersen, 253–79. Hawthorne, N.Y.: Aldine de Gruyter.

Hall, G. S. 1904. *Adolescence: Its Psychology and Its Relations to Physiology, Anthropology, Sociology, Sex, Crime, Religion, and Education.* New York: Appleton.

Hamburg, B. A. 1974. "Early Adolescence: A Specific and Stressful Stage of the Life Cycle." In *Coping and Adaptation.* Ed. G. V. Coelho, D. A. Hamburg, and J. E. Adams, 102–24. New York: Basic Books.

Hembry, K. F. 1988. "Little Women: Repeat Childbearing among Black, Never-Married Adolescent Mothers." Ph.D. dissertation, University of California, Berkeley.

Hippler, A. E. 1971. *Hunter's Point: A Black Ghetto.* New York: Basic Books.

Hogan, D. P. 1978. "The Variable Order of Events in the Life Course." *American Sociological Review.* 43: 573–86.

Hogan, D. P., and E. M. Kitagawa. 1985. "The Impact of Social Status, Family Structure, and Neighborhood on the Fertility of Black Adolescents. *American Journal of Sociology* 90: 825–55.

Hollingshead, A. B. 1949. *Elmtown's Youth.* New York: Wiley.

Jackson, J. J. 1988. "Growing Old In Black America: Research on Aging in Black Populations." In J. Jackson, ed., *The Black American,* 3–16. New York: Springer.

Jarrett, R. L. 1990. *A Comparative Examination of Socialization Patterns among Low-Income African Americans, Chicanos, Puerto Ricans, and Whites: A Review of the Ethnographic Literature.* New York: Social Science Research Council.

———. 1994. "Living Poor: Family Life among Single Parent, African-American Women." *Social Problems* 41: 30–49.

———. 1995. "Growing Up Poor: The Family Experiences of Socially Mobile Youth in Low-Income African-American Neighborhoods. *Journal of Adolescent Research* 10:111–135.

Jeffers, C. 1967. *Living Poor: A Participant Observer Study of Choices and Priorities.* Ann Arbor, Mich.: Ann Arbor.

Jessor, R. 1993. "Successful Adolescent Development among Youth in High-Risk Settings." *American Psychologist* 48: 117–26.

Jones, R. L., ed. 1989. *Black Adolescents.* Berkeley, Calif.: Cobb and Henry.

Keating, D. 1990. "Adolescent Thinking." In *At the Threshold: The Developing Adolescent.* Ed. S. S. Feldman and G. R. Elliott, 54–89. Cambridge, Mass.: Harvard University Press.

Kett, J. 1977. *Rites of Passage: Adolescence in America, 1790 to the Present.* New York: Basic Books.

Kotlowitz, A. 1991. *There Are No Children Here.* New York: Doubleday.

Ladner, J. A. 1971. *Tomorrow's Tomorrow: The Black Woman.* Garden City, N.Y.: Doubleday.

Lerner, R. M. 1987. "A Life-Span Perspective for Early Adolescence." In *Biological-Psychosocial Interactions in Early Adolescence.* Ed. Lerner and T. T. Foch, 9–34. Hillsdale, N.J.: Erlbaum.

Lerner, J. V., and R. M. Lerner. 1983. "Temperament and Adaptation across Life: Theoretical and Empirical Issues." In *Life-Span Development and Behavior.* Vol. 5. Ed. P. B. Baltes and O. G. Brin Jr., 46–67. New York: Academic Press.

Linton, R. 1942. "Age and Sex Categories." *American Sociological Review* 7: 589–603.

MacLeod, J. 1987. *Ain't No Making It: Leveled Aspirations in a Low-Income Neighborhood.* Boulder, Colo.: Westview Press.

Masten, A. 1988. "Toward a Developmental Psychopathology of Early Adolescence." In *Early Adolescent Transitions.* Ed. M. D. Levine and E. R. McAnarney, 261–78. Lexington, Mass.: Lexington Books.

Masten, A., K. Best, and N. Garmezy. 1990. "Resilience and Development: Contributions from the Study of Children Who Overcame Adversity." *Development and Psychopathology* 2: 425–44.

McLoyd, V. C. 1990. "The Impact of Economic Hardship on Black Families and Children: Psychological Distress, Parenting, and Socioemotional Development." *Child Development* 61: 311–46.

Mead, M. 1928. *Coming of Age in Samoa.* New York: Morrow.

Modell, J. 1989. *Into One's Own: From Youth to Adulthood in the United States, 1920–1975.* Berkeley: University of California Press.

Newman, K. S. 1992. *"The View from the Corner": Neighborhood Influences on Children and Adolescents.* New York: Social Science Research Council.

Obeidallah, D. A., S. M. McHale, and R. J. Silbereisen. "Why Some Girls and Not Others? A Study of Early Adolescent Girls' Depressive Symptomatology." Unpublished.

Ogbu, J. 1974. *The Next Generation: An Ethnography of Education in an Urban Neighborhood.* New York: Academic Press.

———. 1981. "The Origins of Human Competence: A Cultural Ecological Perspective." *Child Development* 52: 413–29.

———. 1985. "A Cultural Ecology of Competence among Inner-City Blacks." In *Beginnings: Social and Affective Development of Black Children.* Ed. M. B. Spencer, G. K. Brookins, and W. R. Allen, 45–66. Hillsdale, N.J.: Erlbaum.

Petersen, A. C. 1988. "Adolescent Development." In *Annual Review of Psychology.* Ed. M. R. Rosenzweig. Palo Alto, Calif.: Annual Reviews.

Phelan, P., A. L. Davidson, and H. T. Cao. 1991. "Students' Multiple Worlds: Negotiating the Boundaries of Family, Peer, and School Cultures. *Anthropology and Education Quarterly* 22: 224–50.

Powers, S. I., S. T. Hauser, and L. A. Kilner. 1989. "Adolescent Mental Health." *American Psychologist* 44: 200–208.

Rosenfeld, G. 1971. *Shut Those Thick Lips: A Study of Slum School Failure.* New York: Holt, Rinehart, and Winston.

Savin-Williams, R. C. 1987. *Adolescence: An Ethnological Perspective.* New York: Springer.

Seidman, E. 1991. "Growing Up the Hard Way: Pathways of Urban Adolescents." *American Journal of Community Psychology* 19(2): 173–205.

Silbereisen, R. K., K. Eyferth, and G. Rudinger, eds. 1986. *Development as Action in Context: Problem Behavior and Normal Youth Development.* New York: Springer-Verlag.

Silverstein, B., and R. Krate. 1975. *Children of the Dark Ghetto: A Developmental Psychology.* New York: Praeger.

Simmons, R. G., and Y. Zhou. 1990. "Racial School and Family Context among Adolescents." In S. S. Feldman and G. R. Elliott, eds., *At the Threshold: The Developing Adolescent,* 149–76. Cambridge, Mass.: Harvard University Press.

Spencer, M. B. 1995. "Old Issues and New Theorizing about African-American Youth: A Phenomenological Variant of Ecological Systems Theory." In *Black Youth: Perspectives on Their Status in the United States.* Ed. R. Taylor. Westport, Conn.: Praeger.

Spencer, M. B., S. P. Cole, D. DuPree, A. Glymph, and P. Pierre. 1993. "Self-Efficacy among Urban African American Early Adolescents: Exploring Issues of Risk, Vulnerability, and Resilience." *Development and Psychopathology* 5: 719–39.

Spencer, M. B., and S. M. Dornbusch. 1990. "Challenges in Studying Minority Youth." In *At the Threshold: The Developing Adolescent.* Ed. S. S. Feldman and G. R. Elliott, 123–46. Cambridge, Mass.: Harvard University Press.

Stack, C. B. 1974. *All Our Kin: Strategies for Survival in a Black Community.* New York: Harper and Row.

Stack, C. B., and L. M. Burton. 1993. "Kinscripts." *Journal of Comparative Family Studies* 24: 157–70.

Steinberg, L. 1990. "Autonomy, Conflict, and Harmony in the Family Relationship." In *At the Threshold: The Developing Adolescent.* Ed. S. S. Feldman and G. R. Elliott, 255–76. Cambridge, Mass.: Harvard University Press.

Sullivan, M. 1988. *Getting Paid: Youth Crime and Work in the Inner-City.* Ithaca, N.Y.: Cornell University Press.

Valentine, B. L. 1978. *Hustling and Other Hard Work: Life Styles of the Ghetto.* New York: Free Press.

Weisner, T. S., and R. Gallimore. 1977. "My Brother's Keeper: Child and Sibling Caretaking." *Current Anthropology* 18:169–90.

Williams, M. 1978. "Childhood in an Urban Black Ghetto." *Umoja* 2:169–82.

Williams, T., and W. Kornblum. 1985. *Growing Up Poor.* Lexington, Mass.: Lexington Books.

Youniss, J., and J. Smollar. 1985. *Adolescents' Relations with Mothers, Fathers, and Friends.* Chicago: University of Chicago Press.

19 Transitions in Early Childhood: The Promise of Comparative, Longitudinal Ethnography

WILLIAM A. CORSARO

Recently we have seen the beginnings of a movement away from theories that view development as the solo child's mastery of the world on her own terms to a view of socialization as a collective process that occurs in a public rather than a private realm (Bruner 1986; Corsaro 1992; Gaskins, Miller, and Corsaro 1992). From this view the child is not only active, but socially active—a participant in negotiations with others (adults and other children) in the communal events that are the basis of shared culture. This interpretive approach differs from traditional theories of human development and socialization in a number of important respects.

First, the interpretive approach places special emphasis on language and children's participation in cultural routines. As Ochs has argued, language is central to socialization both as a "symbolic system that encodes local social and cultural structure" and as a "tool for establishing (that is, maintaining, creating) social and psychological realities" (1988:210). These interrelated features of language and language use are "deeply embedded and instrumental in the accomplishment of the concrete routines of social life" (Schieffelin 1990:19). Children's participation in cultural routines is a key element of the interpretive approach. The habitual, taken-for-granted character of routines provides actors with the security and shared understanding of belonging to a social group. On the other hand, this very predictability empowers routines, providing frames within which a wide range of sociocultural knowledge can be produced, displayed, and interpreted (Corsaro 1992).

Second, the emphasis on the importance of language and the accomplishment of everyday cultural routines in the interpretive approach provides an alternative for extending traditional views of learning and development. Traditional views assume that children pass through a transition from purely biological beings through a period of childhood into socially competent membership in a social group and set of social institutions. The emphasis in this linear view is on the end point of development, or the movement from immaturity to adult competence (Cook-Gumperz and Corsaro 1986).

The interpretive approach views development as reproductive rather than linear. Children do not merely internalize individually the external adult culture. Rather, they become part of adult culture—that is, they contribute to its reproduction—through their negotiations with adults and their creative production of a series of peer cultures with other children. Thus the interpretive model extends traditional views of individual linear progression through a series of increasingly complex stages to one in which individual development is embedded in children's collective weaving of their places in the "webs of significance" which constitute their culture (Geertz 1973:5; see also Corsaro 1993 and Corsaro and Rosier 1992 for a description of the "orb web" as a metaphor for conceptualizing the reproductive view of socialization).

Documenting Productive-Reproductive Processes: The Promise of Comparative Longitudinal Ethnography

In this section I discuss features of what I see as an ideal method (comparative, longitudinal ethnography) for documenting productive-reproductive processes in children's lives. I realize, of course, that given practical problems including time, expense, and difficulties in gaining access to target groups and settings, the ideal ethnography is rarely accomplished. My aim is to highlight key aspects of the ethnographic method that make it most appropriate for interpretive studies of children's socialization. In the following section I build on this discussion by providing illustrative examples of these features from my research on the peer cultures of preschool children in the United States and Italy.

I see the ideal ethnography for studying productive-reproductive processes in childhood socialization as one which is *longitudinal and ethnohistorical, multilevel,* and *cross-cultural.* All ethnographic research is *longitudinal* in a general sense in that it involves entering a group, gaining acceptance, and collecting a wide range of observational and interview data over a prolonged period of time. However, the ideal ethnography for documenting productive-reproductive processes is not just prolonged, it is also focused on key developmental or transition periods in children's lives. In this sense the ideal ethnography shares a basic similarity with quantitative longitudinal research in psychology and sociology: a direct focus on the nature and results of changes in children's lives over long periods of time. There are, however, important differences in the two methods regarding how change is conceptualized and measured. While positivist longitudinal studies rely almost exclusively on repeated quantitative measures of discrete variables at distanced points in time (Magnusson et al. 1991), interpretive ethnographies involve intensive, continuous, and often microscopic observations of small samples over prolonged developmental and transition periods (Burton, Obeidallah, and Allison, this volume; Corsaro 1988; Corsaro and Rosier 1992; Heath 1983, and in this volume; Miller, this volume; Ochs 1988; Schieffelin 1990). Quantitative longitudinal studies are far superior to cross-sectional studies for predicting important individual outcomes and for developing intervention strategies and policy. However, such large-scale, longitudinal research can not identify what is actually occurring in family, peer-group, school, and other important settings where children spend their time, nor can they document key processes of continuity or discontinuity in children's transitions from one setting to another. Here ethnographic studies have made important contributions to fill in the sketchy pictures that emerge from more large-scale quantitative research.

The ideal interpretive ethnography is not only longitudinal but ethnohistorical. An ethnography is ethnohistorical when it places the study of a particular group over some limited time period (from one to several years) in a broader historical context (Heath 1983, and in this volume). Many such attempts have appeared in recent interpretive studies. For example, in her study of language socialization of Kaluli children in Papua New Guinea, Schieffelin (1990) combines detailed microanalyses of children's use of language in everyday routines with caregivers and others with her own and other ethnographies of the values, social practices, rituals, and exchange systems making up Kaluli culture. In this way Schieffelin's analysis articulates time in a developmental sense (specific children's language socialization) with time in a sociohistorical sense (1990:21), and in the process weaves the implications of her work into a powerful model of the dynamic relation between language and culture.

While interpretive ethnographies have made important contributions to our understanding of children's socialization, most of these studies limit their focus to one context and fail to effectively link features of the home, neighborhood, community, school, and other settings that directly and indirectly affect children's lives. The ideal ethnography is *multilevel* in that there is an attempt to place the particular groups and setting(s) under study into broader cultural context (see Burton, Obeidallah, and Allison, this volume; Heath, this volume). This goal of multilevel contextualization is especially important in studies of children's transitions across developmental periods and from one major cultural institution to another. Here

Burton et al.'s (this volume) work on economically disadvantaged African-American youths' movement into adolescence and related work on children's transition from home to school by Boggs (1985), Heath (1983), and Watson-Gegeo (1992) can serve as models. Watson-Gegeo's work on the socialization and schooling of Kwara'ae (Solomon Islands) children is particularly illuminating in this regard because she found that societal factors incorporated into her analysis at the macro level could be linked to actual behavior at the micro interactional level where socialization occurs. She found, for example, that while children's home and community contexts for socialization are cognitively rich and demanding, parental frustration with the poor quality of the schools is communicated to the children which negatively affects their motivation and confidence.

Finally, ideal ethnography involves *comparison across cultures or subcultures within societies.* Until recently, most work in child development and socialization has been restricted to children from Western societies (but see Cole et al. 1971, and Whiting and Whiting 1975 for important exceptions), and few of these studies involve comparisons of groups across or within these societies. However, in the last ten years this neglect has been addressed by numerous observational and ethnographic studies of socialization in diverse cultural groups (Rogoff and Morelli 1989; Whiting and Edwards 1988).

Interpretive ethnographies that have contributed to this tradition have involved several types of comparative designs. First, a very few have included intensive observations of two or more cultural or subcultural groups over extended periods of time (Heath 1983; Miller, this volume). Such work is ideal because it allows for direct comparisons of different groups at similar points in historical time. However, the expense and time demands of this ideal model are often difficult to overcome.

A second model involves successive interpretive ethnographies of differing groups. Shweder's work on moral development (Shweder, Mahapatra, and Miller 1987) and my own work on young children's peer cultures are examples of this design. I initiated my research on peer culture with a one-year study of middle- and upper-class American nursery-school children (Corsaro 1985). In this study I identified key aspects of peer culture and developed an interpretive theory of childhood socialization. I later extended this work cross-culturally with a three-year study of peer culture in an Italian nursery school (Corsaro 1988; Corsaro and Rizzo 1988). In the Italian study I identified analogous and divergent routines in the American and Italian children's peer cultures and further developed the more general theoretical importance of peer culture for children's socialization. In a current study I returned to preschool centers in the United States, but now have added a new middle-class sample and a sample of economically disadvantaged children (Corsaro and Rosier 1992; Rosier and Corsaro 1993). Overall, this design has enabled me to search for universal features of peer culture, to identify how elements of the peer and adult cultures interact within children's worlds, and to refine and expand an interpretive theory of childhood socialization (Corsaro 1992).

There is, however, a clear limitation to the successive ethnography design. The groups being compared have participated in processes of social production and reproduction in different sociohistorical periods. Therefore, it is difficult for me to estimate, for example, how the major increase in the number of young children attending preschools since the original study (which was completed in 1975) may affect comparisons with the Italian data collected in 1984–87 and the current study involving economically disadvantaged children.

A third design is an intensive ethnographic case study of children in understudied (usually non-Western) societies with a focus on certain aspects of development (language, cognition, emotions) which includes comparisons with previous research in Western societies (Schieffelin and Ochs 1986; Rogoff 1990). Such research increases our knowledge of uniformities and differences in key developmental processes across social groups and has led to important advances in socialization theory. However, like the second design of successive ethnographies, this design faces the problem of estimating the possible effects of sociohistorical change. Additionally, in this design, interpretations of the comparisons must always be qualified because of differences in the goals and methods of the ethnography and the earlier studies that serve as its comparative base.

I now turn to two illustrative examples of my recent work as a way of providing in-depth illustrations of these features of comparative longitudinal ethnography.

Studying Peer Culture in the Italian *Scuola Materna*

Entering the Peer Culture

Field entry is crucial in ethnography since one of its central goals as an interpretive method is the establishment of membership status and an insider's perspective or point of view (Rizzo, Corsaro, and Bates 1992). Acceptance into the world of children is especially difficult because of obvious differences between adults and children in terms of cognitive and communicative maturity, power (both real and perceived), and physical size. While some ethnographers of children maintain that complete acceptance (of researchers by children) is possible and full participation (by researchers in children's worlds) is desirable (see Mandell 1988), others argue that certain differences between adults and children (especially physical size) can not be fully overcome and thus advise some form of limited or peripheral participation (Corsaro 1985; Fine and Glassner 1979).

Regardless of one's position on degree of participation, documentation of entry, acceptance, and participation is imperative in ethnographic studies of socialization for several reasons. Most obviously such documentation allows for estimates of possible disruptive effects of the research process on the normal flow of cultural routines and practices. Here the concern goes beyond degree of participation to a documentation of the effects of routine practices of data collection (like informal interviewing, note taking, audiovisual recording, and the collection of artifacts).[1] More subtly, since entry, acceptance, and participation are processes with developmental histories, their documentation provides insights to productive and reproductive processes in local cultures (Heath, this volume; Miller, this volume).

Let me try to illustrate the importance of such documentations by considering my entry into the local peer and school cultures of an Italian *scuola materna* where I carried out ethnographic research for a six-month period in 1984 and then returned for further data collection in the spring of 1985 and 1986. While I had some confidence regarding my abilities to enter into the play and peer culture of preschool children because of prior ethnographic work in the United States (Corsaro 1985), I was quite apprehensive about field entry into the *scuola materna* because of my limited abilities in conversational Italian, my lack of knowledge about the Italian early education system, and my unfamiliarity with Italian culture more generally. It turned out that most of these apprehensions were short-lived.

With the help of Italian colleagues, I selected a research site (a *scuola materna* in Bologna named *Le Due Torri*)[2] and presented my research aims to the teachers. I decided on this particular *scuola materna* for several reasons. First, there was a fairly even mix of three-, four-, and five-year-olds which meant that I would be able to follow a number of children over a three-year period as they moved into and prepared to move out of the peer and school culture. Second, all of the teachers had been together at the school for several years and there was no clear status hierarchy among them. Finally, the school was near our rental apartment and our landlord's daughter attended the *scuola materna.*

On my first full day at the school the teachers introduced me to the children as someone from the United States who would be coming to the school to be with them throughout the year. Employing the "reactive" method of field entry I had used in my earlier work (Corsaro 1985), I entered play areas, sat down, and waited for the children to react to me.

They soon began to ask me questions, drew me into their activities, and over time gradually began to define me as an atypical adult.

In many ways my acceptance by the Italian children was much easier and quicker than it had been for the American children I have studied. For the American children it took some getting used to on their part that I was more like a big kid than a normal adult. For the Italian children as soon as I spoke in my fractured Italian I was unusual, funny, and fascinating. I was not just an atypical adult, but also an incompetent adult—not just a big kid but sort of a dumb big kid.[3]

The first thing they noticed was my accent, but they quickly got used to it and then realized that I often used the wrong words (bad grammar) and more than often made little sense (bad semantics). At first they loved to laugh at and correct my pronunciations. But soon the little teachers went beyond simple corrections of my accent and grammar and began to repeat and adjust their own speech when I could not understand them. They would, at times, act out words and frequently consulted in small groups often calling out to other children playing nearby for help. Before long we were doing pretty well and my confidence began to grow. I specifically remember one small triumph.

I was sitting on the floor of a play area with two boys (Felice and Roberto) playing with toy cars. Felice began talking about an Italian race car driver and, while I only understood part of the description, I clearly heard the phrase "Lui è morto," which I knew meant "He's dead." I assumed that Felice had been re-creating a tragic accident in an auto race and it called to mind a particular phrase that I had liked the sound of in one of my first Italian courses: "Che peccato!" (What a pity!). Hearing me produce the expression the two boys looked up in amazement and Felice said: "Bill! Bill! Ha ragione! Bravo, Bill!" (Bill! Bill! He's right! Way to go Bill!). "Bravo, Bill!" Roberto chimed in, and then I heard Felice calling out to other children in the school about my exploits. Several of the children came over and listened attentively as Felice repeated the story of the tragic accident and then added: "And Bill said, 'Che peccato!'" The small group cheered and some even clapped at this news. Not in the least embarrassed by all the attention, I actually felt good—like one of the group. It was only later that I began to realize the significance of this strong emotional reaction in becoming a participant in the local peer culture.

Things were not going as well communicatively with the teachers. In fact, confusions and communicative breakdowns were fairly frequent during my first months in the school. There were a number of reasons for these problems. First, the teachers and I were self-conscious about these language troubles. For them it was because they knew only one language and for me it was because my Italian was so poor. Second, we tried to talk about rather abstract topics (like my research, early education in the United States, and other things) as compared to the more context-bound conversations I had with the children. Third, the teachers did not adjust their speech very well. They would start off talking slow and were careful to avoid difficult constructions and idiomatic expressions. However, after a conversation was under way, things sped up, complicated phrases emerged, and I often got confused. When I expressed such confusion, the teachers would often get a bit flustered and insist we start over, and, as a result, we seldom got very far in these early attempts.

Given these experiences, the teachers were surprised by my apparent communicative successes with the children. On several occasions I saw them call children over to ask them what we had been talking about. The teachers also asked me why things seemed to go more smoothly with the children, and I replied that the children and I talked about simpler and more direct things related to the children's play. While still a bit perplexed, the teachers accepted this explanation and over time the situation improved.

The children's discovery of my communicative problems with the teachers was a important element in their acceptance of me into the peer culture. The children came to see themselves as having a special relationship with me—a relationship that was different from the one I had with the teachers. They could talk with me and I with them with little difficulty, but it was apparent to them that this was not true regarding my communication with the teachers. In short, the children saw my relationship with them in some respects as a partial breakdown of the control of the teachers.

Discovering the School Culture

In this and the next section I present thick descriptions of features of the school and peer cultures as I acquired a sense of them during participant observation in the *scuola materna.* My grasp of both the nature and importance of the school and peer cultures in the children's lives resulted from my gradual entry into and involvement in these cultures and living with my family in Italy over a period of several years. In these descriptions I first provide an ethnohistorical context of the school culture acquired in work with Italian colleagues and my reading of the historical documentation of early childhood education in Italy. I then attempt to capture the meanings of the local peer and school cultures as I experienced them in the *scuola materna.*

Ethnohistorical context of school culture. Recently my colleague Francesca Emiliani and I (Corsaro and Emiliani 1992) have examined the history of child-care legislation in Italy to place the contemporary *scuola materna* in social and political context. Most of the legislation related to child care instituted in the late 1960s and early 1970s was the result of intense periods of social and political struggle which followed the Italian economic miracle of the 1950s and 1960s. Much of the collective and highly public political mobilization of this period was directly tied to the mass migration of Italians from rural areas throughout the country to major cities, primarily in the north. This type of collective action had a long history in certain regions of the north, most especially Emilia Romagna, where the school I studied is located. As a result, child-care issues were caught up in labor militancy, youth movements, the women's movement, and other urban protest movements.

The general orientation of early childhood education in Italy reflects the collective and communal movements from which it was born. The *scuola materna* is seen as a place of life for children. Activities such as playing, eating, debating, and working together are considered just as important as those that focus on individual cognitive or intellectual development. This communal orientation is evident in the organizational structure of the *scuola materna* as well as the wide range of social, verbal, and artistic projects making up the curriculum that stress the relationship of the *scuola materna* with the family, community, and the children's peer culture.

The school, the children, the teachers. The *scuola materna* studied was staffed by five teachers, and thirty-five children attended for approximately eight hours (9:30 until 5:30; some children returned home at 1:00) each weekday. The five teachers worked rotating five-hour shifts (from 8 to 1 and 1 to 6), with three teachers present in the morning and two in the afternoon. The teachers also worked fifteen to twenty additional hours a month due to participation in staff meetings (*collettivo*) and in conferences with parents (*assemblea*). All of the teachers had attained the *magistrale* diploma to teach in the *scuola materna* and had also taken refresher and specialty courses on early education offered by the university. One teacher had extensive university training. All of the women had taught for at least twenty years, three had been at the school for more than thirteen years, and the other three for more than six years.

Although I did not attempt to carry out a detailed study of social stratification in Bologna, it is clear that like most large cities in northern Italy, it is less stratified economically with much less abject poverty than large cities in southern Italy or in the United States (CENSIS 1982; Zangheri 1986). The *scuola materna* I studied was located in a large city park surrounded by a clearly upper-class residential area. However, most of the children and all the teachers lived outside this small zone of large and expensive villas and apartments. The occupational and educational backgrounds of parents ranged from factory workers and owners of small businesses to professionals with the majority of the children coming from middle- to upper-class families.

Although nearly 90 percent of Italian three- to six-year-olds attend *scuola materne,* there is a good deal of variation across individual preschools in the social background of the children, education and experience of the teachers, and structure and organization of the curriculum. Such variation is greatest between the north and south, with more centers, better qualified teachers, and more extensive programs and community involvement in the north (Corsaro and Emiliani 1992). The *scuola materna* I studied was representative of the Emilia Romagna region and, to a large degree, of northern Italy in general.[4]

In addition to the teachers, two other women worked rotating shifts at the school in the morning and afternoon. Although it was clear that these women were not teachers, it took me several weeks to discover the complexity of their place in the school. At first I assumed they were support personnel who cleaned up and served food to the children. The teachers and children called these women *Dada* (in Bologna, *dada* is used in to refer to women who care for young children). In addition to their most visible jobs of cleaning and serving food, I eventually came to see that the role of *Dada* could best be described as surrogate grandmother.

The *dade* formed close bonds with the children and were quick to offer both physical affection and verbal reprimands. The *dade* would at times intervene on the behalf of particular children in their interaction with the teachers. For example, on one occasion a child had become quite upset in a dispute with a peer over possession of a desired object. Three of the teachers had talked to the child, but she continued to cry. The teachers decided it was best if she stay seated while they escorted the rest of the children upstairs to get ready for lunch. As the teachers and children began climbing the stairs, one of the *dade* sat next to the girl and comforted her.

The *dade* also, at times, gave aid to a child or group of children who were having trouble while working on a range of educational tasks. I frequently heard the teachers' refrain of, "Don't help them, *Dada.*" Such incidents do not, however, indicate that there is inherent conflict among the teachers and *dade.* On the contrary, the teachers expect the *dade* to aid the children, to be more like mothers or grandmothers than teachers. In essence that is the *dada's* role, but the role is to be carried out in harmony with that of the teacher. As a result, the children experience a blending of styles in their interactions with the different adults in the *scuola materna.*

This blending of roles was also apparent in the weekly *collettivo.* In these meetings the teachers and *dade* talk about the children, exchange ideas about educational projects, and generally discuss how things were going in the school. I attended several meetings and was struck by the intensity of some of the discussions. However, as I was told by the teachers, the whole point of the *collettivo* is the exploration of the range of viewpoints of the different members of the group. The goal is one of confrontation in a group which stresses the importance of the toleration of a diversity of ideas and personalities (Manini 1984).

General orientation and curriculum. During my early months at the school, the elements of the curriculum that I found most striking were projects that involved observations, discussion, action, and reconstruction. These projects had many of the characteristics of those discussed by the American educator, Lilian Katz (1987:162–64), in that they involved a planning, an implementation, and a reporting or reproduction stage. The projects were of three types that stressed either the children's relationship to their physical environment, community, or larger culture. For example, during my first months at the school the teachers introduced the children and me to the process of hibernation. We looked at several books that described the process and talked about the different animals that hibernate. As I found to be usual in this phase of a project, the children engaged in a great deal of discussion and argumentation among themselves about the information. The teachers encouraged such debate and sometimes actively joined in taking the side of one child or another. The discussion phase was followed by the production of a large mural that depicted animals in hibernation with all of the children making individual contributions (fig. 1). Once the mural was completed, there was again a great deal of talk about the process as the children admired their contributions. There were even more discussions when the children later showed the mural and explained hibernation to their parents and grandparents when they visited the school.

A second project is worthy of extended discussion because it blended a number of themes and experiences important to the children at the level of the peer and school culture, the home, and the community. The project involved planning for, making, and reconstructing visits to the homes of the older children during the spring of their final year at the school. Early in the spring each of the older children talked to us about their families, homes, and where they lived in the community. About a week before an actual visit a particular child described the preparations his or her family was making for the visit. On the important day we walked as a group to the home of one of the older children.

I especially remember the walk to Felice's house. His home was very near the school and located in a residential and shopping area near my apartment. Thus I knew many of the merchants with whom we stopped

Figure 1.   Children's collective representation of animals in hibernation.

and chatted along the way. The storekeepers knew about these annual outings and looked forward to the opportunity to talk with and admire the children. In many ways this mundane event of "walking to Felice's house" manifested much of the dramatic flair of public life in Italian culture.

As we continued our journey we left a busy thoroughfare, walking down a small side street that came to an end in front of the large apartment building where Felice's family lived. Looking to my right I noticed several cats lounging in the shade under one of the cars parked along the narrow street. "Guardate i gatti," cried Luisa, pointing to the cars ahead of the one where I had spied the cats. As I bent down to look I saw four more cats, then five, six—"Molti! Molti!" one of the children shouted. Indeed, there were many; I counted fifteen. We all went over to get a closer look with my partner, Antonia, tugging at my arm because I was moving too slow. The cats scurried further back under the cars and the teachers cautioned us about touching these street animals. The beautiful felines did not appear dangerous to me, but strays are often well-fed by the local community in Italy so their looks can be deceiving. "Andiamo! Dai!" commanded one of the teachers, and we reluctantly moved on.

When Antonia and I reached the front door of Felice's building, several children were taking turns pressing the bell. Antonia pushed forward to get her turn. Swept up in the moment, when Antonia finished I reached out a gave the bell a long ring. Everyone laughed and one of the teachers said, "That Bill, always one of the kids. Enough. Let's go in."

Felice and his younger brother, Marco, peered down over the railing at us as we climbed the four flights of stairs to their apartment. When we arrived we were greeted by his parents who escorted the other adults to the kitchen while I was pulled off to Felice's room with the other children. We inspected all of Felice's toys which included an impressive collection of "I Puffi" (small replicas of cartoon characters—Smurfs, in the United States—that were very popular among the children at that time). Eventually we all went off to the kitchen where Felice's mother served a wide variety of scrumptious snacks. Before we left Felice's father presented me with homemade wine and salami. That evening after I summarized the event in my notes I again reflected on my strong emotional reactions to the event and I wrote, "It was a good day!"

For several days after a home visit, the teachers and children first verbally and then artistically reconstruct the experience. The artwork contained a series of pictures that visually captured the major phases of the event with each child contributing in some way to each picture. The detail of the pictures was striking. In a depiction of our walk to the child's home, some children drew the cars on the street, others drew individual members of the group (teachers, *dade,* children, and me), while still others drew shops while their classmates designed clothes to put in the shop windows. These pictures were then prominently displayed in the school until the end of the year, when they were taken home by the older children to keep as mementos (fig. 2).

In this project the children think about, discuss, and artistically reconstruct their relations with the school, family, community and each other. They collectively reaffirm the emotional security of these bonds while reflecting on how the nature of these attachments change as they grow older. In the process the children gain insight into their changing positions in the developing webs of significance that constitute their culture.

Documenting the Peer Culture: Discussione and La Cantilena

By a "peer culture" I mean a stable set of activities or routines, artifacts, values, and concerns that children produce and share. Although peer culture was manifested in a variety of ways in the preschool settings I have studied, two central themes have appeared consistently in the children's peer activities: the children made persistent attempts to gain control of their lives and to share that control with each other (Corsaro 1985).

Since the peer culture of preschool children is shared primarily in the course of its production, it is extremely difficult to capture using methods such as formal interviews or surveys that require children to reflect on their peer relations and experiences. Interpretive methods such as ethnography and intensive interviewing are necessary to document the children's production and sharing of peer culture. However, even traditional ethnography, which relies heavily on participant observation and the collection of fieldnotes over prolonged periods of time, is often not sufficient for overcoming differences between the perspectives of adults and children. I have found that the collection and microanalysis of audiovisual recordings of peer activities and routines is essential for capturing subtle aspects of children's cultures.

In Italy, as in my earlier research, the collection of audiovisual materials was embedded in a prolonged period of traditional ethnography and participant observation. During the last few weeks of my first year at the *scuola materna* I collected audio- and videotaped specimens of different types of peer routines that I had earlier documented and summarized in fieldnotes. I then returned to the school the following two springs and collected additional videotape data over six-week periods. These materials, grounded in background ethnographic observations and interview data, served as a basis for the comparative analysis of young children's peer culture in Italy and the United States.

Figure 2.   Children's collective representation of the trip to Felice's house.

I identified numerous analogous routines in the American and Italian data including: joke and riddle routines, insult and teasing routines, routines to evade and mock adult rules, and approach-avoidance routines. This finding provides some evidence for the possible universality of some elements of the peer culture of young children. Approach-avoidance, a fantasy routine involving pretend fear of a threatening agent, is an especially interesting candidate for universality. I have observed children producing the routine both spontaneously and in more rule-like games in several different settings in both the United States and Italy over nearly a twenty-year period (Corsaro 1988; Corsaro and Heise 1990). Variants of approach-avoidance play have also been reported in many cross-cultural studies of children's play (Barlow 1985).

Although some aspects of peer culture are best seen as innovative productions that are in many ways unique to children's worlds, many others are directly related to features of the adult culture. Shirley Heath has argued that a central aspect of the socialization process is how children learn to make sense of the social world and how they "adapt to its dynamic social interactions and role relations" (1989:367). The art of verbal negotiation and debate is deeply valued in Italian society. Public debate (or *discussione*) in bars, public squares, and shopping area is an integral part of everyday life. My earlier discussion of the *collettivo* provided a glimpse of the importance of verbal debate for the teachers. Children also engage in *discussione* with adults and peers from an early age. In fact, during my first days in the *scuola materna* I was struck by the frequency and complexity of discussion and debate among the children.

I have presented detailed analyses of the sociolinguistic features of *discussione* elsewhere (Corsaro 1994; Corsaro and Rizzo 1988, 1990), here I focus on brief discussion between two young girls that demonstrates some important aspects of the routine in peer culture. In this videotaped example, Franca and Carla (both around four and a half years old) are playing in the outside yard of the *scuola materna*. They have been rubbing small pieces of chalk against a large stone and in the process are producing a fine white powder. Franca shows some concern about a need for new chalk when the present pieces are used up. This concern leads to a debate about who will buy the new chalk and where she will buy them.

(1) *F:* E quando si consuma—quando si consuma—tutt'e due—
lo compriamo, tutt'e due, va bene?
(And when it's used up—when it's used up, both of us—we buy it, both of us, okay?)

(2) *C:* No, quando si—si—domani le compro tutto io.
(No, when it—it—tomorrow I will buy them all.)

(3) *F:* Noo, tu ne compri tre e io tre, non tutte quelle del negozio.

(Noo, you buy three of them and I buy three, not all of them that are in the store.)

(4) *C:* Ma va'che non l'ho comprate nel negozio—l'ho comprato nel 'nanen.' L'ho comprato nella banca.
(Oh come on! I didn't buy them at the store—I bought it at the 'bad.' I bought it at the bank.)

(5) *F:* Be'ma la banca non vende.
(Well, but the bank does not sell them.)

(6) *C:* Io l'ho comprato alla banca. Io l'ho comprato alla banca.
(I bought it at the bank. I bought it at the bank.)

(7) *F:* Be'alla banca—ci da i soldi. Non si vendono le cose alla banca.
(Well, at the bank—we get money there. They do not sell things at the bank.)

(8) *C:* Si, si vendono! Ci danno anche questo—hai visto che a me—me l'hanno dati. Si sta consumando—fai piano. Mettilo qua.
(Yes, they do sell things! They gave us even this—did you see that—they gave them to me. It is getting worn out—go easy. Put it here.)

The sequence begins with Franca proposing that she and Carla buy new chalk together (1). Carla, however, rejects this idea, saying that she will buy the chalk alone. Franca is insistent in her attempt to get Carla to agree to her proposal of joint action (3), and in the process claims that they will buy some but not all of the items at the store.

Carla's turn at (4) is interesting for several reasons. First, she introduces her opposition to Franca's claim with the slang expression "Ma va'che" (Oh, come on), which is, in this case, a predisagreement marking the coming challenge of Franca's claim. Predisagreements and other stylized grammatical markings or frequently used to aggravate opposition in *discussione* (Corsaro and Rizzo 1990). Second, the last part of the challenge (beginning with "l'ho comprato—") is produced in a sing-song cadence which in Italian is known as *la cantilena*.

The *cantilena* is a tonal device or sing-song which the children often produce in *discussione* and with less frequency in other peer routines and activities. The chanting is often accompanied rhythmically with nonverbal gestures such as hitting one's fists or the sides of one's open hands together. Although the sing-song cadence and rhythmic gestures usually signal opposition such as in this example, the *cantilena* can be used to mark agreement and communal sharing of an aesthetic production (Corsaro and Molinari 1990). As is the case in this example, the introduction of the *cantilena* in *discussione* often energizes the debate, providing excitement and dramatic flair.

Here Carla's use of the cantilena involves: (1) the denial of Franca's claim about the store; (2) a temporary nonsense claim that she bought things at the *nanen* (general expression meaning "bad"); and (3) a final claim that she bought it at the bank. Carla wants to challenge Franca, and, therefore, produces the *cantilena* to stress her opposition. But once into the rhythm of the *cantilena*, Carla seems to become unsure regarding where exactly you might buy chalk if not at the store. So she says she bought them at the "bad," which, of course, does not make sense. Such a claim is like an American child saying she bought them at the "yucky." Carla then continues with the rhythm of the *cantilena*, repeating the phrase "l'ho comprato—" and eventually comes up with the a more acceptable (but still quite implausible) place of purchase, the bank.

Without using the *cantilena*, Franca counters Carla's challenge pointing out correctly that the bank doesn't sell these things. Carla again responds in the *cantilena*, repeating the phrase twice. At (7) Franca tries to come up with an argument about what does go on at banks ("you get money there"), and then she again denies that chalk is sold there. Franca's position here nicely demonstrates the children's use of developing conceptions of social knowledge during the course of *discussione*. Finally, Carla tries to close off the debate by claiming that she bought the chalk in her hand at the bank. This is, of course, an obvious untruth. But before Franca can challenge her, Carla goes on to shift the topic by suggesting to Franca to go easy so that the chalks are not used up.

Discussione is highly valued in the peer culture for several reasons. First, it provides an arena for participation in and sharing of peer culture. The children debate things that are important to them (for example, friendship, play activities, monsters), and in the process develop a shared sense of control over their social world. Second, *discussione* is a highly communal activity. It has a participant structure that has relatively easy entry requirements (for example, simple denials like "No, non è vero," or repetition of previous strings), but also the attraction of multiple opportunities for embellishment and individual creativity. In fact, given the simple participant structure of the routine I was often able to join debates, but most often by way of simple contributions like "No, non è vero," or "Si, si è vero," produced in the sing-song of the *cantilena*. However, even this minimal participation was appreciated by the children and it made me feel part of the group.

Third, *discussione* is important in the peer culture because it can accompany and even take over teacher-suggested or controlled activities like drawing, play with materials, and even eating at snack and lunchtimes. In this way the initiation and sustaining of a *discussione* of their choosing gives the children a sense of power and control over their environment and caretakers. Finally, producing, embellishing, and simply enjoying bouts of *discussione* is especially powerful and satisfying for the children because the general activity of *discussione* is highly valued in the adult culture. Thus, through *discussione* the children produce, maintain, and often extend peer culture and simultaneously contribute to the reproduction of the adult world.

Discussion

In this section I have attempted to capture how my entry into the ethnographic setting, acceptance by the children and teachers, and participation in the local school and peer cultures over an extended period of time are key processes in gaining a better understanding of human development in cultural context. Cultural context from this interpretive perspective is not a variable or a static environmental niche that affects development. Rather, cultural context is a dynamic that is continually constituted in routine practices collectively produced at various levels of organization (see the chapters by Heath, McDermott, Miller, Saxe, and Schweder in this volume for similar views on the centrality of routine practices for culture and development). Children develop through their *participation* in these routine practices.

Given my initial limited competence in Italian and lack of knowledge of the school and peer culture in the *scuola materna,* I was in many ways like the three-year-old Italian child entering the school for the first time. Over time, like the younger children, I developed as a participating member of these local cultures by engaging in *discussione,* producing *cantilene,* and relishing the experiences embedded in the various school projects. Also like these younger children, I felt strong positive emotional reactions to my successes and to my developing membership in the group.

These positive emotions are especially useful for capturing the notion of development as degrees and types of participation in the productive-reproductive practices through which culture is constituted and maintained. Especially important among these reproductive practices is what I refer to as *priming activities* that prepare children for coming transitions in their lives.

Consider, for example, the participation of the children of the three age groups in the home visits like the one we made to Felice's family. For me and the children in their first year, this project was new and enticing. We were fascinated with the discussions of the coming visits and excited by the opportunity to participate in an activity that seemed so highly valued by the older children and teachers. This project, like several others we had already experienced over the school term, offered opportunities for participation in planning, doing, and reconstructing. Further, since there were several visits we had multiple chances to vary and embellish the nature of our participatory roles in the event. Over the course of the visits, this project, which had begun as a novel activity with a seemingly restricted participatory structure, was transformed into something familiar, comfortable, and open to personal embellishment. It also became with repetition an activity we could look forward to in our next year in the school as seasoned veterans rather than rookies.

For the children in their second year at the school, the home visits project was marked by a high degree of participation that was filtered through a frame of spirited anticipation. Given their introduction to the project in the previous year, they were well prepared to take on very active roles in the familiar participatory structure of the activities. However, embedded in every comment they made in discussion, every experience they had in the homes of their older peers, and every contribution they made in the artistic reproductions of the visits was a foreshadowing, a prospective savoring of the coming year when they would be the oldest children and their teachers and peers would visit *their* homes.

In the home-visits project, as in most transition events, the spotlight shines most brightly on the children about to begin an important change in their lives. For the children in their third year at the *scuola materna,* the home-visits project is the culmination of a year when they were often in leadership roles. In this project each of the older children are singled out as their teachers and peers come to their neighborhoods and homes to share directly in their lives outside the school. However, now having reached the peak of participation and at a time when they feel most at home in the local school and peer cultures, these children become acutely aware of coming changes in their lives. They discover a basic tenet of development as cultural participation: the fuller the participation, the more likely that change and transition is imminent and necessary.

Documenting One Child's Transition from Home to Formal Schooling

My current research with economically disadvantaged children in the United States began as one component of a larger, comparative study that examines preschool children's peer cultures in three settings: an Italian nursery school, a private upper-middle-class American developmental learning center, and an American Head Start center. It is the first step toward expanding the earlier research to include more features of the ideal ethnography described above. My three-year study of nine families from the Head Start center expands the earlier work both longitudinally to cover the crucial years in children's transition from home to school, and ethnohistorically by documenting important changes in the lives of the families (employment history, family structure and kin networks, and community and residential patterns), and in the curriculum, staffing, and administrative policy of the schools. In this section I first discuss my entry into the school and peer culture at the Head Start center and then present a narrative case history of one child's transition from home to school.

The Head Start Study

The Head Start center is one of three sites in a large midwestern city. It is located in a converted old elementary school. The lower floor houses a gymnasium, a library, a kitchen, and nine classrooms, while the upper level contains administrative offices. Each of the two classrooms I studied (one which met in the morning, the other in the afternoon) was staffed by a head teacher and an assistant, and met for approximately three and a half hours, Monday through Thursday. Although attendance varied greatly, there were normally around sixteen children present on any given day. All of the children in both groups were four years old at the beginning of the school year, and most had turned five by the time the study was completed.

Head Start is a federally sponsored compensatory preschool education program that stresses the development of cognitive and social skills. Parents must meet income eligibility criteria in order to enroll their children in this free program. Many of the families of the children I observed were former or current welfare recipients, although most of the families had at least one employed member. The children attending this particular center reflected the population of its inner-city location in that the overwhelming majority of the children attending were black.[5] In fact, in the two classrooms studied, only one child was not (this exception was a Hispanic child). Likewise, very nearly all of the employees at the center were also black.

The Head Start center itself is best described as a small community that emphasizes collective values and provides something approaching an "extended family" for the children. On a typical day, the average child comes into contact with a wide range of adults: teachers and teaching assistants in the nine classrooms, bus drivers, administrative staff, speech therapists, custodians, and cooks. Although the children spend the overwhelming majority of their time at the center with the teacher and assistant in their particular classrooms, they know all the adults' last names and frequently exchange greetings and playful talk with them everyday. These adults also knew all of the children and would call out to them by name when they entered classrooms or passed them in the hallways. It was not unusual to see these adults and children engaging in teasing and joking banter or hugging and exchanging kisses. The classrooms I observed reflected the communal atmosphere of the center and exhibited the type of collective ethos that has been observed in other ethnographic studies of Head Start programs (Lubeck 1985; Suransky 1982).

The Head Start study, like my earlier work, involved careful field entry and acceptance by the children and teachers, several months of participant observation, and the collection of fieldnotes and audiovisual recordings of representative episodes of peer and teacher-student interaction. Field entry in this setting was complicated by the fact that the children were at the center for so few hours each day. Also, because of limited research funds, I was able to visit the center only a day or two each week. Therefore, both the children's production of peer culture and my acceptance and entry into their peer world proceeded at a slower rate than in my previous work.

Early on, the teachers were highly skeptical of my plan to visit the classroom regularly throughout the year. In fact, upon my announcement of this plan, one teacher responded, "Why on earth would you want to do that for!" She was convinced that I would soon tire of what she saw as an enjoyable but highly demanding job.[6] I did not, of course, tire of observing in the center, and over a period of several weeks I was able to develop close and enduring relations with the teachers and children. One incident in particular seemed very important in solidifying my acceptance into the school and peer culture.

One of several problems the teachers faced due to the center's location in an old elementary school was that washrooms and toilets were not located in classrooms. Given the recency of toilet training of the children and the general nature of the activities in the preschool, this ecology demanded that the teachers had to spend quite a bit of time taking children to and from the washrooms. It was clear that this was not a pleasant task. The children, while normally on their best behavior on the walk through the center, often began to act up once they got into the washrooms. They would shout at one another to hurry up in negotiations for use of the facilities, engage in water fights, and pummel each other with rolled-up paper towels. The teachers frequently had to enter into the washrooms, put a halt to such misbehavior, and herd the children outside for the trip back to their classrooms.

During my third week at the center the head teachers in both classrooms nearly simultaneously enlisted my help in this dreaded chore. I found myself in a bit of a spot with this request. I had explained earlier to the teachers that the purpose of my research was to study the children's culture and that I did not want to be seen as an authority figure. On the other hand, I had accompanied the class on these washroom trips and it was hard to argue that the task ranked very high in the teachers' overall responsibilities. I also wanted to maintain the growing rapport with the teachers. So I accepted.

My first experiences with this new charge pretty much set a tone for things. The children were little angels as we publicly marched through the hallways to the washroom. They also lined up nicely and waited patiently as another class finished up and left the washroom. A few minutes after several boys and girls entered for their turns, all hell seemed to be breaking loose on the boys' side. When I entered I saw that one boy had another in a headlock while a third pushed both, two others huddled over one urinal pushing together and laughing about their poor aims even though two other urinals were unoccupied, a third boy stood near one of the sinks calmly flipping water at all the others.

When I tried to bring some order to this scene, I was quickly told that I was not a teacher and could not tell them what to do. I knew this was coming and had tried to minimize the tone of my directives because I did not want them to see me as an authority figure. Therefore, I agreed with their premise, but told them we would all get in trouble if they didn't calm down and hurry up. Knowing that other teachers could happen by at any time and that their teacher would be suspicious if we took too long, they all smiled at one another and reluctantly complied with my plea. When we moved back outside I then heard a great deal of commotion coming from the girls' side. I stuck my head in and was immediately told to stay out because I was a boy and also not a teacher. I agreed on both counts and then used the same strategy I did with the boys with the same eventual success.

Over time my trips to the washrooms with the children became almost a ritual in which the children would always push me a little further without letting things get out of hand. In fact, these washroom trips came to symbolize our relationship. I was seen as a quasi-adult, a grown-up friend who had minimal control over their lives. My agreement to take on this task also served to increase my rapport with the teachers. They saw me as a good sport and over time as someone who really cared about them and the children and not just my research aims.

Peer Culture at Head Start. I do not have space to describe adequately the rich variety of routines and activities that the Head Start children displayed in peer interaction. Here I want to focus on a particular aspect of the children's language styles—oppositional or competitive talk—that was related to friendship processes in the peer culture. Like the somewhat older inner-city black children studied by Goodwin (1990), the Head Start children constructed social identities, cultivated friendships, and both maintained and transformed the social order of the peer culture through opposition. Peer interaction and play routines were peppered with oppositional talk like, "Why you following me like that for?" and "Get that block out the way!" Both boys and girls were quick to oppose the untoward behavior of other children with retorts like, "You better get out my face!" Once, after the access attempt of a boy into a group of a two girls and another boy was rejected, one of the girls told me, "That boy always be messing with us!" These responses differed from my observations of the reactions of middle- and upper-class American children who most often relied on references to friendship ("Go away, you're not our friend," or "We don't like you") in similar circumstances (Corsaro 1994).

The children seldom reacted negatively to oppositional talk, nor did they run to complain to teachers. Rather, the children normally responded in kind, and serious verbal or physical disputes were rare. In fact, oppositional talk and teasing were valued (much like the Italian children's *discussione*) as part of the verbal enrichment of everyday play routines. Particularly clever oppositions or retorts were often marked as such with appreciative laughter and comments like "good one," or "you sure told her," by the audience and, at times, even the target child.

During participant observation in the peer culture I was also fascinated by the children's incorporation of many issues and themes relevant to their families' economic status into their play. For example, I observed role play in which children pretended to be employees in fast-food establishments, harried single mothers frustrated by their children's constant demands and misbehavior, parents taking sick baby dolls to the clinic, and police ordering suspected drug dealers against the wall to be searched (Corsaro 1994). I decided that my understanding of the social worlds of the children would be greatly enhanced by completing interviews with their parents and observing in their homes and communities. Thus I initiated an intensive study of a small sample of families whose children attended the Head Start center. The purpose of this study (which I carried out with my colleague, Katherine Rosier) was to examine the strategies that these low-income families employ, and the obstacles that they face, as their children make the transition from the home, to preschool, and on to first grade.

Nine of the ten mothers we contacted agreed to tape-recorded interviews that were conducted in their homes during the summer of 1990 and normally lasted ninety minutes to two hours. In addition to requesting demographic information, our open-ended interviews encouraged the respondents to talk extensively about their families' circumstances and their children's daily lives. The mothers were gracious and candid in response to our inquiries, and the first set of interviews provided us with a wealth of information about the families. Encouraged by the mothers' willingness to share their experiences, we collected additional sets of interviews with these families as their children moved into the early elementary grades. We also made informal observations in their homes, joining them for dinner or spending time with the children as they have gone about their daily activities. We attended a variety of church and school activities with the families: songfests and holiday programs, as well as regular services in local churches, graduation ceremonies in the children's classrooms, and evening programs in the schools. Finally, we interviewed the children's kindergarten teachers in the spring of 1991 and first-grade teachers one year later. We also were able to carry out some limited observations in several of the children's first-grade classrooms. Our relationships with these families are ongoing through phone calls, informal visits, and conversations, and an annual picnic (Corsaro and Rosier 1992; Rosier and Corsaro 1993).

We now have rich longitudinal data on the day-to-day lives of these families. While I do not have space here to discuss fully the major themes we have isolated in these data, I can highlight key features of these themes through the presentation of a detailed narrative of one girl's (Zena's) transition from home to formal schooling. At a more concrete level, this narrative captures the complexity of Zena's conscious and unconscious attempts to link the routines, experiences, and values in her family, peer group, and the classroom to the objective demands she faces in this crucial transition period in her life.

A Case Study of One's Girl's Transition from Home to Formal Schooling

Zena attended the Head Start program on a regular basis, settled in well to the school routine, and developed a good rapport with the teachers. Zena was an active participant in the peer culture and clearly held her own with her playmates. She stood out among her peers for organizing and playing a leadership role in complex dramatic role-play episodes. Many of these episodes involved activities and themes that reflected Zena's family experiences. For example, in one highly complex episode that we recorded on videotape, Zena and another girl, Debra, pretend to be mothers talking on the telephone in the family living area of the classroom. The telephone talk is impressive because it is doubly metacommunicative in nature. The children are producing their own interpretation of their mothers' telephone conversations about their mothers' parenting demands and problems.

In one segment of the episode, Debra dials the phone and asks Zena what she is doing. Zena responds:

> *Zena:* Hah. Cookin'. Now I need to go to the grocery store.
> *Debra:* Got to take my kids to the party store, they told me—I said—
> *Zena:* My kids—my kids want me to take them to the park.
> *Debra:* What?
> *Zena:* My kids told me to take them to the park, and then, and then the bus had to come and get 'em. That's gonna be a long walk for to here! And then the bus would have to come and get us!
> *Debra:* Well, we have to wait for transfers, then I have to buy groceries, we have to buy some groceries. And um—
> *Zena:* Guess where my kids told me to take them? To the store. When the bus comes by—my kids waitin' for it. I don't got time to do that.

In this segment the girls skillfully build coherent discourse by using "format tying" (Goodwin 1990) to establish shared agreement regarding a general topic for their telephone talk. According to Goodwin, format tying involves the systematic use of phonological, syntactic, or semantic elements of the surface structure of speech for orderly sequencing in informal talk (1990:177). For example, we see that Zena picks up on Debra's prior introduction of kids, using the same exact phrase "my kids" and noting that they want to be taken to the park. Zena expands her description by introducing the information that the kids will have to take the bus because it is too far to walk to the park. Debra continues the orderly sequencing by semantically tying her turn to Zena's earlier mention of the bus by stressing the requirement of having to "wait for transfers." Finally, Zena ties her turn to Debra's prior turn by noting that she does not have *time* to be waiting for the bus. The girls' skillful building of coherent discourse through the repetition of syntactic features of prior turns and the semantic linkage of developing ideas or information in the discourse is important because it enables the collaborative construction of a shared topic: problems of parenting in poverty.

Zena's role play in this instance is striking in her ability to capture the frustrations of trying to meet the demands of one's children when you do not have a car and must deal with a limited and time-consuming bus service. These are problems her mother faces every day. Through participation in such role play, Zena gains insight into both her own and her mother's perceptions and feelings about parenting.

Zena's academic performance at Head Start could be best rated as slightly above average. Like many of the other children who were active participants in the peer culture, Zena was ill at ease with the structured nature of the routine language and cognitive drills that were a part of the Head Start curriculum. Zena did well when called on in these drills, but she was often anxious, seldom volunteered answers, and seemed to dread being singled out to provide a response. While Zena displayed doubts about her abilities and was reserved in structured tasks, she was very active and talkative in free play, during meals, and on field trips. Like a number of the other children, she was, at times, corrected for talking too loud, not following directions, or for arguing.

While keenly aware of Zena's and the other children's anxiety in structured language and cognitive tasks, the emotion that I felt most strongly was frustration. In observing these drills I noted that while the children fidgeted and diverted their gaze from the teacher, they would often mumble the correct answer to themselves and nearby peers. While the pedagogical aim of these lessons can be seen as a collective learning experience through individual performances, the children did not see them this way. For the children, the overwhelming concern seemed to be discovering the "correct" answer and having confidence in their knowledge. Most of the children did fairly well regarding the former, but not the latter. They often lacked confidence even after correct performance and praise.

Because of family problems including a period of time in which Zena, her siblings, and mother lived in a homeless shelter, Zena missed the first several weeks of kindergarten (which is not mandatory in this city). Nevertheless, the kindergarten teacher (Mrs. Hill, a black educator with several years experience working with economically disadvantaged children) described Zena as one of the quieter students in her class, who listened and followed directions well. She was quite satisfied with Zena's progress, rating it satisfactory. Overall, the teacher felt that given Zena's late start, she was very capable, with guidance, of doing above-average work. The teacher also described Zena's mother as a "very concerned" and "very supportive" parent who continually asked how her daughter was doing and how she could help her.

Zena had to contend with several important changes when she entered first grade. First, although she began her day at a leisurely pace during her Head Start and kindergarten years since she attended afternoon sessions, in first grade she had to get up to catch a 7:45 A.M. bus each day and arrived home at 4:00 P.M., spending nearly an hour each day in transit. Second, there were twenty-two children in Zena's first-grade class, a considerable increase in size over the Head Start and kindergarten classrooms. Third, Zena had to adjust to the mostly white student population of the school and in her classroom. Her teacher and all but six of her classmates were white. Only two other girls were black and same-gender friendships seemed to be the rule among the children, so Zena had few options for playmates. Finally, the philosophy and style of Zena's first-grade teacher, Mrs. Majors, was considerably more flexible and tolerant than the no-nonsense style of Zena's kindergarten and Head Start teachers. While she gave students considerable freedom in the classroom, Mrs. Majors also had high expectations regarding their use of that freedom. While the children seemed to benefit from the opportunities for independent activity this freedom provided, many of them also, at times, exploited their freedom to engage in a number of types of horseplay and off-task behaviors that often led to peer disputes and conflict.

Zena's frequent participation in disputes and conflicts affected both her standing in the peer culture and, to some extent, her academic performance. She had difficultly interacting with the other girls who did not respond well to the oppositional style that had served Zena well in her previous peer groups. Mrs. Majors described Zena as an "outsider" who did not fit in with the "sweet and innocent" group of girls who were "just cutey-cute." This clique of around seven girls often complained to the teacher about Zena's bossiness and offensive manner. In fact, two of the girls approached me on the day we observed bemoaning the fact that Zena "thinks she knows it all" and is "always telling us what to do." While our observations on peer interaction in this setting were limited, Zena clearly faced a new set of challenges in relating to peers in first grade that negatively affected her social adjustment and academic performance.

Mrs. Majors felt that such misbehavior, conflict, and attitudinal problems among the children were serious matters that needed to be reported to parents. She wrote to Zena's mother about her conflicts with peers noting that Zena had a bad attitude and was often moody. She also asked if Zena was getting enough sleep, a possible explanation that certainly could be related to Zena's new schedule.

In our interview with Mrs. Majors she noted that she felt race and "race awareness" was a factor in Zena's problems. She said that she wished there were more black children (especially girls) for Zena to interact with. In particular, she noted that Zena grumbled about the "white" girls getting her in trouble and acting too good to play with her. An important thing here is that differences in interactive and communicative styles can be crucial not only for explaining interpersonal conflicts, but could also affect developing racial attitudes. A cycle can develop where these differences in style are misinterpreted, leading children to limit further interaction and to also articulate these differences into personal characteristics or traits (aggressive, bossy, conceited, or stuck up) that are then linked to race (see Schofield 1982 for similar findings among older children).

Academically, Zena's marks in first grade did not meet the expectations of her parents, who considered her an excellent student. While her parents and teacher agreed that Zena's behavior influenced her academic achievement, they differed in their perceptions of the magnitude and the directness of the relationship. Zena's mother said that she did not understand why her daughter did not make the honor roll, but noted that the teacher "had a remark on the back [of her report card] about Zena's behavior, [and] it coulda been that." She felt that making the honor roll was not just classroom performance but was also related to personality and getting along with other children. We shared these perceptions with Mrs. Majors, and she acknowledged that some of Zena's failure to achieve academic honors may have been related to her behavior, but the relationship was indirect. Mrs. Majors said that Zena was a "good, solid student," but her grades were marked down because she often failed to finish her assignments on time. Although Zena completed her work "beautifully" when she was not distracted, Mrs. Majors felt her moodiness and temper interfered with her ability to complete her work at times because she was "always fussing with somebody."

In our observations in the classroom we noted that Zena tore up her work on the day's major project three different times and began anew. On each occasion she became upset with a minor error. However, it was clear that she had displayed an understanding of the assignment. She finally completed the project near the end of allotted time, after Mrs. Majors had asked her several times "to finish up." Later, when we pointed out to Mrs. Majors that Zena had started over several times, she expressed surprise, noting that she assumed the delay was because Zena was into the business of others. In fact, Zena had stopped several times to comment on the work of others, but the major reason for the delay in finishing seemed more related to a sort of perfectionism in her standards for the project. Such perfectionism on structured tasks was reported in interviews of several of the other teachers we interviewed and may derive from the children's earlier anxious behaviors on structured tasks in Head Start.

Since Zena completed first grade, we have learned through informal conversations with her mother of two changes in Zena's life, one possibly disruptive, the other clearly positive. First, her parents have again separated. Her mother has gone back on Aid to Families with Dependent Children (AFDC), is enrolled in a mandatory training program, and plans to again seek full-time employment once the program is completed. She claims and appears to be happy with these developments. No doubt the children once again miss their father.

Second, a woman who runs a small day-care home not far from their house is now caring for the children five days a week while Zena's mother attends her classes. Because of the location of this day-care provider's home on the other side of the school district line, Zena will return to the neighborhood school where she attended kindergarten for second grade.

Discussion

Earlier I outlined an interpretive approach to childhood socialization in which individual development is seen as embedded in children's collective weaving of their places in the "webs of significance" that constitute their culture. This collective weaving is the product of children's interactions with adults and other children in the various institutional locales or fields making up their culture. Through the examination of Zena's transition we get a glimpse of the intricacy of her life as she moves from the family (the hub of her developing web) to formal schooling. Zena has faced a complex array of obstacles in her path as she moved from Head Start to kindergarten and then on to first grade. While many of these problems are related to her family's circumstances, others pertain to the school system and features of her classroom environments. Clearly Zena has been affected by her family's many moves, her late start in kindergarten, and the unstable relationship between her parents. In addition, the transition was made more difficult by school policies such as court-ordered busing to achieve racial desegregation and half-day kindergarten. Zena has had to begin each school year with the task of accustoming herself to new schedules and locales. Furthermore, her movement into first grade presented her with culturally dissimilar classmates. While peer relations was an area in which Zena excelled in Head Start, her attempts to cope with the demands of this new and unfamiliar peer culture appear to have been largely unsuccessful and possibly disruptive to her academic performance.

In sum, while these preliminary findings from a small pilot study must be interpreted with caution, they do demonstrate the value of longitudinal ethnographic studies of key transitions points in children's live. The rich longitudinal data allowed us to employ what Mishler (this volume) refers to as case-based analyses, in which we construct individual narratives that capture the complexity and dynamics of human development in cultural context. This case-based approach is crucial in cases like Zena's where both continuities and discontinuities in the transition from home to school are related to cultural differences and economic inequalities (Rosier 1996). In this sense Zena's transition narrative helps us to "understand context as a product of the work people do in the course of making sense with each other and the preconstructed materials of their culture, materials filled with biases and inequalities of the social structure" (McDermott and Varenne, this volume).

Conclusion

In this chapter I have outlined key features of longitudinal, comparative ethnography and illustrated the potential of the method by considering examples of my recent work in Italy and the United States. These comparative studies have important implications for doing ethnographies of children, building a comparative data base for further developing an interpretive theory of socialization, and documenting children's transitions from the family to schooling.

Doing Ethnographies of Children

The voices of children are rarely heard in traditional theories of socialization. The focus in most theories is on adult conceptions of the child or how the child becomes an adult. A major strength of ethnographic studies of children is their potential for capturing children's words, actions, and perspectives for revitalizing our theories of socialization and human development. However, doing ethnographies of children is not easy. Entering children's worlds, overcoming their suspicion of and resistance to adult control, and gaining their acceptance and trust are difficult tasks.

In general I have found that the more different I am from other adults in the ethnographic setting, the quicker and easier it is for the children to define me as an atypical adult and accept me into their peer relations. The fact that I was male, foreign, and far from fluent in Italian led the Italian children to define me as an incompetent adult who needed their help. Furthermore, the fact that I could communicate better with children than I could with the teachers strengthened our relationship, and gave them a small sense of control over the teachers' power. Although clearly seen as a competent adult at the American Head Start center, I was still atypical because I was a white adult male among primarily black adult females and children. I was, thus, initially something of a curiosity at the Head Start center, but I still had to work hard to overcome the children's perceptions of my adult power. Seizing the opportunity to supervise washroom trips, my lax style in carrying out this assignment led the Head Start children to see me as grown-up friend who had little control over their lives.

Gaining children's acceptance and definition as an atypical adult is only the first step in doing ethnographies of children. Adult ethnographers must work to become active participants in children's peer cultures. As Mandell argues, such active participation is accomplished by engaging "in joint action with the children, thus creating mutual understanding" (1988:436). But how can adults engage in joint action with children without being obtrusive and controlling? How can adults suspend their knowledge and preconceptions of children's worlds? How can they compensate the sheer force and power of their physical presence?

In my twenty years of ethnographic study of young children, I have crafted and continually refined a participant observation style that has several elements. First, there is the issue of physical size. Being big is always a problem, but a simple willingness to sit on the floor or small chairs, to crawl into tight spaces, to roll on the ground, and to engage in bouts of rough-and-tumble play can go a long way in breaking down the barriers of physical size. Second, my style is reactive. I try not to initiate or terminate activities, settle disputes, or direct interaction. As a result, I have referred to myself as a peripheral participant in children's peer cultures. Although my participation has been peripheral, I do pick my spots and I do participate.

In the Italian preschool I expanded my general participation style. Although still sensitive to the problems of obtrusiveness by disrupting or influencing peer interactions, I discovered that my linguistic incompetence and my limited knowledge of the adult and school culture enabled me to move gradually from peripheral to a fuller and more active participation in the peer culture. My entry into the school and peer culture was much like that of the three-year-old children in their first year in the *scuola materna*. Like these children, I made mistakes, accepted aid, and learned the ropes.

During this first year apprenticeship, we *bimbi nuovi* struggled with the uncertainty of separation from familial bonds, watched the whirl of complex activities and interactions, and listened to the many voices of the rich verbal traditions. Over time we felt more comfortable, saw patterns in developing webs of meaning, and participated in and contributed to the school and peer cultures. Our early participation was often rudimentary, involving the reproduction of the actions of others or of the most basic elements of routines. However, participating in routines, contributing to the collective production of artifacts, and sharing concerns and values is what the production and reproduction of local cultures is all about. These acts of participation, contribution, and sharing, regardless of their sophistication or originality, generated in us a basic emotion of belonging to a group, of feeling at home in a culture. This process of capturing the children's experienced worlds is essential to the validity of ethnographic research (Becker, this volume).

My experiences in Italy made me more aware of the drawbacks of my earlier reliance on peripheral participation in American preschools. However, later in the Head Start center I found that it was not easy to duplicate my success at fuller participation in Italy. Although the Head Start children saw me as a grown-up friend and different from the teachers, I was not able to go much beyond peripheral participation in their peer activities. First, for practical reasons I could only observe at the school once or twice a week. However, even if I had been present everyday, the children themselves were at the school for only a few hours a day, four days a week. In short, the school and peer cultures of the Head Start center were less developed than those in the Italian *scuola materna,* and my grasp of the Head Start children's perspectives were less firm and satisfying. Second, unlike the situation in Italy, I found it more difficult to suspend my adult preconceptions of the Head Start center and children. The compensatory nature of the Head Start program may have been a factor in this regard, as I frequently thought about what the children's present activities, communicative styles, and peer relations might portend for their futures in formal schooling.

These problems aside, I learned a great deal about the school and peer cultures at the Head Start center, and I have pursued important comparative analyses using these data (Corsaro 1994). Nevertheless, I often recorded feelings of discomfort with my observations of the Head Start children in fieldnotes. In particular, I felt I needed to know more about their lives outside the center. Therefore, we interviewed some of the parents of the Head Start children, observed the children in their homes and communities, and followed them (through observations and interviews) as the moved on to kindergarten and first grade. Overall, my experiences in these settings contributed importantly to my evolving conception and practice of longitudinal, comparative ethnography.

Building a Comparative Data Base

The careers of comparative ethnographers usually involve a series of carefully sampled case studies. In this approach, ethnographers attempt to document both similarities, or what Erickson (1986) calls "concrete universals," and differences as a way of generating and refining theory (Ragin 1994). Crucial to this process is the theoretical sampling of specific cases and the general representativeness of the cases selected. For example, over the last twenty years I have carried out several ethnographies of preschool children which have enabled me to document the nature and extensiveness of peer culture at this age and its implications for the further development of an interpretive theory of childhood socialization.

I began my work with a study of a private middle- to upper-class nursery school on the West Coast of the United States in 1974–75, a time when only a small minority of American preschoolers regularly attended such programs. I moved my work in a cross-national direction in 1984–85, selecting Italy, an industrialized country with a long history of government involvement in child care and early childhood education. In 1989–92, now in the American Midwest, I selected an inner-city Head Start center (the only nationally supported early education program) and an upper-middle-class private nursery school. The general rationale of my sampling was to pursue the importance of peer culture in children's lives and how government policies and cultural values regarding child care and early education was effecting children's cultures and socialization more generally.

In this essay, I have focused on work in process from the Italian and American Head Start case studies. These cases are generally representative of their two countries in terms of government supported early education programs. The *scuola materna* in Bologna was typical of such programs in northern Italy and generally representative of all of Italy given that 90 percent of Italian three- to five-year-olds regularly attend programs with similar structure and orientation. The two Head Start classrooms I studied were generally representative of other classrooms of a Head Start program that served around 50 percent of the eligible inner-city children in the midwestern city where it was located. On the other hand, I am well aware that the economically disadvantaged children who attend Head Start in this city are different from those who do not in regard to the simple fact that their parents have taken the initiative to enroll them in this program.

We see then that the case studies were generally representative of government-supported early education programs in the two countries. However, the cases do differ in important ways, most obviously in terms of the racial, ethnic, and economic background of the children. These differences were, of course, directly related to the compensatory character of American early education policies and are thus not easily disentangled in the cross-national comparisons I make. Nevertheless, obvious differences in social class and ethnicity in the two cases must be kept in mind in drawing inferences in comparison across the two cases, especially when comparing individual performances. However, in this chapter and other reports (Corsaro 1994) I have focused on general group comparisons of similarities and differences in peer culture and how the preschool experience may affect children's transitions on to formal schooling. Comparisons of the importance of race, ethnicity, and class regarding these issues are best addressed through subcultural comparisons within the American data sets (that is, comparison of the of Head Start and private middle- to upper-class nursery school children). Analyses of these differences are currently underway.

Priming Activities, Transitions, and Interpretive Reproduction in Early Childhood

My ethnographic work with preschool children involves the collection of threads or strands in the children's ongoing collective weaving of the webs of significance of their cultures. These threads are sampled across situations and over time and preserved first in fieldnotes and then on audio- or videotape. For example, in my ethnography of Italian children, the interpretive analysis of particular preserved threads of activities such as the visits to the homes of the children in their last year at the *scuola materna* or dramatic enactments of peer routines like *discussione* capture the nature of productive-reproductive processes without distortion or disruption of the integrity of the collective and public local cultures within which they are embedded. My preservation of the interactive, communicative, and emotional elements of these activities in fieldnotes and on videotape have enabled me to cultivate a deep appreciation of their complexity as cultural productions as well as their reproductive force as repeated and varied instantiations of cultural meaning (see Miller, this volume). Although longitudinal data on the Italian children's later transition to formal schooling is needed for confirmation, I propose that the children's everyday, relentless involvement in these *priming* activities paves the way for a smooth, almost natural transition from the family to the wider peer and adult culture.

Recent work with economically disadvantaged American black children adds several new wrinkles to my repertoire of ethnographic procedures, as well as the further development of a theory of interpretive reproduction. While still relying primarily on participant observation and audiovisual recording of productive-reproductive processes in a particular cultural setting, I have added a more extensive longitudinal design and the collection of intensive interview data from important adults in the children's lives at different points in time. This new design and additional data have enabled me to generate a number of case-study narratives that provide information about the key transitions of early childhood in the lives of these economically disadvantaged children. Much analysis needs to be completed, and I am working with a small sample. Nevertheless, it appears that the children's routine involvement in culturally meaningful activities with adults and peers in the home, community, and Head Start center do not always have desirable priming effects for later transitions to formal schooling and the wider culture. In fact, in some instances what worked well in the home and at the Head Start center contributed to unanticipated (and often misunderstood) problems in kindergarten or first grade. I believe that longitudinal, comparative ethnography can help us greatly in better understanding the complexity of transitions in the lives of young children, most especially economically disadvantaged children like Zena.

Notes

1. In my research I have found that instruments of data collection like microphones, cameras, VCRs, and tape recorders can be disruptive, and I have outlined techniques for estimating and minimizing such effects (Corsaro 1982). However, even more mundane and everyday objects like pens and notebooks seldom escape children's attention. Many times children request to see and write in my notebooks and I have found that allowing them to do so quickly dissipates the attractiveness of these objects.

2. Cover names for places and individuals are used throughout.

3. The children's awareness of my limitations in speaking Italian continued long after my Italian improved. I was continually teased about my mistakes and failure to understand something someone had said. The youngest children most especially enjoyed such teasing. In fact, the children often extended my incompetence in language to other areas of social and cultural knowledge. Once on a field trip to a park that had scale models of dinosaurs, I pointed out to a small group (in very good Italian, I might add) that the particular dinosaur we were looking at had lived in the same place that I now did in the United States (actually, I knew I was correct about this because the sign with the exhibit said as much). The children laughed uproariously and one, Romano, said, "Bill, he's crazy! He says the dinosaur lived in the United States." Then, pointing to the dinosaur, he added, "But you can see it lived right here!"

4. In addition to my work in this school, I also observed (for periods of two days to a week) in several other *scuola materne* throughout Italy (Bologna, Pesaro, Rome, Salerno, and Trento). Although I found clear differences between the two schools in the south (in Rome and Salerno) and the three schools in the north in the teacher's training and experience and structural aspects of the program (such as the length of the school day, the number of teachers, and parental involvement), I observed a great deal of similarity regarding the collective emphasis of the curriculum and the frequent engagement of teachers and children in extensive and complex *discussioni.*

5. Throughout this article, I use *black* rather than *African American* or some other term. I recognize that there is controversy over this issue. However, my choice of terminology reflects the children's, parents', and teachers' own usage and their self-identification at the time the data were collected.

6. The job was extremely demanding when compared to that of the teacher in the Italian *scuola materna.* Each Head Start teacher had one assistant and was responsible for a morning and afternoon class of about seventeen children each. They arrived at the school around 7:30 A.M. each day and seldom left much before 4:30 P.M. They were also supervised by a number of assistant directors and a director, all of whom had offices in the same building. They had much less autonomy in their work, they received lower pay, and a had many more children from eco-

nomically disadvantaged and often troubled families in their classrooms as compared to the teachers in the *scuola materna*.

References

Barlow, K. 1985. "Play and Learning in a Sepik Society." Paper presented at the Eighty-Fourth Annual Meeting of the American Anthropological Association, Washington, D.C.

Boggs, S. T. 1985 *Speaking, Relating, Learning: A Study of Hawaiian Children at Home and at School.* Norwood, N.J.: Ablex.

Bruner, J. 1986. *Actual Minds, Possible Worlds.* Cambridge, Mass.: Harvard University Press.

CENSIS. *Bologna: Stili di vita e istituzioni in una società consolidata.* Bologna: Il Mulino.

Cole, M., J. Gay, J. A. Glick, and D. W. Sharp. 1971. *The Cultural Context of Learning and Thinking.* New York: Basic Books.

Cook-Gumperz, J., and W. A. Corsaro. 1986. Introduction to *Children's Language and Children's Worlds.* Ed. J. Cook-Gumperz, W. A. Corsaro, and J. Streeck, 1–11. Berlin: Mouton.

Corsaro, W. A. 1982. "Something Old and Something New: The Importance of Prior Ethnography in the Collection and Analysis of Audiovisual Data." *Sociological Research and Methods* 11: 145–66.

———. 1985. *Friendship and Peer Culture in the Early Years.* Norwood, N.J.: Ablex.

———. 1988. "Routines in the Peer Culture of American and Italian Nursery School Children." *Sociology of Education* 61: 1–14.

———. 1992. "Interpretive Reproduction in Children's Peer Cultures." *Social Psychology Quarterly* 58: 160–77.

———. 1993. "Interpretive Reproduction in the *Scuola Materna*." *European Journal of Educational Psychology* 8: 345–62.

———. 1994. "Discussion, Debate and Friendship Processes: Peer Discourse in Nursery Schools in the United States and Italy." *Sociology of Education* 67: 1–26.

Corsaro, W. A., and D. J. Eder. 1990. "Children's Peer Cultures." *Annual Review of Sociology* 16: 197–220.

Corsaro, W. A., and F. Emiliani. 1992. "Child Care, Early Education and Children's Peer Culture in Italy." In *Child Care in Context.* Ed. M. Lamb, K. Sternberg, C. Hwang, and A. Broberg, 81–115. Hillsdale, N.J.: Erlbaum.

Corsaro, W. A., and D. R. Heise. 1990. "Event Structure Models From Ethnographic Data." *Sociological Methodology* 20: 1–57.

Corsaro, W. A., and L. Molinari. 1990. "From *Seggiolini* to *Discussione:* The Generation and Extension of Peer Culture among Italian Preschool Children." *International Journal of Qualitative Studies in Education* 3: 213–30.

Corsaro, W. A., and T. A. Rizzo. 1988. "*Discussione* and Friendship: Socialization Processes in the Peer Culture of Italian Nursery School Children." *American Sociological Review* 53: 879–94.

————. "Disputes in the Peer Culture of American and Italian Nursery School Children." 1990. In *Conflict Talk*. Ed. A. D. Grimshaw, 21–66. New York: Cambridge University Press.

Corsaro, W. A., and K. B. Rosier. 1992. "Documenting Productive an Reproductive Processes in Children's Lives: Transition Narratives of a Black Family Living in Poverty." In *Interpretive Approaches to Children's Socialization*. Ed. W. A. Corsaro and P. J. Miller, 67–91. New Directions for Child Development no. 58. San Francisco: Jossey-Bass.

Erickson, F. D. 1986. "Qualitative Research." In vol. 3 of *Handbook of Research on Teaching*. Ed. M. C. Wittrock, 119–61. New York: Macmillian.

Fine, G. A., and B. Glassner. 1979. "Participant Observation with Children: Promise and Problems." *Urban Life* 8: 153–74.

Gaskins, S., P. J. Miller, and W. A. Corsaro. 1992. "Theoretical and Methodological Perspectives in the Interpretive Study of Children." In *Interpretive Approaches to Children's Socialization*. Ed. W. A. Corsaro and P. J. Miller, 5–23. New Directions for Child Development no. 58. San Francisco: Jossey-Bass.

Geertz, C. 1973. *The Interpretation of Cultures*. New York: Basic Books.

Goodwin, M. H. 1990. *He-Said-She-Said: Talk as Social Organization among Black Children*. Bloomington: Indiana University Press.

Heath, S. B. 1983. *Ways with Words: Language, Life, and Work in Communities and Classrooms*. New York: Cambridge University Press.

————. 1989. "Oral and Literate Traditions among Black Americans Living in Poverty." *American Psychologist* 44: 367–72.

Katz, L. 1987. "Early Education: What Should Young Children Be Doing." In *Early Schooling: The National Debate*. Ed. S. Kagan and E. Zigler. New Haven, Conn.: Yale University Press.

Lubeck, S. 1985. *Sandbox Society: Early Education in Black and White American*. Philadelphia: Falmer.

Magnusson, D., L. R. Bergman, G. Rudinger, and B. Torestadd, eds. 1991. *Problems and Methods in Longitudinal Research: Stability and Change*. Cambridge: Cambridge University Press.

Mandell, N. 1988. "The Least-Adult Role in Studying Children." *Journal of Contemporary Ethnography* 16: 433–67.

Manini, M. 1984. "La Scuola del'Infanzia dagli Orientamenti al Curricolo: Motivazioni Socioeducative e Considerazioni Operative." In *La Scuola dell'Infanzia Verso il 2000*. Ed. P. Bertolini, 106–21. Florence: La Nuova Italia Editric.

Ochs, E. 1988. *Culture and Language Development: Language Acquisition and Language Socialization in a Samoan Village*. New York: Cambridge University Press.

Ragin, C. C. 1994. *Constructing Social Research*. Thousand Oaks, Calif.: Pine Forge.

Rizzo, T. A., W. A. Corsaro, and J. E. Bates. 1992. "Ethnographic Methods and Interpretive Analysis: Expanding the Methodological Options of Psychologists." *Developmental Review* 12: 101–23.

Rogoff, B. 1990. *Apprenticeship in Thinking: Cognitive Development in Social Context*. New York: Oxford University Press.

Rogoff, B., and G. Morelli. 1989. "Perspectives on Children's Development From Cultural Psychology." *American Psychologist* 44: 343–48.

Rosier, K. B. 1996. "Competent Parents, Complex Lives: A Longitudinal Study of Low-Income Black Mothers and Their Children's Transition into Schooling." Ph.D. diss., Indiana University.

Rosier, K. B., and W. A. Corsaro. 1993. "Competent Parents, Complex Lives: Managing Parenthood in Poverty." *Journal of Contemporary Ethnography* 22: 171–204.

Schofield, J. 1982. *Black and White in School.* New York: Praeger.

Schieffelin, B. 1990. *The Give and Take of Everyday Life: Language Socialization of Kaluli Children.* New York: Cambridge University Press.

Schieffelin, B. B., and E. Ochs. 1986. *Language Socialization across Cultures.* New York: Cambridge University Press.

Shweder, R. A., M. Mahapatra, and J. Miller. 1987. "Culture and Moral Development. In *Cultural Psychology: Essays on Comparative Human Development.* Ed. J. Stigler, Shweder, and G. Herdt, 130–204. New York: Cambridge University Press.

Suransky, V. P. 1982. *The Erosion of Childhood.* Chicago: University of Chicago Press.

Watson-Gegeo, K. A. 1992. "Thick Explanation in the Ethnographic Study of Child Socialization: A Longitudinal Study of the Problem of Schooling for Kwara'ae (Solomon Islands) Children." In *Interpretive Approaches to Children's Socialization.* Ed. W. A. Corsaro and P. J. Miller, 51–66. New Directions for Child Development, no. 58. San Francisco: Jossey-Bass.

Whiting, B. B., and C. P. Edwards. 1988. *Children of Different Worlds: The Formation of Social Behavior.* Cambridge, Mass.: Harvard University Press.

Whiting, B. B., and J. W. Whiting. 1975. *Children of Six Cultures.* Cambridge, Mass.: Harvard University Press.

Zangheri, Renato. 1986. *Bologna: Storia delle città italiane.* Bari: Gius. Laterza and Figli.

20 Nature, Second Nature, and Individual Development: An Ethnographic Opportunity

WILLIAM DAMON

The appeal of this volume is that it promises a new joining of two distinguished social science research traditions, the ethnographic and the developmental. Each tradition has had its share of success in forging insights about human behavior, yet each tradition also has been constrained by certain inherent limitations in perspective and method. Because of such limitations, the two traditions often have overlooked one another—or, when they have noticed one another, they often have clashed. In the past, in fact, developmentalists and ethnographers have been among each other's harshest critics. The hope for the present is that, with some broader thinking on the matter, the two perspectives may prove complementary rather than contradictory. If so, a joining of the two may help to overcome the limitations of each. In the process—and this is the focus of my commentary—the two together could launch a productive conceptual assault on some of the vexing social problems surrounding young people growing up in contemporary society.

I shall argue that ethnographic approaches to youth development already have demonstrated the potential to further our understanding about social problems such as antisocial behavior and educational failure among today's young. Social problems such as these are difficult to understand because they are deeply entrenched in multiple layers of personal and social causation. At the same time, we need to gain better understanding of such problems; for not only have they become increasingly serious in recent times, but they also have proven highly resistant to remediation. In my view, this is why some of the lines of research presented in this volume have a special significance at this time.

Why Join Developmental and Ethnographic Perspectives?

From its beginnings over a century ago, developmental research has made great strides in charting the formation of behavior, affect, and intelligence in the individual over time and under a variety of personal and social conditions. In recent years, developmental research has taught us much about processes of psychological change, about the dynamics of social influence, and about the particular natural endowment with which humans enter the world.

As a social science discipline, however, developmental psychology has had its blind spots. Writing from an anthropological perspective, LeVine (1989) noted three. The first is an *optimality assumption* that favors Western, middle-class environments. This assumption holds that the kinds of parenting, school, and community arrangements that are available to most modern Western children provide the optimal conditions for human development and that any deviation from this ideal constitutes a deficiency. The second is what LeVine calls the *assumption of endogenous development.* This is the belief that normative ontogenetic trends established in studies of Western children reveal fixed, universal capacities that are triggered through maturational processes. The third is an assumption of *methodological rigor* that gives credence only to findings that are obtainable—and replicable—through standardized testing or strict experimental controls.

I would add a fourth blind spot to LeVine's list: the assumption that variation in social contexts may be represented as a developmental "factor" which exerts an external impact on the formation of mind, behavior, or emotion, rather than as an intrinsic part of any psychological process, whether within or between individuals. For example, many developmental studies have been designed around the notion that culture and class may have "effects" on children's intellectual growth that are somehow independent from children's evolving understanding of the social world and their participation in it. This common research design separates social influence from personal meaning, reduces complex experiences like culture or class to unidimensional "marker" variables, and removes the key process of interpersonal communication from the developmental mix entirely.

All four of these assumptions prevent a balanced, comprehensive view of today's most challenging social problems. The optimality assumption restricts our understanding of the diverse populations of young people that are growing up in today's society. The assumption of endogenous development obstructs our vision of human potential and deters us from investigating all the multiple pathways of human adaptation; it also deters us from exploring all the possible avenues of progressive change. The assumption of methodological rigor, when narrowly framed in LeVine's sense, makes it impossible to capture the interweaving set of forces that shape behavior in a particular community at a particular time: the community's "living spirit," to use one sociologist's intentionally less-than-rigorous phrase for it (Etzioni 1993).

The assumption that social influence is extraneous to mind and behavior is the most misleading of all, because it leads to a mechanistic formulation that seriously mistakes the nature of thought, action, communication, social interaction, and developmental change. Thought and action are expressed in social contexts, whether proximal or distant. From the time of birth, a person's psychological experience always takes its shape with reference to some present or past experience of the other. Central elements of psychological experience, such as meaning, belief, understanding, and intention, are at the same time social as well as personal.

Like thought and action, communication and social influence are played out in social contexts of one sort or another. Contexts are social because they bring together (not necessarily on the same here-and-now spot) people who are mutually aware of one another's intentional capacities. It is mutual intentionality that makes possible communication, which in turn makes possible social influence. In this manner, thought and action are formed in the course of multiple social interactions over the course of development. Social influence is part and parcel of mind and behavior from the start. It cannot be treated as a "factor" to be isolated or analyzed. Research designs that do so are ill equipped to examine the very phenomenon that they are trying explain: the dynamic relations between social experience and personal development.

Ethnographic studies, which generally have come out of sociology or anthropology, have succeeded in giving us more interactive accounts of social contexts, often in the form of rich and vivid portraits of particular communities. Moreover, studies from the ethnographic tradition have revealed much about the diversity of human experience and have shown us some widely varied forms of human adaptation. In so doing, they have brought us inner views of perspectives that otherwise would have remained foreign to us. All of this has been accomplished through a quite different sort of "methodological rigor" than developmental psychologists are accustomed to. In ethnographic study, concerns for replicability, standardized testing, and experimental control have given way to concerns for authenticity, meaning, and systemic validity (Cole 1992). As I shall show later in this commentary, these ethnographer's methodological concerns are essential for capturing the complexities of social problems as well as the life experiences of young people who are trying to adapt to troubled social conditions.

At the same time, disciplines that have used ethnographic methods have had their own blind spots. Neither sociology nor anthropology has found a way to ask, or answer, the central questions of human development. They have described the settings for human behavior and have shown how these settings determine the behavioral moment; but they have not been concerned with continuities in the individual across settings or across time. Nor have they been concerned with the legacy that social participation leaves on the individual. What does a person bring away from a social experience? How does that legacy affect the person's next social engagement? In short, what, and how, do people *learn* from the social settings that surround them? Without grappling with the central questions of learning and developmental change, it is difficult to imagine how we can understand key societal issues such as how culture is transmitted (or transformed) from one generation to the next.

In order to grapple with questions of learning and development, we need to appreciate something else that sociology and anthropology have been slow to recognize (or, if not slow, certainly resistant): the nature of the developing child. There are at least two ways that nature must be considered if we are to understand the development of social behavior. Some have found it helpful to refer to these as first and second nature.[1]

First, recent studies in developmental psychology have taught us that infants enter the world with well-defined predispositions (Kagan 1984; Trevarthen 1993). In fact, research uncovering the multiple facets of our natural endowments have been among developmental psychology's strongest contributions during the past decade. We now know that basic thought patterns, emotional reactions, and personal styles already are organized at birth. Categories of perception, social and linguistic sensitivities, and capacities for learning and self-referencing are active and ready for further elaboration. Because all social environments for childrearing must adapt to these natural predispositions, it is as accurate to say that these shape culture as it is to say that culture shapes the child.

Recent infant research has even provided us with strong evidence that children are born with specific moral reactions such as empathy and sympathy (Eisenberg 1989). If so, the implications are that human culture has a biological basis that provides, at the very least, undeniable universal constraints on social construction (Trevarthen 1993). Early empathy and sympathy are universal "natural events" that provide a foundation and a direction for the formation of a child's altruistic goals and intentions. The particular natural events of empathy and sympathy are elemental parts of what James Wilson has called the endemic moral sense of our species (Wilson 1993).

Life provides some people with other such natural events, neither universal or inborn. For example, a serious illness or physical handicap, even incurred late in life, may predispose a person toward empathic responding. But not all afflicted adults turn their bout with illness into a charitable orientation, just as not all children turn their empathic reactions into moral goals. The natural event gains its meaning, and its ultimate developmental effect, through processes of social communication and reflection (Damon 1994).

In other words, a natural life event may provide a disposition or an opportunity for reflection but cannot in itself seal the direction of change. At all ages, people learn from their social experience, and this learning transforms them. Much that is learned is not sustained in any meaningful way. But some transformations set the stage for further developmental acquisitions. These turn into relatively stable personal characteristics that persist over time and influence the course of the individual's future social behavior and communications (Caspi, Bem, and Elder 1989). Any social setting that comes in contact with the person must, in some way, come to terms with these individual characteristics (even as the infant's social environment by necessity molds itself to the infant's early dispositions). It is in this sense that the child's developing characteristics constitute a kind of "second nature," whatever other biogenetic distinctions there may be between these and the child's original endowment.

The point for the present is that fundamental developmental processes, experiential legacies, and behavioral continuities do reside in the individual, no matter how powerful the forces of culture and society may be. A child who has learned to greet others with hostility and suspicion will create a different sort of developmental pathway for himself than a child who has learned more positive and friendly modes of responding. Although not necessarily permanently entrenched—there is always the possibility of change—the child's behavior sustains itself across time and settings, because it has the capacity to at least partly shape the nature of those settings. (In this example, the hostile greeting provokes a hostile response, which further feeds the child's suspicious orientation). The individual's behavior is affected by the individual's particular history; and, in this sense, there are behavioral continuities that reside in the individual and contribute to the direction of the individual's future development. The social construction of mind and behavior is important for us to recognize, but it does not capture the whole story of how young people grow and act in society. Scholarly approaches that are constrained by too rigid or extreme a position on social constructionism tend to lose sight of this fundamental truth.

Developmental and ethnographic perspectives need one another to correct each other's biases. Social science needs both if it is to capture the whole story of youth in society—and if, in the end, it is to contribute to our comprehension and improvement of today's social problems. We need to understand both the nature of the environments that young people are faced with today and the nature of the young people who are living in and interacting with these environments. We need to understand both the dynamics of social change and the dynamics of individual change. The great hope is that these scholarly enterprises may be conducted together rather than separately, that the insights which they produce may be joined rather than added in some patchwork fashion. Only in this way will the full implications of findings from either tradition become apparent. In order to achieve this hope, a new discipline must be created, residing at the intersection of the various fields that traditionally have conducted developmental and ethnographic work. One attractive feature of the present volume is that it presages precisely this possibility.

Some Early Fruits of a New Tradition

The present volume presents some initial steps toward a joining of developmental and ethnographic study around major societal problems such as youth crime, community dissolution, violence, and poverty. Although much of the work reported in this volume is still in progress, there is much in it to suggest the value of this sort of effort. In order to highlight this potential, I shall focus on some informative findings in three chapters that pertain to youth development in the inner city: Sullivan's, Heath's, and the chapter by Burton, Allison, and Obeidallah. I also shall refer to other published work by these authors, particularly when the material is more elaborated elsewhere, as well as to the work of sociologist Elijah Anderson, who has used ethnographic methods to study the environments for youth development that today's inner cities provide.

Sullivan's chapter refers to his landmark study of youth crime in the inner city, published under the title *Getting Paid* (Sullivan 1989). Among other things, Sullivan's study offers unparalleled insights into the life choices of urban teenagers who drift into criminal pursuits. I quote here from one of the cases that Sullivan mentions in his chapter, a seventeen-year-old boy, code-named Arturo Morales, who lives in Brooklyn, New York. On his own initiative, the boy wrote the following document to explain his motivations for engaging in crime:

> Let's say it was right before the burglary with a serious armed robbery charge on me and pending. How was I thinking then? If I was to write my thinking about myself in a scale of 1 to 10, it was a 2 if 1 was lucky.

1. Didn't care if I got caught by police, prepared to do any crime. Down to shoot, stab, not fatal thoughts though, mug, rob anybody, burglarize any property.
2. No job at all.
3. No girlfriend or person to count on.
4. School, I gave up on that.
5. Family, let down.
6. Real tight dirty relationships.
7. Try to get over on cheap shit (crime in general).
8. Thinking to do a job for some money.
9. Wasting time on absolutely nothing but to think of nasty and dirty things to do.
10. Damaging myself physically on a day-to-day basis without doing any positive thinking for myself.
11. Almost every penny to get high or find dumb pleasures.
12. Didn't handle boredom the right way.
13. Being in the neighborhood 90 percent of the time.
14. Hanging out with the wrong people 85 percent of the time I hang out.
15. Thinking that I had authority to rob and steal.
16. Not think about the future at all, or serious thing not to do especially at such a young age.
17. Just falling into hell.
18. Not using nothing at all as lessons.
19. Not knowing all I was doing was wrong and later going to be punished for it.
20. Letting money problems get to me thinking I was slick, having a let's-do-it attitude.
21. Nothing to be happy about.

I find this to be a remarkable document because the boy opens a window onto some ways of growing up in today's troubled urban environments. In the boy's list, we can observe the boy's own reflections on the goals and values that have influenced his life choices. These reflections are powerfully revealing of both this boy's troubles and the shortcomings in the social condition that he is living within.

The first thing that the list reveals is the striking absence of supportive relationships in the boy's life. Who does the boy have to keep him on the right track, to comfort him when he's been wronged, to set him straight when he is wrong? Not his family, not a girlfriend, no sign of people who genuinely care for one another. Just "real tight dirty relationships"—associations in which, in all likelihood, people are treated like objects for one another's gratification and/or exploitation. It is almost impossible for a child to develop respect either for others or the self in a social world where people are treated as means to ends rather than ends in themselves (Damon 1988).

What the boy does develop respect (and affection) for is money—as well as for the instant pleasures that it can bring. As one observer has written, in the absence of communities that provide more spiritual values, "the result is lives of what we might call 'random nows,' of fortuitous and fleeting moments preoccupied with 'getting over' with acquiring pleasure, property, and power by any means necessary" (West 1993). Arturo is well aware how empty such goods and pleasures turn out to be. Yet acquiring such things is the only goal that Arturo has found in his young life to motivate his energies. School certainly has not motivated him; nor has he found inspiration in any future "calling" or occupation.

This lack of future prospect quickly leads Arturo to boredom, self-destruction, and despair. Arturo is self-reflective enough to understand this. He has some awareness of another standard of existence against which he compares his own spiritually impoverished circumstances. He knows that something is wrong, that there is a better way—otherwise he could not decry his lack of good relationships, his sense of lawlessness, his failure to learn from his mistakes. He could not complain about "falling into hell" unless he had some intimation of a better course. Arturo will not let himself be fooled into thinking that his materialism could ever lead to happiness. There is an astuteness, a wisdom in his comments that belies the common stereotype of a savage youth, of an all-around loser as short on wits as he is on conscience.

In an insightful attack on this misleading stereotype, Sullivan points out how bright and adaptable these "wayward" youth really are. "Some of these youths' criminal activities were indeed reckless and thrill-seeking, but others displayed considerable and often successful ingenuity. *The assumptions of low intelligence and blind pathological motivation as the chief driving forces of criminality do not square well with such evidence*" (Sullivan 1989:2). The problem is not in the adaptive capabilities of these young people but in the direction in which they are heading.

Burton, Allison, and Obeidallah's study reveals further dimensions of adaptiveness among disadvantaged inner-city youth. Burton and her colleagues show a more hopeful side of inner-city life than does Sullivan's study of criminality. The African-American teens in the Burton, Allison, and Obeidallah study demonstrate impressive competence, strong values, and a clear sense of themselves. These dimensions of character and competence, however, would be hidden to observers who are unprepared to recognize the diverse developmental outcomes expressed by young people today's inner-city communities. In the ethnographic approach that Burton and her colleagues employ, we are provided with an inside view of what these outcomes mean for young people and their families. Emerging from Burton's interviews with African-American youth are a wide variety of developmental goals and sources of personal pride. These include material goods, cultural and gender identifications, survival skills, creativity, spirituality, and good citizenship within the community. Young people who might be considered at risk for social failure are seen in a more favorable light when these diverse developmental outcomes are considered. For example, a nineteen-year-old school dropout named Anthony is described this way: "Anthony may not have finished high school, and he may not have a job, but he is the treasure of our community. He helps young mothers around the neighborhood with their kids. He does the grocery shopping for some of the old folks here who can't get out. And he keeps the peace between rival street gangs in the community."

One of the great shortcomings of traditional work in developmental psychology is that, because of its reliance on standardized tests and narrowly defined developmental outcomes, it obscures the potential of children from minority and non-Western populations. Both the Sullivan study and the Burton, Allison, and Obeidallah study show how an ethnographic approach can overcome this shortcoming. These studies do so by obtaining subjects' perspectives on their own development and by broadening the range of developmental outcomes by which young people's personal growth is gauged. With such an approach, the Sullivan study is able to detect the true adaptive competence of the young delinquents that he studies; and the Burton, Allison, and Obeidallah study is able to observe an impressive array of intellectual and moral achievements on the part of disadvantaged African-American teenagers. Although these studies depart from the methodological conventions of normative research in developmental psychology, they are framed in developmental terms and ask important developmental questions—for example, about how children acquire skills and values in a variety of life conditions. Because the studies combine ethnographic and developmental perspectives in this manner, they are able to forge insights that would be unavailable to either tradition by itself.

Sullivan and the Burton group offer us new understandings of how inner-city youths display their impressive potentials for adaptation and growth. These new understandings offer valuable information for those who would educate and work with young people from similar backgrounds. At the same time, we should not let these positive new appraisals of youth potential obscure the severe disadvantages that many of these young people face. Some of our inner-city communities have deteriorated to such a grave degree that they are unable to sustain the growth of even the hardiest youngster.

In his ethnographic study *Streetwise,* Elijah Anderson has documented some powerful examples of this in an urban community similar to those studied by Burton and her colleagues (Anderson 1990). Anderson's cases demonstrate how an unfortunate mix of deteriorating economic and social conditions can rob children of the guidance they need from concerned adults. Anderson's focus is on the disappearance of "old heads"—informal mentors for young people—from the disadvantaged neighborhoods that he has studied. The community no longer supports the presence of these extrafamilial adult guides, and without them many young people wind up lost, directionless, and in constant trouble. Anderson's examples also show how the same combination can devastate the community's capacity to support a religious presence and maintain a spiritual or moral core.

More evidence of this is provided in the work of Shirley Brice Heath and her frequent collaborator, Milbrey McLaughlin. In an examination of three inner-city neighborhoods, Heath and McLaughlin have documented the loss of what they call "nurturing settings" for youth development (McLaughlin 1993). They have described how violence has made neighborhoods into threatening environments for children rather than places for them to find friends and mentors:

> The notion of neighborhood as a nurturing setting where older members watch out for and over neighborhood youth and where networks of "local knowledge" and intergenerational intimacy weave sturdy systems of support for young people and their developing identities is far from the reality that contemporary inner-city youth experience. Such notions of nurturing neighborhoods embody, at best, times gone by. (McLaughlin 1993:54)

Heath and McLaughlin also show how the schools, churches, and workplaces no longer hold much attraction for young people. The schools have crumbled, many of the churches are gone, and the workplaces no longer offer good jobs. These once valuable contexts for growth, writes McLaughlin, "do not add up to much for inner-city youth." As a result, children develop neither a sense of what it is like to work nor an inner system of values and beliefs that supports work. They cannot imagine themselves as people who can handle serious responsibilities, enjoy working hard, and contribute something of value to society. "In this context, the deep pessimism, low self-esteem, and destructive behavior that corresponds to this (disconnected) sense of personhood are not surprising, nor is the hope of the youth advocate that they 'just live, just duck the bullet.'"

But the same young people can come alive if given even a small bit of opportunity. These may be young people whom everyone has given up on. Yet they look wholly different when they find engagements that galvanize their natural strengths. In new settings that present them with tasks that they can understand and take seriously, their astonishing array of natural intelligences shines through. The histories of disappointments and failures that they bring with them recede into the background. Eventually, they build upon their earlier strengths, they acquire new ones, and they adopt reinvigorated beliefs in their own potential. Their newly hopeful views become shared with others in their social worlds, and in turn this reinforces the positive directions that their lives have now taken.

Scattered throughout our cities and towns are a few remaining settings that do still provide nurturing environments for young people. In chapter 11 of this volume, Heath examines some of these—in particular, grassroots organizations that shelter young people and offer them worthwhile activities, safe peer relations, and informal counseling from concerned adults. Boys and girls clubs, theater groups, sports teams, charities, and local community centers are among the organizations that provide nurturant settings for youth development. Heath's analysis of these successful youth organizations is instructive, in part because it pinpoints what is missing in the other, less successful settings; and in part because it provides clues about what kinds of settings we need to create if we are to reclaim the future prospects of all our young.

First and foremost, successful youth organizations ensure the physical survival of the children who attend them. They provide safe havens from the perils of the streets and, for some children, from the unpredictable hazards of their own homes. For one thing, the organization gives the child a place to go to get away from trouble. Just as importantly, it gives the child an identity as a member of an organized group that will look out for him. Youth workers are aware of the protective value of such an identity and use it freely. One worker is quoted as saying: "As long as you are involved in something—school, sports—the gangs will leave you alone. It's the unaffiliated youth that they are after."

Other characteristics of organizations that work include local credibility in the community and stability of staff. Workers who know the local scene well and are committed enough to remain on the job year after year are able to reach even the most difficult youth because they can be *trusted*— a feeling that is sorely missing in so many of the young people's lives. Trustworthy organizations also take pains to include all the youths who seek them out, as long as they follow the rules and are not disruptive of the group. And they engage youths in activities that reflect a sense of purpose. The purpose may be relatively narrow—such as winning the basketball game—or broad, such as providing food for the needy. Either way, the purpose creates a sense of solidarity within the organization and serves to bring youngsters out of their own self-centered concerns.

Perhaps most striking of the characteristics that mark a successful youth organization is the nature of its expectations for youth. They hold a high positive regard for their young members. They hold high expectations for their behavior, requiring strict adherence to community regulations. The organizations also hold high expectations for their young members' abilities, giving them demanding tasks to perform. Most importantly, they give their young members real responsibilities without doubting that they can shoulder them. All of this stands in sharp contrast to the approach that many other organizations in our society take when they come in contact with young people.

Some Obstacles and Further Opportunities

The work that I have discussed above offers us valuable new information about important populations of youth that are little understood today. It also offers us unmatched insights into the developmental potential of these young people, about the kinds of settings that bring out this potential, and about the kinds of settings where they are likely to run into trouble. Such insight is desperately needed if we are to work with all our diverse groups of today's young people in a constructive way.

At the same time, there are still limitations in the efforts presented here. Some of these limitations derive from conceptual obstacles that still must be overcome if developmental and ethnographic perspectives are to be truly joined. With reference to chapters in this section, I shall note two such limitations that particularly trouble me.

First, there is an inattention to learning. After reading rich ethnographic descriptions of the environments in which young people are conducting their daily affairs, one naturally wonders how these environments are affecting those young people's skills, values, and behavioral patterns. This is the "developmental legacy" question that I raised earlier in this commentary: What do children bring away with them from their social experience? I find it a question that is mostly begged in the present set of papers. Reading Sullivan (chap. 10 in this volume) or Anderson (1990), the implicit assumption seems to be that dissolute environments lead to dissolute youth behavior. But no empirical connections are explicitly made; and, in any case, this is far too simplified and generalized an assumption to serve the purpose of identifying exactly what it is in children's lives that makes a difference, for good or for ill. After all, some children come through the bleakest circumstances in fine shape, whereas others fail to develop strong skills or virtue in even the most advantaged conditions.

We need to know more about how particular sorts of relationships and experiences foster particular sorts of capacities and dispositions. We need to know more about what happens to the young people in Shirley Heath's study once they have "graduated" from the grass-roots youth organizations that have nurtured them. In my rendition of the Heath line of research, I have indicated my belief that participation in these organizations can turn a young person's life around. But this belief has not yet been well tested or well defined. There remain a number of important and unanswered questions.

How are these young people different than they would have been if they had never participated in such organizations? What exactly have they learned from this participation? How does their experience in these organizations interact with other experiences—in schools, in families, in communities? (Does it, for example, affect what they are able to learn in these other settings?) Are there differences among young people in how they respond to these organizations? In what they are able to gain from their participation? In what they have learned and what they take away with them into their own futures? It would be a straightforward matter to design a longitudinal study following these young people through their participation in such organizations. These young people could be compared with others who have been living in places where such participation is unavailable. Such an effort would greatly expand the usefulness as well as the theoretical scope of this ethnographic work.

In his commentary for this volume, my friend John Modell worries that the perspective implicit in such a strategy rests on a view of the individual taken out of context: "Seen thus," he writes, "the person engages in society and returns to herself" (chap. 21). As Modell suggests, it surely would be foolish, after all we have learned from ethnographic study, to isolate people from the systems of cultural meaning that at all time shape their awareness. But it is well known in social science that we must choose a level of analysis that best serves our purpose, and we cannot always examine everything at once. If we are interested in understanding a person's life through time, the right level of analysis is the individual—for, although people do not exactly "engage in society and return to themselves," they do engage in particular social interactions and relationships and then move on to others. And it is the individual who does the moving, bringing along only the vestiges of those interactions and relations that *this individual's* knowledge, memory, and other systems of psychological awareness will allow.

What is more—and I will up the ante here—if we are interested in understanding a young person's life through time, we must commit ourselves not only to an individual level of analysis but also to a developmental perspective. Otherwise we shall never be able to make sense out of the pattern of transitions within, among, and across social contexts that occur in the course of growing up. What helps us make sense of these patterns is the notion of directionality, a notion that defines the developmental enterprise and distinguishes it from studies of mere change. I shall elaborate on this point in the following section.

The second troubling limitation is a failure to articulate developmental directions. If there is one prerequisite for developmental analysis it is having some prior sense of what the investigator considers to be a developmental change. What sort of movement represents progress, and toward what end? Without a clear sense of the directions that are being studied, one may as well dispense with the concept of "development" entirely. A change without any direction—without movement toward (or away from) something—is simply a change. If one wishes to study directionless changes, that's fine, but then there is no need to introduce an additional notion called development. One only needs the concept of development when one wishes to determine what represents an advance or a decline, a positive or a negative change, progress or regression, an optimal or a suboptimal state of being.

Out of egalitarian concerns about invidious comparisons between people, some social scientists argue that a nondevelopmental focus on simple change is preferable to a developmental orientation that looks for progress and directionality in behavior. I do not wish to engage the ideological implications of this debate here. But I do wish to state that developmental analysis, complete with assumptions of progress and direction, is an essential perspective when it comes to understanding the challenges and opportunities of young people growing up in any society. The notion of developmental direction is an inescapable part of the story of youth— personally, phenomenologically, socially, and, when admitted with a wide enough spectrum of variation, culturally as well.

Let me give an example here; it is a hypothetical example, but it has parallels in any number of personal testimonials from people who have grown up in disadvantaged conditions and gone on to do well in life. Suppose Arturo from Mercer Sullivan's study were taken under the wing of a mentor who could inspire him to settle down, acquire employable skills, stay on the right side of the law, and develop sustained relationships with people whom he can count on. Suppose, too, that in the process Arturo acquires a sense of service to others, a motivating set of goals and aspirations, and a hopeful sense of his own future. These would all be changes in a direction that I suggest is unambiguously positive. They represent movement and growth: in short, personal and social development. They are quite different from other sorts of changes that Arturo could experience—for example, acquiring a dislike for the police or learning a new way to steal cars. Their difference can only be fully understood in relation to their meaning for Arturo's development as an individual who must learn to function well in a particular social world. Without understanding the nature of the developmental directions that will enable Arturo to function well, we shall never be able to make sense of his—or other young people's—hopes, fears, frustrations, joys, beliefs, or behavioral fluctuations. The developmental directions that define progressive change are an integral part of growing up in any social setting.

Defining developmental directions is *not,* in any sense, an empirical endeavor. It is impossible to derive from a data set, post hoc, any criteria for defining advances in the formation of behavior. Rather, one must begin by postulating directions that one considers to represent progress and then go on to determine how, whether, and under what conditions people gravitate toward these directions. As developmental psychologists have long argued, any other approach can yield nothing more than uninterpretable ontogenetic trends (Lerner 1986; Damon 1991).

Now, I should make clear that developmental directions do not exist independent of the social contexts in which they play themselves out. Acquiring, say, quantitative competence in New Guinea need not look anything like acquiring quantitative competence at the Bronx High School of Science. Different sorts of means, ends, and evaluative standards would apply. In order to determine what constitutes progress in any domain— intellectual, social, moral—we must always take into consideration the social context in which the individual operates. But within any social context, all outcomes are not equal. Some yield better adaptation, deeper understanding, finer values, more accurate knowledge, stronger competence, and so on. Development means gravitating toward these higher outcomes.

Too many ethnographic studies seem unaware of this principle. One result is a confusion between the perspectives of investigator and subject. For example, the Burton, Allison, and Obeidallah study gives equal status to a range of "developmental outcomes" that include material reward, survival, spiritual growth, and community service. Exactly what is developing here, and in what direction? Are these personal outcomes? Survival outcomes? Moral ones? One can not have it all ways; because an advance, say, in material acquisitiveness might mitigate against an advance in one's moral inclinations. It may well be—in fact, it is most likely the case—that the various outcomes described by Burton, Allison, and Obeidallah bear dramatically different significance for young people's future lives. Pursuing material goals will not lead a young person in the same direction as pursuing spiritual ones. Some of the young subjects in ethnographic studies may be confused about this, but there is no reason for researchers to be.

Doing developmental work means taking positions on value-laden issues regarding direction and progress. It is impossible to conduct cogent developmental analyses without being clear about one's criteria for assessing development. For a number of historical reasons related to its roots in anthropology, ethnographic study often has refrained from examining anything that could be considered an advance along some predefined dimension of progress. In order to fulfill its potential for contributing to our understanding of human development, ethnographic study must become freed from its historical constraints and directed toward the central questions of progressive change.

Acknowledgments

This commentary was completed while the author was a fellow at the Center for Advanced Study in the Behavioral Sciences, in Stanford, California. I am grateful for financial support provided by the John D. and Catherine T. MacArthur Foundation (grant no. 8900078). The ideas expressed in this commentary are the sole responsibility of the author. Sections of this commentary pertaining to ethnographic analyses of contemporary youth problems are drawn from Damon, *Greater Expectations* (1995), and many of the points are further elaborated there. I am grateful to all three editors of this book—Anne Colby, Dick Jessor, and Rick Shweder—for their constructive comments on earlier drafts of this chapter.

Notes

1. I am grateful to Michael Cole for the phrasing of this distinction.

References

Anderson, E. 1990. *Streetwise: Race, Class, and Change in an Urban Community.* Chicago: University of Chicago Press.
Caspi, A., D. Bem, and G. Elder. 1989. "Continuities and Consequences of Interactional Styles across the Life Course." *Journal of Personality* 57: 376–406.
Cole, M. 1992. "Culture in Development." In *Developmental Psychology: An Advanced Textbook.* Ed. M. Bornstein and M. Lamb. Hillsdale, N.J.: Erlbaum.
Damon, W. 1988. *The Moral Child.* New York: Free Press.
———. 1991. "Problems of Direction in Socially Shared Cognition." In *Perspectives on Socially Shared Cognition.* Ed. L. Resnick and J. Levine. New York: Plenum.

————. 1994. "The Lifelong Transformation of Moral Goals through Social Influence." In *Interactive Minds: Life-Span Perspectives on Social Influence and Psychological Development.* Ed. P. Baltes and U. Staudinger. Chicago: University of Chicago Press.

Eisenberg, N., ed. 1989. *Empathy and Related Emotional Responses.* San Francisco: Jossey-Bass.

Etzioni, A. 1993. *The Spirit of Community.* New York: Crown.

Kagan, J. 1984. *The Nature of the Child.* New York: Basic Books.

Lerner, R. 1986. *Concepts and Theories of Human Development.* 2d ed. New York: Random House.

LeVine, R. 1989. "Cultural Environments in Child Development." In *Child Development Today and Tomorrow.* Ed. W. Damon. San Francisco: Jossey-Bass.

McLaughlin, M. 1993. "Embedded Identities: Enabling Balance in Urban Contexts." In *Identity and Inner-City Youth: Beyond Ethnicity and Gender.* Ed. S. B. Heath and M. W. McLaughlin. New York: Teacher's College Press.

Sullivan, M. L. 1989. *Getting Paid: Youth Crime and Work in the Inner City.* Ithaca, N.Y.: Cornell University Press.

Trevarthen, C. 1993. "Culture and Emotion: A Nativistic Interpretation." *Nature* 81: 1119–42.

West, C. 1993. *Race Matters.* Boston: Beacon Press.

Wilson, J. Q. 1993. *The Moral Sense.* New York: Free Press.

PART FOUR

Concluding Overview

21 The Uneasy Engagement of Human Development and Ethnography

JOHN MODELL

The encounter of developmentalists and ethnographers recorded in this volume responds to a moment when the characteristic scientism of American work in child development has begun to appear confining to many in the field. Ethnographers and other practitioners of interpretive approaches have for their parts begun to seek insight into the processes by which individuals come to be as they are. The engagement of human development and ethnography is, however, not an easy one.

Developmentalists have traveled a considerable distance from a natural science mode of thinking toward the *sciences humaines* notion that has recently so enlivened the humanities and "soft" social sciences. Normative Piagetian accounts of individual development now open out toward Vygotskian dialectics in which the social production of learning is seen at the heart of the movement of the organism through life (Wertsch 1985a; Forman, Minick, and Stone 1993). Developmental psychology has taken something of a retrospective turn, looking back upon its own history in a self-reflexive way and seeking in its classics a source of renewed inspiration (Bronfenbrenner et al. 1986; Kessen 1990). Such notable practitioners as Jerome Bruner (1986, 1990) have taken a decided interest in the contributions that narrative theory and other linguistically oriented humanities can bring to the study of human lives

Participants in Oakland generally found that a number of polarities no longer polarized. Most simplistic, and most easily gotten out of the way, was the distinction between *quantitative* and *qualitative,* the former term no longer uniquely valorized. Survey techniques in particular (and "laboratory" settings in general) now seem marked as much by what they cannot find out, while ethnographic techniques seem to offer at least provisional access to "the action," for the action now is seen to take the form of agency rather than structure, to take place thus in a historical setting rather than a timeless one, and to occur in a world in which transactions must be understood linguistically and not just behaviorally. Open for discussion, but not so easily consensual, is the notion that culture is enacted and at risk[1] rather than transmitted and inert, within which the ways individuals come to be as they are, are seen to depend upon culture, not only for the content of these ways but also the manner of their unfolding.

Postmodernism, though, has provoked a profound uncertainty, in effect, about the meaning of meaning. The superb contrast within these covers between the positions of Becker and Denzin is not just a disagreement about method or even epistemology, but also reflects a disagreement over how shared and public is the sense of "why" and "should" with which actors go about their daily lives in society. Each time a social text is deconstructed, unitary notions of culture weaken, and the presumptive fit between the concepts "individual" and "actor" seems less compelling. Even as this suggests to interpretive social scientists that they need a developmental theory of the individual, it heightens their wariness of normative assumptions. Developmentalists open to new empirical methods sometimes have trouble discerning quite what they are.

As a social historian, an outsider to both fields from a famously eclectic discipline, I am at ease although not at home in the interdisciplinary ground being explored here. Social historians, like historians generally, ask how individuals interact with institutions, an approach, I think, that offers a good way of situating ethnography historically, and a good site for relevant ethnographic observation of age-graded phenomena. Although until recently I have usually tended to examine modal life-course tendencies (and deviations from the mode) within populations, rather than looking at individual development per se, as my orientation to issues of childhood and youth has deepened, I have myself begun to seek a theoretically grounded understanding about individual-level processes, and to read in the literature of human development.

Interdisciplinary courtship is a sweetly and dangerously ambiguous game: some seductions, some small deceits, some delicate misdirections are inevitable and necessary if curiosity is to lead to understanding by bringing the disciplines onto one another's home ground. My reflective task, on the other hand, is that of the skeptic, seeking to identify and perhaps elucidate imperfect understandings.

Ethnography as Risky Partner: The Problem of Validity

The strategically naive assertion of the July 1991 proposal for the conference at which these essays were first presented maintained that we have come to "recognize" that lives are mediated by intention, and that with positivism in retreat, methods that claim to discern "meaning" can be perhaps even more "valid" than those that don't. The conference cannot be said to have ratified this assertion, but there is a sense the notion of validity in which it may be said to have held among participants.

Validity is generally said to include three analytically separable components. The first of these, called "apparent" validity by Kirk and Miller (1986), depends on the fit of the measurement to the commonsense understanding of the content upon which the evidence is sought.[2] Historians commonly assess validity according to this criterion, and often document their arguments through the persuasive presentation of apparently valid verbal evidence in the form of quotations. Concepts that are not readily discernible at the surface of social behavior, however, cannot so easily rest on evidence that is assessed mainly for apparent validity. Apparent validity could be what the conference call had in mind.

Evidence for scientific understandings, however, ordinarily must satisfy one or both of two other criteria, which Kirk and Miller render "instrumental" and "theoretical." The first of these refers to the success of an indicator of a given theoretical concept in fitting empirically with available "criterion" measures as do other, putatively already validated indicators of the same concept. The final aspect of validity refers to the strength of the explicit theoretical reasons according to which the indicator *should* track the underlying concept.

American developmental psychology has depended heavily upon instrumental validity. This sense of validity fits well with a view of scientific cumulation in which right knowledge is gradually accomplished through incrementing accurate and precise measurement, fostering and being fostered by tighter theoretical structures, as facilitated by a growing battery of standard, proven instruments whose validity has been assured by explicit quantitative assessment. "Instruments" in social and behavioral science, as in natural science, are concrete instantiations of shared disciplinary perspectives on how to proceed with the gathering of knowledge. The essays collected in this volume offer a number of instances of innovative formalized techniques used to process field data that minutely break down observed behavioral (or narrative) passages into components for analytic purposes, to the end of enhancing the validity of the resultant evidence. Mishler, for instance, adopted optimal matching techniques in order to preserve in considerable detail the time-dependent qualities of individual developmental patterns without falling back on ad hoc characterizations of each individual's career, which would render comparison or even summary suspect.

On the whole, however, the conference's concern for "meaning" shifts our sense of validity to its third aspect, toward evidence that can be seen as linked to the underlying concepts not just empirically but by explicit theoretical ties. Since the shift to a concern for "meaning" is part and parcel of a shift toward actor-centered and, ultimately, intentional explanations for theoretical validity, however, this in practice means making explicit the meanings according to which the actors intend their actions. And here is the rub: insofar as intention is understood in a commonsense way, it is very difficult indeed to distinguish "theoretical" validity from "apparent" validity. Of course, middle-age Japanese wives, like Orissa householders, or like inner-city black children (and perhaps like all children) do not entirely share our meanings. But a part of the ethnographer's task is commonly taken to be to draw her readers within the frame of reference of her otherwise exotic subjects in order to make intuitively plausible to readers the implausible native theories according to which their subjects act. So success in this realm is tantamount once again to drawing back together theoretical and apparent validity. This reduces the persuasiveness of such accounts to many developmentalists, as long as there is no methodological specification for the ethnographer's (indeed, the reader's) intuitions of common sense.

At the Oakland conference whenever developmentalists asked ethnographers how to assess the validity of claimed knowledge, the ethnographers cited conscientious field methods and thoughtful methods for collating field observations.[3] In essence, they echoed the formulations that Becker offered in his effort to explain why qualitative methods might be said to be more credible than quantitative methods. Becker values data that "are accurate, in the sense of being based on close observation of what is being talked about [rather than] only on remote indicators . . . [and] are precise, in the sense of being close to the thing discussed and thus being ready to take account of matters not anticipated in the original formulation of the problem." Since the nature of what is "out there" is not fully known *a priori,* instrumental validity may be an irrelevant criterion. Sought too eagerly, theoretical validity, too, may preempt understanding. If we focus our concern for validity upon the process of gathering evidence, then we may assess how persuasive the evidence ought to be about the phenomena under discussion, without predetermining its nature.

Becker writes in the mode of objectivity, of "seeing the real world of everyday life," but for many ethnographers subjectivity, too, plays an essential role in producing the knowledge gained in the field. Perception ("seeing") isn't all there is to it.[4] Both Corsaro and Shweder, for example, depend explicitly upon the ethnographer's own subjectivity for discerning and validating their access to others' culturally shared subjectivities.

Corsaro's essay recounts a handful of fieldwork stories. These illustrate his personal engagement in the daily practices he observed and lend a sense of immediacy to readers, a persuasive technique that suggests apparent validity. He also makes explicit the grounding of theoretical validity in these same fieldwork incidents. "Over time like the younger children, I developed as a participating member of these local [children's] cultures. . . . Also like these younger children I felt strong positive emotional reactions to my successes and to my developing membership in the group. These positive emotions are especially useful for capturing the notion of development as degrees and types of participation in the productive-reproductive practices through which culture is constituted and maintained." To credit Corsaro's emotion as a mark of validity, we need to accept him as an acute self-observer, even as he tries to fit in as a kind of big kid, and also being enough like a kid that his emotions upon acceptance do in fact parallel those of Italian three-year-olds.

Shweder proposes that the fieldworker's subjectivity participates in the production of valid ethnographic knowledge by permitting a self-conscious, conceptual analysis of the "mental state language" (emotions, feelings, beliefs) of others. "Your own mental life is very complex, and major aspects of your mental life are hidden from your view and direct experience and in desperate need of anthropological excavation. The same is true of the mental life of others, . . . [who share with us] a universal original multiplicity, which makes each of us so variegated that 'others' become accessible and imaginable to us through some aspect or other of our own complex self." The selection of emphasis within these shared aspects of humanity to produce the "native" within different cultures is, in Shweder's account, the work of the "moral community" in which one lives. The moral community is external and observable in the analytic process that Shweder provocatively calls mind reading. But the subjective element is no less a part of this analytic process: the "excavation" that will enable the construction of a plausible model of the mental life of the other takes place also upon one's self.

Corsaro's and Shweder's arguments need be confronted if ethnography and human development are to pursue their engagement. If validity is to be distinguished from persuasiveness, on the one hand, and conscientiousness, on the other, then some version of the kind of subjective basis of knowledge that Corsaro and Shweder lay out must be accepted as grounding for theoretical validity of a sort—not merely as apparent validity. Should this happen, however, the identification of validity with sure reproducibility will be generally weakened, and, with it, some of the sense of the building of knowledge through gradual accretion and modification. How, then, may knowledge grow? How, indeed, has knowledge grown?

Have We Been Here Before?

> One night the boys' aunts were bathing them. James offered to
> teach one of the sisters the song "Clementine," but said that he
> wanted to be paid for the job. They agreed upon twopence. After
> she had gone out of the bathroom, her sister heard Denis (5:3)
> say quietly to James: "James, you shouldn't say how much you
> want now, because you can't tell how long you're going to take to
> teach her." When she returned James insisted upon a fresh ar-
> rangement; twopence every time he had to go over the song.
> (Isaacs 1930:355)

We may well have been here before, or nearly here. Seventy years ago,
Susan Isaacs began her three years of participant observation at the Malt-
ing House School, Cambridge, England, moved by a conviction that child
psychology not only rested too heavily upon experimental method, but,
even when observational, was too committed to *a priori* schemes of abstraction. This inevitably led, Isaacs held, to "oversimplification of the
problem . . . through the overlooking of qualifying differences—qualifying differences which most unacademic persons [read, "natives"] used to
observing children and parents would know to be vital" (1933:6). Isaacs
maintained that the study of children's development would instead ideally
conform to the model of "an anthropologist among a primitive people,
watching but not entering into the life he observes" (1930:9). "It would
not be possible for anyone who had lived with the children while these
records were being made, and had felt the continuous impact of their
minds upon things and events and each other, to rest content with any
formal scheme of relations or relation-finding, or types of judgment or
reasoning. The children themselves compel us to look at the problem of
cognition in terms of process, and of genetic history" (1930:49). The children *themselves*.

Isaacs's own direction in fact led away from ethnography toward the
more conventional case-based approaches of psychoanalysis. Interpretations of developing child and responsive context—of James, James's sister,
and Denis—were left behind. Although Isaacs notes the "hair-trigger action of external events . . . causing a profound redistribution of internal
forces" (1933:9), the nature of the shared understandings that coordinate
intentional action did not engage her imagination. Her anthropologist-
observer disregarded much of what ethnography offers to development
that might really matter—or might prove unacceptable. Proceeding from
psychoanalytic presumptions, Isaacs made a sharp distinction between
fantasy and reality: the constitution of that "reality" was not of great concern to her. Children's development, she maintained, contrasting her no-